AIA

Foundation Level

FINANCIAL ACCOUNTING

LEARNING AND PRACTICE WORKBOOK

In this 2021 edition

- A **user-friendly format** for easy navigation
- **Exam-centred topic coverage**, directly linked to AIA's syllabus
- **Exam focus points** showing you what the examiner will want you to do
- Regular **fast forward** summaries emphasising the key points in each chapter
- **Questions** and **quick quizzes** to test your understanding
- **Practice question bank** containing exam-standard questions with answers
- **Exam question bank** containing recent exam questions with answers
- 2 Mock exams
- A full index

FOR EXAMS FROM 2025

Second edition October 2024
ISBN 9781 0355 2573 7
eISBN 9781 0355 2601 7

British Library Cataloguing-in-Publication Data
A catalogue record for this book is available from the British Library

Published by
BPP Learning Media Ltd
BPP House, Aldine Place
142-144 Uxbridge Road
London W12 8AA

learningmedia.bpp.com

Printed in the United Kingdom

All rights reserved. No part of this publication may be reproduced, stored in a retrieval system or transmitted in any form or by any means, electronic, mechanical, photocopying, recording or otherwise, without the prior written permission of BPP Learning Media.

Contains public sector information licensed under the Open Government Licence v3.0.

The contents of this book are intended as a guide and not professional advice. Although every effort has been made to ensure that the contents of this book are correct at the time of going to press, BPP Learning Media makes no warranty that the information in this book is accurate or complete and accept no liability for any loss or damage suffered by any person acting or refraining from acting as a result of the material in this book.

We are grateful to the Association of International Accountants for permission to reproduce past examination questions. The suggested solutions in the exam answer bank have been prepared by BPP Learning Media Ltd.

BPP Learning Media is grateful to the IASB for permission to reproduce extracts from IFRS® Accounting Standards, IAS® Standards, SIC and IFRIC. This publication contains copyright © material and trademarks of the IFRS Foundation®. All rights reserved. Used under license from the IFRS Foundation®. Reproduction and use rights are strictly limited. For more information about the IFRS Foundation and rights to use its material please visit www.IFRS.org.

Disclaimer: The IASB, the International Financial Reporting Standards (IFRS) Foundation, the authors and the publishers do not accept responsibility for any loss caused by acting or refraining from acting in reliance on the material in this publication, whether such loss is caused by negligence or otherwise to the maximum extent permitted by law.

©
BPP Learning Media Ltd
2025

A note about copyright

Dear Customer

What does the little © mean and why does it matter?

Your market-leading BPP books, course materials and e-learning materials do not write and update themselves. People write them on their own behalf or as employees of an organisation that invests in this activity. Copyright law protects their livelihoods. It does so by creating rights over the use of the content.

Breach of copyright is a form of theft – as well as being a criminal offence in some jurisdictions, it is potentially a serious breach of professional ethics.

With current technology, things might seem a bit hazy but, basically, without the express permission of BPP Learning Media:

- Photocopying our materials is a breach of copyright
- Printing our digital materials in order to share them with or forward them to a third party or use them in any way other than in connection with your BPP studies is a breach of copyright.

You can, of course, sell your books, in the form in which you have bought them – once you have finished with them. (Is this fair to your fellow students? We update for a reason.) Please note the e-products are sold on a single user licence basis: we do not supply 'unlock' codes to people who have bought them secondhand.

And what about outside the UK? BPP Learning Media strives to make our materials available at prices students can afford by local printing arrangements, pricing policies and partnerships which are clearly listed on our website. A tiny minority ignore this and indulge in criminal activity by illegally photocopying our material or supporting organisations that do. If they act illegally and unethically in one area, can you really trust them?

NO AI TRAINING. Unless otherwise agreed in writing, the use of BPP material for the purpose of AI training is not permitted. Any use of this material to "train" generative artificial intelligence (AI) technologies is prohibited, as is providing archived or cached data sets containing such material to another person or entity.

Copyright © IFRS Foundation

All rights reserved. Reproduction and use rights are strictly limited. No part of this publication may be translated, reprinted or reproduced or utilised in any form either in whole or in part by any electronic, mechanical or other means, now known or hereafter invented, including photocopying and recording, or in any information storage and retrieval system, without prior permission in writing from the IFRS Foundation. Contact the IFRS Foundation for further details.

The Foundation has trade marks registered around the world (Trade Marks) including 'IAS®', 'IASB®', 'IFRIC®', the IFRS® logo, 'IFRS for SMEs®', IFRS for SMEs® logo, the 'Hexagon Device', 'International Financial Reporting Standards®', NIIF® and 'SIC®'.

Further details of the Foundation's Trade Marks are available from the Licensor on request.

Contents

Page

Introduction

> The introductory pages contain lots of valuable advice and information. They include tips on studying for and passing the exam, also the content of the syllabus and what has been examined.

How the BPP Learning Media Learning & Practice Workbook can help you pass – Help yourself study for your AIA exams – Syllabus – Command words and learning outcomes – The exam paper

Part A Financial accounting
1 Introduction to accounting 3
2 The regulatory framework 15
3 Accounting conventions 25

Part B Accounting records and procedures
4 Sources, records and books of prime entry 49
5 Ledger accounts and double entry 63
6 From trial balance to financial statements 93
7 Value added tax 109
8 Accruals and prepayments 119
9 Bank reconciliations 133
10 Control accounts 145
11 Correction of errors 167
12 Incomplete records 179

Part C Practical application of accounting theory
13 Inventory 211
14 Irrecoverable debts and allowances 237
15 Provisions and contingencies 253
16 Tangible non-current assets 263
17 Intangible non-current assets 299

Part D Financial reporting, analysis and interpretation
18 Business entity 311
19 Preparation of financial statements for sole traders 341
20 Preparation of financial statements under IAS 1 353
21 Accounting ratios 371
22 Statements of cash flows 397

Practice exam question bank 417
Practice exam answer bank 459
Exam question bank 495
Exam answer bank 521
Mock exam 1 555
Mock exam 2 569
Bibliography 583
Index 587

How the BPP Learning Media Learning & Practice Workbook can help you pass

> It provides you with the knowledge and understanding, skills and application techniques that you need to be successful in your exams

This Learning & Practice Workbook has been targeted at the **Financial Accounting** syllabus.

- It is **comprehensive**. It covers the syllabus content. No more, no less.
- It is written at the **right level**. Each Chapter is written with AIA's syllabus in mind.
- It is aimed at the **exam**. We have taken account of recent exams, guidance the examiner has given and the assessment methodology.

> It allows you to study in the way that best suits your learning style and the time you have available, by following your personal Study Plan (see page vii)

You may be studying at home on your own or you may be attending a course. You may like to read every word, or you may prefer to do a fast read through and learn through doing practice questions the rest of the time. However you study, you will find the BPP Learning Media Learning & Practice Workbook meets your needs in designing and following your personal Study Plan.

Help yourself study for your AIA exams

Exams for professional bodies such as AIA are very different from those you have taken at college or university. You will be under **greater time pressure before** the exam – as you may be combining your study with work. Here are some hints and tips.

The right approach

1   **Develop the right attitude**

Believe in yourself	Yes, there is a lot to learn. But thousands have succeeded before and you can too.
Remember why you're doing it	You are studying for a good reason: to advance your career.

2   **Focus on the exam**

Read through the Syllabus	This tells you what you are expected to know and is supplemented by **Exam focus points** in the text.
Study the Exam paper section	Past papers are likely to be good guides to what you should expect in the exam.

3   **The right method**

See the whole picture	Keeping in mind how all the detail you need to know fits into the whole picture will help you understand it better. • The **Introduction** of each Chapter puts the material in context. • The **Syllabus content** and **Exam focus points** show you what you need to **grasp**.
Use your own words	To absorb the information (and to practise your written communication skills), you need to **put it into your own words**. • **Take notes**. • Answer the **questions** in each Chapter. • Draw **mind maps**. • Try '**teaching**' **a subject** to a colleague or friend.
Give yourself cues to jog your memory	The Learning & Practice Workbook uses **bold** to **highlight key points**. • Try **colour coding** with a highlighter pen. • Write **key points** on cards.

4   **The right recap**

Review, review, review	Regularly reviewing a topic in summary form can **fix it in your memory**. The Learning & Practice Workbook helps you review in many ways. • **Chapter roundups** summarise the 'Fast forward' key points in each Chapter. Use them to recap each study session. • The **Quick quiz** actively tests your grasp of the essentials. • Go through the **Examples** in each Chapter a second or third time.

INTRODUCTION

Developing your personal Study Plan

BPP recommends that you follow a study plan. Planning and sticking to the plan are key elements of learning successfully.

Step 1   **How do you learn?**

What types of intelligence do you display when learning? You might be advised to brush up on certain study skills before launching into this Learning & Practice Workbook but refer to the 'tackling your studies' section below which will help.

Step 2   **What do you prefer to do first?**

If you prefer to get to grips with a theory before seeing how it is applied, we suggest you concentrate first on the explanations we give in each Chapter before looking at the examples and case studies. If you prefer to see first how things work in practice, read through the detail in each Chapter, and concentrate on the examples and case studies, before supplementing your understanding by reading the detail.

Step 3   **How much time do you have?**

Work out the time you have available per week, given the following:

- The standard you have set yourself
- The other exam(s) you are sitting
- Practical matters such as work, travel, exercise, sleep and social life

		Hours
Note your time available in box A.	A	

Step 4   **Allocate your time**

- Take the time you have available per week for this Learning & Practice Workbook shown in box A, multiply it by the number of weeks available and insert the result in box B.   **B** [ ]

- Divide the figure in box B by the number of Chapters in this text and insert the result in box C.   **C** [ ]

Remember that this is only a rough guide. Some of the Chapters in this book are longer and more complicated than others, and you will find some subjects easier to understand than others.

Step 5   **Implement**

Set about studying each Chapter in the time shown in box C, following the key study steps in the order suggested by your particular learning style.

This is your personal **Study Plan**. You should try to combine it with the study sequence outlined below. You may want to modify the sequence to adapt it to your **personal style**.

Tackling your studies

The best way to approach this Learning & Practice Workbook is to tackle the chapters in order. Taking into account your individual learning style, you could follow this sequence for each chapter.

Key study steps	Activity
Step 1 **Topic list**	This topic list helps you navigate each chapter; each numbered topic is a numbered section in the chapter.
Step 2 **Introduction**	This sets your objectives for study by giving you the big picture in terms of the context of the chapter. The content is referenced to the syllabus, and Exam guidance shows how the topic is likely to be examined. The Introduction tells you **why** the topics covered in the chapter need to be studied.
Step 3 **Fast forward**	Fast forward boxes give you a quick summary of the content of each of the main chapter sections. They are listed together in the roundup at the end of each chapter to help you review each chapter quickly.
Step 4 **Explanations**	Proceed methodically through each chapter, particularly focusing on areas highlighted as significant in the chapter introduction, or areas that are frequently examined.
Step 5 **Key terms and Exam focus points**	• Key terms are definitions of important concepts that you really need to know and understand before the exam. • Exam focus points highlight areas or topics that may be examined.
Step 6 **Note taking**	Take brief notes, if you wish. Don't copy out too much. Remember that being able to record something yourself is a sign of being able to understand it. Your notes can be in whatever format you find most helpful; lists, diagrams, mind maps.
Step 7 **Examples**	Work through the examples very carefully as they illustrate key knowledge and techniques.
Step 8 **Case studies**	Study each one and try to add flesh to them from your own experience. They are designed to show how the topics you are studying come alive in the real world.
Step 9 **Questions**	Attempt each one, as they will illustrate how well you've understood what you've read.
Step 10 **Answers**	Check yours against ours, and make sure you understand any discrepancies.
Step 11 **Chapter roundup**	Review it carefully, to make sure you have grasped the significance of all the important points in the chapter.
Step 12 **Quick quiz**	Use the Quick quiz to check how much you have remembered of the topics covered and to practise questions in a variety of formats.
Step 13 **Question practice**	Attempt the multiple choice questions contained in the question bank at the end of this Learning & Practice Workbook.

AIA Achieve Academy

AIA provides an interactive course of study AIA Achieve Academy, which offers students the tools, resources and learning environment to study for the exams. The study tools include a course of study e-book, marked practice questions, marked mock exam paper and feedback and technical advice via an e-Tutor. Contact the Study Support team at: Achieve@aiaworldwide.com

Moving on...

When you are ready to start revising, you should still refer back to this Learning & Practice Workbook.

- As a source of **reference** (you should find the index particularly helpful for this)
- As a way to review (the Fast forwards, Exam focus points, Chapter roundups and Quick quizzes help you here)

PQ Qualification Syllabus

The assessment requirements in the AIA exams at the Foundation, Professional 1 and 2 stages reflect a progression of cognitive levels which successful students are expected to demonstrate in satisfying each stage of the qualification. The levels progress from an emphasis on 'knowledge and comprehension' at the Foundation stage, to a predominance of 'application and analysis' at the subsequent Professional 1 and 2 stages and incorporate 'synthesis and evaluation' at the Professional 2 stage.

Indicative weightings for the cognitive levels at each stage of the qualification are defined in the following table.

Stage of qualification	Cognitive levels of learning*			Associated learning outcomes
	Knowledge and comprehension	Application and Analysis	Synthesis and evaluation	
Foundation Level	90%	10%	0%	Outcomes consistent with the International Education Standards Board (IAESB) standards
Professional 1 Level	50%	50%	0%	
Professional 2 Level	10%	70%	20%	

*The cognitive levels of learning are associated with the following:

'Knowledge and comprehension' refer to

The acquisition of concepts, ideas, terms, facts, practices and techniques in accounting and related disciplines and understanding of how they relate to the conduct, management, reporting and assessment of the activities of business and other organisations.

'Application and analysis' refer to

The ability to apply knowledge and comprehension to actual circumstances and situations and to identify constituent components involved (concepts, ideas, terms, facts, practices, and techniques) and the relationship between these elements.

'Synthesis and evaluation' refer to

The ability to bring together a variety of components in order to form a coherent whole, and to form judgements about the application of and value of those components in a particular context or for a particular purpose. learning outcomes.

Foundation Level Syllabus

The Foundation level examination is intended to establish that students have attained the necessary knowledge of accounting in its economic context and relevant skills to be permitted to commence study for the first Professional stage examinations of the Association. It does so by assessing students in four foundational areas of knowledge and understanding relevant for prospective professional accountants; offered within the Foundation Unit:

In designing the syllabus and the related examination papers AIA has employed 'intended learning outcomes' as the means to communicate expectations to potential students and stakeholders and to inform the specification requirements to be tested in the assessment of students.

The use of learning outcomes:

- Is consistent with what is commonly acknowledged as good practice in the higher education sector; and
- Is consistent with the approach embodied in International Accounting Education Standards

At the Foundation Levels students are expected to demonstrate that they are able to achieve the following:

Intended Learning Outcomes[1] – Description of expectations	
Foundation level	At the Foundation level students are expected to demonstrate that they: ▪ Understand basic principles and concepts underpinning accounting and related practices in organisations ▪ Understand the role of accounting and related practices within the financial and governance context of organisations ▪ Know and can execute basic recording and measurement techniques relevant to accounting, management and assurance ▪ Are able to analyse financial information and interpret it for the purpose of supporting decision making

Foundation level syllabus components

The Foundation Unit is made up of four components:

- Section A: Financial Accounting
- Section B: Corporate Governance and Audit
- Section C: Management Accounting
- Section D: Business Management

---

[1] The description of the levels of proficiency supports the IAESBs use of learning outcomes in its International Education Standards (IESs) 2, 3, and 4.

Relationship to Qualification Structure

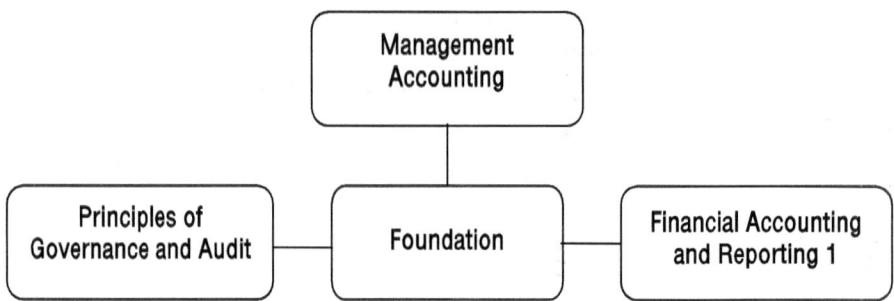

Demonstrating that the learning outcomes associated with the Foundation syllabus have been met is a requirement for all students before they are permitted to proceed to Professional level studies.

Students able to demonstrate they have met the learning outcomes based on prior study and educational qualification can be granted exemption from the Foundation Examination. For those students unable to do so, passing the Foundation Examination is a core requirement to Professional levels studies.

Aims

The aim of a Foundation Level paper is to develop and examine the candidate's knowledge and understanding of:

1. The theory of accounting and its application to the practical situations indicated in the syllabus
2. The fundamental elements of corporate governance and audit and the inter-relationship between these areas
3. The fundamentals of management and cost accounting and their application in cost ascertainment, the control of operations, and the provision of information to assist management decision-making and policy formulation
4. Business management and the role of the manager in modern business organisations

Foundation Level learning outcomes

In order to successfully complete this paper, candidates will demonstrate that they are able to:

FINANCIAL ACCOUNTING

1. Explain and identify accounting concepts and the regulatory purpose of accounting standards and sustainability standards
2. Describe, prepare and summarise basic accounting records
3. Identify accounting concepts in presenting financial statements for sole traders and limited companies
4. Describe and explain the financial position and performance of an organisation

CORPORATE GOVERNANCE AND AUDIT

5. Identify and explain the purpose of corporate governance and auditing
6. Explain the inter-relationship between corporate governance and auditing
7. Relate the contribution of corporate governance and auditing to the safeguarding of capital markets

INTRODUCTION

MANAGEMENT ACCOUNTING

8. Explain the role of management and cost accounting within an organisation

9. Describe the nature of costs and how and why they are classified in different ways for different purposes

10. Calculate material, labour, expense and overhead costs for products, processes, services and functions

11. Identify and discuss appropriate principles and techniques to advise managers on short-term and long-run decision-making

BUSINESS MANAGEMENT

12. Describe the major schools of management thought, their development and their implications

13. Explain the key aspects of organisational structure and design

14. Identify the nature and importance of managerial control, including the main elements and types of control in the business organisation and the role and importance of management information in the control process

15. Describe the use of information technology in modern business management

This Learning & Practice Workbook covers **Section A: Financial Accounting.**

Detailed learning outcomes for Section A: Financial Accounting

A1 ACCOUNTING THEORY AND THE ROLE OF ACCOUNTING STANDARDS (LEARNING OUTCOME1)

Topic weighting 10%

- The conceptual basis of financial accounting, including:
- The objective of financial reporting
- The qualitative characteristics of useful financial information
- The definition, recognition and measurement of the elements from which financial statements are constructed
- The function of financial accounts and management accounts
- The role of financial reporting standards and sustainability standards and standard setting bodies including IASB and ISSB

A2 ACCOUNTING RECORDS AND PROCEDURES (LEARNING OUTCOME 2)

Topic weighting 25%

- The accounting equation
- Double entry bookkeeping
- The accounting cycle
- The trial balance
- Control accounts
- Approach to incomplete records

A3   PRACTICAL APPLICATION OF ACCOUNTING THEORY (LEARNING OUTCOMES 1,2)

Topic weighting 25%

Valuation of current assets

Valuation of non-current assets, including depreciation and impairment:

- tangible non-current assets
- intangible non-current assets
- disposal and depreciation - methods of calculation and accounting

A4   FINANCIAL REPORTING BY LIMITED COMPANIES AND SOLE TRADERS (LEARNING OUTCOME 3)

Topic weighting 25%

- The distinction between a sole trader and a limited company
- An outline of the basic features of limited companies
- The presentation of financial statements for sole trader and limited company
- Statement of profit or loss and other comprehensive income (income and expenditure accounts)
- Statement of financial position (balance sheet)
- Statement of cash flows

A5   USE OF RATIOS IN ANALYSIS OF FINANCIAL STATEMENTS (LEARNING OUTCOME 4)

Topic weighting 15%

The calculation and interpretation of ratios for:

- Profitability - ratios such as return on capital employed
- Cash flow and liquidity – ratios such as the current ratio
- Capital structure – ratios such as the gearing ratio

Note: In examination, the following three titles will be assigned the meanings shown:

The title 'statement of profit or loss and other comprehensive income' will refer to the single statement format by IAS1 as revised in June 2011.

The title 'statement of profit or loss' will refer to that part of the 'statement of profit or loss and other comprehensive income' which excludes other comprehensive income, ie it refers to that part from revenue (or sales or turnover) down to profit or loss for the year.

The title 'other comprehensive income' refers to that part of 'the statement of profit or loss and other comprehensive income' which excludes the calculation of profit for the year.

Structure of the Foundation Level exam

Assessment is by a three-hour 15 minute examination (including 15 minutes of reading time) consisting of 100 questions. There are 25 objective test style questions in the form of multiple-choice questions covering each component area of the syllabus. All questions are compulsory.

The assessment covers the learning outcomes for each of the four component areas of study in the foundation syllabus.

The coverage of questions will reflect the weighting of different areas of syllabus content as specified in the Foundation examination syllabus, but the format of questions associated with each area of study may vary between sittings of the examination.

Relationship to overall AIA syllabus

An accountant in practice and in business needs an understanding of the nature, importance and issues in effective business management. Not only are all accountants by definition managers, but they also have to have a wider appreciation and understanding of how their function and activities relate to other parts of the business. The implications of effective business management are important aspects of the contemporary accountant's function. A professionally qualified accountant must understand the nature of business management in a contemporary business organisation and an awareness of how this understanding can contribute to overall efficiency and effectiveness.

Foundation Level Financial Accounting therefore seeks to ensure that the professional accountant has this necessary understanding and can use this to increase their effectiveness in organisations as accountants.

Ethics

Candidates are advised that the standards outlined in The Code of Ethics for Professional Accountants issued by the International Ethics Standards Board for Accountants (IESBA Code) are implicit in, and examinable throughout, the AIA syllabus. The Code can be accessed via the AIA website at www.aiaworldwide.com.

Recommended reading

This reading list is recommended and not essential for your studies.

You can purchase any of the books listed quickly and easily on the AIA website www.aiaworldwide.com/books

AIA Magazine – International Accountant
ISSN   1465 5144

AIA Learning and Practice Workbooks
Foundation Unit
Publisher: BPP Learning Media

Financial Accounting (16th Edition 2024)
Business Accounting Volume 1
Author: Wood, F and Sangster, A
Publisher: Pearson Education Limited
ISBN: 9781035525874

Free website providing comprehensive information about IFRS: www.iasplus.com

PART A

Financial accounting

Introduction to accounting

Topic list	Syllabus reference
1 The objectives of financial reporting	A1
2 Types of business entity	A1
3 Nature, principles and scope of financial reporting	A1
4 Users' and stakeholders' needs	A1
5 The main elements of financial reports	A1

Introduction

We will begin by looking at the aim of Foundation Level Financial Accounting, as laid out in AIA's syllabus and discussed already in the introductory pages to this text (if you haven't read through the introductory pages, do so now – the information in there is extremely important).

Aim of Foundation Level Financial Accounting

To examine the candidate's knowledge and understanding of the theory of accounting and its application to the practical situations indicated in the syllabus.'

Before you learn **how** to prepare financial reports, it is important to understand **why** they are prepared. Sections 1 to 3 of this chapter introduce some basic ideas about financial reports and give an indication of their purpose. You will also be introduced to the **functions** which accountants carry out: financial accounting and management accounting. These functions will be developed in detail in your later studies for the AIA qualification.

Section 4 identifies the main **users** of financial statements and their **needs**.

Finally, in Section 5, we will look at the **main financial statements: the statement of financial position** and the **statement of profit or loss and other comprehensive income**; as well as the main elements of assets, liabilities, equity, revenue and expense.

PART A FINANCIAL ACCOUNTING

Exam focus point

Students need to study the full breadth of the syllabus.

1 The objectives of financial reporting

1.1 What is financial reporting?

FAST FORWARD

Financial reporting is a way of recording, analysing and summarising financial data.

Financial data is the name given to the actual transactions carried out by a business eg sales of goods, purchases of goods, payment of expenses.

These transactions are **recorded** in **books of prime entry** (which we will study in detail in Chapter 4).

The transactions are **analysed** in the books of prime entry and the totals are posted to the ledger accounts (see Chapter 5).

Finally, the transactions are **summarised** in the financial statements, which we will meet in Section 5 of this chapter (and will study in detail in Chapter 6).

Question — Financial reporting

Financial reporting means the financial statements produced only by a large, quoted company.

Is this statement correct?

A   Yes
B   No

Answer

The correct answer is B. Financial reporting is carried out by all businesses, no matter what their size or structure.

2 Types of business entity

2.1 What is a business?

FAST FORWARD

Businesses of whatever size or nature exist to make a **profit**.

There are a number of different ways of looking at a business. Some ideas are listed below.

- A business is a commercial or industrial concern which exists to deal in the manufacture, re-sale or supply of goods and services.
- A business is an organisation which uses economic resources to create goods or services which customers will buy.
- A business is an organisation providing jobs for people.
- A business invests money in resources (for example: buildings, machinery, employees) in order to make even more money for its owners.

1: INTRODUCTION TO ACCOUNTING

This last definition introduces the important idea of profit. Businesses vary from very small businesses (the local shopkeeper or plumber) to very large ones (Tesco, IKEA and Tata Steel). However, all of them want to earn profits.

Key term

> **Profit** is the excess of revenue (income) over expenditure. When expenditure exceeds revenue, the business is running at a loss.

One of the jobs of an accountant is to measure revenue and expenditure, and so profit. It is not such a straightforward problem as it may seem and in later chapters we will look at some of the theoretical and practical difficulties involved.

2.2 Types of business entity

There are three main types of business entity:

- Sole traders
- Partnerships
- Limited liability companies

Sole traders are people who work for themselves. Examples include the local shopkeeper, a plumber and a hairdresser. The term sole trader refers to the **ownership** of the business; sole traders can have employees.

Partnerships occur when **two or more** people decide to run a business together. Examples include an accountancy practice, a medical practice and a legal practice.

Limited liability companies are incorporated to take advantage of 'limited liability' for their owners (shareholders). This means that, while sole traders and partners are **personally responsible** for the amounts owed by their businesses, the shareholders of a limited liability company are only responsible for the **amount to be paid for their shares**. Limited liability companies are dealt with in more detail in Chapter 18.

In law sole traders and partnerships are not separate entities from their owners. However, a limited liability company is legally a separate entity from its owners and it can issue contracts in the company's name.

For **accounting purposes**, all three entities are treated as separate from their owners. This is called the **business entity concept**. We will see the practical consequence in Chapter 5.

2.3 Advantages of trading as a limited liability company

(a) **Limited** liability makes investment less risky than investing in a sole trader or partnership. However, lenders to a small company may ask for a shareholder's personal guarantee to secure any loans.

(b) It is easier to raise finance because of limited liability and there is no limit on the number of shareholders.

(c) A limited liability company has a separate legal identity from its shareholders. So a company continues to exist regardless of the identity of its owners. In contrast, a partnership ceases, and a new one starts, whenever a partner joins or leaves the partnership.

(d) There are tax advantages to being a limited liability company. The company is taxed as a separate entity from its owners and the tax rate on companies may be lower than the tax rate for individuals.

(e) It is relatively easy to transfer shares from one owner to another. In contrast, it may be difficult to find someone to buy a sole trader's business or to buy a share in a partnership.

2.4 Disadvantages of trading as a limited liability company

(a) Limited liability companies have to **publish annual financial statements**. This means that anyone (including competitors) can see how well (or badly) they are doing. In contrast, sole traders and partnerships do not have to publish their financial statements.

(b) Limited liability company financial statements have to comply with **legal and accounting requirements**. In particular the financial statements have to comply with accounting standards. Sole traders and partnerships may comply with accounting standards, but are not compelled to do so.

(c) The financial statements of larger limited liability companies have to be **audited**. This means that the statements are subject to an independent review to ensure that they comply with legal requirements and accounting standards. This can be inconvenient, time consuming and expensive.

(d) **Share issues** are regulated by law. For example, it is difficult to reduce share capital. Sole traders and partnership can increase or decrease capital as and when the owners wish.

3 Nature, principles and scope of financial reporting

> **FAST FORWARD**
>
> You should be able to distinguish between the following:
> - Financial accounting
> - Management accounting

You may have a wide understanding of what accounting and financial reporting is about. Your job may be in one area or type of accounting, but you must understand the breadth of work which an accountant undertakes.

3.1 Financial accounting

So far in this chapter we have dealt with **financial** accounts. Financial accounting is mainly a method of reporting the results and financial position of a business. It is not primarily concerned with providing information towards the more efficient running of the business. Although financial accounts are of interest to management, their principal function is to satisfy the information needs of persons not involved in running the business. They provide **historical** information.

3.2 Management accounting

The information needs of management go far beyond those of other accounts users. Managers have the responsibility of planning and controlling the resources of the business. Therefore they need much more detailed information. They also need to **plan for the future** (eg budgets, which predict future revenue and expenditure).

Key term

> **Management (or cost) accounting** is a management information system which analyses data to provide information as a basis for managerial action. The concern of a management accountant is to present accounting information in the form most helpful to management.

You need to understand this distinction between management accounting and financial accounting.

 Question — Accountants

They say that America is run by lawyers and Britain is run by accountants, but what do accountants do in your organisation or country? Before moving on to the next section, think of any accountants you know and the kind of jobs they do.

4 Users' and stakeholders' needs

4.1 The need for financial statements

FAST FORWARD

> There are **various groups of people** who need information about the activities of a business.

Why do businesses need to produce financial statements? If a business is being run efficiently, why should it have to go through all the bother of accounting procedures in order to produce financial information?

The International Accounting Standards Board (IASB) states in its document *The Conceptual Framework for Financial Reporting* (which we will examine in detail later in this Workbook):

Key term

> 'The objective of general purpose financial reporting is to provide **financial information** about the **reporting entity** that is useful to existing and potential investors, lenders and other creditors in making decisions about **providing resources to the entity**. Those decisions involve:
>
> (a) buying, selling or holding equity and debt instruments;
>
> (b) providing or settling loans and other forms of credit;
>
> (c) exercising rights to vote on, or otherwise influence, management's actions that affect the use of the entity's economic resources'
>
> *(Conceptual Framework:* para. 1.2)

In other words, a business should produce information about its activities because there are various groups of people who want or need to know that information. This sounds rather vague: to make it clearer, we will study the classes of people who need information about a business. We also need to think about what information in particular is of interest to the members of each class.

Large businesses are of interest to a greater variety of people and so we will consider the case of a large public company, whose shares can be purchased and sold on a stock exchange.

4.2 Users of financial statements and accounting information

The following people are likely to be interested in financial information about a large company with listed shares:

(a) **Managers of the company** appointed by the company's owners to supervise the day-to-day activities of the company. They need information about the company's financial situation as it is currently and as it is expected to be in the future. This is to enable them to manage the business efficiently and to make effective decisions.

(b) **Shareholders of the company**, ie the company's owners, want to assess how well management is performing. They want to know how profitable the company's operations are and how much profit they can afford to withdraw from the business for their own use.

(c) **Trade contacts** include suppliers who provide goods to the company on credit and customers who purchase the goods or services provided by the company. **Suppliers** want to know about the company's ability to pay its debts; **customers** need to know that the company is a secure source of supply and is in no danger of having to close down.

(d) **Providers of finance to the company** might include a bank which allows the company to operate an overdraft, or provides longer-term finance by granting a loan. The bank wants to ensure that the company is able to keep up interest payments, and eventually to repay the amounts advanced.

PART A FINANCIAL ACCOUNTING

(e) **The taxation authorities** want to know about business profits in order to assess the tax payable by the company, including sales taxes.

(f) **Employees of the company** should have a right to information about the company's financial situation, because their future careers and the size of their wages and salaries depend on it.

(g) **Financial analysts and advisers** need information for their clients or audience. For example, stockbrokers need information to advise investors; credit agencies want information to advise potential suppliers of goods to the company; and journalists need information for their reading public.

(h) **Governments and their agencies** are interested in the allocation of resources and therefore in the activities of business entities. They also require information in order to provide a basis for national statistics.

(i) **The public**. Entities affect members of the public in a variety of ways. For example, they may make a substantial contribution to a local economy by providing employment and using local suppliers. Another important factor is the effect of an entity on the environment, for example as regards pollution.

Accounting information is summarised in financial statements to satisfy the **information needs** of these different groups. Not all will be equally satisfied.

4.3 Needs of different users

Managers of a business need the most information, to help them make their planning and control decisions. They obviously have 'special' access to information about the business, because they are able to demand whatever internally produced statements they require. When managers want a large amount of information about the costs and profitability of individual products, or different parts of their business, they can obtain it through a system of cost and management accounting.

Question — Information for managers

Which of the following reports is particularly useful for managers?

A   Financial statements for the last financial year
B   Tax records for the past five years
C   Budgets for the coming financial year
D   Bank statements for the past year

Answer

The correct answer is C. Managers need to look forward and make plans to keep the business profitable. Therefore the most useful information for them would be the budgets for the coming financial year.

In addition to management information, financial statements are prepared (and perhaps published) for the benefit of other user groups, which may demand certain information.

(a) The **national laws** of a country may provide for the provision of some accounting information for shareholders and the public.

(b) **National taxation** authorities will receive the information they need to make tax assessments.

(c) A **bank** might demand a forecast of a company's expected future cash flows as a pre-condition of granting an overdraft.

1: INTRODUCTION TO ACCOUNTING

(d) The **International Accounting Standards Board (IASB)** has been responsible for issuing **International Financial Reporting Standards (IFRSs and IASs)** and these require companies to publish certain additional information. Accountants, as members of professional bodies, are placed under a strong obligation to ensure that company financial statements conform to the requirements of IFRS/IAS or local generally accepted accounting principles (GAAP).

(e) Some companies provide, voluntarily, specially prepared financial information for issue to their employees. These statements are known as '**employee reports**'.

Exam focus point

The needs of users can easily be examined as part of a scenario question. For example, you could be given a list of types of information and asked which user group would be most interested in this information.

5 The main elements of financial reports

FAST FORWARD

The principal financial statements of a business are the **statement of financial position** and the **statement of profit or loss and other comprehensive income**

5.1 Statement of financial position

Key term

The **statement of financial position** is simply a **list** of all the **assets owned** and all the **liabilities owed** by a business as at a particular date. It is a snapshot of the financial position of the business at a particular moment. Monetary amounts are attributed to each of the assets and liabilities.

5.1.1 Assets

Key term

An **asset** is something valuable which a business owns or has the use of.

The *Conceptual Framework* gives the more formal definition: 'An asset is a present economic resource controlled by the entity as a result of past events'. (*Conceptual Framework:* para. 4.1)

Examples of assets are factories, office buildings, warehouses, delivery vans, lorries, plant and machinery, computer equipment, office furniture, cash and goods held in store awaiting sale to customers.

Some assets are held and used in operations for a long time. An office building is occupied by administrative staff for years; similarly, a machine has a productive life of many years before it wears out.

Other assets are held for only a short time. The owner of a newsagent shop, for example, has to sell his newspapers on the same day that he gets them. The more quickly a business can sell the goods it has in store, the more profit it is likely to make; provided, of course, that the goods are sold at a higher price than what it cost the business to acquire them.

5.1.2 Liabilities

Key term

A **liability** is something which is owed to somebody else. 'Liabilities' is the accounting term for the debts of a business.

The *Conceptual Framework* gives the more formal definition: 'A liability is a present obligation of the entity to transfer an economic resource as a result of past events'. (*Conceptual Framework:* para. 4.26)

Examples of liabilities are amounts owed to a supplier for goods bought on credit, amounts owed to a bank (or other lender) for a loan, a bank overdraft and amounts owed to tax authorities (eg in respect of sales tax).

Some liabilities are due to be repaid fairly quickly eg suppliers. Other liabilities may take some years to repay (eg a bank loan).

5.1.3 Capital or equity

The amounts invested in a business by the owner are amounts that the business owes to the owner. This is a special kind of liability, called **capital**. In a limited liability company, capital usually takes form of shares. Share capital is also known as **equity**.

Equity is the residual interest in the assets of the entity after deducting all its liabilities (*Conceptual Framework:* para. 4.63). This will be considered further in Chapter 3.

5.1.4 Form of statement of financial position

A statement of financial position used to be called a balance sheet. The former name is apt because assets will always be equal to liabilities plus capital (or equity). A very simple statement of financial position for a sole trader is shown below.

A TRADER
STATEMENT OF FINANCIAL POSITION AS AT 30 APRIL 20X7

	$	$
Assets		
Plant and machinery		55,000
Inventories	5,000	
Trade receivables (from customers)	1,500	
Cash and cash equivalents	500	
		7,000
Total assets		62,000
Capital		
Retained earnings brought forward		25,000
Profit for the year		10,400
Retained earnings carried forward		35,400
Liabilities		
Bank loan		25,000
Trade and other payables (to suppliers)		1,600
Total capital plus liabilities		62,000

We will be looking at the statement of financial position in a lot more detail later in this Workbook. This example is given simply to illustrate what a statement of financial position looks like.

5.2 Statement of profit or loss and other comprehensive income

Key term

> A **statement of profit or loss and other comprehensive income** is a **record of revenue generated** and **expenditure incurred** over a given period. The statement shows whether the business has had more revenue than expenditure (a profit) or vice versa (a loss).

5.2.1 Revenue and expenses

Revenue is a component of an entity's income for a period. Income is increases in assets or decreases in liabilities that result in increases in equity, other than those relating to contributions from holders of equity claims (*Conceptual Framework:* para. 4.68).

The **expenses** are the costs of running the business for the same period. Expenses are decreases in assets or increases in liabilities that result in decreases in equity, other than those relating to distributions to holders of equity claims (*Conceptual Framework:* para. 4.69). These definitions are complicated at this stage and will be explained further as we progress through this Workbook.

5.2.2 Form of statement of profit or loss and other comprehensive income

The period chosen will depend on the purpose for which the statement is produced. The statement of profit or loss and other comprehensive income which forms part of the published annual financial statements of a **limited liability company** will usually be for the period of a **year**, commencing from the date of the previous year's statements. On the other hand, **management** might want to keep a closer eye on a company's profitability by making up **quarterly or monthly** statements.

A simple statement of profit or loss and other comprehensive income for a sole trader is shown below.

A TRADER
STATEMENT OF PROFIT OR LOSS FOR THE YEAR ENDED
30 APRIL 20X7

	$
Revenue	150,000
Cost of sales	75,000
Gross profit	75,000
Other expenses	64,600
Net profit	10,400

Once again, this example is given purely for illustrative purposes. We will be dealing with the statement of profit or loss and other comprehensive income in detail later in this Workbook.

> **Exam focus point**
>
> The AIA Exam Scheme and Reading List states the following:
>
> In an exam the following three titles will be assigned the meanings shown:
>
> - The title 'statement of profit or loss and other comprehensive income' will refer to the single statement format by IAS 1 as revised in June 2011.
>
> - The title 'statement of profit or loss' will refer to that part of the 'statement of profit or loss and other comprehensive income' which excludes other comprehensive income; ie it refers to that part from Revenue (or sales or turnover) down to profit or loss for the year.
>
> - The title 'other comprehensive income' refers to that part of the 'statement of profit or loss and other comprehensive income' which excludes the calculation of profit for the year.

5.3 Purpose of financial statements

Both the statement of financial position and the statement of profit or loss and other comprehensive income are **summaries of accumulated data**. For example, the statement of profit or loss and other comprehensive income shows a figure for revenue earned from selling goods to customers. This is the total amount of revenue earned from all the individual sales made during the period. One of the jobs of an accountant is to devise methods of recording such individual transactions, so as to produce summarised financial statements from them.

The statement of financial position and the statement of profit or loss and other comprehensive income form the basis of the financial statements of most businesses. For limited liability companies, other information by way of statements and notes may be required by national legislation and/or accounting standards, for example a **statement of cash flows** and a **statement of changes in equity**. These are considered in detail later in this Workbook.

PART A   FINANCIAL ACCOUNTING

Question — Accounting information

The financial statements of a limited liability company will consist solely of the statement of financial position and statement of profit or loss and other comprehensive income.

Is this statement correct?

A   True
B   False

Answer

The correct answer is B. As shown above, other statements, such as a statement of cash flows, and other notes, are usually needed.

Chapter roundup

- **Financial reporting** is a way of recording, analysing and summarising financial data.
- Businesses of whatever size or nature exist to make a **profit**.
- You should be able to distinguish between the following:
  - Financial accounting
  - Management accounting
- There are **various groups of people** who need information about the activities of a business.
- The principal financial statements of a business are the **statement of financial position** (balance sheet) and the **statement of profit or loss and other comprehensive income** (income and expenditure account).

Quick quiz

1. What is financial reporting?

2. A business entity is owned and run by Alpha, Beta and Gamma.

   What type of business is this an example of?

   A Sole trader
   B Partnership
   C Limited liability company
   D Don't know

3. Identify seven user groups who need accounting information.

4. What are the two main financial statements drawn up by accountants?

5. Which of the following is an example of a liability?

   A Inventories
   B Trade receivables
   C Plant and machinery
   D Loan

PART A FINANCIAL ACCOUNTING

Answers to quick quiz

1. A way of recording, analysing and summarising financial data.
2. B A partnership, as it is owned and run by three people.
3. See Section 4.2.
4. The statement of profit or loss and other comprehensive income and the statement of financial position.
5. D A loan. The rest are all assets.

The regulatory framework

Topic list	Syllabus reference
1 The regulatory system	A1
2 The International Accounting Standards Board (IASB)	A1
3 IFRS Accounting Standards	A1
4 The International Sustainability Standards Board (ISSB)	A1

Introduction

In this chapter, we introduce the regulatory system run by the International Accounting Standards Board (IASB). We are concerned with the **IASB's relationship with other bodies**, and with the way the IASB operates.

The newly formed International Sustainability Standards Board is also discussed.

You must try to understand and appreciate the contents of this chapter. The examiner is not only interested in whether you can add up; she wants to know whether you can think about a subject which, after all, is your future career.

PART A   FINANCIAL ACCOUNTING

1 The regulatory system

FAST FORWARD   A number of factors have shaped the **development** of financial accounting.

1.1 Introduction

Although new to the subject, you may know from seeing business news and reports that there have been some considerable upheavals in financial reporting, mainly in response to criticism. The **details** of the regulatory framework of accounting, and the technical aspects of the changes made, will be covered later in this chapter and in your more advanced studies. The purpose of this section is to give a **general picture** of some of the factors which have shaped financial accounting. We will concentrate on the accounts of limited liability companies, as these are the accounts most closely regulated by statute (law) or otherwise.

The following factors can be identified.

- National/local legislation
- Accounting concepts and individual judgement
- Accounting standards
- Other international influences (covered in Section 3)
- Generally accepted accounting principles (GAAP)
- Fair presentation

1.2 National/local legislation

Limited liability companies may be required by law to prepare and publish accounts annually. The form and content of the accounts may be regulated primarily by national legislation, but must also comply with International Financial Reporting Standards (IFRSs) and International Accounting Standards (IASs).

1.3 Accounting concepts and individual judgement

FAST FORWARD   Many figures in financial statements are derived from the **application of judgement** in applying fundamental accounting assumptions and conventions. This can lead to subjectivity.

Financial statements are prepared on the basis of a number of **fundamental accounting assumptions and conventions**. Many figures in financial statements are derived from the application of judgement in putting these assumptions into practice.

It is clear that different people exercising their judgement on the same facts can arrive at very different conclusions.

Case Study

An accountancy training firm has an excellent **reputation** amongst students and employers. How would you value this? The firm may have relatively little in the form of assets that you can touch, perhaps a building, desks and chairs. If you simply drew up a statement of financial position showing the cost of the assets owned, then the business would not seem to be worth much, yet its income earning potential might be high. This is true of many service organisations where the people are among the most valuable assets.

Other examples of areas where the judgement of different people may vary are as follows:

(a) Valuation of buildings in times of rising property prices.

(b) Research and development: is it right to treat this only as an expense? In a sense it is an investment to generate future revenue.

(c) Accounting for inflation.

(d) Brands such as 'Mars' or 'iPad™'. Are they assets in the same way that a fork lift truck is an asset?

Working from the same data, different groups of people produce very different financial statements. If the exercise of judgement is completely unfettered, there will be no comparability between the accounts of different organisations. This will be all the more significant in cases where deliberate manipulation occurs, in order to present accounts in the most favourable light.

1.4 Accounting standards

In an attempt to deal with some of the subjectivity, and to achieve comparability between different organisations, **accounting standards** were developed. These are developed at both a national level (in most countries) and an international level. In this text we are concerned with **International Financial Reporting Standards (IFRS Accounting Standards)**.

1.4.1 IFRS Accounting Standards and the IASB

IFRS Accounting Standards are produced by the **International Accounting Standards Board (IASB)**. The IASB develops IFRS Accounting Standards through an international process that involves the world-wide accountancy profession, the preparers and users of financial statements, and national standard-setting bodies. Prior to 2003, standards were issued as International Accounting Standards (IASs). In 2003 International Financial Reporting Standard (IFRS) 1 was issued and all new standards are now designated as IFRSs. Throughout this Workbook, we will use IFRS Accounting Standards to include **both** IFRSs **and** IASs.

In the UK the consolidated accounts of listed companies have had to be produced in accordance with IFRS Accounting Standards from January 2005.

1.4.2 IFRS Advisory Council

The IFRS Advisory Council assists the IASB in standard setting. It has 50 members (as of November 2018) drawn from organisations all over the world, such as national standard-setting bodies, accountancy firms, the IMF and the World Bank.

The IFRS Advisory Council meets at least two times a year and puts forward the views of its members on current standard-setting projects, helping to identify issues that need addressing and to prioritise the work of the IASB.

1.4.3 IFRS Interpretations Committee

The IFRS Interpretations Committee issues guidance in cases where unsatisfactory or conflicting interpretations of accounting standards have developed. It also addresses newly emerging issues which are not yet covered by IFRS Accounting Standards. In these situations, IFRS Interpretations Committee works closely with similar national committees with a view to reaching consensus on the most appropriate accounting treatment.

1.4.4 The IFRS Foundation

The IFRS Foundation is an independent, not-for-profit body that oversees the IASB.

The objectives of the IFRS Foundation are:

(a) Through the IASB and ISSB (International Sustainability Standards Board), to develop, in the public interest, high-quality, understandable, enforceable and globally accepted standards (referred to as IFRS Standards) for general purpose financial reporting based on clearly articulated principles. The IASB is responsible for developing a set of accounting standards (IFRS Accounting Standards) and the ISSB is responsible for developing a set of sustainability disclosure standards (IFRS Sustainability Disclosure Standards). These complementary sets of IFRS Standards are intended to result in the provision of high-quality, transparent and comparable information in financial statements and in sustainability disclosures that is useful to investors and other participants in the world's capital markets in making economic decisions.

(b) To promote the use and rigorous application of IFRS standards.

(c) In fulfilling the objectives associated with (a) and (b), to take account of, as appropriate, the needs of a range of sizes and types of entities in diverse economic settings.

(d) To promote and facilitate the adoption of IFRS Standards through the convergence of national and regional accounting standards and IFRS Standards.

The overall structure of the IFRS Foundation and its bodies is shown below.

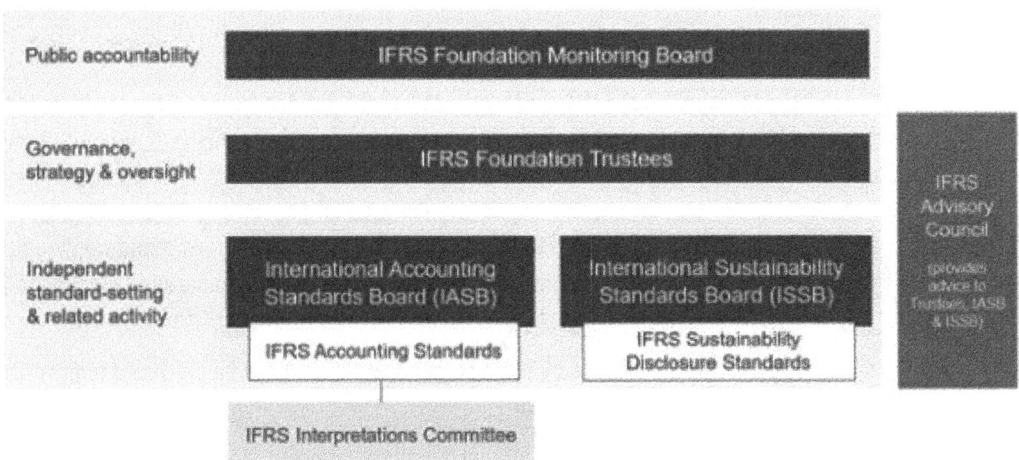

(www.ifrs.org)

Exam focus point

The examiners often comment that this area 'is not given adequate attention'. The examiners also regard this area to be an important part of the syllabus.

1.4.5 The use and application of IFRS Accounting Standards

IFRS Accounting Standards have helped to both improve and harmonise financial reporting around the world. The standards are used in the following ways:

(a) As **national requirements**, often after a national process
(b) As the **basis** for all or some **national requirements**
(c) As an **international benchmark** for those countries which develop their own requirements
(d) By **regulatory authorities** for domestic and foreign companies
(e) **By companies** themselves

1.5 Generally accepted accounting principles (GAAP)

We also need to consider some important terms which you will meet in your financial accounting studies. GAAP, as a term, has sprung up in recent years and signifies all the rules, from whatever source, which govern accounting.

Key term

> **GAAP** is a set of rules governing accounting. The rules may derive from:
> - Local (national) company legislation
> - National and international accounting standards
> - Statutory requirements in other countries (particularly the USA)
> - Stock exchange requirements

1.6 Faithful representation

FAST FORWARD

> Financial statements are required to give a **faithful representation** of the financial position of the organisation or **present fairly in all material respects** the financial results of the entity. These terms are not defined and tend to be decided in courts of law on the facts.

It is a requirement of both national legislation (in some countries) and International Standards on Auditing that the financial statements should be a **faithful representation** of the financial position and performance of the entity as at the end of the financial year.

1.6.1 Faithful representation (or 'true and fair override')

A company's managers may depart from any of the provisions of accounting standards if these are inconsistent with the requirement to give a faithful representation of the financial performance, financial position and cash flows of the organisation. This is commonly referred to as the 'true and fair override' (see Chapter 3).

2 The International Accounting Standards Board (IASB)

FAST FORWARD

> The main objectives of the IASB are to raise the standard of financial reporting and to eventually bring about global harmonisation of accounting standards.

2.1 International harmonisation

The IASB is an **independent private sector body**. Its objective is to achieve **uniformity** in the accounting principles which are used by businesses and other organisations for financial reporting around the world. This is known as **international harmonisation**.

2.2 Current position of the IASB

The IASB's predecessor body, the IASC, had issued 41 International Accounting Standards (IASs) and in 2001 the IASB adopted all of these standards and now issues its own International Financial Reporting Standards (IFRSs). In addition there is *The Conceptual Framework for Financial Reporting*, which is discussed in Chapter 3. A substantial number of multinational companies prepare financial statements in accordance with IFRS. IFRS are also endorsed by many countries as their own standards, either unchanged or with minor amendments.

Since 1 January 2005 listed companies in the EU have been required to prepare consolidated accounts in accordance with IFRS.

3 IFRS Accounting Standards

> **FAST FORWARD** The IASB has an established process for setting IFRSs.

3.1 Standard setting process

The due process in developing an accounting standard is as follows:

Agenda Consultation

The IASB develops a new project work plan every five years after comprehensive review and consultation. The work plan can be updated between agenda consultations if required.

Research programme

The first stage of most projects is research to determine with standard-setting is required. A discussion paper is sometimes issued for public comment.

If a post-implementation review of an issued standard has raised any issues, this might also be an area for research.

Standard-setting programme

If research indicates that a new or amended standards is required, the process for this is:

1. Exposure draft of proposed changes issued for public consultation
2. IASB / IFRSIC review exposure draft responses
3. New/updated IFRS Accounting Standard / IFRIC Interpretation issued

Maintenance programme

The IASB monitor application of all issued standards and if there are any issues with implementation or application of a standard then an IFRIC Interpretation or IFRS Accounting Standard narrow-scope amendment might be recommended.

(www.ifrs.org)

3.2 Interpretation of IFRSs – IFRS Interpretations Committee

The IASB has developed a procedure for issuing interpretations of its standards. In 2001 the IFRS Interpretations Committee was set up.

The IFRS Interpretations Committee considers accounting issues that are likely to receive divergent or unacceptable treatment in the absence of authoritative guidance. Its review will be within the context of existing IFRS Accounting Standards and the IASB's *Conceptual Framework*.

The IFRS Interpretations Committee will deal with issues of reasonably widespread importance, and not issues of concern to only a small set of entities. The interpretations will cover both:

(a) **Mature issues** (unsatisfactory practice within the scope of existing standards); and

(b) **Emerging issues** (new topics relating to an existing standard but not actually considered when the standard was developed).

In developing interpretations, the 14-person IFRS Interpretations Committee will work closely with similar national committees. If it reaches consensus on an interpretation the Committee will ask the Board to approve the interpretation for issue. Interpretations are formally published after approval by the Board.

3.3 Accounting standards and choice

It is sometimes argued that companies should be given a **choice** in matters of financial reporting on the grounds that accounting standards are detrimental to the quality of such reporting. There are arguments on both sides.

In favour of accounting standards (both national and international), the following points can be made:

(a) They **reduce or eliminate** confusing **variations** in the methods used to prepare accounts, increasing comparability.

(b) They provide a **focal point** for debate and discussions about accounting practice.

(c) They oblige companies to **disclose** the accounting policies used in the preparation of accounts.

(d) They are a **less rigid alternative** to enforcing conformity by means of **legislation**.

(e) They have obliged companies to **disclose more accounting information** than they would otherwise have done if accounting standards did not exist, for example IAS 33 *Earnings per Share*.

Many companies are reluctant to disclose information which is not required by national legislation. However, the following arguments may be put forward against standardisation and in **favour of choice**:

(a) A **set of rules** which give backing to one method of preparing accounts **might be inappropriate** in some circumstances.

(b) Standards may be **subject to lobbying** or government pressure (in the case of national standards). For example, in the USA, the accounting standard FAS 19 on the accounts of oil and gas companies led to a powerful lobby of oil companies, which persuaded the SEC (Securities and Exchange Commission) to step in. FAS 19 was then suspended.

(c) Many national standards are **not based on a *Conceptual Framework*** of accounting, although IFRSs are (see Chapter 3).

(d) There may a **trend towards rigidity**, and away from flexibility in applying the rules.

4 The International Sustainability Standards Board (ISSB)

> **FAST FORWARD**
>
> The newly formed ISSB issues IFRS Sustainability Disclosure Standards.

4.1 Sustainability reporting landscape

Sustainability is a concept with the aim of improving people's lives and safeguarding the plant for future generations. The scope of sustainability is large and includes environmental, social and governance (ESG) issues such as biodiversity loss, deterioration of air quality, human rights etc.

Company stakeholders are increasingly more aware of sustainability matters and there has been growing interest/pressure on businesses to consider sustainability matters when taking strategic decisions or considering business risks and opportunities.

A number of different reporting frameworks and standards have been created over the years. This has led to some confusion for businesses and stakeholders. To address this, the IFRS Foundation established the ISSB.

4.2 Creation of the ISSB

The ISSB was established by the IFRS Foundation in 2021 in response to investors' demand for high-quality, transparent, reliable and comparable reporting on climate and other ESG issues.

It has four key objectives:

- To develop standards for a global baseline of sustainability disclosures;
- To meet the information needs of investors;
- To enable companies to provide comprehensive sustainability information to global capital markets; and
- To facilitate interoperability with disclosures that are jurisdiction-specific and/or aimed at broader stakeholder groups.

The ISSB builds on the work of existing market-led investor-focussed reporting initiatives and works closely with other sustainability standard setters, such as the Global Reporting Initiative, which are based at a wider stakeholder group.

4.3 IFRS Sustainability Disclosure Standards

The ISSB publishes IFRS Sustainability Disclosure Standards. The first two standards were issued in June 2023:

- IFRS S1 *General Requirements for Disclosure of Sustainability-related Financial Information*
    - sets out core content areas for a complete set of sustainability-related financial disclosures – governance, strategy, risk management and metrics and targets
    - requires companies to consider and to report on sustainability-related risks and opportunities
    - sets out conceptual foundations
- IFRS *S2 Climate-related Disclosures*
    - First subject-specific standard
    - Climate-related risks and opportunities
    - Reporting of metrics such as greenhouse gas emissions

The ISSB works closely with the IASB, ensuring connections between IFRS Accounting Standards and IFRS Sustainability Disclosure Standards. However, IFRS Sustainability Disclosure Standards can be used by companies following other financial reporting frameworks, such as national GAAP.

Chapter roundup

- A number of factors have shaped the **development** of financial accounting.
- Many figures in financial statements are derived from the **application of judgement** in applying fundamental accounting assumptions and conventions. This can lead to subjectivity.
- Financial statements are required to give a **fair presentation** or **present fairly in all material respects** the financial results of the entity. These terms are not defined and tend to be decided in courts of law on the facts.
- The main objectives of the IASB are to raise the standard of financial reporting and to eventually bring about global harmonisation of accounting standards.
- The IASB has an established process for setting IFRS Accounting Standards.
- The ISSB was set up in 2021 to harmonise the sustainability disclosure reporting framework. The ISSB issues IFRS Sustainability Disclosure Standards.

Quick quiz

1. What are the objectives of the IASB?

    A   To enforce IFRS Accounting Standards
    B   To issue IFRS Accounting Standards

2. Which committee at the IASB aids users' interpretation of IFRS Accounting Standards?

3. Which of the following arguments is not in favour of accounting standards, but is in favour of accounting choice?

    A   They reduce variations in methods used to produce accounts
    B   They oblige companies to disclose their accounting policies
    C   They are a less rigid alternative to legislation
    D   They may tend towards rigidity in applying the rules

4. At which stage of the IFRS Accounting Standards development process can the public first be asked for their initial comments and feedback on proposed changes?

5. The IASB is responsible for the standard-setting process. True or false?

PART A FINANCIAL ACCOUNTING

Answers to quick quiz

1 B The IASB has no powers of enforcement.
2 The IFRS Interpretations Committee.
3 D The other arguments are all in favour of accounting standards.
4 Discussion paper (Exposure Draft is the second stage).
5 True. The IASB is responsible for the standard-setting process.

Accounting conventions

Topic list	Syllabus reference
1 *Conceptual Framework* and GAAP	A1
2 The IASB's *Conceptual Framework*	A1
3 The objective of general purpose financial reporting	A1
4 Qualitative characteristics of useful financial information	A1
5 Financial statements and the reporting entity	A1
6 The elements of financial statements	A1
7 Recognition and derecognition	A1
8 Measurement	A1
9 Presentation and disclosure	A1
10 Capital and capital maintenance	A1

Introduction

The purpose of this chapter is to encourage you to think more deeply about the **assumptions** on which financial statements are prepared.

This chapter deals with the accounting conventions which lie behind accounts preparation and which you will meet in Chapters 5 to 12.

In Chapters 13 to 17, you will see how conventions and assumptions are **put into practice**. You will also deal with certain items which are the subject of accounting standards.

This chapter deals with an important guidance document: the *Conceptual Framework*. Do not neglect these sections as they contain **very important** basic ideas which underpin accounting.

PART A FINANCIAL ACCOUNTING

Exam focus point

Always **read the question carefully** before answering. Make sure that you understand the requirement and have picked out the main points of the question. Remember that you will not score any points if you do not answer the question set, so always **check your answer** before moving on.

1 *Conceptual Framework* and GAAP

FAST FORWARD

There are advantages and disadvantages to having a *Conceptual Framework*.

1.1 The search for a *Conceptual Framework*

A *Conceptual Framework*, in the field we are concerned with, is a statement of generally accepted theoretical principles which form the frame of reference for financial reporting.

These theoretical principles provide the basis for the development of new accounting standards and the evaluation of those already in existence. The financial reporting process is concerned with providing information that is useful in the business and economic decision-making process. Therefore a *Conceptual Framework* will form the **theoretical basis** for determining which events should be accounted for, how they should be measured and how they should be communicated to the user. Although it is theoretical in nature, a *Conceptual Framework* for financial reporting has highly practical final aims.

The **danger of not having a *Conceptual Framework*** is demonstrated in the way some countries' standards have developed over recent years; standards tend to be produced in a haphazard and fire-fighting approach. Where an agreed framework exists, the standard-setting body act as an architect or designer, rather than a fire-fighter, building accounting rules on the foundation of sound, agreed basic principles.

The lack of a *Conceptual Framework* also means that fundamental principles are tackled more than once in different standards, thereby producing **contradictions and inconsistencies** in basic concepts, such as matching. This leads to ambiguity and it affects the true and fair concept of financial reporting.

Another problem with the lack of a *Conceptual Framework* has become apparent in the USA. The large number of **highly detailed standards** produced by the Financial Accounting Standards Board (FASB) has created a financial reporting environment governed by specific rules rather than general principles. This would be avoided if a cohesive set of principles were in place.

A *Conceptual Framework* can also bolster standard setters **against political pressure** from various 'lobby groups' and interested parties. Such pressure would only prevail if it was acceptable under the *Conceptual Framework*.

1.2 Advantages and disadvantages of a *Conceptual Framework*

Advantages

(a) The situation is avoided whereby standards are developed on a patchwork basis, where a particular accounting problem is recognised as having emerged, and resources are then channelled into **standardising accounting practice** in that area, without regard to whether that particular issue was necessarily the most important issue remaining at that time without standardisation.

(b) As stated above, the development of certain standards (particularly national standards) have been subject to considerable **political interference** from interested parties. Where there is a conflict of interest between user groups on which policies to choose, policies deriving from a *Conceptual Framework* will be **less open to criticism** that the standard-setter buckled to external pressure.

(c) Overall a *Conceptual Framework* facilitates the development of consistent and complementary standards.

Disadvantages

(a) Financial statements are intended for a **variety of users**, and it is not certain that a single *Conceptual Framework* can be devised which will suit all users.

(b) Given the diversity of user requirements, there may be a need for a variety of accounting standards, each produced for a **different purpose** (and with different concepts as a basis).

(c) It is not clear that a *Conceptual Framework* makes the task of **preparing and then implementing** standards any easier than without a framework.

Before we look at the IASB's *Conceptual Framework* in detail, we need to consider another term of importance to this debate: generally accepted accounting principles; or GAAP.

1.3 Generally accepted accounting principles (GAAP)

GAAP signifies all the rules, from whatever source, which govern accounting.

In individual countries this is seen primarily as a **combination** of:

- National company law
- National accounting standards
- Local stock exchange requirements

Although those sources are the basis for the GAAP of individual countries, the concept also includes the effects of **non-mandatory sources** such as:

- International accounting standards
- Statutory requirements in other countries

In many countries, like the UK, GAAP does not have any statutory or regulatory authority or definition, unlike other countries, such as the USA. The term is mentioned rarely in legislation, and only then in fairly limited terms.

2 The IASB's *Conceptual Framework*

> **FAST FORWARD**
>
> The IASB produced its revised *Conceptual Framework for Financial Reporting* (*Conceptual Framework*) in 2018.

We will look briefly at the introduction to the *Conceptual Framework* as this will place the document in context with the rest of what you will be studying for this paper and in particular the context of the *Conceptual Framework* in the IASB's approach to developing IFRS Accounting Standards.

As you read through this chapter think about the impact it has had on standards, particularly the definitions.

2.1 Purpose and scope

The purpose of the *Conceptual Framework* is to:

(a) assist the International Accounting Standards Board (Board) to develop IFRS Standards (Standards) that are based on consistent concepts;

(b) assist preparers to develop consistent accounting policies when no Standard applies to a particular transaction or other event, or when a Standard allows a choice of accounting policy; and

(c) assist all parties to understand and interpret the Standards.

(Conceptual Framework: para. SP1)

The *Conceptual Framework* is not Standard and so does not overrule any individual IFRS Accounting Standard. In the (rare) case of conflict between an IFRS Accounting Standard and the *Conceptual Framework*, the **IFRS Accounting Standard will prevail**.

2.1.1 Scope

The *Conceptual Framework* is divided into eight chapters:

1. The objective of general purpose financial reporting
2. Qualitative characteristics of useful financial information
3. Financial statements and the reporting entity
4. The elements of financial statements
5. Recognition and derecognition
6. Measurement
7. Presentation and disclosure
8. Concepts of capital and capital maintenance

We will cover the relevant points from each of the chapters in the following sections.

(*Conceptual Framework*: para. OB2)

3 The objective of general purpose financial reporting

FAST FORWARD

> The *Conceptual Framework* states that 'The objective of general purpose financial reporting is to provide financial information about the reporting entity that is useful to existing and potential **investors, lenders and other creditors** in making **decisions relating to providing resources** to the entity.
>
> Those decisions involve decisions about:
>
> (a) buying, selling or holding equity and debt instruments;
> (b) providing or settling loans and other forms of credit; or
> (c) exercising rights to vote on, or otherwise influence, management's actions that affect the use of the entity's economic resources.'
>
> (*Conceptual Framework*: para. 1.2)

Existing and potential investors, lenders and other creditors are referred to as the '**primary users**' of financial statements (para. 1.5). Primary users may make decisions about buying, selling or holding shares or debt instruments or providing or settling loans (para 1.2).

To make these decisions, the primary users need information about:

(a) the **economic resources of the entity**; **claims against the entity**; and changes in the entity's **economic resources and claims**; and

(b) how efficiently and effectively the entity's management and governing board have discharged their responsibilities to use the entity's economic resources.

(*Conceptual Framework*: para. 1.4)

Information about the entity's **economic resources and the claims against it** helps users to assess the entity's liquidity and solvency and its likely needs for additional financing. Information about a reporting entity's financial performance (the **changes in its economic resources and claims**) helps users to understand the return that the entity has produced on its economic resources. This is an indicator of how efficiently and effectively management has used the resources of the entity and is helpful in predicting future returns.

Question: Users of financial information

Consider the information needs of the users of financial information identified in the *Conceptual Framework*.

Answer

(a) **Investors** are the providers of risk capital.

    (i) Information is required to help make a decision about buying or selling shares, taking up a rights issue and voting.

    (ii) Investors must have information about the level of dividend, past, present and future and any changes in share price.

    (iii) Investors will also need to know whether the management has been running the company efficiently.

    (iv) As well as the position indicated by the statement of profit or loss and other comprehensive income, statement of financial position and earnings per share (EPS), investors will want to know about the liquidity position of the company, the company's future prospects, and how the company's shares compare with those of its competitors.

(b) **Lenders** need information to help them decide whether to lend to a company. They will also need to check that the value of any security remains adequate, that the interest repayments are secure, that the cash is available for redemption at the appropriate time and that any financial restrictions (such as maximum debt/equity ratios) have not been breached.

(c) **Other creditors** such as suppliers need to know whether the company will be a reliable customer and pay its debts on time.

3.1 Accrual accounting

The *Conceptual Framework* makes it clear that accrual accounting should be applied when preparing financial information. Accrual accounting requires transactions and events to be recorded in the period they are entered into rather than when the cash is settled. A more formal definition is provided by the *Conceptual Framework*.

Key term

> **Accruals accounting.** Accrual accounting depicts the effects of transactions and other events and circumstances on a reporting entity's economic resources and claims in the periods in which those effects occur, even if the resulting cash receipts and payments occur in a different period.
>
> (*Conceptual Framework:* para. 1.17)

Accrual accounting is also known as the matching concept.

Applying accrual accounting provides better information about a reporting entity's economic resources and claims and changes in those resources and claims during a period than information solely about cash receipts and payments during that period.

Information about a reporting entity's financial performance during a period helps users to assess the entity's **ability to generate future net cash inflows** and gives users a better understanding of its operations.

3.2 Example: Accrual accounting

Emma prints 20 T-shirts in her first month of trading (May) at a cost of $5 each. She then sells all of them for $10 each. Emma has therefore made a profit of $100, by matching the revenue ($200) earned against the cost ($100) of acquiring them.

If, however, Emma only sells 18 T-shirts, it is incorrect to charge her statement of profit or loss and other comprehensive income with the cost of 20 T-shirts, as she still has 2 T-shirts in inventory. If she sells them in June, she is likely to make a profit on the sale. Therefore, only the purchase cost of 18 T-shirts ($90) should be matched with her sales revenue ($180), leaving her with a profit of $90.

Her statement of financial position will look like this (if no cash has changed hands):

	$
Assets	
Inventory (at cost, ie 2 × $5)	10
Accounts receivable (18 × $10)	180
	190
Capital and liabilities	
Proprietor's capital (profit for the period)	90
Accounts payable (20 × $5)	100
	190

However, if Emma had decided to cease trading, then the going concern assumption (see Section 4.1) no longer applies and the value of the 2 T-shirts in the statement of financial position is break-up valuation not cost. Similarly, if the two unsold T-shirts are unlikely to be sold at more than their cost of $5 each (say, because of damage or a fall in demand) then they should be recorded on the statement of financial position at their net realisable value (ie the likely eventual sales price less any expenses incurred to make them saleable) rather than cost.

4 Qualitative characteristics of useful financial information

FAST FORWARD

> The *Conceptual Framework* states that qualitative characteristics are the attributes that make financial information useful to users.

Information is useful if it is relevant and faithfully represents what it purports to represent. The *Conceptual Framework* therefore identifies **relevance** and **faithful representation** as the **fundamental** qualitative characteristics.

It also identifies the following enhancing qualitative characteristics which make information more useful when they are maximised:

- Comparability
- Verifiability
- Timeliness
- Understandability

4.1 Relevance

Key term

> **Relevance**. Relevant financial information is capable of making a difference in the decisions made by users. Information may be capable of making a difference in a decision even if some users choose not to take advantage of it or are already aware of it. Financial information is capable of making a difference in decisions if it has **predictive value**, **confirmatory value** or both.
>
> (*Conceptual Framework:* para. 2.6–2.7)

The relevance of information is affected by its **materiality**.

> **Key term**
>
> **Materiality.** Information is material if omitting, misstating or obscuring it could reasonably be expected to influence decisions that the users of general purpose financial statements make on the basis of those financial statements.
>
> *(Conceptual Framework: para. QC11)*

In assessing whether or not an item is material, it is not only the value of the transaction or item which needs to be considered. The **context** is also important, in other words transactions or items can be material by nature or by value.

(a) If a statement of financial position shows non-current assets of $2m and inventories of $30,000, an error of $20,000 in the depreciation calculations might not be regarded as material. Whereas an error of $20,000 in the inventory valuation is material. In other words, the specific balance of which the error forms part must be considered.

(b) If a business has a bank loan of $50,000 and a $55,000 balance on its bank deposit account, it will be a material misstatement if these two amounts are displayed on the statement of financial position as 'cash at bank $5,000'. In other words, incorrect presentation may amount to material misstatement even if there is no monetary error.

Question — Materiality

Would you treat the following items as assets in the accounts of a company?

(a) A box file
(b) A computer
(c) A small plastic display stand

Answer

(a) No. You would write it off to the statement of profit or loss and other comprehensive income as an expense.

(b) Yes. You would capitalise the computer and charge depreciation on it.

(c) Your answer depends on the size of the company and whether writing off the item has a material effect on its profits. A larger organisation might well write this item off under the heading of advertising expenses, while a small one might capitalise it and depreciate it over time. This is because the item is material to the small company, but not to the large company.

4.2 Faithful representation

> **Key term**
>
> **Faithful representation.** Financial reports represent **economic phenomena** in words and numbers. To be useful, financial information must not only represent relevant phenomena but it must also **faithfully represent** the phenomena that it purports to represent.
>
> *(Conceptual Framework: para. 2.12)*

To be a perfectly faithful representation information must be **complete, neutral** and **free from error**.

A **complete** depiction includes all information necessary for a user to understand the phenomenon being depicted, including all necessary descriptions and explanations.

A **neutral** depiction is without bias in the selection or presentation of financial information. This means that information must not be manipulated in any way in order to influence the decisions of users. Neutrality is supported by the concept of **prudence**.

Free from error means there are no errors or omissions in the description of the phenomenon and no errors made in the process by which the financial information was produced. It does not mean that no inaccuracies can arise, particularly where estimates have to be made.

4.2.1 Substance over form

This is **not a separate qualitative characteristic** under the *Conceptual Framework*. Faithful representation of a transaction is only possible if it is accounted for according to its **substance and economic reality**.

4.2.2 Prudence

Prudence is exercising caution, particularly within areas where judgement or estimation is required. The exercise of prudence means that assets and income are not overstated and liabilities and expenses are not understated.

(*Conceptual Framework:* para. 2.16)

4.3 Enhancing qualitative characteristics

4.3.1 Comparability

Key term

> **Comparability.** Comparability is the qualitative characteristic that enables users to identify and understand similarities in, and differences among, items. Unlike the other qualitative characteristics, comparability does not relate to a single item. A comparison requires at least two items.
>
> (*Conceptual Framework:* para. 2.25)

Consistency, although related to comparability, **is not the same**. It refers to the use of the same methods for the same items (ie consistency of treatment) either from period to period within a reporting entity or in a single period across entities.

Comparability is **not the same as uniformity**. Entities should change accounting policies if existing policies become inappropriate.

4.3.2 Verifiability

Key term

> **Verifiability.** Verifiability helps assure users that information faithfully represents the economic phenomena it purports to represent. It means that different knowledgeable and independent observers could reach consensus that a particular depiction is a faithful representation.
>
> (*Conceptual Framework:* para. 2.30)

Information can be verified to a model or formula or by direct observation, such as undertaking an inventory count. Independent verification can be carried out, eg a valuation by a specialist.

4.3.3 Timeliness

Key term

> **Timeliness.** Timeliness means having information available to decision-makers in time to be capable of influencing their decisions. Generally, the older information is the less useful it is.
>
> (*Conceptual Framework:* para. 2.33)

Information may become less useful if there is a delay in reporting it. There is a **balance between timeliness and the provision of reliable information**.

If information is reported on a timely basis when not all aspects of the transaction are known, it may not be complete or free from error.

Conversely, if every detail of a transaction is known, it may be too late to publish the information because it has become irrelevant. The overriding consideration is how best to satisfy the economic decision-making needs of the users.

4.3.4 Understandability

Key term

> **Understandability.** Classifying, characterising and presenting information clearly and concisely makes it understandable. *(Conceptual Framework:* para. 2.34)

Financial reports are prepared for users who have a **reasonable knowledge of business and economic activities** and who review and analyse the information diligently. Some phenomena are inherently complex and cannot be made easy to understand. Excluding information on those phenomena might make the information easier to understand, but without it those reports would be incomplete and therefore potentially misleading. Therefore matters should not be left out of financial statements simply due to their difficulty as even well-informed and diligent users may sometimes need the aid of an adviser to understand information about complex economic phenomena.

4.3.5 The cost constraint on useful financial reporting

This is a **pervasive** constraint, not a qualitative characteristic. When information is provided, its benefits must exceed the costs of obtaining and presenting it. This is a **subjective area** and there are difficulties; others, not the intended users, may gain a benefit and the cost may be paid by someone other than the users. It is therefore difficult to apply a cost-benefit analysis, but preparers and users should be aware of the constraint.

5 Financial statements and the reporting entity

5.1 Financial statements

The objective of financial statements is to provide financial information about the reporting entity's assets, liabilities, equity, income and expenses that is useful to users of financial statements. That information is provided:

(a) In the statement of financial position, by recognising assets, liabilities and equity;
(b) In the statement(s) of financial performance,9 by recognising income and expenses; and
(c) In other statements and notes,

The primary financial statements will be discussed in more detail as we progress through this Workbook.

5.2 Going concern underlying assumption

FAST FORWARD

> **Going concern** is the underlying assumption in preparing financial statements.

Key term

> **Going concern.** The financial statements are normally prepared on the assumption that an entity is a going concern and will continue in operation for the foreseeable future. Hence, it is assumed that the entity has neither the intention nor the need to liquidate or curtail materially the scale of its operations.
>
> *(Conceptual Framework:* para. 4.1)

If an entity did have the intention to liquidate or curtail major operations, then the financial statements would be prepared on a **different (disclosed) basis**.

5.3 Example: Going concern

Emma acquires a T-shirt printing machine at a cost of $60,000. The asset has an estimated life of six years, and it is normal to write off the cost of the asset to the statement of profit or loss and other comprehensive income over this time. In this case, a depreciation cost of $10,000 per year is charged.

Using the going concern assumption, it is presumed that the business will continue its operations and so the asset will live out its full six years in use. A depreciation charge of $10,000 is made each year and the value of the asset in the statement of financial position is its cost less the accumulated depreciation charged to date. After one year, the **carrying amount** of the asset is $(60,000 – 10,000) = $50,000, after two years it is $40,000, after three years $30,000 etc, until it is written down to a value of $0 after six years.

This asset has no other operational use outside the business and, in a forced sale, it would only sell for scrap. After one year of operation, its scrap value is $8,000.

The carrying amount of the asset, applying the going concern assumption, is $50,000 after one year, but its immediate sell-off value is only $8,000. It can be argued that the asset is over-valued at $50,000, that it should be written down to its break-up value ($8,000) and the balance of its cost should be treated as an expense. However, provided that the going concern assumption is valid, it is appropriate accounting practice to value the asset at its carrying amount.

Question
Going concern

A retailer commences business on 1 January and buys inventory of 20 washing machines, each costing $100. During the year he sells 17 machines at $150 each. How should the remaining machines be valued at 31 December in the following circumstances?

(a) He is forced to close down his business at the end of the year and the remaining machines will realise only $60 each in a forced sale.

(b) He intends to continue his business into the next year.

Answer

(a) If the business is to be closed down, the remaining three machines must be valued at the amount they will realise in a forced sale, ie 3 × $60 = $180.

(b) If the business is regarded as a going concern, the inventory unsold at 31 December will be carried forward into the following year, when the cost of the three machines will be matched against the eventual sale proceeds in computing that year's profits. The three machines will therefore be valued at cost, 3 × $100 = $300.

6 The elements of financial statements

Transactions and other events are grouped together in broad **classes** and in this way their financial effects are shown in the financial statements. These broad classes are the **elements** of financial statements.

The *Conceptual Framework* lays out these elements as follows.

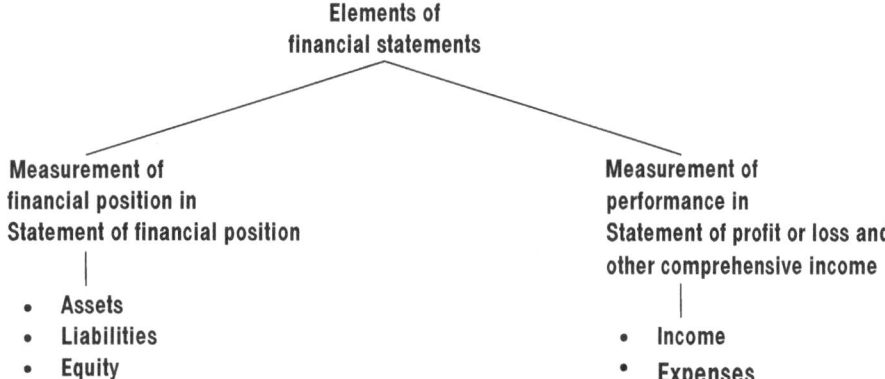

A process of **sub-classification** then takes place for presentation in the financial statements, eg assets are classified by their nature or function in the business to show information in the best way for users to take economic decisions.

6.1 Financial position

We need to define three terms:

Key terms

- **Asset**. A present economic resource controlled by the entity as a result of past events. An economic resource is a right that has the potential to produce economic benefits.
- **Liability**. A present obligation of the entity to transfer an economic resource as a result of past events (para. 4.2).
- **Equity**. The residual interest in the assets of the entity after deducting all its liabilities.

(*Conceptual Framework:* para. 4.2)

These definitions are important, but they do not cover the **criteria for recognition** of any of these items, which are discussed in the next section of this chapter. This means that the definitions may include items which would not actually be recognised in the statement of financial position because they fail to satisfy recognition criteria.

Whether an item satisfies any of the definitions above will depend on the **substance and economic reality** of the transaction, not merely its legal form.

6.2 Assets

We can look in more detail at the components of the definitions given above.

Key terms

Right. Some rights give rise to an obligation in another entity, such as the right to receive cash, other goods or services or other economic resources from another entity. Other rights, such as the right to physical assets or intellectual property, do not result in an obligation for the other entity.

Potential to produce economic benefits. For that potential to exist, it does not need to be certain, or even likely, that the right will produce economic benefit, it just needs to be able to produce those benefits.

> **Control.** An entity controls an economic resource if it has the present ability to direct the use of the economic resource and obtain the economic benefits that may flow from it. This may involve using the resource directly or preventing another entity from obtaining benefits from it.

6.3 Liabilities

Again we can look more closely at some aspects of the definition. An essential characteristic of a liability is that the entity has a **present obligation**.

Key term

> **Obligation.** An obligation is a duty or responsibility that an entity has no practical ability to avoid. An obligation is always owed to another party and involves the transfer of resources to that party. Obligations are established by contract or legislation and are legal enforceable.

It is important to distinguish between a present obligation and a **future commitment**. A management decision to purchase assets in the future does not, in itself, give rise to a present obligation.

Settlement of a present obligation will involve the entity giving up resources embodying economic benefits in order to satisfy the claim of the other party. This may be done in various ways, not just by payment of cash.

Liabilities must arise from **past transactions or events**. In the case of, say, recognition of future rebates to customers based on annual purchases, the sale of goods in the past is the transaction that gives rise to the liability.

6.4 Equity

Equity is defined above as a **residual**, but it may be sub-classified in the statement of financial position (eg into share capital and retained earnings, see Chapter 18). This will indicate legal or other restrictions on the ability of the entity to distribute or otherwise apply its equity. Some reserves are required by statute or other law, eg for the future protection of creditors. The amount shown for equity depends on the **measurement of assets and liabilities**. It has nothing to do with the market value of the entity's shares.

6.5 Performance

Profit is used as a **measure of performance**, or as a basis for other measures (eg earnings per share). It depends directly on the measurement of income and expenses, which in turn depend (in part) on the concepts of capital and capital maintenance adopted.

The elements of income and expense are therefore defined.

Key terms

> - **Income.** Increases in assets or decreases in liabilities that result in increases in equity, other than those relating to contributions from equity participants.
> - **Expenses.** Decreases in assets or increases in liabilities that result in decreases in equity, other than those relating to distributions to equity participants.
>
> *(Conceptual Framework:* para. 4.2)

Income and expenses can be **presented in different ways** in the statement of profit or loss and other comprehensive income, to provide information relevant for economic decision-making. For example, income and expenses which relate to continuing operations are distinguished from the results of discontinued operations.

6.6 Income

Both **revenue** and **gains** are included in the definition of income. **Revenue** arises in the course of ordinary activities of an entity eg sales.

Gains include those arising on the disposal of non-current assets. The definition of income also includes **unrealised gains**, eg on revaluation of marketable securities.

6.7 Expenses

As with income, the definition of expenses includes losses as well as those expenses that arise in the course of ordinary activities of an entity eg wages.

Losses will include those arising on the disposal of non-current assets. The definition of expenses will also include **unrealised losses**, eg the fall in value of an investment.

Exam focus point

Make sure you learn the important definitions.

- Financial position:
    - Assets
    - Liabilities
    - Equity
- Financial performance:
    - Income
    - Expenses

7 Recognition and derecognition

FAST FORWARD

Items which meet the definition of the elements may still not be recognised in financial statements because they must also meet certain **recognition criteria**.

Key terms

Recognition. The process of capturing for inclusion in the statement of financial position or the statement(s) of financial performance an item that meets the definition of one of the elements of financial statements. *(Conceptual Framework:* para. 5.1)

Derecognition. Derecognition normally occurs when the item no longer meets the definition of an element. *(Conceptual Framework:* para. 5.26)

Put simply, recognition means including an item in the financial statements, with a description in words and a number value. Recognising one element requires the recognition or derecognition of one or more other elements. The elements are connected as follows:

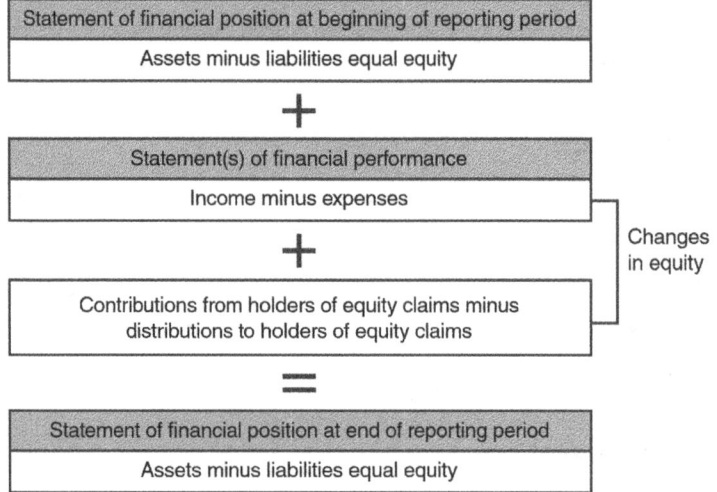

7.1 Recognition

The *Conceptual Framework* requires an item to be recognised in the financial statements if:

(a) The item meets the definition of an **element** (asset, liability, income, expense or equity); and

(b) Recognition of that element provides users of the financial statements with information that is **useful**, ie with:

- **Relevant** information about the element
- A **faithful representation** of the element

Relevance and faithful representation were covered in Section 4 above.

7.2 Derecognition

Derecognition normally occurs:

- For an asset – when control is lost (derecognise part of a recognised asset if control of that part is lost)

- For a liability – when there is no longer a present obligation

8 Measurement

> **FAST FORWARD**
>
> The *Conceptual Framework* considers two measurement bases:
> - Historical cost
> - Current value

Key terms

Historical cost. Measures that provide monetary information about assets, liabilities and related income and expenses, using information derived, at least in part, from the price of the transaction or other event that gave rise to them. *(Conceptual Framework* para. 6.4)

Current value. Current value measures provide monetary information about assets, liabilities and related income and expenses, using information updated to reflect conditions at the measurement date. *(Conceptual Framework* para. 6.10)

8.1 Historical cost

Historical cost is the most commonly adopted measurement basis. The use of historical cost means transactions and balances are recorded at the date of the original transaction which is not updated to reflect current prices. Historical cost is usually combined with other bases, eg inventory is carried at the lower of cost and net realisable value.

8.1.1 Advantages of historical cost

(a) Amounts used are objective, as it is more difficult to manipulate cost-based figures.

(b) Amounts are reliable, they can always be verified, they exist on invoices and documents.

(c) The statement of financial position and statement of cash flows figures are consistent with each other.

(d) There is less possibility for manipulation by using 'creative accounting' in asset valuation.

(e) Cost is a measure which is readily understood.

8.1.1 Disadvantages of historical cost

(a) Overstatement of profit – it shows current revenues less out of date costs. During periods where price inflation is low, profit overstatement will be marginal. The disadvantages of historical cost accounting become most apparent **in periods of inflation**.

(b) Out of date asset values – based on their historical values.

(c) Return on assets/capital employed is **distorted** by both (a) and (b).

(d) Holding gains/losses (ie the fact that something is worth more or costs more over time simply due to price rises) are not measured separately from operating results.

(e) Historical cost does not measure any gain/loss on monetary items arising from the impact of inflation (ie the fact that savers lose because the purchasing power of their savings is eroded, while borrowers gain because they still owe the same nominal amount while earnings have risen due to inflation).

(f) Historical cost gives a **misleading trend of results** since comparative figures are not restated for the effects of inflation.

8.2 Current value

Current value accounting attempts to address some of the problems of HCA by using information updated to reflect conditions at the measurement date. The *Conceptual Framework* recognises four current value measurement bases:

- Fair value
- Value in use for assets/fulfilment value for liabilities
- Current cost

8.2.1 Fair value

Key term

> **Fair value.** Fair value is the price that would be received to sell an asset, or paid to transfer a liability, in an orderly transaction between market participants at the measurement date.
>
> *(Conceptual Framework.* para. 6.12 and IFRS 13: Appendix A)

Fair value is measured in accordance with IFRS 13 *Fair Value Measurement* (the detail of which is outside the scope of thus syllabus)

Fair value is most commonly calculated by taking the open market value. Where there is no active market for the asset or liability, then the following should be used as a basis:

- Estimates of future cash flows
- Time value of money (discounting the future cash flows)

8.2.2 Value in use and fulfilment value

Key terms

> **Value in use.** Value in use is the present value of the cash flows, or other economic benefits, that an entity expects to derive from the use of an asset and from its ultimate disposal.
>
> **Fulfilment value.** Fulfilment value is the present value of the cash, or other economic resources, that an entity expects to be obliged to transfer as it fulfils a liability.
>
> *(Conceptual Framework: para. 6.17)*

Value in use looks at the likely future value to the entity of using the asset and fulfilment value considers the future payments to third parties.

Value in use and fulfilment value both consider entity-specific factors, whereas fair value is market specific.

8.2.3 Current cost

Key terms

> **Current cost of an asset.** The current cost of an asset is the cost of an equivalent asset at the measurement date, comprising the consideration that would be paid at the measurement date plus the transaction costs that would be incurred at that date. *(Conceptual Framework: para. 6.21)*
>
> **Current cost of a liability.** The current cost of a liability is the consideration that would be received for an equivalent liability at the measurement date minus the transaction costs that would be incurred at that date. *(Conceptual Framework: para. 6.21)*

Current cost differs from historical cost as current cost assesses the price to purchase at the reporting date, rather than the date the asset was acquired or liability assumed.

Where the current cost cannot be obtained from information in the market, then the entity can adjust for condition and age to buy a similar model.

8.2.4 Advantages of using current value

(a) Assets are valued after management has considered the expected benefits from their future use. Value in use is therefore a useful guide for management in deciding whether to hold or sell assets.

(b) It is relevant to the needs of information users in:

　　(i) Assessing the stability of the business entity

　　(ii) Assessing the vulnerability of the business (eg to a takeover), or the liquidity of the business

　　(iii) Evaluating the performance of management in maintaining and increasing the business substance

　　(iv) Judging future prospects

8.2.5 Limitations of using current value

(a) The discount factor used to calculate the present value of future cash flows requires subjective judgements by management. Also, the expected benefits from cash flows from the asset will be upon management's best estimates and judgements.

(b) There may be problems in deciding how to provide an estimate of current costs for non-current assets which can only be purchased new, such as a bespoke or specialist piece of machinery.

(c) As the *Conceptual Framework* allows different groups of assets and liabilities to be valued on different bases (which are the most useful to users of the financial statements), this can mean that some assets will be valued at current cost, but others will be valued at value in use or fair value.

9 Presentation and disclosure

A reporting entity communicates information about its assets, liabilities, equity, income and expenses by presenting and disclosing information in its financial statements (*Conceptual Framework:* para. 7.1).

The financial statements should **present fairly** the financial position, financial performance and cash flows of an entity. **Compliance with IFRS Accounting Standards** is presumed to result in financial statements that achieve a fair presentation.

The following points made by IAS 1 expand on this principle:

(a) **Compliance with IFRS Accounting Standards** should be disclosed

(b) **All relevant IFRS** Accounting Standards must be followed if compliance with IFRS is disclosed

(c) Use of an **inappropriate accounting treatment** cannot be rectified either by disclosure of accounting policies or notes/explanatory material

IAS 1 states what is required for a fair presentation.

(a) Selection and application of **accounting policies**

(b) **Presentation of information** in a manner which provides relevant, reliable, comparable and understandable information

(c) **Additional disclosures** where required

There may be (very rare) circumstances when management decides that compliance with a requirement of an IFRS would be misleading. **Departure from the IFRS Accounting Standards** is therefore required to achieve a fair presentation. The following should be disclosed in such an event:

(a) Management confirmation that the financial statements fairly present the entity's financial position, performance and cash flows

(b) Statement that all IFRS have been complied with *except* departure from one IFRS Accounting Standard to achieve a fair presentation

(c) The title of the Standard, details of the nature of the departure, why the IFRS Accounting Standard treatment would be misleading, and the treatment adopted

(d) Financial impact of the departure

This is usually referred to as the 'true and fair override'. IAS 1 is covered on more detail in Chapter 20 of this Workbook.

10 Capital and capital maintenance

There are two concepts of capital:

Key terms

> **Financial capital.** Refers to the monetary amount of net assets of an entity.
>
> **Physical capital.** Refers to the operating capacity of an entity.

10.1 Capital maintenance

Capital maintenance is concerned with whether a profit has been earned in the period. There are two concepts of capital maintenance:

- **Financial capital maintenance** – Under this concept a profit is earned only if the financial (or money) amount of the net assets at the end of the period exceeds the financial (or money) amount of net assets at the beginning of the period.

- **Physical capital maintenance** – Under this concept a profit is earned only if the physical productive capacity (or operating capability) of the entity (or the resources or funds needed to achieve that capacity) at the end of the period exceeds the physical productive capacity at the beginning of the period.

(Conceptual Framework: para. 8.3)

Chapter roundup

- There are advantages and disadvantages to having a *Conceptual Framework*.
- The *Conceptual Framework* was revised in 2018
- The *Conceptual Framework* states that:

    The objective of general purpose financial reporting1 is to provide financial information about the reporting entity that is useful to existing and potential **investors, lenders and other creditors** in making **decisions relating to providing resources** to the entity.' (*Conceptual Framework* para. 1.2)

- **Accrual accounting** should be applied when preparing financial statements.
- The *Conceptual Framework* states that two fundamental and four enhancing qualitative characteristics are the attributes that make financial information useful to users.

    Fundamental – relevance and faithful representation
    Enhancing – comparability, verifiability, timeliness and understandability

- Transactions and other events are grouped together in broad **classes** and in this way their financial effects are shown in the financial statements. These broad classes are the **elements** of financial statements. The financial position elements are **assets, liabilities and equity**. The performance elements are **income** and **expenses**.
- Items which meet the definition of assets or liabilities may still not be recognised in financial statements because they must also meet certain **recognition criteria**.
- Two different measurement bases are noted in the *Conceptual Framework*. They are:
    - **Historical cost**
    - **Current value**
- Current value can either be:
    - **Fair value**
    - **Value in use/fulfilment value**
    - **Current cost**
- There are two concepts of capital and capital maintenance
    - Financial – monetary amount of net assets
    - Physical – operating capacity

PART A   FINANCIAL ACCOUNTING

Quick Quiz

1. Define a '*Conceptual Framework*'.
2. What are the advantages and disadvantages of developing a *Conceptual Framework*?
3. Which parties are identified as the primary users of financial statements?
4. Define 'relevance'.
5. In which two ways should users be able to compare an entity's financial statements?
6. A right only exists where there is an obligation on behalf of another entity. True or false?
7. Define 'recognition'.
8. The cost or value of items in the financial statements is never estimated. True or false?
9. What is the most common basis of measurement used in financial statements?

Answers to quick quiz

1   This is a statement of generally accepted theoretical principles, which form the frame of reference for financial reporting.

2   *Advantages*
    - Standardised accounting practice
    - Less open to criticism/pressure

    Disadvantages
    - Variety of users, so not all will be satisfied
    - Variety of standards for different purposes
    - Preparing and implementing standards not necessarily any easier

3   Investors, creditors and other lenders are the primary users of financial statements

4   Information has relevance if it is capable of influencing the decisions of the users of financial statements.

5   - Through time to identify trends
    - With other entities' statements

6   False. A right to use physical assets such as property, plant and equipment or to use intellectual property does not give rise to an obligation of another entity. The right to, for example, receive case does result in an obligation of another entity.

7   Recognition is the process of capturing for inclusion in the statement of financial position or the statement(s) of financial performance an item that meets the definition of one of the elements of financial statements

8   False. Current values, such as fair value or value in use can involve judgements and estimates.

9   Historical cost continues to be the most widely used measurement basis.

PART A FINANCIAL ACCOUNTING

PART B

Accounting records and procedures

Sources, records and books of prime entry

Topic list	Syllabus reference
1 The role of source documents	A2
2 The need for books of prime entry	A2
3 Sales and purchase day books	A2
4 Cash book	A2
5 Petty cash	A2

Introduction

From your studies of the first three chapters you should have grasped some important points about the nature and purpose of accounting.

- Most organisations provide products and services in the hope of making a profit for their owners, by receiving payment in money for those goods and services.
- The role of the accounting system is to record these monetary effects and create information about them.

You should also, by now, understand the basic principles underlying the statement of financial position and statement of profit or loss and other comprehensive income and have an idea of what they look like.

We now turn our attention to the process by which a business transaction works its way through to the financial statements.

It is usual to record a business transaction on a **document**. Such documents include invoices, orders, credit notes and goods received notes, all of which will be discussed in Section 1 of this chapter. In terms of the accounting system these are known as **source documents**. The information on them is processed by the system by, for example, aggregating (adding together) or classifying.

Records of source documents are kept in 'books of prime entry', which, as the name suggests, are the first stage at which a business transaction enters into the accounting system. The various types of books of prime entry are discussed in Sections 2 to 4. We will also look at the treatment of petty cash in Section 5.

In the next chapter we consider what happens to transactions after the books of prime entry stage.

… PART B ACCOUNTING RECORDS AND PROCEDURES

1 The role of source documents

FAST FORWARD

Business transactions are recorded on **source documents**. Examples include sales and purchase orders, invoices and credit notes.

1.1 Types of source documents

Whenever a business transaction takes place, involving sales or purchases, receiving or paying money, or owing or being owed money, it is usual for the transaction to be recorded on a document. These documents are the source of all the information recorded by a business.

Documents used to record the business transactions in the 'books of account' of the business include the following:

- **Quotation.** A business makes a written offer to a customer to produce or deliver goods or services for a certain amount of money.
- **Sales order.** A customer writes out or signs an order for goods or services he requires.
- **Purchase order.** A business orders from another business goods or services, such as material supplies.
- **Goods received note.** A list of goods that a business has received from a supplier. This is usually prepared by the business's own warehouse or goods receiving area.
- **Goods despatched note.** A list of goods that a business has sent out to a customer.
- **Invoice.** This is discussed further below.
- **Statement.** A document sent out by a supplier to a customer listing all invoices, credit notes and payments received from the customer.
- **Credit note.** A document sent by a supplier to a customer in respect of goods returned or overpayments made by the customer. It is a 'negative' invoice.
- **Debit note.** A document sent by a customer to a supplier in respect of goods returned or an overpayment made. It is a formal request for the supplier to issue a credit note.
- **Remittance advice.** A document sent with a payment, detailing which invoices are being paid and which credit notes offset.
- **Receipt.** A written confirmation that money has been paid. This is usually in respect of cash sales, eg a till receipt from a cash register.

1.2 Invoices

Key term

An **invoice** relates to a sales order or a purchase order.

- When a business sells goods or services on credit to a customer, it sends out an invoice. The details on the invoice should match the details on the sales order. The invoice is a request for the customer to pay what he owes.
- When a business buys goods or services on credit it receives an invoice from the supplier. The details on the invoice should match the details on the purchase order.

The invoice is primarily a demand for payment, but it is used for other purposes as well, as we shall see. Since it has several uses, an invoice is often produced on multi-part stationery, or photocopied, or carbon-copied. The top copy will go to the customer and other copies will be used by various people within the business.

1.2.1 What does an invoice show?

Most invoices are numbered, so that the business can keep track of all the invoices it sends out. Information usually shown on an invoice includes the following:

(a) Name and address of the seller and the purchaser
(b) Date of the sale
(c) Description of what is being sold
(d) Quantity and unit price of what has been sold (eg 20 pairs of shoes at $25 a pair)
(e) Details of trade discount, if any (eg 10% reduction in cost if buying over 100 pairs of shoes)
(f) Total amount of the invoice including (usually) details any of sales tax
(g) Sometimes, the date by which payment is due, and other terms of sale

1.2.2 Uses of multi-part invoices

As stated above invoices may be used for different purposes:

- Top copy to customer as a request for payment
- Second copy to accounts department to match to eventual payment
- Third copy to warehouse to generate a despatch of goods, as evidenced by a goods despatched note
- Fourth copy stapled to sales order and kept in sales department as a record of sales

Please note that businesses will design their own invoices and there may be other copies for other departments. Not all businesses will need four part invoices. A very small business may use the customer copy of the invoice as a despatch note as well. In addition, the sales invoice may be stapled to the sales order and both documents passed to the accounts department.

1.3 The credit note

China Supplies sent out an invoice for 20 dinner plates, but the typist accidentally typed in a total of $162.10, instead of $62.10. The china shop has been **overcharged** by $100. What is China Supplies to do?

Alternatively, when the china shop received the plates it found that they had all been broken in the post and that it was going to send them back. Although the china shop has received an invoice for $62.10, it has no intention of paying it because the plates were useless. Again, what is China Supplies to do?

The answer is that China Supplies sends out a **credit note**. A credit note is sometimes printed in red to distinguish it from an invoice. Otherwise, it will be made out in much the same way as an invoice, but with less detail and 'Credit Note Number' instead of 'Invoice Number'.

Key term

> A **credit note** is a document relating to returned goods or refunds when a customer has been overcharged. It can be regarded as a **negative invoice**.

1.4 Other documents

The following documents are sometimes used in connection with sales and purchases:

(a) Debit notes
(b) Goods received notes

A **debit note** might be issued to **adjust an invoice** already issued. This is also commonly achieved by issuing a revised invoice after raising a credit or debit note purely for internal purposes (ie to keep the records straight).

More commonly, a debit note is issued to a supplier as a means of formally requesting a credit note.

PART B ACCOUNTING RECORDS AND PROCEDURES

Goods received notes (GRNs) record a receipt of goods, most commonly in a warehouse. They may be used in addition to suppliers' advice notes. Often the accounts department will require to see the relevant GRN before paying a supplier's invoice. Even where GRNs are not routinely used, the details of a consignment from a supplier which arrives without an advice note must always be recorded.

Question
Credit note

Fill in the blanks.

'China Supplies sends out a .... to a credit customer in order to correct an error where a customer has been overcharged on an ....'

Answer

Credit note; invoice.

2 The need for books of prime entry

In the course of business, source documents are created. The details on these source documents need to be summarised, as otherwise the business might forget to ask for some money, or forget to pay some, or even accidentally pay something twice. In other words, it needs to keep records of source documents – of transactions – so that it knows what is going on. Such records are made in **books of prime entry**.

Key term

Books of prime entry are books in which we first record transactions.

FAST FORWARD

The main **books of prime entry** are as follows:

(a) Sales day book
(b) Purchase day book
(c) Sales returns day book
(d) Purchase returns day book
(e) Journal (described in the next chapter)
(f) Cash book
(g) Petty cash book

It is worth bearing in mind that, for convenience, this chapter describes books of prime entry as if they are actual books written by hand. However, books of prime entry are often not books at all, but rather files hidden in the memory of a computer. However, the principles remain the same whether they are manual or computerised.

Exam focus point

You may get a question on books of prime entry, also you need to know where the entries to the ledger accounts come from and how they are posted.

4: SOURCES, RECORDS AND BOOKS OF PRIME ENTRY

3 Sales and purchase day books

FAST FORWARD

Invoices and credit notes are recorded in **day books**.

3.1 The sales day book

Key term

The **sales day book** is the book of prime entry for credit sales.

The sales day book is used to keep a list of all invoices sent out to customers each day. An extract from a sales day book might look like this.

SALES DAY BOOK

Date	Invoice	Customer	Total amount invoiced
20X0			$
Jan 10	247	Jones & Co	105.00
	248	Smith Co	86.40
	249	Alex & Co	31.80
	250	Enor College	1,264.60
			1,487.80

Most businesses 'analyse' their sales. For example, this business sells boots and shoes. The sale to Smith was entirely boots, the sale to Alex was entirely shoes, and the other two sales were a mixture of both.

Then the sales day book might look like this.

SALES DAY BOOK

Date	Invoice	Customer	Total amount invoiced	Boot sales	Shoe sales
20X0			$	$	$
Jan 10	247	Jones & Co	105.00	60.00	45.00
	248	Smith Co	86.40	86.40	
	249	Alex & Co	31.80		31.80
	250	Enor College	1,264.60	800.30	464.30
			1,487.80	946.70	541.10

The analysis gives the managers of the business useful information which helps them to decide how best to run the business.

3.2 The purchase day book

A business also keeps a record in the purchase day book of all the invoices it receives.

Key term

The **purchase day book** is the book of prime entry for credit purchases.

An extract from a purchase day book might look like this.

PURCHASE DAY BOOK

Date	Supplier	Total amount Invoiced	Purchases	Electricity etc
20X8		$	$	$
Mar 15	Cook & Co	315.00	315.00	
	W Butler	29.40	29.40	
	EEB	116.80		116.80
	Show Fair Co	100.00	100.00	
		561.20	444.40	116.80

PART B ACCOUNTING RECORDS AND PROCEDURES

Points to note
- There is no 'invoice number' column, because the purchase day book records **other people's invoices**, which have all sorts of different numbers.
- Like the sales day book, the purchase day book analyses the invoices which have been sent in. In this example, three of the invoices related to goods which the business intends to re-sell (called simply 'purchases') and the other invoice was an electricity bill.

3.3 The sales returns day book

When customers return goods for some reason, a credit note is raised. All credit notes are recorded in the sales returns day book. An extract from the sales returns day book follows.

SALES RETURNS DAY BOOK

Date	Credit note	Customer and goods	Amount
20X8			$
30 April	CR008	Owen Plenty	
		3 pairs 'Texas' boots	135.00

Key term

The **sales returns day book** is the book of prime entry for credit notes raised.

Not all sales returns day books analyse what goods were returned, but it makes sense to keep as complete a record as possible. Where a business has very few sales returns, it may record a credit note as a negative entry in the sales day book.

3.4 The purchase returns day book

Not surprisingly, the purchase returns day book records credit notes received in respect of goods which the business sends back to its suppliers.

An extract from the purchase returns day book follows.

PURCHASE RETURNS DAY BOOK

Date	Supplier and goods	Amount
20X8		$
29 April	Boxes Co	
	300 cardboard boxes	46.60

Key term

The **purchase returns day book** is the book of prime entry for credit notes received from suppliers.

Once again, a business with very few purchase returns may record a credit note received as a negative entry in the purchase day book.

4 Cash book

FAST FORWARD

The **cash book** may be a manual record or a computer file. It records all transactions that go through the bank account.

4.1 The cash book

The cash book is also a day book, used to keep a record of money received and money paid out by the business. The cash book deals with money paid into and out of the business **bank account**. This could be money received on the business premises in notes, coins and cheques*, subsequently paid into the bank. There are also receipts and payments made by bank transfer, standing order, direct debit and bank interest and charges, directly by the bank.

Some cash, in notes and coins, is usually kept on the business premises in order to make occasional payments for odd items of expense. This cash is usually accounted for separately in a **petty cash book** (which we will look at shortly).

One side (the left) of the cash book is used to record receipts of cash, and the other side (the right) is used to record payments. The best way to see how the cash book works is to follow through an example. For convenience, we are showing the cash receipts and cash payments sides separately, but they are part of the same book.

*While cheques are still in paper format and have to be physically paid into the bank, the Small Business, Enterprise and Employment Act, 2015 allows 'cheque imaging' whereby a digital image of a cheque can be paid into a bank electronically. Paying in paper cheques to the bank is still possible, but having the additional option of cheque imaging speeds up the cheque clearing process and offers a more convenient form of payment.

Key term

The **cash book** is the book of prime entry for both cash receipts and payments.

4.2 Example: Cash book

At the beginning of 1 September, Robin Plenty had $900 in the bank.

During 1 September 20X7, Robin Plenty had the following receipts and payments:

(a) Cash sale: receipt of $80
(b) Payment from credit customer Hay $380
(c) Payment from credit customer Been $720
(d) Payment from credit customer Seed $140
(e) Cheque received for cash to provide a short-term loan from Len Dinger $1,800
(f) Second cash sale: receipt of $150
(g) Cash received for sale of machine $200
(h) Payment to supplier Kew $120
(i) Payment to supplier Hare $310
(j) Payment of telephone bill $400
(k) Payment of gas bill $280
(l) $100 in cash withdrawn from bank for petty cash
(m) Payment of $1,500 to Hess for new plant and machinery

If you look through these transactions, you will see that seven of them are receipts and six of them are payments.

PART B ACCOUNTING RECORDS AND PROCEDURES

The receipts part of the cash book for 1 September would look like the following:

CASH BOOK (RECEIPTS)

Date 20X7	Narrative	Total $
1 Sept	Balance b/d*	900
	Cash sale	80
	Accounts receivable: Hay	380
	Accounts receivable: Been	720
	Accounts receivable: Seed	140
	Loan: Len Dinger	1,800
	Cash sale	150
	Sale of non-current asset	200
		4,370

* 'b/d' = brought down (ie brought forward)

Points to note

- There is space on the right hand side of the cash book so that the receipts can be analysed under various headings – for example, 'cash from receivables', 'cash sales' and 'other receipts'.

- The cash received in the day amounted to $3,470. Added to the $900 at the start of the day, this comes to $4,370. This is not the amount to be carried forward to the next day, because first we have to subtract all the payments made during 1 September.

The payments part of the cash book for 1 September would look like this.

CASH BOOK (PAYMENTS)

Date 20X7	Narrative	Total $
1 Sept	Accounts payable: Kew	120
	Accounts payable: Hare	310
	Telephone	400
	Gas bill	280
	Petty cash	100
	Machinery purchase	1,500
	Balance c/d (balancing figure)	1,660
		4,370

As you can see, this is very similar to the receipts part of the cash book. The only points to note are as follows:

(a) The analysis on the right would be under headings like 'payments to payables, 'payments into petty cash', 'wages' and 'other payments'.

(b) Payments during 1 September totalled $2,710. We know that the total of receipts was $4,370. That means that there is a balance of $4,370 – $2,710 = $1,660 to be 'carried down' to the start of the next day. As you can see this 'balance carried down' is noted at the end of the payments column, so that the receipts and payments totals show the same figure of $4,370 at the end of 1 September.

With analysis columns completed, the cash book given in the examples above might look as follows.

CASH BOOK (RECEIPTS)

Date 20X7	Narrative	Total $	Accounts receivable $	Cash sales $	Other $
1 Sept	Balance b/d	900			
	Cash sale	80		80	
	Accounts receivable: Hay	380	380		
	Accounts receivable: Been	720	720		
	Accounts receivable: Seed	140	140		

Date 20X7	Narrative	Total $	Accounts receivable $	Cash sales $	Other $
	Loan: Len Dinger	1,800			1,800
	Cash sale	150		150	
	Sale of non-current asset	200			200
		4,370	1,240	230	2,000

CASH BOOK (PAYMENTS)

Date	Narrative	Total $	Accounts payable $	Petty cash $	Wages $	Other $
20X7						
1 Sept	Account payable: Kew	120	120			
	Account payable: Hare	310	310			
	Telephone	400				400
	Gas bill	280				280
	Petty cash	100		100		
	Machinery purchase	1,500				1,500
	Balance c/d	1,660				
		4,370	430	100	–	2,180

4.3 Bank statements

Weekly or monthly, a business will receive a **bank statement**. Bank statements should be used to check that the amount shown as a balance in the cash book agrees with the amount on the bank statement, and that no cash has 'gone missing'. This agreement or 'reconciliation' of the cash book with a bank statement is the subject of a later chapter.

5 Petty cash

FAST FORWARD

> Most businesses keep **petty cash** on the premises, which is topped up from the main bank account. Under the **imprest system**, the petty cash is kept at an agreed sum, so that each topping up is equal to the amount paid out in the period.

5.1 What is petty cash?

Most businesses keep a small amount of cash on the premises to make occasional small payments in cash, eg staff refreshments, postage stamps, to pay the office cleaner, taxi fares, etc. This is often called the cash float or **petty cash** account. The cash float can also be the resting place for occasional small receipts, eg cash paid by a visitor to make a phone call, etc.

5.2 Security

As you will appreciate, keeping cash (even in small amounts) on the premises is a security risk. Therefore a petty cash system is usually subject to strict controls.

- Payment is only made in respect of **authorised** claims.
- All claims are supported by **evidence**.

In addition, the business may use the **imprest system** (see Section 5.4 below).

5.2.1 Authorisation

An employee must complete a **petty cash voucher** detailing the expenses claimed. Usually receipts must be attached to the voucher (see below: evidence). The completed voucher then needs to be signed by (say) the employee's manager to **authorise** payment. Sometimes the petty cashier may be authorised to sign vouchers for small amounts (eg $5 or less) if these are supported by receipts.

5.2.2 Evidence

All petty cash vouchers must have receipts for the expenditure attached, as **evidence** that the employee has really incurred that cost. Sometimes receipts may not be available (eg taxi fares) and the employer may then have systems in place to authorise claims without evidence.

5.3 The petty cash book

> **Key term**
>
> A **petty cash book** is a cash book for small payments.

Although the amounts involved are small, petty cash transactions still need to be recorded; otherwise the cash float could be abused for personal expenses or even stolen.

There are usually more payments than receipts, and petty cash must be 'topped up' from time to time with cash from the business bank account. A typical layout follows.

PETTY CASH BOOK

Receipts $	Date 20X7	Narrative	Total $	Milk $	Postage $	Travel $	Other $
250	1 Sept	Bal b/d					
		Milk bill	25	25			
		Postage stamps	5		5		
		Taxi fare	10			10	
		Flowers for sick staff	15				15
		Bal c/d	195				
250			250	25	5	10	15

5.4 Imprest system

Under what is called the **imprest system**, the amount of money in petty cash is kept at an agreed sum or 'float' (say $250). This is called the **imprest amount**. Expense items are recorded on vouchers as they occur, so that at any time:

	$
Cash still held in petty cash	195
Plus voucher payments (25 + 5 + 10 + 15)	55
Must equal the imprest amount	250

The total float is made up regularly (to $250, or whatever the imprest amount is) by means of a cash payment from the bank account into petty cash. The amount of the 'top-up' into petty cash will be the total of the voucher payments since the previous top-up.

> **Key term**
>
> The **imprest system** makes a refund of the total paid out in a period.

> **Exam focus point**
>
> An exam question may ask students to calculate the imprest amount. In the past, students didn't read the question carefully enough and so arrived at a wrong answer. Make sure that you follow the example below, which demonstrates the correct technique.

5.5 Example: Petty cash and the imprest system

Dozy Co operates an imprest system for petty cash. During February 20X9, the following petty cash transactions took place.

		$
2.2.X9	Stamps	12.00
3.2.X9	Milk	25.00
8.2.X9	Taxi fare	15.00
17.2.X9	Stamps	5.00
18.2.X9	Received from staff for photocopying	8.00
28.2.X9	Stationery	7.50

The amount remaining in petty cash at the end of the month was $93.50. What is the imprest amount?

A $166.00
B $150.00
C $72.50
D $56.50

The solution is B.

	$	
Opening balance (imprest amount)	150.00	(balancing figure)
Add amount received from staff	8.00	
	158.00	
Less expenditure	(64.50)	(12 + 25 + 15 + 5 + 7.50)
Cash in hand at end of month	93.50	

Question   Books of prime entry

State which books of prime entry the following transactions would be entered into.

(a) Your business pays A Brown (a supplier) $450.00.
(b) You send D Smith (a customer) an invoice for $650.
(c) Your accounts manager asks you for $12 urgently in order to buy some envelopes.
(d) You receive an invoice from A Brown for $300.
(e) You pay D Smith $500.
(f) F Jones (a customer) returns goods to the value of $250.
(g) You return goods to J Green to the value of $504.
(h) F Jones pays you $500.

Answer

(a) Cash book
(b) Sales day book
(c) Petty cash book
(d) Purchases day book
(e) Cash book
(f) Sales returns day book
(g) Purchase returns day book
(h) Cash book

Chapter roundup

- Business transactions are recorded on **source documents**. Examples include sales and purchase orders, invoices and credit notes.

- The main **books of prime entry** are as follows:
    (a) Sales day book
    (b) Purchase day book
    (c) Sales returns day book
    (d) Purchase returns day book
    (e) Journal (described in the next chapter)
    (f) Cash book
    (g) Petty cash book

- Invoices and credit notes are recorded in **day books**.

- The **cash book** may be a manual record or a computer file. It records all transactions that go through the bank account.

- Most businesses keep **petty cash** on the premises, which is topped up from the main bank account. Under the **imprest system**, the petty cash is kept at an agreed sum, so that each topping up is equal to the amount paid out in the period.

Quick quiz

1. Name four pieces of information normally shown on an invoice.

2. Which of the following is not a book of prime entry?
   - A Sales invoice
   - B Purchase day book
   - C Sales day book
   - D Journal

3. Which of the following is a source document for petty cash?
   - A Purchase invoice
   - B Quotation
   - C Sales invoice
   - D Receipt and claim form

4. What is the purchase returns day book used to record?
   - A Supplier's invoices
   - B Customer's invoices
   - C Details of goods returned to suppliers
   - D Details of goods returned by customers

5. What is the difference between the cash book and the petty cash book?

6. Petty cash is controlled under an imprest system. The imprest amount is $100. During a period, payments totalling $53 have been made. How much needs to be reimbursed at the end of the period to restore petty cash to the imprest account?
   - A $100
   - B $53
   - C $47
   - D $50

7. All petty cash claims are automatically paid from petty cash. Is this statement true or false?

Answers to quick quiz

1. **Four** from the following:
   - Invoice number
   - Seller's name and address
   - Purchaser's name and address
   - Date of sale
   - Description of goods or services
   - Quantity and unit price
   - Trade discount (if any)
   - Total amount, including sales tax (if any)
   - Any special terms

2. A   Sales invoice is a source document.

3. D   The claim form and receipt form the source document for the petty cash system.

4. C   Supplier's invoices (A) are recorded in the purchase day book, customer's invoices (B) are recorded in the sales day book and goods returned by customers (D) are recorded in the sales returns day book.

5. The cash book records amounts paid into or out of the bank account. The petty cash book records payments of small amounts of cash.

6. B   Under the imprest system, a reimbursement is made of the amount of the vouchers (or payments made) for the period.

7. False. Only **authorised** and **evidenced** petty cash claims are paid out of petty cash.

Ledger accounts and double entry

Topic list	Syllabus reference
1 Why do we need ledger accounts?	A2
2 The nominal ledger	A2
3 The accounting equation	A2
4 Double entry bookkeeping	A2
5 The journal	A2
6 Day book analysis	A2
7 The imprest system	A2
8 The receivables and payables ledgers	A2

Introduction

In the previous chapter we saw how to organise transactions into lists (ie entered into books of prime entry). It is not easy, however, to see how a business is doing from the information scattered throughout these books of prime entry. The lists need to be summarised. This is **ledger accounting**, which we look at in Sections 1 and 2.

The summary is produced in the nominal ledger by a process you may have heard of known as **double entry bookkeeping**. This is the cornerstone of accounts preparation and is surprisingly simple, once you have grasped the rules. We will look at the essentials in Sections 3 and 4.

In Section 5, we will deal with the final book of prime entry: **the journal**.

We will then look in detail at posting transactions from the day books to the ledgers in Sections 6 and 7.

Finally, we will consider how to deal with credit transactions in Section 8.

PART B   ACCOUNTING RECORDS AND PROCEDURES

1 Why do we need ledger accounts?

FAST FORWARD

Ledger accounts **summarise** all the individual transactions listed in the books of prime entry.

A business is continually making transactions, eg buying and selling, and we do not want to prepare a statement of profit or loss and other comprehensive income and a statement of financial position on completion of every individual transaction. To do so would be a time-consuming and cumbersome administrative task.

It is common sense that a business should keep a record of the transactions that it makes, the assets it acquires and liabilities it incurs. When the time comes to prepare a statement of profit or loss and other comprehensive income and a statement of financial position, the relevant information can be taken from those records.

The **records of transactions, assets and liabilities** should be kept in the following ways:

(a)   In **chronological order**, and **dated** so that transactions can be related to a particular period of time.

(b)   Built up in **cumulative totals**.

   (i)   Day by day (eg total sales on Monday, total sales on Tuesday)
   (ii)   Week by week
   (iii) Month by month
   (iv)   Year by year

We have already seen the first step in this process, which is to list all the transactions in various books of prime entry. Now we will look at the method used to summarise these records: **ledger accounting** and **double entry**.

This system of summarising information speeds up the provision of useful information to managers and so helps managers to keep to organisational deadlines (eg provision of monthly profit figures for management purposes).

2 The nominal ledger

FAST FORWARD

The principal accounts are contained in a ledger called the **general** or **nominal ledger**.

Key term

The **nominal ledger** is an accounting record which summarises the financial affairs of a business.

The nominal ledger is sometimes called the **'general ledger'**. The information contained in the books of prime entry (see Chapter 4) is **summarised** and **posted** to accounts in the nominal ledger.

It contains details of assets, liabilities, capital, income and expenditure, and so profit and loss. It consists of a large number of different accounts, each account having its own purpose or 'name' and an identity or code.

There may be various subdivisions, whether for convenience, ease of handling, confidentiality, security, or to meet the needs of computer software design. For example, the ledger may be split alphabetically, with different clerks responsible for sections A–F, G–M, N–R and S–Z. This can help to stop fraud, as there would have to be collusion between the different section clerks.

Examples of accounts in the nominal ledger include the following:

(a)   Plant and machinery at cost (non-current asset)
(b)   Motor vehicles at cost (non-current asset)
(c)   Plant and machinery, allowance for depreciation (liability)

64

(d) Motor vehicles, allowance for depreciation (liability)
(e) Proprietor's capital (liability)
(f) Inventories – raw materials (current asset)
(g) Inventories – finished goods (current asset)
(h) Total trade receivables (current asset)
(i) Total trade payables (current liability)
(j) Wages and salaries (expense item)
(k) Rent and local taxes (expense item)
(l) Advertising expenses (expense item)
(m) Bank charges (expense item)
(n) Motor expenses (expense item)
(o) Telephone expenses (expense item)
(p) Revenue (sales item)
(q) Total cash or bank overdraft (current asset or liability)

When it comes to drawing up the financial statements, the revenue and expense accounts will help to form the statement of profit or loss and other comprehensive income; while the asset and liability accounts go into the statement of financial position.

2.1 The format of a ledger account

If a ledger account were to be kept in an actual book, rather than as a computer record, it might look like this:

ADVERTISING EXPENSES

Date	Narrative	Ref.	$	Date	Narrative	Ref.	$
20X6							
15 April	JFK Agency for quarter to 31 March	PL 348	2,500				

For the rest of this chapter, we will assume that a manual system is being used, in order to illustrate fully the working of the ledger accounts. However, a computerised system performs the same functions although the actual ledger accounts may be 'hidden' inside the computer!

There are two sides to the account, and an account heading on top, and so it is convenient to think in terms of 'T' accounts.

(a) On top of the account is its name.
(b) There is a left hand side, or debit side.
(c) There is a right hand side, or credit side.

NAME OF ACCOUNT

DEBIT SIDE	$	CREDIT SIDE	$

We will look at 'DEBITS' and 'CREDITS' in detail in Section 4, but first we shall consider the accounting equation.

3 The accounting equation

FAST FORWARD

The **accounting equation** emphasises the equality between assets and liabilities (including capital as a liability).

We will start by showing how to account for a business's transactions from the time that trading first begins. We will use an example to illustrate the 'accounting equation', ie the rule that the assets of a business will at all times equal its liabilities. This is also known as the **statement of financial position equation**.

PART B   ACCOUNTING RECORDS AND PROCEDURES

3.1 Example: The accounting equation

Key term

> **Business entity concept.** Regardless of how a business is legally set up, in accounting a business is always treated separately from its owner(s).

Liza Doolittle starts a business. The business begins by owning the cash that Liza has put into it, $2,500. The business is a separate entity in accounting terms and so it owes the money to Liza as **capital**.

Key term

> In accounting, **capital** is an investment of money (funds) with the intention of earning a return. A business proprietor invests capital with the intention of earning profit. As long as that money is invested, accountants will treat the capital as money owed to the proprietor by the business.

When Liza Doolittle sets up her business:
Capital invested   = $2,500
Cash   = $2,500

Capital invested is a form of liability, because it is an amount owed by the business to its owner(s). Adapting this to the idea that assets and liabilities are always equal amounts, we can state the accounting equation as follows.

Formula to learn

> The accounting equation is:
>
> ASSETS = CAPITAL + LIABILITIES

For Liza Doolittle, as at 1 July 20X6:

Assets	=	*Capital*	+	*Liabilities*
$2,500 (cash)	=	$2,500	+	$0

3.2 Example continued

Liza Doolittle purchases a market stall from Len Turnip, who is retiring from his fruit and vegetables business. The cost of the stall is $1,800.

She also purchases some flowers and potted plants from a trader in the wholesale market, at a cost of $650. This leaves $50 in cash, after paying for the stall and goods for resale, out of the original $2,500.

The assets and liabilities of the business have now altered, and at 3 July before trading begins, the state of her business is as follows.

Assets		=	*Capital*	+	*Liabilities*
	$				
Stall	1,800	=	$2,500	+	$0
Flower and plants	650				
Cash	50				
	2,500				

The stall and the flowers and plants are physical items, but they must be given a money value. This money value is usually what they cost the business (called **historical cost** in accounting terms).

3.3 Profit introduced into the accounting equation

On 3 July Liza has a very successful day. She sells all of her flowers and plants for $900 cash.

Since Liza has sold goods costing $650 to earn revenue of $900, we can say that she has **earned a profit of $250 on the day's trading**.

Profits belong to the owners of a business. In this case, the $250 belongs to Liza Doolittle. However, so long as the business retains the profits and does not pay anything out to its owners, the **retained profits** are accounted for as an addition to the proprietor's capital.

5: LEDGER ACCOUNTS AND DOUBLE ENTRY

Assets		=	Capital		+	Liabilities
	$			$		
Stall	1,800		Original investment	2,500		
Flower and plants	0		Retained profit			
Cash (50 + 900)	950		(900 – 650)	250		
	2,750			2,750	+	$0

We can re-arrange the accounting equation to help us to calculate the capital balance.

Assets – liabilities = Capital, which is the same as
Net assets = Capital

At the beginning and end of 3 July 20X6, Liza Doolittle's financial position was as follows.

		Net assets	Capital
(a)	At the beginning of the day:	$(2,500 – 0) = $2,500 =	$2,500
(b)	At the end of the day:	$(2,750 – 0) = $2,750 =	$2,750

There has been an increase of $250 in net assets, which is the amount of profits earned during the day.

3.4 Drawings

Key term

Drawings are amounts of money taken out of a business by its owner.

Since Liza Doolittle has made a profit of $250 from her first day's work, she might want to withdraw some money from the business. After all, business owners, like everyone else, need income for living expenses. Liza decides to pay herself $180 in 'wages'. However, the $180 is not an expense to be deducted in arriving at the figure of net profit. In other words, it is incorrect to calculate the net profit earned by the business as follows.

	$
Profit on sale of flowers etc	250
Less 'wages' paid to Liza	180
Net profit earned by business (incorrect)	70

This is because any amounts paid by a business to its proprietor are treated by accountants as withdrawals of profit (the usual term is **drawings**) and not as expenses incurred by the business. In the case of Liza's business, the true position is that the net profit earned is the $250 surplus on sale of flowers.

	$
Net profit earned by business	250
Less profit withdrawn by Liza	180
Net profit retained in the business	70

Profits are capital as long as they are retained in the business. Once they are **withdrawn**, the business suffers a reduction in capital.

The withdrawals of profit are taken in cash, and so the business loses $180 of its cash assets. After the withdrawals have been made, the accounting equation would be restated.

(a)
Assets		=	Capital		+	Liabilities
	$			$		
Stall	1,800		Original investment	2,500		
Flowers and plants	0		Retained profit			
Cash (950 – 180)	770		(250 – 180)	70		
	2,570			2,570	+	$0

(b) Alternatively Net assets   Capital
                  $(2,570 – 0) = $2,570

The increase in net assets since trading operations began is now only $(2,570 – 2,500) = $70, which is the amount of the retained profits.

Question
Capital

Which of the following is correct?

A   Capital = assets + liabilities
B   Capital = liabilities – assets
C   Capital = assets – liabilities
D   Capital + assets = liabilities

Answer

The correct answer is C. As assets = liabilities + capital, then capital = assets – liabilities

3.5 Example continued

FAST FORWARD You should now be aware that when business transactions are accounted for it should be possible to **restate the assets and liabilities** of the business after the transactions have taken place.

The next market day is on 10 July and Liza purchases more flowers and plants for cash, at a cost of $740. She is not feeling well, because of a heavy cold, and so she decides to accept help for the day from her cousin Ethel. Ethel is to be paid a wage of $40 at the end of the day.

Trading on 10 July was again very brisk, and Liza and Ethel sold all their goods for $1,100 cash. Liza paid Ethel her wage of $40 and drew out $200 for herself.

Required

(a) State the accounting equation before trading began on 10 July.
(b) State the accounting equation at the end of 10 July, after paying Ethel:
    (i) But before drawings are made
    (ii) After drawings have been made

You are reminded that the accounting equation for the business at the end of transactions for 3 July is given in Paragraph 3.4.

Solution

(a) After the purchase of the goods for $740.

Assets		=	Capital	+	Liabilities
	$				
Stall	1,800				
Goods	740				
Cash (770 – 740)	30				
	2,570	=	$ 2,570	+	$0

5: LEDGER ACCOUNTS AND DOUBLE ENTRY

(b) (i) On 10 July, all the goods are sold for $1,100 cash, and Ethel is paid $40. The profit for the day is $320.

	$	$
Revenue		1,100
Less cost of goods sold	740	
Ethel's wage	40	
		780
Profit		320

Assets	$	= Capital	$	+ Liabilities
Stall	1,800	At beginning of 10 July	2,570	
Goods	0	Profits earned on 10 July	320	
Cash (30 + 1,100 – 40)	1,090			
	2,890		2,890	+ $0

(ii) After Liza has withdrawn $200 in cash, retained profits will be only $(320 – 200) = $120.

Assets	$	= Capital	$	+ Liabilities
Stall	1,800	At beginning of 10 July	2,570	
Goods	0	Retained profits	120	
Cash (1,090 – 200)	890	for 10 July		
	2,690		2,690	+ $0

Tutorial note. Trade receivables. It is very important you should understand the principles described so far. Do not read on until you are confident that you understand the solution to this example.

3.6 Trade payables and receivables

FAST FORWARD

Trade payables are **liabilities**. Trade receivables are **assets**.

3.6.1 Trade payables and trade receivables

Key term

A **payable** is a person to whom a business owes money.

A **trade payable** is a person to whom a business owes money for debts incurred in the course of trading operations. In the accounts of a business, debts still outstanding which arise from the purchase of materials, components or goods for resale are called **trade payables**, sometimes abbreviated to 'accounts payable' or 'payables'.

A business does not always pay immediately for goods or services it buys. It is a common business practice to make purchases on credit, with a promise to pay within 30 days, or two months or three months, of the date of the invoice for the goods. For example, A buys goods costing $2,000 on credit from B, B sends A an invoice for $2,000, dated 1 March, with credit terms that payment must be made within 30 days. If A then delays payment until 31 March, B will be a payable of A between 1 and 31 March for $2,000. From A's point of view, the amount owed to B is a **trade payable.**

A trade payable is a **liability** of a business.

Key term

Trade receivable. Just as a business might buy goods on credit, so too might it sell goods to customers on credit.

A customer who buys goods without paying cash for them straight away is a **trade receivable**.

For example, suppose that C sells goods on credit to D for $6,000 on terms that the debt must be settled within two months of the invoice date 1 October. If D does not pay the $6,000 until 30 November, D will be a receivable of C for $6,000 from 1 October until 30 November. In the accounts of the business, amounts owed by receivables are called **trade receivables,** sometimes abbreviated to 'accounts receivable' or 'receivables'.

A trade receivable is an **asset** of a business. When the debt is finally paid, the trade receivable 'disappears' as an asset, to be replaced by 'cash at bank and in hand'.

3.6.2 Example continued

The example of Liza Doolittle's market stall is continued, by looking at the consequences of the following transactions in the week to 17 July 20X6. (See Paragraph 3.5 for the situation as at the end of 10 July.)

(a) Liza Doolittle realises that she is going to need more money in the business and so she makes the following arrangements:

　(i) She invests immediately a further $250 of her own capital.

　(ii) She persuades her Uncle Henry to lend her $500 immediately. Uncle Henry tells her that she can repay the loan whenever she likes, but in the meantime, she must pay him interest of $5 each week at the end of the market day. They agree that it will probably be quite a long time before the loan is eventually repaid.

(b) She decides to buy a second hand van to pick up flowers and plants from her supplier and bring them to her stall in the market. She finds a car dealer, Laurie Loader, who agrees to sell her a van on credit for $700. Liza agrees to pay for the van after 30 days' trial use.

(c) During the week, Liza's Uncle George telephones her to ask whether she would sell him some garden gnomes and furniture for his garden. Liza tells him that she will look for a supplier. After some investigations, she buys what Uncle George has asked for, paying $300 in cash to the supplier. Uncle George accepts delivery of the goods and agrees to pay $350, but he asks if she can wait until the end of the month for payment. Liza agrees.

(d) Liza buys flowers and plants costing $800. Of these purchases $750 are paid in cash, with the remaining $50 on seven days' credit. Liza decides to use Ethel's services again as an assistant on market day, at an agreed wage of $40.

(e) On 17 July, Liza succeeds in selling all her goods earning revenue of $1,250 (all in cash). She decides to withdraw $240 for her week's work. She also pays Ethel $40 in cash. She decides to make the interest payment to her Uncle Henry the next time she sees him.

(f) We shall ignore any van expenses for the week, for the sake of relative simplicity.

Required

State the accounting equation:

(i) After Liza and Uncle Henry have put more money into the business and after the purchase of the van

(ii) After the sale of goods to Uncle George

(iii) After the purchase of goods for the weekly market

(iv) At the end of the day's trading on 17 July, and after withdrawals have been appropriated out of profit

Solution

There are a number of different transactions to account for here. This solution deals with them one at a time in chronological order. (In practice, it is possible to do one set of calculations which combines the results of all the transactions.)

(i) *The addition of Liza's extra capital and Uncle Henry's loan*

An investment analyst might call Uncle Henry's loan a capital investment, on the grounds that it will probably be for the long term. Uncle Henry is not the owner of the business, however, even though he has made an investment of a loan in it. He would only become an owner if Liza offered him a partnership in the business, and she has not done so. To the business, Uncle Henry is a long-term payable, and it is more appropriate to define his investment as a liability of the business and not as business capital.

The accounting equation after $(250 + 500) = \$750$ cash is put into the business will be:

Assets		=	Capital		+	Liabilities	
	$			$			$
Stall	1,800		As at end of 10 July	2,690		Loan	500
Goods	0		Additional capital put in	250			
Cash (890 + 750)	1,640						
	3,440	=		2,940	+		500

The purchase of the van (cost $700) on credit

Assets		=	Capital		+	Liabilities	
	$			$			$
Stall	1,800		As at end of 10 July	2,690		Loan	500
Van	700		Additional capital	250		Trade payables	700
Cash	1,640						
	4,140	=		2,940	+		1,200

(ii) *The sale of goods to Uncle George on credit ($350) which cost the business $300 (cash paid)*

Assets		=	Capital		+	Liabilities	
	$			$			$
Stall	1,800		As at end of 10 July	2,690		Loan	500
Van	700		Additional capital	250		Trade payables	700
Trade receivable	350		Profit on sale to				
Cash			Uncle George (350 – 300)	50			
(1,640 – 300)	1,340						
	4,190	=		2,990	+		1,200

(iii) *After the purchase of goods for the weekly market ($750 paid in cash and $50 of purchases on credit)*

Assets		=	Capital		+	Liabilities	
	$			$			$
Stall	1,800		As at end of 10 July	2,690		Loan	500
Van	700		Additional capital	250		payables (van)	700
Goods	800		Profit on sale to				
Trade receivables	350		Uncle George	50		Trade payables (goods)	50
Cash							
(1,340 – 750)	590						
	4,240	=		2,990	+		1,250

PART B ACCOUNTING RECORDS AND PROCEDURES

(iv) *After market trading on 17 July*

Sales of goods costing $800 earned revenues of $1,250. Ethel's wages were $40 (paid), Uncle Henry's interest charge is $5 (not paid yet) and withdrawals on account of profits were $240 (paid). The profit for 17 July may be calculated as follows, taking the full $5 of interest as a cost on that day.

	$	$
Revenue		1,250
Cost of goods sold	800	
Wages	40	
Interest	5	
		845
Profit earned on 17 July		405
Profit on sale of goods to Uncle George		50
Profit for the week		455
Drawings		240
Retained profit		215

Assets		=	Capital		+	Liabilities	
	$			$			$
Stall	1,800		As at end of 10 July	2,690		Loan	500
Van	700		Additional capital	250		Payable for van	700
Goods (800 – 800)	0		Profits retained	215			
Trade receivables	350					Trade payable for goods	50
Cash (590 + 1,250 – 40 – 240)	1,560					Payable for interest payment	5
	4,410			3,155			1,255

3.7 Matching

> **FAST FORWARD**
>
> The **matching convention** requires that revenue earned is matched with the expenses incurred in earning it.

In the example above, we have 'matched' the revenue earned with the expenses incurred in earning it. So in part (iv), we included all the costs of the goods sold of $800, even though $50 had not yet been paid in cash. Also the interest of $5 was deducted from revenue, even though it had not yet been paid. This is known as the **matching convention**, or accruals convention.

Question

The accounting equation

How would each of these transactions affect the accounting equation?

A Purchasing $800 worth of inventory on credit
B Paying the telephone bill $25
C Selling $450 worth of inventory for $650
D Paying $800 to the supplier

Answer

A	Increase in liabilities (payables)	$800
	Increase in assets (inventory)	$800
B	Decrease in assets (cash)	$25
	Decrease in capital (profit)	$25
C	Decrease in assets (inventory)	$450
	Increase in assets (cash)	$650
	Increase in capital (profit)	$200
D	Decrease in liabilities (payables)	$800
	Decrease in assets (cash)	$800

4 Double entry bookkeeping

FAST FORWARD

Double entry bookkeeping is based on the idea that each transaction has an equal but opposite effect. Every accounting event must be entered in ledger accounts both as a debit and as an equal but opposite credit.

4.1 Dual effect (duality concept)

Double entry bookkeeping is the method used to transfer our weekly/monthly totals from our books of prime entry into the nominal ledger.

Central to this process is the idea that every transaction has two effects, the **dual effect**. This feature is not something peculiar to businesses. If you were to purchase a car for $1,000 cash for instance, you would be affected in two ways:

(a) You own a car worth $1,000.
(b) You have $1,000 less cash.

If instead you got a bank loan to make the purchase:

(a) You own a car worth $1,000.
(b) You owe the bank $1,000.

A month later if you pay a garage $50 to have the exhaust replaced:

(a) You have $50 less cash.
(b) You have incurred a repairs expense of $50.

Ledger accounts, with their debit and credit sides, are kept in a way which allows the two-sided nature of every transaction to be recorded. This is known as the **'double entry'** system of bookkeeping, because **every transaction is recorded twice** in the accounts.

4.2 The rules of double entry bookkeeping

FAST FORWARD

A debit entry will:

- Increase an asset
- Decrease a liability
- Increase an expense

A credit entry will:

- Decrease an asset
- Increase a liability
- Increase income

The basic rule, which must always be observed, is that **every financial transaction gives rise to two accounting entries, one a debit and the other a credit**. The total value of debit entries in the nominal ledger is therefore always equal at any time to the total value of credit entries. Which account receives the credit entry and which receives the debit depends on the nature of the transaction.

Key terms

- An **increase** in an **expense** (eg a purchase of stationery) or an **increase in an asset** (eg a purchase of office furniture) is a **debit**.
- An **increase** in **revenue** (eg a sale) or an **increase in a liability** (eg buying goods on credit) is a **credit**.
- A **decrease** in an **asset** (eg making a cash payment) is a **credit**.
- A **decrease** in a **liability** (eg paying a creditor) is a **debit**.

In terms of 'T' accounts:

ASSET			LIABILITY			CAPITAL		
DEBIT	$	CREDIT $	DEBIT	$	CREDIT $	DEBIT	$	CREDIT $
Increase		Decrease	Decrease		Increase	Decrease		Increase

For income and expenses, think about profit. Profit retained in the business increases capital. Income increases profit and expenses decrease profit.

INCOME			EXPENSE		
DEBIT	$	CREDIT $	DEBIT	$	CREDIT $
Decrease		Increase	Increase		Decrease

Have a go at the question below before you learn about this topic in detail.

Question — Debits and credits

Complete the following table relating to the transactions of a bookshop. (The first two are done for you.)

(a) Purchase of books on credit

    (i)   Trade payables increase   CREDIT   trade payables   (increase in liability)

    (ii)   Purchases expense increases   DEBIT   purchases   (item of expense)

(b) Purchase of cash register

    (i)   Own a cash register   DEBIT   cash register   (increase in asset)

    (ii)   Cash at bank decreases   CREDIT   cash at bank   (decrease in asset)

(c) Payment received from a credit customer

    (i)   Trade receivables decrease

    (ii)   Cash at bank increases

(d) Purchase of van
  (i) Own a van
  (ii) Cash at bank decreases

Answer

(c) Payment received from a credit customer
  (i) Trade receivables decrease   CREDIT trade receivables   decrease in asset
  (ii) Cash at bank increases   DEBIT   cash at bank   increase in asset
(d) Purchase of van
  (i) Own a van   DEBIT   van   increase in asset
  (ii) Cash at bank decreases   CREDIT cash at bank   decrease in asset

How did you get on? Students coming to the subject for the first time often have difficulty in knowing where to begin. A good starting point is the cash account, ie the nominal ledger account in which receipts and payments of cash are recorded. The rule to remember about the cash account is as follows:

(a) A cash **payment** is a **credit** entry in the cash account. Here the **asset is decreasing**. Cash may be paid out, for example, to pay an expense (such as tax) or to purchase an asset (such as a machine). The matching debit entry is therefore made in the appropriate expense or asset account.

(b) A cash **receipt** is a **debit** entry in the cash account. Here the **asset is increasing**. Cash might be received, for example, by a retailer who makes a cash sale. The credit entry would then be made in the revenue account.

Key term

> **Double entry bookkeeping** is the method by which a business records financial transactions. An account is maintained for every asset, liability, income and expense. Every transaction is recorded twice so that every **debit** is balanced by a **credit**.

4.3 Example: Double entry for cash transactions

In the cash book of a business, the following transactions have been recorded:

(a) A cash sale (ie a receipt) of $250
(b) Payment of a rent bill totalling $150
(c) Buying some goods for cash at $100
(d) Buying some shelves for cash at $200

How would these four transactions be posted to the ledger accounts and to which ledger accounts should they be posted? Don't forget that each transaction will be posted twice, in accordance with the rule of double entry.

Solution

(a) The two sides of the transaction are:
  (i) Cash is received (debit entry in the cash at bank account)
  (ii) Revenue increase by $250 (credit entry in the revenue account)

CASH AT BANK ACCOUNT

	$		$
Revenue a/c	250		

REVENUE ACCOUNT

	$		$
		Cash a/c	250

(Note how the entry in the cash at bank account is cross-referenced to the revenue account and vice-versa. This enables a person looking at one of the accounts to trace where the other half of the double entry can be found.)

(b) The two sides of the transaction are:

    (i)   Cash is paid (credit entry in the cash at bank account)
    (ii)   Rent expense increases by $150 (debit entry in the rent account)

CASH AT BANK ACCOUNT

	$		$
		Rent a/c	150

RENT ACCOUNT

	$		$
Cash at bank a/c	150		

(c) The two sides of the transaction are:

    (i)   Cash is paid (credit entry in the cash at bank account)
    (ii)   Purchases increase by $100 (debit entry in the purchases account)

CASH AT BANK ACCOUNT

	$		$
		Purchases a/c	100

PURCHASES ACCOUNT

	$		$
Cash at bank a/c	100		

(d) The two sides of the transaction are:

    (i)   Cash is paid (credit entry in the cash at bank account)
    (ii)   Assets – In this case, shelves – Increase by $200 (debit entry in shelves account)

CASH AT BANK ACCOUNT

	$		$
		Shelves a/c	200

SHELVES (ASSET) ACCOUNT

	$		$
Cash at bank a/c	200		

4.4 Credit transactions

FAST FORWARD

Some accounts in the nominal ledger represent the total of very many smaller balances. For example, the **trade receivables account** represents all the balances owed by individual customers of the business while the **trade payables account** represents all money owed by the business to its suppliers.

Not all transactions are settled immediately in cash or by cheque. A business can purchase goods or non-current assets on credit terms, so that the suppliers would be trade payables until settlement was made in cash. Equally, the business might grant credit terms to its customers who would then be trade receivables of the business. Clearly no entries can be made in the cash book when a credit transaction occurs, because no cash has been received or paid, so where can the details of the transactions be entered?

The solution to this problem is to use **trade receivables and trade payables accounts**. When a business acquires goods or services on credit, the credit entry is made in an account designated 'trade payables' instead of in the cash at bank account. The debit entry is made in the appropriate expense or asset account, exactly as in the case of cash transactions. Similarly, when a sale is made to a credit customer the entries made are a debit to the total trade receivables account (instead of cash at bank account) and a credit to revenue account.

4.5 Example: Credit transactions

Recorded in the sales day book and the purchase day book are the following transactions.

(a) The business sells goods on credit to a customer Mr A for $2,000.
(b) The business buys goods on credit from a supplier B Inc for $100.

How and where are these transactions posted in the ledger accounts?

Solution

(a)

TRADE RECEIVABLES

	$		$
Revenue a/c	2,000		

REVENUE ACCOUNT

	$		$
		Trade receivables	2,000

(b)

TRADE PAYABLES

	$		$
		Purchases a/c	100

PURCHASES ACCOUNT

	$		$
Trade payables	100		

4.5.1 When cash is paid to suppliers or by customers

What happens when a credit transaction is eventually settled? Suppose that, in the example above, the business paid $100 to B Inc one month after the goods were acquired. The two sides of this new transaction are as follows:

(a) Cash is paid (credit entry in the cash at bank account)
(b) The amount owing to the trade payable is reduced (debit entry in the trade payables account)

CASH AT BANK ACCOUNT

	$		$
		Trade payables a/c	100

TRADE PAYABLE A/C

	$		$
Cash a/c	100		

If we now bring together the two parts of this example, the original purchase of goods on credit and the eventual settlement in cash, we find that the accounts appear as follows:

CASH AT BANK ACCOUNT

	$		$
		Trade payable a/c	100

PURCHASES ACCOUNT

	$		$
Trade payable a/c	100		

TRADE PAYABLES A/C

	$		$
Cash at bank a/c	100	Purchases a/c	100

The two entries in the trade payables account cancel each other out, indicating that no money is owing to suppliers any more. We are left with a credit entry of $100 in the cash at bank account and a debit entry of $100 in the purchases account. These are exactly the same as the entries used to record a **cash** purchase of $100 (compare example above). This is what we would expect: after the business has paid off its trade payable, it is in exactly the same position as if it had made a cash purchase, and the accounting records reflect this similarity.

Similar reasoning applies when a customer settles his debt. In the example above when Mr A pays his debt of $2,000 the two sides of the transaction are:

(a) Cash is received (debit entry in the cash at bank account).
(b) The amount owed by the trade receivable is reduced (credit entry in the trade receivables account).

CASH AT BANK ACCOUNT

	$		$
Trade receivables a/c	2,000		

TRADE RECEIVABLES A/C

	$		$
		Cash at bank a/c	2,000

The accounts recording this sale to, and payment by, Mr A now appear as follows.

CASH AT BANK ACCOUNT

	$		$
Trade receivable a/c	2,000		

REVENUE ACCOUNT

	$		$
		Trade receivable a/c	2,000

TRADE RECEIVABLE

	$		$
Revenue a/c	2,000	Cash at bank a/c	2,000

The two entries in the trade receivables cancel each other out; while the entries in the cash at bank account and revenue account reflect the same position as if the sale had been made for cash (see above).

Now try the following questions.

Question — Debit and credit

See if you can identify the debit and credit entries in the following transactions:

(a) Bought a machine on credit from A, cost $8,000
(b) Bought goods on credit from B, cost $500
(c) Sold goods on credit to C, value $1,200
(d) Paid D (a credit supplier) $300
(e) Collected $180 from E, a credit customer
(f) Paid wages $4,000
(g) Received rent bill of $700 from landlord G
(h) Paid rent of $700 to landlord G
(i) Paid insurance premium $90
(j) Received a credit note for $450 from supplier, H
(k) Sent out a credit note for $200 to customer, I

Answer

				$	$
(a)	DEBIT	Machine account (non-current asset)		8,000	
	CREDIT	Trade payables			8,000
(b)	DEBIT	Purchases account		500	
	CREDIT	Trade payables			500
(c)	DEBIT	Trade receivables		1,200	
	CREDIT	Revenue			1,200

PART B ACCOUNTING RECORDS AND PROCEDURES

			$	$
(d)	DEBIT	Trade payables	300	
	CREDIT	Cash at bank		300
(e)	DEBIT	Cash at bank	180	
	CREDIT	Trade receivables		180
(f)	DEBIT	Wages account	4,000	
	CREDIT	Cash at bank		4,000
(g)	DEBIT	Rent account	700	
	CREDIT	Trade payables		700
(h)	DEBIT	Trade payables	700	
	CREDIT	Cash at bank		700
(i)	DEBIT	Insurance costs	90	
	CREDIT	Cash at bank		90
(j)	DEBIT	Trade payables	450	
	CREDIT	Purchase returns		450
(k)	DEBIT	Sales returns	200	
	CREDIT	Trade receivables		200

Question   Ledger entries

See now whether you can record the ledger entries for the following transactions. Ron Knuckle set up a business selling keep fit equipment, trading under the name of Buy Your Biceps Shop. He put $7,000 of his own money into a business bank account (transaction A) and in his first period of trading, the following transactions occurred.

Transaction		$
B	Paid rent of shop for the period	3,500
C	Purchased equipment (inventories) on credit	5,000
D	Raised loan from bank	1,000
E	Purchase of shop fittings (for cash)	2,000
F	Sales of equipment: cash	10,000
G	Sales of equipment: on credit	2,500
H	Payments for trade payables	5,000
I	Payments from trade receivables	2,500
J	Interest on loan (paid)	100
K	Other expenses (all paid in cash)	1,900
L	Drawings	1,500

Try to do as much of this question as you can by yourself before reading the solution.

Answer

Clearly, there should be an account for cash at bank, trade receivable, trade payable, purchases, a shop fittings account, revenue, a loan account and a proprietor's capital account. It is also useful to keep a separate account for **drawings** until the end of each accounting period. Other accounts should be set up as they seem appropriate and in this exercise, accounts for rent, bank interest and other expenses would seem appropriate.

It has been suggested to you that the cash at bank account is a good place to start, if possible. You should notice that cash transactions include the initial input of capital by Ron Knuckle, subsequent drawings, the payment of rent, the loan from the bank, the interest, some cash sales and cash purchases, and payments for trade payables and from trade receivables. (The transactions are identified below by their reference, to help you to find them.)

CASH AT BANK

	$		$
Capital – Ron Knuckle (A)	7,000	Rent (B)	3,500
Bank loan (D)	1,000	Shop fittings (E)	2,000
Revenue (F)	10,000	Trade payables (H)	5,000
Trade receivables (I)	2,500	Bank loan interest (J)	100
		Other expenses (K)	1,900
		Drawings (L)	1,500

CAPITAL (RON KNUCKLE)

	$		$
		Cash at bank (A)	7,000

BANK LOAN

	$		$
		Cash at bank (D)	1,000

PURCHASES

	$		$
Trade payables (C)	5,000		

TRADE PAYABLES

	$		$
Cash at bank (H)	5,000	Purchases (C)	5,000

RENT

	$		$
Cash at bank (B)	3,500		

NON-CURRENT ASSETS (SHOP FITTINGS)

	$		$
Cash at bank (E)	2,000		

REVENUE

	$		$
		Cash at bank (F)	10,000
		Trade receivables (G)	2,500

TRADE RECEIVABLES

	$		$
Revenue (G)	2,500	Cash at bank (I)	2,500

BANK LOAN INTEREST

	$		$
Cash at bank (J)	100		

OTHER EXPENSES

	$		$
Cash at bank (K)	1,900		

DRAWINGS ACCOUNT

	$		$
Cash at bank (L)	1,500		

(a) If you want to make sure that this solution is complete, you should go through the transactions A to L and tick off each of them twice in the ledger accounts, once as a debit and once as a credit. When you have finished, all transactions in the 'T' account should be ticked.

(b) In fact, there is an easier way to check that the solution to this sort of problem does 'balance' properly, which we will meet in the next chapter.

(c) On asset and liability accounts, the debit or credit balance represents the amount of the asset or liability outstanding at the period end. For example, on the cash at bank account, debits exceed credits by $6,500 and so there is a debit balance of cash in hand of $6,500. On the capital account, there is a credit balance of $7,000 and so the business owes Ron $7,000.

(d) The balances on the revenue and expense accounts represent the total of each revenue or expense for the period. For example, sales for the period total $12,500.

5 The journal

FAST FORWARD

The **journal** is the record of prime entry for transactions which are not recorded in any of the other books of prime entry.

You should remember that one of the books of prime entry was the **journal**.

Key term

The **journal** keeps a record of unusual movement between accounts. It is used to record any double entries made which do not arise from the other books of prime entry. For example, journal entries are made when errors are discovered and need to be corrected.

Whatever type of transaction is being recorded, the **format of a journal entry** is.

Date	Debit	Credit
	$	$
Account to be debited	X	
Account to be credited		X
(Narrative to explain the transaction)		

(Remember: in due course, the ledger accounts will be written up to include the transactions listed in the journal.)

5: LEDGER ACCOUNTS AND DOUBLE ENTRY

A **narrative explanation** must accompany each journal entry. It is required for audit and control, to indicate the purpose and authority of every transaction which is not first recorded in a book of original entry.

Exam focus point

> An examination question might ask you to 'journalise' transactions which would not in practice be recorded in the journal at all. If you are faced with such a problem, you should simply record the debit and credit entries for every transaction.

5.1 Examples: Journal entries

The following is a summary of the transactions of Hair by Fiona Middleton hairdressing business of which Fiona is the sole proprietor.

1 January	Put in cash of $2,000 as capital
	Purchased brushes and combs for cash $50
	Purchased hair driers from Gilroy Ltd on credit $150
30 January	Paid three months' rent to 31 March $300
	Collected and paid in takings $600
31 January	Gave Mrs Sullivan a perm, highlights etc on credit $80

Show the transactions by means of journal entries.

Solution

JOURNAL

			$	$
1 January	DEBIT	Cash at bank	2,000	
	CREDIT	Fiona Middleton – capital account		2,000
	Initial capital introduced			
1 January	DEBIT	Brushes and combs account	50	
	CREDIT	Cash at bank		50
	The purchase for cash of brushes and combs as non-current assets			
1 January	DEBIT	Hair dryer account	150	
	CREDIT	Sundry payables*		150
	The purchase on credit of hair driers as non-current assets			
30 January	DEBIT	Rent account	300	
	CREDIT	Cash at bank		300
	The payment of rent to 31 March			
30 January	DEBIT	Cash at bank	600	
	CREDIT	Revenue		600
	Cash takings			
31 January	DEBIT	Trade receivables	80	
	CREDIT	Revenue		80
	The provision of a hair-do on credit			

* **Note.** Suppliers who have supplied non-current assets are included amongst sundry payables, as distinct from trade suppliers (who have supplied raw materials or goods for resale) who are trade payables. It is quite common to have separate 'total payable' accounts, one for trade payables and another for sundry other payables.

5.2 The correction of errors

The journal is most commonly used to record corrections to errors that have been made in writing up the nominal ledger accounts. Errors corrected by the journal must be **capable of correction by means of a**

double entry in the ledger accounts. In other words the error must not have caused total debits and total credits to be unequal.

Special rules apply when errors are made which break the rule of double entry.

We will deal with errors in Chapter 11.

6 Day book analysis

FAST FORWARD

Entries in the day books are totalled and analysed before posting to the nominal ledger.

6.1 Sales day book

In the previous chapter, we used the following example of four transactions entered into the sales day book.

SALES DAY BOOK

Date 20X0	Invoice	Customer	Total amount invoiced $	Boot sales $	Shoe sales $
Jan 10	247	Jones & Co	105.00	60.00	45.00
	248	Smith Ltd	86.40	86.40	
	249	Alex & Co	31.80		31.80
	250	Enor College	1,264.60	800.30	464.30
			1,487.80	946.70	541.10

We have already seen that in theory these transactions are posted to the ledger accounts as follows.

DEBIT	Trade receivables	$1,487.80	
CREDIT	Revenue		$1,487.80

However a total revenue account is not very informative, particularly if the business sells lots of different products. So, using our example, the business might open up a 'sale of shoes' account and a 'sale of boots' account. Then the ledger account postings are:

		$	$
DEBIT	Trade receivables	1,487.80	
CREDIT	Sale of shoes account		541.10
	Sale of boots account		946.70

That is why the analysis of sales is kept. Exactly the same reasoning lies behind the analyses kept in the other books of prime entry.

6.2 Sales returns day book

We will now look at the sales returns day book from Chapter 4.

SALES RETURNS DAY BOOK

Date 20X8	Credit note	Customer and goods	Amount $
30 April	CR008	Owen Plenty 3 pairs 'Texas' boots	135.00

This will be posted as follows:

		$	$
DEBIT	Sales returns book	135.00	
CREDIT	Trade receivables		135.00

6.3 Purchase day book and purchases returns day book

The purchase day book and purchases returns day book in Chapter 4 can be posted in a similar way.

6.3.1 Purchases

		$	$
DEBIT	Purchases	444.40	
	Electricity	116.80	
CREDIT	Trade payables		561.20

6.3.2 Purchase returns

		$	$
DEBIT	Trade payable	46.60	
CREDIT	Purchases returns		46.60

7 The imprest system

FAST FORWARD

The imprest system is operated through the petty cash book using **double entry**.

The concept of the imprest system in petty cash was introduced in Chapter 4. This is reviewed in more detail by looking at how the journals are used to update the accounting records.

A business starts with a cash float on 1.3.20X7 of $250. This will be a payment from cash at bank to petty cash, ie:

DEBIT	Petty cash	$250	
CREDIT	Cash at bank		$250

Five payments were made out of petty cash during March 20X7. The petty cash book might look as follows.

Receipts $	Date	Narrative	Total $	Payments Postage $	Travel $
250.00	1.3.X7	Cash			
	2.3.X7	Stamps	12.00	12.00	
	8.3.X7	Stamps	10.00	10.00	
	19.3.X7	Travel	16.00		16.00
	23.3.X7	Travel	5.00		5.00
	28.3.X7	Stamps	11.50	11.50	
250.00			54.50	33.50	21.00

At the end of each month (or at any other suitable interval) the total payments in the petty cash book are **posted** to ledger accounts. For March 20X7, $33.50 would be debited to postage account and $21.00 to travel account. The total payments of $54.50 are credited to the petty cash account. This completes the double entry.

The cash float needs to be topped up by a payment of $54.50 from the main cash book, ie:

		$	$
DEBIT	Petty cash	54.50	
CREDIT	Cash		54.50

PART B ACCOUNTING RECORDS AND PROCEDURES

So the rules of double entry have been satisfied, and the petty cash book for the month of March 20X7 will look like this.

Receipts $	Date	Narrative	Total $	Payments Postage $	Travel $
250.00	1.3.X7	Cash			
	2.3.X7	Stamps	12.00	12.00	
	8.3.X7	Stamps	10.00	10.00	
	19.3.X7	Travel	16.00		16.00
	23.3.X7	Travel	5.00		5.00
	28.3.X7	Stamps	11.50	11.50	
	31.3.X7	Balance c/d	195.50		
250.00			250.00	33.50	21.00
195.50	1.4.X7	Balance b/d			
54.50	1.4.X7	Cash			

As you can see, the cash float is back up to $250 on 1.4.X7, ready for more payments to be made.

The petty cash account in the ledger will appear as follows.

PETTY CASH

			$			$
1.3.20X7	Cash		250.00	31.3.20X7	Payments	54.50
1.4.20X7	Cash		54.50	1.4.20X7	Balance c/d	250.00
			304.50			304.50
1.4.20X7	Balance b/d		250.00			

Question
Petty cash

Summit Glazing operates an imprest petty cash system. The imprest amount is $150.00. At the end of the period the totals of the four analysis columns in the petty cash book were as follows.

	$
Column 1	23.12
Column 2	6.74
Column 3	12.90
Column 4	28.50

How much cash is required to restore the imprest amount?

Answer

$71.26. This is the total amount of cash that has been used.

8 The trade receivables and payables ledgers

FAST FORWARD

The trade receivables and payables ledgers contain the **personal accounts** of individual customers and suppliers. They do not normally form part of the double-entry system.

8.1 Impersonal accounts and personal accounts

The accounts in the nominal ledger (ledger accounts) relate to types of income, expense, asset, liability – rent, revenue, trade receivables, payables etc – rather than to the person to whom the money is paid or

from whom it is received. They are therefore called **impersonal** accounts. However, there is also a need for **personal** accounts, most commonly for trade receivables and payables, and these are contained in the trade receivables ledger and trade payables ledger.

8.2 The trade receivables ledger

The sales day book provides a chronological record of invoices sent out by a business to credit customers. For many businesses, this might involve very large numbers of invoices per day or per week. The same customer might appear in several different places in the sales day book, for sales made on credit at different times. So a customer may owe money on several unpaid invoices.

In addition to keeping a chronological record of invoices, a business should also keep a record of how much money each individual credit customer owes, and what this total debt consists of. The need for a **personal account for each customer** is a practical one.

(a) A customer might telephone, and ask how much he currently owes. Staff must be able to tell him.

(b) It is a common practice to send out statements to credit customers at the end of each month, showing how much they still owe, and itemising new invoices sent out and payments received during the month.

(c) The managers of the business will want to keep a check on the credit position of an individual customer, and to ensure that no customer is exceeding his credit limit by purchasing more goods.

(d) Most important is the need to match payments received against debts owed. If a customer makes a payment, the business must be able to set off the payment against the customer's debt and establish how much he still owes on balance.

Key term

> The **trade receivables ledger** is a ledger for customers' personal accounts.

Trade receivables ledger accounts are written up as follows:

(a) When entries are made in the sales day book (invoices sent out), they are subsequently also made in the **debit side** of the relevant customer account in the trade receivables ledger.

(b) Similarly, when entries are made in the cash book (payments received), or in the sales returns day book, they are also made in the **credit side** of the relevant customer account.

Each customer account is given a reference or code number, and it is that reference which appears in the **sales day book**. We say that amounts are **posted** from the sales day book to the trade receivables ledger.

Here is an example of how a trade receivables ledger account is laid out.

ENOR COLLEGE

A/c no: RL 9

		$		$
Balance b/f		250.00		
10.1.X0	Revenue – SDB 48			
	(invoice no 250)	1,264.60	Balance c/d	1,514.60
		1,514.60		1,514.60
11.1.X0	Balance b/d	1,514.60		

The debit side of this personal account, then, shows amounts owed by Enor College. When Enor pays some of the money it owes it will be entered into the cash book (receipts) and subsequently 'posted' to the credit side of the personal account. For example, if the college paid $250 on 10.1.20X0, it would appear as follows.

ENOR COLLEGE

A/c no: RL 9

		$			$
Balance b/f		250.00	10.1.X0	Cash	250.00
10.1.X0	Revenue – SDB 48				
	(invoice no 250)	1,264.60		Balance c/d	1,264.60
		1,514.60			1,514.60
11.1.X0	Balance b/d	1,264.60			

The opening balance owed by Enor College on 11.1.X0 is now $1,264.60 instead of $1,514.60, because of the $250 receipt which came in on 10.1.X0.

8.3 The trade payables ledger

The trade payables ledger, like the trade receivables ledger, consists of a number of personal accounts. These are separate accounts for **each individual supplier**, and they enable a business to keep a continuous record of how much it owes each supplier at any time.

Key term

> The **trade payables ledger** is a ledger for suppliers' personal accounts.

After entries are made in the purchase day book, cash book, or purchase returns day book – ie after entries are made in the books of prime entry – they are also made in the relevant supplier account in the payables ledger. Again we say that the entries in the purchase day book are **posted** to the suppliers' personal accounts in the payables ledger.

Here is an example of how a payables ledger account is laid out.

COOK & CO

A/c no: PL 31

	$		$
Balance c/d	515.00	Balance b/f	200.00
		15 Mar 20X8	
		Invoice received	
		PDB 37	315.00
	515.00		515.00
		16 March 20X8	
		Balance b/d	515.00

The credit side of this personal account, then, shows amounts owing to Cook & Co. If the business paid Cook & Co some money, it would be entered into the cash book (payments) and subsequently be posted to the debit side of the personal account. For example, if the business paid Cook & Co $100 on 15 March 20X8, it would appear as follows:

COOK & CO

A/c no: PL 31

		$			$
15.3.X8	Cash	100.00		Balance b/f	200.00
			15.3.X8	Invoice received	
	Balance c/d	415.00		PDB 37	315.00
		515.00			515.00
			16.3.X8	Balance b/d	415.00

The opening balance owed to Cook & Co on 16 March 20X8 is now $415.00 instead of $515.00 because of the $100 payment made during 15 March 20X8.

The remainder of the balance brought forward of $100.00 ($200.00 brought forward less payment of $100.00) is in dispute and Cook & Co send the business a credit note for $100.00 on 17 March 20X8.

5: LEDGER ACCOUNTS AND DOUBLE ENTRY

COOK & CO

A/c no: PL 31

		$			$
17.3.X8	Credit note received	100.00	16.3.X8	Balance b/f	415.00
	Balance c/d	315.00			
		415.00			415.00
			12.3.X8	Balance b/d	315.00

The business now owes Cook & Co the amount of the invoice received on 15 March 20X8.

Tutorial note. Please note that, in a manual system, the account is not 'balanced off' after each transaction. It is more likely to be done once a month. However, we have done this to show the effect of the transactions.

Chapter roundup

- Ledger accounts **summarise** all the individual transactions listed in the books of prime entry.
- The principal accounts are contained in a ledger called the **general** or **nominal ledger**.
- The **accounting equation** emphasises the equality between assets and liabilities (including capital as a liability).
- You should now be aware that when business transactions are accounted for it should be possible to **restate the assets and liabilities** of the business after the transactions have taken place.
- **Trade payables** are **liabilities**. **Trade receivables** are **assets.**
- The **matching convention** requires that revenue earned is matched with the expenses incurred in earning it.
- **Double entry bookkeeping** is based on the idea that each transaction has an equal but opposite effect. Every accounting event must be entered in ledger accounts both as a debit and as an equal but opposite credit.
- A debit entry will:
    - Increase an asset
    - Decrease a liability
    - Increase an expense

  A credit entry will:
    - Decrease an asset
    - Increase a liability
    - Increase income
- Some accounts in the nominal ledger represent the total of very many smaller balances. For example, the **trade receivable account** represents all the balances owed by individual customers of the business while the **trade payable account** represents all money owed by the business to its suppliers.
- The **journal** is the record of prime entry for transactions which are not recorded in any of the other books of prime entry.
- Entries in the day books are totalled and analysed before posting to the nominal ledger.
- The imprest system is operated through the petty cash book using **double entry**.
- The trade receivables and payables ledgers contain the **personal accounts** of individual customers and suppliers. They do not normally form part of the double-entry system.

Quick quiz

1. What is the double entry to record a cash sale of $50?

2. What is the double entry to record a credit sale of $50?

    A   Debit cash $50, credit revenue $50
    B   Debit trade receivables $50, credit revenue $50
    C   Debit revenue $50, credit trade receivables $50
    D   Debit revenue $50, credit cash $50

3. What is the double entry to record a purchase of office chairs for $1,000?

    A   Debit non-current assets $1,000, credit cash $1,000
    B   Debit cash $1,000, credit purchases $1,000

4. What is the double entry to record a credit sale of $500 to A?

    A   Debit trade receivables $500, credit revenue $500
    B   Debit trade receivables ledger (A's account) $500, credit revenue $500

5. Name one reason for making a journal entry.

6. Individual customer accounts are kept in which ledger?

    A   General ledger
    B   Trade receivable account
    C   Trade receivables ledger
    D   Nominal ledger

PART B ACCOUNTING RECORDS AND PROCEDURES

Answers to quick quiz

1 | | | $ | $ |
  | DEBIT | Cash a/c | 50 | |
  | CREDIT | Revenue a/c | | 50 |

2   B

3   A

4   A   The trade receivables ledger is a memorandum account and not part of the double entry system.

5   Most commonly to correct an error, although it can be used to make any entry that is not recorded in a book of prime entry (eg prepayments, accrued expenses, depreciation).

6   C   The trade receivables ledger contains the individual customer accounts. The general ledger (A) and nominal ledger (D) are different names for the same ledger. This contains the trade receivable account (B) which is the **total** of all the individual customer accounts.

From trial balance to financial statements

Topic list	Syllabus reference
1 The trial balance	A2
2 The statement of profit or loss and other comprehensive income	A2
3 The statement of financial position	A2
4 Balancing accounts and preparing financial statements	A2

Introduction

In the previous chapter you learned the principles of double entry and how to post to the ledger accounts. The next step in our progress towards the financial statements is the **trial balance**.

Before transferring the relevant balances at the year end to the statement of profit or loss and other comprehensive income and putting closing balances carried forward into the statement of financial position, it is usual to test the accuracy of double entry bookkeeping records by preparing **a list of account balances**. This is done by taking all the balances on every account; because of the self-balancing nature of the system of double entry, **the total of the debit balances will be exactly equal to the total of the credit balances**.

In very straightforward circumstances, where no complications arise and where the records are complete, it is possible to prepare accounts directly from a trial balance. This is covered in Section 4.

PART B   ACCOUNTING RECORDS AND PROCEDURES

1 The trial balance

FAST FORWARD

> At suitable intervals, the entries in each **ledger account** are totalled and a **balance** is struck. Balances are usually collected in a **trial balance** which is then used as a basis for preparing a statement of profit or loss and other comprehensive income and a statement of financial position.

You have a list of transactions, and have been asked to post them to the relevant ledger accounts. You do it as quickly as possible and find that you have a little time left over at the end of the day. How do you check that you have posted all the debit and credit entries properly?

There is no foolproof method, but a technique which shows up the more obvious mistakes is to prepare a **trial balance**.

Key term

A **trial balance** is a list of ledger balances shown in debit and credit columns.

1.1 The first step

Before you draw up a list of account balances, you must have a collection of ledger accounts. For the sake of convenience, we will use the accounts of Ron Knuckle, which we drew up in the previous chapter.

CASH AT BANK

	$		$
Capital: Ron Knuckle	7,000	Rent	3,500
Bank loan	1,000	Shop fittings	2,000
Revenue	10,000	Trade payable control a/c	5,000
Trade receivable control a/c	2,500	Bank loan interest	100
		Other expenses	1,900
		Drawings	1,500

CAPITAL (RON KNUCKLE)

	$		$
		Cash at bank	7,000

BANK LOAN

	$		$
		Cash at bank	1,000

PURCHASES

	$		$
Trade payable control a/c	5,000		

TRADE PAYABLE CONTROL A/C

	$		$
Cash at bank	5,000	Purchases	5,000

RENT

	$		$
Cash at bank	3,500		

SHOP FITTINGS

	$		$
Cash at bank	2,000		

REVENUE

	$		$
		Cash at bank	10,000
		Trade receivable control a/c	2,500

TRADE RECEIVABLE CONTROL A/C

	$		$
Revenue	2,500	Cash at bank	2,500

BANK LOAN INTEREST

	$		$
Cash at bank	100		

OTHER EXPENSES

	$		$
Cash at bank	1,900		

DRAWINGS

	$		$
Cash at bank	1,500		

The next step is to 'balance' each account.

1.2 Balancing ledger accounts

At the end of an accounting period, a balance is struck on each account in turn. This means that all the debits on the account are totalled and so are all the credits. **If the total debits exceed the total credits there is said to be a debit balance on the account; if the credits exceed the debits then the account has a credit balance.**

In our simple example, there is very little balancing to do.

(a) Both the trade payable control account and the trade receivable control account balance off to zero.
(b) The cash at bank account has a debit balance of $6,500.
(c) The total on the revenue account is $12,500, which is a credit balance.

CASH AT BANK

	$		$
Capital: Ron Knuckle	7,000	Rent	3,500
Bank loan	1,000	Shop fittings	2,000
Revenue	10,000	Trade payable control a/c	5,000
Trade receivable control a/c	2,500	Bank loan interest	100
		Other expenses	1,900
		Drawings	1,500
			14,000

PART B ACCOUNTING RECORDS AND PROCEDURES

	$		$
		Balancing figure – the amount of cash left over after payments have been made	6,500
	20,500		20,500

TRADE PAYABLE CONTROL A/C

	$		$
Cash at bank	5,000	Purchases	5,000

REVENUE

	$		$
		Cash at bank	10,000
		Trade accounts receivable	2,500
			12,500

TRADE RECEIVABLE CONTROL A/C

	$		$
Revenue	2,500	Cash at bank	2,500

Otherwise, the accounts have only one entry each, so there is no totalling to do to arrive at the balance on each account.

1.3 Collecting the balances

If the basic principle of double entry has been correctly applied throughout the period it will be found that the credit balances equal the debit balances in total. This can be illustrated by collecting together the balances on Ron Knuckle's accounts.

	Debit	Credit
	$	$
Cash at bank (asset = debit balance)	6,500	
Capital (capital = credit balance)		7,000
Bank loan (liability = credit balance)		1,000
Purchases (expense = debit balance)	5,000	
Trade payable control a/c	–	–
Rent (expense)	3,500	
Shop fittings (asset)	2,000	
Revenue (income = credit balance)		12,500
Trade receivable control a/c	–	–
Bank loan interest (expense)	100	
Other expenses (expense)	1,900	
Drawings	1,500	
	20,500	20,500

This is called a **trial balance**. It does not matter in what order the various accounts are listed. It is just a method used to test the accuracy of the double entry bookkeeping.

1.4 What if the trial balance shows unequal debit and credit balances?

FAST FORWARD

A trial balance can be used to test the accuracy of the accounting records. It lists the balances on ledger accounts and totals them. Total debits should equal total credits.

If the two columns of the list are not equal, there must be an error in recording the transactions in the accounts. A list of account balances, however, will **not** disclose the following types of errors:

(a) The **complete omission** of a transaction, because neither a debit nor a credit is made.
(b) The posting of a debit or credit to the correct side of the ledger, but to a **wrong account**.

(c) **Compensating errors** (eg an error of $100 is exactly cancelled by another $100 error elsewhere).
(d) **Errors of principle**, eg cash from receivables being debited to trade receivables and credited to cash at bank instead of the other way round.

1.5 Example: Trial balance

As at 30.3.20X7, your business has the following balances on its ledger accounts.

Accounts	Balance $
Bank loan	12,000
Cash at bank	11,700
Capital	13,000
Local business taxes	1,880
Trade payables	11,200
Purchases	12,400
Revenue	14,600
Sundry payables	1,620
Trade receivables	12,000
Bank loan interest	1,400
Other expenses	11,020
Vehicles	2,020

During the year the business made the following transactions.

(a) Bought materials for $1,000, half for cash and half on credit
(b) Made $1,040 sales, $800 of which was for credit
(c) Paid wages to shop assistants of $260 in cash

You are required to draw up a trial balance showing the balances as at the end of 31.3.X7.

Solution

First it is necessary to decide which of the original balances are debits and which are credits.

Account	Dr $	Cr $
Bank loan (liability)		12,000
Cash at bank (asset; overdraft = liability)	11,700	
Capital (liability)		13,000
Local taxes (expense)	1,880	
Trade payables (liability)		11,200
Purchases (expense)	12,400	
Revenue (income)		14,600
Sundry payables (liability)		1,620
Trade receivables (asset)	12,000	
Bank loan interest (expenses)	1,400	
Other expenses	11,020	
Vehicles (non-current asset)	2,020	
	52,420	52,420

Now we must take account of the effects of the three transactions which took place on 31.3.X7.

				$	$
(a)	DEBIT	Purchases		1,000	
	CREDIT	Cash at bank			500
		Trade payables			500
(b)	DEBIT	Cash at bank		240	
		Trade receivables		800	
	CREDIT	Revenue			1,040

PART B ACCOUNTING RECORDS AND PROCEDURES

				$	$
(c)	DEBIT	Other expenses		260	
	CREDIT	Cash at bank			260

When these figures are included in the trial balance, it becomes:

Account	Dr	Cr
	$	$
Bank loan		12,000
Cash at bank (11,700 + 240 – 500 – 260)	11,180	
Capital		13,000
Local taxes	1,880	
Trade payables (11,200 + 500)		11,700
Purchases (12,400 + 1,000)	13,400	
Revenue (14,600 + 1,040)		15,640
Sundry payables		1,620
Trade receivables (12,000 + 800)	12,800	
Bank loan interest	1,400	
Other expenses (11,020 + 260)	11,280	
Vehicles	2,020	
	53,960	53,960

2 The statement of profit or loss and other comprehensive income

FAST FORWARD

> A **profit or loss ledger account** is opened up to gather all items relating to income and expenses. When **rearranged**, these items make up the **statement of profit or loss and other comprehensive income**.

The first step in the process of preparing the financial statements is to open up another ledger account, called the **profit or loss account**. In it a business summarises its results for the period by gathering together all the ledger account balances relating to the statement of profit or loss and other comprehensive income. This account is still part of the double entry system, so the basic rule of double entry still applies: every debit must have an equal and opposite credit entry.

This profit or loss account contains the same information as the financial statement we are aiming for, ie the statement of profit or loss and other comprehensive income, and in fact there are very few differences between the two. However, the statement of profit or loss and other comprehensive income lays the information out differently and it may be much less detailed.

So what do we do with this new ledger account? The first step is to look through the ledger accounts and identify which ones relate to income and expenses. In the case of Ron Knuckle, these accounts consist of purchases, rent, revenue, bank loan interest, and other expenses.

The balances on these accounts are transferred to the new profit or loss account. For example, the balance on the purchases account is $5,000 DR. To balance this to zero, we write in $5,000 CR. But to comply with the rule of double entry, there has to be a debit entry somewhere, so we write $5,000 DR in the profit or loss (P/L) account. Now the balance on the purchases account has been moved to the profit or loss account.

If we do the same thing with all the separate accounts of Ron Knuckle dealing with income and expenses, the result is as follows:

PURCHASES

	$		$
Trade payables	5,000	P/L a/c	5,000

RENT

	$		$
Cash at bank	3,500	P/L a/c	3,500

REVENUE

	$		$
P/L a/c	12,500	Cash at bank	10,000
		Trade receivables	2,500
	12,500		12,500

BANK LOAN INTEREST

	$		$
Cash at bank	100	P/L a/c	100

OTHER EXPENSES

	$		$
Cash at bank	1,900	P/L a/c	1,900

PROFIT OR LOSS ACCOUNT

	$		$
Purchases	5,000	Revenue	12,500
Rent	3,500		
Bank loan interest	100		
Other expenses	1,900		

(Note that the profit or loss account has not yet been balanced off but we will return to that later.)

If you look at the items we have gathered together in the profit or loss account, they should strike a chord in your memory. They are the same items that we need to draw up the statement of profit or loss and other comprehensive income.

Question — Statement of profit or loss and other comprehensive income

Draw up Ron Knuckle's statement of profit or loss and other comprehensive income.

Answer

RON KNUCKLE: STATEMENT OF PROFIT OR LOSS AND OTHER COMPREHENSIVE INCOME (SPLOCI)

	$	$	
Revenue		12,500	Trading
Cost of sales (= purchases in this case)		(5,000)	account
Gross profit		7,500	
Expenses			
Rent	3,500		
Bank loan interest	100		
Other expenses	1,900		
		(5,500)	
Net profit		2,000	

Note that the first part of the SPLOCI is also known as the trading account and gross profit is also known as trading profit.

PART B   ACCOUNTING RECORDS AND PROCEDURES

3 The statement of financial position

FAST FORWARD

The balances on all **remaining ledger accounts** (including the profit or loss account) can be listed and **rearranged** to form the **statement of financial position**.

Look back at the ledger accounts of Ron Knuckle. Now that we have dealt with those relating to income and expenses, which ones are left? The answer is that we still have to find out what to do with the cash, capital, bank loan, trade payables, shop fittings, trade receivables and the drawings accounts.

Are these the only ledger accounts left? No, don't forget there is still the last one we opened up, called the **profit or loss account**. The balance on this account represents the profit earned by the business, and if you go through the arithmetic, you will find that it has a credit balance – a profit – of $2,000. (Not surprisingly, this is the figure that is shown in the statement of profit or loss and other comprehensive income.)

These remaining accounts must also be balanced and ruled off, but since they represent assets and liabilities of the business (not income and expenses) their balances are not transferred to the income and expense account. Instead they are **carried down** in the books of the business. This means that they become opening balances for the next accounting period and indicate the value of the assets and liabilities at the end of one period and the beginning of the next.

The conventional method of ruling off a ledger account at the end of an accounting period is illustrated by the bank loan account in Ron Knuckle's books.

BANK LOAN ACCOUNT

	$		$
Balance carried down (c/d)	1,000	Cash (D)	1,000
		Balance brought down (b/d)	1,000

Ron Knuckle therefore begins the new accounting period with a credit balance of $1,000 on this account. A **credit balance brought down** denotes a liability. An asset would be represented by a **debit balance brought down**.

One further point is worth noting before we move on to complete this example. You will remember that a proprietor's capital comprises any cash introduced by him, plus any profits made by the business, less any drawings made by him. At the stage we have now reached, these three elements are contained in different ledger accounts: cash introduced of $7,000 appears in the capital account; drawings of $1,500 appear in drawings; and the profit made by the business is represented by the $2,000 credit balance on the profit or loss account. It is convenient to gather together all these amounts into one **capital account**, in the same way as we earlier gathered together income and expense accounts into one P/L account.

If we go ahead and gather the three amounts together, the results are as follows:

DRAWINGS

	$		$
Cash at bank	1,500	Capital a/c	1,500

PROFIT OR LOSS ACCOUNT

	$		$
Purchases	5,000	Revenue	12,500
Rent	3,500		
Bank loan interest	100		
Other expenses	1,900		
Capital a/c	2,000		
	12,500		12,500

CAPITAL

	$		$
Drawings	1,500	Cash at bank	7,000
Balance c/d	7,500	P/L a/c	2,000
	9,000		9,000
		Balance b/d	7,500

Question — Statement of financial position

You can now complete Ron Knuckle's simple statement of financial position.

Answer

RON KNUCKLE
STATEMENT OF FINANCIAL POSITION AT END OF FIRST TRADING PERIOD

	$
Assets	
Non-current assets	
Shop fittings	2,000
Current assets	
Cash at bank	6,500
Total assets	8,500
Capital and liabilities	
Proprietor's capital	7,500
Non-current liabilities	
Bank loan	1,000
Total capital and liabilities	8,500

When a statement of financial position is drawn up for an accounting period which is not the first one, then it ought to show the capital at the start of the accounting period and the capital at the end of the accounting period. This will be illustrated in the next example.

In an examination question, you might not be given the ledger accounts – you might have to draw them up in the first place. That is the case with the following exercise – see if you can do it by yourself before looking at the solution.

4 Balancing accounts and preparing financial statements

The exercise which follows is by far the most important in this text so far. It uses all the accounting steps from entering up ledger accounts to preparing the financial statements. It is **very important that you try the question by yourself!** If you do not, you will be missing out a vital part of this Workbook.

Exam focus point

Examiners have emphasised the need to practise full length questions in order to fully understand the techniques involved.

PART B ACCOUNTING RECORDS AND PROCEDURES

Question — Financial statements

A business is established with capital of $2,000, and this amount is paid into a business bank account by the proprietor. During the first year's trading, the following transactions occurred:

	$
Purchases of goods for resale, on credit	4,300
Payments to trade payables	3,600
Revenue, all on credit	5,800
Payments from trade receivables	3,200
Non-current assets purchased for cash	1,500
Other expenses, all paid in cash	900

The bank has provided an overdraft facility of up to $3,000.

Required

Prepare the ledger accounts, a statement of profit or loss and other comprehensive income for the year and a statement of financial position as at the end of the year.

Answer

(1) The first thing to do is to **open ledger accounts** so that the transactions can be entered up. The relevant accounts which we need for this example are: cash at bank; capital; trade payables; purchases; non-current assets; revenue; trade receivables and other expenses.

(2) The next step is to work out the **double entry** bookkeeping for each transaction. Normally you would write them straight into the accounts, but to make this example easier to follow, they are first listed below.

		DEBIT	CREDIT
(a)	Establishing business ($2,000)	Cash at bank	Capital
(b)	Purchases ($4,300)	Purchases	Trade payables
(c)	Payments to trade payables ($3,600)	Trade payables	Cash at bank
(d)	Revenue ($5,800)	Trade receivables	Revenue
(e)	Payments from trade receivables ($3,200)	Cash at bank	Trade receivables
(f)	Non-current assets ($1,500)	Non-current assets	Cash at bank
(g)	Other (cash) expenses ($900)	Other expenses	Cash at bank

So far, the ledger accounts will look like this.

CASH AT BANK

	$		$
Capital	2,000	Trade payables	3,600
Trade receivables	3,200	Non-current assets	1,500
		Other expenses	900

CAPITAL

	$		$
		Cash at bank	2,000

TRADE PAYABLES CONTROL A/C

	$		$
Cash at bank	3,600	Purchases	4,300

PURCHASES

	$		$
Trade accounts payable	4,300		

NON-CURRENT ASSETS

	$		$
Cash at bank	1,500		

REVENUE

	$		$
		Trade receivables	5,800

TRADE RECEIVABLES CONTROL A/C

	$		$
Revenue	5,800	Cash at bank	3,200

OTHER EXPENSES

	$		$
Cash at bank	900		

(3) The next thing to do is to **balance** all these accounts. It is at this stage that you could, if you wanted to, draw up a trial balance to make sure the double entry is accurate. There is not very much point in this simple example, but if you did, it would look like this.

	Debit	Credit
	$	$
Cash at bank		800
Capital		2,000
Trade payables		700
Purchases	4,300	
Non-current assets	1,500	
Revenue		5,800
Trade receivables	2,600	
Other expenses	900	
	9,300	9,300

(4) After balancing the accounts, the profit or loss account should be opened. Into it should be **transferred all the balances** relating to income and expense (ie purchases, other expenses, and revenue). At this point, the ledger accounts will be as follows.

CASH AT BANK

	$		$
Capital	2,000	Trade payables	3,600
Trade receivables	3,200	Non-current assets	1,500
Balance c/d	800	Other expenses	900
	6,000		6,000
		Balance b/d	800*

* A credit balance b/d means that this cash item is a liability, not an asset. This indicates a bank overdraft of $800, with cash income of $5,200 falling short of payments of $6,000 by this amount.

PART B ACCOUNTING RECORDS AND PROCEDURES

CAPITAL

	$		$
Balance c/d	2,600	Cash at bank	2,000
		P/L a/c	600
	2,600		2,600

TRADE PAYABLES CONTROL A/C

	$		$
Cash at bank	3,600	Purchases	4,300
Balance c/d	700		
	4,300		4,300
		Balance b/d	700

PURCHASES ACCOUNT

	$		$
Trade payables	4,300	P/L a/c	4,300

NON-CURRENT ASSETS

	$		$
Cash at bank	1,500	Balance c/d	1,500
Balance b/d	1,500		

REVENUE

	$		$
P/L a/c	5,800		5,800

TRADE RECEIVABLES

	$		$
Revenue	5,800	Cash at bank	3,200
		Balance c/d	2,600
	5,800		5,800
Balance b/d	2,600		

OTHER EXPENSES

	$		$
Cash at bank	900	P/L a/c	900

PROFIT OR LOSS ACCOUNT

	$		$
Purchases account	4,300	Revenue	5,800
Gross profit c/d	1,500		
	5,800		5,800
Other expenses	900	Gross profit b/d	1,500
Net profit (transferred to capital account)	600		
	1,500		1,500

So the statement of profit or loss and other comprehensive income will be:

STATEMENT OF PROFIT OR LOSS AND OTHER COMPREHENSIVE INCOME FOR THE ACCOUNTING PERIOD

	$
Revenue	5,800
Cost of sales (purchases)	4,300
Gross profit	1,500
Expenses	900
Net profit	600

Listing and then rearranging the balances on the ledger accounts gives the statement of financial position as:

STATEMENT OF FINANCIAL POSITION AS AT THE END OF THE PERIOD

	$	$
Assets		
Non-current assets		1,500
Current assets		
Trade receivables		2,600
Total assets		4,100
Capital and liabilities		
Capital		
At start of period	2,000	
Net profit for period	600	
At end of period		2,600
Current liabilities		
Bank overdraft	800	
Trade payables	700	
		1,500
Total capital and liabilities		4,100

Exam focus point

The above example is highly detailed. This detail is given to help you to work through the example properly. You may wish to do things this way yourself until you get more practised in accounting techniques and are confident enough to take short cuts.

The techniques are worth practising as you may well get a question requiring you to calculate a figure for the statement of profit or loss and other comprehensive income or statement of financial position from a trial balance.

PART B   ACCOUNTING RECORDS AND PROCEDURES

Question — Opening trial balance

Alpha has the following opening balances on its ledger accounts.

	$
Fixtures	5,000
Trade receivables	2,000
Bank account	1,000
Loan	3,000

(a)   What is the total assets figure?
- A $6,000
- B $5,000
- C $8,000
- D $3,000

(b)   What is the opening figure for capital?
- A $6,000
- B $5,000
- C $8,000
- D $3,000

Answer

(a)   C   Assets = 5,000 + 2,000 + 1,000
              = 8,000

(b)   B   Capital = assets – liabilities
              = (5,000 + 2,000 + 1,000) – 3,000
              = 5,000

Chapter roundup

- At suitable intervals, the entries in each **ledger account** are totalled and a **balance** is struck. Balances are usually collected in a **trial balance** which is then used as a basis for preparing a statement of profit or loss and other comprehensive income and a statement of financial position.

- A trial balance can be used to test the accuracy of the accounting records. It lists the balances on ledger accounts and totals them. Total debits should equal total credits.

- A **profit or loss ledger account** is opened up to gather all items relating to income and expenses. When **rearranged**, the items make up the **statement of profit or loss and other comprehensive income**.

- The balances on all **remaining ledger accounts** (including the profit or loss account) can be listed and **rearranged** to form the **statement of financial position**.

Quick quiz

1. What is the purpose of a trial balance?

2. A trial balance may still balance if some of the balances are wrong.
   Is this statement correct?
   A   Yes
   B   No

3. In a period, sales are $140,000, purchases $75,000 and other expenses $25,000. What is the figure for net profit to be transferred to the capital account?
   A $40,000
   B $65,000
   C $75,000
   D $140,000

4. The balance on an expense account will go to the statement of profit or loss account. However, the balance on a liability account is written off to capital.
   Is this statement correct?
   A   Yes
   B   No

5. The balance brought forward on the bank account is a debit figure. This means that the balance is overdrawn. True or false?

PART B ACCOUNTING RECORDS AND PROCEDURES

Answers to quick quiz

1. To test the accuracy of the double entry bookkeeping.

2. A See Section 1.4.

3. A

    PROFIT OR LOSS ACCOUNT

	$		$
Purchases	75,000	Revenue	140,000
Gross profit c/d	65,000		
	140,000		140,000
Other expenses	25,000	Gross profit b/d	65,000
Net profit – to capital a/c	40,000		
	65,000		65,000

    B is the **gross** profit figure, while C is the figure for purchases and D revenue.

4. B When an expense account is balanced off, the balance is transferred to the profit or loss account. When a liability account is balanced off, the balance is carried forward to the next accounting period.

5. False. A debit balance b/f is an asset and means that the bank account is **not** overdrawn.

Value added tax

Topic list	Syllabus reference
1 The nature of value added tax (VAT) and how it is collected	A2
2 Accounting for VAT	A2

Introduction

Many business transactions involve sales tax, known as value added tax (VAT) in the UK. Invoices and bills show any VAT charged separately.

VAT is charged on the supply of goods and services. It is an **indirect tax**.

Section 1 explains how VAT works.

Section 2 deals with the accounting treatment of sales tax. If you understand the principle behind the tax and how it is collected, you will understand the accounting treatment.

Note. A VAT rate of 20% has been used throughout this chapter and any examples.

PART B ACCOUNTING RECORDS AND PROCEDURES

1 The nature of value added tax (VAT) and how it is collected

FAST FORWARD

VAT is an indirect tax levied on the sale of goods and services. It is usually administered by the local tax authorities.

1.1 How is VAT levied?

VAT is a cumulative tax, collected at various stages of a product's life. In the illustrative example below, a manufacturer of a television buys materials and components and then sells the television to a wholesaler, who in turn sells it to a retailer, who then sells it to a customer. It is assumed that the rate for VAT is 20% on all items. All the other figures are for illustration only.

1.2 Example

			Price net of sales tax $	VAT 20% $	Total price $
(a)	(i)	Manufacturer purchases raw materials and components	40	8	48
	(ii)	Manufacturer sells the completed television to a wholesaler	200	40	240
		The manufacturer hands over to tax authorities		32	
(b)	(i)	Wholesaler purchases television for	200	40	240
	(ii)	Wholesaler sells television to a retailer	320	64	384
		Wholesaler hands over to tax authorities		24	
(c)	(i)	Retailer purchases television for	320	64	384
	(ii)	Retailer sells television	480	96	576
		Retailer hands over to tax authorities		32	
(d)		Customer purchases television for	480	96	576

The total tax of $96 is borne by the ultimate consumer. However, the tax is handed over to the authorities in stages. If we assume that the sales tax of $8 on the initial supplies to the manufacturer is paid by the supplier, the tax authorities would collect the VAT as follows:

	$
Supplier of materials and components	8
Manufacturer	32
Wholesaler	24
Retailer	32
Total sales tax paid	96

1.3 Input and output VAT

Key term

VAT charged on goods and services sold by a business is referred to as **output VAT**. VAT paid on goods and services 'bought in' by a business is referred to as **input VAT**.

FAST FORWARD

If output VAT exceeds input VAT, the business pays the difference in tax to the authorities. If output VAT is less than input VAT in a period, the tax authorities will refund the difference to the business.

The example above assumes that the supplier, manufacturer, wholesaler and retailer are all VAT registered traders.

7: VALUE ADDED TAX

A VAT registered trader must carry out the following tasks:

(a) Charge VAT on the goods and services sold at the rate prescribed by the government. This is output VAT.

(b) Pay VAT on goods and services purchased from other businesses. This is input VAT.

(c) Pay to the tax authorities the difference between the VAT collected on sales and the VAT paid to suppliers for purchases. Payments are made at quarterly intervals.

1.4 Irrecoverable VAT

There are some circumstances in which traders are not allowed to reclaim VAT paid on their inputs. In these cases the trader must bear the cost of VAT and account for it accordingly. So the cost of expenses and any non-current assets purchased will include any irrecoverable VAT.

FAST FORWARD

> Where VAT is not recoverable it must be regarded as part of the cost of the items purchased and included as part of the expense in the statement of profit or loss or as part of the asset in the statement of financial position as appropriate.

2 Accounting for VAT

FAST FORWARD

> Registered businesses charge output VAT on sales and suffer input VAT on purchases. VAT does not affect the statement of profit or loss and other comprehensive income, but is simply being collected on behalf of the tax authorities to whom a quarterly payment is made.

2.1 Statement of profit or loss and other comprehensive income

A business does not make any profit out of the VAT it charges. It therefore follows that its statement of profit or loss and other comprehensive income figures should not include VAT. For example, if a business sells goods for $600 + VAT $120, ie for $720 total price, the sales account should only record the $600 excluding VAT. The accounting entries to record the sale would be as follows:

DEBIT	Cash or trade receivables	$720	
CREDIT	Revenue		$600
CREDIT	VAT payable (output VAT)		$120

If input VAT is recoverable, the cost of purchases should exclude the VAT and be recorded net of tax. For example, if a business purchases goods on credit for $400 + VAT $80, the transaction would be recorded as follows:

DEBIT	Purchases	$400	
DEBIT	VAT payables (input VAT recoverable)	$80	
CREDIT	Trade payables		$480

If the input VAT is not recoverable, the cost of purchases must include the tax, because it is the business itself which must bear the cost of the tax.

Exam focus point

Statement of profit or loss and other comprehensive income

Purchases   *Revenue*

Irrecoverable input VAT: include   Exclude VAT
Recoverable input VAT: exclude

2.2 VAT in the cash book, sales day book and purchase day book

When a business makes a credit sale the total amount invoiced, including VAT, will be recorded in the sales day book. The analysis columns will then separate the VAT from the sales income of the business as follows.

Date	Total	Sales income	VAT
	$	$	$
A Detter and Sons	240	200	40

When a business is invoiced by a supplier the total amount payable, including VAT, will be recorded in the purchase day book. The analysis columns will then separate the recoverable input VAT from the net purchase cost to the business as follows.

Date	Total	Purchase	VAT
	$	$	$
A Splier (Merchants)	192	160	32

When trade receivables pay what they owe, or payables are paid, there is **no need to show** the VAT in an analysis column of the cash book, because input and output VAT arise when the sale is made, not when the debt is settled.

However, VAT charged on **cash sales** or VAT paid on **cash purchases** will be analysed in a separate column of the cash book. This is because output VAT has just arisen from the cash sale and must be credited to the VAT payables in the ledger accounts. Similarly input VAT paid on cash purchases, having just arisen, must be debited to the VAT payable.

For example, the receipts side of a cash book might be written up as follows.

				Analysis columns	
Date	Narrative	Total	Sales ledger	Cash sales	Output sales tax on cash sales
		$	$	$	$
	A Detter & Sons	240	240		
	Owen	660	660		
	Cash sales	336		280	56
	Newgate Merchants	184	184		
	Cash sales	96		80	16
		1,516	1,084	360	72

The payments side of a cash book might be written up as follows.

				Analysis columns	
Date	Narrative	Total	Purchase ledger	Cash purchases and sundry items	Input sales tax on cash purchases
		$	$	$	$
	A Splier (Merchants)	192	192		
	Telephone bill paid	144		120	24
	Cash purchase of stationery	48		40	8
	VAT paid to tax authorities	1,400		1,400	
		1,784	192	1,560	32

7: VALUE ADDED TAX

Question
VAT

Are trade receivables and trade payables shown in the accounts inclusive of VAT or exclusive of VAT?

Answer

They are shown **inclusive** of VAT, as the statement of financial position must reflect the total amount due from receivables and due to payables.

Exam focus point

A small element of VAT is quite likely in questions. It is worth spending a bit of time ensuring that you understand the logic behind the way VAT is accounted for, rather than trying to learn the rules by rote. This will ensure that even if you forget the rules, you will be able to work out what should be done.

2.3 VAT payable/receivable

FAST FORWARD

An outstanding payable for VAT will appear as a current liability in the statement of financial position.

The VAT paid to the authorities each quarter is the difference between recoverable input VAT on purchases and output VAT charged on sales. For example, if a business is invoiced for input VAT of $8,000 and charges VAT of $15,000 on its credit sales and VAT of $2,000 on its cash sales, the VAT payable account would be as follows.

VAT PAYABLE

	$		$
Trade payables (input VAT)	8,000	Trade receivables (output sales tax invoiced)	15,000
Cash (payment to authorities)	9,000	Cash (output VAT on cash sales)	2,000
	17,000		17,000

Payments to the authorities do not coincide with the end of the accounting period of a business, and so at the reporting date there will be a balance on the VAT payable account. If this balance is for an amount payable to the authorities, the outstanding payable for VAT will appear as a current liability in the statement of financial position.

Occasionally, a business will be owed money back by the authorities, and in such a situation, the VAT refund owed by the authorities would be a VAT receivable current asset in the statement of financial position.

Question
Sales tax payable

A business in its first period of trading charges $4,000 of VAT on its sales and suffers $3,500 of VAT on its purchases which include $250 VAT on business entertaining. Prepare the VAT payable account.

Answer

VAT PAYABLE ACCOUNT

	$		$
Trade payables	3,250	Trade receivables	4,000
Balance c/d (owed to tax authorities)	750		
	4,000		4,000
		Balance b/d	750

> **The main points**
>
> (a) **Credit sales**
>   (i) Include VAT in sales day book; separately
>   (ii) Include gross receipts from receivables in cashbook; no need to show VAT separately
>   (iii) Exclude VAT element from statement of profit or loss and other comprehensive income
>   (iv) Credit VAT payable with output VAT element of receivables invoiced
>
> (b) **Credit purchases**
>   (i) Include VAT in purchases day book; show it separately
>   (ii) Include gross payments in cashbook; no need to show VAT separately
>   (iii) Exclude recoverable VAT from statement of profit or loss and other comprehensive income
>   (iv) Include irrecoverable VAT in statement of profit or loss and other comprehensive income
>   (v) Debit VAT payable with recoverable input VAT element of credit purchases
>
> (c) **Cash sales**
>   (i) Include gross receipts in cashbook; show VAT separately
>   (ii) Exclude VAT element from statement of profit or loss and other comprehensive income
>   (iii) Credit VAT payable with output VAT element of cash sales
>
> (d) **Cash purchases**
>   (i) Include gross payments in cashbook: show VAT separately
>   (ii) Exclude recoverable VAT from statement of profit or loss and other comprehensive income
>   (iii) Include irrecoverable VAT in statement of profit or loss and other comprehensive income
>   (iv) Debit VAT payable with recoverable input VAT element of cash purchases

Exam focus point

In VAT questions, remember to check the tax rate used. If you are required to calculate VAT, the rate will always be given.

Chapter roundup

- **VAT** is an indirect tax levied on the sale of goods and services. It is usually administered by the local tax authorities.
- If output VAT exceeds input VAT, the business pays the difference in tax to the authorities. If output VAT is less than input VAT in a period, the tax authorities will refund the difference to the business.
- Where VAT is not recoverable it must be regarded as part of the cost of the items purchased and included in the statement of profit or loss charge or in the statement of financial position as appropriate.
- Registered businesses charge output VAT on sales and suffer input VAT on purchases. VAT does not affect the statement of profit or loss and other comprehensive income, but is simply being collected on behalf of the tax authorities to whom a quarterly payment is made.
- An outstanding payable for VAT will appear as a current liability in the statement of financial position.

Quick quiz

1 VAT is:

    A   A direct tax levied on sales of goods and services
    B   An indirect tax levied on the sales of goods and services
    C   Administered by the Treasury
    D   Charged by businesses on taxable supplies

2 VAT is due on all sales. Is this statement correct?

    A   Yes
    B   No

3 When VAT is not recoverable on the cost of a motor car, it should be treated in which of the following ways?

    A   Deducted from the cost of the asset capitalised
    B   Included in the cost of the asset capitalised
    C   Deducted from output tax for the period
    D   Written off to statement of profit or loss as an expense

4 Purchases of goods costing $500 subject to VAT at 20% occur. Which of the following correctly records the **credit purchase**?

A	DEBIT	Purchases	$500.00	
	DEBIT	VAT	$100.00	
	CREDIT	Trade payables		$600.00
B	DEBIT	Purchases	$600.00	
	CREDIT	Payables		$600.00
C	DEBIT	Purchases	$400.00	
	DEBIT	VAT	$100.00	
	CREDIT	Trade payables		$500.00
D	DEBIT	Purchases	$500.00	
	CREDIT	VAT		$100.00
	CREDIT	Trade payables		$400.00

PART B ACCOUNTING RECORDS AND PROCEDURES

5   A business purchases goods valued at $400. VAT is charged at 20%. The double entry to record the purchase is:

    DEBIT   .... $...............
    DEBIT   .... $...............
    CREDIT   .... $...............

6   Fill in the blanks.

Input VAT is ...., output VAT is ....

7   When a cash sale is made for $120.00 (including VAT at 20%) the entries made are:

    DEBIT   .... account $...............
    CREDIT   .... account $...............
    CREDIT   .... account $...............

8   When a cash purchase of $120.00 is made (including VAT at 20%) the entries are:

A	DEBIT	Purchases	120.00	
	CREDIT	Cash		120.00
B	DEBIT	Purchases	100.00	
	DEBIT	VAT	20.00	
	CREDIT	Cash		120.00
C	DEBIT	Cash	100.00	
	DEBIT	VAT	20.00	
	CREDIT	Purchases		120.00
D	DEBIT	Cash	120.00	
	CREDIT	Purchases		120.00

9   The VAT paid to the tax authorities each quarter is the difference between ....
.... and ....

Answers to quick quiz

1. **B** Correct.

   A Incorrect, the consumer has a choice as to whether or not to consume so VAT is only chargeable when this choice is exercised.

   C Incorrect, VAT is administrated by the tax authorities.

   D Only VAT registered traders can charge VAT.

2. **B** VAT is only due on taxable outputs.

3. **B** Correct, the statement of financial position value will therefore include VAT and the depreciation charge will rise accordingly.

   A Incorrect, it must be added.

   C Incorrect.

   D Incorrect, the motor car is a non-current asset not an expense, VAT will form part of the depreciable amount of the asset.

4. **A** Correct, recoverable input tax is debited to the VAT account and the purchases account is debited net of VAT.

   B Incorrect, the VAT has not been reclaimed.

   C Incorrect, the $500 is subject to VAT.

   D Incorrect, reversal of the VAT transaction has occurred.

5.
DEBIT	PURCHASES	$400	
	VAT	$80	
CREDIT	CASH or TRADE PAYABLES		$480

6. Input VAT is **VAT suffered on goods and services brought by a business**, output VAT is the **VAT collected on sales**.

7.
DEBIT	Cash account	$120.00	
CREDIT	Revenue account		$100.00
CREDIT	VAT account		$20.00

8. **B**

9. The VAT paid to the tax authorities each quarter is the difference between **output VAT collected on sales** and **input VAT suffered on purchases and expenses**.

PART B ACCOUNTING RECORDS AND PROCEDURES

Accruals and prepayments

Topic list	Syllabus reference
1 Accruals and prepayments	A2

Introduction

In Chapter 13, we will look at the adjustments needed for inventory in cost of sales. This chapter deals with the adjustments which may need to be made to the **expenses** in the statement of profit or loss and other comprehensive income.

PART B ACCOUNTING RECORDS AND PROCEDURES

1 Accruals and prepayments

FAST FORWARD

Accrued expenses (accruals) are expenses which relate to an accounting period but have not been paid for. They are shown in the statement of financial position as a **liability**.

Prepaid expenses (prepayments) are expenses which have already been paid but relate to a future accounting period. They are shown in the statement of financial position as an **asset**.

1.1 Introduction

Accruals and prepayments are required as a result of the application of accrual accounting as required by the *Conceptual Framework* (see Chapter 3). We have already seen that the gross profit for a period should be calculated by **matching** sales and the cost of goods sold. In the same way, the net profit for a period should be calculated by charging the expenses which relate to that period. For example, in preparing the statement of profit or loss and other comprehensive income of a business for a period of, say, six months, it would be appropriate to charge six months' expenses for rent and local taxes, insurance costs and telephone costs, etc.

Expenses might not be paid for during the period to which they relate. For example, a business rents a shop for $20,000 per annum and pays the full annual rent on 1 April each year. If we calculate the profit of the business for the first six months of the year 20X7, the correct charge for rent in the statement of profit or loss and other comprehensive income is $10,000, even though the rent paid is $20,000 in that period. Similarly, the rent charge in the statement of profit or loss and other comprehensive income for the second six months of the year is $10,000, even though no rent was actually paid in that period.

Key terms

Accruals or accrued expenses are expenses which are charged against the profit for a particular period, even though they have not yet been paid for.

Prepayments are payments which have been made in one accounting period, but should not be charged against profit until a later period, because they relate to that later period.

Accruals and prepayments might seem difficult at first, but the following examples should help to clarify the principle involved, that expenses should be matched against the period to which they relate. We can regard accruals and prepayments as the means by which we move charges into the correct accounting period. If we pay in this period for something which relates to the next accounting period, we use a prepayment to transfer that charge forward to the next period. If we have incurred an expense in this period which will not be paid for until next period, we use an accrual to bring the charge back into this period.

1.2 Example: Accruals

Horace Goodrunning, trading as Goodrunning Motor Spares, ends his financial year on 28 February each year. His telephone was installed on 1 April 20X6 and he receives his telephone account quarterly at the end of each quarter. On the basis of the following data, you are required to calculate the telephone expense to be charged to the statement of profit or loss and other comprehensive income for the year ended 28 February 20X7.

Goodrunning Motor Spares – telephone expense for the three months ended:

	$
30.6.20X6	23.50
30.9.20X6	27.20
31.12.20X6	33.40
31.3.20X7	36.00

Solution

The telephone expenses for the year ended 28 February 20X7 are:

	$
1 March – 31 March 20X6 (no telephone)	0.00
1 April – 30 June 20X6	23.50
1 July – 30 September 20X6	27.20
1 October – 31 December 20X6	33.40
1 January – 28 February 20X7 (two months)	24.00
	108.10

The charge for the period 1 January – 28 February 20X7 is two-thirds of the quarterly bill received on 31 March. As at 28 February 20X7, no telephone bill has been received because it is not due for another month. However, it is inappropriate to ignore the telephone expenses for January and February, and so an accrued charge of $24 is made, being two-thirds of the quarter's bill of $36.

The accrued charge will also appear in the statement of financial position of the business as at 28 February 20X7, as a current liability.

1.3 Example: Accrual

Cleverley started in business as a paper plate and cup manufacturer on 1 January 20X2, making up accounts to 31 December 20X2. Electricity bills received were as follows:

	20X2 $	20X3 $	20X4 $
31 January	–	6,491.52	6,753.24
30 April	5,279.47	5,400.93	6,192.82
31 July	4,663.80	4,700.94	5,007.62
31 October	4,117.28	4,620.00	5,156.40

What should the electricity charge be for the year ended 31 December 20X2?

Solution

The three invoices received during 20X2 totalled $14,060.55, but this is not the full charge for the year: the November and December electricity charge was not invoiced until the end of January. To show the correct charge for the year, it is necessary to **accrue** the charge for November and December based on January's bill. The charge for 20X2 is:

	$
Paid in year	14,060.55
Accrual ($2/3 \times \$6,491.52$)	4,327.68
	18,388.23

The double entry for the accrual (using the **journal**) will be:

DEBIT	Electricity account	$4,327.68	
CREDIT	Accruals (liability)		$4,327.68

1.4 Example: Prepayment

A business opens on 1 January 20X4 in a shop which is on a 20 year lease. The rent is $20,000 per year and is payable quarterly in advance. Payments were made on what are known as the 'quarter-days' (except the first payment) as follows:

	$
1 January 20X4	5,000.00
25 March 20X4	5,000.00
24 June 20X4	5,000.00
29 September 20X4	5,000.00
25 December 20X4	5,000.00

What will the rental charge be for the year ended 31 December 20X4?

Solution

The total amount paid in the year is $25,000. The yearly rental, however, is only $20,000. The last payment was almost entirely a prepayment (give or take a few days) as it is payment in advance for the first three months of 20X5. The charge for 20X4 is therefore:

	$
Paid in year	25,000.00
Prepayment	(5,000.00)
	20,000.00

The double entry for this prepayment is:

DEBIT	Prepayments (asset)	$5,000.00	
CREDIT	Rent account		$5,000.00

1.5 Double entry for accruals and prepayments

You can see from the double entry shown for both these examples that the other side of the entry is taken to an asset or a liability account.

- **Prepayments** are included in **trade receivables** in current assets in the statement of financial position. They are **assets** as they represent money that has been paid out in advance of the expense being incurred.
- **Accruals** are included in **trade payables** in **current liabilities** as they represent liabilities which have been incurred but for which no invoice has yet been received.

Transaction	DEBIT	CREDIT	Description
Accrual	Expense	Liability	Expense incurred in period, not recorded
Prepayment	Asset	(Reduction in) expense	Expense recorded in period, not incurred until next period

1.5.1 Reversing accruals and prepayments in subsequent periods

In each of the above examples, as with all prepayments and accruals, the double entry will be **reversed** in the following period, otherwise the organisation will charge itself twice for the same expense (accruals) **or** will never charge itself (prepayments). It may help to see the accounts in question (SPLOCI = statement of profit or loss and other comprehensive income).

ELECTRICITY ACCOUNT

20X2		$	20X2		$
30.4	Cash	5,279.47	31.12	SPLOCI	18,388.23
31.7	Cash	4,663.80			
31.10	Cash	4,117.28			
31.12	Balance c/d (accrual)	4,327.68			
		18,388.23			18,388.23
20X3			20X3		
31.1	Cash	6,491.52	1.1	Balance b/d	
30.4	Cash	5,400.93		(accrual reversed)	4,327.68
31.7	Cash	4,700.94	31.12	SPLOCI	21,387.87
31.10	Cash	4,620.00			
31.12	Balance c/d (accrual)	4,502.16			
		25,715.55			25,715.55

The statement of profit or loss and other comprehensive income charge and accrual for 20X3 can be checked as follows:

Invoice paid		Proportion charged in 20X3	$
31.1.X3	6,491.52	1/3	2,163.84
30.4.X3	5,400.94	all	5,400.93
31.7.X3	4,700.94	all	4,700.94
31.10.X3	4,620.00	all	4,620.00
31.1.X4	6,753.24	2/3	4,502.16
Charge to SPLOCI in 20X3			21,387.87

It should be clear to you here that the $5,000 rent prepaid in 20X2 will be added to by the payments in 20X3, and then reduced at the end of 20X3 in the same way.

Question — Accruals

Ratsnuffer is a business dealing in pest control. Its owner, Roy Dent, employs a team of eight who were paid $12,000 per annum each in the year to 31 December 20X5. At the start of 20X6 he raised salaries by 10% to $13,200 per annum each.

On 1 July 20X6, he hired a trainee at a salary of $8,400 per annum.

He pays his work force on the first working day of every month, one month in arrears, so that his employees receive their salary for January on the first working day in February, etc.

Required

(a) Calculate the cost of salaries which would be charged in the statement of profit or loss and other comprehensive income of Ratsnuffer for the year ended 31 December 20X6.
(b) Calculate the amount actually paid in salaries during the year (ie the amount of cash received by the work force).
(c) State the amount of accrued charges for salaries which would appear in the statement of financial position of Ratsnuffer as at 31 December 20X6.

Answer

(a) *Salaries cost in the statement of profit or loss and other comprehensive income*

	$
Cost of 8 employees for a full year at $13,200 each	105,600
Cost of trainee for a half year	4,200
	109,800

(b) *Salaries actually paid in 20X6*

	$
December 20X5 salaries paid in January (8 employees × $1,000 per month)	8,000
Salaries of 8 employees for January – November 20X6 paid in February – December (8 employees × $1,100 per month × 11 months)	96,800
Salaries of trainee (for July – November paid in August – December 20X6: 5 months × $700 per month)	3,500
Salaries actually paid	108,300

(c) *Accrued salaries costs as at 31 December 20X6*
(ie costs charged in the SPLOCI, but not yet paid)

	$
8 employees × 1 month × $1,100 per month	8,800
1 trainee × 1 month × $700 per month	700
	9,500

1.6 Example: Prepayments

The Square Wheels Garage pays fire insurance annually in advance on 1 June each year. The firm's financial year end is 28 February. From the following record of insurance payments you are required to calculate the charge to statement of profit or loss and other comprehensive income for the financial year to 28 February 20X8.

Insurance paid

	$
1.6.20X6	600
1.6.20X7	700

Insurance cost for:

		$
(a)	The 3 months, 1 March – 31 May 20X7 (3/12 × $600)	150
(b)	The 9 months, 1 June 20X7 – 28 February 20X8 (9/12 × $700)	525
	Insurance cost for the year, charged to the SPLOCI	675

At 28 February 20X8 there is a prepayment for fire insurance, covering the period 1 March – 31 May 20X8. This insurance premium was paid on 1 June 20X7, but only nine months worth of the full annual cost is chargeable to the accounting period ended 28 February 20X8. The prepayment of (3/12 × $700) $175 as at 28 February 20X8 will appear as a current asset in the statement of financial position of the Square Wheels Garage as at that date.

In the same way, there was a prepayment of (3/12 × $600) $150 in the statement of financial position one year earlier as at 28 February 20X7.

Summary

	$
Prepaid insurance premiums as at 28 February 20X7	150
Add insurance premiums paid 1 June 20X7	700
	850
Less insurance costs charged to the SPLOCI for the year ended 28 February 20X8	675
Equals prepaid insurance premiums as at 28 February 20X8 (asset)	175

Question — Accruals and prepayments

The Batley Print Shop rents a photocopying machine from a supplier for which it makes a quarterly payment as follows:

(a) Three months' rental in advance
(b) A further charge of 2 cents per copy made during the quarter just ended

The rental agreement began on 1 August 20X4 and the first six quarterly bills were as follows.

Bills dated and received	Rental	Costs of copies taken	Total
	$	$	$
1 August 20X4	2,100	0	2,100
1 November 20X4	2,100	1,500	3,600
1 February 20X5	2,100	1,400	3,500
1 May 20X5	2,100	1,800	3,900
1 August 20X5	2,700	1,650	4,350
1 November 20X5	2,700	1,950	4,650

The bills are paid promptly, as soon as they are received.

(a) Calculate the charge for photocopying expenses for the year to 31 August 20X4 and the amount of prepayments and/or accrued charges as at that date.

(b) Calculate the charge for photocopying expenses for the following year to 31 August 20X5, and the amount of prepayments and/or accrued charges as at that date.

Answer

(a) Year to 31 August 20X4 $

One months' rental (1/3 × $2,100) *	700
Accrued copying charges (1/3 × $1,500) **	500
Photocopying expense (SPLOCI)	1,200

* From the quarterly bill dated 1 August 20X4
** From the quarterly bill dated 1 November 20X4

There is a prepayment for two months' rental ($1,400) as at 31 August 20X4.

(b) Year to 31 August 20X5

	$	$
Rental from 1 September 20X4 – 31 July 20X5 (11 months at $2,100 per quarter or $700 per month)		7,700
Rental from 1 August – 31 August 20X5 (1/3 × $2,700)		900
Rental charge for the year		8,600
Copying charges:		
1 September – 31 October 20X4 (2/3 × $1,500)	1,000	
1 November 20X4 – 31 January 20X5	1,400	
1 February – 30 April 20X5	1,800	
1 May – 31 July 20X5	1,650	
Accrued charges for August 20X5 (1/3 × $1,950)	650	
		6,500
Total photocopying expenses (SPLOCI)		15,100

There is a prepayment for two months' rental ($1,800) as at 31 August 20X5.

Summary of year 1 September 20X4 – 31 August 20X5

	Rental charges $	Copying costs $
Prepayments as at 31.8.20X4	1,400	
Accrued charges as at 31.8.20X4		(500)
Bills received during the year		
1 November 20X4	2,100	1,500
1 February 20X5	2,100	1,400
1 May 20X5	2,100	1,800
1 August 20X5	2,700	1,650
Prepayment as at 31.8.20X5	(1,800)	
Accrued charges as at 31.8.20X5		650
Charge to the SPLOCI for the year	8,600	6,500
Financial position items as at 31 August 20X5		
Prepaid rental (current asset)	1,800	
Accrued copying charges (current liability)		650

1.7 Further example: Accruals

Willie Woggle opens a shop on 1 May 20X6 to sell hiking and camping equipment. The rent of the shop is $12,000 per annum, payable quarterly in arrears (with the first payment on 31 July 20X6). Willie decides that his accounting period should end on 31 December each year.

The rent account as at 31 December 20X6 will record only two rental payments (on 31 July and 31 October) and there will be two months' accrued rental expenses for November and December 20X6 ($2,000), since the next rental payment is not due until 31 January 20X7.

The charge to the statement of profit or loss and other comprehensive income for the period to 31 December 20X6 will be for eight months' rent (May–December inclusive) and so it follows that the total rental cost should be $8,000.

So far, the rent account appears as follows:

RENT ACCOUNT

20X6		$	20X6		$
31 July	Cash	3,000			
31 Oct	Cash	3,000	31 Dec	SPLOCI	8,000

To complete the picture, the accrual of $2,000 has to be put in, to bring the balance on the account up to the full charge for the year. At the beginning of the next year the accrual is reversed:

RENT ACCOUNT

20X6		$	20X6		$
31 July	Cash *	3,000			
31 Oct	Cash *	3,000			
31 Dec	Balance c/d (accruals)	2,000	31 Dec	SPLOCI	8,000
		8,000			8,000
			20X7		
			1 Jan	Balance b/d (accrual reversed)	2,000

* The corresponding credit entry would be cash if rent is paid without the need for an invoice – eg with payment by standing order or direct debit at the bank. If there is always an invoice where rent becomes payable, the double entry would be:

DEBIT	Rent account	$2,000	
CREDIT	Payables		$2,000

Then when the rent is paid, the ledger entries would be:

DEBIT	Payables	$2,000	
CREDIT	Bank		$2,000

The rent account for the **next** year to 31 December 20X7, assuming no increase in rent in that year, would be as follows:

RENT ACCOUNT

20X7		$	20X7		$
31 Jan	Cash	3,000	1 Jan	Balance b/d (accrual reversed)	2,000
30 Apr	Cash	3,000			
31 Jul	Cash	3,000			
31 Oct	Cash	3,000			
31 Dec	Balance c/d (accruals)	2,000	31 Dec	SPLOCI	12,000
		14,000			14,000
			20X8		
			1 Jan	Balance b/d (accrual reversed)	2,000

A full 12 months' rental charges are taken as an expense to the statement of profit or loss and other comprehensive income.

1.8 Further example: Prepayments of income

Terry Trunk commences business as a landscape gardener on 1 September 20X5. He immediately decides to join his local trade association, the Confederation of Luton Gardeners, for which the annual membership subscription is $180, payable annually in advance. He paid this amount on 1 September. The Confederation makes up its accounts to 30 June each year.

In the first period to 30 June 20X6, Terry has paid a full year's membership, but only ten twelfths of the subscription should be charged to the period (ie 10/12 × $180 = $150). There is a prepayment of two months of membership subscription (ie 2/12 × $180 = $30).

The prepayment is recognised in the Confederation's ledger account for subscriptions. For simplicity, only Terry's subscription is shown. This is done in much the same way as accounting for accruals, by using the balance carried down/brought down technique.

DEBIT	Subscriptions account with prepayment as a balance c/d	$30
CREDIT	Subscriptions account with the same balance b/d	$30

Remember that the prepaid subscription is a liability because, theoretically, this amount could be repaid to Terry.

The remaining expenses in the subscriptions account should then be taken to the statement of profit or loss and other comprehensive income. The balance on the account will appear as a current liability (prepaid subscriptions) in the statement of financial position as at 30 June 20X6.

SUBSCRIPTIONS ACCOUNT

			$				$
20X6				20X5			
30 Jun	SPLOCI		150	1 Sept	Cash		180
30 Jun	Balance c/d (prepayment)		30				
			180				180
				20X6			
				1 Jul	Balance b/d (prepayment reversed)		30

The subscription account for the next year, assuming no increase in the annual charge, will be:

SUBSCRIPTIONS ACCOUNT

			$				$
20X7				20X6			
30 Jun	SPLOCI		180	1 Jul	Balance b/d		30
30 Jun	Balance c/d (prepayment)		30	1 Sep	Cash		180
			210				210
				20X7			
				1 Jul	Balance b/d (prepayment reversed)		30

Again, the charge to the statement of profit or loss and other comprehensive income is for a full year's subscriptions. Remember that the prepaid subscription b/d is, theoretically, repayable if Terry ceases to be a member. Therefore, it is a liability.

Exam focus point

You will almost certainly have to deal with accruals and/or prepayments in the exam. Make sure you understand the logic, then you will be able to do whatever question comes up.

PART B ACCOUNTING RECORDS AND PROCEDURES

1.9 Effect on profit and net assets

You may find the following table a useful summary of the effects of accruals and prepayments.

	Effect on income/expenses	Effect on profit	Effect on assets/liabilities
Accruals	Increases expenses	Reduces profit	Increases liabilities
Prepayments	Reduces expenses	Increases profit	Increases assets
Prepayments of income	Reduces income	Reduces profit	Increases liabilities

Question
SPLOCI and statement of financial position

The Umbrella Shop has the following trial balance as at 30 September 20X8.

	$	$
Revenue		156,000
Purchases	65,000	
Land and buildings – carrying amount at 30.9.X8	125,000	
Plant and machinery – carrying amount at 30.9.X8	75,000	
Inventory at 1.10.X7	10,000	
Cash at bank	12,000	
Trade receivables	54,000	
Trade payables		40,000
Selling expenses	10,000	
Cash in hand	2,000	
Administration expenses	15,000	
Finance expenses	5,000	
Carriage inwards	1,000	
Carriage outwards	2,000	
Capital account at 1.10.X7		180,000
	376,000	376,000

The following information is available:

(a) Closing inventory at 30.9.X8 is $13,000, after writing off damaged goods of $2,000.

(b) Included in administration expenses is machinery rental of $6,000 covering the year to 31 December 20X8.

(c) A late invoice for $12,000 covering rent for the year ended 30 June 20X9 has not been included in the trial balance.

Prepare a statement of profit or loss and other comprehensive income and statement of financial position for the year ended 30 September 20X8.

Answer

THE UMBRELLA SHOP
STATEMENT OF PROFIT OR LOSS AND OTHER COMPREHENSIVE INCOME FOR THE YEAR END 30 SEPTEMBER 20X8

	$	$
Revenue		156,000
Opening inventory	10,000	
Purchases	65,000	
Carriage inwards	1,000	
	76,000	
Closing inventory (W1)	13,000	

	$	$
Cost of goods sold		63,000
Gross profit		93,000
Selling expenses	10,000	
Carriage outwards	2,000	
Administration expenses (W2)	16,500	
Finance expenses	5,000	
		33,500
Net profit for the period		59,500

THE UMBRELLA SHOP
STATEMENT OF FINANCIAL POSITION AS AT 30 SEPTEMBER 20X8

	$	$
Assets		
Non-current assets		
Land and buildings		125,000
Plant and machinery		75,000
		200,000
Current assets		
Inventories (W1)	13,000	
Trade receivables	54,000	
Prepayments (W4)	1,500	
Cash at bank and in hand	14,000	
		82,500
		282,500
Capital and liabilities		
Proprietor's capital		
Balance brought forward	180,000	
Profit for the period	59,500	
		239,500
Current liabilities		
Trade payables	40,000	
Accruals (W3)	3,000	
		43,000
		282,500

Workings

1   *Closing inventory*

    As the figure of $13,000 is **after** writing off damaged goods, no further adjustments are necessary. Remember that you are effectively crediting closing inventory to statement of profit or loss and other comprehensive income and the corresponding debit is to the statement of financial position.

2   *Administration expenses*

	$
Per trial balance	15,000
Add: accrual (W3)	3,000
	18,000
Less: prepayment (W4)	(1,500)
	16,500

3   *Accrual*

	$
Rent for year to 30 June 20X9	12,000
Accrual for period to 30 September 20X8 ($3/12 \times \$12,000$)	3,000

4   *Prepayment*

	$
Machinery rental for the year to 31 December 20X8	6,000
Prepayment for period 1 October to 31 December 20X8 ($3/12 \times \$6,000$)	1,500

Chapter roundup

- **Accrued expenses (accruals)** are expenses which relate to an accounting period but have not yet been paid for. They are shown in the statement of financial position as a **liability**.
- **Prepaid expenses (prepayments)** are expenses which have already been paid but relate to a future accounting period. They are shown in the statement of financial position as an **asset**.

Quick quiz

1 How is the cost of goods sold calculated?

   A Opening inventory + purchases + closing inventory
   B Opening inventory + closing inventory – purchases
   C Opening inventory + purchases – closing inventory
   D Closing inventory + purchases – closing inventory

2 Electricity paid during the year is $14,000. There was an opening accrual b/f of $500. A bill for the quarter ended 31 January 20X7 was $900. What is the electricity charge in the statement of profit or loss and other comprehensive income for the year ended 31 December 20X6?

   A $14,000
   B $14,100
   C $13,900
   D $14,400

3 If a business has paid rent of $1,000 for the year to 31 March 20X9, what is the prepayment in the accounts for the year to 31 December 20X8?

   A $250
   B $750

4 What is the correct journal for an electricity prepayment of $500?

   A DEBIT   prepayment $500
      CREDIT expense $500
   B DEBIT   expense $500
      CREDIT prepayment $500

5 An accrual is an expense charged against profit for a period, even though it has not yet been paid or invoiced.

   This statement is:

   A True
   B False

Answers to quick quiz

1. C

2. B

ELECTRICITY

	$		$
Cash	14,800	Accrual b/f	500
Accrual c/f (2/3 × 900)	600	SPLOCI	14,100
	14,600		14,600

3. A 3/12 × $1,000 = $250

4. A A prepayment needs to reduce the expense and set up an asset in the statement of financial position.

5. A True

Bank reconciliations

Topic list	Syllabus reference
1 Bank statement and cash book	A2
2 The bank reconciliation	A2
3 Worked examples	A2

Introduction

It is very likely that you will have had to do bank reconciliation at work. If not, you will probably have done one on your own bank account without even being aware of it.

The first two sections of this chapter explain why we need a bank reconciliation, and the sort of differences that need to be reconciled.

The third section takes you through some examples of increasing complexity.

PART B ACCOUNTING RECORDS AND PROCEDURES

1 Bank statement and cash book

FAST FORWARD

In theory, the entries appearing on a business's **bank statement** should be exactly the same as those in the business cash book. The balance shown by the bank statement should be the same as the **cash book** balance on the same date.

The cash book of a business is the record of **how much cash the business believes** that it **has in the bank**. In the same way, you might keep a private record of how much you think you have in your own bank account, perhaps by making a note in your cheque book of income received and the cheques you write. If you do keep such a record, you will probably agree that your bank statement balance is rarely exactly the same as your own figure.

Why might your own estimate of your bank balance be different from the amount shown on your bank statement? There are three common explanations:

(a) **Error**. Errors in calculation, or recording income and payments, are more likely to have been made by you than by the bank, but it is conceivable that the bank has made a mistake too.

(b) **Bank charges or bank interest**. The bank might deduct charges for interest on an overdraft or for its services, which you are not informed about until you receive the bank statement.

(c) **Time differences**

 (i) There might be some cheques that you have received and paid into the bank, but which have not yet been '**cleared**' and added to your account. So although your own records show that some cash has been added to your account, it has not yet been acknowledged by the bank – although it will be soon once the cheque has cleared.

 (ii) Similarly, you might have made some payments by cheque, and reduced the balance in your account in the record that you keep, but the person who receives the cheque might not bank it for a while. Even when it is banked, it takes a day or two for the banks to process it and for the money to be deducted from your account.

If you do keep a personal record of your cash position at the bank, and if you do check your periodic bank statements against what you think you should have in your account, you will be doing a bank reconciliation.

Key term

A **bank reconciliation** is a comparison of a bank statement (sent monthly, weekly or even daily by the bank) with the cash book. Differences between the balance on the bank statement and the balance in the cash book will be errors or timing differences, and they should be identified and satisfactorily explained.

2 The bank reconciliation

FAST FORWARD

Differences between the **cash book** and the bank statement arise for three reasons:

- Errors – usually in the cash book
- Omissions – such as bank charges not posted in the cash book
- Timing differences – such as unpresented cheques

2.1 The bank statement

It is a common practice for a business to issue a monthly statement to each credit customer, itemising:

(a) The **balance** owed at the **beginning** of the month
(b) **New debts** incurred during the month

(c) **Payments** made during the month
(d) The **balance** owed at the **end** of the month

In the same way, a bank statement is sent by a bank to its short-term receivables and payables – ie customers with bank overdrafts and customers with money in their account – itemising the balance on the account at the beginning of the period, receipts into the account and payments from the account during the period, and the balance at the end of the period.

It is necessary to remember, however, that if a customer has money in his account, the bank owes him that money, and the customer is therefore a **payable** of the bank (hence the phrase 'to be in credit' means to have money in your account). This means that if a business has $8,000 cash in the bank, it will have a debit balance in its own cash book, but the bank statement, if it reconciles exactly with the cash book, will state that there is a credit balance of $8,000. (The bank's records are a 'mirror image' of the customer's own records, with debits and credits reversed.)

2.2 Why is a bank reconciliation necessary?

A bank reconciliation is needed to identify and account for the differences between the cash book and the bank statement.

Question — Differences

These differences fall into three categories. What are they?

Answer

Look back to the beginning of this section.

2.3 What to look for when doing a bank reconciliation

The cash book and bank statement will rarely agree at a given date. If you are doing a bank reconciliation, you may have to look for the following items:

(a) **Corrections and adjustments to the cash book**

   (i) Payments made into the account or from the account by way of standing order, which have not yet been entered in the cash book

   (ii) Dividends received (on investments held by the business), paid direct into the bank account but not yet entered in the cash book

   (iii) Bank interest and bank charges, not yet entered in the cash book

(b) **Items reconciling the correct cash book balance to the bank statement**

   (i) Cheques drawn (ie paid) by the business and credited in the cash book, which have not yet been presented to the bank, or 'cleared', and so do not yet appear on the bank statement

   (ii) Cheques received by the business, paid into the bank and debited in the cash book, but which have not yet been cleared and entered in the account by the bank, and so do not yet appear on the bank statement

Exam focus point: If asked to prepare a bank reconciliation, you may have to adjust the cash book, the bank balance or both.

PART B ACCOUNTING RECORDS AND PROCEDURES

3 Worked examples

FAST FORWARD When the differences between the bank statement and the cash book are identified, the cash book must be corrected for any errors or omissions. Any remaining difference can then be shown to be due to timing differences.

3.1 Example: Bank reconciliation

At 30 September 20X6, the balance in the cash book of Wordsworth Co was $805.15 debit. A bank statement on 30 September 20X6 showed Wordsworth Co to be in credit by $1,112.30.

On investigation of the difference between the two sums, it was established that:

(a) The cash book had been undercast by $90.00 on the debit side*
(b) Cheques paid in not yet credited by the bank amounted to $208.20, called outstanding lodgements
(c) Cheques drawn not yet presented to the bank amounted to $425.35 called unpresented cheques

* **Note.** 'Casting' is an accountant's term for adding up.

Required

(a) Show the correction to the cash book.
(b) Prepare a statement reconciling the balance per bank statement to the balance per cash book.

Solution

(a)

	$
Cash book balance brought forward	805.15
Add: Correction of undercast	90.00
Corrected balance	895.15

(b)

	$
Balance per bank statement	1,112.30
Add outstanding lodgements	208.20
	1,320.50
Less: Unpresented cheques	(425.35)
Balance per cash book	895.15

Question Reconciliation

On 31 January 20X8 a company's cash book showed a credit balance of $150 on its current account which did not agree with the bank statement balance. In performing the reconciliation the following points come to light.

	$
Not recorded in the cash book	
Bank charges	36
Transfer from deposit account to current account	500
Not recorded on the bank statement	
Unpresented cheques	116
Outstanding lodgements	630

It was also discovered that the bank had debited the company's account with a cheque for $400 in error. What was the original balance on the bank statement?

Answer

CASH ACCOUNT

	$		$
		Balance b/d	150
Transfer from deposit a/c	500	Charges	36
		Balance c/d	314
	500		500

	$
Balance per cash book	314
Add unpresented cheques	116
Less outstanding lodgements	(630)
Less error by bank*	(400)
Balance per bank statement	(600)

*Note. On the bank statement a debit is a payment out of the account.

Exam focus point

You could be asked to reconstruct opening figures in the exam. If so, then you may need to reverse the usual workings, as illustrated in the example above.

Question — Bank statement

A company's bank statement shows $715 direct debits and $353 investment income not recorded in the cash book. The bank statement does not show a customer's cheque for $875 entered in the cash book on the last day of the accounting period. If the cash book shows a credit balance of $610, what balance appears on the bank statement?

A $1,847 debit
B $1,847 credit
C $972 credit
D $972 debit

Answer

A

	$	$
Balance per cash book		(610)
Items on statement, not in cash book		
Direct debits	(715)	
Investment income	353	
		(362)
Corrected balance per cash book		(972)
Item in cash book not on statement:		
Customer's cheque		(875)
Balance per bank statement		(1,847)

As the balance is overdrawn, this is a debit on the bank statement.

PART B   ACCOUNTING RECORDS AND PROCEDURES

Question
Bank balance

Given the facts in the question above, what is the figure for the bank balance to be reported in the final accounts?

- A $1,847 credit
- B $972 credit
- C $972 debit
- D $1,847 debit

Answer

B   The figure to go in the statement of financial position is the corrected cash book figure. This is $972 credit (or overdrawn). So the bank figure will appear in liabilities.

3.2 Example: More complicated bank reconciliation

On 30 June 20X0, Cook's cash book showed that he had an overdraft of $300 on his current account at the bank. A bank statement as at the end of June 20X0 showed that Cook was in credit with the bank by $65.

On checking the cash book with the bank statement you find the following:

(a) Cheques drawn, amounting to $500, had been entered in the cash book but had not been presented.

(b) Cheques received, amounting to $400, had been entered in the cash book, but had not been credited by the bank.

(c) On instructions from Cook the bank had transferred interest received on his deposit account amounting to $60 to his current account, recording the transfer on 5 July 20X0. This amount had, however, been credited in the cash book as on 30 June 20X0.

(d) Bank charges of $35 shown in the bank statement had not been entered in the cash book.

(e) The payments side of the cash book had been undercast by $10.

(f) Dividends received amounting to $200 had been paid direct to the bank and not entered in the cash book.

(g) A cheque for $50 drawn on deposit account had been shown in the cash book as drawn on current account.

(h) A cheque issued to Jones for $25 was replaced when out of date. It was entered again in the cash book, no other entry being made. Both cheques were included in the total of unpresented cheques shown above.

Required

(a) Indicate the appropriate adjustments in the cash book.
(b) Prepare a statement reconciling the amended balance with that shown in the bank statement.

Solution

(a) The errors to correct are given in notes (c) (e) (f) (g) and (h) of the problem. Bank charges (note (d)) also call for an adjustment.

(Note that debit entries add to the cash balance and credit entries are deductions from the cash balance.)

9: BANK RECONCILIATIONS

		Adjustments in cash book	
		Debit	Credit
		$	$
Item			
(c)	Cash book incorrectly credited with interest on 30 June. It should have been debited with the receipt	60	
(c)	Debit cash book (current a/c) with transfer of interest from deposit a/c (Note 1)	60	
(d)	Bank charges		35
(e)	Undercast on payments (credit) side of cash book		10
(f)	Dividends received should be debited in the cash book	200	
(g)	Cheque drawn on deposit account, not current account. Add cash back to current account	50	
(h)	Cheque paid to Jones is out of date and so cancelled. Cash book should now be debited, since previous credit entry is no longer valid (Note 2)	25	
		395	45

	$	$
Cash book: balance on current account as at 30 June 20X0		(300)
Adjustments and corrections:		
Debit entries (adding to cash)	395	
Credit entries (reducing cash balance)	(45)	
Net adjustments		350
Corrected balance in the cash book		50

Notes

1. Item (c) is rather complicated. The transfer of interest from the deposit to the current account was presumably given as an instruction to the bank on or before 30 June 20X0. Since the correct entry is to debit the current account (and credit the deposit account) the correction in the cash book should be to debit the current account with 2 × $60 = $120 – ie to cancel out the incorrect credit entry in the cash book and then to make the correct debit entry. However, the bank does not record the transfer until 5 July, and so it will not appear in the bank statement.

2. Item (h). Two cheques have been paid to Jones, but one is now cancelled. Since the cash book is credited whenever a cheque is paid, it should be debited whenever a cheque is cancelled. The amount of cheques paid but not yet presented should be reduced by the amount of the cancelled cheque.

(b) BANK RECONCILIATION STATEMENT AT 30 JUNE 20X0

	$	$
Balance per bank statement		65
Add: Outstanding lodgements	400	
Deposit interest not yet credited	60	
		460
		525
Less: Unpresented cheques	500	
Less cheque to Jones cancelled	(25)	
		475
Balance per corrected cash book		50

Notice that in preparing a bank reconciliation it is good practice to begin with the balance shown by the bank statement and end with the balance shown by the cash book. It is this corrected cash book balance

PART B ACCOUNTING RECORDS AND PROCEDURES

which will appear in the statement of financial position as 'cash at bank'. However examination questions sometimes ask for the reverse order: as always, read the question carefully.

You might be interested to see the adjustments to the cash book in part (a) of the problem presented in the 'T' account format, as follows:

CASH BOOK

20X0		$	20X0		$
Jun 30	Bank interest – reversal of incorrect entry	60	Jun 30	Balance brought down	300
	Bank interest account	60		Bank charges	35
	Dividends paid direct to bank	200		Correction of undercast	10
	Cheque drawn on deposit account written back	50		Balance carried down	50
	Cheque issued to Jones cancelled	25			
		395			395

Question — Bank reconciliation

From the information given below relating to PWW Co you are required:

(a) To make such additional entries in the cash at bank account of PWW Co as you consider necessary to show the correct balance at 31 October 20X2.

(b) To prepare a statement reconciling the correct balance in the cash at bank account as shown in (a) above with the balance at 31 October 20X2 that is shown on the bank statement from Z Bank Co.

CASH AT BANK ACCOUNT IN THE LEDGER OF PWW CO

20X2 October		$	20X2 October		$
1	Balance b/f	274	1	Wages	3,146
8	Q Manufacturing	3,443	1	Petty Cash	55
8	R Cement	1,146	8	Wages	3,106
11	S Co	638	8	Petty Cash	39
11	T & Sons	512	15	Wages	3,029
11	U & Co	4,174	15	Petty Cash	78
15	V Co	1,426	22	A & Sons	929
15	W Electrical	887	22	B Co	134
22	X and Associates	1,202	22	C & Company	77
26	Y Co	2,875	22	D & E	263
26	Z Co	982	22	F Co	1,782
29	ABC Co	1,003	22	G Associates	230
29	DEE Corporation	722	22	Wages	3,217
29	GHI Co	2,461	22	Petty Cash	91
31	Balance c/f	14	25	H & Partners	26
			26	J Sons & Co	868
			26	K & Co	107
			26	L, M & N	666
			28	O Co	112
			29	Wages	3,191
			29	Petty Cash	52
			29	P & Sons	561
		21,759			21,759

140

Z BANK CO – STATEMENT OF ACCOUNT WITH PWW CO

20X2 October		Payments $	Receipts $		Balance $
1					1,135
1	cheque	55			
1	cheque	3,146			
1	cheque	421		O/D	2,487
2	cheque	73			
2	cheque	155		O/D	2,715
6	cheque	212		O/D	2,927
8	sundry credit		4,589		
8	cheque	3,106			
8	cheque	39		O/D	1,483
11	sundry credit		5,324		3,841
15	sundry credit		2,313		
15	cheque	78			
15	cheque	3,029			3,047
22	sundry credit		1,202		
22	cheque	3,217			
22	cheque	91			941
25	cheque	1,782			
25	cheque	134		O/D	975
26	cheque	929			
26	sundry credit		3,857		
26	cheque	230			1,723
27	cheque	263			
27	cheque	77			1,383
29	sundry credit		4,186		
29	cheque	52			
29	cheque	3,191			
29	cheque	26			
29	dividends on investments		2,728		
29	cheque	666			4,362
31	bank charges	936			3,426

Answer

(a)

CASH BOOK

		$			$
31 Oct	Dividends received	2,728	31 Oct	Unadjusted balance b/f (overdraft)	14
			31 Oct	Bank charges	936
			31 Oct	Adjusted balance c/f	1,778
		2,728			2,728

(b) **BANK RECONCILIATION STATEMENT AT 31 OCTOBER 20X2**

	$	$
Corrected balance as per cash book		1,778
Cheques paid out but not yet presented	1,648	
Cheques paid in but not yet cleared by bank	0	
		1,648
Balance as per bank statement		3,426

PART B ACCOUNTING RECORDS AND PROCEDURES

Workings

1. Payments shown on bank statement but not in cash book*
   $(421 + 73 + 155 + 212)$ — $861
   * Presumably recorded in cash book before 1 October 20X2 but not yet presented for payment as at 30 September 20X2

2. Payments in the cash book and on the bank statement
   $(3,146 + 55 + 3,106 + 39 + 78 + 3,029 + 3,217 + 91 + 1,782 + 134 + 929 + 230 + 263 + 77 + 52 + 3,191 + 26 + 666)$ — $20,111

3. Payments in the cash book but not on the bank statement = Total payments in cash book $21,759 – $20,111 = — $1,648

		$
Alternatively	J & Sons	868
	K & Co	107
	O Co	112
	P & Sons	561
		1,648

4. Bank charges, not in the cash book — $936

5. Receipts recorded by bank statement but not in cash book:
   dividends on investments — $2,728

6. Receipts in the cash book and also bank statement
   (8 Oct $4,589; 11 Oct $5,324; 15 Oct $2,313; 22 Oct $1,202;
   26 Oct $3,857; 29 Oct $4,186) — $21,471

7. Receipts recorded in cash book but not bank statement — None

Chapter roundup

- In theory, the entries appearing on a business's **bank statement** should be exactly the same as those in the business cash book. The balance shown by the bank statement should be the same as the **cash book** balance on the same date.
- Differences between the **cash book** and the bank statement arise for three reasons:
  - Errors – usually in the cash book
  - Omissions – such as bank charges not posted in the cash book
  - Timing differences – such as unpresented cheques
- When the differences between the bank statement and the cash book are identified, the cash book must be corrected for any errors or omissions. Any remaining difference can then be shown to be due to timing differences.

Quick quiz

1. Which of the following are common reasons for differences between the cash book and the bank statements?
   - (i) Timing differences
   - (ii) Errors
   - (iii) Omissions
   - (iv) Contra entries

   A (i) and (ii)
   B (i) and (iv)
   C (ii), (iii) and (iv)
   D (i), (ii) and (iii)

2. A cash book and a bank statement will never agree.
   Is this statement?

   A True
   B False

3. A bank statement shows a balance of $1,200 in credit. An examination of the statement shows a $500 cheque paid in per the cash book but not yet on the bank statement and a $1,250 cheque paid out but not yet on the statement. In addition the cash book shows deposit interest received of $50 but this is not yet on the statement. What is the balance per the cash book?

   A $1,900 overdrawn
   B $500 overdrawn
   C $1,900 in hand
   D $500 in hand

4. Comparing the cash book with the bank statement is called a .... (complete the blanks).

5. Why is it necessary to compare the cash book and bank statement?

Answers to quick quiz

1. D   Contra entries only occur between the receivables and payables control account.

2. B   False. In very small businesses, with few transactions, the cash book and bank statement could well agree.

3. D

	$	$
Balance per bank statement		1,200
Add outstanding lodgements	500	
deposit interest not yet credited	50	550
	1,750	
Less unpresented cheques		(1,250)
Balance per cash book		500

4. Comparing the cash book with the bank statement is called a **bank reconciliation**.

5. It highlights errors and omissions in the cash book and helps to prevent fraud. It also checks the bank figure and helps to spot any bank errors.

Control accounts

Topic list	Syllabus reference
1 What are control accounts?	A2
2 Discounts	A2
3 The operation of control accounts	A2
4 The purpose of control accounts	A2

Introduction

So far in this text we have assumed that the bookkeeping and double entry (and subsequent preparation of financial accounts) has been carried out by a business without any mistakes. This is not likely to be the case in real life: even the bookkeeper of a very small business with hardly any accounting entries to make will be prone to human error. If a debit is written as $123 and the corresponding credit as $321, then the books of the business are immediately out of balance by $198.

Once an error has been detected, it has to be corrected.

In this chapter and the next chapter we explain how errors can be **detected**, what kinds of error might **exist**, and how to post **corrections** and adjustments to produce final accounts.

PART B ACCOUNTING RECORDS AND PROCEDURES

1 What are control accounts?

FAST FORWARD

A control account keeps a total record of a number of individual items. It is an **impersonal** account which is part of the double entry system.

Key terms

A **control account** is an account in the general ledger in which a record is kept of the total value of a number of similar but individual items. Control accounts are used chiefly for trade receivables and payables.

- A **trade receivables control account** is an account in which records are kept of transactions involving all receivables in total. The balance on the receivables control account at any time will be the total amount due to the business at that time from its receivables.
- A **trade payables control account** is an account in which records are kept of transactions involving all payables in total, and the balance on this account at any time will be the total amount owed by the business at that time to its payables.

Although control accounts are used mainly in accounting for trade receivables and payables, they can also be kept for other items, such as inventories, wages and salaries, and cash. The first important idea to remember, however, is that a control account is an account which keeps a total record for a collective item (eg trade receivables), which in reality consists of many individual items (eg individual customer trade receivables).

A control account is an (impersonal) ledger account which will appear in the general ledger.

1.1 Control accounts and personal accounts

The personal accounts of individual customers of the business are kept in the trade receivables ledger, and the amount owed by each receivable will be a balance on his personal account. The amount owed by all the receivables together (ie all the trade receivables) will be a balance on the trade receivables control account.

At any time the balance on the trade receivables control account should be equal to the sum of the individual balances on the personal accounts in the receivables ledger.

For example, a business has three trade accounts receivable: A Arnold owes $80, B Bagshaw owes $310 and C Cloning owes $200. The debit balances on the various accounts would be:

Receivables ledger (personal accounts)

	$
A Arnold	80
B Bagshaw	310
C Cloning	200
	590

General ledger: receivables control account   590

What has happened here is that the three entries of $80, $310 and $200 were first entered into the sales day book. They were also recorded in the three personal accounts of Arnold, Bagshaw and Cloning in the receivables ledger – but remember that this is not part of the double entry system.

Later, the **total** of $590 is posted from the sales day book by a debit into the trade receivables (control) account and a credit to revenue. If you add up all the debit figures on the personal accounts, they also total $590, as shown above.

2 Discounts

FAST FORWARD

Discounts can be defined as follows:

- **Trade discount** is a reduction in the list price of an article, given by a wholesaler or manufacturer to a retailer. It is often given in return for bulk purchase orders.
- **Settlement discount (also known as a prompt payment discount)** is a reduction in the amount payable for the purchase of goods or services in return for payment in cash, or within an agreed period.

Before looking at control accounts for accounts receivable and payable, we need to consider the accounting treatment for discounts.

A discount is a reduction in the price of goods below the amount at which those goods would normally be sold to other customers. There are two types of discount.

- **Trade discount**
- **Settlement or prompt payment discount**

2.1 Trade discount

Key term

Trade discount is a reduction in the cost of goods owing to the nature of the trading transaction. It usually results from buying goods in bulk.

2.1.1 Examples of trade discount

(a) A customer is quoted a price of $1 per unit for a particular item, but a lower price of 95 cents per unit if the item is bought in quantities of 100 units or more at a time.

(b) An important customer or a regular customer is offered a discount on all the goods he buys, regardless of the size of each individual order, because the total volume of his purchases over time is so large.

2.1.2 Accounting for trade discounts

FAST FORWARD

Trade discounts received are deducted from the cost of purchases. **Trade discounts allowed** are deducted from revenue.

A trade discount is a reduction in the amount of money **demanded** from a customer.

(a) If a trade discount is **received** by a business for goods purchased from a supplier, the **amount of money demanded from the business** by the supplier will be **net of discount** (ie it will be the normal sales value less the discount).

(b) Similarly, if a trade discount is given by a business for goods sold to a customer, the amount of money demanded by the business will be **after deduction of the discount**.

Trade discounts should therefore be accounted for as follows.

(a) **Trade discounts received** will already have been accounted for in the invoice received, and therefore will be deducted to arrive at the purchases cost.

(b) **Trade discounts allowed** should be deducted from the gross sales price, so that revenue for the period will be reported in the trading account at the invoiced value.

Essentially, the figures in the statement of profit or loss will reflect the invoiced value in both cases.

2.2 Settlement discounts

Key term

Settlement discount is a reduction in the amount payable to the supplier, in return for immediate payment in cash, rather than purchase on credit, or for payment within an agreed period.

For example, a supplier charges $1,000 for goods, but offers a discount of 5% if the goods are paid for within 14 days of the invoice date.

FAST FORWARD

Settlement discounts are deducted from revenue. If a customer is expected to take advantage of the discount, the discount will be deducted from revenue at the point of recording. If the customer is not expected to take advantage of the discount, revenue will initially be recorded without the discount and an adjustment will subsequently be made.

2.2.1 Settlement discounts received

When a business is given the opportunity to take advantage of a settlement discount for prompt payment, the decision as to whether or not to take the discount is a matter of financing policy, not of trading policy.

These are usually offered as an inducement to settle a debt early, for example a 5% discount if settled within 14 days.

2.2.2 Example: Settlement discounts received

Ascot Co buys goods from Beverley Co, on the understanding that Ascot Co will be allowed a period of credit before having to pay for the goods. The terms of the transaction are as follows:

(a) Date of sale: 1 July 20X6
(b) Credit period allowed: 30 days
(c) Invoice price of the goods: $2,000
(d) Settlement discount offered: 4% discount for prompt payment

Ascot Co has the following choices:

(a) Holding on to their money for 30 days and then paying the full $2,000
(b) Paying $2,000 less 4% – ie $1,920 now

This is a **financing decision** about whether it is worthwhile for Ascot Co to save $80 by paying its debts sooner, or whether it can employ its cash more usefully for 30 days, and pay the debt at the latest acceptable moment.

If Ascot Co decides to take the settlement discount, they will pay $1,920, instead of the invoiced amount of $2,000. The cash discount received ($80) will be accounted for in the books of Ascot Co as follows:

(a) In the purchases account, the cost of purchases will be at the invoiced price (or 'full trade' price) of $2,000. When the invoice for $2,000 is received by Ascot Co, it will be recorded in its books of account at that price, and the subsequent financing decision about accepting the cash discount is ignored.

(b) In the statement of profit or loss, the cash discount received is shown as though it were income received. There is no expense in the statement of profit or loss from which the cash discount can be deducted, and so there is no alternative other than to show the discount received as income.

In our example

	$
Cost of purchase from Beverley Co by Ascot Co	2,000
Discount received (income in the statement of profit or loss)	(80)
Net cost	1,920

Question | Discounts

Soft Supplies Co recently purchased from Hard Imports Co ten printers originally priced at $200 each. A 10% trade discount was negotiated together with a 5% cash discount if payment was made within 14 days. Calculate the following.

(a) The total of the trade discount
(b) The total of the settlement discount

Answer

(a) $200 ($200 × 10 × 10%)
(b) $90 ($200 × 10 × 90% × 5%)

2.2.3 Settlement discounts allowed

IFRS 15 *Revenue from Contracts with Customers* uses a five step approach to recognising revenue. Step 3 of the approach is to determine the transaction price. In respect of discounts, the seller needs to determine how likely it is that the customer will take the discount. If it is **probable that the customer will take the discount**, the transaction price, and so the revenue recorded, is **net of the discount offered**.

2.2.4 Example: Settlement discounts allowed

Xavier Co sells goods on credit to Yankee Co at a price of $5,000. Yankee Co is offered a discount of 2% for payment within 10 days of the invoice date.

Historically, Yankee Co has taken advantage of settlement discounts offered and so Xavier Co considers it probable that Yankee Co will also take this discount. Therefore, Xavier Co should record revenue net of the discount, ie $4,900:

		$
DEBIT	Trade receivables	4,900
CREDIT	Revenue	4,900

If as expected, Yankee Co does pay within 10 days, no adjustments are necessary. However, if Yankee Co does **not** pay within 10 days and so does not take advantage of the discount, an adjustment to revenue will be needed:

		$
DEBIT	Trade receivables	100
CREDIT	Revenue	100

Now suppose Xavier Co sells goods to Zebra Co for $2,600. Zebra Co is also offered a settlement discount of 2% for payment within 10 days. However, Zebra Co is a new customer and Xavier Co considers it unlikely that Zebra Co will take the settlement discount. As the probability of Zebra Co taking the settlement discount is low, Xavier Co should record the revenue at the full amount of $2,600:

		$
DEBIT	Trade receivables	2,600
CREDIT	Revenue	2,600

If as expected, Zebra Co does not pay within 10 days, no adjustments are necessary. However, if Zebra Co does pay within 10 days and so does take the settlement discount, an adjustment to revenue is required:

		$
DEBIT	Revenue	52
CREDIT	Trade receivables	52

PART B ACCOUNTING RECORDS AND PROCEDURES

3 The operation of control accounts

FAST FORWARD

The two most important **control accounts** are those for **trade receivables** and **trade payables**. They are part of the double entry system.

3.1 Example: Accounting for trade receivables

You might still be uncertain why we need to have control accounts at all. Before turning our attention to this question, it will be useful first of all to see how transactions involving trade receivables are accounted for by means of an illustrative example. Reference numbers are shown in the accounts to illustrate the cross-referencing that is needed, and in the example reference numbers beginning:

(a) SDB, refer to a page in the sales day book
(b) RL, refer to a particular account in the trade receivables ledger
(c) GL, refer to a particular account in the general ledger
(d) CB, refer to a page in the cash book

At 1 July 20X2, the Outer Business Company had no trade accounts receivable. During July, the following transactions affecting credit sales and customers occurred.

(a) July 3: invoiced A Arnold for the sale on credit of hardware goods: $100. The customer was offered a 10% early settlement discount and was expected to take advantage of the discount at the date of invoice.

(b) July 11: invoiced B Bagshaw for the sale on credit of electrical goods: $150

(c) July 15: invoiced C Cloning for the sale on credit of hardware goods: $250

(d) July 10: received payment from A Arnold of $90, in settlement of his debt in full, having taken advantage of a settlement discount of $10 for payment within seven days

(e) July 18: received a payment of $72 from B Bagshaw in part settlement of $80 of his debt

(f) July 28: received a payment of $120 from C Cloning, who was unable to claim any discount

Account numbers are as follows:

RL 4   Personal account: A Arnold
RL 9   Personal account: B Bagshaw
RL 13 Personal account: C Cloning
GL 6   Trade receivables control account
GL 21 Revenue: hardware
GL 22 Revenue: electrical
GL 1   Cash at bank

Solution

The accounting entries would be as follows.

SALES DAY BOOK   SDB 35

Date 20X2		Name	Ref.	Total $	Hardware $	Electrical $
July	3	A Arnold	RL 4 Dr	90.00	90.00	
	11	B Bagshaw	RL 9 Dr	150.00		150.00
	15	C Cloning	RL 13 Dr	250.00	250.00	
				490.00	340.00	150.00
				NL 6 Dr	NL 21 Cr	NL 22 Cr

Note. The personal accounts in the trade receivables ledger are debited on the day the invoices are sent out. The double entry in the ledger accounts might be made at the end of each day, week or month; here it is made at the end of the month, by posting from the sales day book as follows.

			$	$
DEBIT	GL 6	Trade receivables control account	490	
CREDIT	GL 21	Revenue: hardware		340
	GL 22	Revenue: electrical		150

CASH BOOK EXTRACT
RECEIPTS – JULY 20X2
CB 23

Date 20X2	Narrative	Ref.	Total $	Accounts receivable $
July 10	A Arnold	RL 4 Cr	90.00	90.00
18	B Bagshaw	RL 9 Cr	72.00	80.00
28	C Cloning	RL 13 Cr	120.00	120.00
			282.00	290.00
			GL 1 Dr	GL 6 Cr

MEMORANDUM TRADE RECEIVABLES LEDGER
A ARNOLD
A/c no: RL 4

Date 20X2	Narrative	Ref.	$	Date 20X2	Narrative	Ref.	$
July 3	Revenue	SDB 35	90.00	July 10	Cash	CB 23	90.00
			90.00				90.00

B BAGSHAW
A/c no: RL 9

Date 20X2	Narrative	Ref.	$	Date 20X2	Narrative	Ref.	$
July 11	Revenue	SDB 35	150.00	July 18	Cash	CB 23	72.00
				July 31	Balance	c/d	78.00
			150.00				150.00
Aug 1	Balance	b/d	78.00				

C CLONING
A/c no: RL 13

Date 20X2	Narrative	Ref.	$	Date 20X2	Narrative	Ref.	$
July 15	Revenue	SDB 35	250.00	July 28	Cash	CB 23	120.00
				July 31	Balance	c/d	130.00
			250.00				250.00
Aug 1	Balance	b/d	130.00				

In the general ledger, the accounting entries are made from the books of prime entry to the ledger accounts, in this example at the end of the month.

PART B ACCOUNTING RECORDS AND PROCEDURES

GENERAL LEDGER (EXTRACT)
TRADE RECEIVABLES LEDGER CONTROL ACCOUNT A/c no: GL 6

Date 20X2	Narrative	Ref.	$	Date 20X2	Narrative	Ref.	$
July 31	Revenue	SDB 35	490.00	July 31	Cash	CB 23	282.00
				July 31	Balance	c/d	208.00
			490.00				490.00
Aug 1	Balance	b/d	200.00				

Note. At 31 July the closing balance on the trade receivables control account ($208) is the same as the total of the individual balances on the personal accounts in the trade receivables ledger ($0 + $78 + $130). This is an important check which should be done every month. If the balance on the control account does not equal the sum of the individual balances, an error has been made.

BANK CONTROL ACCOUNT A/c no: GL 1

Date 20X2	Narrative	Ref.	$	Date	Narrative	Ref.	$
July 31	Cash received	CB 23	282.00				

REVENUE: HARDWARE A/c no: GL 21

Date	Narrative	Ref.	$	Date 20X2	Narrative	Ref.	$
				July 31	Trade receivables	SDB 35	340.00

REVENUE: ELECTRICAL A/c no: GL 22

Date	Narrative	Ref.	$	Date 20X2	Narrative	Ref.	$
				July 31	Trade receivables	SDB 35	150.00

If we take the balance on the accounts shown in this example as at 31 July 20X2, the trial balance is as follows.

TRIAL BALANCE

	Debit $	Credit $
Cash (all receipts)	282	
Trade receivables	208	
Revenue: hardware		340
Revenue: electrical		150
	490	490

The trial balance is shown here to emphasise the point that a trial balance includes the balances on control accounts, but excludes the balances on the personal accounts in the trade receivables ledger and payables ledger.

3.2 Accounting for trade payables

If you are able to follow the example above dealing with the trade receivables control account, you should have no difficulty in dealing with similar examples relating to purchases/payables. If necessary refer back to revise the entries made in the purchase day book and purchase ledger personal accounts.

One of the key ways that businesses can verify what monies are outstanding to suppliers is by regularly reconciling their accounting records to statements from the suppliers.

3.2.1 Supplier statements

A supplier will usually send a monthly statement showing invoices issued, credit notes, payments received and discounts given. It is **vitally important** that these statements are compared to the supplier's personal account in the payables ledger. Any discrepancies need to be identified and any errors corrected.

A statement of account is reproduced as follows.

STATEMENT OF ACCOUNT

Pickett (Handling Equipment) Co
Unit 7, Western Industrial Estate
Dunford DN2 7RJ

Tel: (01990) 72101   Fax: (01990) 72980   VAT Reg No 982 7213 49

Accounts Department
Finstar Co
67 Laker Avenue
Dunford DN4 5PS

RECEIVED 1 JUN X1

Date: 31 May 20X1

A/c No: F023

Date	Details	Debit $ c	Credit $ c	Balance $ c
30/4/X1	Balance brought forward from previous statement			492 22
3/5/X1	Invoice no. 34207	129 40 ✓		621 62
4/5/X1	Invoice no. 34242	22 72 ✓		644 34
5/5/X1	Payment received - thank you		412 17 ✓	232 17
17/5/X1	Invoice no. 34327	394 95 ✓		627 12
18/5/X1	Credit note no. 00192		64 40 ✓	562 72
21/5/X1	Invoice no. 34392	392 78		955 50
28/5/X1	Credit note no. 00199		107 64 ✓	847 86

Amount now due $ 847 86

Terms: 30 days net, 1% discount for payment in 7 days. E & OE

Registered office: 4 Arkwright Road, London E16 4PQ Registered in England No 2182417

The statement is received on 1 June 20X1 and is passed to Linda Kelly who is the purchase ledger clerk at Finstar Co. Linda obtains a printout of the transactions with Pickett (Handling Equipment) Co from Finstar's purchase ledger system. (The reason why Linda has made ticks on the statement and on the printout which follows will be explained as follows.)

PART B ACCOUNTING RECORDS AND PROCEDURES

FINSTAR CO		PURCHASE LEDGER
ACCOUNT NAME:	PICKETT (HANDLING EQUIPMENT) CO	
ACCOUNT REF:	P042	
DATE OF REPORT:	1 JUNE 20X1	
Date	Transaction	(Debit)/Credit $
16.03.X1	Invoice 33004	350.70
20.03.X1	Invoice 33060	61.47
06.04.X1	Invoice 34114	80.05
03.05.X1	Invoice 34207	129.40 ✓
04.05.X1	Payment	(412.17) ✓
06.05.X1	Invoice 34242	22.72 ✓
19.05.X1	Invoice 34327	394.95 ✓
19.05.X1	Credit note 00192	(64.40) ✓
28.05.X1	Payment	(117.77)
30.05.X1	Credit note 00199	(107.64) ✓
	Balance	337.31

The purchase ledger of Finstar shows a balance due to Pickett of $337.31, while Pickett's statement shows a balance due of $847.86.

3.2.2 Supplier statement reconciliations

Linda wants to be sure that her purchase ledger record for Pickett is correct and so she prepares a **supplier statement reconciliation**.

These are the steps to follow.

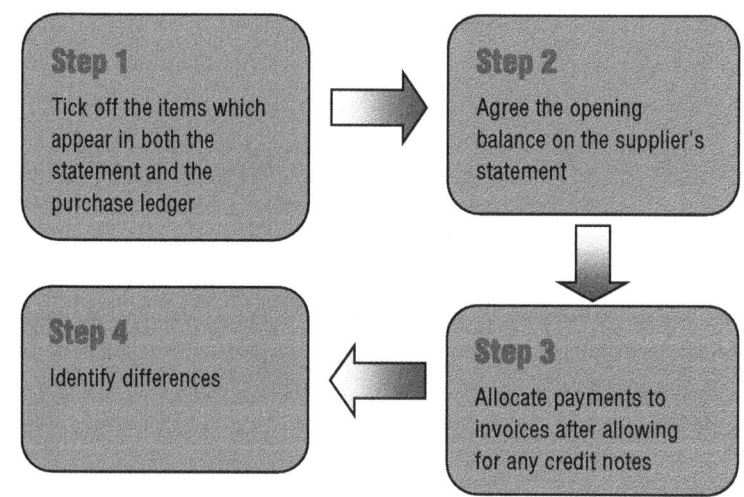

Step 1 Tick off the items which appear in both the statement and the purchase ledger

Step 2 Agree the opening balance on the supplier's statement

Step 3 Allocate payments to invoices after allowing for any credit notes

Step 4 Identify differences

3.2.3 Example: Supplier reconciliation

Linda applies the above steps to Pickett's statement.

Step 1 The common items have been ticked off on the statement and purchase ledger above.

Step 2 The balance brought forward at 30.4.X1 consists of three invoices.

		$
33004		350.70
33060		61.47
34114		80.05
		492.22

Step 3 Invoices 33004 and 33060 were paid on 4 May and 34114 was part of the payment on 28 May.

Step 4 Pickett's statement does not show the payment of $117.77 made on 28 May. However this is reasonable, as the cheque was probably still in the post. The statement also shows an invoice 34392 dated 21 May, which is not in the purchase ledger. This is surprising. Finstar needs to check if the invoice has been received (using the purchase day book), if so has it been posted to the wrong account? If it has not been received, Linda will need to contact Pickett and ask for a duplicate.

SUPPLIER STATEMENT RECONCILIATION

ACCOUNT: PICKETT (HANDLING EQUIPMENT) CO (P042)

	$
Balance per supplier's statement	847.86
Less: Payment (28 May) not on statement	(117.77)
Invoice (supplier no 34392) on statement, not on purchase ledger	(392.78)
Balance per purchase ledger	337.31

3.2.4 The reasons for reconciling items

Reconciling items may occur as a result of the following items.

Reconciling item	Effect	Status
Payments in transit	A payment will go in the purchase ledger when the cheque is issued or when a bank transfer instruction is made. There will be delay (postal, processing) before this payment is entered in the records of the supplier. Any statement of account received by post will also be out of date by the length of time taken to deliver it.	Timing difference
Omitted invoices and credit notes	Invoices or credit notes may appear in the ledger of one business but not in that of the other due to error or omission. However, the most common reason will be a timing difference in recording the items in the different ledgers.	Error or omission or timing difference
Other errors	Addition errors can occur, particularly if a statement of account is prepared manually. Invoice, credit note or payment amounts can be mis-posted. Regular reconciliation of supplier statements will minimise the possibility of missing such errors.	Error

3.3 Entries in control accounts

Typical entries in the control accounts are listed below. Reference 'Jnl' indicates that the transaction is first lodged in the journal before posting to the control account and other accounts indicated. References SRDB and PRDB are to sales returns and purchase returns day books.

TRADE RECEIVABLES CONTROL ACCOUNT

	Ref.	$		Ref.	$
Opening debit balances	b/d	7,000	Opening credit balances		
Revenue	SDB	53,640	(if any)	b/d	200
Dishonoured bills or Cheques	Jnl	1,000	Cash received	CB	52,250

	Ref.	$		Ref.	$
Cash paid to clear credit balances	CB	110	Returns inwards from customers	SRDB	800
			Irrecoverable debts	Jnl	300
			Closing debit balances	C/d	8,200
		61,750			61,750
Debit balances b/d		8,200	Credit balances b/d		

Note. Opening credit balances are unusual in the receivables control account. They represent debtors to whom the business owes money, probably as a result of the over-payment of debts or for advance payments of debts for which no invoices have yet been sent.

TRADE PAYABLES CONTROL ACCOUNT

	Ref.	$		Ref.	$
Opening debit balances (if any)	b/d	70	Opening credit balances	b/d	8,300
Cash paid	CB	29,840	Purchases	PDB	31,000
Discounts received	CB	30	Cash received clearing debit balances	CB	20
Returns outwards to suppliers	PRDB	60	Closing debit balances (if any)	c/d	
Closing credit balances	c/d	9,400			
		39,400			39,400
Debit balances	b/d	80	Credit balances	b/d	9,400

Note. Opening debit balances in the trade payables control account would represent suppliers who owe the business money, perhaps because the business has overpaid or because a credit note is awaited for returned goods.

Posting from the journal to the memorandum trade receivables or trade payables ledgers and to the general ledger may be effected at the same time; as in the following example, where C Cloning has returned goods with a sales value of $50.

Journal entry	Ref.	Dr $	Cr $
Revenue	GL 21	50	
To trade receivables control	GL 6		50
To C Cloning (memorandum)	GL 13	–	50
Return of electrical goods inwards			

3.4 Contra entries

Sometimes the same business may be both a trade receivable and a trade payable. For example, C Cloning buys hardware from you and you buy stationery from C Cloning. In the trade receivables ledger, C Cloning owes you $130. However, you owe C Cloning $250. You may reach an agreement to offset the balances trade receivable and trade payable. This is known as a 'contra'. The double entry is as follows:

DEBIT	Trade payables control	$130	
CREDIT	Trade receivables control		$130

You will also need to make the appropriate entries in the memorandum trade receivables and payables ledger. After this, C Cloning will owe you nothing and you will owe C Cloning $120 ($250 – $130).

Question — Trade payables control account

A trade payables control account contains the following entries:

	$
Bank	79,500
Credit purchases	83,200
Credit notes on returned goods received	3,750
Contra with trade receivables control account	4,000
Balance c/f at 31 December 20X8	12,920

There are no other entries in the account. What was the opening balance brought forward at 1 January 20X8?

Answer

TRADE PAYABLES CONTROL

	$		$
Bank payments	79,500	Balance b/f (balancing figure)	16,970
Contra with trade receivables	4,000	Purchases	83,200
Balance c/f	12,920		
	100,170		100,170

Question — Receivables control account

The total of the balances in a company's trade receivables ledger is $800 more than the debit balance on its trade receivables control account. Which one of the following errors could by itself account for the discrepancy?

A   The sales day book has been undercast by $800

B   Credit notes sent to customers totalling $800 have been omitted from the general ledger

C   One trade receivables ledger account with a credit balance of $800 has been treated as a debit balance

D   The cash receipts book has been undercast by $800

Answer

A   The total of sales invoices in the day book is debited to the control account. If the total is understated by $800, the debits in the control account will also be understated by $800. Options B and D would have the opposite effect: credit entries in the control account would be understated. Option C would lead to a discrepancy of 2 × $800 = $1,600.

3.5 Summary of entries

It may help you to see how the trade receivables ledger and trade receivables control account are used, by means of a flowchart.

PART B ACCOUNTING RECORDS AND PROCEDURES

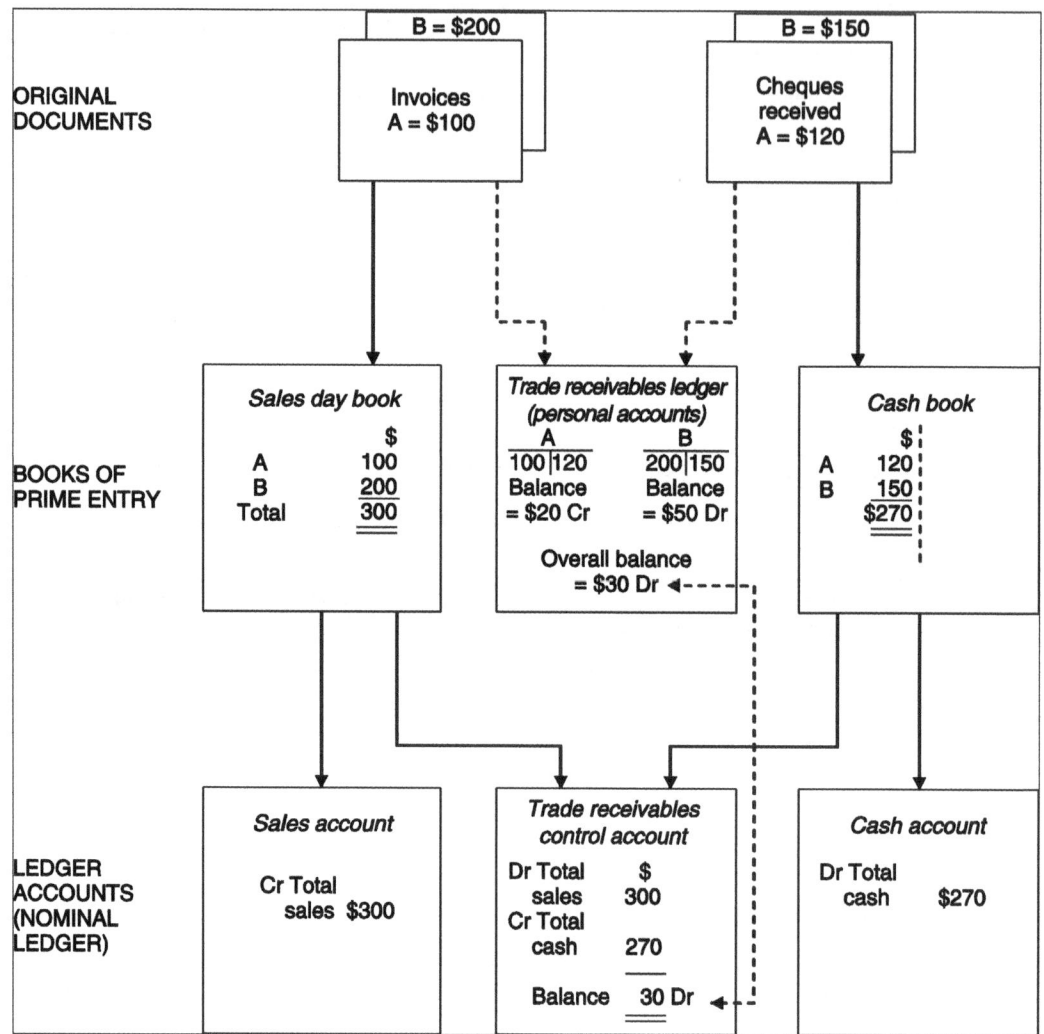

Notes

1 The trade receivables ledger is not part of the double entry system (it is not used to post the ledger accounts).

2 Nevertheless, the total balance on the trade receivables ledger (ie all the personal account balances added up) should equal the balance on the trade receivables control account.

Attention!

> The diagram shows the personal accounts being written up from the original documents. An alternative way is to transfer the information from the books of prime entry. The system shown has the advantage of helping to reduce errors (as an error made in the books of prime entry will not be transferred to the personal accounts and so will be spotted in the control account reconciliation).

See now whether you can do the following question yourself.

 Question　　　　　　　　　　　　　　　　　　　　**Receivables and payables control accounts**

On examining the books of Exports Co, you ascertain that on 1 October 20X8 the trade receivables ledger balances were $8,024 debit and $57 credit, and the trade payables ledger balances on the same date $6,235 credit and $105 debit.

For the year ended 30 September 20X9 the following particulars are available:

	$
Revenue	63,728
Purchases	38,499
Cash from trade accounts receivable	55,212
Cash to trade accounts payable	37,307
Customer returns not yet accounted for	3,330
Returns inwards	1,002
Returns outwards	535
Irrecoverable debts written off	326
Cash received in respect of debit balances in trade payables ledger	105
Amount due from customer as shown by trade receivables ledger, offset against amount due to the same firm as shown by payables ledger (settlement by contra)	434
Allowances to customers on goods damaged in transit	212

On 30 September 20X9 there were no credit balances in the trade receivables ledger except those outstanding on 1 October 20X8, and no debit balances in the trade payables ledger.

You are required to write up the following accounts recording the above transactions bringing down the balances as on 30 September 20X9:

(a) Trade receivables control account
(b) Trade payables control account

Answer

(a)

TRADE RECEIVABLES CONTROL ACCOUNT

			$			$
20X8				20X8		
Oct 1	Balances b/f		8,024	Oct 1	Balances b/f	57
20X9				20X9		
Sept 30	Revenue		63,728	Sept 30	Cash received from credit customers	55,212
	Balances c/f		57			
					Customer returns	3,330
					Irrecoverable debts written off	326
					Contra trade payables control account	434
					Allowances on goods damaged	212
					Balances c/f	12,238
			71,809			71,809

(b)

TRADE PAYABLES CONTROL ACCOUNT

		$			$
20X8			20X8		
Oct 1	Balances b/f	105	Oct 1	Balances b/f	6,235
20X9			20X9		
Sept 30	Cash paid to credit suppliers	37,307	Sept 30	Purchases	38,499
				Cash	105
	Returns outwards	535			
	Contra trade receivables control account	434			
	Balances c/f	6,458			
		44,839			44,839

PART B   ACCOUNTING RECORDS AND PROCEDURES

4 The purpose of control accounts

FAST FORWARD

Cash books and day books are totalled periodically and the totals posted to the control accounts. At suitable intervals, the balances on the **personal accounts** (also referred to as **memorandum accounts**) are extracted and totalled. These balance totals should agree to the balance on the control account. In this way, errors can be located and corrected.

4.1 Reasons for having control accounts

The reasons for having control accounts are as follows:

(a) They provide a **check on the accuracy** of entries made in the personal accounts in the trade receivables ledger and trade payables ledger. It is very easy to make a mistake in posting entries, because there might be hundreds of entries to make. Figures can get transposed. Some entries might be omitted altogether, so that an invoice or a payment transaction does not appear in a personal account as it should. By comparing (i) and (ii) below, it is possible to identify that fact that errors have been made.

   (i) The total balance on the trade receivables control account with the total of individual balances on the personal accounts in the trade receivables ledger.

   (ii) The total balance on the trade payables control account with the total of individual balances on the personal accounts in the trade payables ledger.

(b) The control accounts also assist in the **location of errors**, where postings to the control accounts are made daily or weekly, or even monthly. If a clerk fails to record an invoice or a payment in a personal account, or makes a transposition error, it would be a formidable task to locate the error or errors at the end of a year, say, given the number of transactions. By using the control account, a comparison with the individual balances in the trade receivables or payables ledger can be made for every week or day of the month, and the error found much more quickly than if control accounts did not exist.

(c) Where there is a separation of clerical (bookkeeping) duties, the control account provides an **internal check**. The person posting entries to the control accounts will act as a check on a different person(s) whose job it is to post entries to the trade receivables and payables ledger accounts.

(d) To provide total trade receivables and payables balances more quickly for producing a trial balance or statement of financial position. A single balance on a control account is obviously **extracted more simply and quickly** than many individual balances in the trade receivables or payables ledger. This means also that the number of accounts in the double entry bookkeeping system can be kept down to a manageable size, since the **personal accounts are memorandum accounts only**.

However, particularly in computerised systems, it may be feasible to use trade receivables and payables ledgers without the need for operating separate control accounts. In such a system, the trade receivables or payables ledger printouts produced by the computer constitute the list of individual balances as well as providing a total balance which represents the control account balance.

Exam focus point

A question may ask which errors would be revealed by a trade receivables control account reconciliation.

4.2 Balancing and agreeing control accounts with trade receivables and trade payables ledgers

The control accounts should be **balanced regularly** (at least monthly), and the balance on the account agreed with the sum of the individual debtors' or suppliers' balances extracted from the trade receivables

or trade payables ledgers respectively. It is one of the sad facts of an accountant's life that more often than not the balance on the control account does not agree with the sum of balances extracted, for one or more of the following reasons:

(a) An **incorrect amount** may be **posted** to the control account because of a **miscast** of the total in the book of original entry (ie adding up incorrectly the total value of invoices or payments). The general ledger debit and credit postings will then balance, but the control account balance will not agree with the sum of individual balances extracted from the (memorandum) trade receivables ledger or trade payables ledger. A journal entry must then be made in the general ledger to correct the control account and the corresponding sales or expense account.

(b) A **transposition error** may occur in posting an individual's balance from the book of prime entry to the memorandum ledger, eg a sale to C Cloning of $250 might be posted to his account as $520. This means that the sum of balances extracted from the memorandum ledger must be corrected. No accounting entry would be required to do this, except to alter the figure in C Cloning's account.

(c) A transaction may be **recorded in the control account** and *not* **in the memorandum ledger**, or vice versa. This requires an entry in the ledger that has been missed out which means a double posting if the control account has to be corrected, and a single posting if it is the individual's balance in the memorandum ledger that is at fault.

(d) The sum of balances extracted from the memorandum ledger may be **incorrectly extracted or miscast**. This would involve simply correcting the total of the balances.

4.3 Example: Agreeing control account balances with the trade receivables and payables ledgers

Reconciling the control account balance with the sum of the balances extracted from the (memorandum) trade receivables ledger or trade payables ledger should be done in two stages.

(a) Correct the total of the balances extracted from the memorandum ledger. (The errors must be located first of course.)

	$	$
Trade receivables ledger total		
Original total extracted		15,320
Add difference arising from transposition error ($95 written as $59)		36
		15,356
Less: Credit balance of $60 extracted as a debit balance ($60 × 2)	120	
Overcast of list of balances	90	
		210
		15,146

(b) Bring down the balance before adjustments on the control account, and adjust or post the account with correcting entries.

TRADE RECEIVABLES CONTROL ACCOUNT

	$		$
Balance before adjustments	15,091	Petty cash: posting omitted	10
		Returns inwards: individual posting omitted from control account	35
Undercast of total invoices issued in sales day book	100	Balance c/d (now in agreement with the corrected total of individual balances in (a))	15,146
	15,191		15,191
Balance b/d	15,146		

PART B ACCOUNTING RECORDS AND PROCEDURES

Question — Receivables control account

April Showers sells goods on credit to most of its customers. In order to control its trade receivables collection system, the company maintains a trade receivables control account. In preparing the accounts for the year to 30 October 20X3 the accountant discovers that the total of all the personal accounts in the trade receivables ledger amounts to $12,802, whereas the balance on the trade receivables control account is $12,550.

Upon investigating the matter, the following errors were discovered.

(a) Sales for the week ending 27 March 20X3 amounting to $850 had been omitted from the control account.

(b) A customer's account balance of $300 had not been included in the list of balances.

(c) Cash received of $750 had been entered in a personal account as $570.

(d) Returns from customers totalling $100 had not been entered in the control account.

(e) A personal account balance had been undercast by $200.

(f) A contra item of $400 with the payables ledger had not been entered in the control account.

(g) An irrecoverable debt of $500 had not been entered in the control account.

(h) Cash received of $250 had been debited to a personal account.

(i) Credit note from a supplier of $50 had been debited to Bell's receivables ledger account.

(j) Returns inwards valued at $200 had not been included in the control account.

(k) Cash received of $80 had been credited to a personal account as $8.

(l) A cheque for $300 received from a customer had been dishonoured by the bank, but no adjustment had been made in the control account.

Required

(a) Prepare a corrected trade receivables control account, bringing down the amended balance as at 1 November 20X3.

(b) Prepare a statement showing the adjustments that are necessary to the list of personal account balances so that it reconciles with the amended trade receivables control account balance.

Answer

(a)

TRADE RECEIVABLES CONTROL ACCOUNT

	$		$
Uncorrected balance b/f	12,550	Returns from customers (d)	100
Sales omitted (a)	850	Contra entry omitted (f)	400
Bank: cheque dishonoured (l)	300	Irrecoverable debt omitted (g)	500
		Returns inwards omitted (j)	200
		Amended balance c/d	12,500
	13,700		13,700
Balance b/d	12,500		

Note. Items (b), (c), (e), (h), (i) and (k) are matters affecting the personal accounts of customers. They have no effect on the control account.

10: CONTROL ACCOUNTS

(b) STATEMENT OF ADJUSTMENTS TO LIST OF PERSONAL ACCOUNT BALANCES

	$	$
Original total of list of balances		12,802
Add: Debit balance omitted (b)	300	
Debit balance understated (e)	200	
		500
		13,302
Less: Transposition error (c): understatement of cash received	180	
Cash debited instead of credited (2 × $250) (h)	500	
Credit note from supplier wrongly posted to Bell (i)	50	
Understatement of cash received (k)	72	
		802
		12,500

Question — Payables control account

ABC has a trade payables control account balance of $12,500 at 31 December 20X6. However the extract of balances from the trade payables ledger totals $12,800. Investigation finds the following errors: purchases for week 52 of $1,200 had been omitted form the control account; a supplier account of $900 had been omitted from the list of balances.

What is the correct trade payables balance at 31 December 20X6?

A $12,500
B $13,400
C $12,800
D $13,700

Answer

D

TRADE PAYABLES CONTROL

	$		$
		Bal b/f	12,500
Bal c/f	13,700	Purchases – week 52	1,200
	13,700		13,700

Corrected list of balances:

	$
Original	12,800
Omitted account	900
	13,700

Chapter roundup

- A control account keeps a total record of a number of individual items. It is an **impersonal** account which is part of the double entry system.
- Discounts can be defined as follows:
  - **Trade discount** is a reduction in the list price of an article, given by a wholesaler or manufacturer to a retailer. It is often given in return for bulk purchase orders.
  - **Settlement discount** is a reduction in the amount payable for the purchase of goods or services in return for payment within an agreed period.
- **Trade discounts** are deducted from the cost of purchases. **Trade discounts allowed** are deducted from revenue.
- **Settlement discounts** are deducted from revenue. If a customer is expected to take advantage of the discount, the discount will be deducted from revenue at the point of recording. If the customer is not expected to take advantage of the discount, revenue will initially be recorded without the discount and an adjustment will subsequently be made.
- The two most important **control accounts** are those for **trade receivables** and **trade payables**. They are part of the double entry system.
- Cash books and day books are totalled periodically and the totals posted to the control accounts. At suitable intervals, the balances on the **personal accounts** (also referred to as **memorandum accounts**) are extracted and totalled. These balance totals should agree to the balance on the control account. In this way, errors can be located and corrected.

Quick quiz

1. Which of the following accounting items may have control accounts in the general ledger?
   - (i) Trade receivables and payables
   - (ii) Inventories
   - (iii) Cash
   - (iv) Salaries and wages

   A (i) and (ii)
   B (i), (ii) and (iv)
   C (i), (ii) and (iii)
   D (i), (ii), (iii) and (iv)

2. Sales of $4,000 have been omitted from the trade receivables control account. What is the entry to correct this?

   A Debit RCA $4,000
   B Credit RCA $4,000

3. During a period, Angela Co has the following transactions on trade receivables control account. Revenue $123,000, cash received $50,000. The balance carried forward is $95,000. What was the opening balance at the beginning of the period?

   A $22,000 debit
   B $22,000 credit
   C $18,000 debit
   D $20,000 debit

4. An invoice amount has been incorrectly posted to the sales day book. The memorandum accounts are posted direct from the invoices. A trade receivables control account reconciliation will reveal this error. True or false?

5. Charlie Co has a trade payables control account balance of $25,000 at 31 March 20X6. However the extract of balances from the trade payables ledger totals $25,600. However, purchases for week 52 of $2,400 had been omitted form the control account; and purchase invoices of $1,800 had been omitted from the list of balances.

   What is the correct trade payables balance at 31 March 20X6?

   A $25,000
   B $26,800
   C $27,400
   D $25,600

PART B ACCOUNTING RECORDS AND PROCEDURES

Answers to quick quiz

1 D

2 A

3 A

TRADE RECEIVABLES CONTROL

	$		$
Bal b/f (bal figure)	22,000	Cash	50,000
Revenue	123,000		
		Bal c/f	95,000
	145,000		145,000

If you had answer B, you reversed the double entry and so produced a trade payables control account. In answer D, you omitted the discounts allowed figure; while in answer C you put discounts allowed on the debit instead of the credit side of the control account.

4 True. However, if the memorandum accounts were posted from the sales day book, then the answer would be false.

5 C

TRADE PAYABLES CONTROL

	$		$
		Bal b/f	25,000
Bal c/f	27,400	Purchases – week 52	2,400
	27,400		27,400

Corrected list of balances:

	$
Original	25,600
Omitted invoices	1,800
	27,400

Correction of errors

Topic list	Syllabus reference
1 Types of error in accounting	A2
2 The correction of errors	A2

Introduction

This chapter continues the subject of errors in accounts. You have already learned about errors which arise in the context of the cash book or the trade receivables and trade payables ledgers and control accounts.

Here we deal with errors that may be corrected by means of the journal or a suspense account.

By the end of this chapter you should be able to prepare a set of final accounts for a sole trader from a trial balance after incorporating adjustments to profits for errors.

PART B   ACCOUNTING RECORDS AND PROCEDURES

Exam focus point

It is important that you are familiar with clearing suspense accounts and correcting errors. This is often included as part of a longer question in the exam. Ensure you understand the different types of error, and how they may be identified.

1 Types of error in accounting

FAST FORWARD

There are five main types of error. Some can be corrected by journal entry, some require the use of a suspense account.

It is not really possible to draw up a complete list of all the errors which might be made by bookkeepers and accountants. Even if you tried, it is more than likely that as soon as you finished, someone would commit a completely new error that you had never even dreamed of! However, it is possible to describe **five types of error** which cover most of the errors which might occur. They are as follows:

- Errors of **transposition**
- Errors of **omission**
- Errors of **principle**
- Errors of **commission**
- **Compensating errors**

Once an error has been detected, it needs to be put right.

- If the correction **involves a double entry** in the ledger accounts, then it is done by using a **journal entry** in the journal.

- When the error **breaks the rule of double entry**, then it is corrected by the use of a **suspense account** as well as a journal entry.

Topics covered in this chapter

- The five common types of error
- Review journal entries (which we briefly looked at earlier in this Workbook)
- Define a **suspense account**, and describe how it is used

1.1 Errors of transposition

Key term

An **error of transposition** is when two digits in an amount are accidentally recorded the wrong way round.

For example, suppose that a sale is recorded in the sales account as $6,843, but it has been incorrectly recorded in the total trade receivables account as $6,483. The error is the transposition of the 4 and the 8. The consequence is that total debits will not be equal to total credits. You can often detect a transposition error by checking whether the difference between debits and credits can be divided exactly by 9. For example, $6,843 – $6,483 = $360; $360 ÷ 9 = 40.

1.2 Errors of omission

Key term

An **error of omission** means failing to record a transaction at all, or making a debit or credit entry, but not the corresponding double entry.

Here is an example.

(a) If a business receives an invoice from a supplier for $250, the transaction might be omitted from the books entirely. As a result, both the total debits and the total credits of the business will be out by $250.

(b) If a business receives an invoice from a supplier for $300, the trade payables control account might be credited, but the debit entry in the purchases account might be omitted. In this case, the total credits would not equal total debits (because total debits are $300 less than they ought to be).

1.3 Errors of principle

Key term

An **error of principle** involves making a double entry in the belief that the transaction is being entered in the correct accounts, but subsequently finding out that the accounting entry breaks the 'rules' of an accounting principle or concept.

A typical example of such an error is to treat certain revenue expenditure incorrectly as capital expenditure.

(a) For example, repairs to a machine costing $150 should be treated as revenue expenditure, and debited to a repairs account. If, instead, the repair costs are added to the cost of the non-current asset (capital expenditure) an error of principle would have occurred. As a result, although total debits still equal total credits, the repairs account is $150 less than it should be and the cost of the non-current asset is $150 greater than it should be.

(b) Similarly, suppose that the proprietor of the business sometimes takes cash out of the till for his personal use and during a certain year these withdrawals on account of profit amount to $280. The book-keeper states that he has reduced cash sales by $280 so that the cash book could be made to balance. This would be an error of principle, and the result of it would be that the withdrawal account is understated by $280, and so is the total value of sales in the sales account.

1.4 Errors of commission

Key term

Errors of commission are where the bookkeeper makes a mistake in carrying out his or her task of recording transactions in the accounts.

Here are two common types of errors of commission.

(a) **Putting a debit entry or a credit entry in the wrong account**. For example, if telephone expenses of $540 are debited to the electricity expenses account, an error of commission would have occurred. The result is that although total debits and total credits balance, telephone expenses are understated by $540 and electricity expenses are overstated by the same amount.

(b) **Errors of casting (adding up)**. The total daily credit sales in the sales day book should be $28,425, but are incorrectly added up as $28,825. The total sales in the sales day book are then used to credit total sales and debit total receivables in the ledger accounts. Although total debits and total credits are still equal, they are incorrect by $400.

1.5 Compensating errors

Key term

Compensating errors are errors which are, coincidentally, equal and opposite to one another.

For example, two transposition errors of $540 might occur in extracting ledger balances, one on each side of the double entry. In the administration expenses account, $2,282 might be written instead of $2,822, while in the sundry income account, $8,391 might be written instead of $8,931. Both the debits and the credits would be $540 too low, and the mistake would not be apparent when the trial balance is cast. Consequently, compensating errors hide the fact that there are errors in the trial balance.

1.6 Summary: Errors that can be detected by a trial balance

- Errors of transposition
- Errors of omission (if the omission is one-sided)
- Errors of commission (if one-sided, or two debit entries are made, for example)

Other errors will not be detected by extracting a trial balance, but may be spotted by other controls (such as bank or control account reconciliations).

2 The correction of errors

FAST FORWARD

Errors which leave total debits and credits in the ledger accounts in balance can be corrected by using **journal entries**. Otherwise a suspense account has to be opened first, and later cleared by a journal entry.

2.1 Journal entries

Some errors can be corrected by journal entries. To remind you, the format of a journal entry is:

Date	Debit $	Credit $
Account to be debited	X	
Account to be credited		X
(Narrative to explain the transaction)		

Exam focus point

As already indicated, in the exam you are often required to present answers in the form of journal entries. It is important to show the double entry if you are asked to do this, rather than just making the correction within the financial statements.

The journal requires a debit and an equal credit entry for each 'transaction', ie for each correction. This means that if total debits equal total credits before a journal entry is made then they will still be equal after the journal entry is made. This would be the case if, for example, the original error was a debit wrongly posted as a credit and *vice versa*.

Similarly, if total debits and total credits are unequal before a journal entry is made, then they will still be unequal (by the same amount) after it is made.

For example, a bookkeeper accidentally posts a bill for $40 to the local taxes account instead of to the electricity account. A trial balance is drawn up, and total debits are $40,000 and total credits are $40,000. A journal entry is made to correct the misposting error as follows.

1.7.20X7

DEBIT	Electricity account	$40	
CREDIT	Local taxes account		$40

To correct a misposting of $40 from the local taxes account to electricity account

After the journal has been posted, total debits will still be $40,000 and total credits will be $40,000. Total debits and totals credits are still equal.

Now suppose that, because of some error which has not yet been detected, total debits were originally $40,000 but total credits were $39,900. If the same journal correcting the $40 is put through, total debits will remain $40,000 and total credits will remain $39,900. Total debits were different by $100 **before** the journal, and they are still different by $100 **after** the journal.

This means that journals can only be used to correct errors which require both a credit and (an equal) debit adjustment.

2.2 Example: Journal entries

Listed below are five errors which were used as examples earlier in this chapter. Write out the journal entries which would correct these errors.

(a) A business receives an invoice for $250 from a supplier which was omitted from the books entirely.

(b) Repairs worth $150 were incorrectly debited to the non-current asset (machinery) account instead of the repairs account.

(c) The bookkeeper of a business reduces cash sales by $280 because he was not sure what the $280 represented. In fact, it was a withdrawal on account of profit.

(d) Telephone expenses of $540 are incorrectly debited to the electricity account.

(e) A page in the sales day book has been added up to $28,425 instead of $28,825.

Solution

(a) DEBIT   Purchases $250
    CREDIT   Trade payables ledger $250
    A transaction previously omitted

(b) DEBIT   Repairs account $150
    CREDIT   Non-current asset (machinery) a/c $150
    The correction of an error of principle: Repairs costs incorrectly added to non-current asset costs

(c) DEBIT   Withdrawals on account $280
    CREDIT   Sales $280
    An error of principle, in which sales were reduced to compensate for cash withdrawals not accounted for

(d) DEBIT   Telephone expenses $540
    CREDIT   Electricity expenses $540
    Correction of an error of commission: telephone expenses wrongly charged to the electricity account

(e) DEBIT   Trade receivables ledger $400
    CREDIT   Sales $400
    The correction of a casting error in the sales day book
    ($28,825 – $28,425 = $400)

2.3 Use of journal entries in examinations

Occasionally an examination question might ask you to 'journalise' a transaction (ie select one of two, three or four journal entries), even though the transaction is perfectly normal and nothing to do with an error. This is just the examiner's way of finding out whether you know your debits and credits. For example:

Question — Journal

A business sells $500 of goods on credit. What is the correct journal to reflect this transaction?

A   Debit sales $500, credit trade receivables $500
B   Debit trade receivables $500, credit sales $500

Answer

B	DEBIT	Trade receivables	$500	
	CREDIT	Sales		$500

No error has occurred here, just a normal credit sale of $500. By asking you to select a journal, the examiner can see that you understand the double-entry bookkeeping.

2.4 Suspense accounts

FAST FORWARD

Suspense accounts, as well as being used to correct some errors, are also opened when it is not known immediately where to post an amount. When the mystery is solved, the suspense account is closed and the amount correctly posted using a journal entry.

Key term

A **suspense account** is an account showing a balance equal to the difference in a trial balance.

A suspense account is a **temporary** account which can be opened for a number of reasons. The most common reasons are as follows:

(a) A trial balance is drawn up which does not balance (ie total debits do not equal total credits).

(b) The bookkeeper of a business knows where to post the credit side of a transaction, but does not know where to post the debit (or vice versa). For example, a cash payment might be made and must obviously be credited to cash. But the bookkeeper may not know what the payment is for, and so will not know which account to debit.

In both these cases, a temporary suspense account is opened up until the problem is sorted out. The next few paragraphs explain exactly how this works.

2.5 Use of suspense account: When the trial balance does not balance

When an error has occurred which results in an imbalance between total debits and total credits in the ledger accounts, the first step is to open a suspense account. For example, an accountant draws up a trial balance and finds that total debits exceed total credits by $162.

He knows that there is an error somewhere, but for the time being he opens a suspense account and enters a credit of $162 in it. This serves two purposes:

(a) As the suspense account now exists, the accountant will not forget that there is an error (of $162) to be sorted out.

(b) Now that there is a credit of $162 in the suspense account, the trial balance balances.

When the cause of the $162 discrepancy is tracked down, it is corrected by means of a journal entry. For example, the credit of $162 should be to purchases. The journal entry would be:

DEBIT	Suspense a/c	$162	
CREDIT	Purchases		$162

To close off suspense a/c and correct error

Whenever an error occurs which results in total debits not being equal to total credits, the first step an accountant makes is to open up a suspense account. Three more examples are given below.

2.6 Example: Transposition error

The bookkeeper of Mixem Gladly Co made a transposition error when entering an amount for sales in the sales account. Instead of entering the correct amount of $37,453.60 he entered $37,543.60, transposing

the 4 and 5. The trade receivables were posted correctly, and so when total debits and credits on the ledger accounts were compared, it was found that credits exceeded debits by $(37,543.60 – 37,453.60) = $90.

The initial step is to equalise the total debits and credits by posting a debit of $90 to a suspense account.

When the cause of the error is discovered, the double entry to correct it should be logged in the journal as:

DEBIT	Sales	$90	
CREDIT	Suspense a/c		$90

To close off suspense a/c and correct transposition error

2.7 Example: Error of omission

When Guttersnipe Builders paid the monthly salary cheques to its office staff, the payment of $5,250 was correctly entered in the cash account, but the bookkeeper omitted to debit the office salaries account. As a consequence, the total debit and credit balances on the ledger accounts were not equal, and credits exceeded debits by $5,250.

The initial step in correcting the situation is to debit $5,250 to a suspense account, to equalise the total debits and total credits.

When the cause of the error is discovered, the double entry to correct it should be logged in the journal as:

DEBIT	Office salaries account	$5,250	
CREDIT	Suspense a/c		$5,250

To close off suspense account and correct error of omission

2.8 Example: Error of commission

A bookkeeper might make a mistake by entering what should be a debit entry as a credit, or vice versa. For example, a credit customer pays $460 of the $660 he owes to Ashdown Tree Felling Contractors, but Ashdown's bookkeeper debits $460 on the trade receivables account in the nominal ledger by mistake instead of crediting the payment received.

The total debit balances in Ashdown's ledger accounts would now exceed the total credits by 2 × $460 = $920. The initial step in correcting the error would be to make a credit entry of $920 in a suspense account. When the cause of the error is discovered, it should be corrected as follows.

DEBIT	Suspense a/c	$920	
CREDIT	Trade receivables		$920

To close off suspense account and correct error of commission

In the receivables control account in the nominal ledger, the correction would appear therefore as follows.

TRADE RECEIVABLES CONTROL ACCOUNT

	$		$
Balance b/f	660	Suspense a/c: error corrected	920
Payment incorrectly debited	460	Balance c/f	200
	1,120		1,120

2.9 Use of suspense account: Not knowing where to post a transaction

Another use of suspense accounts occurs when a bookkeeper does not know where to post one side of a transaction. Until the mystery is sorted out, the entry can be recorded in a suspense account. A typical example is when the business receives cash through the post from a source which cannot be determined. The double entry in the accounts would be a debit in the cash book, and a credit to a suspense account.

2.9.1 Example: Not knowing where to post a transaction

Windfall Garments received a cheque in the post for $620. The name on the cheque is R J Beasley, but Windfall Garments have no idea who this person is, nor why he should be sending $620. The bookkeeper decides to open a suspense account, so that the double entry for the transaction is:

DEBIT	Cash	$620	
CREDIT	Suspense a/c		$620

Eventually, it transpires that the cheque was in payment for a debt owed by the Haute Couture Corner Shop and paid out of the proprietor's personal bank account. The suspense account can now be cleared, as follows.

DEBIT	Suspense a/c	$620	
CREDIT	Trade receivables		$620

2.10 Suspense accounts might contain several items

If more than one error or unidentifiable posting to a ledger account arises during an accounting period, they will all be merged together in the same suspense account. Indeed, until the causes of the errors are discovered, the bookkeepers are unlikely to know exactly how many errors there are. An examination question might give you a balance on a suspense account, together with enough information to make the necessary corrections, leaving a nil balance on the suspense account and correct balances on various other accounts. In practice, of course, finding these errors is far from easy!

2.11 Suspense accounts are temporary

FAST FORWARD

Suspense accounts are only temporary. None should exist when it comes to drawing up the financial statements at the end of the accounting period.

It must be stressed that a **suspense account should only be temporary**. Postings to a suspense account are only made when the bookkeeper doesn't know yet what to do, or when an error has occurred. Mysteries must be solved, and errors must be corrected. **There should not be a suspense account when it comes to preparing the statement of financial position of a business. The suspense account must be cleared and all the correcting entries made before the final accounts are drawn up.**

Question — Errors

At the year end of T Down & Co, an imbalance in the trial balance was revealed which resulted in the creation of a suspense account with a credit balance of $1,040.

Investigations revealed the following errors:

(i)   A sale of goods on credit for $1,000 had been omitted from the sales account.

(ii) Delivery and installation costs of $240 on a new item of plant had been recorded as a revenue expense.

(iii) Settlement discount of $150 on paying a supplier, JW, had been taken, even though the payment was made outside the time limit.

(iv) Inventory of stationery at the end of the period of $240 had been ignored.

(v)   A purchase of raw materials of $350 had been recorded in the purchases account as $850.

(vi) The purchase returns day book included a sales credit note for $230 which had been entered correctly in the acccount of the customer concerned, but included with purchase returns in the nominal ledger.

11: CORRECTION OF ERRORS

Required

(a) Prepare journal entries to correct **each** of the above errors. Narratives are **not** required.
(b) Open a suspense account and show the corrections to be made.
(c) Prior to the discovery of the errors, T Down & Co's gross profit for the year was calculated at $35,750 and the net profit for the year at $18,500.

Calculate the revised gross and net profit figures after the correction of the errors.

Answer

(a)

				Dr $	Cr $
(i)	DEBIT	Suspense a/c		1,000	
	CREDIT	Revenue			1,000
(ii)	DEBIT	Plant		240	
	CREDIT	Delivery cost			240
(iii)	DEBIT	Purchases		150	
	CREDIT	JW a/c			150
(iv)	DEBIT	Inventory of stationery		240	
	CREDIT	Stationery expense			240
(v)	DEBIT	Suspense a/c		500	
	CREDIT	Purchases			500
(vi)	DEBIT	Purchase returns		230	
	DEBIT	Sales returns		230	
	CREDIT	Suspense a/c			460

(b)

SUSPENSE A/C

		$			$
(i)	Revenue	1,000		End of year balance	1,040
(v)	Purchases	500	(vi)	Purchase returns/sales returns	460
		1,500			1,500

(c)

	$
Gross profit originally reported	35,750
Sales omitted	1,000
Plant costs wrongly allocated	240
Incorrect recording of purchases	500
Sales credit note wrongly allocated	(460)
Adjusted gross profit	37,030
Net profit originally reported	18,500
Adjustments to gross profit $(37,030 – 35,750)	1,280
Cash discount incorrectly taken	(150)
Stationery inventory	240
Adjusted net profit	19,870

Note. It has been assumed that the delivery and installation costs on plant have been included in purchases.

Exam focus point

A question may ask you to calculate the balance remaining on the suspense account after certain errors had been adjusted. The key to this type of question is recognising which errors affected the suspense account, then putting the adjustments through correctly, as in the above example.

PART B ACCOUNTING RECORDS AND PROCEDURES

Chapter roundup

- There are five main types of error. Some can be corrected by journal entry, some require the use of a suspense account.

- Errors which leave total debits and credits in the ledger accounts in balance can be corrected by using **journal entries**. Otherwise a suspense account has to be opened first, and later cleared by a journal entry.

- **Suspense accounts**, as well as being used to correct some errors, are also opened when it is not known immediately where to post an amount. When the mystery is solved, the suspense account is closed and the amount correctly posted using a journal entry.

- **Suspense accounts are only temporary**. None should exist when it comes to drawing up the financial statements at the end of the accounting period.

Quick quiz

1. List five types of error made in accounting.

2. What is a journal used for?
    - A To correct errors
    - B To correct errors and post unusual transactions
    - C To correct errors and clear suspense account
    - D To make adjustments to the double entry

3. A suspense account is a temporary account to make the Trial Balance balance.
   Is this statement:
    - A True
    - B False

4. What must be done with a suspense account before preparing a statement of financial position?
    - A Include in assets
    - B Clear it to nil
    - C Include in liabilities
    - D Write it off to capital

5. Sales returns of $460 have inadvertently been posted to the purchase returns, although the correct entry has been made to the accounts receivable control. A suspense account needs to be set up for how much?
    - A $460 debit
    - B $460 credit
    - C $920 debit
    - D $920 credit

Answers to quick quiz

1. Transposition, omission, principle, commission and compensating errors.

2. D   Although A, B and C are correct as far as they go, they don't cover everything. Selection D is the most comprehensive answer.

3. A   The statement is true.

4. B   All errors must be identified and the suspense account cleared to nil.

5. C   The sales returns of $460 have been credited to trade receivables and also $460 has been credited to purchase returns. Therefore the trial balance needs a debit of 2 × $460 = $920 to balance.

PART B ACCOUNTING RECORDS AND PROCEDURES

Incomplete records

Topic list	Syllabus reference
1 Incomplete records questions	A2
2 The opening position	A2
3 Credit sales and trade receivables	A2
4 Purchases and trade payables	A2
5 Establishing cost of sales	A2
6 Stolen goods or goods destroyed	A2
7 The cash book	A2
8 Accruals and prepayments	A2
9 Drawings	A2
10 The business equation	A2
11 Comprehensive worked examples	A2

Introduction

So far in your work on preparing the final accounts for a sole trader we have assumed that a full set of records are kept. In practice many sole traders do not keep a full set of records and you must apply certain techniques to arrive at the necessary figures.

Incomplete records questions are a very good test of your understanding of the way in which a set of accounts is built up.

In most countries, limited liability companies are obliged by national laws to keep proper accounting records.

PART B ACCOUNTING RECORDS AND PROCEDURES

1 Incomplete records questions

FAST FORWARD

Incomplete records questions may test your ability to prepare accounts in the following situations.

- A trader **does not maintain a ledger** and therefore has no continuous double entry record of transactions.
- Accounting records are **destroyed** by accident, such as fire.
- Some essential figure is **unknown** and must be calculated as a balancing figure. This may occur as a result of inventory being damaged or destroyed, or because of misappropriation of assets.

Incomplete records problems occur when a business does not have a full set of accounting records, for one of the following reasons:

- The proprietor of the business does not keep a full set of accounts.
- Some of the business accounts are accidentally lost or destroyed.

The problem for the accountant is to prepare a set of year-end accounts for the business; ie a statement of profit or loss and other comprehensive income and a statement of financial position. Since the business does not have a full set of accounts, preparing the final accounts is not a simple matter of closing off accounts and transferring balances to the profit or loss account, or showing outstanding balances in the statement of financial position. The task of preparing the final accounts involves the following:

(a) Establishing the **cost of purchases** and other expenses
(b) Establishing the **total amount of sales**
(c) Establishing the amount of **trade payables, accruals, trade receivables and prepayments** at the end of the year

Examination questions often take incomplete records problems a stage further, by introducing an 'incident', such as fire or burglary which leaves the owner of the business uncertain about how much inventory has been destroyed or stolen.

The great merit of incomplete records problems is that they focus attention on the relationship between cash received and paid, sales and accounts receivable, purchases and accounts payable, and inventory, as well as calling for the preparation of final accounts from basic principles.

To understand what incomplete records are about, it will obviously be useful now to look at what exactly might be incomplete. The items we shall consider in turn are:

(a) The opening position
(b) Credit sales and trade receivables
(c) Purchases and trade payables
(d) Purchases, inventory and the cost of sales
(e) Stolen goods or goods destroyed
(f) The cash book
(g) Accruals and prepayments
(h) Drawings

Exam focus point

Incomplete records questions are a good test of your understanding of the accounting equation (Chapter 5) and whether you have a really thorough grasp of double entry. It is important to practise these questions to become familiar with the style and to understand the impact of the adjustments.

2 The opening position

In practice there should not be any missing item in the opening statement of financial position of the business, because it should be available from the preparation of the previous year's final accounts. However, an examination problem might provide information about the assets and liabilities of the business at the beginning of the period under review, but then leave the balancing figure (ie the proprietor's business capital) unspecified. If you remember the accounting equation (A = C + L), the problem is quite straightforward.

2.1 Example: Opening statement of financial position

Suppose Joe Han's business has the following assets and liabilities as at 1 January 20X3.

	$
Fixtures and fittings at cost	7,000
Allowance for depreciation, fixtures and fittings	4,000
Motor vehicles at cost	12,000
Allowance for depreciation, motor vehicles	6,800
Inventories	4,500
Trade receivables	5,200
Cash at bank and in hand	1,230
Trade payables	3,700
Prepayment	450
Accrued rent	2,000

You are required to prepare a statement of financial position for the business, inserting a balancing figure for proprietor's capital.

Solution

STATEMENT OF FINANCIAL POSITION AS AT 1 JANUARY 20X3

	$	$
Assets		
Non-current assets		
Fixtures and fittings at cost	7,000	
Less accumulated depreciation	4,000	
		3,000
Motor vehicles at cost	12,000	
Less accumulated depreciation	6,800	
		5,200
Current assets		
Inventories	4,500	
Trade receivables	5,200	
Prepayment	450	
Cash	1,230	
		11,380
Total assets		19,580
Capital and liabilities		
Proprietor's capital as at 1 January 20X3 (balancing figure)		13,880
Current liabilities		
Trade payables	3,700	
Accruals	2,000	
		5,700
Total capital and liabilities		19,580

PART B   ACCOUNTING RECORDS AND PROCEDURES

3 Credit sales and trade receivables

FAST FORWARD

> The approach to incomplete records questions is to build up the information given so as to complete the necessary **double entry**. This may involve reconstructing **control accounts** for:
> - Cash and bank
> - Trade receivables and trade payables

If a business does not keep a record of its sales on credit, the value of these sales can be derived from the opening balance of trade receivables, the closing balance of trade receivables, and the payments received from customers during the period.

Formula to learn: credit sales

	$
Payments from trade receivables	X
Plus closing balance of trade receivables (since these represent sales in the current period for which cash payment has not yet been received)	X
Less opening balance of trade receivables (these represent credit sales in a previous period)	(X)
Credit sales in the period	X

For example, suppose that Joe Han's business had trade receivables of $1,750 on 1 April 20X4 and trade receivables of $3,140 on 31 March 20X5. If payments received from trade receivables during the year to 31 March 20X5 were $28,490, and if there are no irrecoverable debts, then credit sales for the period would be:

	$
Cash from trade receivables	28,490
Plus closing trade receivables	3,140
Less opening trade receivables	(1,750)
Credit sales	29,880

If there are irrecoverable debts during the period, the value of sales will be increased by the amount of irrecoverable debts written off, no matter whether they relate to opening trade receivables or credit sales during the current period.

Question   Calculating sales

The calculation above could be made in a T-account, with credit sales being the balancing figure to complete the account. Prepare the T-account.

Answer

TRADE RECEIVABLES CONTROL ACCOUNT

	$		$
Opening balance b/f	1,750	Cash received	28,490
Credit sales (balancing fig)	29,880	Closing balance c/f	3,140
	31,630		31,630

The same interrelationship between credit sales, cash from trade receivables, and opening and closing trade receivables balances can be used to derive a missing figure for cash from trade receivables, or opening or closing trade receivables, given the values for the three other items. For example, if we know that opening trade receivables are $6,700, closing trade receivables are $3,200 and credit sales for the period are $69,400, then cash from trade receivables during the period would be as follows:

TRADE RECEIVABLES CONTROL ACCOUNT

	$		$
Opening balance	6,700	Cash received (balancing figure)	72,900
Sales (on credit)	69,400	Closing balance c/f	3,200
	76,100		76,100

An alternative way of presenting the same calculation would be:

	$
Opening balance of trade receivables	6,700
Credit sales during the period	69,400
Total money owed to the business	76,100
Less closing balance of trade receivables	(3,200)
Equals cash received during the period	72,900

4 Purchases and trade payables

A similar relationship exists between purchases of inventory during a period, the opening and closing balances for trade payables, and amounts paid to suppliers during the period.

If we wish to calculate an unknown amount for purchases, the amount would be derived as follows:

	$
Payments to trade payables during the period	X
Plus closing balance of trade payables (since these represent purchases in the current period for which payment has not yet been made)	X
Less opening balance of trade payables (these debts, paid in the current period, relate to purchases in a previous period)	(X)
Purchases during the period	X

For example, suppose that Joe Han's business had trade payables of $3,728 on 1 October 20X5 and trade payables of $2,645 on 30 September 20X6. If payments to trade payables during the year to 30 September 20X6 were $31,479, then purchases during the year would be:

	$
Payments to trade payables	31,479
Plus closing balance of trade payables	2,645
Less opening balance of trade payables	(3,728)
Purchases	30,396

Question

Calculating purchases 1

Again, the calculation above could be made in a T-account, with purchases being the balancing figure to complete the account. Prepare the T-account.

Answer

TRADE PAYABLE CONTROL ACCOUNT

	$		$
Cash payments	31,479	Opening balance b/f	3,728
Closing balance c/f	2,645	Purchases (balancing figure)	30,396
	34,124		34,124

PART B ACCOUNTING RECORDS AND PROCEDURES

Question
Calculating purchases 2

Mr Harmon does not keep full accounting records, but the following information is available in respect of his accounting year ended 31 December 20X9.

	$
Cash purchases in year	3,900
Cash paid for goods supplied on credit	27,850
Trade payables at 1 January 20X9	970
Trade payables at 31 December 20X9	720

In his statement of profit or loss for 20X9, what will be Harmon's figure for purchases?

Answer

Credit purchases = $(27,850 + 720 – 970) = $27,600. Therefore total purchases = $(27,600 + 3,900) = $31,500.

5 Establishing cost of sales

FAST FORWARD

Where inventory, sales or purchases is the unknown figure it will be necessary to use information on **gross profit percentages** so as to construct a working for gross profit in which the unknown figure can be inserted as a balance.

When the value of purchases is not known, a different approach might be required to find out what they were, depending on the nature of the information given to you.

One approach would be to use information about the cost of sales, and opening and closing inventory rather than trade accounts payable to find the cost of purchases.

Formula to learn

		$
Since	opening inventory	X
	plus purchases	X
	less closing inventory	(X)
	equals the cost of goods sold	X
then	the cost of goods sold	X
	plus closing inventory	X
	less opening inventory	(X)
	equals purchases	X

Suppose that the inventory of Joe Han's business on 1 July 20X6 has a value of $8,400, and an inventory count at 30 June 20X7 showed inventory to be valued at $9,350. Sales for the year to 30 June 20X7 are $80,000, and the business makes a mark-up of $33^1/_3\%$ on cost for all the items that it sells. What were the purchases during the year?

The cost of goods sold can be derived from the value of sales, as follows:

		$
Sales	($133^1/_3\%$)	80,000
Gross profit (mark-up)	($33^1/_3\%$)	20,000
Cost of goods sold	(100%)	60,000

The cost of goods sold is 75% of sales value.

	$
Cost of goods sold	60,000
Plus closing inventory	9,350
Less opening inventory	(8,400)
Purchases	60,950

It is worth mentioning here that two different terms may be given to you in the exam for the calculation of profit.

Key terms

- **Mark-up** is the profit as a percentage of **cost**.
- **Gross profit margin** is the profit as a percentage of **sales**.

Looking at the above example:

(a) The mark-up on cost is $33\frac{1}{3}\%$
(b) The gross profit margin percentage is 25% (ie $33\frac{1}{3}/133\frac{1}{3} \times 100\%$)

Question — Calculating purchases 3

Harry has budgeted sales for the coming year of $175,000. He achieves a constant gross **mark-up** of 40% on cost. He plans to reduce his inventory level by $13,000 over the year.

What will Harry's purchases be for the year?

Answer

Cost of sales = 100/140 × $175,000
 = $125,000

Since the inventory level is being allowed to fall, it means that purchases will be $13,000 less than $125,000 = $112,000.

Question — Calculating purchases 4

Using the same facts as in the question above, calculate Harry's purchases for the year if he achieves a constant **margin** of 40% on sales.

Answer

Gross profit = 40% of sales, so cost of sales = 60% of sales.

Cost of sales = $\frac{60}{100} \times \$175,000$

 = $105,000

Since the inventory level is being allowed to fall, it means purchases will be $13,000 less than $105,000 = $92,000.

6 Stolen goods or goods destroyed

A similar type of calculation might be required to derive the value of goods stolen or destroyed. When an unknown quantity of goods is lost, whether they are stolen, destroyed in a fire, or lost in any other way such that the quantity lost cannot be counted, then the cost of the goods lost is the difference between (a) and (b).

(a) The **cost of goods sold**

(b) **Opening inventory of the goods** (at cost) plus **purchases** less **closing inventory of the goods** (at cost)

In theory, (a) and (b) should be the same. However, if (b) is a larger amount than (a), it follows that the difference must be the cost of the goods purchased and neither sold nor remaining in inventory, ie the cost of the goods lost.

6.1 Example: Cost of goods destroyed

Orlean Flames is a shop which sells fashion clothes. On 1 January 20X5, it had trade inventory which cost $7,345. During the nine months to 30 September 20X5, the business purchased goods from suppliers costing $106,420. Sales during the same period were $154,000. The shop makes a gross profit of 40% on cost for everything it sells. On 30 September 20X5, there was a fire in the shop which destroyed most of the inventory in it. Only a small amount of inventory, known to have cost $350, was undamaged and still fit for sale.

How much of the inventory was lost in the fire?

Solution

(a)

	$
Sales (140%)	154,000
Gross profit (40%)	44,000
Cost of goods sold (100%)	110,000

(b)

	$
Opening inventory, at cost	7,345
Plus purchases	106,420
	113,765
Less closing inventory, at cost	350
Equals cost of goods sold and goods lost	113,415

(c)

	$
Cost of goods sold and lost	113,415
Cost of goods sold	110,000
Cost of goods lost	3,415

6.2 Example: Cost of goods stolen

Beau Gullard runs a jewellery shop in the High Street. On 1 January 20X9, his trade inventory, at cost, amounted to $4,700 and his trade payables were $3,950.

During the six months to 30 June 20X9, sales were $42,000. Beau Gullard makes a gross profit of $33^{1}/3\%$ on the sales value of everything he sells.

On 30 June, there was a burglary at the shop, and all the inventory was stolen.

In trying to establish how much inventory had been taken, Beau Gullard was only able to say that:

(a) He knew from his bank statements that he had paid $28,400 to trade payables in the six month period to 30 June 20X9.

(b) He currently had trade payables due of $5,550.

Required

(a) Calculate the amount of inventory stolen.
(b) Calculate gross profit for the six months to 30 June 20X9.

Solution

Step 1 The first 'unknown' is the amount of purchases during the period. This is established by the method previously described in this chapter.

TRADE PAYABLES CONTROL ACCOUNT

	$		$
Payments to trade payables	28,400	Opening balance b/f	3,950
Closing balance c/f	5,550	Purchases (balancing figure)	30,000
	33,950		33,950

Step 2 The cost of goods sold is also unknown, but this can be established from the gross profit margin and the sales for the period.

		$
Sales	(100%)	42,000
Gross profit	(33$\frac{1}{3}$%)	14,000
Cost of goods sold	(66$\frac{2}{3}$%)	28,000

Step 3 The cost of the goods stolen is:

	$
Opening inventory at cost	4,700
Purchases	30,000
	34,700
Less closing inventory (after burglary)	0
Cost of goods sold and goods stolen	34,700
Cost of goods sold (see (b) above)	28,000
Cost of goods stolen	6,700

Step 4 The cost of the goods stolen will not be included in cost of sales, and so the gross profit for the period is as follows.

BEAU GULLARD
GROSS PROFIT FOR THE SIX MONTHS TO 30 JUNE 20X9

	$	$
Sales		42,000
Less cost of goods sold		
Opening inventory	4,700	
Purchases	30,000	
	34,700	
Less inventory stolen	6,700	
		28,000
Gross profit		14,000

6.3 Accounting for inventory destroyed, stolen or otherwise lost

When inventory is stolen, destroyed or otherwise lost, the loss must be accounted for somehow. Since the loss is not a trading loss, the cost of the goods lost is not included in the cost of sales, as the previous example showed. The accounting double entry is therefore:

DEBIT   See below
CREDIT   Cost of sales

The account that is to be debited is one of two possibilities, depending on whether or not the lost goods were insured against the loss.

(a) If the lost goods were not insured, the business must bear the loss, and the loss is shown in the statement of profit or loss and other comprehensive income, ie:

DEBIT   Expenses (eg administrative expenses)
CREDIT   Cost of sales

(b) If the lost goods were insured, the business will not suffer a loss, because the insurance will pay back the cost of the lost goods. This means that there is no charge at all in the statement of profit or loss and other comprehensive income, and the appropriate double entry is:

DEBIT   Insurance claim account (receivable account)
CREDIT   Cost of sales

with the cost of the loss. The insurance claim will then be a current asset, and shown in the statement of financial position of the business as such. When the claim is paid, the account is then closed by:

DEBIT   Cash
CREDIT   Insurance claim account

7 The cash book

FAST FORWARD

> The construction of a cash book, largely from bank statements showing receipts and payments of a business during a given period, is often an important feature of incomplete records problems.

Exam focus point

> In an examination, the purpose of an incomplete records question is largely to test the understanding of candidates about how various items of receipts or payments relate to the preparation of a final set of accounts for a business.

We have already seen in this chapter that information about cash receipts or payments might be needed to establish:

(a) The amount of purchases during a period
(b) The amount of credit sales during a period

Other items of receipts or payments might be relevant to establishing:

(a) The amount of cash sales
(b) The amount of certain expenses in the statement of profit or loss and other comprehensive income
(c) The amount of withdrawals on account of profit by the business proprietor

It might therefore be helpful, if a business does not keep a cash book day-to-day, to construct a cash book at the end of an accounting period. A business which typically might not keep a day-to-day cash book is a shop.

(a) Many sales, if not all sales, are cash sales (ie with payment by notes and coins, cheques, or credit cards at the time of sale).

(b) Some payments are made in notes and coins out of the till rather than by payment out of the business bank account by cheque.

Where there appears to be a sizeable volume of receipts and payments in cash (ie notes and coins), then it is also helpful to construct a two column cash book.

Key term

> A **two column cash book** is a cash book with one column for receipts and payments, and one column for money paid into and out of the business bank account.

An example will illustrate the technique and the purpose of a two column cash book.

7.1 Example: Two column cash book

Jonathan Slugg owns and runs a shop selling fishing tackle, making a gross profit of 25% on the cost of everything he sells. He does not keep a cash book.

On 1 January 20X7 the statement of financial position of his business was as follows.

	$	$
Current assets		
Inventories	10,000	
Cash in the bank	3,000	
Cash in the till	200	
		13,200
Net long-term assets		20,000
		33,200
Trade payables		1,200
Proprietor's capital		32,000
		33,200

In the year to 31 December 20X7:

(a) There were no sales on credit.

(b) $41,750 in receipts were banked.

(c) The bank statements of the period show the payments:

		$
(i)	To trade payables	36,000
(ii)	Sundry expenses	5,600
(iii)	To drawings	4,400

(d) Payments were also made in cash out of the till:

		$
(i)	For trade payables	800
(ii)	Sundry expenses	1,500
(iii)	To drawings	3,700

At 31 December 20X7, the business had cash in the till of $450 and trade payables of $1,400. The cash balance in the bank was not known and the value of closing inventory has not yet been calculated. There were no accruals or prepayments. No further long-term assets were purchased during the year. The depreciation charge for the year is $900.

Required

(a) Prepare a two column cash book for the period.
(b) Prepare the statement of profit or loss and other comprehensive income for the year to 31 December 20X7 and the statement of financial position as at 31 December 20X7.

7.2 Discussion and solution

A two column cash book is completed as follows:

Step 1 Enter the opening cash balances.

Step 2 Enter the information given about cash payments (and any cash receipts, if there had been any such items given in the problem).

Step 3 The cash receipts banked are a 'contra' entry, being both a debit (bank column) and a credit (cash in hand column) in the same account.

Step 4 Enter the closing cash in hand (cash in the bank at the end of the period is not known).

CASH BOOK

	Cash in hand $	Bank $		Cash in hand $	Bank $
Balance b/f	200	3,000	Trade		
Cash receipts			payables	800	36,000
banked (contra)		41,750	Sundry expenses	1,500	5,600
Sales*	48,000		Drawings	3,700	4,400
			Cash receipts		
			banked (contra)	41,750	
Balance c/f		*1,250	Balance c/f	450	
	48,200	46,000		48,200	46,000

* Balancing figure

Step 5 The closing balance of money in the bank is a balancing figure.

Step 6 Since all sales are for cash, a balancing figure that can be entered in the cash book is sales, in the cash in hand (debit) column.

It is important to notice that since not all receipts from cash sales are banked, the value of cash sales during the period is:

	$
Receipts banked	41,750
Plus expenses and withdrawals paid out of the till in cash	
$(800 + 1,500 + 3,700)$	6,000
Plus any cash stolen (here there is none)	0
Plus the closing balance of cash in hand	450
	48,200
Less the opening balance of cash in hand	(200)
Equals cash sales	48,000

The cash book constructed in this way has enabled us to establish both the closing balance for cash in the bank and also the volume of cash sales. The statement of profit or loss and other comprehensive income and the statement of financial position can also be prepared, once a value for purchases has been calculated.

TRADE PAYABLES CONTROL ACCOUNT

	$		$
Cash book: payments from bank	36,000	Balance b/f	1,200
Cash book: payments in cash	800	Purchases (balancing figure)	37,000
Balance c/f	1,400		
	38,200		38,200

The gross profit margin of 25% on cost indicates that the cost of the goods sold is $38,400, ie:

	$
Sales (125%)	48,000
Gross profit (25%)	9,600
Cost of goods sold (100%)	38,400

The closing inventory is now a balancing figure in the trading account.

JONATHAN SLUGG
STATEMENT OF PROFIT OR LOSS AND OTHER COMPREHENSIVE INCOME
FOR THE YEAR ENDED 31 DECEMBER 20X7

	$	$
Revenue		48,000
Less cost of goods sold		
Opening inventory	10,000	
Purchases	37,000	
	47,000	
Less closing inventory (balancing figure)	8,600	
		38,400
Gross profit (25/125 × $48,000)		9,600
Expenses		
Sundry $(1,500 + 5,600)	7,100	
Depreciation	900	
		8,000
Net profit		1,600

JONATHAN SLUGG
STATEMENT OF FINANCIAL POSITION AS AT 31 DECEMBER 20X7

	$	$
Assets		
Current assets		
Inventories	8,600	
Cash in the till	450	
		9,050
Net long-term assets $(20,000 – 900)		19,100
Total assets		28,150
Capital and liabilities		
Proprietor's capital		
Balance b/f	32,000	
Net profit for the year	1,600	
Withdrawals on account $(3,700 + 4,400)	(8,100)	
Balance c/f		25,500
Current liabilities		
Bank overdraft	1,250	
Trade payables	1,400	
		2,650
Total capital and liabilities		28,150

7.3 Theft of cash from the till

When cash is stolen from the till, the amount stolen will be a credit entry in the cash book, and a debit in either the net profit section (profit or loss account) or insurance claim account, depending on whether the business is insured. The missing figure for cash sales, if this has to be calculated, must not ignore cash received but later stolen – see above.

8 Accruals and prepayments

Where there is an accrued expense or a prepayment, the charge to be made in the statement of profit or loss and other comprehensive income for the item concerned should be found from the opening balance b/f, the closing balance c/f, and cash payments for the item during the period. The charge in the statement of profit or loss and other comprehensive income is perhaps most easily found as the balancing figure in a T-account.

For example, suppose that on 1 April 20X6 a business had prepaid rent of $700 which relates to the next accounting period. During the year to 31 March 20X7 it pays $9,300 in rent, and at 31 March 20X7 the prepayment of rent is $1,000. The cost of rent in the statement of profit or loss account for the year to 31 March 20X7 would be the balancing figure in the following T-account. (Remember that a prepayment is a current asset, and so is a debit balance b/f.)

RENT

	$		$
Prepayment: balance b/f	700	SPL a/c (balancing figure)	9,000
Cash	9,300	Prepayment: balance c/f	1,000
	10,000		10,000
Balance b/f	1,000		

Similarly, if a business has accrued telephone expenses as at 1 July 20X6 of $850, pays $6,720 in telephone bills during the year to 30 June 20X7, and has accrued telephone expenses of $1,140 as at 30 June 20X7, then the telephone expense to be shown in the statement of profit or loss and other comprehensive income for the year to 30 June 20X7 is the balancing figure in the following T-account. (Remember that an accrual is a current liability, and so is a credit balance b/f.)

TELEPHONE EXPENSES

	$		$
Cash	6,720	Balance b/f (accrual)	850
Balance c/f (accrual)	1,140	SPL a/c (balancing figure)	7,010
	7,860		7,860
		Balance b/f	1,140

9 Drawings

FAST FORWARD

> **Drawings** often feature as the missing item in an incomplete records problem. The trader has been drawing money but does not know how much.

Drawings would normally represent no particular problem at all in preparing a set of final accounts from incomplete records, but it is not unusual for examination questions to contain complicating situations.

(a) The business owner may pay income into his bank account which has nothing whatever to do with the business operations. For example, the owner might pay dividend income, or other income from investments into the bank, from stocks and shares which he owns personally, separate from the business itself. (In other words, there are no investments in the business statement of financial position, and so income from investments cannot possibly be income of the business.) These amounts will be credited to his drawings.

(b) The business owner may pay money out of the business bank account for items which are not business expenses, such as life insurance premiums or a payment for his family's holidays etc. These will be treated as drawings.

Where such **personal items of receipts or payments** are made the following adjustments should be made.

(a) Receipts should be set off against drawings. For example, if a business owner receives $600 in dividend income and pays it into his business bank account, although the dividends are from investments not owned by the business, then the accounting entry is:

DEBIT   Cash
CREDIT   Drawings

(b) Payments should be charged to drawings on account, ie:

DEBIT   Drawings
CREDIT   Cash

9.1 Beware of the wording in an examination question

You should note that:

(a) If a question states that a proprietor's drawings during a given year are 'approximately $40 per week' then you should assume that drawings for the year are $40 × 52 weeks = $2,080.

(b) However, if a question states that drawings in the year are 'between $35 and $45 per week', do not assume that the drawings average $40 per week and so amount to $2,080 for the year. You could not be certain that the actual withdrawals did average $40, and so you should treat the withdrawals figure as a missing item that needs to be calculated.

10 The business equation

FAST FORWARD

Where no trading records have been kept, profit can be derived from opening and closing net assets by use of the **business equation**.

The most obvious incomplete records situation is that of a sole trader who has kept no trading records. It may not be possible to reconstruct his whole statement of profit or loss and other comprehensive income, but it will be possible to compute his profit for the year using the **business equation**.

Here is the basic statement of financial position format:

Assets		XX
Capital	X	
Liabilities	X	XX

This can be rearranged as:

Assets	XX	
Liabilities	(X)	X
Capital		X

So this gives us a figure for capital – assets less liabilities, or **net assets**.

What will increase or decrease capital?

Capital is changed by:

(a) Money paid in by the trader
(b) Drawings by the trader
(c) Profits or losses

So, if we are able to establish the traders net assets at the beginnings and end of the period, we can compute profits as follows:

Profit (loss) = movement in net assets – capital introduced + drawings

We want to eliminate any movement caused by money paid in or taken out for personal use by the trader. So we take out capital introduced and add back in drawings.

10.1 Example: Business equation

Joe starts up his camera shop on 1 January 20X1, from rented premises, with $5,000 inventory and $3,000 in the bank. All of his sales are for cash. He keeps no record of his takings.

At the end of the year he has inventory worth $6,600 and $15,000 in the bank. He owes $3,000 to suppliers. He had paid in $5,000 he won on the lottery and drawn out $2,000 to buy himself a motorbike. The motorbike is not used in the business. He has been taking drawings of $100 per week. What is his profit at 31 December 20X1?

Solution

	$
Opening net assets	
Inventories	5,000
Cash	3,000
	8,000
Closing net assets	
Inventories	6,600
Cash	15,000
Trade payables	(3,000)
	18,600
Movement in capital (net assets)	10,600
Less capital paid in	(5,000)
Plus drawings ((100 × 52) + 2000)	7,200
Profit	12,800

11 Comprehensive worked examples

A suggested approach to dealing with incomplete records problems brings together the various points described so far in this chapter. The nature of the 'incompleteness' in the records will vary from problem to problem, but the approach, suitably applied, should be successful in arriving at the final accounts whatever the particular characteristics of the problem might be.

The approach is as follows:

Step 1 If possible, and if it is not already known, establish the opening statement of financial position and the proprietor's interest.

Step 2 Open up four accounts.
- Profit or loss account
- A cash book, with two columns if cash sales are significant and there are payments in cash out of the till
- A trade receivables account
- A trade payables account

Step 3 Enter the opening balances in these accounts.

Step 4 Work through the information you are given line by line; and each item should be entered into the appropriate account if it is relevant to one or more of these four accounts.

You should also try to recognise each item as an 'income or expense item' or a 'closing statement of financial position item'.

It may be necessary to calculate an amount for withdrawals on account and an amount for non-current asset depreciation.

Step 5 Look for the balancing figures in your accounts. In particular you might be looking for a value for credit sales, cash sales, purchases, the cost of goods sold, the cost of goods stolen or destroyed, or the closing bank balance. Calculate these missing figures, and make any necessary double entry (eg to the profit or loss account from trade payables for purchases, to the profit or loss account from the cash book for cash sales, and to the profit or loss account from trade receivables for credit sales).

Step 6 Now complete the statement of profit or loss and other comprehensive income and statement of financial position. Working T-accounts might be needed where there are accruals or prepayments.

Remember

> The business equation [Profit = increase in net assets – capital introduced + drawings] may be useful as a check on the profit figure.

An example will illustrate this approach.

11.1 Example: An incomplete records problem

John Snow is the sole distribution agent in the Branton area for Diamond floor tiles. Under an agreement with the manufacturers, John Snow purchases the Diamond floor tiles and annually in May receives an agency commission of 1% of his purchases for the year ended on the previous 31 March.

For several years, John Snow has obtained a gross profit of 40% on all sales. In a burglary in January 20X1 John Snow lost inventory costing $4,000 as well as many of his accounting records. However, after careful investigations, the following information has been obtained covering the year ended 31 March 20X1.

(a) Assets and liabilities at 31 March 20X0 were as follows:

		$
Buildings:	at cost	10,000
	accumulated depreciation	6,000
Motor vehicles:	at cost	5,000
	accumulated depreciation	2,000
Inventory: at cost		3,200
Trade receivables (for sales)		6,300
Agency commission due		300
Prepayments (trade expenses)		120
Balance at bank		4,310
Trade payables		4,200
Accrued vehicle expenses		230

(b) John Snow has been notified that he will receive an agency commission of $440 on 1 May 20X1.

(c) Inventory, at cost, at 31 March 20X1 was valued at an amount $3,000 more than a year previously.

(d) In October 20X0 inventory costing $1,000 was damaged by dampness and had to be scrapped as worthless.

(e) Trade payables at 31 March 20X1 related entirely to goods received whose list prices totalled $9,500.

(f) Trade expenses prepaid at 31 March 20X1 totalled $80.

(g) Vehicle expenses for the year ended 31 March 20X1 amounted to $7,020.

(h) Trade receivables (for sales) at 31 March 20X1 were $6,700.

(i) All receipts are passed through the bank account.

PART B ACCOUNTING RECORDS AND PROCEDURES

(j) Depreciation is charged annually at the following rates.

Buildings 5% on cost
Motor vehicles 20% on cost.

(k) Commissions received are paid directly to the bank account.

(l) In addition to the payments for purchases, the bank payments were:

	$
Vehicle expenses	6,720
Drawings	4,300
Trade expenses	7,360

(m) John Snow is not insured against loss of inventory owing to burglary or damage to inventory caused by damp.

Required

Prepare John Snow's statement of profit or loss and other comprehensive income for the year ended 31 March 20X1 and a statement of financial position on that date.

11.2 Discussion and solution

This is an incomplete records problem because we are told that John Snow has lost many of his accounting records. In particular we do not know sales for the year, purchases during the year, or all the cash receipts and payments.

The first step is to find the opening statement of financial position, if possible. In this case, it is. The proprietor's capital is the balancing figure.

JOHN SNOW
STATEMENT OF FINANCIAL POSITION AS AT 31 MARCH 20X0

	$	$
Assets		
Non-current assets		
Buildings: Cost	10,000	
Accumulated deprecation	6,000	
		4,000
Motor vehicles: Cost	5,000	
Accumulated depreciation	2,000	
		3,000
Current assets		
Inventories	3,200	
Trade receivables	6,300	
Commission due	300	
Prepayments	120	
Cash and bank	4,310	
		14,230
Total assets		21,230
Capital and liabilities		
Proprietor's capital (balance)		16,800
Current liabilities		
Trade payables	4,200	
Accrued expenses	230	
		4,430
Total capital and liabilities		21,230

The next step is to open up a profit or loss account, cash book, trade receivables account and trade payables account and to insert the opening balances, if known. Cash sales and payments in cash are not a feature of the problem, and so a single column cash book is sufficient.

The problem should then be read line by line, identifying any transactions affecting those accounts.

Statement of profit or loss account

	$	$
Revenue (note 5)		60,000
Opening inventory	3,200	
Purchases (note 1)	44,000	
	47,200	
Less: Damaged inventory written off (note 3)	(1,000)	
Inventory stolen (note 4)	(4,000)	
	42,200	
Less closing inventory (note 2)	(6,200)	
Cost of goods sold		36,000
Gross profit (note 5)		24,000

CASH BOOK

	$		$
Opening balance	4,310	Trade payables	
Trade receivables (see below)	59,600	(see trade payables)	40,600
Agency commission (note 6)	300	Trade expenses	7,360
		Vehicle expenses	6,720
		Drawings	4,300
		Balance c/f	5,230
	64,210		64,210

TRADE ACCOUNTS RECEIVABLE

	$		$
Opening balance b/f	6,300	Cash received (balancing figure)	59,600
Revenue (note 5)	60,000	Closing balance c/f	6,700
	66,300		66,300

TRADE ACCOUNTS PAYABLE

	$		$
		Opening balance b/f	4,200
Cash paid (balancing figure)	40,600	Purchases (note 1)	44,000
Closing balance c/f	7,600		
	48,200		48,200

VEHICLE EXPENSES

	$		$
Cash	6,720	Accrual b/f	230
Accrual c/f (balancing figure)	530	SPL account	7,020
	7,250		7,250

The trading account is complete already, but now the statement of profit or loss and other comprehensive income and statement of financial position can be prepared. Remember not to forget items such as the inventory losses and commission earned on purchases

JOHN SNOW
STATEMENT OF PROFIT OR LOSS AND OTHER COMPREHENSIVE INCOME
FOR THE YEAR ENDED 31 MARCH 20X1

	$	$
Revenue (note 5)		60,000
Opening inventory	3,200	
Purchases (note 1)	44,000	
	47,200	
Less: Damaged inventory written off (note 3)	(1,000)	
Inventory stolen (note 4)	(4,000)	
	42,200	

PART B ACCOUNTING RECORDS AND PROCEDURES

	$	$
Less closing inventory (note 2)	6,200	
Cost of goods sold		36,000
Gross profit (note 5)		24,000
Add: Commission on purchases		440
		24,440
Expenses		
Trade expenses (note 7)	7,400	
Inventory damaged	1,000	
Inventory stolen	4,000	
Vehicle expenses	7,020	
Depreciation		
Buildings	500	
Motor vehicles	1,000	
		20,920
Net profit (to capital account)		3,520

JOHN SNOW
STATEMENT OF FINANCIAL POSITION AS AT 31 MARCH 20X1

	$	$
Assets		
Non-current assets		
Buildings: Cost	10,000	
Accumulated depreciation	6,500	
		3,500
Motor vehicles: Cost	5,000	
Accumulated depreciation	3,000	
		2,000
Current assets		
Inventories	6,200	
Trade receivables	6,700	
Commission due	440	
Prepayments (trade expenses)	80	
Cash and bank	5,230	
		18,650
Total assets		24,150
Capital and liabilities		
Proprietor's capital		
As at 31 March 20X0	16,800	
Net profit for year to 31 March 20X0	3,520	
Less drawings	(4,300)	
As at 31 March 20X0		16,020
Current liabilities		
Trade payables	7,600	
Accrued expenses	530	
		8,130
Total capital and liabilities		24,150

Notes

1. The agency commission due on 1 May 20X1 indicates that purchases for the year to 31 March 20X1 were:

    100%/1% × $440 = $44,000.

2. Closing inventory at cost on 31 March 20X1 was $(3,200 + 3,000) = $6,200.

3. Inventory scrapped ($1,000) is accounted for by:

    CREDIT   Cost of sales
    DEBIT   Statement of profit or loss account

4   Inventory lost in the burglary is accounted for by:
    CREDIT   Cost of sales
    DEBIT   Statement of profit or loss account

5   The trade discount of 20% has already been deducted in arriving at the value of the purchases. The gross profit margin is 40% on sales, so with cost of sales = $36,000.

		$
Cost	(60%)	36,000
Profit	(40%)	24,000
Revenue	(100%)	60,000

(It is assumed that trade expenses are not included in the cost of sales, and so should be ignored in this calculation.)

6   The agency commission of $300 due on 1 May 20X0 would have been paid to John Snow at that date.

7   The SPL expenditure for trade expenses and closing balance on vehicle expenses account are as follows:

TRADE EXPENSES

	$		$
Prepayment	120	SPL account (balancing figure)	7,400
Cash	7,360	Prepayment c/f	80
	7,480		7,480

11.3 Using trade receivables to calculate both cash sales and credit sales

A final point which needs to be considered is how a missing value can be found for cash sales and credit sales, when a business has both, but takings banked by the business are not divided between takings from cash sales and takings from credit sales.

11.4 Example: Using trade receivables

Suppose, for example, that a business had, on 1 January 20X8, trade receivables of $2,000, cash in the bank of $3,000, and cash in hand of $300.

During the year to 31 December 20X8 the business banked $95,000 in takings.

It also paid out the following expenses in cash from the till:

Drawings	$1,200
Sundry expenses	$800

On 29 August 20X8 a thief broke into the shop and stole $400 from the till.

At 31 December 20X8 trade receivables amounted to $3,500, cash in the bank $2,500 and cash in the till $150.

What was the value of sales during the year?

Solution

If we tried to prepare a trade receivables control account and a two column cash book, we would have insufficient information, in particular about whether the takings which were banked related to cash sales or credit sales.

TRADE RECEIVABLES CONTROL ACCOUNT

	$		$
Balance b/f	2,000	Cash from receivables (credit sales)	Unknown
Credit sales	Unknown		
		Balance c/f	3,500

PART B ACCOUNTING RECORDS AND PROCEDURES

CASH BOOK

	Cash $	Bank $		Cash $	Bank $
Balance b/f	300	3,000	Drawings	1,200	
			Sundry expenses	800	
Cash from trade receivables		Unknown	Cash stolen	400	
Cash sales	Unknown		Balance c/f	150	2,500

All we do know is that the combined sums from trade receivables and cash takings banked is $95,000.

The value of sales can be found instead by using the trade receivables control account, which should be used to record cash takings banked as well as payments from trade receivables. The balancing figure in the trade receivables account will then be a combination of credit sales and some cash sales. The cash book only needs to be a single column.

TRADE RECEIVABLE CONTROL ACCOUNT

	$		$
Balance b/f	2,000	Cash banked	95,000
Revenue: to trading account	96,500	Balance c/f	3,500
	98,500		98,500

CASH (EXTRACT)

	$		$
Balance in hand b/f	300	*Payments in cash*	
Balance in bank b/f	3,000	Drawings	1,200
Trade receivables a/c	95,000	Expenses	800
		Other payments	?
		Cash stolen	400
		Balance in hand c/f	150
		Balance in bank c/f	2,500

The remaining 'undiscovered' amount of cash sales is now found as follows:

	$	$
Payments in cash out of the till		
Drawings	1,200	
Expenses	800	
		2,000
Cash stolen		400
Closing balance of cash in hand		150
		2,550
Less opening balance of cash in hand		(300)
Further cash sales		2,250

(This calculation is similar to the one described above for calculating cash sales.)

Total revenue for the year is:

	$
From trade receivables	96,500
From cash book	2,250
Total revenue	98,750

Question Incomplete records

Mary Grimes, wholesale fruit and vegetable merchant, does not keep a full set of accounting records. However, the following information has been produced from the business's records.

12: INCOMPLETE RECORDS

(a) Summary of the bank account for the year ended 31 August 20X8

	$		$
1 Sept 20X7 balance b/f	1,970	Payments to suppliers	72,000
Cash from trade receivables	96,000	Purchase of motor van (E471 KBR)	13,000
Sale of private yacht	20,000	Rent and local taxes	2,600
Sale of motor van (A123 BWA)	2,100	Wages	15,100
		Motor vehicle expenses	3,350
		Postages and stationery	1,360
		Drawings	9,200
		Repairs and renewals	650
		Insurances	800
		31 August 20X8 balance c/f	2,010
	120,070		120,070
1 Sept 20X8 balance b/f	2,010		

(b) Assets and liabilities, other than balance at bank

		1 Sept 20X7	31 Aug 20X8
		$	$
Trade payables		4,700	2,590
Trade receivables		7,320	9,500
Rent and local taxes accrued		200	260
Motor vans:			
A123 BWA:	At cost	10,000	–
	Accumulated depreciation	8,000	–
E471 KBR:	At cost	–	13,000
	Accumulated depreciation	–	To be determined
Inventories		4,900	5,900
Insurance prepaid		160	200

(c) All receipts are banked and all payments are made from the business bank account.

(d) A trade debt of $300 owing by John Blunt and included in the trade receivables at 31 August 20X8 (see (b) above), is to be written off as an irrecoverable debt.

(e) It is Mary Grimes' policy to charge depreciation at the rate of 20% on the cost of motor vans held at the end of each financial year; no depreciation is charged in the year of sale or disposal of a motor van.

(f) Discounts received during the year ended 31 August 20X8 from trade payables amounted to $1,100.

Required

(a) Prepare Mary Grimes' statement of profit or loss and other comprehensive income for the year ended 31 August 20X8.

(b) Prepare Mary Grimes' statement of financial position as at 31 August 20X8.

Answer

(a) STATEMENT OF PROFIT OR LOSS AND OTHER COMPREHENSIVE INCOME
FOR THE YEAR ENDED 31 AUGUST 20X8

	$	$
Revenue (W1)		98,180
Opening inventory	4,900	
Purchases (W2)	70,990	
	75,890	
Less closing inventory	5,900	
		69,990

	$	$
Gross profit		28,190
Discounts received		1,100
Profit on sale of motor vehicle ($2,100 – $(10,000 – 8,000))		100
		29,390
Rent and local taxes (W3)	2,660	
Wages	15,100	
Motor vehicle expenses	3,350	
Postages and stationery	1,360	
Repairs and renewals	650	
Insurances (W4)	760	
Irrecoverable debt	300	
Depreciation of van (20% × $13,000)	2,600	
		26,780
		2,610

(b) STATEMENT OF FINANCIAL POSITION AS AT 31 AUGUST 20X8

	$	$
Assets		
Non-current assets		
Motor van: cost	13,000	
Depreciation	2,600	
		10,400
Current assets		
Inventories	5,900	
Trade receivables ($9,500 – $300 irrecoverable debt)	9,200	
Prepayment	200	
Cash at bank	2,010	
		17,310
Total assets		27,710
Capital and liabilities	$	$
Capital account		
Balance at 1 September 20X7 (W5)	11,450	
Additional capital: proceeds on sale of yacht	20,000	
Net profit for the year	2,610	
Less drawings	(9,200)	
Balance at 31 August 20X8		24,860
Current liabilities		
Trade payables	2,590	
Accrual	260	
		2,850
Total capital and liabilities		27,710

Workings

1   Revenue

	$
Cash received from customers	96,000
Add trade receivables at 31 August 20X8	9,500
	105,500
Less trade receivables at 1 September 20X7	7,320
Sales in year	98,180

2 Purchases

	$	$
Payments to suppliers		72,000
Add: Trade payables at 31 August 20X8	2,590	
Discounts granted by suppliers	1,100	
		3,690
		75,690
Less trade payables at 1 September 20X7		4,700
		70,990

3 Rent and local taxes

	$
Cash paid in year	2,600
Add accrual at 31 August 20X8	260
	2,860
Less accrual at 1 September 20X7	200
Charge for the year	2,660

4 Insurances

	$
Cash paid in year	800
Add prepayment at 1 September 20X7	160
	960
Less prepayment at 31 August 20X8	200
	760

Workings 1–4 could also be presented in ledger account format as follows.

TRADE RECEIVABLES CONTROL ACCOUNT

	$		$
Balance b/f	7,320	Bank	96,000
∴ Revenue	98,180	Balance c/f	9,500
	105,500		105,500

TRADE PAYABLES CONTROL ACCOUNT

	$		$
Bank	72,000	Balance b/f	4,700
Discounts received	1,100	∴ Purchases	70,990
Balance c/f	2,590		
	75,690		75,690

RENT AND LOCAL TAXES

	$		$
Bank	2,600	Balance b/f	200
Balance c/f	260	∴ SPL charge	2,660
	2,860		2,860

INSURANCES

	$		$
Balance b/f	160	∴ SPL charge	760
Bank	800	Balance c/f	200
	960		960

5   Capital at 1 September 20X7

	$	$
Assets		
Bank balance		1,970
Trade receivables		7,320
Motor van $(10,000 – 8,000)		2,000
Inventories		4,900
Prepayment		160
		16,350
Liabilities		
Trade payables	4,700	
Accrual	200	
		4,900
		11,450

> **Exam focus point**
>
> You may be asked to prepare a full set of accounts in the exam. Therefore, it is essential that you practise on full questions, so that you can easily calculate any missing figure that you need in the exam.

Chapter roundup

- **Incomplete records** questions may test your ability to prepare accounts in the following situations.
    - A trader **does not maintain a ledger** and therefore has no continuous double entry record of transactions.
    - Accounting records are **destroyed** by accident, such as fire.
    - Some essential figure is **unknown** and must be calculated as a balancing figure. This may occur as a result of inventory being damaged or destroyed, or because of misappropriation of assets.

- The approach to incomplete records questions is to build up the information given so as to complete the necessary **double entry**. This may involve reconstructing **control accounts** for:
    - Cash and bank
    - Trade receivables and trade payables

- Where inventory, revenue or purchases is the unknown figure it will be necessary to use information on **gross profit percentages** so as to construct a working for gross profit in which the unknown figure can be inserted as a balance.

- The construction of a cashbook, largely from bank statements showing receipts and payments during the period, is often an important feature of incomplete records problems.

- **Drawings** often feature as the missing item in an incomplete records problem. The trader has been drawing money but does not know how much.

- Where no trading records have been kept, profit can be derived from opening and closing net assets by use of the **business equation**.

PART B   ACCOUNTING RECORDS AND PROCEDURES

Quick quiz

1. In the absence of a revenue account or sales day book, how can a figure for revenue for the year be computed?

2. A business has opening trade payables of $75,000 and closing trade payables of $65,000. Cash paid to suppliers was $65,000 and discounts received $3,000. What is the figure for purchase?
    - A $58,000
    - B $78,000
    - C $52,000
    - D $55,000

3. What is the difference between 'mark-up' and 'gross profit percentage'?

4. What is the accounting double entry to record the loss of inventory by fire or burglary?
    - A   DR Statement of profit or loss, CR revenue
    - B   DR revenue, CR Statement of profit or loss

5. In what circumstances is a two-column cash book useful?

6. If a business proprietor pays his personal income into the business bank account, what is the accounting double entry to record the transaction?
    - A   DR drawings, CR cash
    - B   DR cash, CR drawings

7. A business has net assets of $70,000 at the beginning of the year and $80,000 at the end of the year. Drawings were $25,000 and a lottery win of $5,000 was paid into the business during the year. What was the profit for the year?
    - A $10,000 loss
    - B $30,000 profit
    - C $10,000 profit
    - D $30,000 loss

8. A business usually has a mark-up of 20% on cost of sales. During a year, its revenue was $90,000. What was cost of sales?
    - A $15,000
    - B $72,000
    - C $18,000
    - D $75,000

Answers to quick quiz

1. By using the trade accounts receivable control account to calculate revenue as a balancing figure.

2. A

    TRADE PAYABLES CONTROL

	$		$
Bank	65,000	Opening trade payables	75,000
Discounts received	3,000	Purchases (bal fig)	58,000
Closing trade payables	65,000		
	133,000		133,000

3. Mark-up is the profit as a percentage of cost. Gross profit percentage is the profit as a percentage of sales.

4. A   DEBIT   Statement of profit or loss a/c
       CREDIT Cost of sales

    Assuming that the goods were not insured.

5. Where a large amount of receipts and payments are made in cash.

6. B   DEBIT   Cash
       CREDIT Drawings

7. B   Profit = movement in net assets – capital introduced + drawings
       = (80,000 – 70,000) – 5,000 + 25,000
       = 30,000

8. D

	$
Revenue	90,000
Cost of sales (bal fig)	75,000
Profit $\left(\dfrac{20}{120} \times 90,000\right)$	15,000

PART B ACCOUNTING RECORDS AND PROCEDURES

Practical application of accounting theory

13

Inventory

Topic list	Syllabus reference
1 Cost of goods sold	A3
2 Accounting for opening and closing inventories	A3
3 Counting inventories	A3
4 Valuing inventories	A3
5 IAS 2 *Inventories*	A3

Introduction

Inventory is one of the most important assets in a company's statement of financial position. As we will see, it also affects the statement of profit or loss and other comprehensive income, having a direct impact on gross profit.

So far you have come across inventories in the preparation of a simple statement of financial position. Here we will look at in the calculation of the cost of goods sold. This chapter also explores the **difficulties of valuing inventories**.

This is the first time that you will be required to consider the impact of the relevant International Accounting Standard on the valuation and presentation of an item in the accounts: IAS 2 *Inventories*.

PART C PRACTICAL APPLICATION OF ACCOUNTING THEORY

1 Cost of goods sold

FAST FORWARD

The **cost of goods sold** is calculated as:
Opening inventory + purchases – closing inventory

1.1 Unsold goods in inventory at the end of an accounting period

Goods might be unsold at the end of an accounting period and so still be **held in inventory**. The purchase cost of these goods should not be included therefore in the cost of sales of the period.

1.2 Example: Closing inventory

Perry P Louis, trading as the Umbrella Shop, ends his financial year on 30 September each year. On 1 October 20X4 he had no goods in inventory. During the year to 30 September 20X5, he purchased 30,000 umbrellas costing $60,000 from umbrella wholesalers and suppliers. He resold the umbrellas for $5 each, and sales for the year amounted to $100,000 (20,000 umbrellas). At 30 September there were 10,000 unsold umbrellas left in inventory, valued at $2 each.

What was Perry P Louis's gross profit for the year?

Solution

Perry P Louis purchased 30,000 umbrellas, but only sold 20,000. Purchase costs of $60,000 and sales of $100,000 do not represent the same quantity of goods.

The gross profit for the year should be calculated by 'matching' the sales value of the 20,000 umbrellas sold with the cost of those 20,000 umbrellas. The cost of sales in this example is therefore the cost of purchases minus the cost of goods in inventory at the year end.

	$	$
Revenue (20,000 units)		100,000
Purchases (30,000 units)	60,000	
Less closing inventory (10,000 units @ $2)	20,000	
Cost of sales (20,000 units)		40,000
Gross profit		60,000

1.3 Example continued

We shall continue the example of the Umbrella Shop into its next accounting year, 1 October 20X5 to 30 September 20X6. During the course of this year, Perry P Louis purchased 40,000 umbrellas at a total cost of $95,000. During the year he sold 45,000 umbrellas for $230,000. At 30 September 20X6 he had 5,000 umbrellas left in inventory, which had cost $12,000.

What was his gross profit for the year?

Solution

In this accounting year, he purchased 40,000 umbrellas to add to the 10,000 he already had in inventory at the start of the year. He sold 45,000, leaving 5,000 umbrellas in inventory at the year end. Once again, gross profit should be calculated by matching the value of 45,000 units of sales with the cost of those 45,000 units.

The cost of sales is the value of the 10,000 umbrellas in inventory at the beginning of the year, plus the cost of the 40,000 umbrellas purchased, less the value of the 5,000 umbrellas in inventory at the year end.

	$	$
Revenue (45,000 units)		230,000
Opening inventory (10,000 units) *	20,000	
Add purchases (40,000 units)	95,000	
	115,000	
Less closing inventory (5,000 units)	12,000	
Cost of sales (45,000 units)		103,000
Gross profit		127,000

* Taken from the closing inventory value of the previous accounting year, see Paragraph 1.2.

1.4 The cost of goods sold

The cost of goods sold is found by applying the following formula.

Formula to learn

	$
Opening inventory value	X
Add cost of purchases (or, in the case of a manufacturing company, the cost of production)	X
	X
Less closing inventory value	(X)
Equals cost of goods sold	X

In other words, to match 'sales' and the 'cost of goods sold', it is necessary to adjust the cost of goods manufactured or purchased to allow for increases or reductions in inventory levels during the period.

The 'formula' above is based on a logical idea. You should learn it, because it is fundamental among the principles of accounting.

Test your knowledge of the formula with the following example.

1.5 Example: Cost of goods sold and variations in inventory levels

On 1 January 20X6, the Grand Union Food Stores had goods in inventory valued at $6,000. During 20X6 its proprietor purchased supplies costing $50,000. Sales for the year to 31 December 20X6 amounted to $80,000. The cost of goods in inventory at 31 December 20X6 was $12,500.

Calculate the gross profit for the year.

Solution

GRAND UNION FOOD STORES
TRADING ACCOUNT FOR THE YEAR ENDED 31 DECEMBER 20X6

	$	$
Revenue		80,000
Opening inventory	6,000	
Add purchases	50,000	
	56,000	
Less closing inventory	12,500	
Cost of goods sold		43,500
Gross profit		36,500

PART C PRACTICAL APPLICATION OF ACCOUNTING THEORY

1.6 The cost of carriage inwards and outwards

FAST FORWARD

Carriage inwards is included in the cost of purchases.
Carriage outwards is a selling expense.

'Carriage' refers to the **cost of transporting purchased goods** from the supplier to the premises of the business which has bought them. Someone has to pay for these delivery costs: sometimes the supplier pays, and sometimes the purchaser pays. When the purchaser pays, the cost to the purchaser is carriage inwards (**into** the business). When the supplier pays, the cost to the supplier is known as carriage outwards (**out** of the business).

The **cost of carriage inwards** is usually added to the **cost of purchases**.

The **cost of carriage outwards** is a **selling and distribution expense** in the **statement of profit or loss and other comprehensive income**.

1.7 Example: Carriage inwards and carriage outwards

Gwyn Tring, trading as Clickety Clocks, imports and resells clocks. He pays for the costs of delivering the clocks from his supplier in Switzerland to his shop in Wales.

He resells the clocks to other traders throughout the country, paying the costs of carriage for the consignments from his business premises to his customers.

On 1 July 20X5, he had clocks in inventory valued at $17,000. During the year to 30 June 20X6 he purchased more clocks at a cost of $75,000. Carriage inwards amounted to $2,000. Sales for the year were $162,100. Other expenses of the business amounted to $56,000 excluding carriage outwards which cost $2,500. Gwyn Tring took drawings of $20,000 from the business during the course of the year. The value of the goods in inventory at the year end was $15,400.

Required

Prepare the statement of profit or loss and other comprehensive income of Clickety Clocks for the year ended 30 June 20X6.

Solution

CLICKETY CLOCKS
STATEMENT OF PROFIT OR LOSS AND OTHER COMPREHENSIVE INCOME
FOR THE YEAR ENDED 30 JUNE 20X6

	$	$
Revenue		162,100
Opening inventory	17,000	
Purchases	75,000	
Carriage inwards	2,000	
	94,000	
Less closing inventory	15,400	
Cost of goods sold		78,600
Gross profit		83,500
Carriage outwards	2,500	
Other expenses	56,000	
		58,500
Net profit (transferred to statement of financial position)		25,000

1.8 Goods written off or written down

A trader might be unable to sell all the goods that he purchases, because a number of things might happen to the goods before they can be sold. For example:

(a) Goods might be lost or stolen.
(b) Goods might be damaged, become worthless and so be thrown away.
(c) Goods might become obsolete or out of fashion. These might be thrown away, or sold off at a very low price in a clearance sale.

When goods are **lost, stolen or thrown away** as worthless, the business will make a loss on those goods because their **'sales value' will be $nil**.

Similarly, when goods lose value because they have become **obsolete** or out of fashion, the business will **make a loss** if their clearance sales value is less than their cost. For example, if goods which originally cost $500 are now obsolete and could only be sold for $150 the business would suffer a loss of $350.

If, at the end of an accounting period, a business still has goods in inventory which are either worthless or worth less than their original cost, the value of the inventories should be **written down** to:

(a) Nothing, if they are worthless
(b) Their net realisable value, if this is less than their original cost

This means that the loss will be reported as soon as the loss is foreseen, even if the goods have not yet been thrown away or sold off at a cheap price.

The costs of inventory written off or written down should not usually cause any problems in calculating the gross profit of a business, because the cost of goods sold will include the cost of inventories written off or written down, as the following example shows.

1.9 Example: Inventory written off and written down

Lucas Wagg, trading as Fairlock Fashions, ends his financial year on 31 March. At 1 April 20X5 he had goods in inventory valued at $8,800. During the year to 31 March 20X6, he purchased goods costing $48,000. Fashion goods which cost $2,100 were still held in inventory at 31 March 20X6, and Lucas Wagg believes that these could only now be sold at a sale price of $400. The goods still held in inventory at 31 March 20X6 (including the fashion goods) had an original purchase cost of $7,600. Sales for the year were $81,400.

Required

Calculate the gross profit of Fairlock Fashions for the year ended 31 March 20X6.

Solution

Initial calculation of closing inventory values:

INVENTORY COUNT

	At cost $	Realisable value $	Amount written down $
Fashion goods	2,100	400	1,700
Other goods (balancing figure)	5,500	5,500	–
	7,600	5,900	1,700

FAIRLOCK FASHIONS
STATEMENT OF PROFIT OR LOSS FOR THE YEAR ENDED 31 MARCH 20X6

	$	$
Revenue		81,400
Value of opening inventory	8,800	
Purchases	48,000	
	56,800	
Less closing inventory	5,900	
Cost of goods sold		50,900
Gross profit		30,500

By using the figure of $5,900 for closing inventory, the cost of goods sold automatically includes the inventory written down of $1,700.

Question
Gross profit

Gross profit for 20X7 can be calculated from:

A Purchases for 20X7, plus inventory at 31 December 20X7, less inventory at 1 January 20X7
B Purchases for 20X7, less inventory at 31 December 20X7, plus inventory at 1 January 20X7
C Cost of goods sold during 20X7, plus sales during 20X7
D Net profit for 20X7, plus expenses for 20X7

Answer

The correct answer is D. Gross profit less expenses = net profit. Therefore net profit plus expenses = gross profit.

2 Accounting for opening and closing inventories

FAST FORWARD

Opening inventory brought forward in the inventory account are **transferred to the statement of profit or loss**, and so at the end of the accounting year, the balance on the inventory account ceases to be the opening inventory value b/f, and becomes instead the closing inventory value c/f.

2.1 Recap

In Section 1, we saw that in order to calculate **gross profit** it is necessary to work out the **cost of goods sold**, and in order to calculate the cost of goods sold it is necessary to have values for the **opening inventory** (ie inventory in hand at the beginning of the accounting period) and **closing inventory** (ie inventory in hand at the end of the accounting period).

You should remember, in fact, that the trading part of a statement of profit or loss and other comprehensive income includes:

	$
Opening inventory	X
Plus purchases	X
Less closing inventory	(X)
Equals cost of goods sold	X

However, just writing down this formula hides three basic problems.

(a) How do you manage to get a **precise count** of inventory in hand at any one time?
(b) Even once it has been counted, how do you **value** the inventory?
(c) Assuming the inventory is given a value, how does the **double entry bookkeeping** for inventory work?

The purpose of this chapter is to answer all three of these questions. In order to make the presentation a little easier to follow, it is convenient to take the last one first.

2.2 Ledger accounting for inventory

FAST FORWARD

> The value of **closing inventory** is accounted for in the **general ledger** by debiting an inventory account and crediting the statement of profit or loss at the end of an accounting period. The inventory will therefore always have a debit balance at the end of a period, and this balance will be shown in the statement of financial position as a current asset for inventories.

It has already been shown that purchases are introduced to the statement of profit or loss and other comprehensive income by means of the double entry:

DEBIT	Statement of profit or loss	$X
CREDIT	Purchases account	$X

But what about opening and closing inventories? How are their values accounted for in the double entry bookkeeping system? The answer is that an inventory account must be kept. This inventory account is only ever used **at the end of an accounting period**, when the business counts up and values the inventory in hand, in an inventory count.

(a) When an inventory count is made, the business will have a value for its closing inventory, and the double entry is:

DEBIT	Inventory account (closing inventory value)	$X
CREDIT	Statement of profit or loss	$X

However, rather than show the closing inventory as a 'plus' value in the trading account (by adding it to sales) it is usual to show it as a 'minus' figure in arriving at cost of sales. This is illustrated in Paragraph 2.1 above. The debit balance on an inventory account represents an asset, which will be shown as part of current assets in the statement of financial position.

(b) Closing inventory at the end of one period becomes opening inventory at the start of the next period. The inventory account remains unchanged until the end of the next period, when the value of opening inventory is taken to the profit or loss account:

DEBIT	Statement of profit or loss	$X
CREDIT	Inventory account (value of opening inventory)	$X

Partly as an example of how this ledger accounting for inventories works, and partly as revision on ledger accounting in general, try the following exercise. It is an example from an earlier part of this text which has had a closing inventory figure included.

PART C PRACTICAL APPLICATION OF ACCOUNTING THEORY

Question
Inventories

A business is established with capital of $2,000 and this amount is paid into a business bank account by the proprietor. During the first year's trading, the following transactions occurred.

	$
Purchases of goods for resale, on credit	4,300
Payments for trade accounts payable	3,600
Sales, all on credit	4,000
Payments from trade receivables	3,200
Non-current assets purchased for cash	1,500
Other expenses, all paid in cash	900

The bank has provided an overdraft facility of up to $3,000.

All 'other expenses' relate to the current year.

Closing inventory is valued at $1,800. (Because this is the first year of the business, there are no opening inventories.)

Ignore depreciation and withdrawals on account of profit.

Required

Prepare the ledger accounts, a statement of profit or loss for the year and a statement of financial position as at the end of the year.

Answer

CASH

	$		$
Capital	2,000	Trade payables	3,600
Trade receivables	3,200	Non-current assets	1,500
Balance c/d	800	Other expenses	900
	6,000		6,000
		Balance b/d	800

CAPITAL

	$		$
		Cash	2,000
Balance c/d	2,600	Statement of profit or loss	600
	2,600		2,600
		Balance b/d	2,600

TRADE PAYABLES

	$		$
Cash	3,600		
Balance c/d	700	Purchases	4,300
	4,300		4,300
		Balance b/d	700

PURCHASES ACCOUNT

	$		$
Trade payables	4,300	Statement of profit or loss	4,300

NON-CURRENT ASSETS

	$		$
Cash	1,500	Balance c/d	1,500
Balance b/d	1,500		

REVENUE

	$		$
Statement of profit or loss	4,000	Trade receivables	4,000

TRADE RECEIVABLES

	$		$
		Cash	3,200
Revenue	4,000	Balance c/d	800
	4,000		4,000
Balance b/d	800		

OTHER EXPENSES

	$		$
Cash	900	Statement of profit or loss	900

STATEMENT OF PROFIT OR LOSS

	$		$
Purchases account	4,300	Revenue	4,000
Gross profit c/d	1,500	Closing inventory (inventory a/c)	1,800
	5,800		5,800
Other expenses	900	Gross profit b/d	1,500
Net profit (transferred to capital account)	600		
	1,500		1,500

Alternatively, closing inventory could be shown as a minus value on the debit side of the statement of profit or loss, instead of a credit entry, giving purchases $4,300 less closing inventory $1,800 equals cost of goods sold $2,500.

INVENTORY ACCOUNT

	$		$
Statement of profit or loss (closing inventory)	1,800	Balance c/d	1,800
Balance b/d (opening inventory)	1,800		

STATEMENT OF FINANCIAL POSITION AS AT THE END OF THE PERIOD

	$	$
Assets		
Non-current assets		1,500
Current assets		
Inventory	1,800	
Trade receivables	800	
		2,600
Total assets		4,100
Capital and liabilities		
Capital		
At start of period	2,000	
Profit for period	600	
At end of period		2,600

	$	$
Current liabilities		
Bank overdraft	800	
Trade payables	700	
		1,500
Total capital and liabilities		4,100

Make sure you can see what has happened here. The balance on the inventory account was $1,800, which appears in the statement of financial position as a current asset. As it happens, the $1,800 closing inventory was the only entry in the inventory account – there was no figure for opening inventory.

If there had been, it would have been eliminated by transferring it as a debit balance to the statement of profit or loss, ie:

DEBIT   Statement of profit or loss (with value of opening inventory)
CREDIT   Inventory account (with value of opening inventory)

The debit in the statement of profit or loss would then have increased the cost of sales, ie opening inventory is added to purchases in calculating cost of sales. Again, this is illustrated in Paragraph 2.1 above.

So if we can establish the value of inventories on hand, the above paragraphs and exercise show us how to account for that value. That takes care of one of the problems noted at the beginning of this chapter. But now another of those problems becomes apparent – how do we establish the **value** of inventories on hand? The first step must be to establish **how much inventory is held**.

3 Counting inventories

FAST FORWARD

The **quantity** of inventories held at the year end is established by means of a **physical count** of inventory in an annual counting exercise, or by a 'continuous' inventory count.

Business trading is a continuous activity, but accounting statements must be drawn up at a particular date. In preparing a statement of financial position it is necessary to **'freeze'** the activity of a business so as to determine its assets and liabilities at a given moment. This includes establishing the quantities of inventories on hand, which can create problems.

In simple cases, when a business holds easily counted and relatively small amounts of inventory, quantities of inventories on hand at the reporting date can be determined by physically counting them in an **inventory count**.

In more complicated cases, where a business holds considerable quantities of varied inventory, an alternative approach to establishing quantities is to maintain **continuous inventory records**. This means that a card is kept for every item of inventory, showing receipts and issues from the stores, and a running total (some businesses may use an IT system to record this information). A few inventory items are counted each day to make sure their record cards are correct – this is called a 'continuous' count because it is spread out over the year rather than completed in one count at a designated time.

One obstacle is overcome once a business has established how much inventory is on hand. But another of the problems noted in the introduction immediately raises its head. What value should the business place on those inventories?

4 Valuing inventories

FAST FORWARD

The value of inventories is calculated at the lower **cost** and **net realisable value** for each separate item or group of items. **Cost** can be arrived at by using **FIFO** (first-in, first-out) or **AVCO** (weighted average costing).

4.1 The basic rule

There are **several methods** which, in theory, might be used for the valuation of inventory.

(a) Inventory might be valued at its **expected selling price**.

(b) Inventory might be valued at its expected selling price, less any costs still to be incurred in getting it ready for sale and then selling them. This amount is referred to as the **net realisable value** (NRV) of the inventories.

(c) Inventory might be valued at its **historical cost** (ie the cost at which they were originally bought).

(d) Inventory might be valued at the amount it would cost to replace it. This amount is referred to as the **current replacement cost** of inventory.

Current replacement costs are not used in the type of accounts dealt with in this syllabus.

The use of selling prices in inventory valuation is ruled out because this would create a profit for the business before the inventory has been sold.

A simple example might help to explain this. A trader buys two items of inventory, each costing $100. He can sell them for $140 each, but in the accounting period we shall consider, he has only sold one of them. The other is closing inventory in hand.

Since only one item has been sold, you might think it is common sense that profit ought to be $40. But if closing inventory is valued at selling price, profit would be $80, ie profit would be taken on the closing inventory as well.

This would contradict the accounting concept of **faithful representation**, ie to claim a profit before the item has actually been sold.

The same objection **usually** applies to the use of NRV in inventory valuation. The item purchased for $100 requires $5 of further expenditure in getting it ready for sale and then selling it (eg $5 of processing costs and distribution costs). If its expected selling price is $140, its NRV is $(140 – 5) = $135. To value it at $135 in the statement of financial position would still be to anticipate a $35 profit.

	$	$
Revenue		140
Opening inventory	–	
Purchases (2 × $100)	200	
	200	
Less closing inventory (at selling price)	140	
Cost of sale		60
Profit		80

We are left with **historical cost** as the normal basis of inventory valuation. **The only time when historical cost is not used is in the exceptional case where the neutrality concept requires a lower value to be used.**

Staying with the example above, suppose that the market in this kind of product suddenly slumps and the item's expected selling price is only $90. The item's NRV is then $(90 – 5) = $85 and the business has in effect made a loss of $15($100 – $85). The concept of faithful representation requires that losses should be recognised as soon as they are foreseen. This can be achieved by valuing the inventory item in the statement of financial position at its NRV of $85.

The argument developed above suggests that the rule to follow is that inventories should be valued at cost, or if lower, net realisable value. The accounting treatment of inventory is governed by an accounting

PART C PRACTICAL APPLICATION OF ACCOUNTING THEORY

standard, IAS 2 *Inventories*. IAS 2 states that **inventory should be valued at the lower of cost and net realisable value** as we will see below. This is an important rule and one which you should learn by heart.

Rule to learn | Inventory should be valued at the lower of cost and net realisable value.

4.2 Applying the basic valuation rule

If a business has many inventory items on hand the comparison of cost and NRV should theoretically be carried out for each item separately. It is not sufficient to compare the total cost of all inventory items with their total NRV. An example will show why.

Suppose a company has four items of inventory on hand at the end of its accounting period. Their cost and NRVs are as follows.

Inventory item	Cost $	NRV $	Lower of cost/NRV $
1	27	32	27
2	14	8	8
3	43	55	43
4	29	40	29
	113	135	107

It would be incorrect to compare total costs ($113) with total NRV ($135) and to state inventory at $113 in the statement of financial position. The company can foresee a loss of $6 on item 2 and this should be recognised. If the four items are taken together in total the loss on item 2 is masked by the anticipated profits on the other items. By performing the cost/NRV comparison for each item separately the valuation of $107 can be derived. This is the value which should appear in the statement of financial position.

However, for a company with large amounts of inventory this procedure may be impracticable. In this case it is acceptable to group similar items into categories and perform the comparison of cost and NRV category by category, rather than item by item.

Question — Valuation

The following figures relate to inventory held at the year end.

	A $	B $	C $
Cost	20	9	12
Selling price	30	12	22
Modification cost to enable sale	–	2	8
Marketing costs	7	2	2
Units held	200	150	300

Required

Calculate the value of inventory held.

Answer

Item	Cost $	NRV $	Valuation $	Quantity Units	Total value $
A	20	23	20	200	4,000
B	9	8	8	150	1,200
C	12	12	12	300	3,600
					8,800

So have we now solved the problem of how a business should value its inventories? It seems that all the business has to do is to choose the lower of cost and net realisable value. This is true as far as it goes, but there is one further problem, perhaps not so easy to foresee: for a given item of inventory, **what was the cost?**

4.3 Determining the purchase cost

Inventories may be **raw materials** or components bought from suppliers, **finished goods** which have been made by the business but not yet sold, or work in the process of production, but only part-completed (this type of inventory is called **work in progress** or WIP). It will simplify matters, however, if we think about the historical cost of purchased raw materials and components, which ought to be their purchase price.

A business may be continually purchasing consignments of a particular component. As each consignment is received from suppliers they are stored in the appropriate bin or on the appropriate shelf or pallet, where they will be mingled with previous consignments. When the storekeeper issues components to production he will simply pull out from the bin the nearest components to hand, which may have arrived in the latest consignment or in an earlier consignment or in several different consignments. Our concern is to devise a pricing technique, a rule of thumb which we can use to attribute a cost to each of the components issued from stores.

There are several techniques which are used in practice.

Key terms

- **FIFO (first-in, first-out).** Using this technique, we assume that components are used in the order in which they are received from suppliers. The components issued are deemed to have formed part of the oldest consignment still unused and are costed accordingly.
- **AVCO (average cost).** As purchase prices change with each new consignment, the average price of components in the bin is constantly changed. Each component in the bin at any moment is assumed to have been purchased at the average price of all components in the bin at that moment.

If you are preparing **financial accounts** you would normally expect to use FIFO or average costs for the valuation of inventory. **IAS 2 does not permit the use of LIFO (last-in, first-out).** You should note furthermore that terms such as AVCO and FIFO refer to **pricing techniques** only. The **actual** components can be used in any order.

To illustrate the various pricing methods, the following transactions will be used in each case.

TRANSACTIONS DURING MAY 20X7

	Quantity Units	Unit cost $	Total cost $	Market value per unit on date of transactions $
Opening balance 1 May	100	2.00	200	
Receipts 3 May	400	2.10	840	2.11
Issues 4 May	200			2.11
Receipts 9 May	300	2.12	636	2.15
Issues 11 May	400			2.20
Receipts 18 May	100	2.40	240	2.35
Issues 20 May	100			2.35
Closing balance 31 May	200			2.38
			1,916	

Receipts mean goods are received into store and issues represent the issue of goods from store. The problem is to put a valuation on the following.

(a) The issues of materials
(b) The closing inventory

PART C PRACTICAL APPLICATION OF ACCOUNTING THEORY

How would issues and closing inventory be valued using each of the following in turn?

(a) FIFO
(b) AVCO

4.4 FIFO (first-in, first-out)

FIFO assumes that materials are **issued out of inventory in the order in which they were delivered into inventory**, ie issues are priced at the cost of the earliest delivery remaining in inventory.

The cost of issues and closing inventory value in the example, using FIFO, would be as follows (note that OI stands for opening inventory).

Date of issue	Quantity Units	Value issued	Cost of issues $	$
4 May	200	100 OI at $2	200	
		100 at $2.10	210	
				410
11 May	400	300 at $2.10	630	
		100 at $2.12	212	
				842
20 May	100	100 at $2.12		212
				1,464
Closing inventory value	200	100 at $2.12	212	
		100 at $2.40	240	
				452
				1,916

Note that the cost of materials issued plus the value of closing inventory equals the cost of purchases plus the value of opening inventory ($1,916).

4.5 AVCO (average cost)

There are various ways in which average costs may be used in pricing inventory issues. The most common (cumulative weighted average pricing) is illustrated below.

The **cumulative weighted average pricing method** calculates a weighted average price for all units in inventory. Issues are priced at this average cost, and the balance of inventory remaining would have the same unit valuation.

A new weighted average price is calculated whenever a new delivery of materials into store is received. This is the key feature of cumulative weighted average pricing.

In our example, issue costs and closing inventory values would be as follows.

Date	Received Units	Issued Units	Balance Units	Total inventory value $	Unit cost $	Price of issue $
Opening inventory			100	200	2.00	
3 May	400			840	2.10	
			500	1,040	2.08 *	
4 May		200		(416)	2.08 **	416
			300	624	2.08	
9 May	300			636	2.12	
			600	1,260	2.10 *	
11 May		400		(840)	2.10 **	840
			200	420	2.10	
18 May	100			240	2.40	
			300	660	2.20 *	

Date	Received Units	Issued Units	Balance Units	Total inventory value $	Unit cost $	Price of issue $
20 May		100		(220)	2.20 **	220
						1,476
Closing inventory value			200	440	2.20	440
						1,916

* A new unit cost of inventory is calculated whenever a new receipt of materials occurs.

** Whenever inventory is issued, the unit value of the items issued is the current weighted average cost per unit at the time of the issue.

For this method too, the cost of materials issued plus the value of closing inventory equals the cost of purchases plus the value of opening inventory ($1,916).

4.6 Inventory valuations and profit

In the previous descriptions of FIFO and AVCO the example used raw materials as an illustration. Each method of valuation produced different costs both of closing inventories and also of material issues. Since raw material costs affect the cost of production, and the cost of production works through eventually into the cost of sales, it follows that different methods of inventory valuation will provide different profit figures. An example may help to illustrate this point.

4.7 Example: Inventory valuations and profit

On 1 November 20X2 a company held 300 units of finished goods item No 9639 in inventory. These were valued at $12 each. During November 20X2 three batches of finished goods were received into store from the production department, as follows.

Date	Units received	Production cost per unit
10 November	400	$12.50
20 November	400	$14
25 November	400	$15

Goods sold out of inventory during November were as follows.

Date	Units sold	Sale price per unit
14 November	500	$20
21 November	500	$20
28 November	100	$20

What was the profit from selling inventory item No 9639 in November 20X2, applying the following principles of inventory valuation?

(a) FIFO
(b) AVCO (using cumulative weighted average costing)

Ignore administration, sales and distribution costs.

PART C PRACTICAL APPLICATION OF ACCOUNTING THEORY

Solution

(a) FIFO

Date	Issue costs	Issue cost Total $	Closing inventory $
14 November	300 units × $12 plus		
	200 units × $12.50	6,100	
21 November	200 units × $12.50 plus		
	300 units × $14	6,700	
28 November	100 units × $14	1,400	
Closing inventory	400 units × $15		6,000
		14,200	6,000

(b) AVCO (cumulative weighted average cost)

			Unit cost $	Balance in inventory $	Total cost of issues $	Closing inventory $
1 November	Opening inventory	300	12.000	3,600		
10 November	400		12.500	5,000		
	700		12.286	8,600		
14 November	500		12.286	6,143	6,143	
	200		12.286	2,457		
20 November	400		14.000	5,600		
	600		13.428	8,057		
21 November	500		13.428	6,714	6,714	
	100		13.428	1,343		
25 November	400		15.000	6,000		
	500		14.686	7,343		
28 November	100		14.686	1,469	1,469	
30 November	400		14.686	5,874	14,326	5,874

Summary: profit

	FIFO $	AVCO $
Opening inventory	3,600	3,600
Cost of production	16,600	16,600
	20,200	20,200
Closing inventory (deduct)	6,000	5,874
Cost of sales	14,200	14,326
Revenue (1,100 × $20)	22,000	22,000
Profit	7,800	7,674

Different inventory valuations have produced different cost of sales figures, and therefore different profits. In our example opening inventory values are the same, therefore the difference in the amount of profit under each method is the same as the difference in the valuations of closing inventory.

The profit differences are only temporary. In our example, the opening inventory in December 20X2 will be $6,000 or $5,874, depending on the inventory valuation used. Different opening inventory values will affect the cost of sales and profits in December, so that in the long run inequalities in cost of sales each month will even themselves out.

Question

FIFO

A firm has the following transactions with its product R.

Year 1
Opening inventory: nil
Buys 10 units at $300 per unit
Buys 12 units at $250 per unit
Sells 8 units at $400 per unit
Buys 6 units at $200 per unit
Sells 12 units at $400 per unit

Year 2
Buys 10 units at $200 per unit
Sells 5 units at $400 per unit
Buys 12 units at $150 per unit
Sells 25 units at $400 per unit

Required

Using FIFO, calculate the following on an item by item basis for both year 1 and year 2.

(i) The closing inventory
(ii) The sales
(iii) The cost of sales
(iv) The gross profit

Answer

Year 1

Purchases (units)	Sales (units)	Balance (units)	Inventory value $	Unit cost $	Cost of sales $	Sales $
10		10	3,000	300		
12			3,000	250		
		22	6,000			
	8		(2,400)		2,400	3,200
		14	3,600			
6			1,200	200		
		20	4,800			
	12		(3,100)*		3,100	4,800
		8	1,700		5,500	8,000

* (2 @ $300) + (10 @ $250) = $3,100

Year 2

Purchases (units)	Sales (units)	Balance (units)	Inventory value $	Unit cost $	Cost of sales $	Sales $
B/f		8	1,700			
10			2,000	200		
		18	3,700			
	5		(1,100)*		1,100	2,000
		13	2,600			

PART C PRACTICAL APPLICATION OF ACCOUNTING THEORY

Purchases (units)	Sales (units)	Balance (units)	Inventory value $	Unit cost $	Cost of sales $	Sales $
12		25	1,800	150		
			4,400			
	25		(4,400)**		4,400	10,000
		0	0		5,500	12,000

* (2 @ $250) + (3 @ $200) = $1,100
** (13 @ $200) + (12 @ $150) = $4,400

Statement of profit or loss

	FIFO $	$
Year 1		
Sales		8,000
Opening inventory	0	
Purchases	7,200	
	7,200	
Closing inventory	1,700	
Cost of sales		5,500
Gross profit		2,500
Year 2		
Sales		12,000
Opening inventory	1,700	
Purchases	3,800	
	5,500	
Closing inventory	0	
Cost of sales		5,500
Gross profit		6,500

5 IAS 2 *Inventories*

> **FAST FORWARD**
>
> Inventory should be valued at the lower of cost and net realisable value.

IAS 2 lays out the required accounting treatment for inventories (sometimes called stocks). The major area of contention is the cost **value of inventory** to be recorded. This is recognised as an asset of the enterprise until the related revenues are recognised (ie the item is sold) at which point the inventory is recognised as an expense (ie cost of sales). Part or all of the cost of inventories may also be expensed if a write-down to **net realisable value** is necessary.

In other words, the fundamental accounting assumption of **accrual** requires costs to be matched with associated revenues. In order to achieve this, costs incurred for goods which remain unsold at the year end must be carried forward in the statement of financial position and matched against future revenues.

5.1 Scope

The following items are **excluded** from the scope of the standard.

- **Financial instruments** (ie shares, bonds)
- **Biological assets** (eg agricultural and forest products)

5.2 Definitions

The standard gives the following important definitions.

Key terms

- **Inventories** are assets:
  - held for sale in the ordinary course of business;
  - in the process of production for such sale; or
  - in the form of materials or supplies to be consumed in the production process or in the rendering of services.
- **Net realisable value** is the estimated selling price in the ordinary course of business less the estimated costs of completion and the estimated costs necessary to make the sale. (IAS 2: para. 6)

Inventories can **include** any of the following.

- **Goods purchased and held for resale**, eg goods held for sale by a retailer, or land and buildings held for resale
- **Finished goods** produced
- **Work in progress** being produced
- Materials and supplies awaiting use in the production process (**raw materials**)

5.3 Measurement of inventory

The standard states that '**Inventories should be measured at the lower of cost and net realisable value**' (IAS 2: para. 9).

Exam focus point

This is a very important rule and you will be expected to apply it in the exam.

5.4 Cost of inventory

The cost of inventories will consist of all the following costs.

(a) **Purchase**
(b) **Costs of conversion**
(c) Other costs incurred in bringing the inventories to their **present location and condition**

5.4.1 Costs of purchase

The standard lists the following as comprising the costs of purchase of inventories.

(a) **Purchase price**; *plus*
(b) **Import duties** and other taxes; *plus*
(c) Transport, handling and any other cost **directly attributable** to the acquisition of finished goods, materials and services; *less*
(d) **Trade discounts**, rebates and other similar amounts.

5.4.2 Costs of conversion

Costs of conversion of inventories consist of two main parts.

(a) Costs **directly related** to the units of production, eg direct materials, direct labour.
(b) Fixed and variable **production overheads** that are incurred in converting materials into finished goods, allocated on a systematic basis.

You may have come across the terms 'fixed production overheads' or 'variable production overheads' elsewhere in your studies. The standard defines them as follows.

Key terms

- **Fixed production overheads** are those indirect costs of production that remain relatively constant regardless of the volume of production, eg the cost of factory management and administration.
- **Variable production overheads** are those indirect costs of production that vary directly, or nearly directly, with the volume of production, eg indirect materials and labour. (IAS 2: para.12)

The standard emphasises that fixed production overheads must be allocated to items of inventory on the basis of the **normal capacity of the production facilities**. This is an important point.

(a) **Normal capacity** is the expected achievable production based on the average over several periods/seasons, under normal circumstances.

(b) The above figure should take account of the capacity lost through **planned maintenance**.

(c) If it approximates to the normal level of activity then the **actual level of production** can be used.

(d) **Low production** or **idle plant** will *not* result in a higher fixed overhead allocation to each unit.

(e) **Unallocated overheads** must be recognised as an expense in the period in which they were incurred.

(f) When production is **abnormally high**, the fixed production overhead allocated to each unit will be reduced, so avoiding inventories being stated at more than cost.

(g) The allocation of variable production overheads to each unit is based on the **actual use** of production facilities.

5.4.3 Other costs

Any other costs should only be recognised if they are incurred in bringing the inventories to their **present location and condition**.

The standard lists types of cost which **would not be included** in cost of inventories. Instead, they should be recognised as an **expense** in the period they are incurred.

- **Abnormal amounts** of wasted materials, labour or other production costs
- **Storage costs** (except costs which are necessary in the production process before a further production stage)
- **Administrative overheads** not incurred to bring inventories to their present location and condition
- **Selling costs**

5.4.4 Techniques for the measurement of cost

Two techniques are mentioned by the standard, both of which produce results which **approximate to cost**, and so both of which may be used for convenience.

(a) **Standard costs** are set up to take account of normal production values: amount of raw materials used, labour time etc. They are reviewed and revised on a regular basis.

(b) **Retail method**: this is often used in the retail industry where there is a large turnover of inventory items, which nevertheless have similar profit margins. The only practical method of inventory valuation may be to take the total selling price of inventories and deduct an overall average profit margin, thus reducing the value to an approximation of cost. The percentage will take account of reduced price lines. Sometimes different percentages are applied on a departmental basis.

5.5 Cost formulas

Cost of inventories should be assigned by **specific identification** of their individual costs for:

(a) Items that are **not ordinarily interchangeable**
(b) Goods or services produced and segregated for **specific projects**

Specific costs should be attributed to individual items of inventory when they are segregated for a specific project, but not where inventories consist of a large number of interchangeable (ie identical or very similar) items. In the latter circumstance, one of **two approaches** may be taken.

The cost formula is that the cost of inventories should be assigned by using the **first-in, first-out (FIFO)** or **weighted average** cost formulas.

Under the weighted average cost method, a recalculation can be made after each purchase (as we calculated in Section 4), **or alternatively only at the period end**.

Last-in, first-out (LIFO) is not permitted under IAS 2.

Question — Inventory valuation

You are the accountant at Water Pumps Co, and you have been asked to calculate the valuation of the company's inventory at cost at its year end of 30 April 20X5.

Water Pumps manufactures a range of pumps. The pumps are assembled from components bought by Water Pumps (the company does not manufacture any parts).

The company does not use a standard costing system, and work in progress and finished goods are valued as follows.

(a) Material costs are determined from the product specification, which lists the components required to make a pump.

(b) The company produces a range of pumps. Employee's record the hours spent on assembling each type of pump, this information is input into the payroll system which prints the total hours spent each week assembling each type of pump. All employees assembling pumps are paid at the same rate and there is no overtime.

(c) Overheads are added to the inventory value in accordance with IAS 2 *Inventories*. The financial accounting records are used to determine the overhead cost, and this is applied as a percentage based on the direct labour cost.

For direct labour costs, you have agreed that the labour expended for a unit in work in progress is half that of a completed unit.

The draft accounts show the following materials and direct labour costs in inventory.

	Raw materials	Work in progress	Finished goods
Materials ($)	74,786	85,692	152,693
Direct labour ($)		13,072	46,584

The costs incurred in April, as recorded in the financial accounting records, were as follows.

	$
Direct labour	61,320
Selling costs	43,550
Depreciation and finance costs of production machines	4,490
Distribution costs	6,570
Factory manager's wage	2,560
Other production overheads	24,820
Purchasing and accounting costs relating to production	5,450
Other accounting costs	7,130
Other administration overheads	24,770

PART C PRACTICAL APPLICATION OF ACCOUNTING THEORY

For your calculations assume that all work in progress and finished goods were produced in April 20X5 and that the company was operating at a normal level of activity.

Required

Calculate the value of overheads which should be added to work in progress and finished goods in accordance with IAS 2 *Inventories*.

Note. You should include details and a description of your workings and all figures should be calculated to the nearest $.

Answer

Calculation of overheads for inventory

Production overheads are as follows.

	$
Depreciation/finance costs	4,490
Factory manager's wage	2,560
Other production overheads	24,820
Accounting/purchase costs	5,450
	37,320

Direct labour = $61,320

$\therefore$ Production overhead rate = $\dfrac{37,320}{61,320}$ = 60.86%

Inventory valuation

	Raw materials $	WIP $	Finished goods $	Total $
Materials	74,786	85,692	152,693	313,171
Direct labour	–	13,072	46,584	59,656
Production overhead (at 60.86% of labour)	–	7,956	28,351	36,307
	74,786	106,720	227,628	409,134

Variable overheads will be included in the cost of inventory.

5.6 Net realisable value (NRV)

As a general rule assets should not be carried at amounts greater than those expected to be realised from their sale or use. In the case of inventories this amount could fall below cost when items are **damaged or become obsolete**, or where the **costs to completion have increased** in order to make the sale.

In fact we can identify the principal situations in which **NRV is likely to be less than cost**.

(a) An **increase in costs to complete** or a **fall in selling price**
(b) A **physical deterioration** in the condition of inventory
(c) **Obsolescence** of products
(d) A decision as part of the company's marketing strategy to manufacture and sell products at a **loss**
(e) **Errors in production or purchasing**

A write down of inventories would normally take place on an item by item basis, but similar or related items may be **grouped together**. This grouping together is acceptable for, say, items in the same product line, but it is not acceptable to write down inventories based on a whole classification (eg finished goods) or a whole business.

The assessment of NRV should take place **at the same time** as estimates are made of selling price, using the most reliable information available. Fluctuations of price or cost should be taken into account if they relate directly to **events after the reporting period,** which confirm conditions existing at the end of the period.

The reasons why inventory is held must also be taken into account. Some inventory, for example, may be held to satisfy a firm contract and its NRV will therefore be the **contract price**. Any additional inventory of the same type held at the period end will, in contrast, be assessed according to general sales prices when NRV is estimated.

Net realisable value must be reassessed at the end of each period and compared again with cost. If the NRV has risen for inventories held over the end of more than one period, then the previous write-down must be **reversed** to the extent that the inventory is then valued at the lower of cost and the new NRV. This may be possible when selling prices have fallen in the past and then risen again.

On occasion a write-down to NRV may be of such size, incidence or nature that it must be **disclosed separately**.

5.7 Recognition as an expense

The following treatment is required **when inventories are sold**.

(a) The **carrying amount** is recognised as an expense in the period in which the related revenue is recognised.

(b) The amount of any **write-down of inventories** to NRV and all losses of inventories are recognised as an expense in the period the write-down or loss occurs.

(c) The amount of any **reversal of any write-down of inventories**, arising from an increase in NRV, is recognised as a reduction in the amount of inventories recognised as an expense in the period in which the reversal occurs.

Chapter roundup

- The **cost of goods sold** is calculated as:

    Opening inventory + purchases – closing inventory

- **Carriage inwards** is included in the cost of purchases.

    Carriage outwards is a selling expense.

- **Opening inventory** brought forward in the inventory account are **transferred to the statement of profit or loss**, and so at the end of the accounting year, the balance on the inventory account ceases to be the opening inventory value b/f, and becomes instead the closing inventory value c/f.

- The value of **closing inventory** is accounted for in the **general ledger** by debiting an inventory account and crediting the statement of profit or loss at the end of an accounting period. The inventory will therefore always have a debit balance at the end of a period, and this balance will be shown in the statement of financial position as a current asset for inventories.

- The **quantity** of inventory held at the year end is established by means of a **physical count** of inventory in an annual counting exercise, or by a 'continuous' inventory count.

- The value of inventories is calculated at the lower **cost** and **net realisable value** for each separate item or group of items. **Cost** can be arrived at by using **FIFO** (first-in, first-out) or **AVCO** (weighted average costing).

- Inventory should be valued at the lower of cost and net realisable value.

Quick quiz

1. When is an inventory account used?

2. How is closing inventory incorporated in the financial statements?
   - A DEBIT: statement of profit or loss   CREDIT: statement of financial position
   - B DEBIT: statement of financial position   CREDIT: statement of profit or loss

3. What is 'continuous' inventory counting?

4. An item of inventory was purchased for $10. However, due to a fall in demand, its selling price will be only $8. In addition further costs will be incurred prior to sale of $1. What is the net realisable value?
   - A $7
   - B $8
   - C $10
   - D $11

5. Why is inventory not valued at expected selling price?

6. When valuing inventory at historical cost, the following methods are available.
   - (i)   FIFO
   - (ii) AVCO
   - (iii) LIFO
   - (iv) Standard cost

   Which methods are allowable under IAS 2 *Inventories*?
   - A (i), (ii), (iii)
   - B (i), (ii), (iii), (iv)
   - C (i) only
   - D (i), (ii)

7. What is included in the cost of purchase of inventories according to IAS 2 *Inventories*?
   - A Purchase price less trade discount
   - B Purchase price plus transport costs less trade discount
   - C Purchase price less import duties less trade discount
   - D Purchase price plus import duties plus transport costs less trade discount

8. What type of costs should be recognised as an expense, not as part of the cost of inventory?

9. What are the most likely situations when the NRV of inventory falls below cost?

Answers to quick quiz

1. Only at the end of an accounting period.

2. B   DEBIT: Inventory in hand (statement of financial position)
   CREDIT: Closing inventory (statement of profit or loss)

3. A card is kept for every item of inventory. It shows receipts and issues, with a running total. A few inventory items are counted each day to test that the records are correct.

4. A   Net realisable value is selling price ($8) less further costs to sell ($1), ie $7.

5. Mainly because this would result in the business taking a profit before the goods have been sold.

6. D   Only FIFO and AVCO are allowed.

7. D   Purchase price plus import duties (and other taxes) plus transport costs less trade discount.

8. See Paragraph 5.4.3.

9.
   - Increase in costs to sell or a fall in selling price
   - Physical deterioration of inventory
   - Obsolescence
   - Marketing strategy
   - Errors in production or purchasing

Irrecoverable debts and allowances

Topic list	Syllabus reference
1 Irrecoverable debts	A3
2 Allowances for trade receivables	A3
3 Accounting for irrecoverable debts and trade receivables allowances	A3

Introduction

In this chapter we move even closer to our goal of preparing the financial statements. We look at two types of adjustment which need to be made in respect of credit sales.

- Irrecoverable debts
- Allowance for receivables

Important note:

In past exam papers you will see reference to 'allowance for doubtful debts'. This is now known as the 'receivables allowances' or 'allowance for receivables' and that is the terminology used in this text.

In addition, 'bad debts' are now usually referred to as 'irrecoverable debts' in accordance with IASB terminology.

PART C PRACTICAL APPLICATION OF ACCOUNTING THEORY

1 Irrecoverable debts

FAST FORWARD

Irrecoverable debts are specific debts owed to a business which it decides are never going to be paid. They are written off as an expense in the statement of profit or loss and other comprehensive income.

1.1 Introduction

Very few businesses expect to be paid immediately in cash, unless they are retail businesses on the high street. Most businesses buy and sell to one another on credit terms. This has the **benefit** of allowing businesses to keep trading without having to provide cash 'up front'. So a business will allow credit terms to customers and receive credit terms from its suppliers. Ideally a business wants to receive money from its customers as quickly as possible, but delay paying its suppliers for as long as possible. This can lead to problems.

Most businesses aim to control such problems by means of **credit control**. A customer will be given a **credit limit**, which cannot be exceeded (compare an overdraft limit or a credit card limit). If an order would take the account over its credit limit, it will not be filled until a payment is received.

Another tool in **credit control** is the **aged receivables analysis**. This shows how long invoices have been outstanding and may indicate that a customer is unable to pay. Most credit controllers will have a system of chasing up payment for long outstanding invoices.

Customers might fail to pay, perhaps out of dishonesty or because they have gone bankrupt and cannot pay. Customers in another country might be prevented from paying by the unexpected introduction of foreign exchange control restrictions by their country's government during the credit period. Therefore, the **costs** of offering credit facilities to customers can include:

(a) Interest costs of an overdraft, if customers do not pay promptly
(b) Costs of trying to obtain payment
(c) Court costs

For one reason or another, a business might decide to give up expecting payment and to write the debt off.

Key term

An **irrecoverable debt** is a debt which is not expected to be paid.

1.2 Writing off irrecoverable debts

When a business decides that a particular debt is unlikely to be paid, the amount of the debt is '**written off**' as an expense in the statement of profit or loss and other comprehensive income:

DR Irrecoverable debts
CR Trade receivables control account

Alfred's Mini-Cab Service sends an invoice for $300 to a customer who subsequently does a 'moonlight flit' from his office premises, never to be seen or heard of again. The debt of $300 must be written off. It might seem sensible to record the business transaction as:

Revenue $(300 – 300) = $0.

However, irrecoverable debts written off are accounted for as follows.

(a) **Sales** are shown at their invoice value in the **statement of profit or loss and other comprehensive income**. The sale has been made, and gross profit should be earned. The subsequent failure to collect the debt is a separate matter, which is reported in the statement of profit or loss and other comprehensive income under expenses.

(b) Irrecoverable debts written off are shown as an expense in the statement of profit or loss.

(c) The credit entry removes the trade receivable from the trade receivables account. (We also need to update the personal account in the trade receivables ledger.)

In our example of Alfred's Mini-Cab Service:

	$
Revenue (in the SPLOCI)	300
Irrecoverable debt written off (expense in the SPLOCI)	300
Net profit on this transaction	0

Obviously, when a debt is written off, the value of the receivable as a current asset falls to zero. If the debt is expected to be uncollectable, its **'net realisable value'** is nil, and so it has a zero value in the statement of financial position.

1.3 Irrecoverable debts written off and subsequently paid

An irrecoverable debt which has been written off might occasionally be unexpectedly paid. Regardless of when the payment is received, the account entries are as follows.

DR Cash account
CR Irrecoverable debts expense

For example, a statement of profit or loss and other comprehensive income for the Blacksmith's Forge for the year to 31 December 20X5 could be prepared as shown below from the following information.

	$
Inventory, 1 January 20X5	6,000
Purchases of goods	122,000
Inventory, 31 December 20X5	8,000
Cash sales	100,000
Credit sales	70,000
Irrecoverable debts written off	9,000
Debts paid in 20X5 which were previously written off as irrecoverable in 20X4	2,000
Other expenses	31,800

BLACKSMITH'S FORGE
STATEMENT OF PROFIT OR LOSS AND OTHER COMPREHENSIVE INCOME FOR THE YEAR ENDED 31.12.20X5

	$	$
Revenue		170,000
Opening inventory	6,000	
Purchases	122,000	
	128,000	
Less closing inventory	8,000	
Cost of goods sold		120,000
Gross profit		50,000
Expenses		
Irrecoverable debts written off (9,000 – 2,000)	7,000	
Other expenses	31,800	
		38,800
Net profit		11,200

PART C   PRACTICAL APPLICATION OF ACCOUNTING THEORY

2 Allowances for trade receivables

FAST FORWARD

> In addition to irrecoverable debts, a business may make an **allowance for receivables** as a precaution to account for the fact that some receivables balances might not be collectable.
>
> An increase in the allowance for trade receivables is shown as an expense in the statement of profit or loss and other comprehensive income.
>
> Trade receivables in the statement of financial position are shown **net** of any receivables allowance.

When irrecoverable debts are written off, specific debts owed to the business are identified as unlikely ever to be collected.

However, because of the risks involved in selling goods on credit, it might be accepted that a certain amount of outstanding debts at any time are unlikely to be collected. Although it might be determined that, say, 5% of debts will prove irrecoverable, the business will not know until later which specific debts are irrecoverable.

A business commences operations on 1 July 20X4, and in the 12 months to 30 June 20X5 makes sales of $300,000 (all on credit) and writes off irrecoverable debts amounting to $6,000. Cash received from customers during the year is $244,000, so that at 30 June 20X5, the business has outstanding trade receivables of $50,000.

	$
Credit sales during the year	300,000
Add trade receivables at 1 July 20X4	0
Total debts owed to the business	300,000
Less cash received from credit customers	244,000
	56,000
Less irrecoverable debts written off	6,000
Trade receivables outstanding at 30 June 20X5	50,000

Now, some of these outstanding debts might turn out to be irrecoverable. The business does not know on 30 June 20X5 which specific debts in the total $50,000 owed will be irrecoverable, but it might determine that 5% of debts will eventually be found to be irrecoverable.

When a business expects irrecoverable debts amongst its current receivables, but does not yet know which specific debts will be irrecoverable, it can make an **allowance for receivables**.

Key term

> An **allowance for trade receivables** is an **impairment** amount in relation to trade receivables that reduces the receivables asset to its **recoverable amount** in the statement of financial position. It is offset against trade receivables, which are shown at the net amount.

An allowance for trade receivables accounts for potential irrecoverable debts, as a precaution by the business. The business will be more likely to avoid claiming profits which subsequently fail to materialise because some debts turn out to be irrecoverable.

(a) When an allowance is first made, the amount of this initial allowance is charged as an expense in the statement of profit or loss and other comprehensive income, in the period in which the allowance is created.

(b) When an allowance already exists, but is subsequently increased in size, the amount of the **increase** in allowance is charged as an **expense** in the statement of profit or loss and other comprehensive income in the period in which the increased allowance is made.

(c) When an allowance already exists, but is subsequently reduced in size, the amount of the **decrease** in allowance is credited back to the statement of profit or loss and other comprehensive income for the period in which the reduction in allowance is made.

14: IRRECOVERABLE DEBTS AND ALLOWANCES

Exam focus point

> In an exam you may well be required to calculate the increase or decrease in the allowance for trade receivables.

The statement of financial position, as well as the statement of profit or loss and other comprehensive income of a business, must be adjusted to show the allowance.

Important!

> The value of trade accounts receivable in the statement of financial position must be shown after deducting the allowance for trade receivables.

This is because the net realisable value of all the receivables of the business is estimated to be less than their 'sales value'. After all, this is the reason for making the allowance in the first place. The net realisable value of trade accounts receivable is the total value of receivables minus the receivables allowance.

In the example above the newly created allowance for trade receivables at 30 June 20X5 will be 5% of $50,000 = $2,500. This means that although total trade accounts receivable are $50,000, eventual payment of only $47,500 is expected.

(a) In the statement of profit or loss and other comprehensive income, the newly created allowance of $2,500 will be shown as an expense.

(b) In the statement of financial position, trade accounts receivable will be shown as:

	$
Total trade receivables at 30 June 20X5	50,000
Less allowance for receivables	2,500
	47,500

2.1 Example: Allowance for trade receivables

Corin Flakes owns and runs the Aerobic Health Foods Shop in Dundee. He commenced trading on 1 January 20X1, selling health foods to customers, most of whom make use of a credit facility that Corin offers. (Customers are allowed to purchase up to $200 of goods on credit but must repay a certain proportion of their outstanding debt every month.)

This credit system gives rise to a large number of irrecoverable debts, and Corin Flake's results for his first three years of operations are as follows.

Year to 31 December 20X1
Gross profit	$27,000
Irrecoverable debts written off	$8,000
Debts owed by customers as at 31 December 20X1	$40,000
Allowance for trade receivables	2.5% of outstanding receivables
Other expenses	$20,000

Year to 31 December 20X2
Gross profit	$45,000
Irrecoverable debts written off	$10,000
Debts owed by customers as at 31 December 20X2	$50,000
Allowance for trade receivables	2.5% of outstanding receivables
Other expenses	$28,750

Year to 31 December 20X3
Gross profit	$60,000
Irrecoverable debts written off	$11,000
Debts owed by customers as at 31 December 20X3	$30,000
Allowance for trade receivables	3% of outstanding receivables
Other expenses	$32,850

PART C PRACTICAL APPLICATION OF ACCOUNTING THEORY

Required

For each of these three years, prepare the statement of profit or loss and other comprehensive income of the business, and state the value of trade accounts receivable appearing in the statement of financial position as at 31 December.

Solution

AEROBIC HEALTH FOODS SHOP
STATEMENT OF PROFIT OR LOSS AND OTHER COMPREHENSIVE INCOME
FOR THE YEARS ENDED 31 DECEMBER

	20X1		20X2		20X3	
	$	$	$	$	$	$
Gross profit		27,000		45,000		60,000
Expenses:						
Irrecoverable debts written off	8,000		10,000		11,000	
Increase/decrease in allowance for receivables*	1,000		250		(350)	
Other expenses	20,000		28,750		32,850	
		29,000		39,000		43,500
Net (loss)/profit		(2,000)		6,000		16,500

* At 1 January 20X1 when Corin began trading the allowance for receivables was nil. At 31 December 20X1 the allowance required was 2½% of $40,000 = $1,000. The increase in the allowance is therefore $1,000. At 31 December 20X2 the allowance required was 2½% of $50,000 = $1,250. The 20X1 allowance must therefore be increased by $250. At 31 December 20X3 the allowance required is 3% × $30,000 = $900. The 20X2 allowance is therefore reduced by $350.

VALUE OF TRADE ACCOUNTS RECEIVABLE IN THE STATEMENT OF FINANCIAL POSITION

	As at 31.12.20X1	As at 31.12.20X2	As at 31.12.20X3
	$	$	$
Total value of trade receivables	40,000	50,000	30,000
Less allowance for trade receivables	1,000	1,250	900
Statement of financial position value	39,000	48,750	29,100

You should now try to use what you have learned to attempt a solution to the following exercise, which involves preparing a statement of profit or loss and other comprehensive income and statement of financial position.

Question Newbegin Tools

The financial affairs of Newbegin Tools prior to the commencement of trading were as follows.

NEWBEGIN TOOLS
STATEMENT OF FINANCIAL POSITION AS AT 1 AUGUST 20X5

	$	$
Assets		
Non-current assets		
Motor vehicle	2,000	
Shop fittings	3,000	
		5,000
Current assets		
Inventory	12,000	
Cash	1,000	
		13,000
		18,000

		$	$
Equity and liabilities			
Equity			12,000
Current liabilities			
Bank overdraft		2,000	
Trade payables		4,000	
			6,000
Total capital and liabilities			18,000

At the end of six months trading the business had made the following transactions.

(a) Goods were purchased on credit at a gross amount of $10,000.

(b) Closing inventory was valued at $5,450.

(c) Cash sales and credit sales together totalled $27,250.

(d) Outstanding trade receivables balance at 31 January 20X6 amounted to $3,250 of which $250 were to be written off.

(e) An allowance for trade receivables is to be made amounting to 2% of the remaining outstanding receivables.

(f) Cash payments were made in respect of the following expenses.

		$
(i)	Stationery, postage and wrapping	500
(ii)	Telephone charges	200
(iii)	Electricity	600
(iv)	Cleaning and refreshments	150
(v)	Suppliers	8,000

(g) Cash drawings by the proprietor, Alf Newbegin, amounted to $6,000.

(h) The outstanding overdraft balance as at 1 August 20X5 was paid off. Interest charges and bank charges on the overdraft amounted to $40.

Alf Newbegin knew the balance of cash on hand at 31 January 20X6 but he wanted to know if the business had made a profit for the six months that it had been trading, and so he asked his friend, Harry Oldhand, if he could tell him.

Prepare the statement of profit or loss and other comprehensive income of Newbegin Tools for the six months to 31 January 20X6 and a statement of financial position as at that date.

Answer

The statement of profit or loss and other comprehensive income should be fairly straightforward.

NEWBEGIN TOOLS
STATEMENT OF PROFIT OR LOSS AND OTHER COMPREHENSIVE INCOME
FOR THE SIX MONTHS ENDED 31 JANUARY 20X6

	$	$
Revenue		27,250
Opening inventory	12,000	
Purchases	10,000	
	22,000	
Less closing inventory	5,450	
Cost of goods sold		16,650
Gross profit		10,700

PART C PRACTICAL APPLICATION OF ACCOUNTING THEORY

	$	$
Electricity (note 1)	600	
Stationery, postage and wrapping	500	
Irrecoverable debts written off	250	
Allowance for receivables (note 2)	60	
Telephone charges	200	
Cleaning and refreshments	150	
Interest and bank charges	40	
		1,800
Net profit		8,900

Notes

1 Expenses are grouped into sales and distribution expenses (here assumed to be electricity, stationery, postage and wrapping, irrecoverable debts and allowance for trade receivables) administration expenses (here assumed to be telephone charges and cleaning) and finance charges.

2 2% of $3,000 = $60.

The preparation of a statement of financial position is not so easy, because we must calculate the value of trade payables and cash in hand.

(a) **Trade payables as at 31 January 20X6**

The amount owing on trade accounts is the sum of the amount owing at the beginning of the period, plus the cost of purchases during the period (net of all discounts), less the payments already made for purchases. If you think carefully about this, you might see that this calculation is logical. What is still owed is the total amount of costs incurred less payments already made.

	$
Trade payables as at 1 August 20X5	4,000
Add purchases during the period	10,000
	14,000
Less payments to suppliers accounts during the period	(8,000)
	6,000

(b) **Cash at bank and in hand at 31 January 20X6**

This too requires a fairly lengthy calculation. You need to identify cash payments received and cash payments made.

(i) Cash received from sales

	$
Total sales in the period	27,250
Add trade receivables as at 1 August 20X5	0
	27,250
Less unpaid debts as at 31 January 20X6	3,250
Cash received	24,000

(ii) Cash paid

	$
Trade payables	8,000
Stationery, postage and wrapping	500
Telephone charges	200
Electricity	600
Cleaning and refreshments	150
Bank charges and interest	40
Bank overdraft repaid	2,000
Drawings by proprietor	6,000
	17,490

Note. It is easy to forget some of these payments, especially drawings.

			$
(iii)	Cash in hand at 1 August 20X5		1,000
	Cash received in the period		24,000
			25,000
	Cash paid in the period		(17,490)
	Cash at bank and in hand as at 31 January 20X6		7,510

(c) When irrecoverable debts are written off, the value of outstanding trade receivables must be reduced by the amount written off. This is because the customers are no longer expected to pay, and it would be misleading to show them in the statement of financial position as current assets of the business for which cash payment is expected within one year. Trade receivables will be valued at $3,000 less the allowance for receivables of $60 – ie at $2,940.

NEWBEGIN TOOLS
STATEMENT OF FINANCIAL POSITION AS AT 31 JANUARY 20X6

	$	$
Assets		
Non-current assets		
Motor vehicles	2,000	
Shop fittings	3,000	
		5,000
Current assets		
Inventory	5,450	
Trade receivables	2,940	
Cash and bank	7,510	
		15,900
		20,900
Equity and liabilities		
Equity		
Capital at 1 August 20X5	12,000	
Net profit for the period	8,900	
Less drawings	(6,000)	
Capital at 31 January 20X6		14,900
Current liabilities		
Trade payables		6,000
Total capital and liabilities		20,900

The bank overdraft has now been repaid and is therefore not shown.

3 Accounting for irrecoverable debts and trade receivables allowances

3.1 Irrecoverable debts written off: Ledger accounting entries

For irrecoverable debts written off, there is an irrecoverable debts account. The double-entry bookkeeping is fairly straightforward, but there are two separate transactions to record.

(a) When it is decided that a particular debt will not be paid, the customer is no longer called an outstanding receivable, and becomes an irrecoverable debt.

DEBIT   Irrecoverable debts account (expense)
CREDIT Trade receivables

PART C PRACTICAL APPLICATION OF ACCOUNTING THEORY

(b) At the end of the accounting period, the balance on the irrecoverable debts account is transferred to the statement of profit or loss and other comprehensive income (SPLOCI) ledger account (like all other expense accounts).

DEBIT   SPLOCI account
CREDIT Irrecoverable debts account

However, where an irrecoverable debt is subsequently recovered, the accounting entries will be as follows.

DEBIT   Cash account
CREDIT Irrecoverable debts account (expense)

3.2 Example: Irrecoverable debts written off

At 1 October 20X5 a business had total outstanding debts of $8,600. During the year to 30 September 20X6 the following transaction took place.

(a) Credit sales amounted to $44,000.

(b) Payments from various customers (accounts receivable) amounted to $49,000.

(c) Two debts, for $180 and $420, were declared irrecoverable and the customers are no longer purchasing goods from the company. These are to be written off.

Required

Prepare the trade receivables account and the irrecoverable debts account for the year.

Solution

TRADE RECEIVABLES

	$		$
Opening balance b/f	8,600	Cash	49,000
Revenue	44,000	Irrecoverable debts	180
		Irrecoverable debts	420
		Closing balance c/d	3,000
	52,600		52,600
Opening balance b/d	3,000		

IRRECOVERABLE DEBTS

	$		$
Trade receivables	180	SPL a/c: irrecoverable debts written off	600
Trade receivables	420		
	600		600

In the trade receivables ledger, personal accounts of the customers whose debts are irrecoverable will be taken off the ledger. The business should then take steps to ensure that it does not sell goods on credit to those customers again.

3.3 Allowance for trade receivables: Ledger accounting entries

FAST FORWARD

Only **the movement** on the trade receivables allowance is debited or credited to irrecoverable debts in the statement of profit or loss and other comprehensive income.

A business might determine that 2% of trade receivables balances are unlikely to be collected, ie doubtful debts. Since they are doubtful debts rather than irrecoverable, it would not be appropriate to write off any individual customer balances as irrecoverable debts. The procedure is then to leave the total trade receivables balance completely untouched, but to open up an allowance account by the following entries:

DEBIT   Irrecoverable debts account (expense in SPLOCI)
CREDIT   Allowance for receivables

Important!

When preparing a statement of financial position, the credit balance on the allowance account is deducted from the total debit balances in the receivables ledger.

In subsequent years, adjustments may be needed to the amount of the allowance. The procedure to be followed then is as follows.

(a) Calculate the new allowance required.

(b) Compare it with the existing balance on the allowance account (ie the balance b/f from the previous accounting period).

(c) Calculate increase or decrease required.

   (i) If a higher allowance is required now:

      CREDIT   Allowance for receivables
      DEBIT   Irrecoverable debts expense

      with the amount of the increase.

   (ii) If a lower allowance is needed now than before:

      DEBIT   Allowance for receivables
      CREDIT   Irrecoverable debts expense

      with the amount of the decrease.

3.4 Example: Accounting entries for allowance for receivables

Alex Gullible has total receivables outstanding at 31 December 20X2 of $28,000. He determines that about 1% of these balances will not be collected and wishes to make an appropriate allowance. Before now, he has not made any allowance for receivables.

On 31 December 20X3 his trade receivables amount to $40,000. He reviews the allowance for receivables and determines that the allowance should be adjusted to 5% of trade receivables.

What accounting entries should Alex make on 31 December 20X2 and 31 December 20X3, and what figures for trade receivables will appear in his statements of financial position as at those dates?

Solution

At 31 December 20X2

Allowance required = 1% × $28,000
                             = $280

Alex will make the following entries:

DEBIT	Irrecoverable debts expense	$280
CREDIT	Allowance for receivables	$280

PART C PRACTICAL APPLICATION OF ACCOUNTING THEORY

Trade receivables will appear as follows under current assets.

	$
Trade receivables ledger balances	28,000
Less allowance for trade receivables	280
	27,720

At 31 December 20X3

Following the procedure described above, Alex will calculate as follows.

	$
Allowance required now (5% × $40,000)	2,000
Existing allowance	(280)
∴ Additional allowance required	1,720

He will make the following entries:

DEBIT	Irrecoverable debts expense	$1,720	
CREDIT	Allowance for receivables		$1,720

The allowance account will by now appear as follows.

ALLOWANCE FOR RECEIVABLES

20X2		$	20X2		$
31 Dec	Balance c/d	280	31 Dec	SPL account	280
20X3			20X3		
31 Dec	Balance c/d	2,000	1 Jan	Balance b/d	280
			31 Dec	SPL account	1,720
		2,000			2,000
			20X4		
			1 Jan	Balance b/d	2,000

Trade receivables will be valued as follows.

	$
Trade receivables ledger balances	40,000
Less allowance for receivables	2,000
	38,000

In practice, it is unnecessary to show the total receivables balances and the allowance as separate items in the statement of financial position. Normally it shows only the net figure ($27,720 in 20X2, $38,000 in 20X3).

Now try the following question on allowance for receivables for yourself.

Question — Receivables allowance

Horace Goodrunning fears that his business will suffer an increase in defaulting receivables in the future and so he determines that an allowance for receivables should be made of 2% of outstanding trade receivables at the reporting date from 28 February 20X6. On 28 February 20X8, Horace reviews the allowance and determines that the allowance should be adjusted to 1% of outstanding trade receivables. Outstanding receivables balances at the various reporting dates are as follows.

	$
28.2.20X6	15,200
28.2.20X7	17,100
28.2.20X8	21,400

You are required to show extracts from the following accounts for each of the three years above.

(a) Trade receivables
(b) Allowance for trade receivables
(c) Statement of profit or loss

Show how trade receivables would appear in the statement of financial position at the end of each year.

Answer

The entries for the three years are denoted by (a), (b) and (c) in each account.

TRADE ACCOUNTS RECEIVABLE (EXTRACT)

			$
(a)	28.2.20X6	Balance	15,200
(b)	28.2.20X7	Balance	17,100
(c)	28.2.20X8	Balance	21,400

ALLOWANCE FOR RECEIVABLES

			$				$
(a)	28.2.20X6	Balance c/d (2% of 15,200)	304	28.2.20X6	P/L account		304
			304				304
(b)	28.2.20X7	Balance c/d (2% of 17,100)	342	1.3.20X6	Balance b/d		304
				28.2.20X7	P/L account (note 1)		38
			342				342
(c)	28.2.20X8	P/L account (note 2)	128	1.3.20X7	Balance b/d		342
	28.2.20X8	Balance c/d (1% of 21,400)	214				
			342				342
				1.3.20X8	Balance b/d		214

PROFIT OR LOSS (EXTRACT)

		$			$
28.2.20X6	Allowance for receivables	304			
28.2.20X7	Allowance for receivables	38			
			28.2.20X8	Allowance for receivables	128

Notes

1. The increase in the allowance is $(342 – 304) = $38
2. The decrease in the allowance is $(342 – 214) = $128
3. We calculate the net receivables figure for inclusion in the statement of financial position as follows.

	20X6	20X7	20X8
	$	$	$
Current assets			
Trade accounts receivable	15,200	17,100	21,400
Less allowance for receivables	304	342	214
	14,896	16,758	21,186

Exam focus point

There may well be a question on irrecoverable debts and the allowance for receivables in the exam. The examiners have commented that this was one of the areas that have been answered particularly badly in the past. Work through the question shown below to practise the correct technique.

3.5 Example: Combined entries

Fatima's receivables at 31 May 20X7 were $723,800. The balance on the allowance for trade receivables account at 1 June 20X6 was $15,250. At 31 May 20X7, Fatima reviewed the trade receivables allowance and determined that the allowance should be adjusted to 1.5% of receivables.

PART C PRACTICAL APPLICATION OF ACCOUNTING THEORY

On 14 May 20X7 Fatima received $540 in final settlement of an amount written off during the year ended 31 May 20X6.

What total amount should be recognised for receivables in the statement of profit or loss and other comprehensive income for the year ended 31 May 20X7?

The exam question gave four options for 2 marks. However we will concentrate on calculating the correct answer.

Solution

First, note the requirement's wording 'recognised for trade receivables in the statement of profit or loss and other comprehensive income'. This means that the examiner wants to know the total charge (or recovery) in respect of irrecoverable debts and the allowance for receivables.

Second, consider the allowance for receivables.

	$
Closing allowance required (723,800 × 1.5%)	10,857
Opening allowance	(15,250)
Adjustment needed	(4,393)

Third, the amount received of $540 had already been written off the previous year and now needs to be credited to irrecoverable debts.

Total credit to SPLOCI = $540 + $4,393

= $4,933

Chapter roundup

- Irrecoverable debts are specific debts owed to a business which it decides are never going to be paid. They are written off as an expense in the statement of profit or loss and other comprehensive income.

- In addition to irrecoverable debts, a business may make an **allowance for receivables** as a precaution to account for the fact that some receivables balances might not be collectable.

  An increase in the allowance for receivables is shown as an expense in the statement of profit or loss and other comprehensive income.

  Trade receivables in the statement of financial position are shown **net** of any receivables allowance.

- Only **movement** on the receivables allowance is debited or credited to irrecoverable debts in the statement of profit or loss and other comprehensive income.

Quick quiz

1. An irrecoverable debt arises in which of the following situations?
   - A   A customer pays part of the account
   - B   An invoice is in dispute
   - C   The customer goes bankrupt
   - D   The invoice is not yet due for payment

2. Irrecoverable debts are $5,000. Excluding this amount, trade receivables at the year end are $120,000. If an allowance for receivables of 5% is required, what is the entry for irrecoverable debts and allowance for receivables in the statement of profit or loss and other comprehensive income?
   - A $5,000
   - B $11,000
   - C $6,000
   - D $10,750

3. An allowance for receivables of 2% is required. Trade receivables at the period end are $200,000 and the allowable for receivables brought forward from the previous period is $2,000. What movement is required this year?
   - A   Increase by $4,000
   - B   Decrease by $4,000
   - C   Increase by $2,000
   - D   Decrease by $2,000

4. If a receivables allowance is increased, what is the effect on the statement of profit or loss and other comprehensive income?
   - A   Reduction in expenses
   - B   Increase in expenses

5. What is the double entry to record an irrecoverable debt written off?
   - A   DEBIT: expenses   CREDIT: trade receivables
   - B   DEBIT: trade receivables   CREDIT: expenses

Answers to quick quiz

1. C
2. B $5,000 + (5% × $120,000).
3. C   2% of $200,000 = $4,000. Therefore the allowable needs to be increased by $2,000.
4. B   The increase in the allowance is charged as an expense in the statement of profit or loss and other comprehensive income.
5. A   DEBIT: Irrecoverable debts account (expenses)
            CREDIT: Trade receivables

Provisions and contingencies

Topic list	Syllabus reference
1 Provisions and contingencies (IAS 37)	A3

Introduction

You are required here to consider accounting issues which are the subject of an international accounting standard (IAS 37).

IAS 37 *Provisions, Contingent Liabilities and Contingent Assets* is important standard that you will meet again later in your studies. At this stage, you need to understand the basic definitions and whether an item needs to be disclosed in the financial statements.

PART C PRACTICAL APPLICATION OF ACCOUNTING THEORY

Exam focus point

Provisions are one of the areas consistently answered badly in the exam, so make sure you study this chapter closely.

1 Provisions and contingencies (IAS 37)

1.1 Provisions

FAST FORWARD

A **provision** should be recognised:

- When an entity has incurred a **present obligation**
- When it is **probable** that a **transfer of economic benefits** will be required to settle it
- When a **reliable estimate** can be made of the amount involved

IAS 37 views a provision as a liability.

Key terms

A **provision** is a **liability** of uncertain timing or amount.

A **liability** is a present obligation of the entity arising from past events, the settlement of which is expected to result in an outflow from the entity of resources embodying economic benefits.

(IAS 37: para. 10)

Note that the IAS 37 definition of a liability in IAS 37 was not revised when the *Conceptual Framework* was revised in 2018.

IAS 37 distinguishes provisions from other liabilities such as trade payables and accruals. This is on the basis that for a provision there is **uncertainty** about the timing or amount of the future expenditure. Whilst uncertainty is clearly present in the case of certain accruals the uncertainty is generally much less than for provisions.

A provision is made for something which will **probably** happen. It should be recognised when there is a present obligation as a result of a past event, when it is probable that a transfer of economic events will take place and when its amount can be estimated reliably.

A provision is accounted for as follows:

DEBIT   Expense account (SPLOCI)
CREDIT   Provision account (SOFP)

1.2 Example of provisions

A business has been told by its lawyers that it is likely to have to pay $10,000 damages for a product that failed. The business duly set up a provision at 31 December 20X7. However, the following year, the lawyers found that damages were more likely to be $50,000. How is the provision treated in the accounts at:

(a) 31 December 20X7?
(b) 31 December 20X8?

Solution

(a) The business needs to set up a provision as follows:

DEBIT   Damages (SPLOCI) $10,000
CREDIT   Provision (SOFP) $10,000

EXTRACT FROM STATEMENT OF PROFIT OR LOSS AND OTHER COMPREHENSIVE INCOME

	$
Expenses	
Provision for damages	10,000

EXTRACT FROM STATEMENT OF FINANCIAL POSITION

	$
Non-current liabilities	
Provision for damages	10,000

(b) The business needs to increase the provision.

DEBIT	Damages (SPLOCI)	$40,000	
CREDIT	Provision (SOFP)		$40,000

Do not forget that the provision account has already got a balance brought forward of $10,000, so that we only need to account for the **increase** in the provision.

EXTRACT FROM STATEMENT OF PROFIT OR LOSS AND OTHER COMPREHENSIVE INCOME

	$
Expenses	
Provision for damages	40,000

EXTRACT FROM STATEMENT OF FINANCIAL POSITION

	$
Non-current liabilities	
Provision for damages (10,000 + 40,000)	50,000

1.3 Legal or constructive obligation

A provision is set up when there is a legal or constructive obligation. This means that the business is obliged to pay an amount as a result of this obligation. Examples include warranties, guarantees and sales returns.

Warranties are given on new items, for example cars, promising that they will be repaired free of charge if something goes wrong during an initial period of ownership, for example two years. Extended warranties may be granted on payment of a premium.

Guarantees may be given to a bank to help another company in a group to obtain a loan.

Sales returns may arise on a regular basis and it may be prudent to make a provision to cover these.

1.4 Example of sales returns

Apple Co has noticed that sales returns average 5% of sales during a year. It has decided to make a provision for these sales returns. During the year ended 30 April 20X8, sales are $500,000 and sales for the year ended 30 April 20X9 are projected to be $750,000. Set up a provision as at 30 April 20X8.

Solution

The provision is to be set up to meet **future** liabilities. It is likely that any returns for the year ended 30 April 20X8 have already been made. Therefore the provision must be based on projected sales for the following year ie 5% × $750,000 ($37,500).

1.5 Contingent liabilities

An entity **should not recognise a contingent asset or liability** but they **should be disclosed in certain circumstances**.

Contingent liabilities are defined as follows.

Key term

IAS 37 defines a **contingent liability** as:

- A possible obligation that arises from past events and whose existence will be confirmed only by the occurrence or non-occurrence of one or more uncertain future events not wholly within the control of the entity; or
- A present obligation that arises from past events but is not recognised because:
  - It is not probable that a transfer of resources embodying economic benefits will be required to settle the obligation; or
  - The amount of the obligation cannot be measured with sufficient reliability.

(IAS 37: para.10)

As a rule of thumb, probable means more than 50% likely. **If an obligation is probable, it is not a contingent liability** – instead, a **provision is needed**.

1.6 Treatment of contingent liabilities

Contingent liabilities **should not be recognised in financial statements** but they **should be disclosed unless an outflow of resources is remote**.

1.6.1 Disclosure: Contingent liabilities

Where a transfer of resources in relation to a material contingent liability is not likely to be remote, disclose:

- A description of the nature of the contingent liability
- An estimate of their **financial effect**
- An indication of the **uncertainties** that exist
- The possibility of any **reimbursement**

1.7 Contingent assets

Key term

IAS 37 defines a **contingent asset** as:

A possible asset that arises from past events and whose existence will be confirmed only by the occurrence or non-occurrence of one or more uncertain future events not wholly within the control of the entity.

(IAS 37: para.10)

A contingent asset must not be recognised. Only when the realisation of the related economic benefits is **virtually certain** should recognition take place. At that point, **the asset is no longer a contingent asset**!

Contingent assets must be disclosed in the notes if they are **probable**.

1.7.1 Disclosure: Contingent assets

A brief description of a probable contingent asset should be provided along with an estimate of its likely financial effect.

15: PROVISIONS AND CONTINGENCIES

You must practise the questions below to get the hang of the IAS 37 rules on contingencies. But first, study the flow chart, taken from the IAS 37 implementation guidance, which is a good summary of its requirements.

Exam focus point

If you learn this flow chart you should be able to deal with most questions you are likely to meet in an exam.

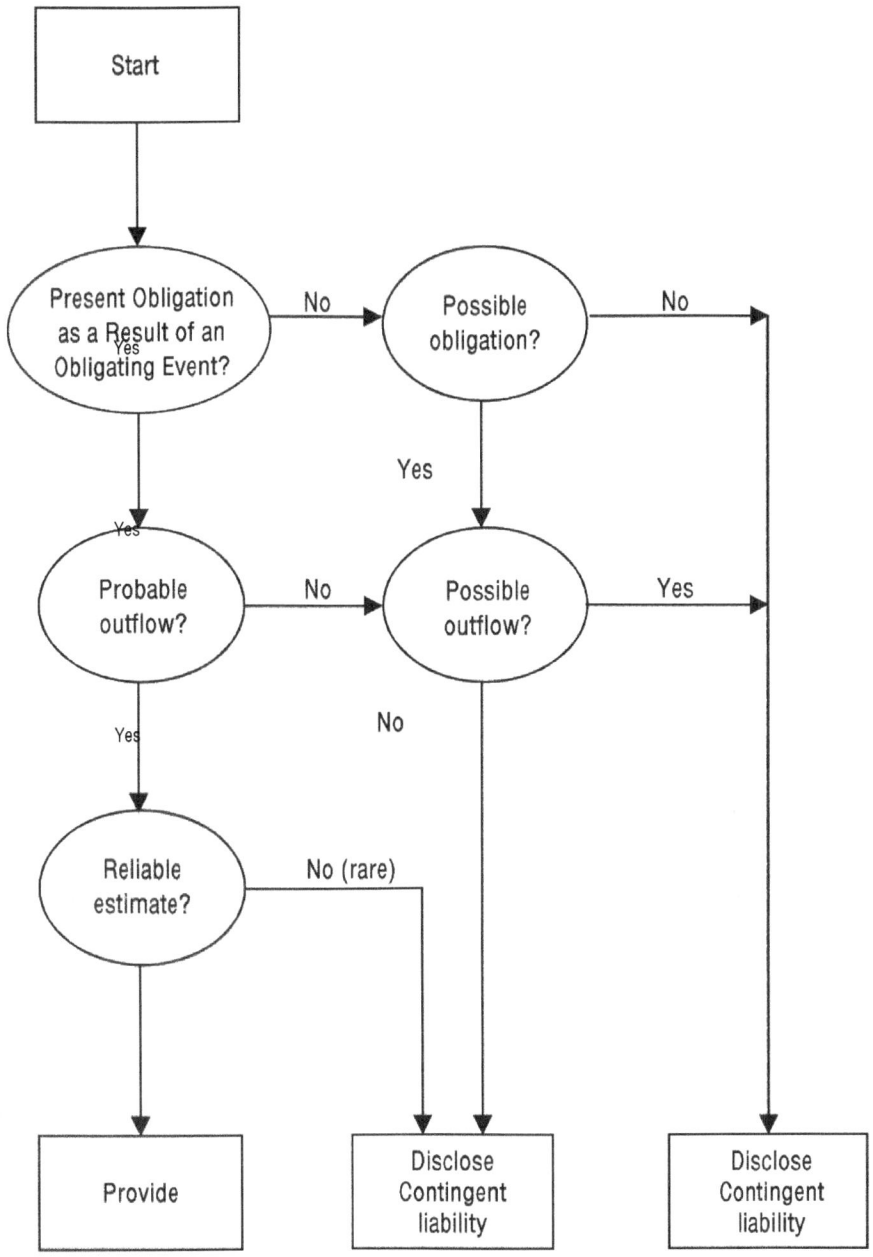

Question

Contingencies 1

During 20X9 Smock Co gives a guarantee of certain borrowings of Penny Co, whose financial condition at that time is sound. During 20Y0, the financial condition of Penny Co deteriorates and at 30 June 20Y0 Penny Co files for protection from its creditors.

What accounting treatment is required:

(a) At 31 December 20X9?
(b) At 31 December 20Y0?

Answer

(a) At 31 December 20X9

There is a present obligation as a result of a past obligating event. The obligating event is the giving of the guarantee, which gives rise to a legal obligation. However, at 31 December 20X9 no transfer of economic benefits is probable in settlement of the obligation.

No provision is recognised. The guarantee is disclosed as a contingent liability unless the probability of any transfer is regarded as remote.

An appropriate note to the accounts would be as follows.

Contingent liability

The company has given a guarantee in respect of the bank borrowings (currently $500,000) of Penny Co. At the reporting date, Penny Co was sound and it is unlikely that the company will be required to fulfil its guarantee.

(b) At 31 December 20Y0

As above, there is a present obligation as a result of a past obligating event, namely the giving of the guarantee.

At 31 December 20Y0 it is probable that a transfer of economic events will be required to settle the obligation. A provision is therefore recognised for the best estimate of the obligation.

Question   Contingencies 2

After a wedding in 20X0 ten people died, possibly as a result of food poisoning from products sold by Callow Co. Legal proceedings are started seeking damages from Callow but it disputes liability. Up to the date of approval of the financial statements for the year to 31 December 20X0, Callow's lawyers advise that it is probable that it will not be found liable. However, when Callow prepares the financial statements for the year to 31 December 20X1 its lawyers advise that, owing to developments in the case, it is probable that it will be found liable.

What is the required accounting treatment:

(a) At 31 December 20X0?
(b) At 31 December 20X1?

Answer

(a) At 31 December 20X0

On the basis of the evidence available when the financial statements were approved, there is no obligation as a result of past events. No provision is recognised. The matter is disclosed as a contingent liability unless the probability of any transfer is regarded as remote.

(b) At 31 December 20X1

On the basis of the evidence available, there is a present obligation. A transfer of economic benefits in settlement is probable and a provision is required assuming the liability can be measured reliably.

Question — Contingencies 3

An oil company causes environmental contamination in the course of its operations, but cleans up only when required to do so under the laws of the country in which it is operating. One country in which it has been operating for several years has up to now had no legislation requiring cleaning up. However, there is now an environmental lobby in this country. At the date of the company's year end, it is virtually certain that a draft law requiring clean up of contaminated land will be enacted very shortly. The oil company will then be obliged to deal with the contamination it has caused over the past several years.

What accounting treatment is required at the year end?

Answer

At the year end there is a **present obligation** as a result of a **past obligating event**. Because the passage of the Act is 'virtually certain', the past contamination becomes an obligating event. It is highly probable that an **outflow of economic resources** will be required to settle this. A provision should therefore be made of the best estimate of the costs involved.

PART C   PRACTICAL APPLICATION OF ACCOUNTING THEORY

Chapter roundup

- A **provision** should be recognised:
    - When an entity has incurred a **present obligation**
    - When it is **probable** that a **transfer of economic benefits** will be required to settle it
    - When a **reliable estimate** can be made of the amount involved
- An entity **should not recognise a contingent asset or liability** but they **should be disclosed in certain circumstances.**

Quick quiz

1   A company is being sued for $10,000 by a customer. The company's lawyers reckon that it is likely that the claim will be upheld. Legal fees are currently $5,000.
    How should the company account for this?
    A   Provision
    B   Contingent liability

2   Given the facts in 1 above, how much of a provision should be made if further legal fees of $2,000 are likely to be incurred?
    A $10,000
    B $5,000
    C $15,000
    D $12,000

3   A company has a provision for warranty claims b/f of $50,000. It does a review and decides that the provision needed in future should be $45,000. What is the effect on the financial statements?

	SPLOCI	Statement of financial position
A	Increase expenses by $5,000	Provision $50,000
B	Increases expenses by $5,000	Provision $45,000
C	Decrease expenses by $5,000	Provision $50,000
D	Decrease expenses by $5,000	Provision $45,000

4   A contingent liability is always disclosed on the face of the statement of financial position.
    Is this statement:
    A   True
    B   False

5   How does a company account for a contingent asset that is not probable?
    A   By way of note
    B   As an asset in the statement of financial position
    C   It does nothing

Answers to quick quiz

1. A
2. D The legal fees incurred to date of $5,000 is a current liability and should already be included in the accounts. The provision is for the claim of $10,000 plus the additional legal fees of $2,000.
3. D

PROVISION ACCOUNT

	$		$
P/L account	5,000	Bal b/f	50,000
Bal c/f	45,000		
	50,000		50,000

Note. We are debiting provision account $5,000 and so crediting the statement of profit or loss and other comprehensive income $5,000. Therefore, we are **decreasing** expenses.

4. B False. A contingent liability is disclosed by way of notes to the statements.
5. C

PART C PRACTICAL APPLICATION OF ACCOUNTING THEORY

Tangible non-current assets

Topic list	Syllabus reference
1 Capital and revenue expenditure	A3
2 Depreciation accounting	A3
3 Depreciation: the mechanics	A3
4 Revaluation of non-current assets	A3
5 Non-current asset disposals	A3
6 IAS 16 *Property, Plant and Equipment*	A3
7 The asset register	A3
8 Worked example	A3

Introduction

We start by looking at capital and revenue expenditure and the distinction between **non-current and current assets**, a non-current asset being one bought for ongoing use in the business.

Non-current assets might be held and used by a business for a number of years, but they **wear out** or lose their usefulness in the course of time. Every tangible non-current asset has a limited life; the only exception is land.

The accounts of a business try to recognise that the cost of a non-current asset is gradually consumed as the asset wears out. This is done by gradually **writing off the asset's cost in the statement of profit or loss and other comprehensive income over several accounting periods**. For example, in the case of a machine costing $1,000 and expected to wear out after ten years, it might be appropriate to reduce the value by $100 each year. This process is known as **depreciation**. We will look at the definitions, before going on to the mechanics in Sections 2 and 3.

Occasionally, particularly in the case of land or buildings, the market value of a non-current asset will rise with time. The asset may then be **revalued**. The accounting treatment of revaluations and the effect on depreciation are considered in Section 4. Section 5 deals with disposals of non-current assets. A profit may arise on the sale of a non-current asset if too much depreciation has been charged.

The main categories of non-current tangible assets are governed by IAS 16 *Property, Plant and Equipment*, which codifies much of the information in Sections 2, 4 and 5. In particular see the disclosure requirements on revaluations in Section 6.9.

Non-current assets need to be controlled, as they are usually valuable. One way of doing this is by an **asset register**. This is looked at in Section 7. We bring everything together in a worked example on the **final accounts for a sole trader** in Section 8.

PART C PRACTICAL APPLICATION OF ACCOUNTING THEORY

1 Capital and revenue expenditure

FAST FORWARD

Capital expenditure is expenditure which results in the **acquisition of non-current assets**.
Revenue expenditure is expenditure incurred for the **purpose of the trade** or to **maintain non-current assets**.

You need to be familiar with an important distinction, the distinction between **capital and revenue expenditure**.

Key terms

Capital expenditure is expenditure which results in the acquisition of non-current assets, or an improvement in their earning capacity.

(a) Capital expenditure is not charged as an expense in the statement of profit or loss and other comprehensive income, although a depreciation charge will usually be made to write off the capital expenditure gradually over time. Depreciation charges are expenses in the statement of profit or loss and other comprehensive income.

(b) Capital expenditure on non-current assets results in the appearance of a non-current asset in the statement of financial position of the business.

Revenue expenditure is expenditure which is incurred for either of the following reasons.

(a) For the purpose of the trade of the business. This includes expenditure classified as selling and distribution expenses, administration expenses and finance charges.

(b) To maintain the existing earning capacity of non-current assets.

Revenue expenditure is charged to the statement of profit or loss and other comprehensive income of a period, provided that it relates to the trading activity and sales of that particular period. For example, if a business buys ten steel bars for $200 ($20 each) and sells eight of them during an accounting period, it will have two steel bars left in inventory at the end of the period. The full $200 is revenue expenditure but only $160 is a cost of goods sold during the period. The remaining $40 (cost of two units) will be included in the statement of financial position in inventory, ie as a current asset valued at $40.

A business purchases a building for $30,000. It then adds an extension to the building at a cost of $10,000. The building needs to have a few broken windows mended, its floors polished and some missing roof tiles replaced. These cleaning and maintenance jobs cost $900.

In this example, the original purchase ($30,000) and the cost of the extension ($10,000) are capital expenditures, because they are incurred to acquire and then improve a non-current asset. The other costs of $900 are revenue expenditure, because these merely maintain the building and thus the 'earning capacity' of the building.

1.1 Capital income and revenue income

Capital income is the proceeds from the sale of non-trading assets (ie proceeds from the sale of non-current assets, including long-term investments). The profits (or losses) from the sale of non-current assets are included in the statement of profit or loss and other comprehensive income of a business, for the accounting period in which the sale takes place. For instance, the business may sell vehicles or machinery which it no longer needs – the proceeds will be capital income.

Revenue income is income derived from the following sources.

(a) The sale of trading assets, such as goods held in inventory
(b) The provision of services
(c) Interest and dividends received from investments held by the business

1.2 Capital transactions

The categorisation of capital and revenue items given above does not mention raising additional capital from the owner(s) of the business, or raising and repaying loans.

(a) These transactions add to the cash assets of the business, thereby creating a corresponding liability (capital or loan).

(b) When a loan is repaid, it reduces the liabilities (loan) and the assets (cash).

None of these transactions would be reported through the statement of profit or loss and other comprehensive income.

1.3 Why is the distinction between capital and revenue items important?

Revenue expenditure results from the purchase of goods and services for one of the following reasons.

(a) To be used fully in the accounting period in which they are purchased, and so be a cost or expense in the statement of profit or loss and other comprehensive income; or

(b) To result in a current asset as at the end of the accounting period because the goods or services have not yet been consumed or made use of. The current asset would be shown in the statement of financial position and is not yet a cost or expense in the statement of profit or loss and other comprehensive income.

For instance, inventory which is purchased for resale will either be sold during the period as per (a) or still be in inventory as per (b).

Capital expenditure results in the **purchase or improvement of non-current assets**, which are assets that will provide benefits to the business in more than one accounting period, and which are not acquired with a view to being resold in the normal course of trade. The cost of purchased non-current assets is not charged in full to the statement of profit or loss and other comprehensive income of the period in which the purchase occurs. Instead, the non-current asset is gradually depreciated over a number of accounting periods.

Examples of non-current assets are computers for the office, delivery vans, and factory machines.

Since revenue items and capital items are accounted for in different ways, the correct and consistent calculation of profit for any accounting period depends on the correct and consistent classification of items as revenue or capital.

This may seem rather confusing at the moment, but things will become clearer in the next few chapters. You must get used to the terminology used as these words appear in the accounting standards themselves, as we will see.

Question   Capital or revenue

State whether each of the following items should be classified as 'capital' or 'revenue' expenditure or income for the purpose of preparing the statement of profit or loss and other comprehensive income and the statement of financial position of the business.

(a) The purchase of a property (eg an office building)

(b) The annual depreciation of such a property

(c) Solicitors' fees in connection with the purchase of such a property

(d) The costs of adding extra storage capacity to a mainframe computer used by the business

PART C PRACTICAL APPLICATION OF ACCOUNTING THEORY

(e) Computer repairs and maintenance costs
(f) Profit on the sale of an office building
(g) Revenue from sales by credit card
(h) The cost of new plant
(i) Customs duty charged on the plant when imported into the country
(j) The 'carriage' costs of transporting the new plant from the supplier's factory to the premises of the business purchasing the plant
(k) The cost of installing the new plant in the premises of the business
(l) The wages of the machine operators

Answer

(a) Capital expenditure
(b) Depreciation of a non-current asset is a revenue expenditure.
(c) The legal fees associated with the purchase of a property may be added to the purchase price and classified as capital expenditure. The cost of the property in the statement of financial position of the business will then include the legal fees.
(d) Capital expenditure (enhancing an existing non-current asset)
(e) Revenue expenditure
(f) Capital income (net of the costs of sale)
(g) Revenue income
(h) Capital expenditure
(i) If customs duties are borne by the purchaser of the non-current asset, they may be added to the cost of the machinery and classified as capital expenditure.
(j) Similarly, if carriage costs are paid for by the purchaser of the non-current asset, they may be included in the cost of the non-current asset and classified as capital expenditure.
(k) Installation costs of a non-current asset are also added to the non-current asset's cost and classified as capital expenditure.
(l) Revenue expenditure

Exam focus point

Exam questions are highly likely on the distinction between capital and revenue expenditure.

2 Depreciation accounting

FAST FORWARD

The **cost** of a non-current asset, less its **estimated residual value**, is allocated fairly between accounting periods by means of **depreciation**. Depreciation is both:

- Charged against profit; and
- Deducted from the value of the non-current asset in the statement of financial position.

Where assets held by an entity have a **limited (finite) useful life**, it is necessary to apportion the value of an asset used in a period against the consumption of the asset's economic benefits. If an asset's life extends over more than one accounting period, it earns profits over more than one period. It is a **non-current asset**. **Current assets**, such as inventory and cash, are continually being used and replaced. **Non-current assets** such as plant and vehicles are intended for long-term use in the business.

With the exception of land held on freehold or very long leasehold, **every non-current asset eventually wears out over time**. Machines, cars and other vehicles, fixtures and fittings, and even buildings do not last forever. When a business acquires a non-current asset, it will have some idea about how long its useful life is intended to be.

(a) To keep on using the non-current asset until it becomes **completely worn out**, useless, and worthless

(b) To **sell off** the non-current asset at the end of its useful life, as a second-hand item or as scrap

Since a non-current asset has a cost, a limited useful life, and its value eventually declines, it follows that a charge should be made in the statement of profit or loss and other comprehensive income to reflect the use that is made of the asset by the business. This charge is called **depreciation**.

Depreciation accounting is governed by IAS 16 *Property, Plant and Equipment*, which will be looked at in detail in Section 6 of this chapter. However, this section will deal with some of the IAS 16 definitions of depreciation.

Key terms

> - **Depreciation** is the systematic allocation of the depreciable amount of an asset over its estimated useful life. Depreciation for the accounting period is charged to net profit or loss for the period either directly or indirectly.
> - **Depreciable assets** are assets which:
>   – are expected to be used during more than one accounting period;
>   – have a limited useful life; and
>   – are held by an entity for use in the production or supply of goods and services, for rental to others, or for administrative purposes.
> - **Useful life** is either:
>   – the period over which a depreciable asset is expected to be available for use by the entity; or
>   – the number of production or similar units expected to be obtained from the asset by the entity.
> - **Depreciable amount** of a depreciable asset is the cost or other amount substituted for cost in the financial statements, less its residual value. (IAS 16)

An 'amount substituted for cost' will normally be a **current market value** after a revaluation has taken place.

2.1 Depreciation

IAS 16 requires the depreciable amount to be allocated on a **systematic basis** to each accounting period during the useful life of the asset.

One way of defining depreciation is to describe it as a means of **spreading the cost** of a non-current asset over its useful life, and so matching the cost against the full period during which it the economic benefits of the asset are consumed by the business. Depreciation charges are an example of the application of the accrual assumption to calculate profits.

There are situations where, over a period, an asset has **increased in value**, ie its current fair value is greater than the carrying amount in the financial statements. You might think that in such situations it would not be necessary to depreciate the asset. The standard states, however, that this is irrelevant, and that depreciation should still be charged to each accounting period, based on the depreciable amount, irrespective of a rise in fair value.

2.2 Useful life

The following factors should be considered when **estimating the useful life** of a depreciable asset.

- Expected **usage**
- Expected **physical wear and tear**
- **Obsolescence**
- Legal or other **limits** on the use of the asset

Once decided, the useful life should be **reviewed periodically** and depreciation rates adjusted for the current and future periods if expectations vary significantly from the original estimates. The effect of the change should be disclosed in the accounting period in which the change takes place.

The assessment of useful life requires **judgement** based on previous experience with similar assets or classes of asset. When a completely new type of asset is acquired (ie through technological advancement or through use in producing a brand new product or service) it is still necessary to estimate useful life, even though the exercise will be much more difficult.

The standard also points out that the physical life of the asset might be longer than its useful life to the entity in question. One of the main factors to be taken into consideration is the **physical wear and tear** the asset is likely to endure. This will depend on various circumstances, including the number of shifts for which the asset will be used, the entity's repair and maintenance programme and so on. Other factors to be considered include obsolescence (due to technological advances/improvements in production/reduction in demand for the product/service produced by the asset) and legal restrictions, eg length of a related lease.

2.3 Residual value

In most cases the residual value of an asset is **likely to be immaterial**. If it is likely to be of any significant value, that value must be estimated at the date of purchase and reviewed at each year end. The amount of residual value should be estimated based on the current situation with other similar assets, used in the same way, which are now at the end of their useful lives. Any expected costs of disposal should be offset against the gross residual value.

(a) A non-current asset costing $20,000 which has an expected life of five years and an expected residual value of $nil should be depreciated by $20,000 in total over the five year period.

(b) A non-current asset costing $20,000 which has an expected life of five years and an expected residual value of $3,000 should be depreciated by $17,000 in total over the five year period.

2.4 Depreciation methods

Consistency is important. The depreciation method selected should be applied consistently from period to period unless there is a significant change in the expected pattern of consumption of future economic benefits. When the method **is** changed, the effect should be quantified and disclosed as a change in accounting estimate in accordance with IAS 8 and the reason for the change should be stated.

Various methods of allocating depreciation to accounting periods are available, but whichever is chosen must be applied **consistently** to ensure comparability from period to period (as required by the *Conceptual Framework*: see Chapter 3). Change of policy is not allowed simply because of the profitability situation of the entity.

The various accepted methods of allocating depreciation and the relevant calculations and accounting treatments are discussed in the next section.

2.5 Disclosure

An accounting policy note should disclose the **measurement bases** used for determining the amounts at which depreciable assets are stated, along with the other accounting policies: see IAS 1.

IAS 16 also requires the following to be disclosed in respect of depreciation for each major class of depreciable asset.

- **Depreciation methods** used
- **Useful lives** or the depreciation rates used
- **Total depreciation** allocated for the period
- **Gross amount** of depreciable assets and the related accumulated depreciation at the beginning and end of the period

2.6 What is depreciation?

The need to depreciate non-current assets arises from **accrual accounting**. If money is expended in purchasing an asset then the amount must at some time be charged against profits. Since the entity consumes economic benefits from the asset over a number of accounting periods it would be inappropriate to charge any single period (eg the period in which the asset was acquired) with the whole of the expenditure. Instead, some method must be found of spreading the cost of the asset over its useful life.

This view of depreciation as a process of allocation of the cost of an asset over several accounting periods is the view adopted by IAS 16. It is worth mentioning here two **common misconceptions** about the purpose and effects of depreciation.

(a) It is sometimes thought that the carrying amount of an asset is equal to its net realisable value and that the object of charging depreciation is to **reflect the fall in value of an asset over its life**. This misconception is the basis of a common, but incorrect, argument which says that freehold properties (say) need not be depreciated in times when property values are rising. It is true that historical cost statements of financial position often give a misleading impression when a property's carrying amount is much below its market value, but in such a case it is open to a business to incorporate a revaluation into its books, or even to prepare its accounts based on current costs. This is a separate problem from that of allocating the property's cost over successive accounting periods.

(b) Another misconception is that depreciation is provided **so that an asset can be replaced at the end of its useful life**. This is not the case.

    (i)   If there is no intention of replacing the asset, it could then be argued that there is no need to provide for any depreciation at all.

    (ii)   If prices are rising, the replacement cost of the asset will exceed the amount of depreciation provided.

PART C PRACTICAL APPLICATION OF ACCOUNTING THEORY

3 Depreciation: The mechanics

FAST FORWARD

Two methods of depreciation are specified in your syllabus:
- The straight-line method
- The reducing balance method

3.1 Methods of depreciation

When a non-current asset is depreciated, two things must be accounted for.

(a) The **charge for depreciation** is a cost or expense of the accounting period. For the time being, we shall charge depreciation as an expense in the statement of profit or loss and other comprehensive income.

(b) At the same time, the non-current asset is wearing out and diminishing in value, and so the value of the non-current asset in the statement of financial position must be reduced by the amount of depreciation charged. The value of the non-current asset will be its '**carrying amount**' which is its cost less accumulated depreciation.

The amount of depreciation deducted from the cost of a non-current asset to arrive at its carrying amount will build up (or 'accumulate') over time, as more depreciation is charged in each successive accounting period. This accumulated depreciation is an allowance for the fall in the remaining future economic benefit of the non-current asset.

For example, if a non-current asset costing $40,000 has an expected life of four years and an estimated residual value of nil, it might be depreciated by $10,000 per annum.

	Depreciation charge for the year (SPL) (A) $	Aggregate depreciation at end of year (B) $	Cost of the asset (C) $	Carrying amount at end of year (C − B) $
At beginning of its life	–	–	40,000	40,000
Year 1	10,000	10,000	40,000	30,000
Year 2	10,000	20,000	40,000	20,000
Year 3	10,000	30,000	40,000	10,000
Year 4	10,000	40,000	40,000	0
	40,000			

At the end of year 4, the full $40,000 of depreciation charges have been made in the statements of profit or loss and other comprehensive income of the four years. The carrying amount of the non-current asset is now nil. In theory (although perhaps not in practice) the business will no longer use the non-current asset, which now needs replacing.

There are several different methods of depreciation. Of these, the ones which are specified in the P1 syllabus are:

- Straight-line method
- Reducing balance method

3.2 The straight-line method

This is the most commonly used method of all. The total depreciable amount is charged in equal instalments to each accounting period over the expected useful life of the asset. (In this way, the carrying amount of the non-current asset declines at a steady rate, or in a 'straight-line' over time).

The annual depreciation charge is calculated as: $\dfrac{\text{Cost of asset minus residual value}}{\text{Expected useful life of the asset}}$

3.3 Example: Straight-line depreciation

(a) A non-current asset costing $20,000 with an estimated life of ten years and no residual value would be depreciated at the rate of:

$$\frac{\$20,000}{10 \text{ years}} = \$2,000 \text{ per annum}$$

(b) A non-current asset costing $60,000 has an estimated life of five years and a residual value of $7,000. The annual depreciation charge using the straight line method would be:

$$\frac{\$(60,000 - 7,000)}{5 \text{ years}} = \$10,600 \text{ per annum}$$

The carrying amount of the non-current asset would be:

	After 1 year $	After 2 years $	After 3 years $	After 4 years $	After 5 years $
Cost of the asset	60,000	60,000	60,000	60,000	60,000
Accumulated depreciation	10,600	21,200	31,800	42,400	53,000
Carrying amount	49,400	38,800	28,200	17,600	7,000 *

* ie its estimated residual value.

Since the depreciation charge per annum is the same amount every year with the straight-line method, it is often convenient to state that depreciation is charged at the rate of x per cent per annum on the cost of the asset. In the example in Paragraph 3.3(a) above, the depreciation charge per annum is 10% of cost (ie 10% of $20,000 = $2,000).

Examination questions often describe straight-line depreciation in this way.

The straight-line method of depreciation is a fair allocation of the total depreciable amount between the different accounting periods, **provided that** it is reasonable to assume that the business enjoys equal benefits from the use of the asset in every period throughout its life. An example of this could be shelving (fixtures and fittings) in the accounts department.

3.4 Assets acquired in the middle of an accounting period

A business can purchase new non-current assets at any time during the course of an accounting period. It might seem fair to charge an amount for depreciation, in the period when the purchase occurs, which reflects the limited use the business has had from the asset in that period.

3.5 Example: Assets acquired in the middle of an accounting period

A business which has an accounting year which runs from 1 January to 31 December purchases a new non-current asset on 1 April 20X1, at a cost of $24,000. The expected life of the asset is four years, and its residual value is $nil. What should be the depreciation charge for 20X1?

Solution

The annual depreciation charge will be $\frac{\$24,000}{4 \text{ years}} = \$6,000$ per annum

However, since the asset was acquired on 1 April 20X1, the business has only benefited from the use of the asset for nine months instead of a full 12 months. It would therefore seem fair to charge depreciation in 20X1 of only:

$$\frac{9}{12} \times \$6,000 = \$4,500$$

PART C PRACTICAL APPLICATION OF ACCOUNTING THEORY

Exam focus point

> If an examination question gives you the purchase date of a non-current asset, which is in the middle of an accounting period, you should generally assume that depreciation should be calculated in this way as a 'part-year' amount.

In practice, many businesses ignore the niceties of part-year depreciation, and charge a full year's depreciation on non-current assets in the year of their purchase, regardless of the time of year they were acquired.

3.6 The reducing balance method

The **reducing balance method** of depreciation calculates the annual depreciation charge as a fixed percentage of the carrying amount of the asset, as at the end of the previous accounting period.

For example, a business purchases a non-current asset at a cost of $10,000. Its expected useful life is three years and its estimated residual value is $2,160. The business wishes to use the reducing balance method to depreciate the asset, and calculates that the rate of depreciation should be 40% of the reducing (carrying) value of the asset. (The method of deciding that 40% is a suitable annual percentage is a problem of mathematics, not financial accounting, and is not described here.)

The total depreciable amount is $(10,000 – 2,160) = $7,840.

The depreciation charge per annum and the carrying amount of the asset as at the end of each year will be as follows.

	$	Accumulated depreciation $
Asset at cost	10,000	
Depreciation in year 1 (40%)	4,000	4,000
Carrying amount at end of year 1	6,000	
Depreciation in year 2 (40%)	2,400	6,400 (4,000 + 2,400)
Carrying amount at end of year 2	3,600	
Depreciation in year 3 (40%)	1,440	7,840 (6,400 + 1,440)
Carrying amount at end of year 3	2,160	

You should note that with the reducing balance method, the annual charge for depreciation is higher in the earlier years of the asset's life, and lower in the later years. In the example above, the annual charges for years 1, 2 and 3 are $4,000, $2,400 and $1,440 respectively.

The reducing balance method might therefore be used when it is considered fair to allocate a greater proportion of the total depreciable amount to the earlier years and a lower proportion to later years, on the assumption that the benefits obtained by the business from using the asset decline over time. An example of this could be machinery in a factory, where productivity falls as the machine gets older.

3.7 Applying a depreciation method consistently

It is up to the business concerned to decide which method of depreciation to apply to its non-current assets. Once that decision has been made the chosen method of depreciation should be applied **consistently from year to year**. The depreciation method must be reviewed at each year end and if there has been a significant change in the expected pattern of consumption of future economic benefits, the method should be updated and the impact of and reasons for the change disclosed.

Similarly, it is up to the business to decide what a sensible life span for a non-current asset should be. Again, once that life span has been chosen, it should not be changed unless something unexpected happens to the asset. If this is the found to be the case when the year end review required by IAS 16, is performed, the change should be made and the impact and reasons for the change disclosed.

It is permissible for a business to depreciate different categories of non-current assets in different ways. For example, if a business owns three cars, then each car would normally be depreciated in the same way (eg by the straight-line method); but another category of non-current asset, say, photocopiers, might be depreciated using a different method (eg by the reducing balance method).

Question — Depreciation methods

A lorry bought for a business cost $17,000. It is expected to last for five years and then be sold for scrap for $2,000.

Required

Work out the depreciation to be charged each year under:

(a) The straight-line method
(b) The reducing balance method (using a rate of 35%)

Answer

(a) Under the straight-line method, depreciation for each of the five years is:

$$\text{Annual depreciation} = \frac{\$(17{,}000 - 2{,}000)}{5} = \$3{,}000$$

(b) Under the reducing balance method, depreciation for each of the five years is:

Year	Depreciation	
1	35% × $17,000	= $5,950
2	35% × ($17,000 – $5,950) = 35% × $11,050	= $3,868
3	35% × ($11,050 – $3,868) = 35% × $7,182	= $2,514
4	35% × ($7,182 – $2,514) = 35% × $4,668	= $1,634
5	Balance to bring carrying amount down to $2,000 = $4,668 – $1,634 – $2,000	= $1,034

3.8 Change in method of depreciation

Having made the above comments about consistency, the depreciation method should be reviewed for appropriateness. If there are any changes in the expected pattern of use of the asset (and hence economic benefit), then the method used should be changed. In such cases, the remaining carrying amount is depreciated under the new method, ie only current and future periods are affected; the change is not retrospective.

3.9 Example: Change in method of depreciation

Jakob Co purchased an asset for $100,000 on 1.1.X1. It had an estimated useful life of five years and it was depreciated using the reducing balance method at a rate of 40%. On 1.1.X3 it was decided to change the method to straight line.

Show the depreciation charge for each year (to 31 December) of the asset's life.

Solution

Year		Depreciation charge $	Aggregate depreciation $
20X1	$100,000 × 40%	40,000	40,000
20X2	$60,000 × 40%	24,000	64,000
20X3	$\dfrac{\$100{,}000 - \$64{,}000}{3}$	12,000	76,000
20X4		12,000	88,000
20X5		12,000	100,000

3.10 Change in expected useful life or residual value of an asset

The depreciation charge on a non-current asset depends not only on the cost (or value) of the asset and its estimated residual value, but also on its estimated useful life.

A business purchased a non-current asset costing $12,000 with an estimated life of four years and no residual value. If it used the straight-line method of depreciation, it would make an annual allowance of 25% of $12,000 = $3,000.

Now what would happen if the business decided after two years that the useful life of the asset has been underestimated, and it still had five more years in use to come (making its total life seven years)?

For the first two years, the asset would have been depreciated by $3,000 per annum, so that its carrying amount after two years would be $(12,000 – 6,000) = $6,000. If the remaining life of the asset is now revised to five more years, the remaining amount to be depreciated (here $6,000) should be spread over the remaining life, giving an annual depreciation charge for the final five years of:

$$\frac{\text{Carrying amount at time of life readjustment, minus residual value}}{\text{New estimate of remaining useful life}} = \frac{\$6,000}{5 \text{ years}} = \$1,200 \text{ per year}$$

Formula to learn

$$\text{New depreciation} = \frac{\text{CA less residual value}}{\text{Revised useful life}}$$

Similar adjustments are made when there is a change in the expected residual value of the asset.

3.11 Depreciation is not a cash expense

Depreciation spreads the cost of a non-current asset (less its estimated residual value) over the asset's life. The cash payment for the non-current asset will be made when, or soon after, the asset is purchased. Annual depreciation of the asset in subsequent years is not a cash expense – rather it allocates costs to those later years for a cash payment that has occurred previously.

For example, a business purchased some shop fittings for $6,000 on 1 July 20X5 and paid for them in cash on that date.

Subsequently, depreciation may be charged at $600 every year for ten years. So each year $600 is deducted from profits and the carrying amount of the fittings goes down, but no actual cash is being paid. The cash was all paid on 1 July 20X5. So annual depreciation is not a cash expense, but rather an allocation of the original cost to later years.

Question
Depreciation

(a) What are the purposes of providing for depreciation?

(b) In what circumstances is the reducing balance method more appropriate than the straight-line method? Give reasons for your answer.

Answer

(a) The accounts of a business try to recognise that the cost of a non-current asset is gradually consumed as the asset wears out. This is done by gradually writing off the asset's cost in the statement of profit or loss and other comprehensive income over several accounting periods. This process is known as depreciation, and is an example of the accrual assumption. IAS 16 *Property, Plant and Equipment* requires that depreciation should be allocated on a systematic basis to each accounting period during the useful life of the asset.

With regard to the accrual principle, it is fair that the profits should be reduced by the depreciation charge; this is not an arbitrary exercise. Depreciation is not, as is sometimes supposed, an attempt to set aside funds to purchase new non-current assets when required. Depreciation is not generally provided on freehold land because it does not 'wear out' (unless it is held for mining etc).

(b) The reducing balance method of depreciation is used instead of the straight-line method when it is considered fair to allocate a greater proportion of the total depreciable amount to the earlier years and a lower proportion to the later years, on the assumption that the benefits obtained by the business from using the asset decline over time.

In favour of this method it may be argued that it links the depreciation charge to the costs of maintaining and running the asset. In the early years these costs are low and the depreciation charge is high, while in later years this is reversed.

3.12 Accumulated depreciation

Key term

Accumulated depreciation in the statement of financial position is the cumulative amount set aside as a charge for the wearing out of non-current assets.

There are two basic aspects of accumulated depreciation to remember.

(a) A depreciation charge is made in the statement of profit or loss and other comprehensive income in each accounting period for every depreciable non-current asset. Nearly all non-current assets are depreciable, the most important exceptions being freehold land and non-current investments.

(b) The total accumulated depreciation on a non-current asset builds up as the asset gets older. The total accumulated depreciation is always getting larger, until the non-current asset is fully depreciated.

The ledger accounting entries for depreciation are as follows.

(a) There is an accumulated depreciation account for each separate category of non-current assets, for example, plant and machinery, land and buildings, fixtures and fittings.

(b) The depreciation charge for an accounting period is a charge against profit. It is accounted for as follows.

DEBIT   SPLOCI (depreciation expense)
CREDIT   Accumulated depreciation account (statement of financial position)

with the depreciation charge for the period.

(c) The balance on the statement of financial position depreciation account is the total accumulated depreciation. This is always a credit balance brought forward in the ledger account for depreciation.

(d) The non-current asset accounts are unaffected by depreciation. Non-current assets are recorded in these accounts at cost (or, if they are revalued, at their revalued amount).

(e) In the statement of financial position of the business, the total balance on the accumulated depreciation account is set against the value of non-current asset accounts (ie non-current assets at cost or revalued amount) to derive the carrying amount of the non-current assets.

This is how the non-current asset accounts might appear in a trial balance:

	DR	CR
Freehold building – cost	2,000,000	
Freehold building – accumulated depreciation		500,000
Motor vehicles – cost	70,000	
Motor vehicles – accumulated depreciation		40,000
Office equipment – cost	25,000	
Office equipment – accumulated depreciation		15,000

PART C PRACTICAL APPLICATION OF ACCOUNTING THEORY

And this is how they would be presented in the statement of financial position:

Non-current assets	
Freehold building	1,500,000
Motor vehicles	30,000
Office equipment	10,000

3.13 Example: Depreciation

Brian Box set up his own computer software business on 1 March 20X6. He purchased a computer system on credit from a manufacturer, at a cost of $16,000. The system has an expected life of three years and a residual value of $2,500. Using the straight-line method of depreciation, the non-current asset account, accumulated depreciation account and statement of profit or loss and other comprehensive income (extract) and statement of financial position (extract) would be as follows, for each of the next three years, 28 February 20X7, 20X8 and 20X9.

NON-CURRENT ASSET: COMPUTER EQUIPMENT

	Date		$	Date		$
(a)	1.3.X6	Accounts payable	16,000	28.2.X7	Balance c/d	16,000
(b)	1.3.X7	Balance b/d	16,000	28.2.X8	Balance c/d	16,000
(c)	1.3.X8	Balance b/d	16,000	28.2.X9	Balance c/d	16,000
(d)	1.3.X9	Balance b/d	16,000			

In theory, the non-current asset has now lasted out its expected useful life. However, until it is sold off or scrapped, the asset will still appear in the statement of financial position at cost (less accumulated depreciation) and it should remain in the ledger account for computer equipment until it is eventually disposed of.

ACCUMULATED DEPRECIATION

	Date		$	Date		$
(a)	28.2.X7	Balance c/d	4,500	28.2.X7	P/L account	4,500
(b)	28.2.X8	Balance c/d	9,000	1.3.X7	Balance b/d	4,500
				28.2.X8	P/L account	4,500
			9,000			9,000
(c)	28.2.X9	Balance c/d	13,500	1.3.X8	Balance b/d	9,000
				28.2.X9	P/L account	4,500
			13,500			13,500
				1.3.X9	Balance b/d	13,500

The annual depreciation charge is $\dfrac{\$(16,000 - 2,500)}{3 \text{ years}} = \$4,500$ pa

At the end of three years, the asset is fully depreciated down to its residual value ($16,000 − $13,500 = $2,500). If it continues to be used by Brian Box, it will not be depreciated any further (unless its estimated residual value is reduced).

STATEMENT OF PROFIT OR LOSS AND OTHER COMPREHENSIVE INCOME (EXTRACT)

	Date		$
(a)	28 Feb 20X7	Depreciation	4,500
(b)	28 Feb 20X8	Depreciation	4,500
(c)	28 Feb 20X9	Depreciation	4,500

STATEMENT OF FINANCIAL POSITION (EXTRACT) AS AT 28 FEBRUARY

	20X7	20X8	20X9
	$	$	$
Computer equipment at cost	16,000	16,000	16,000
Less accumulated depreciation	4,500	9,000	13,500
Carrying amount	11,500	7,000	2,500

3.14 Example: Allowance for depreciation with assets acquired part-way through the year

Brian Box prospers in his computer software business, and before long he purchases a car for himself, and later for his chief assistant Bill Ockhead. Relevant data is as follows.

	Date of purchase	Cost	Estimated life	Estimated residual value
Brian Box car	1 June 20X6	$20,000	3 years	$2,000
Bill Ockhead car	1 June 20X7	$8,000	3 years	$2,000

The straight-line method of depreciation is to be used.

Prepare the motor vehicles account and motor vehicle depreciation account for the years to 28 February 20X7 and 20X8. (You should allow for the part-year's use of a car in computing the annual charge for depreciation.)

Calculate the carrying amount of the motor vehicles as at 28 February 20X8.

Solution

(a) (i) Brian Box car Annual depreciation $\frac{\$(20,000 - 2,000)}{3 \text{ years}}$ = $6,000 pa

Monthly depreciation = $500
Depreciation: 1 June–20X6 – 28 February 20X7 (9 months) $4,500
1 March 20X7 – 28 February 20X8 $6,000

(ii) Bill Ockhead car Annual depreciation $\frac{\$(8,000 - 2,000)}{3 \text{ years}}$ = $2,000 pa

Depreciation 1 June 20X7 – 28 February 20X8 (9 months) $1,500

(b)
MOTOR VEHICLES

Date		$	Date		$
1 Jun 20X6	Payables (or cash) (car purchase)	20,000	28 Feb 20X7	Balance c/d	20,000
1 Mar 20X7	Balance b/d	20,000			
1 Jun 20X7	Payables (or cash) (car purchase)	8,000	28 Feb 20X8	Balance c/d	28,000
		28,000			28,000
1 Mar 20X8	Balance b/d	28,000			

MOTOR VEHICLES – ACCUMULATED DEPRECIATION

Date		$	Date		$
28 Feb 20X7	Balance c/d	4,500	28 Feb 20X7	P/L account	4,500
			1 Mar 20X7	Balance b/d	4,500
28 Feb 20X8	Balance c/d	12,000	28 Feb 20X8	P/L account (6,000 + 1,500)	7,500
		12,000			12,000
			1 Mar 20X8	Balance b/d	12,000

STATEMENT OF FINANCIAL POSITION (WORKINGS) AS AT 28 FEBRUARY 20X8

	Brian Box car		Bill Ockhead car		Total
	$	$	$	$	$
Asset at cost		20,000		8,000	28,000
Accumulated depreciation					
Year to 28 Feb 20X7	4,500		–		
Year to 28 Feb 20X8	6,000		1,500		
		10,500		1,500	12,000
Carrying amount		9,500		6,500	16,000

PART C PRACTICAL APPLICATION OF ACCOUNTING THEORY

4 Revaluation of non-current assets

FAST FORWARD

When a non-current asset is **revalued**, depreciation is charged on the **revalued amount**.

It is quite common for the market value of certain non-current assets to **go up, in spite of the asset getting older**. The most obvious example of rising market values is land and buildings. The *Conceptual Framework* identifies current value as a measurement basis for the financial statements and some entities will choose to measure their assets at fair value, which is a current value measure.

A business which owns non-current assets which are rising in value is not obliged to revalue those assets in its statement of financial position. However, in order to give a more 'true and fair view' of the position of the business, it might be decided that some non-current assets should be revalued upwards; otherwise the total value of the assets of the business might seem unrealistically low. When non-current assets are revalued, depreciation should be charged on the **revalued amount**.

4.1 Example: The revaluation of non-current assets

When Ira Vann commenced trading as a car hire dealer on 1 January 20X1, he purchased business premises at a cost of $50,000.

For the purpose of accounting for depreciation, he decided the following.

(a) The land part of the business premises was worth $20,000; this would not be depreciated.

(b) The building part of the business premises was worth the remaining $30,000. This would be depreciated by the straight-line method to a $nil residual value over 30 years.

After five years of trading on 1 January 20X6, Ira decides that his business premises are now worth $150,000, divided into:

	$
Land	75,000
Building	75,000
	150,000

He estimates that the building still has a further 25 years of useful life remaining.

Calculate the annual charge for depreciation in each of the 30 years of its life, and the carrying amount of the land and building as at the end of each year.

Solution

Before the revaluation, the annual depreciation charge is $1,000 per annum on the building. This charge is made in each of the first five years of the asset's life.

The carrying amount of the asset will decline by $1,000 per annum, to:

(a) $49,000 as at 31.12.X1
(b) $48,000 as at 31.12.X2
(c) $47,000 as at 31.12.X3
(d) $46,000 as at 31.12.X4
(e) $45,000 as at 31.12.X5

When the revaluation takes place, the amount of the revaluation is:

	$
New asset value (to be shown in statement of financial position)	150,000
Carrying amount as at end of 20X5 ($20,000 + ($30,000 – $5,000))	45,000
Amount of revaluation	105,000

The asset will be revalued upwards by $105,000 to $150,000. If you remember the accounting equation, that the total value of assets must be equalled by the total value of capital and liabilities, you should recognise that if assets go up in value by $105,000, capital or liabilities must also go up by the same

amount. Since the increased value benefits the owners of the business, the amount of the revaluation is added to capital in the form of a revaluation surplus.

However, the gain on revaluation cannot be recognised in profit or loss (in the top part of the statement of profit or loss and other comprehensive income), as it has not been realised. Instead it is recognised in **other** comprehensive income (in the bottom part of the statement of profit or loss and other comprehensive income – see Chapter 20). From here, the 'gain' is transferred to a **revaluation surplus**. This treatment may surprise you at first. However, to achieve faithful representation, a profit can not be anticipated before it is realised. Therefore, the 'profit' cannot be dealt with as income in profit or loss. **If the building were to be subsequently sold for the revalued amount, the profit would be realised and could be recognised in profit or loss.**

4.2 Accounting entries

The accounting treatment for the revaluation above will be:

DEBIT	Building	– cost ($75,000 – $30,000)	$45,000	
	Building	– accumulated depreciation	$5,000	
	Land	– cost ($75,000 – $20,000)	$55,000	
CREDIT	Revaluation surplus			$105,000

The effect of these entries is as follows:

BUILDING – COST

	$		$
Bal b/f	30,000	Bal c/f	75,000
Revaluation surplus	45,000		
	75,000		75,000

BUILDING – ACCUMULATED DEPRECIATION

	$		$
Revaluation surplus	5,000	Bal b/f	5,000
Bal c/f	–		
	5,000		5,000

LAND – COST

	$		$
Bal b/f	20,000	Bal c/f	75,000
Revaluation surplus	55,000		
	75,000		75,000

REVALUATION SURPLUS

	$		$
Bal c/f	105,000	Building – cost	45,000
		Building – acc dep'n	5,000
		Land – cost	55,000
	105,000		105,000

4.3 Depreciation on revalued assets

After the revaluation, depreciation will be charged on the building at a new rate of:

$$\frac{\text{Revalued amount}}{\text{Remaining useful life}}$$

$$\frac{\$75,000}{25 \text{ years}} = \$3,000 \text{ per year}$$

The carrying amount of the property will then fall by $3,000 per year over 25 years, from $150,000 as at 1 January 20X6 to only $75,000 at the end of the 25 years, ie the building part of the property value will have been fully depreciated.

The consequence of a revaluation is therefore a higher annual depreciation charge.

4.4 Revaluation downwards

After some years, it may become apparent that the building is overvalued and needs to be revalued downwards.

Using the example above five years later, the land is still valued at $75,000 but the building is now valued at $25,000.

BUILDING COST

	$		$
Balance b/f	75,000	Revaluation surplus	50,000
		Bal c/d	25,000

BUILDING-ACCUMULATED DEPRECIATION

	$		$
Revaluation surplus	15,000	Balance b/f (5 × $3,000)	15,000

LAND COST

	$		$
Balance b/f	75,000	Balance c/f	75,000

REVALUATION SURPLUS

	$		$
Cost	50,000	Balance b/f	105,000
Bal c/f	70,000	Excess depreciation	15,000
	120,000	(accumulated depreciation)	120,000

5 Non-current asset disposals

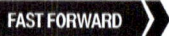

When a non-current asset is **sold**, there is likely to be a **profit or loss on disposal**. This is the difference between the net sale price of the asset and its carrying amount at the time of disposal.

5.1 The disposal of non-current assets

Non-current assets are not purchased by a business with the intention of reselling them in the normal course of trade. However, they might be sold off at some stage during their life, either when their useful life is over or before then. A business might decide to sell off a non-current asset long before its useful life has ended.

Whenever a business sells something, it will make a profit or a loss. When non-current assets are disposed of, there will be a profit or loss on disposal. As it is a capital item being sold, the profit or loss will be a capital gain or a capital loss. These gains or losses are reported in the net profit/loss section of the statement of profit or loss and other comprehensive income of the business (rather than in the trading profit/loss or gross profit/loss section). They are commonly referred to as '**profit on disposal of non-current assets**' or '**loss on disposal**'.

Examination questions on the disposal of non-current assets are likely to ask for ledger accounts to be prepared, showing the entries in the accounts to record the disposal. But before we look at the ledger accounting for disposing of assets, we had better look at the principles behind calculating the profit (or loss) on disposing of assets.

5.2 The principles behind calculating the profit or loss on disposal

The profit or loss on the disposal of a non-current asset is the difference between (a) and (b) below.

(a) The carrying amount of the asset at the time of its sale
(b) Its net sale price, which is the price minus any costs of making the sale

A profit is made when the sale price exceeds the carrying amount, and a loss is made when the sale price is less than the carrying amount.

5.3 Example: Disposal of a non-current asset

A business purchased a non-current asset on 1 January 20X1 for $25,000. It had an estimated life of six years and an estimated residual value of $7,000. The asset was eventually sold after three years on 1 January 20X4 to another trader who paid $17,500 for it.

What was the profit or loss on disposal, assuming that the business uses the straight line method for depreciation?

Solution

Annual depreciation = $\dfrac{\$(25,000 - 7,000)}{6 \text{ years}}$ = $3,000 per annum

	$
Cost of asset	25,000
Less accumulated depreciation (three years)	9,000
Carrying amount at date of disposal	16,000
Sale price	17,500
Profit on disposal	1,500

This profit will be shown in the statement of profit or loss and other comprehensive income of the business where it will be an item of other income added to the gross profit brought down from the trading account.

5.4 Second example: Disposal of a non-current asset

A business purchased a machine on 1 July 20X1 at a cost of $35,000. The machine had an estimated residual value of $3,000 and a life of eight years. The machine was sold for $18,600 on 31 December 20X4, the last day of the accounting year of the business. To make the sale, the business had to incur dismantling costs and costs of transporting the machine to the buyer's premises. These amounted to $1,200.

The business uses the straight-line method of depreciation. What was the profit or loss on disposal of the machine?

Solution

Annual depreciation $\dfrac{\$(35,000 - 3,000)}{8 \text{ years}}$ = $4,000 per annum

It is assumed that in 20X1 only one-half year's depreciation was charged, because the asset was purchased six months into the year.

	$	$
Non-current asset at cost		35,000
Depreciation in 20X1 (½ year)	2,000	
20X2, 20X3 and 20X4	12,000	
Accumulated depreciation		14,000
Carrying amount at date of disposal		21,000
Sale price	18,600	
Costs incurred in making the sale	(1,200)	
Net sale price		17,400
Loss on disposal		(3,600)

This loss will be shown as an expense in the statement of profit or loss and other comprehensive income of the business. It is a capital loss, not a trading loss, and it should not therefore be shown in the trading account (ie it is not part of the gross profit/loss section of the statement of profit or loss and other comprehensive income).

5.5 The disposal of non-current assets: Ledger accounting entries

We have already seen how the profit or loss on disposal of a non-current asset should be computed. A profit on disposal is an item of 'other income' in the statement of profit or loss and other comprehensive income, and a loss on disposal is an item of expense in the statement of profit or loss and other comprehensive income.

It is customary in ledger accounting to record the disposal of non-current assets in a **disposal of non-current assets account**.

(a) The profit or loss on disposal is the difference between:

  (i) The sale price of the asset (if any); and
  (ii) The carrying amount of the asset at the time of sale.

(b) The following items must appear in the disposal of non-current assets account:

  (i) The value of the asset (at cost, or revalued amount*)
  (ii) The accumulated depreciation up to the date of sale
  (iii) The sale price of the asset

  *To simplify the explanation of the rules, we will assume now that the non-current assets disposed of are valued at cost.

(c) The ledger accounting entries are as follows.

  (i) DEBIT   Disposal of non-current asset account
      CREDIT   Non-current asset account

  with the cost of the asset disposed of.

  (ii) DEBIT   Accumulated depreciation account
       CREDIT   Disposal of non-current asset account

  with the accumulated depreciation on the asset as at the date of sale.

  (iii) DEBIT   Receivable account or cash book
        CREDIT   Disposal of non-current asset account

  with the sale price of the asset. The sale is therefore not recorded in a sales account, but in the disposal of non-current asset account itself. You will notice that the effect of these entries is to remove the asset, and its accumulated depreciation, from the statement of financial position.

  The balance on the disposal account is the profit or loss on disposal and the corresponding double entry is recorded in the P/L account itself.

5.6 Example: Disposal of assets: Ledger accounting entries

A business has $110,000 worth of machinery at cost. Its policy is to make an allowance for depreciation at 20% per annum straight-line. The total allowance now stands at $70,000. The business sells for $19,000 a machine which it purchased exactly two years ago for $30,000.

Show the relevant ledger entries.

Solution

PLANT AND MACHINERY ACCOUNT

	$		$
		Plant disposals account	30,000
Balance b/d	110,000	Balance c/d	80,000
	110,000		110,000
Balance b/d	80,000		

PLANT AND MACHINERY ACCUMULATED DEPRECIATION

	$		$
Plant disposals (20% of $30,000 for 2 years)	12,000		
Balance c/d	58,000	Balance b/d	70,000
	70,000		70,000
		Balance b/d	58,000

PLANT DISPOSALS

	$		$
Plant and machinery account	30,000	Accumulated depreciation	12,000
SPL (profit on sale)	1,000	Cash	19,000
	31,000		31,000

Check

	$
Asset at cost	30,000
Accumulated depreciation at time of sale	12,000
Carrying amount at time of sale	18,000
Sale price	19,000
Profit on sale	1,000

5.7 Example continued: Part exchange

Taking the example above assume that, instead of the machine being sold for $19,000, it was exchanged for a new machine costing $60,000, a credit of $19,000 being received upon exchange. In other words $19,000 is the trade-in price of the old machine. Now what are the relevant ledger account entries?

Solution

PLANT AND MACHINERY ACCOUNT

	$		$
Balance b/d	110,000	Plant disposal	30,000
Cash $(60,000 – 19,000)	41,000	Balance c/d	140,000
Plant disposals	19,000		
	170,000		170,000
Balance b/d	140,000		

The new asset is recorded in the non-current asset account at cost $(41,000 + 19,000) = $60,000.

PLANT AND MACHINERY ACCUMULATED DEPRECIATION

	$		$
Plant disposals (20% of $30,000 for 2 years)	12,000	Balance b/d	70,000
Balance c/d	58,000		
	70,000		70,000
		Balance b/d	58,000

PART C PRACTICAL APPLICATION OF ACCOUNTING THEORY

PLANT DISPOSALS

	$		$
Plant and machinery	30,000	Accumulated depreciation	12,000
Profit transferred to SPL	1,000	Plant and machinery-part exchange	19,000
	31,000		31,000

Question — Non-current asset ledger accounts

A business purchased two rivet-making machines on 1 January 20X5 at a cost of $15,000 each. Each had an estimated life of five years and a $nil residual value. The straight-line method of depreciation is used.

Owing to an unforeseen slump in market demand for rivets, the business decided to reduce its output of rivets, and switch to making other products instead. On 31 March 20X7, one rivet-making machine was sold (on credit) to a buyer for $8,000.

Later in the year, however, it was decided to abandon production of rivets altogether, and the second machine was sold on 1 December 20X7 for $2,500 cash.

Prepare the machinery account, depreciation of machinery account and disposal of machinery account for the accounting year to 31 December 20X7.

Answer

MACHINERY ACCOUNT

20X7		$	20X7		$
1 Jan	Balance b/f	30,000	31 Mar	Disposal of machinery account	15,000
			1 Dec	Disposal of machinery account	15,000
		30,000			30,000

MACHINERY – ACCUMULATED DEPRECIATION

20X7		$	20X7		$
31 Mar	Disposal of machinery account*	6,750	1 Jan	Balance b/f	12,000
1 Dec	Disposal of machinery account**	8,750	31 Dec	SPL ***	3,500
		15,500			15,500

* Depreciation at date of disposal = $6,000 + $750
** Depreciation at date of disposal = $6,000 + $2,750
*** Depreciation charge for the year = $750 + $2,750

DISPOSAL OF MACHINERY

20X7		$	20X7		$
31 Mar	Machinery account	15,000	31 Mar	Account receivable (sale price)	8,000
			31 Mar	Accumulated depreciation	6,750
1 Dec	Machinery	15,000	1 Dec	Cash (sale price)	2,500
			1 Dec	Accumulated depreciation	8,750
			31 Dec	SPL (loss on disposal)	4,000
		30,000			30,000

You should be able to calculate that there was a loss on the first disposal of $250, and on the second disposal of $3,750, giving a total loss of $4,000.

Workings

1. At 1 January 20X7, accumulated depreciation on the machines will be:

   2 machines × 2 years × $\frac{\$15,000}{5}$ per machine p.a. = $12,000, or $6,000 per machine.

2. Monthly depreciation is $\frac{\$3,000}{12}$ = $250 per machine per month.

3. The machines are disposed of in 20X7.

   (a) On 31 March – after 3 months of the year.
   Depreciation for the year on the machine = 3 months × $250 = $750.

   (b) On 1 December – after 11 months of the year.
   Depreciation for the year on the machine = 11 months × $250 = $2,750.

5.8 Example: Disposal of a revalued asset

Returning to the case of the revalued asset in Sections 4.2 and 4.3, suppose that two years later the land and property is sold for $200,000. What is the profit on disposal?

BUILDING – COST

	$		$
Bal b/f	75,000	Disposal account	75,000

BUILDING – ACCUMULATED DEPRECIATION

	$		$
Disposal account	6,000	Bal b/f ($3,000 × 2)	6,000

LAND – COST

	$		$
Bal b/f	75,000	Disposal account	75,000

REVALUATION SURPLUS

	$		$
Disposal account	105,000	Bal b/f	105,000

DISPOSAL ACCOUNT

	$		$
Building – cost	75,000	Cash	200,000
Land – cost	75,000	Building – acc dep'n	6,000
Profit on disposal	161,000	Revaluation surplus	105,000
	311,000		311,000

Ignoring the revaluation:

	$
Original cost of building	30,000
Original cost of land	20,000
	50,000
Depreciation ($5,000 + $6,000)	(11,000)
Carrying amount	39,000
Sale proceeds	200,000
Profit on sale	161,000

6 IAS 16 *Property, Plant and Equipment*

> **FAST FORWARD**
>
> IAS 16 covers all aspects of accounting for property, plant and equipment. This represents the bulk of items which are **'tangible' non-current assets**.

6.1 Scope

IAS 16 should be followed when accounting for property, plant and equipment *unless* another international accounting standard requires a **different treatment**.

IAS 16 **does not apply** to the following.

(a) Biological assets related to agricultural activity eg forests and other regenerative natural resources.
(b) Mineral rights, exploration for and extraction of minerals, oil, gas and other non-regenerative resources.
(c) Assets held for sale.

6.2 Definitions

The standard gives a large number of definitions.

Key terms

- **Property, plant and equipment** are tangible items that:
  - Are held for use in the production or supply of goods or services, for rental to others, or for administrative purposes; and
  - Are expected to be used during more than one period.
- **Cost** is the amount of cash or cash equivalents paid or the fair value of the other consideration given to acquire an asset at the time of its acquisition or construction.
- **Residual value** is the estimated amount that an entity would currently obtain from disposal of the asset, after deducting the estimated costs of disposal, if the asset were already of the age and in the condition expected at the end of its useful life.
- **Fair value** is the price that would be received to sell an asset or paid to transfer a liability in an orderly transaction between market participants at the measurement date.
- **Carrying amount** is the amount at which an asset is recognised after deducting any accumulated depreciation and accumulated impairment losses.
- **Recoverable amount** is the higher of an asset's fair value less costs to sell and its value in use.

(IAS 16)

6.3 Recognition

In this context, recognition simply means incorporation of the item in the business's accounts, in this case as a non-current asset. The recognition of property, plant and equipment depends on two criteria.

(a) It is probable that **future economic benefits** associated with the item will flow to the entity.
(b) The cost of the item can be **measured reliably**.

Property, plant and equipment can amount to **substantial amounts** in financial statements, affecting both the presentation of the company's statement of financial position and the profitability of the entity as shown in the statement of profit or loss and other comprehensive income. Smaller items such as tools are often written off as expenses of the period. Most companies have their own policy on this – items below a certain value are charged as expenses.

16: TANGIBLE NON-CURRENT ASSETS

6.4 Initial measurement

Once an item of property, plant and equipment qualifies for recognition as an asset, it will initially be **measured at cost**.

Exam focus point

> From your studies of double entry in Chapter 5, you should remember that the entries to record an acquisition are:
>
> DEBIT   Non-current asset – cost   X
> CREDIT   Cash (or payable if credit transaction)   X

6.4.1 Components of cost

The standard lists the components of the cost of an item of property, plant and equipment.

- **Purchase price**, plus import duties less any trade discount or rebate
- **Directly attributable costs** of bringing the asset to working condition for its intended use, eg:
    - The cost of site preparation
    - Initial delivery and handling costs
    - Installation costs
    - Testing costs
    - Professional fees (architects, engineers)
    - Wages and salaries eg directly spent on construction
- **Initial estimate of the costs of dismantling and removing the item and restoring the site on which it is located**

The following costs **will not be part of the cost** of property, plant and equipment unless they can be attributed directly to the asset's acquisition, or bringing it into its working location and condition.

- Expenses of operations that are incidental to the construction or development of the item
- Administration and other general overhead costs
- Start-up and similar pre-production costs
- Initial operating losses before the asset reaches planned performances
- Training

All of these will be recognised as an **expense** rather than an asset.

6.4.2 Exchanges of assets

Exchange or part exchange of assets occurs frequently for items of property, plant and equipment. IAS 16 states that the cost of an item obtained through (part) exchange is the **fair value of the asset received (unless this cannot be measured reliably)**.

6.5 Subsequent expenditure

How should we treat any subsequent expenditure on long-term assets, after their purchase and recognition? **Subsequent expenditure is added to the carrying amount** of the asset, but only when it is probable that future economic benefits, in excess of the originally assessed standard of performance of the existing asset, will flow to the entity. All other subsequent expenditure is simply recognised as an expense in the period in which it is incurred.

The important point here is whether any subsequent expenditure on an asset **improves** the condition of the asset beyond the previous performance. The following are examples of such improvements.

(a) **Modification** of an item of plant to extend its useful life, including increased capacity
(b) **Upgrade** of machine parts to improve the quality of output
(c) Adoption of a **new production process** leading to large reductions in operating costs

Normal repairs and maintenance on property, plant and equipment items merely maintain or restore value, they do **not** improve or increase it, so such costs are recognised as an expense when incurred.

6.6 Measurement subsequent to initial recognition

The standard offers two possible treatments here, essentially a choice between keeping an asset recorded at **cost** or revaluing it to **fair value**.

(a) **Cost model.** Carry the asset at its cost less accumulated depreciation and any accumulated impairment losses.

(b) **Revaluation model.** Carry the asset at a revalued amount, being its fair value at the date of the revaluation less any subsequent accumulated depreciation and any subsequent accumulated impairment losses. Revaluations should be made regularly enough so that the carrying amount approximates to fair value at the reporting date. The revaluation model is only available if the item can be measured reliably.

6.6.1 Revaluations

The fair value of non-current assets is determined in accordance with IFRS 13 *Fair Value Measurement*. This standard is not within your syllabus and you do not need to know how it is applied. It is, however, normally the case that the fair value of non-current assets is their market value.

Valuations are usually carried out by professionally qualified valuers. The frequency of valuation depends on the **volatility of the fair values** of individual items of property, plant and equipment. The more volatile the fair value, the more frequently revaluations should be carried out. Where the current fair value is very different from the carrying amount then a revaluation should be carried out.

Most importantly, when an item of property, plant and equipment is revalued, **the whole class of assets to which it belongs should be revalued**.

All the items within a class should be **revalued at the same time**, to prevent selective revaluation of certain assets and to avoid disclosing a mixture of costs and values from different dates in the financial statements. A rolling basis of revaluation is allowed if the revaluations are kept up to date and the revaluation of the whole class is completed in a short period of time.

How should any **increase in value** be treated when a revaluation takes place? The debit will be the increase in value in the statement of financial position, but what about the credit? IAS 16 requires the increase to be credited to other comprehensive income as a **revaluation surplus** and accumulated within owners' equity in the statement of financial position. There is an exception to this rule where the increase reverses a previous decrease which was recognised as an expense. To the extent that this offset is made, the increase is recognised as income in profit or loss; any excess is recognised as other comprehensive income and taken to the revaluation surplus.

IAS 16 makes further statements about revaluation, but these are beyond the scope of your syllabus.

6.7 Depreciation

The standard reflects the following approach to depreciation.

- The **depreciable amount** of an item of property, plant and equipment should be allocated on a systematic basis over its useful life.
- The **depreciation method** used should reflect the pattern in which the asset's future economic benefits are expected to be consumed by the entity.
- The **depreciation charge** for each period would be recognised as an expense unless it is included in the carrying amount of another asset.

Most of the comments on depreciation in IAS 16 are dealt with in Section 2.

Land and buildings are dealt with separately even when they are acquired together because land normally has an unlimited life and is therefore not depreciated. In contrast buildings do have a limited life and must be depreciated. Any increase in the value of land on which a building is standing will have no impact on the determination of the building's carrying amount.

Depreciation is usually treated as an **expense**, but not where it is absorbed by the entity in the process of producing other assets. For example, depreciation of plant and machinery is incurred in the production of goods for sale (inventory items). In such circumstances, the depreciation is included in the cost of the new assets produced.

6.7.1 Review of useful life

A review of the **useful life** of property, plant and equipment should be carried out at least **annually** and the depreciation charge for the current and future periods should be adjusted if expectations have changed significantly from previous estimates. The change should be accounted for as a **change in accounting estimate**.

6.7.2 Review of depreciation method

The **depreciation method** should also be reviewed at least **annually** and, if there has been a significant change in the expected pattern of consumption of economic benefits from those assets, the method should be changed to suit this changed pattern. When such a change in depreciation method takes place the change should be accounted for as a **change in accounting estimate** and the depreciation charge for the current and future periods should be adjusted.

6.7.3 Impairment of asset values

The **carrying amount** of an item or group of identical items of property, plant and equipment should also be reviewed **periodically** (ie at each period end). This is to assess whether the recoverable amount has declined below the carrying amount. When there has been such a decline, the carrying amount should be reduced to the **recoverable amount**.

Recoverable amounts should be considered on an **individual asset basis** or for **groups of identical assets**.

6.8 Retirements and disposals

When an asset is permanently **withdrawn from use, or sold or scrapped**, and no future economic benefits are expected from its disposal, it should be withdrawn from the statement of financial position (derecognised).

Gains or losses are the difference between the estimated net disposal proceeds and the carrying amount of the asset. They should be recognised as income or expense in the statement of profit or loss and other comprehensive income.

6.9 Disclosure

The standard has a long list of disclosure requirements, required by class of assets, only some of which are relevant to your syllabus.

- **Measurement bases** for determining the gross carrying amount (if more than one, the gross carrying amount for that basis in each category)
- **Depreciation methods** used
- **Useful lives** or depreciation rates used
- **Gross carrying amount** and accumulated depreciation at the beginning and end of the period

- **Reconciliation** of the carrying amount at the beginning and end of the period showing:
    - Additions
    - Disposals
    - Increases/decreases from revaluations
    - Reductions in carrying amount (ie impairments)
    - Depreciation
    - Any other movements.

The financial statements should also disclose the following.

- Existence and amounts of **restrictions on title**, and items pledged as security for liabilities
- Amount of expenditures on account of **items in the course of construction**
- Amount of commitments to **acquisitions**

Revalued assets require further disclosures.

- **Effective date** of the revaluation
- Whether an **independent valuer** was involved
- **Carrying amount** of each class of property, plant and equipment that would have been included in the financial statements had the assets been carried at cost less depreciation
- **Revaluation surplus**, indicating the movement for the period and any restrictions on the distribution of the balance to shareholders.

The standard also **encourages disclosure** of additional information, which the users of financial statements may find useful.

- The carrying amount of temporarily idle property, plant and equipment
- The gross carrying amount of any fully depreciated property, plant and equipment that is still in use
- The carrying amount of property, plant and equipment retired from active use and not held for disposal
- When the cost model is used, the fair value of property, plant and equipment when this is materially different from the carrying amount

The following format (with notional figures) is commonly used to disclose non-current assets movements.

	Total $	Land and buildings $	Plant and equipment $
Cost or valuation			
At 1 January 20X4	50,000	40,000	10,000
Revaluation surplus	12,000	12,000	–
Additions in year	4,000	–	4,000
Disposals in year	(1,000)	–	(1,000)
At 31 December 20X4	65,000	52,000	13,000
Depreciation			
At 1 January 20X4	16,000	10,000	6,000
Charge for year	4,000	1,000	3,000
Eliminated on disposals	(500)	–	(500)
At 31 December 20X4	19,500	11,000	8,500
Carrying amount			
At 31 December 20X4	45,500	41,000	4,500
At 1 January 20X4	34,000	30,000	4,000

Note that this format is only required for company accounts.

Question — Carrying amount

(a) In a statement of financial position prepared in accordance with IAS 16, what does the carrying amount represent?

(b) In a set of financial statements prepared in accordance with IAS 16, is it correct to say that the carrying amount figure in a statement of financial position cannot be greater than the market (net realisable) value of the partially used asset as at the reporting date? Explain your reasons for your answer.

Answer

(a) In simple terms the carrying amount of an asset is the cost of an asset less the 'accumulated depreciation', that is all depreciation charged so far. It should be emphasised that the main purpose of charging depreciation is to ensure that profits are fairly reported. Thus depreciation is concerned with the statement of profit or loss and other comprehensive income rather than the statement of financial position. In consequence the carrying amount figure in the statement of financial position can be quite arbitrary. In particular, it does not necessarily bear any relation to the market value of an asset and is of little use for planning and decision making.

An obvious example of the disparity between carrying amount and market value is found in the case of buildings, which may be worth more than ten times as much as their carrying amount.

(b) Carrying amount can in some circumstances be higher than market value (net realisable value). IAS 16 *Property, Plant and Equipment* states that the value of an asset cannot be greater than its 'recoverable amount'. However 'recoverable amount' as defined in IAS 16 is the amount recoverable from further use. This may be higher than the market value.

This makes sense if you think of a specialised machine which could not fetch much on the second-hand market but which will produce goods which can be sold at a profit for many years.

7 The asset register

FAST FORWARD

An **asset register** is used to record all non-current assets and is an **internal check** on the accuracy of the general ledger.

Nearly all organisations keep an asset register. This is a listing of all non-current assets owned by the organisation, broken down perhaps by department, location or asset type.

An asset register is maintained primarily for internal purposes. It shows an organisation's investment in capital equipment. The register is also part of the **internal control system**. The asset registers are sometimes called **real accounts**.

7.1 Data kept in an asset register

Details about each non-current asset may include the following.

- The internal reference number (for physical identification purposes)
- Manufacturer's serial number (for maintenance purposes)
- Description of asset
- Location of asset
- Department which 'owns' asset
- Purchase date (for calculation of depreciation)
- Cost
- Depreciation method and estimated useful life (for calculation of depreciation)
- Carrying amount (or written down value)

PART C PRACTICAL APPLICATION OF ACCOUNTING THEORY

7.2 Use of asset register

From time to time, the asset register should be checked to the accounting records. Any discrepancies must be investigated and the records corrected. For example, an asset may have been scrapped and the asset register updated, but the asset had not yet been written off in the accounting records.

Periodically, all physical non-current assets should be checked to the current register. This helps to deter theft.

8 Worked example

You have already had practice at preparing a statement of profit or loss and other comprehensive income and statement of financial position from a simple trial balance. Now see if you can do the same thing but at a more advanced level, taking account of adjustments for depreciation and inventory. Have a go at the following question.

Exam focus point

> The examiners recommend working full length questions not only to become familiar with the techniques involved, but also as a good grounding for your future studies at the higher levels.

Question — Final accounts

The following list of account balances was extracted from the ledger of Kevin Webster, a sole trader, as at 31 May 20X1, the end of his financial year.

KEVIN WEBSTER
TRIAL BALANCE AS AT 31 MAY 20X1

	Dr $	Cr $
Property, at cost	120,000	
Equipment, at cost	80,000	
Accumulated depreciation (as at 1 June 20X0)		
– on property		20,000
– on equipment		38,000
Purchases	250,000	
Sales		402,200
Inventory, as at 1 June 20X0	50,000	
Returns out (purchase returns)		15,000
Wages and salaries	58,800	
Selling expenses	22,600	
Loan interest	5,100	
Other operating expenses	17,700	
Trade accounts payable		36,000
Trade accounts receivable	38,000	
Cash in hand	300	
Bank	1,300	
Drawings	24,000	
17% long-term loan		30,000
Capital, as at 1 June 20X0		126,600
	667,800	667,800

The following additional information as at 31 May 20X1 is available.

(a) Inventory as at the close of business has been valued at cost at $42,000.
(b) Depreciation for the year ended 31 May 20X1 has still to be charged as follows:

Property: 1.5% per annum using the straight-line method
Equipment: 25% per annum using the reducing balance method

Required

Prepare Kevin Webster's statement of profit or loss and other comprehensive income for the year ended 31 May 20X1 and his statement of financial position as at that date.

Answer

KEVIN WEBSTER
STATEMENT OF PROFIT OR LOSS AND OTHER COMPREHENSIVE INCOME
FOR THE YEAR ENDED 31 MAY 20X1

	$	$
Revenue		402,200
Cost of sales		
Opening inventory	50,000	
Purchases	250,000	
Purchases returns	(15,000)	
	285,000	
Closing inventory	42,000	
		243,000
Gross profit		159,200
Expenses		
Wages and salaries	58,800	
Selling expenses	22,600	
Loan interest	5,100	
Depreciation (W1)	12,300	
Other operating expenses	17,700	
		116,500
Net profit for the year		42,700

KEVIN WEBSTER
STATEMENT OF FINANCIAL POSITION AS AT 31 MAY 20X1

	$	$
Assets		
Non-current assets		
Property: Cost	120,000	
Accumulated depreciation (W1)	21,800	
		98,200
Equipment: Cost	80,000	
Accumulated depreciation (W1)	48,500	
		31,500
Current assets		
Inventories	42,000	
Trade receivables	38,000	
Bank	1,300	
Cash in hand	300	
		81,600
Total assets		211,300

Capital and liabilities	$	$
Capital		
Balance at 1 June 20X0	126,600	
Net profit for the year	42,700	
Drawings	(24,000)	
Balance at 31 May 20X1		145,300
Non-current liabilities		
17% loan		30,000
Current liabilities		
Trade payables		36,000
Total capital and liabilities		211,300

Working

1 Depreciation

Property	$
Opening balance	20,000
Charge for the year (1.5% × 120,000)	1,800
Closing balance	21,800
Equipment	
Opening balance	38,000
Charge for the year (25% × 42,000)	10,500
Closing balance	48,500
Depreciation charge in SPLOCI (1,800 + 10,500)	12,300

Chapter roundup

- **Capital expenditure** is expenditure which results in the **acquisition of non-current assets**.

  Revenue expenditure is expenditure incurred for the **purpose of the trade** or to **maintain non-current assets**.

- The **cost** of a non-current asset, less its **estimated residual value**, is allocated fairly between accounting periods by means of **depreciation**. Depreciation is both:
  - Charged against profit; and
  - Deducted from the value of the non-current asset in the statement of financial position.

- Two methods of depreciation are specified in your syllabus:
  - The straight-line method
  - The reducing balance method

- When a non-current asset is **revalued**, depreciation is charged on the **revalued amount**.

- When a non-current asset is **sold**, there is likely to be a **profit or loss on disposal**. This is the difference between the net sale price of the asset and its carrying amount at the time of disposal.

- IAS 16 covers all aspects of accounting for property, plant and equipment. This represents the bulk of items which are **'tangible' non-current assets**.

- An **asset register** is used to record all non-current assets and is an **internal check** on the accuracy of the general ledger.

PART C PRACTICAL APPLICATION OF ACCOUNTING THEORY

Quick quiz

1   Which of the following statements regarding non-current asset accounting is correct?

    A   All non-current assets should be revalued each year.
    B   Non-current assets may be revalued at the discretion of management. Once revaluation has occurred it must be repeated regularly for all non-current assets in a class.
    C   Management can choose which non-current assets in a class of non-current assets should be revalued.
    D   Non-current assets should be revalued to reflect rising prices.

2   Which of the following statements regarding depreciation is correct?

    A   All non-current assets must be depreciated.
    B   Straight-line depreciation is usually the most appropriate method of depreciation.
    C   A change in the chosen depreciation method is a change in accounting policy which should be disclosed.
    D   Depreciation charges must be based upon the carrying amount of an asset (less residual value if appropriate).

3   What is an asset's carrying amount?

    A   Its cost less annual depreciation
    B   Its cost less accumulated depreciation
    C   Its net realisable value
    D   Its replacement value

4   Give two common depreciation methods.

5   A non-current asset (cost $10,000, depreciation $7,500) is given in part exchange for a new asset costing $20,500. The agreed trade-in value was $3,500. The statement of profit or loss and other comprehensive income will include…?

    A   A loss on disposal $1,000
    B   A profit on disposal $1,000
    C   A loss on purchase of a new asset $3,500
    D   A profit on disposal $3,500

6   What details about a non-current asset might be included in an asset register?

7   Why might the asset register not reconcile with the non-current assets?

    A   Asset stolen or damaged
    B   New asset, not yet recorded in the register
    C   Errors in the register
    D   All of the above

Answers to quick quiz

1. **B** Correct.
   - A Non-current assets may be revalued, there is no requirement to do so in IAS 16.
   - C Incorrect, all non-current assets in a class must be revalued.
   - D Incorrect, non-current assets may be reduced in value as well as being increased.

2. **D** Correct, carrying amount
   - A Incorrect, some non-current assets are not depreciated eg land.
   - B Incorrect, management should choose the most appropriate method.
   - C Incorrect, a method change is not a change in accounting policy.

3. **B** Its cost less accumulated depreciation.

4. Straight-line and reducing balance.

5. **B**

	$
Carrying amount at disposal (10,000 – 7,500)	2,500
Trade-in allowance	3,500
Profit	1,000

6.
   - Date of purchase
   - Description
   - Original cost
   - Depreciation rate and method
   - Accumulated depreciation to date
   - Date and amount of any revaluation

7. **D** Other reasons include an asset that is obsolete and so scrapped or improvements not yet recorded in the register.

PART C PRACTICAL APPLICATION OF ACCOUNTING THEORY

Intangible non-current assets

Topic list	Syllabus reference
1 Intangible assets	A3
2 Research and development costs	A3

Introduction

Intangible non-current assets are long-term assets which have a value to the business because they have been paid for, but which do not have any physical substance. The most significant of such intangible assets are research and deferred development costs.

In many companies, especially those which produce food or 'scientific' products such as medicines or 'high technology' products, the expenditure on **Research and Development (R&D)** is considerable. When R&D is a large item of cost its accounting treatment may have a significant influence on the profits of a business and its statement of financial position valuation. Because of this attempts have been made to standardise the treatment via IAS 38 *Intangible Assets*, and these are discussed in this chapter.

PART C PRACTICAL APPLICATION OF ACCOUNTING THEORY

> **Exam focus point**
>
> The examiners have highlighted intangible non-current assets as one of the areas that are consistently answered poorly in the exam.

1 Intangible assets

1.1 Intangible assets

'Intangible assets' means assets that literally cannot be touched, as opposed to tangible assets (such as plant and machinery) which have a physical existence. Intangible assets include goodwill, intellectual rights (eg patents, performing rights and authorship rights), computer software, as well as research and development costs.

1.2 Accounting treatment

Intangible assets are usually capitalised in the accounts and amortised (another word for depreciation but referring specifically to intangible assets). Amortisation is intended to write off the asset over its economic life (under the accruals concept).

1.3 Example: Patent

A business buys a patent for $50,000. It expects to use the patent for the next ten years, after which it will be valueless. Amortisation is calculated in the same way as for tangible assets:

$$\frac{\text{Cost} - \text{residual value}}{\text{Estimated useful life}}$$

In this case, amortisation will be $5,000 per annum ($50,000/10).

1.4 Internally generated goodwill

When a business has been trading for some time, it will have built up a loyal customer base and, hopefully, a reputation for good service. If the business was sold, a purchaser would usually be willing to pay a price in excess of the book value of the business to acquire these intangible assets. This is called **internally generated goodwill**. However, until the business is actually sold, there is no reliable method of valuing this goodwill and so it is **not recognised in the financial statements**.

2 Research and development costs

> **FAST FORWARD**
>
> Expenditure on **research** must always be written off in the period in which it is incurred.
>
> **Development costs** are also usually written off. However, if the criteria laid down by IAS 38 are satisfied, development expenditure can be capitalised as an **intangible asset**. If it has a **finite useful life**, it should then be amortised over that life.

2.1 Introduction to R&D

Large companies may spend significant amounts of money on Research and Development (R&D) activities. Obviously, any amounts so expended must be credited to cash and debited to an account for R&D expenditure. The accounting problem is **how to treat the debit balance on the R&D account** at the reporting date.

There are two possibilities.

(a) The debit balance may be classified as an **expense** and transferred to the statement of profit or loss and other comprehensive income. This is referred to as 'writing off' the expenditure. The argument here is that it is an expense just like rent or wages and its accounting treatment should be the same.

(b) The debit balance may be classified as an **asset** and included in the statement of financial position. This is referred to as 'capitalising' or 'carrying forward' or 'deferring' the expenditure. This argument is based on the accruals assumption. If R&D activity eventually leads to new or improved products which generate revenue, the costs should be carried forward and written off to match the pattern of economic benefits from the asset consumed by the business.

So the main question surrounding R&D costs is whether they should be treated as an expense or capitalised as an asset. This question is dealt with in IAS 38 *Intangible assets*.

2.2 Definitions

The following definitions are given by the standard.

Key terms

- An **intangible asset** is an identifiable non-monetary asset without physical substance.
- An asset is a resource:
    - controlled by an entity as a result of past events; and
    - from which future economic benefits are expected to flow to the entity
- **Research** is original and planned investigation undertaken with the prospect of gaining new scientific or technical knowledge and understanding.
- **Development** is the application of research findings or other knowledge to a plan or design for the production of new or substantially improved materials, devices, products, processes, systems or services before the start of commercial production or use.
- **Amortisation** is the systematic allocation of the depreciable amount of an intangible asset over its useful life. The standard also requires that amortisation period and amortisation method should be reviewed at each financial year end.
- **Depreciable amount** is the cost of an asset, or other amount substituted for cost, less its residual value.
- **Useful life** is:
    (a) the period over which an asset is expected to be available for use by an entity; or
    (b) the number of production or similar units expected to be obtained from the asset by an entity.
    (IAS 38: para. 9)

Although these definitions are usually well-understood, **in practice** it may not be so easy to identify the activities encompassed by R&D and the dividing line between the categories may be indistinct. Identification often depends on the type of business involved, the projects it undertakes and how it is organised.

The standard gives examples of activities which might be included in either research or development, or which are neither but may be closely associated with both.

- **Research**
    - Activities aimed at obtaining new knowledge
    - The search for applications of research findings or other knowledge
    - The search for product or process alternatives
    - The formulation and design of possible new or improved product or process alternatives

- **Development**
    - The design, construction and testing of pre-production prototypes and models
    - The design of tools, jigs, moulds and dies involving new technology
    - The design, construction and operation of a pilot plant that is not of a scale economically feasible for commercial production
    - The design construction and testing of a chosen alternative for new/improved materials, devices, products, processes, systems or services

2.3 Components of research and development costs

Research and development costs will include all costs that are **directly attributable** to research and development activities, or that can be **allocated on a reasonable basis**.

The standard gives examples of the costs which may be included in R&D, where applicable (note that **selling costs are excluded**).

- **Salaries, wages** and other employment related costs of personnel engaged in R&D activities
- Costs of **materials and services** consumed in R&D activities
- **Depreciation** of property, plant and equipment to the extent that these assets are used for R&D activities
- **Overhead costs**, other than general administrative costs, related to R&D activities; these cost are allocated on bases similar to those used in allocating overhead costs to inventories (see IAS 2 *Inventories*)
- **Other costs**, such as the amortisation of patents and licences, to the extent that these assets are used for R&D activities

2.4 Recognition of R&D costs

The relationship between the R&D costs and the **economic benefit** expected to derive from then will determine the allocation of those costs to different periods. Recognition of the costs as an asset will only occur where it is probable that the cost will produce future economic benefits for the entity and where the costs can be measured reliably.

(a) In the case of **research costs**, this will not be the case due to uncertainty about the resulting benefit from them; and so they should be expensed in the period in which they arose.

(b) **Development activities** tend to be much further advanced than the research stage and so it may be possible to determine the likelihood of future economic benefit. Where this can be determined, the development costs should be carried forward as an asset.

2.4.1 Research costs

Research costs should be recognised as an **expense in the period in which they are incurred**. They should not be recognised as an asset in a later period.

2.4.2 Development costs

Alternative treatments are given for development costs, the use of which depends on the situation. Most of the time, development costs will be recognised as an **expense in the period in which they are incurred** unless the criteria for asset recognition identified below are met. Development costs initially recognised as an expense should not be recognised as an asset in a later period.

Development expenditure should be recognised as an asset only when the business can demonstrate **all** of the following. Where the criteria are met, development expenditure **must** be capitalised.

- The technical feasibility of **completing** the intangible asset so that it will be available for use or sale
- Its intention to complete the intangible asset and **use or sell** it
- Its **ability** to use or sell the intangible asset
- How the intangible asset will generate **probable future economic benefits**. Among other things, the entity can demonstrate the existence of a market for the output of the intangible asset or the intangible asset itself or, if it is to be used internally, the usefulness of the intangible asset
- The availability of adequate technical, financial and other **resources** to complete the development and to use or sell the intangible asset
- Its ability to **measure reliably** the expenditure attributable to the intangible asset during its development

There is also an important point about the carrying amount of the asset and recoverability. The development costs of a project recognised as an asset should not exceed the amount that it is probable will be **recovered from related future economic benefits**, after deducting further development costs, related production costs, and selling and administrative costs directly incurred in marketing the product.

2.5 Amortisation of development costs

Once capitalised as an asset, development costs must be **amortised** and recognised as an expense to match the consumption of economic benefits. This must be done on a systematic basis, so as to reflect the pattern in which the related economic benefits are recognised.

It is unlikely to be possible to **match exactly** the economic benefits obtained with the costs which are held as an asset simply because of the nature of development activities. The entity should consider the period of time over which the product/process is expected to be sold/used, or, **in very limited circumstances**, the revenue from the sale/use of the product/process.

Point to note | If the pattern cannot be determined reliably, the straight-line method should be used.

The amortisation will begin when the **asset is available for use**.

If the intangible asset is considered to have an **indefinite** useful life, it should not be amortised but should be subjected to an annual impairment review.

2.6 Impairment of development costs

As with all assets, impairment (fall in value of an asset) is a possibility, but perhaps even more so in cases such as this. The development costs should be **written down** to the extent that the unamortised balance (taken together with further development costs, related production costs, and selling and administrative costs directly incurred in marketing the product) is no longer probable of being recovered from the expected future economic benefit.

2.7 Disclosure

The standard has fairly extensive disclosure requirements for intangible assets. The financial statements should disclose the **accounting policies** for intangible assets that have been adopted.

For **each class of intangible assets** (including development costs), disclosure is required of the following.
- Whether useful lives are indefinite or finite
- Where finite, the **method of amortisation** used
- The **useful life** of the assets or the amortisation rate used
- The **gross carrying amount**, the **accumulated amortisation** and the **accumulated impairment losses** at the beginning and end of the period

PART C PRACTICAL APPLICATION OF ACCOUNTING THEORY

- A **reconciliation of the carrying amount** as at the beginning and at the end of the period (showing additions, retirements/disposals, revaluations, impairment losses, impairment losses reversed, amortisation charge for the period, net exchange differences, other movements)
- The carrying amount of **internally generated intangible assets** in each class

Question | Research and development 1

Y Co is a research company which specialises in developing new materials and manufacturing processes for the furniture industry. The company receives payments from a variety of manufacturers, which pay for the right to use the company's patented fabrics and processes.

Research and development costs for the year ended 30 September 20X5 can be analysed as follows.

	$
Expenditure on continuing research projects	1,420,000
Amortisation of development expenditure capitalised in earlier years	240,000

New projects started during the year:

	$
Project A	280,000

New flame-proof padding. Expected to cost a total of $800,000 to develop. Expected total revenue $2,000,000 once work completed – probably late 20X6.

	$
Project B	150,000

New colour-fast dye. Expected to cost a total of $3,000,000 to complete. Future revenues are likely to exceed $5,000,000. The completion date is uncertain because external funding will have to be obtained before research work can be completed.

	$
Project C	110,000

Investigation of new adhesive recently developed in aerospace industry. If this proves effective then Y Co may well generate significant income because it will be used in place of existing adhesives.

	$
	2,200,000

The company has a policy of capitalising all development expenditure where permitted by IAS 38.

Explain how the three research projects A, B and C will be dealt with in Y Co's statement of profit or loss and other comprehensive income and statement of financial position.

In each case, explain your proposed treatment in terms of IAS 38 *Intangible Assets* and, where relevant, in terms of the fundamental accounting assumptions of going concern and accruals.

Answer

Project A

This project meets the criteria in IAS 38 for development expenditure to be recognised as an asset. These are as follows.

(a) The product or process is clearly defined and the costs attributable to the product or process can be separately identified and measured reliably.

(b) The technical feasibility of the product or process can be demonstrated.

(c) The entity intends to produce and market, or use, the product or process and has the ability to do so.

(d) The existence of a market for the product or process or, if it is to be used internally rather than sold, its usefulness to the enterprise, can be demonstrated.

(e) Adequate resources exist, or their availability can be demonstrated, to complete the project and market or use the product or process.

The capitalisation of development costs in a company which is a going concern means that these are accrued in order that they can be matched against the consumption of the asset's economic benefits.

Hence the costs of $280,000 incurred to date should be transferred from research and development costs to capitalised development expenditure and carried forward until revenues are generated; they should then be matched with the consumption of the asset's economic benefits.

Project B

Whilst this project meets most of the criteria discussed above which would enable the costs to be carried forward it fails on the requirement that 'adequate resources exist, or their availability can be demonstrated, to complete the project'.

Hence it would be prudent to write off these costs. Once funding is obtained the situation can then be reassessed and future costs may be capitalised.

Project C

This is a research project according to IAS 38, ie original and planned investigation undertaken with the prospect of gaining new scientific or technical knowledge or understanding.

There is no certainty as to its ultimate success or commercial viability and therefore it cannot be considered to be a development project. IAS 38 therefore requires that costs be written off as incurred.

Question — Research and development 2

Show how the research and development costs in the previous question will be disclosed in the accounts of Y Co. Assume the cost of capitalised development expenditure brought forward is $1,480,000, and that accumulated amortisation of $240,000 was brought forward at the beginning of the year.

(a) Statement of profit or loss and other comprehensive income
(b) Statement of financial position
(c) Notes to the accounts

Answer

(a) STATEMENT OF PROFIT OR LOSS AND OTHER COMPREHENSIVE INCOME (EXTRACT)

	$
Research expenditure (Project C + 1,420,000)	1,530,000
Development costs (Project B)	150,000
Amortisation of capitalised development costs	240,000

(b) STATEMENT OF FINANCIAL POSITION (EXTRACT)

	$
Non current assets	
Intangible assets	
Deferred development costs	1,280,000

(c) NOTE TO ACCOUNTS
DEFERRED DEVELOPMENT COSTS

	$
Cost	
Balance b/f	1,480,000
Additions during year (Project A)	280,000
Balance c/f	1,760,000
Amortisation	
Balance b/f	240,000
Charge during year	240,000
Balance c/f	480,000
Carrying amount at 30 September 20X5	1,280,000
Carrying amount at 30 September 20X4	1,240,000

Chapter roundup

- Expenditure on **research** must always be written off in the period in which it is incurred.

  Development costs are also usually written off. However, if the criteria laid down by IAS 38 are satisfied, development expenditure can be capitalised as an **intangible asset**. If it has a **finite useful life**, it should then be amortised over that life.

Quick quiz

1. What is the required accounting treatment for expenditure on research?
   - A Write off as an expense in the period it is incurred
   - B Capitalise and carry for ward as an asset

2. Which of the following items is an intangible asset?
   - A Land
   - B Patents
   - C Buildings
   - D Van

3. Research expenditure is incurred in the application of knowledge for the production of new products.
   Is this statement:
   - A True
   - B False

4. XY Co has development expenditure of $500,000. Its policy is to amortise development expenditure at 2% per annum. Accumulated amortisation brought forward is $20,000. What is the charge in the statement of profit or loss and other comprehensive income for the year's amortisation?
   - A $10,000
   - B $400
   - C $20,000
   - D $9,600

5. Given the facts in 4 above, what is the amount shown in the statement of financial position for development expenditure?
   - A $500,000
   - B $480,000
   - C $470,000
   - D $490,000

PART C PRACTICAL APPLICATION OF ACCOUNTING THEORY

Answers to quick quiz

1. A   Research expenditure is always written off as it is incurred.
2. B   All the others are tangible assets.
3. B   False. This is a definition of development expenditure.
4. A   2% × $500,000 = $10,000
5. C   Deferred development expenditure b/f is $480,000 (cost $500,000 – accumulated amortisation $20,000), then deduct annual amortisation of $10,000 to give figure c/f of $470,000.

Financial reporting, analysis and interpretation

Business entity

Topic list	Syllabus reference
1 Limited liability and accounting records	A4
2 Share capital	A4
3 Reserves	A4
4 Bonus and rights issues	A4
5 Ledger accounts and limited liability companies	A4
6 Company accounts for internal purposes	A4
7 Branch accounting	A4
8 Published accounts	A4

Introduction

We begin this chapter by considering the **status of limited** liability companies and the type of accounting records they maintain in order to prepare financial statements.

Then we will look at those accounting entries unique to limited liability companies: share capital, reserves, and bonus and rights issues.

PART D FINANCIAL REPORTING, ANALYSIS AND INTERPRETATION

1 The distinction between a sole trader and a limited company

> **FAST FORWARD**
>
> There are some important differences between the accounts of a **limited liability company** and those of sole traders.

So far, this Workbook has dealt mainly with the accounts of businesses in general. In this chapter we shall turn our attention to the accounts of limited liability companies. As we should expect, the accounting rules and conventions for recording the business transactions of limited liability companies and then preparing their final accounts are much the same as for sole traders. For example, companies will have a cash book, sales day book, purchase day book, journal, sales ledger, purchase ledger and general ledger. They will also prepare a statement of profit or loss and other comprehensive income annually and a statement of financial position at the end of the accounting year.

Below is a table that illustrates the differences between the two different types of entity:

Details	Sole Trader	Limited Company
Ownership	If you are a sole trader, you run your own business as an individual and are self-employed. You can keep all your business' profits after you have paid tax on them. You are personally responsible for any losses your business makes.	If you decide to set up your own limited company, you'll be a director and a shareholder of the business. You can be paid a salary and/or dividends from the company's available profits. The company must make various annual returns and file annual accounts with statutory bodies. It is your responsibility as a director of the company to ensure this happens.
Capital	A sole trader invests personal funds into the business. The funds invested may have been taken from a personal bank loan; this remains the liability of the person.	The share capital in a Limited company is the amount of money invested by its owners in exchange for shares of ownership. Company directors are typically shareholders in their own companies. Shareholders exercise certain powers over how the company is run.
Liability	There is little distinction between the owner and the business. Any business debts become the debts of the owner. Personal assets (for example the owner's house) is not protected.	Its own legal identity, so a shareholder's liability is limited.
Managed by	The sole trader – the business, owner, manager and/or proprietor.	Shareholder – hold all or a proportion of the company's share capital and own the business. Directors – are responsible for the running of the business. Directors often own shares. Company directors are not personally responsible for the company's debts.

Details	Sole Trader	Limited Company
Setup costs	Cost of business name registration. Overall the cost is inexpensive.	Can become expensive – once specialist services are enlisted such as hiring an accountant. The cost of a company formation itself is typically inexpensive, usually between $30 and $150 with extra costs incurred should you visit an accountant for tax or business advice.
Regulations	Sole traders are not legally required to produce annual accounts or file accounts for inspection. Business expenses and personal income records are required for personal tax returns.	Limited companies must produce annual accounts from the company records at the end of the financial year. These should be accompanied by notes to the accounts which include accounting policies adopted by the company. Accounts must be prepared in line with accounting standards.
Raising funds	A sole trader relies on personal credit ratings to borrow capital which is used to grow their business.	A limited company can establish its own credit rating, which can support borrowing to invest in the business.
Tax	**High tax:** Once your sole trader business is particularly, tax rates can be higher than those running as a limited company. Tax does not appear in the sole traders Statement of Profit or Loss – this is done by self-assessment.	**Tax incentives:** Typically, limited companies are more tax efficient than sole trading. They would pay Corporation Tax on your profits rather than income tax, and often this can be more profitable. There are frequently a wider range of allowances and tax-deductibles involved here too. Limited companies pay tax, this is charged to the statement of Profit or Loss as an expense. The tax is not paid until after the year end so the charge for the year is treated as a liability.

2 An outline of the basic features of a limited company

In the table above you have seen the differences between the sole trader and a limited company. It is important that you remember this as well as the basic features of a limited company which are:

- Separate legal entity
- Limited liability
- Separation of ownership and management

3 Limited liability and accounting records

There are, however, some **fundamental differences** in the accounts of limited liability companies, of which the following are perhaps the most significant.

(a) The **national legislation** governing the activities of limited liability companies tends to be very extensive. Amongst other things such legislation may define certain minimum accounting records which must be maintained by companies; they may specify that the annual accounts of a company must be filed with a government bureau and so available for public inspection; and they often contain detailed requirements on the minimum information which must be disclosed in a company's accounts. Businesses which are not limited liability companies (non-incorporated businesses) often enjoy comparative freedom from statutory regulation.

(b) The **owners of a company** (its **members** or **shareholders**) may be **very numerous**. Their capital is shown differently from that of a sole trader; and similarly the 'appropriation account' of a company is different.

UK Small Business, Enterprise and Employment Act 2015

In the UK, the Small Business, Enterprise and Employment Act 2015 made changes to the law applying to UK companies. The changes are intended to reduce the administrative burden on smaller companies and to encourage entrepreneurship. The changes include:

- The annual return filed with Companies House is replaced with a much simpler 'confirmation statement' to be submitted at least once a year. This confirmation statement contains information relating to the company's registered office, directors and shareholders.
- The information required on the statement of capital is simplified and only needs to be filed with Companies House if changes are made during the year.
- More protection for directors has been introduced by no longer making the date of birth of directors publically available.
- Various processes and procedures have been streamlined, such as the procedures required when appointing a director.

PSC register

The Act introduces the requirement for certain UK entities (UK companies, Societates Europaeae, limited liability partnerships and eligible Scottish partnerships) to maintain a public **register of people with significant control** over the company (the **'PSC register'**). The Act sets out the definitions for persons with significant control, which may include an individual who owns more than 25% of the shares or voting rights within a company, or has the right to appoint or remove the majority of directors.

Previously it was only necessary for companies to record the immediate, legal owners of their shares. The introduction of the PSC register means that companies must now look past the immediate shareholders and identify the persons who have significant control over the company. This will provide transparency over how companies are owned, assist law enforcement agencies in money laundering investigations and assist potential investors in deciding whether to invest.

3.1 Limited liability

Key term

> **Unlimited liability** means that if the business runs up debts that it is unable to pay, the proprietors will become personally liable for the unpaid debts and would be required, if necessary, to sell their private possessions to repay them.

It is worth recapping on the relative **advantages and disadvantages** of limited liability (which we have mentioned in earlier parts of the Text). Sole traders and partnerships are, with some significant exceptions, generally fairly small concerns. The amount of capital involved may be modest, and the proprietors of the business usually participate in managing it. Their liability for the debts of the business is

unlimited, which means that if the business runs up debts that it is unable to pay, the proprietors will become personally liable for the unpaid debts, and would be required, if necessary, to sell their private possessions in order to repay them. For example, if a sole trader has some capital in his business, but the business now owes $40,000 which it cannot repay, the trader might have to sell his house to raise the money to pay off his business debts.

Limited liability companies offer limited liability to their owners.

Key term

> **Limited liability** means that the maximum amount that an owner stands to lose in the event that the company becomes insolvent and cannot pay off its debts, is his share of the capital in the business.

Thus, limited liability is a **major advantage** of turning a business into a limited liability company. However, in practice, banks will normally seek personal guarantees from shareholders before making loans or granting an overdraft facility and so the advantage of limited liability is lost to a small owner-managed business.

3.1.1 Disadvantages

(a) Compliance with national legislation
(b) Compliance with national accounting standards and/or IFRSs
(c) Any formation and annual registration costs

These are needed to avoid the privilege of limited liability being abused.

As a business grows, it needs **more capital** to finance its operations, and significantly more than the people currently managing the business can provide themselves. One way of obtaining more capital is to invite investors from outside the business to invest in the ownership or equity of the business. These new co-owners would not usually be expected to help with managing the business. To such investors, limited liability is very attractive.

Investments are always risky undertakings, but with limited liability the investor knows the maximum amount that he stands to lose when he puts some capital into a company.

3.2 The accounting records of limited companies

There is almost always a **national legal requirement** for companies to keep accounting records which are sufficient to show and explain the company's transactions. The records will probably have the following qualities.

(a) Disclose the company's current financial position at any time.

(b) Contain:

   (i) Day-to-day entries of money received and spent
   (ii) A record of the company's assets and liabilities
   (iii) Where the company deals in goods:

       (1) A statement of inventories held at the year end, and supporting inventory count records

       (2) With the exception of retail sales, statements of goods bought and sold which identify the sellers and buyers of those goods

(c) Enable the managers of the company to ensure that the final accounts of the company give a true and fair view of the company's total comprehensive income and statement of financial position.

The detailed requirements of accounting records which must be maintained will vary from country to country.

PART D   FINANCIAL REPORTING, ANALYSIS AND INTERPRETATION

Question Companies

How are limited liability companies regulated in your country?

4 Share capital

FAST FORWARD

In preparing a statement of financial position you must be able to deal with:

- Ordinary and preference share capital
- Reserves
- Loan stock

4.1 The capital of limited liability companies

The proprietors' capital in a limited liability company consists of **share capital**. When a company is set up for the first time, it issues shares, which are paid for by investors, who then become shareholders of the company. Shares are denominated in units of 25 cents, 50 cents, $1 or whatever seems appropriate. The 'face value' of the shares is called their **par value** or **legal value** (or sometimes the **nominal value**).

For example, when a company is set up with a share capital of, say, $100,000, it may be decided to issue:

(a) 100,000 shares of $1 each par value;
(b) 200,000 shares of 50c each;
(c) 400,000 shares of 25c each; or
(d) 250,000 shares of 40c each, etc.

The amount at which the shares are issued may exceed their par value. For example, a company might issue 100,000 $1 shares at a price of $1.20 each. Subscribers will then pay a total of $120,000. The issued share capital of the company would be shown in its accounts at par value, $100,000; the excess of $20,000 is described not as share capital, but as **share premium** or **capital paid-up in excess of par value**.

4.2 Authorised, issued, called-up and paid-up share capital

A distinction must be made between authorised, issued, called-up and paid-up share capital.

(a) **Authorised (or legal) capital** is the maximum amount of share capital that a company is empowered to issue. The amount of authorised share capital varies from company to company, and can change by agreement.

Not all jurisdictions require authorised share capital. The Companies Act 2006 in the UK abolished the requirement for UK companies to have authorised share capital.

For example, a company's authorised share capital might be 5,000,000 ordinary shares of $1 each. This would then be the maximum number of shares it could issue, unless the maximum were to be changed by agreement.

(b) **Issued capital** is the par amount of share capital that has been issued to shareholders. The amount of issued capital cannot exceed the amount of authorised capital.

Continuing the example above, the company with authorised share capital of 5,000,000 ordinary shares of $1 might have issued 4,000,000 shares. This would leave it the option to issue 1,000,000 more shares at some time in the future.

When share capital is issued, shares are allotted to shareholders. The term 'allotted' share capital means the same thing as issued share capital.

(c) **Called-up capital.** When shares are issued or allotted, a company does not always expect to be paid the full amount for the shares at once. It might instead call up only a part of the issue price, and wait until a later time before it calls up the remainder.

For example, if a company allots 400,000 ordinary shares of $1, it might call up only, say, 75 cents per share. The issued share capital would be $400,000, but the called-up share capital would only be $300,000.

(d) **Paid-up capital.** Like everyone else, investors are not always prompt or reliable payers. When capital is called up, some shareholders might delay their payment (or even default on payment). Paid-up capital is the amount of called-up capital that has been paid.

For example, if a company issues 400,000 ordinary shares of $1 each, calls up 75 cents per share, and receives payments of $290,000, we would have:

	$
Allotted or issued capital	400,000
Called-up capital	300,000
Paid-up capital	290,000
Capital not yet paid-up	10,000

The statement of financial position of the company would appear as follows.

	$
Assets	
Called-up capital not paid	10,000
Cash (called-up capital paid)	290,000
	300,000
Equity	
Called-up share capital	
(400,000 ordinary shares of $1, with 75c per share called up)	300,000

Notice that in a limited liability company's statement of financial position the owners' capital is called **equity**. In your reading, you may find that shares are called **equities**.

4.3 Ordinary shares and preference (preferred) shares

At this stage it is relevant to distinguish between the two types of shares most often encountered: **preference shares** and **ordinary shares**.

4.3.1 Preference shares

Key term

> **Preference shares** are shares which confer certain preferential rights on their holder.

Preference shares carry the right to a final dividend which is expressed as a percentage of their par value: eg a 6% $1 preference share carries a right to an annual dividend of 6 cents. Preference dividends have priority over ordinary dividends; in other words, if the managers of a company wish to pay an ordinary dividend (which they are not obliged to do) they must pay any preference dividend first. Otherwise, no ordinary dividend may be paid.

The rights attaching to preference shares are set out in the company's constitution. They may vary from company to company and country to country, but typically:

(a) Preference shareholders have a **priority right** over ordinary shareholders to a return of their capital if the company goes into liquidation.

(b) Preference shares do **not carry a right to vote**.

(c) If the preference shares are **cumulative**, it means that before a company can pay an ordinary dividend it must not only pay the current year's preference dividend, but must also make good any arrears of preference dividends unpaid in previous years.

4.3.2 Classification of preference shares

Preference shares may be classified in one of two ways.

- Redeemable
- Irredeemable

Redeemable preference shares mean that the company will redeem (repay) the nominal value of those shares at a later date. For example, 'redeemable 5% $1 preference shares 20X9' means that the company will pay these shareholders $1 for every share they hold on a certain date in 20X9. The shares will then be cancelled and no further dividends paid. Redeemable preference shares are treated like loans and are included as non-current liabilities in the statement of financial position. Remember to reclassify as current liabilities if the redemption is due within 12 months. Dividends paid on redeemable preference shares are treated like interest paid on loans and are included in finance costs in the statement of profit or loss and other comprehensive income.

Irredeemable (or non-redeemable) preference shares are treated just like other shares. They form part of equity and their dividends are treated as appropriations of profit.

> **Exam focus point**
>
> In the exam, the question will specifically state whether the shares are redeemable or irredeemable preference shares.

4.3.3 Ordinary shares

Ordinary shares are by far the most common. They carry no right to a fixed dividend but are entitled to all profits left after payment of any preference dividend. Generally, however, only a part of such remaining profits is distributed, the rest being kept in reserve (see below).

> **Key term**
>
> **Ordinary shares** are shares which are not preferred with regard to dividend payments. Thus a holder only receives a dividend after fixed dividends have been paid to preference shareholders.

The amount of ordinary dividends fluctuates although there is a general expectation that it will increase from year to year. Should the company be wound up, any surplus not distributed is shared between the ordinary shareholders. Ordinary shares normally carry voting rights.

Ordinary shareholders are thus the effective **owners** of a company. They own the 'equity' of the business, and any reserves of the business (described later) belong to them. Ordinary shareholders are sometimes referred to as **equity shareholders**. Preference shareholders are in many ways more like payables of the company (although legally they are members, not payables). It should be emphasised, however, that the precise rights attached to preference and ordinary shares may vary, the distinctions noted above are generalisations.

4.4 Example: Dividends on ordinary shares and preference shares

Garden Gloves Co has issued 50,000 ordinary shares of 50 cents each and 20,000 7% preference shares of $1 each. Its profits after taxation for the year to 30 September 20X5 were $8,400. The management board has decided to pay an ordinary dividend (ie a dividend on ordinary shares) which is 50% of profits after tax and preference dividend.

Required

Show the amount in total of dividends and of retained profits, and calculate the dividend per share on ordinary shares.

Solution

	$
Profit after tax	8,400
Preference dividend (7% of $1 × 20,000)	1,400
Earnings (profit after tax and preference dividend)	7,000
Ordinary dividend (50% of earnings)	3,500
Retained earnings (also 50% of earnings)	3,500

The ordinary dividend is 7 cents per share ($3,500 ÷ 50,000 ordinary shares).

The appropriation of profit would be as follows:

	$	$
Profit after tax		8,400
Dividends: preference	1,400	
ordinary	3,500	
		4,900
Retained profit		3,500

As we will see later, appropriations of profit do not appear in the statement of profit or loss and other comprehensive income, but are shown as movements on reserves.

4.5 The market value of shares

The par value of shares will be different from their market value, which is the price at which someone is prepared to purchase shares in the company from an existing shareholder. If Mr A owns 1,000 $1 shares in Z Co he may sell them to Mr B for $1.60 each.

This transfer of existing shares does not affect Z Co's own financial position in any way whatsoever, and apart from changing the register of members, Z Co does not have to bother with the sale by Mr A to Mr B at all. There are certainly no accounting entries to be made for the share sale.

Shares in private companies do not change hands very often, hence their market value is often hard to estimate. Companies listed on a stock exchange are quoted, ie it is the market value of the shares which is quoted.

4.6 Loan stock or bonds

Limited liability companies may issue loan stock or bonds. These are long-term liabilities and in some countries they are described as **loan capital** because they are a means of raising finance, in the same way as issuing share capital raises finance. They are different from share capital in the following ways.

(a) **Shareholders** are **members** of a company, while **providers of loan capital** are **creditors**.

(b) **Shareholders** receive **dividends** (appropriations of profit) whereas the **holders of loan capital** are entitled to a **fixed rate of interest** (an expense charged against revenue).

(c) Loan capital holders can take legal action against a company if their interest is not paid when due, whereas **shareholders cannot enforce the payment of dividends**.

(d) Loan stock is **often secured on company assets**, whereas shares are not.

The holder of loan capital is generally in a less risky position than the shareholder. He has greater security, although his income is fixed and cannot grow, unlike ordinary dividends. As remarked earlier, preference shares are in practice very similar to loan capital, not least because the preference dividend is normally fixed.

Interest is calculated on the par or legal value of loan capital, regardless of its market value. If a company has $700,000 (par value) 12% loan stock in issue, interest of $84,000 will be charged in the statement of profit or loss and other comprehensive income per year. Interest is usually paid half-yearly; examination questions often require an accrual to be made for interest due at the year end.

For example, if a company has $700,000 of 12% loan stock in issue, pays interest on 30 June and 31 December each year, and ends its accounting year on 30 September, there would be an accrual of three months' unpaid interest (3/12 × $84,000) = $21,000 at the end of each accounting year that the loan stock is still in issue.

Question — Share capital

Distinguish between authorised, issued, called-up and paid-up capital.

Answer

Authorised share capital: The maximum amount of share capital that a company is empowered to issue.

Issued share capital: The amount of share capital that has been issued to shareholders.

Called-up share capital: The amount the company has asked shareholders to pay, for the time being, on shares issued to them.

Paid-up share capital: The amount actually paid by shareholders on shares issued to them.

5 Reserves

FAST FORWARD

Share capital and reserves are 'owned' by the shareholders. They are known collectively as 'shareholders' equity'.

Shareholders' equity consists of the following.

(a) The par value of issued capital (minus any amounts not yet called up on issued shares)
(b) Other equity

The share capital itself might consist of both ordinary shares and preference shares. All reserves, however, are owned by the ordinary shareholders, who own the 'equity' in the company. We looked at share capital in detail above.

'Other equity' consists of four elements.

(a) Capital paid-up in excess of par value (share premium)
(b) Revaluation surplus
(c) Reserves
(d) Retained earnings

We will look at each in turn.

5.1 The share premium account

In this context, 'premium' means the difference between the issue price of the share and its par value. The account is sometimes called 'capital paid-up in excess of par value'. When a company is first incorporated (set up) the issue price of its shares will probably be the same as their par value and so there would be no share premium. If the company does well, the market value of its shares will increase, but not the par value. The price of any new shares issued will be approximately their market value.

The difference between cash received by the company and the par value of the new shares issued is transferred to the **share premium account**. For example, if X Co issues 1,000 $1 ordinary shares at $2.60 each the book entry will be:

		$	$
DEBIT	Cash	2,600	
CREDIT	Ordinary shares		1,000
	Share premium account		1,600

A share premium account only comes into being when a company issues shares at a price in excess of their par value. The market price of the shares, once they have been issued, has no bearing at all on the company's accounts, and so if their market price goes up or down the share premium account would remain unaltered.

Key term

> A **share premium account** is an account into which sums received as payment for shares in excess of their nominal value must be placed.

Once established, the share premium account constitutes capital of the company which cannot be paid out in dividends, ie it is a capital reserve. The share premium account will increase in value if and when new shares are issued at a price above their par value. The share premium account can be 'used' – and so decrease in value – only in certain very limited ways, which are largely beyond the scope of your basic financial accounting syllabus. One common use of the share premium account, however, is to 'finance' the issue of bonus shares, which are described later in this chapter. Other uses of this account may depend on national legislation.

Exam focus point

> The share premium account cannot be distributed as dividends under any circumstances.

The reason for creating such non-distributable reserves is to maintain the capital of the company. This capital 'base' provides some security for the company's creditors, bearing in mind that the liability of shareholders is limited in the event that the company cannot repay its debts. It would be most unjust – and illegal – for a company to pay its shareholders a dividend out of its base capital when it is not even able to pay back its debts.

Question
Share issue

AB Co issues 5,000 50 cent shares for $6,000. What are the entries for share capital and share premium in the statement of financial position?

	Share capital	Share premium
A	$5,000	$1,000
B	$1,000	$5,000
C	$3,500	$3,500
D	$2,500	$3,500

> **Answer**
>
> Did you notice that the shares are 50 cents each, not $1? The shares were issued for $1.20 each ($6,000/5,000 shares). Of this 50 cents is share capital and 70 cents is share premium. Therefore option D is the correct answer.
>
> Note that some jurisdictions no longer require share capital to be split into ordinary and premium elements. The Singapore Companies (Amendment) Act 2005 (CAA 2005) removed the notion of nominal/par value of shares and therefore effectively abolished the use of share premium accounts in Singapore.

5.2 Revaluation surplus

We looked at the revaluation of non-current assets in Chapter 16. The result of an upward revaluation is a '**revaluation surplus**'. This is **non-distributable** as it represents unrealised profits on the revalued assets. It is another capital reserve. The relevant part of a revaluation surplus can only become realised if the asset in question is sold, thus realising the gain. The revaluation surplus may fall, however, if an asset which had previously been revalued upwards suffered a fall in value in the next revaluation.

5.3 Reserves

In most countries, a distinction must be made between the following.

(a) **Statutory reserves**, which are reserves which a company is required to set up by law, and which are not available for the distribution of dividends.

(b) **Non-statutory reserves**, which are reserves consisting of profits which are distributable as dividends, if the company so wishes.

Statutory reserves are capital reserves (share premium, revaluation) and non-statutory reserves are revenue reserves.

We are concerned here with the latter type, which the company managers may choose to set up. These may have a specific purpose (eg plant and machinery replacement reserve) or not (eg general reserve). The creation of these reserves usually indicates a general intention not to distribute the profits involved at any future date, although legally any such reserves, being non-statutory, remain available for the payment of dividends.

Profits are transferred to these reserves by making an appropriation out of profits, usually profits for the year. Typically, you might come across the following.

	$	$
Profit after taxation		100,000
Appropriations of profit		
Dividend	60,000	
Transfer to general reserve	10,000	
		70,000
Retained earnings for the year		30,000
Retained earnings b/f		250,000
Retained earnings c/f		280,000

5.3.1 Dividends

Key term

Dividends are appropriations of profit after tax.

Shareholders who are also managers of their company will receive a salary as a manager. They are also entitled to a share of the profits made by the company.

Many companies pay dividends in two stages during the course of their accounting year.

(a) In mid year, after the half-year financial results are known, the company might pay an **interim dividend**.

(b) At the end of the year, the company might propose a further **final dividend**.

The total dividend for the year is the sum of the interim and the final dividend. (Not all companies by any means pay an interim dividend. Interim dividends are, however, commonly paid out by larger limited liability companies.)

At the end of an accounting year, when the financial statements have been prepared, a company's managers may propose a final dividend payment, but this will not have been approved or paid by the reporting date. The final dividend **does not appear in the accounts** but will be disclosed in the notes.

Exam focus point

Dividends which have been **paid** are shown in the statement of changes in equity (see Section 3.6). They are not shown in the statement of profit or loss and other comprehensive income, although they are deducted from retained earnings in the statement of financial position. **Proposed** dividends not approved before the reporting date are not adjusted for, they are simply disclosed by note.

The terminology of dividend payments can be confusing, since they may be expressed either in the form, as 'x cents per share' or as 'y%'. In the latter case, the meaning is always 'y% of the *par value* of the shares in issue'. For example, suppose a company's issued share capital consists of 100,000 50 cent ordinary shares which were issued at a premium of 10 cent per share. The company's statement of financial position would include the following.

		$
Ordinary shares:	100,000 50c ordinary shares	50,000
Share premium account	(100,000 × 10c)	10,000

If the managers wish to pay a dividend of $5,000, they may propose either:

(a) A dividend of 5 cent per share (100,000 × 5c = $5,000); or
(b) A dividend of 10% (10% × $50,000 = $5,000).

Not all profits are distributed as dividends; some will be retained in the business to finance future projects.

Question   **Dividend**

A company has authorised share capital of 1,000,000 50 cent ordinary shares and an issued share capital of 800,000 50 cent ordinary shares. If an ordinary dividend of 5% is declared, what is the amount payable to shareholders?

A $50,000
B $20,000
C $40,000
D $25,000

Answer

B   800,000 × 50c × 5% = $20,000.

5.4 Retained earnings

This is the **most significant reserve** and is variously described as:

(a) Revenue reserve
(b) Retained profits
(c) Accumulated profits
(d) Undistributed profits
(e) Unappropriated profits

These are **profits** earned by the company and not appropriated by dividends, taxation or transfer to another reserve account.

Provided that a company is earning profits, this reserve generally increases from year to year, as most companies do not distribute all their profits as dividends. Dividends can be paid from it: even if a loss is made in one particular year, a dividend can be paid from previous years' retained earnings.

For example, if a company makes a loss of $100,000 in one year, yet has unappropriated profits from previous years totalling $250,000, it can pay a dividend not exceeding $150,000. One reason for retaining some profit each year is to enable the company to pay dividends even when profits are low (or non-existent). Another reason is usually shortage of cash.

Very occasionally, you might come across a debit balance on the retained earnings account. This would indicate that the company has accumulated losses.

5.5 Distinction between reserves and provisions

Key terms

A **reserve** is an appropriation of distributable profits for a specific purpose (eg plant replacement) while a provision is an amount charged against revenue as an expense. A provision relates either to a diminution in the value of an asset or a known liability (eg legal claim for damages), the amount of which cannot be established with any accuracy.

Provisions or allowances (for depreciation etc) are dealt with in company accounts in the same way as in the accounts of other types of business.

5.6 Statement of changes in equity

In the published accounts, a company has to provide a statement of changes in equity which details the movements on its capital and reserves.

5.6.1 Example: Statement of changes in equity

	Share capital	Share premium	Revaluation surplus	Retained earnings	Total
Balance at 1.1.X6	X	X	X	X	X
Changes in accounting policy	–	–	–	(X)	(X)
Restated balance	X	X	X	X	X
Changes in equity for 20X6					
Total comprehensive income for the year	–	–	X	X	X
Transactions with owners					
Dividends	–	–	–	(X)	(X)
Issue of share capital	X	X	–	–	X
Balance at 31.12.X6	X	X	X	X	X

Note that the statement of changes in equity simply takes the equity section of the statement of financial position and shows the movements during the year. The bottom line shows the amounts for the current statement of financial position. Total comprehensive income for the year is taken from the statement of profit or loss and other comprehensive income.

Dividends paid during the year are not shown on the statement of profit or loss and other comprehensive income; they are shown in the statement of changes in equity.

Question — USB 1

USB, a limited liability company, has the following trial balance at 31 December 20X9.

	Debit $'000	Credit $'000
Cash at bank	100	
Inventory at 1 January 20X9	2,400	
Administrative expenses	2,206	
Distribution costs	650	
Non-current assets at cost:		
Buildings	10,000	
Plant and equipment	1,400	
Motor vehicles	320	
Suspense		1,500
Accumulated depreciation		
Buildings		4,000
Plant and equipment		480
Motor vehicles		120
Retained earnings		560
Trade receivables	876	
Purchases	4,200	
Dividend paid	200	
Sales revenue		11,752
Sales tax payable		1,390
Trade payables		1,050
Share premium		500
$1 ordinary shares		1,000
	22,352	22,352

The following additional information is relevant.

(a) Inventory at 31 December 20X9 was valued at $1,600,000. While doing the inventory count, errors in the previous year's inventory count were discovered. The inventory brought forward at the beginning of the year should have been $2.2m, not $2.4m as above.

(b) No final dividend is being proposed.

(c) 1 million new ordinary shares were issued at $1.50 on 1 December 20X9. The proceeds have been left in a suspense account.

(d) The profit for the period was $3,246,000.

Required

Prepare a statement of changes in equity for the year to 31 December 20X9.

Answer

USB
STATEMENT OF CHANGES IN EQUITY FOR THE YEAR ENDED 31 DECEMBER 20X9

	Share capital $'000	Share premium $'000	Retained earnings $'000	Total $'000
Balance at 1 January 20X9	1,000	500	560	2,060
Prior period adjustment*	–	–	(200)	(200)
Restated balance	1,000	500	360	1,860
Profit for the period	–	–	3,246	3,246
Transactions with owners				
Dividends paid	–	–	(200)	(200)
Share issue	1,000	500	–	1,500
	2,000	1,000	3,406	6,406

* The previous year's closing inventory was revalued by $200,000. This means that the profits for that period were overstated by $200,000 and this needs to be adjusted.

6 Bonus and rights issues

FAST FORWARD

A company can increase its share capital by means of a **bonus issue** or a **rights issue**.

6.1 Bonus (capitalisation) issues

A company may wish to increase its share capital without needing to raise additional finance by issuing new shares. For example, a profitable company might expand from modest beginnings over a number of years. Its profitability would be reflected in large balances on its reserves, while its original share capital might look like that of a much smaller business.

It is open to such a company to **re-classify some of its reserves as share capital**. This is purely a paper exercise which raises no funds. Any reserve may be re-classified in this way, including a share premium account or other reserve. Such a re-classification increases the capital base of the company and gives creditors greater protection.

6.1.1 Advantages

- Increases capital without diluting current shareholders' holdings
- Capitalises reserves, so they cannot be paid as dividends

6.1.2 Disadvantages

- Does not raise any cash
- Could jeopardise payment of future dividends if profits fall

6.2 Example: Bonus issue

BUBBLES CO
STATEMENT OF FINANCIAL POSITION (EXTRACT)

	$'000	$'000
Shareholders' equity		
Share capital		
$1 ordinary shares (fully paid)		1,000
Reserves		
Share premium	500	
Retained earnings	2,000	
		2,500
		3,500

Bubbles decided to make a '3 for 2' bonus issue (ie 3 new shares for every 2 already held). The double entry is:

		$'000	$'000
DEBIT	Share premium	500	
	Retained earnings	1,000	
CREDIT	Ordinary share capital		1,500

After the issue the statement of financial position is as follows.

	$'000
Share capital: $1 ordinary shares (fully paid)	2,500
Retained earnings	1,000
Shareholders' equity	3,500

1,500,000 new ('bonus') shares are issued to existing shareholders, so that if Mr X previously held 20,000 shares he will now hold 50,000. The total value of his holding should theoretically remain the same however, since the net assets of the company remain unchanged and his share of those net assets remains at 2% (ie 50,000/2,500,000; previously 20,000/1,000,000).

6.3 Rights issues

A **rights issue** (unlike a bonus issue) is **an issue of shares for cash**. The 'rights' are offered to existing shareholders, who can sell them if they wish. This is beneficial for existing shareholders in that the shares are usually issued at a discount to the current market price.

6.3.1 Advantages

- Raises cash for the company
- Keeps reserves available for future dividends

6.3.2 Disadvantages

- Dilutes shareholders' holdings if they do not take up rights issue

6.4 Example: Rights issue

Bubbles Co (above) decides to make a rights issue, shortly after the bonus issue. The terms are '1 for 5 @ $1.20' (ie one new share for every five already held, at a price of $1.20). Assuming that all shareholders take up their rights (which they are not obliged to) the double entry is:

		$'000	$'000
DEBIT	Cash (2,500 ÷ 5 × $1.20)	600	
CREDIT	Ordinary share capital		500
	Share premium		100

Mr X, who previously held 50,000 shares, will now hold 60,000 (assuming he takes up his rights), and the value of his holding should increase (all other things being equal) because the net assets of the company will increase. The new statement of financial position will show:

	$'000
$1 ordinary shares	3,000
Share premium	100
Retained earnings	1,000
Shareholders' equity	4,100

The increase in funds of $600,000 represents the cash raised from the issue of 500,000 new shares at a price of $1.20 each.

Rights issues are a popular way of raising cash by issuing shares and they are cheap to administer. In addition, shareholders retain control of the business as their holding is not diluted.

Question — Bonus and rights issue

X Co has the following capital structure:

	$
400,000 ordinary shares of 50c	200,000
Share premium account	70,000
Retained earnings	230,000
Shareholders' equity	500,000

Show its capital structure following:

(a) A '1 for 2' bonus issue; and then
(b) A rights issue of '1 for 3' at 75 cents following the bonus issue, assuming all rights taken up

Answer

(a)

	$
600,000 ordinary shares of 50c	300,000
Retained earnings	200,000
Shareholders equity	500,000

(b)

	$
800,000 ordinary shares of 50c	400,000
Share premium account	50,000
Retained earnings	200,000
Shareholders equity	650,000

The bonus issue was financed by the whole of the share premium account and $30,000 retained earnings. The share premium account has funds again following the rights issue. Note that the bonus issue leaves shareholders equity unchanged. The rights issue will have brought in cash of $150,000 (200,000 × 75c) and shareholders equity is increased by this amount.

7 Ledger accounts and limited liability companies

Limited companies keep ledger accounts, and the only difference between the ledger accounts of companies and sole traders is the nature of some of the transactions, assets and liabilities for which accounts need to be kept.

For example, there will be an account for each of the following items:

(a) *Taxation*

    (i)   Tax charged against profits will be accounted for by:

           DEBIT   SPLOCI
           CREDIT   Taxation account

    (ii)   The outstanding balance on the taxation account will be a liability in the statement of financial position, until eventually paid, when the accounting entry would be:

           DEBIT   Taxation account
           CREDIT   Cash

(b) *Dividends*

A separate account will be kept for the dividends for each different class of shares (eg preference, ordinary).

    (i)   Dividends are disclosed in the notes if they are declared after the reporting date

    (ii)   When dividends are declared, we:

           DEBIT   Retained earnings
           CREDIT   Dividend payable

    (iii) When dividends are paid, we:

           DEBIT   Dividend payable
           CREDIT   Cash

(c) *Loan stock*

Loan stock being a long-term liability will be shown as a credit balance in a loan stock or borrowings account.

Interest payable on such loans is not credited to the loan account, but is credited to a separate payables account for interest until it is eventually paid, ie:

    DEBIT   Interest account (an expense, chargeable against profits)
    CREDIT   Interest payable (a current liability until eventually paid)

(d) *Share capital and reserves*

There will be a separate account for:

    (i)   Each different class of share capital (always a credit balance b/f)
    (ii)   Each different type of reserve (nearly always a credit balance b/f)

8 Company accounts for internal purposes

The large amount of information in this chapter so far has really been geared towards the financial statements companies produce for external reporting purposes. In particular, the IFRSs discussed here are all concerned with external disclosure. **Companies do produce financial accounts for internal purposes, however.**

It will often be the case that internal use financial accounts look very similar to those produced for external reporting for various reasons.

(a) The information required by internal users is similar to that required by external users. Any additional information for managers is usually provided by management accounts.

(b) Financial accounts produced for internal purposes can be used for external reporting with very little further adjustment.

It remains true, nevertheless, that **financial accounts for internal use can follow whichever format managers wish**. They may be more detailed in some areas than external financial accounts (perhaps giving breakdown of sales and profits by region or by product), but may also exclude some items, for example the taxation charge may be missed out of the statement of profit or loss and other comprehensive income.

You should always read question requirements carefully to discover whether you are being asked to produce accounts for external or internal purposes. Even when producing the latter, however, it is a good idea to stick to the external statement formats as these show best practice.

Now try this exercise.

Question — Internal accounts

The accountant of Zabit Co has prepared the following trial balance as at 31 December 20X7.

	$'000
50c ordinary shares (fully paid)	350
7% $1 preference shares (fully paid)	100
10% loan stock (secured)	200
Retained earnings 1.1.X7	242
General reserve 1.1.X7	171
Land and buildings 1.1.X7 (cost)	430
Plant and machinery 1.1.X7 (cost)	830
Accumulated depreciation	
Buildings 1.1.X7	20
Plant and machinery 1.1.X7	222
Inventory 1.1.X7	190
Sales	2,695
Purchases	2,152
Preference dividend	7
Ordinary dividend (interim)	8
Loan interest	10
Wages and salaries	254
Light and heat	31
Sundry expenses	113
Suspense account	135
Trade receivables	179
Trade payables	195
Cash	126

Notes

1. Sundry expenses include $9,000 paid in respect of insurance for the year ending 1 September 20X8. Light and heat does not include an invoice of $3,000 for electricity for the three months ended 2 January 20X8, which was paid in February 20X8. Light and heat also includes $20,000 relating to salesmen's commission.

2. The suspense account is in respect of the following items.

	$'000
Proceeds from the issue of 100,000 ordinary shares	120
Proceeds from the sale of plant	300
	420
Less consideration for the acquisition of Mary & Co	285
	135

3. The net assets of Mary & Co were purchased on 3 March 20X7. Assets were valued as follows.

	$'000
Investments	231
Inventory	34
	265

   All the inventory acquired was sold during 20X7. The investments were still held by Zabit at 31 December 20X7.

4. The property was acquired some years ago. The buildings element of the cost was estimated at $100,000 and the estimated useful life of the assets was 50 years at the time of purchase. As at 31 December 20X7 the property is to be revalued at $800,000.

5. The plant which was sold had cost $350,000 and had a carrying amount of $274,000 as on 1.1.X7. $36,000 depreciation is to be charged on plant and machinery for 20X7.

6. The loan stock has been in issue for some years. The 50 cent ordinary shares all rank for dividends at the end of the year.

7. The management wish to provide for:
   (i) Loan stock interest due
   (ii) A transfer to general reserve of $16,000
   (iii) Audit fees of $4,000

8. Inventory as at 31 December 20X7 was valued at $220,000 (cost).

9. Taxation is to be ignored.

Required

Prepare the financial statements of Zabit Co as at 31 December 20X7 including the statement of changes in equity. No other notes are required.

Answer

(a) Normal adjustments are needed for accruals and prepayments (insurance, light and heat, loan interest and audit fees). The loan interest accrued is calculated as follows.

	$'000
Charge needed in SPLOCI (10% × $200,000)	20
Amount paid so far, as shown in list of account balances	10
Accrual: presumably six months' interest now payable	10

PART D FINANCIAL REPORTING, ANALYSIS AND INTERPRETATION

The accrued expenses shown in the statement of financial position comprise:

	$'000
Loan interest	10
Light and heat	3
Audit fee	4
	17

The insurance payment includes eight months of the following financial year. A prepayment should therefore be created and $6,000 excluded from sundry expenses.

(b) The misposting of $20,000 to light and heat is also adjusted, by reducing the light and heat expense, but charging $20,000 to salesmen's commission.

(c) Depreciation on the building is calculated as $\frac{\$100,000}{50} = \$2,000$.

The carrying amount of the property is then $430,000 – $20,000 – $2,000 = $408,000 at the end of the year. When the property is revalued a reserve of $800,000 – $408,000 = $392,000 is then created.

(d) The profit on disposal of plant is calculated as proceeds $300,000 (per suspense account) less carrying amount of $274,000, ie $26,000. The cost of the remaining plant is calculated at $830,000 – $350,000 = $480,000. The depreciation allowance at the year end is:

	$'000
Balance 1.1.X7	222
Charge for 20X7	36
Less depreciation on disposals (350 – 274)	(76)
	182

(e) Goodwill arising on the purchase of Mary & Co is:

	$'000
Consideration (per suspense account)	285
Assets at valuation	265
Goodwill	20

This is shown as an asset on the statement of financial position. The investments, being owned by Zabit at the year end, are also shown on the statement of financial position, whereas Mary's inventory, acquired and then sold, is added to the purchases figure for the year.

(f) The other item in the suspense account is dealt with as follows.

	$'000
Proceeds of issue of 100,000 ordinary shares	120
Less nominal value 100,000 × 50c	50
Excess of consideration over par value (= share premium)	70

(g) The transfer to general reserve increases it to $171,000 + $16,000 = $187,000.

We can now prepare the financial statements.

ZABIT CO
STATEMENT OF PROFIT OR LOSS AND OTHER COMPREHENSIVE INCOME
FOR THE YEAR ENDED 31 DECEMBER 20X7

	$'000	$'000	$'000
Revenue			2,695
Less: Cost of sales			
Opening inventory		190	
Purchases		2,186	
		2,376	
Less closing inventory		220	
			2,156
Gross profit			539
Profit on disposal of plant			26
			565
Expenses			
Wages, salaries and commission		274	
Sundry expenses		107	
Light and heat		14	
Depreciation: buildings		2	
plant		36	
Audit fees		4	
Loan interest		20	
			457
Profit for the year			108
Other comprehensive income:			
Revaluation of non-current assets			392
Total comprehensive income for the year			500

ZABIT CO
STATEMENT OF CHANGES IN EQUITY FOR THE YEAR ENDED 31 DECEMBER 20X7

	Share capital $'000	Share premium $'000	Revaluation surplus $'000	General reserve $'000	Retained earnings $'000	Total $'000
Balance at 1.1.X7	450	–	–	171	242	863
Total comprehensive income for the year	–	–	392	–	108	500
Transactions with owners						
Issue of shares	50	70	–	–	–	120
Dividends paid	–	–	–	–	(15)	(15)
Transfer to general reserve	–	–	–	16	(16)	–
Balance at 31.12.X7	500	70	392	187	319	1,468

ZABIT CO
STATEMENT OF FINANCIAL POSITION AS AT 31 DECEMBER 20X7

	$'000	$'000
ASSETS		
Non-current assets		
Property, plant land and equipment		
Property at valuation		800
Plant: cost	480	
depreciation	182	
		298
Goodwill		20
Investments		231
Current assets		
Inventories	220	
Trade receivables	179	
Prepayments	6	
Cash and cash equivalents	126	
		531
Total assets		1,880
EQUITY AND LIABILITIES		
Equity		
50c ordinary shares	400	
7% $1 preference shares	100	
Share premium	70	
Revaluation surplus	392	
General reserve	187	
Retained earnings	319	
		1,468
Non-current liabilities		
10% loan stock (secured)		200
Current liabilities		
Trade payables	195	
Accrued expenses	17	
		212
Total equity and liabilities		1,880

Tutorial note. A lot of information has been shown on the face of the statement of profit or loss and other comprehensive income and statement of financial position. However, for external purposes, most of this would be hidden in the notes.

9 Branch accounting

Where an organisation is increasing in size and/or is intending to diversify its activities, it may find it necessary or advantageous to control operations more precisely by instituting a system of departmental or branch accounting. As each department or branch is established as a separate cost and/or accounting centre, the net profit per branch can be found and accumulated to arrive at the profit for the whole business.

Various types of organisations may operate through branches; for example, banks, building societies, estate agents, accountants, travel agents and retail outlets.

Branch accounts may be considered to fall into two main categories of accounting problem.

(a) Branch accounts may be prepared to show the performance of both a main trading centre (the head office) and subsidiary trading centres (the branches), but with all accounting records being maintained by the head office.

(b) 'Separate entity' branch accounts are prepared where branches maintain their own records, which must therefore be combined with head office records in order to prepare accounts for the whole business.

9.1 Separate entity branch accounting

Where a complete and independent set of records is maintained by the branch (or branches), accounting records will be maintained for each branch and for the head office. Accounts for the business as a whole can then be produced by combining the individual accounts.

In most cases, the head office sets up the branch, transferring to it necessary assets and recording the details in its own ledger through a branch current account. The branch, in opening its ledger, records the receipt of the assets through a head office current account. So, from the start of the operation, the branch current account balance in the head office statement of financial position is an asset representing the investment in the net worth of the branch. In the branch statement of financial position, the credit balance on the head office current account shows the proprietorship, the 'capital' of the branch.

Usually a central buying policy is adopted by organisations (which thereby may benefit from bulk discounts, standardised product ranges etc) and sales are made to the general public by the branch(es) and, often, the head office. In addition to making normal sales to outsiders, the head office transfers goods to the branch(es) either at cost or, more often, at a marked-up price which enables both the head office and the branch to make a profit.

As the branch becomes fully operational, any transfers of goods, cash, other assets or liabilities, expenses recharged and the branch profit or loss, will be entered in the respective ledgers through the current accounts. The balance (usually debit) in the head office accounting records should equal the balance (usually credit) in the branch accounting records but, in practice, the records will not always agree because of:

(a) **Errors or differences in the local ledger**, which must be corrected in the appropriate ledger, but occasionally may happen where goods are purchased locally by the branch (eg out of takings), they should be entered in the branch inventory control account at selling price, the mark-up being credited to the branch mark-up account.

(b) **Transit items** (eg goods in transit to the branch, cash in transit to head office), which have been recorded in the accounting records of one of either the head office or the branch, but not in the other, at the end of an accounting period. The branch current account balance in the head office records must be reconciled in the head office figure in the branch records.

- Goods in transit may have been recorded in the head off records as being sent to the branch. If the closing inventory figure (in the branch control account) is based on a physical inventory take, you must remember to push forward the inventory in transit into the branch's accounting records before calculating the 'unknown' balance.

- Transfers of goods are sometimes made between the various branches in the organisation. As the head office maintains a current account for each branch, the transfers can be recorded as if they were, in effect, a return to head office by branch A followed by despatch to branch B.

PART D FINANCIAL REPORTING, ANALYSIS AND INTERPRETATION

10 Published accounts

Now work through this example to give you practice in preparing financial statements in accordance with IAS 1.

Note that very little detail appears in the statement of profit or loss and other comprehensive income – all items of income and expenditure are accumulated under the standard headings. Write out the standard proformas and then go through the workings, inserting figures as you go. We have already prepared the SOCIE in the Question USB at the end of Section 3.6 of this Chapter.

Question   USB 2

USB, a limited liability company, has the following trial balance at 31 December 20X9.

	Debit $'000	Credit $'000
Cash at bank	100	
Inventory at 1 January 20X9	2,400	
Administrative expenses	2,206	
Distribution costs	650	
Non-current assets at cost:		
Buildings	10,000	
Plant and equipment	1,400	
Motor vehicles	320	
Suspense		1,500
Accumulated depreciation		
Buildings		4,000
Plant and equipment		480
Motor vehicles		120
Retained earnings		560
Trade receivables	876	
Purchases	4,200	
Dividend paid	200	
Sales revenue		11,752
Sales tax payable		1,390
Trade payables		1,050
Share premium		500
$1 ordinary shares		1,000
	22,352	22,352

The following additional information is relevant.

(a) Inventory at 31 December 20X9 was valued at $1,600,000. While doing the inventory count, errors in the previous year's inventory count were discovered. The inventory brought forward at the beginning of the year should have been $2.2m, not $2.4m as above.

(b) Depreciation is to be charged as follows:

  (i) Buildings at 5% straight-line, charged to administrative expenses
  (ii) Plant and equipment at 20% on the reducing balance basis, charged to cost of sales
  (iii) Motor vehicles at 25% on the reducing balance basis, charged to distribution costs

(c) No final dividend is being proposed.

(d) A customer has gone bankrupt owing $76,000. This debt is not expected to be recovered and an adjustment should be made. An allowance for receivables of 5% is to be set up.

(e) 1 million new ordinary shares were issued at $1.50 on 1 December 20X9. The proceeds have been left in a suspense account.

18: BUSINESS ENTITY

Required

Prepare the statement of profit or loss and other comprehensive income for the year to 31 December 20X9, and a statement of financial position at that date in accordance with the requirements of IFRSs. Ignore taxation.

Answer

USB
STATEMENT OF PROFIT OR LOSS AND OTHER COMPREHENSIVE INCOME FOR THE YEAR ENDED 31 DECEMBER 20X9

	$'000
Revenue	11,752
Cost of sales (W2)	4,984
Gross profit	6,768
Administrative expenses (W3)	2,822
Distribution costs (650 + 50 (W1))	700
Profit for the year	3,246

USB
STATEMENT OF FINANCIAL POSITION AS AT 31 DECEMBER 20X9

	$'000	$'000
Non-current assets		
Property, plant and equipment (W4)		6,386
Current assets		
Inventories	1,600	
Trade receivables (876 – 76 – 40)	760	
Cash and cash equivalents	100	
		2,460
Total assets		8,846
Equity and liabilities		
Equity		
Share capital (1,000 + 1,000 (W5))		2,000
Share premium (500 + 500 (W5))		1,000
Retained earnings (W6)		3,406
Current liabilities		
Sales tax payable	1,390	
Trade payables	1,050	
		2,440
Total equity and liabilities		8,846

Workings

1   Depreciation

	$'000
Buildings (10,000 × 5%)	500
Plant (1,400 – 480) × 20%	184
Motor vehicles (320 – 120) × 25%	50

2   Cost of sales

	$'000
Opening inventory	2,200
Purchases	4,200
Depreciation (W1)	184
Closing inventory	(1,600)
	4,984

PART D FINANCIAL REPORTING, ANALYSIS AND INTERPRETATION

3 Administrative expenses

	$'000
Per T/B	2,206
Depreciation (W1)	500
Irrecoverable debt	76
Receivables allowance ((876 – 76) × 5%)	40
	2,822

4 Property, plant and equipment

	Cost $'000	Acc Dep $'000	Dep chg $'000	Carrying amount $'000
Buildings	10,000	4,000	500	5,500
Plant	1,400	480	184	736
Motor vehicles	320	120	50	150
	11,720	4,600	734	6,386

5 Suspense account

	$'000
B/f per T/B	1,500
Share capital account	(1,000)
Share premium account	(500)
	NIL

6 Retained earnings

	$'000
B/f per T/B	560
Prior period adjustment (inventory)	(200)
Profit for period	3,246
Dividend paid	(200)
	3,406

Chapter roundup

- There are some important differences between the accounts of a **limited liability company** and those of sole traders or partnerships.

- In preparing a statement of financial position you must be able to deal with:
    - Ordinary and preference share capital
    - Reserves
    - Loan stock

- Share capital and reserves are 'owned' by the shareholders. They are known collectively as 'shareholders' equity'.

- A company can increase its share capital by means of a **bonus issue** or a **rights issue**.

Quick quiz

1. What is the meaning of limited liability?

    A   Shareholders are responsible for the company's debts.
    B   Shareholders are responsible only for the amount paid on the shares.

2. What is the difference between issued capital and called-up capital?

3. What are the differences between ordinary shares and preferred shares?

4. What are the differences between loan stock and share capital?

5. A company issues 50,000 $1 shares at a price of $1.25 per share. How much should be posted to the share premium account?

    A $50,000
    B $12,500
    C $62,500
    D $60,000

6. Distinguish between a bonus (capitalisation) issue and a rights issue.

7. A company has a balance on its share premium account of $50,000 and on retained earnings of $75,000. Issued share capital is 400,000 25c shares. The company decides to make a bonus issue of one for one. What are the closing balances on share premium and retained earnings?

	Share premium	Retained earnings
A	$25,000	$Nil
B	$10,000	$15,000
C	$Nil	$25,000
D	$Nil	$(275,000)

8. In the published accounts of XYZ Co, the profit for the period is $3,500,000. The balance of retained earnings at the beginning of the year is $500,000. If dividends of $2,500,000 were paid, what is the closing balance of retained earnings?

    A $4,000,000
    B $1,500,000
    C $500,000
    D $1,000,000

PART D FINANCIAL REPORTING, ANALYSIS AND INTERPRETATION

Answers to quick quiz

1. **B** The maximum amount that a shareholder has to pay is the amount paid on his shares.

2. Issued share capital is the par value of shares issued to shareholders. Called-up share capital is the amount payable to date by the shareholders.

3. Ordinary shares can be paid any or no dividend. The dividend attaching to preferred shares is set from the start.

4. Loan stock are long-term loans, and so loan note holders are long-term payables. Equity shareholders own the company.

5. **B** (50,000 × 25c)

6. A bonus issue is financed by capitalising revenue reserves. A rights issue is paid for by the shareholders taking up the shares.

7. **C** Capitalisation of 1:1 means a further 400,000 25c share are issued. This represents $100,000. This $100,000 is taken from share premium account first ($50,000) and the balance of $50,000 is taken from retained earnings.

8. **B**

	$'000
Retained earnings	
Opening balance	500
Profit for the period	3,500
	4,000
Dividends paid	(2,500)
Closing balance	1,500

Preparation of financial statements for sole traders

Topic list	Syllabus reference
1 Preparation of financial statements	A4

Introduction

We have now reached our goal of preparing of the final accounts of a sole trader!

We will deal with the case of a trial balance and then making adjustments to produce final accounts.

This chapter also acts as a revision of what we have covered to date. Use this period to review all the work covered to date. If you have any problems with the examples and questions, thoroughly revise the appropriate chapter before proceeding to the next part.

PART D FINANCIAL REPORTING, ANALYSIS AND INTERPRETATION

Exam focus point

The examiners have emphasised the need to practise full questions particularly in certain key areas. One of these key areas was accounts preparation. Therefore, do not neglect this chapter. It will also serve as a good foundation for your later studies.

1 Preparation of financial statements

FAST FORWARD

You should now be able to prepare a set of financial statements (final accounts) for a sole trader from a trial balance after incorporating period end adjustments for depreciation, inventory, prepayments, accruals, irrecoverable debts, and allowances for receivables.

1.1 Adjustments to accounts

You should now use what you have learned to produce a solution to the following exercise, which involves preparing a statement of profit or loss and other comprehensive income and statement of financial position. We have met Newbegin Tools before, but now we add a lot more information.

Question — Adjustment to accounts

The financial affairs of Newbegin Tools prior to the commencement of trading were as follows.

NEWBEGIN TOOLS
STATEMENT OF FINANCIAL POSITION AS AT 1 AUGUST 20X5

	$	$
Non-current assets		
Motor vehicle		2,000
Shop fittings		3,000
		5,000
Current assets		
Inventory		12,000
Cash and bank		1,000
		18,000
Capital		12,000
Current liabilities		
Bank overdraft	2,000	
Trade payables	4,000	
		6,000
		18,000

At the end of six months the business had made the following transactions.

(a) Goods were purchased on credit at a list price of $10,000.

(b) Trade discount received was 2% on list price. These were the only payments to suppliers in the period.

(c) Closing inventory of goods was valued at $5,450.

(d) All sales were on credit and amounted to $27,250.

(e) Outstanding trade receivables balances at 31 January 20X6 amounted to $3,250 of which $250 were to be written off. An allowance for receivables is to be made amounting to 2% of the remaining outstanding receivables.

(f) Cash payments were made in respect of the following expenses.

		$
(i)	Stationery, postage and wrapping	500
(ii)	Telephone charges	200
(iii)	Electricity	600
(iv)	Cleaning and refreshments	150

(g) Cash drawings by the proprietor, Alf Newbegin, amounted to $6,000.

(h) The outstanding overdraft balance as at 1 August 20X5 was paid off. Interest charges and bank charges on the overdraft amounted to $40.

Prepare the statement of profit or loss and other comprehensive income of Newbegin Tools for the six months to 31 January 20X6 and a statement of financial position as at that date. Ignore depreciation.

Answer

STATEMENT OF PROFIT OR LOSS AND OTHER COMPREHENSIVE INCOME
FOR THE SIX MONTHS ENDED 31 JANUARY 20X6

	$	$
Revenue		27,250
Opening inventory	12,000	
Purchases (Note 1)	9,800	
	21,800	
Less closing inventory	5,450	
Cost of goods sold		16,350
Gross profit		10,900
Electricity (Note 2)	600	
Stationery, postage and wrapping	500	
Irrecoverable debts written off	250	
Allowance for receivables (Note 3)	60	
Telephone charges	200	
Cleaning and refreshments	150	
Interest and bank charges	40	
		1,800
Net profit		9,100

Notes

1 Purchases at cost $10,000 less 2% trade discount.

2 Expenses are grouped into sales and distribution expenses (here assumed to be electricity, stationery and postage, irrecoverable debts and allowances for trade receivables) administration expenses (here assumed to be telephone charges and cleaning) and finance charges.

3 2% of $3,000 = $60.

The preparation of a statement of financial position is not so easy, because we must calculate the value of trade payables and cash in hand.

(a) Trade payables as at 31 January 20X6

The amount owing to payables is the sum of the amount owing at the beginning of the period, plus the cost of purchases during the period (net of all discounts), less the payments already made for purchases.

PART D FINANCIAL REPORTING, ANALYSIS AND INTERPRETATION

	$
Trade payables as at 1 August 20X5	4,000
Add purchases during the period, net of trade discount	9,800
	13,800
Less settlement discounts received	(400)
	13,400
Less payments to trade payables during the period*	(7,600)
	5,800

* $8,000 less cash discount of $400.

(b) Cash at bank and in hand at 31 January 20X6

You need to identify cash payments received and cash payments made.

(i) *Cash received from sales*

	$
Total sales in the period	27,250
Add trade receivables as at 1 August 20X5	0
	27,250
Less unpaid debts as at 31 January 20X6	3,250
Cash received	24,000

(ii) *Cash paid*

	$
Trade payables (note)	7,600
Stationery, postage and wrapping	500
Telephone charges	200
Electricity	600
Cleaning and refreshments	150
Bank charges and interest	40
Bank overdraft repaid	2,000
Drawings by proprietor	6,000
	17,090

Note. It is easy to forget some of these payments, especially drawings.

(iii)

	$
Cash in hand at 1 August 20X5	1,000
Cash received in the period	24,000
	25,000
Cash paid in the period	(17,090)
Cash at bank and in hand as at 31 January 20X6	7,910

(c) When irrecoverable debts are written off, the value of outstanding trade receivables must be **reduced by the amount written off**. Trade receivables will be valued at $3,250 less irrecoverable debts of $250 and the allowance for receivables of $60 – ie at $2,940.

(d) Non-current assets should be depreciated. However, in this exercise depreciation has been ignored.

NEWBEGIN TOOLS
STATEMENT OF FINANCIAL POSITION AS AT 31 JANUARY 20X6

	$	$
Non-current assets		
Motor vehicles	2,000	
Shop fittings	3,000	
		5,000
Current assets		
Inventory	5,450	
Trade receivables, less allowance for receivables	2,940	
Cash and bank	7,910	
		16,300
		21,300

	$
Capital	
Capital at 1 August 20X5	12,000
Net profit for the period	9,500
	21,500
Less drawings	6,000
Capital at 31 January 20X6	15,500
Current liabilities	
Trade payables	5,800
	21,300

The opening bank overdraft was repaid during the year and is therefore not shown at the year end.

Exam focus point

You might be given a lot of information and asked to calculate a figure to go in the statement of profit or loss and other comprehensive income and/or statement of financial position. Therefore, calculating account balances and preparing financial statements must become second nature to you.

1.2 Example: Accounts preparation from a trial balance

The following trial balance was extracted from the ledger of Stephen Chee, a sole trader, as at 31 May 20X1 – the end of his financial year.

STEPHEN CHEE
TRIAL BALANCE AS AT 31 MAY 20X1

	Debit $	Credit $
Property, at cost	120,000	
Equipment, at cost	80,000	
Allowances for depreciation (as at 1 June 20X0)		
– on property		20,000
– on equipment		38,000
Purchases	250,000	
Revenue		402,200
Inventory, as at 1 June 20X0	50,000	
Customer returns	18,000	
Commission from suppliers		4,800
Returns out		15,000
Wages and salaries	58,800	
Irrecoverable debts	4,600	
Loan interest	5,100	
Other operating expenses	17,700	
Trade payables		36,000
Trade receivables	38,000	
Cash in hand	300	
Bank	1,300	
Drawings	24,000	
Allowance for receivables		500
17% non-current loan		30,000
Capital, as at 1 June 20X0		121,300
	667,800	667,800

PART D FINANCIAL REPORTING, ANALYSIS AND INTERPRETATION

The following additional information as at 31 May 20X1 is available.

(a) Inventory as at the close of business has been valued at cost at $42,000.
(b) Wages and salaries need to be accrued by $800.
(c) Other operating expenses are prepaid by $300.
(d) The allowance for receivables is to be adjusted so that it is 2% of trade receivables.
(e) Depreciation for the year ended 31 May 20X1 has still to be charged as follows.
    Property: 1.5% per annum using the straight line method; and
    Equipment: 25% per annum using the reducing balance method.

Required

Prepare Stephen Chee's statement of profit or loss and other comprehensive income for the year ended 31 May 20X1 and his statement of financial position as at that date.

Tutorial note. Again you have met a simplified form of this question before. However, this version contains a lot more information for you to deal with before you can prepare the accounts.

Solution

STEPHEN CHEE
STATEMENT OF PROFIT OR LOSS AND OTHER COMPREHENSIVE INCOME
FOR THE YEAR ENDED 31 MAY 20X1

	$	$
Revenue ($402,200−$18,000)		384,200
Cost of sales		
Opening inventory	50,000	
Purchases	250,000	
Purchases returns	(15,000)	
	285,000	
Closing inventory	42,000	
		243,000
Gross profit		141,200
Other income – discounts received		4,800
		146,000
Expenses		
Operating expenses		
Wages and salaries ($58,800 + $800)	59,600	
Irrecoverable debts (W1)	4,860	
Loan interest	5,100	
Depreciation (W2)	12,300	
Other operating expenses ($17,700 − $300)	17,400	
		99,260
Net profit for the year		46,740

STEPHEN CHEE
STATEMENT OF FINANCIAL POSITION AS AT 31 MAY 20X0

	Cost $	Accumulated depn. $	Net book value $
Non-current assets			
Property	120,000	21,800	98,200
Equipment	80,000	48,500	31,500
	200,000	70,300	129,700
Current assets			
Inventory		42,000	
Trade receivables net of allowance for receivables ($38,000 – 760 (W1))		37,240	
Prepayments		300	
Bank		1,300	
Cash in hand		300	
			81,140
			210,840
Capital			
Balance at 1 June 20X0			121,300
Net profit for the year			46,740
			168,040
Drawings			24,000
			144,040
Non-current liabilities			
17% loan			30,000
Current liabilities			
Trade payables		36,000	
Accruals		800	
			36,800
			210,840

Workings

1. Irrecoverable debts

	$
Previous allowance	500
New allowance (2% × 38,000)	760
Increase	260
Per trial balance	4,600
Statement of profit or loss and other comprehensive income	4,860

2. Depreciation

Property
	$
Opening allowance	20,000
Charge for the year (1.5% × 120,000)	1,800
Closing allowance	21,800

Equipment
	$
Opening allowance	38,000
Charge for the year (25% × 42,000)	10,500
Closing allowance	48,500
Total charge in SPLOCI	12,300

PART D FINANCIAL REPORTING, ANALYSIS AND INTERPRETATION

Question | Final accounts

Donald Brown, a sole trader, extracted the following trial balance on 31 December 20X0.

TRIAL BALANCE AS AT 31 DECEMBER 20X0

	Debit $	Credit $
Capital at 1 January 20X0		26,094
Trade receivables	42,737	
Cash in hand	1,540	
Trade payables		35,404
Fixtures and fittings at cost	42,200	
Inventory at 1 January 20X0	18,460	
Revenue		491,620
Purchases	387,936	
Motor vehicles at cost	45,730	
Lighting and heating	6,184	
Motor expenses	2,862	
Rent	8,841	
General expenses	7,413	
Bank overdraft		19,861
Allowance for depreciation		
Fixtures and fittings		2,200
Motor vehicles		15,292
Drawings	26,568	
	59,471	590,471

The following information as at 31 December is also available.

(a) $218 is owing for motor expenses.

(b) $680 has been prepaid for rent.

(c) Depreciation is to be charged for the year as follows.

   Motor vehicles: 20% on cost
   Fixtures and fittings: 10% reducing balance method

(d) Inventory at the close of business was valued at $19,926.

Required

Prepare Donald Brown's statement of profit or loss and other comprehensive income for the year ended 31 December 20X0 and his statement of financial position at that date.

Answer

Tutorial note. You should note these points.

(a) Discounts allowed are an expense of the business and should be shown as a deduction from gross profit. Similarly, discounts received is a revenue item and should be added to gross profit.

(b) The figure for depreciation in the trial balance represents accumulated depreciation up to and including 20W9. You have to calculate the charge for the year 20X0 for the statement of profit or loss and other comprehensive income and add this to the trial balance figure to arrive at the accumulated depreciation figure to be included in the statement of financial position.

DONALD BROWN
STATEMENT OF PROFIT OR LOSS AND OTHER COMPREHENSIVE INCOME
FOR THE YEAR ENDED 31 DECEMBER 20X0

	$	$
Revenue		491,620
Less cost of sales		
Opening inventory	18,460	
Purchases	387,936	
	406,396	
Closing inventory	19,926	
		386,470
Gross profit		105,150
Less expenses:		
lighting and heating	6,184	
motor expenses (2,862 + 218)	3,080	
rent (8,841 – 680)	8,161	
general expenses	7,413	
depreciation (W)	13,146	
		37,984
Net profit		67,166

Working: depreciation charge

Motor vehicles: $\$45,730 \times 20\% = \$9,146$
Fixtures and fittings: $10\% \times \$(42,200 - 2,200) = \$4,000$
Total: $\$4,000 + \$9,146 = \$13,146$.

DONALD BROWN
STATEMENT OF FINANCIAL POSITION AS AT 31 DECEMBER 20X0

	Cost $	Depreciation $	Net $
Non-current assets			
Fixtures and fittings	42,200	6,200	36,000
Motor vehicles	45,730	24,438	21,292
	87,930	30,638	57,292
Current assets			
Inventories		19,926	
Trade receivables		42,737	
Prepayments		680	
Cash in hand		1,540	
			64,883
			122,175
Capital			
Balance b/f			26,094
Net profit for year			67,166
			93,260
Less drawings			26,568
			66,692
Current liabilities			
Trade payables		35,404	
Accruals		218	
Bank overdraft		19,861	
			55,483
			122,175

PART D FINANCIAL REPORTING, ANALYSIS AND INTERPRETATION

Exam focus point

There may be a question giving a number of adjustments and asking for the effect on profit. You need to follow the procedure shown in the question below.

Question
Effect on profit

Given the facts in Final accounts (Donald Brown) above, what is the net effect on profit of the adjustments in (a) to (c)?

Answer

(a) Motor expenses accrual – $218 additional expense, so reduction in profit
(b) Rent prepayment – $680 reduction in expense, so increase in profit
(c) Depreciation – total charge $13,146 additional expense, so reduction in profit

Total effect on net profit = + 680 – 218 – 13,146
= 12,684 reduction

19: PREPARATION OF FINANCIAL STATEMENTS FOR SOLE TRADERS

Chapter roundup

- You should now be able to prepare a set of final accounts for a sole trader from a trial balance after incorporating period end adjustments for depreciation, inventory, prepayments, accruals, irrecoverable debts, and allowances for receivables.

Quick quiz

1   Which of the following is the correct formula for cost of sales?
    A   Opening inventory – purchases + closing inventory
    B   Purchases – closing inventory + sales
    C   Opening inventory – closing inventory + purchases
    D   Opening inventory + closing inventory – purchases

2   If an owner takes goods out of inventory for his own use, how is this dealt with?
    A   Credited to drawings at cost
    B   Credited to drawings at selling price
    C   Debited to drawings at cost
    D   Debited to drawings at selling price

3   A business starts trading on 1 September 20X0. During the year, it has sales of $500,000, purchases of $250,000 and closing inventory of $75,000. What is the gross profit for the year?
    A $175,000
    B $675,000
    C $325,000
    D $250,000

4   Mario's trial balance includes the following items: non-current assets $50,000, inventory $15,000, trade payables $10,000, trade receivables $5,000, bank $110,000, allowance for receivables $1,000.
    What is the figure for current assets?
    A $180,000
    B $170,000
    C $129,000
    D $134,000

5   Using the information in Question 4 above, what is the figure for total assets?
    A $184,000
    B $179,000

PART D   FINANCIAL REPORTING, ANALYSIS AND INTERPRETATION

Answers to quick quiz

1   C   Correct, this is a version of the more normal formula: opening inventory + purchases – closing inventory.
    A   Incorrect.
    B   Incorrect. Sales should never form part of cost of sales.
    C   Incorrect.

2   C   Although we have not specifically covered this point, you should have realised that goods for own use must be treated as drawings (and so debited to drawings). Thinking about prudence, if the goods were transferred at selling price, the business would show a profit on the sale of the goods that it has not made. So the transaction must be shown at cost. (Now think about where the credit entry goes before trying the question from the EQB.)

3   C

	$	$
Revenue		500,000
Purchases	250,000	
Closing inventory	(75,000)	
Cost of sales		175,000
Gross profit		325,000

4   C

	$
Current assets	
Inventory	15,000
Trade receivables (5,000 – 1,000)	4,000
Bank	110,000
	129,000

5   B   Total assets = non-current assets + current assets
        = 50,000 + 129,000
        = 179,000

Preparation of financial statements under IAS 1

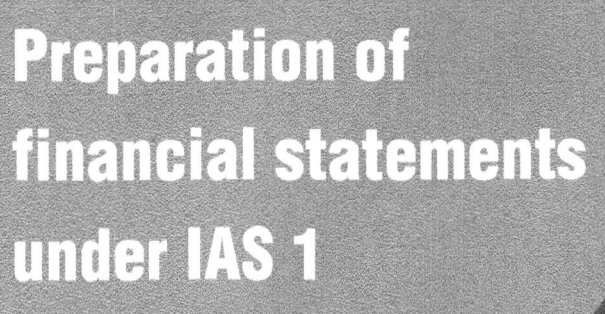

Topic list	Syllabus reference
1 IAS 1 *Presentation of Financial Statements*	A4
2 Items in the statement of profit or loss and other comprehensive income	A4
3 IFRS 15 *Revenue from Contracts with Customers*	A4
4 Items in the statement of financial position	A4
5 The current/non-current distinction	A4

Introduction

You now come to the point in your studies when you can look at the form and content of the financial statements of **limited liability companies**. Your later financial accounting studies will be concerned almost entirely with company accounts so it is vital that you acquire a sound understanding of the basic concepts now.

The financial statements of limited liability companies are usually governed by national legislation and accounting standards. From an international standpoint, however, the **general content** of financial statements is governed by IAS 1 *Presentation of Financial Statements*. We will look at the standard and explain those items in the financial statements which have not yet appeared in the Workbook.

We will look at another accounting standard which has a significant impact on the content and form of company accounts, IFRS 15 *Revenue from Contracts with Customers*.

The standards are concerned with financial statements produced for external reporting purposes (ie to external users), but companies also produce financial accounts for internal purposes, and we will look at the different approach in preparing accounts for internal as well as external use.

1 IAS 1 *Presentation of Financial Statements*

FAST FORWARD

IAS 1 lists the required contents of a company's statement of profit or loss and other comprehensive income and statement of financial position. It also gives guidance on how items should be presented in the financial statements.

As well as covering accounting policies and other general considerations governing financial statements, IAS 1 *Presentation of Financial Statements* give substantial guidance on the form and content of published financial statements.

A full set of financial statements comprises:

- Statement of financial position
- Statement of profit or loss and other comprehensive income
- Statement of changes in equity
- Statement of cash flows
- Notes to the financial statements
- Comparative information

IAS 1 looks at the statement of financial position, statement of profit or loss and other comprehensive income, and statement of changes in equity. The statement of cash flows is covered by IAS 7 and will be dealt with in a later chapter. First of all, some general points are made about financial statements.

1.1 Profit or loss for the period

The statement of profit or loss (the top part of the statement of profit or loss and other comprehensive income) is the most significant indicator of a company's financial performance. So, it is important to ensure that it is not misleading.

The statement of profit or loss will be misleading if costs incurred in the current year are deducted not from the current year profits but from the balance of accumulated profits brought forward. This presents the current year's results more favourably.

IAS 1 stipulates that all items of income and expense recognised in a period shall be included in profit or loss unless a **standard** requires otherwise.

Circumstances where items may be excluded from profit or loss for the current year include the correction of errors and the effect of changes in accounting policies, but these are **outside the scope of your syllabus**.

1.2 Other comprehensive income

The part of the statement of profit or loss and other comprehensive income that deals with other comprehensive income takes the profit or loss for the period and adjusts it for certain gains and losses. At this level, this just means gains on property revaluations. The idea is to present all gains and losses, both those recognised in profit or loss as well as those recognised through reserves (other comprehensive income).

1.3 How items are disclosed

IAS 1 specifies disclosures of certain items in certain ways.

- Some items must appear on the **face of the statement of financial position or statement of profit or loss and other comprehensive income**.
- Other items can appear in a **note to the financial statements** instead.
- **Recommended formats** are given which entities may or may not follow, depending on their circumstances.

Obviously, disclosures specified by **other standards** must also be made, and we will mention the necessary disclosures when we cover each statement in turn. Disclosures in both IAS 1 and other standards must be made either on the face of the statement or in the notes unless otherwise stated, ie disclosures cannot be made in an accompanying commentary or report.

1.4 Identification of financial statements

As a result of the above point, it is most important that entities **distinguish the financial statements** very clearly from any other information published with them. This is because IFRSs apply **only** to the financial statements (ie the main statements and related notes), so readers of the annual report must be able to differentiate between the parts of the report which are prepared under IFRSs, and other parts which are not.

The entity should **identify each component** of the financial statements very clearly. IAS 1 also requires disclosure of the following information in a prominent position. If necessary it should be repeated wherever it is felt to be of use to the reader in his understanding of the information presented.

- **Name** of the reporting entity (or other means of identification)
- Whether the financial statements cover the **single entity** only or a group of entities
- The **reporting date** or the period covered by the financial statements (as appropriate)
- The **reporting currency**
- The **level of precision** used in presenting the figures in the financial statements

Judgement must be used to determine the best method of presenting this information. In particular, the standard suggests that the approach to this will be very different when the financial statements are communicated electronically.

The **level of precision** is important, as presenting figures in thousands or millions of units makes the figures more understandable. The level of precision must be disclosed, however, and it should not obscure necessary details or make the information less relevant.

1.5 Reporting period

It is normal for entities to present financial statements **annually** and IAS 1 states that they should be prepared at least as often as this.

> **Exam focus point**
>
> IFRSs do not set out an **obligatory** format for financial statements but it would be best practice to use the **suggested format** of IAS 1 for published financial statements.

1.6 Statement of financial position

The following is a simplified version of the statement of financial position format provided in IAS 1.

ABC CO
STATEMENT OF FINANCIAL POSITION AS AT 31 DECEMBER 20X2

	20X2		20X1	
	$'000	$'000	$'000	$'000
Assets				
Non-current assets				
Property, plant and equipment	X		X	
Goodwill	X		X	
Other intangible assets	X		X	
		X		X

PART D FINANCIAL REPORTING, ANALYSIS AND INTERPRETATION

	20X2 $'000	20X2 $'000	20X1 $'000	20X1 $'000
Current assets				
Inventories	X		X	
Trade receivables	X		X	
Other current assets	X		X	
Cash and cash equivalents	X		X	
		X		X
Total assets		X		X
Equity and liabilities				
Equity				
Share capital	X		X	
Retained earnings	X		X	
Other components of equity	X		X	
		X		X
Non-current liabilities				
Long-term borrowings	X		X	
Long-term provisions	X		X	
		X		X
Current liabilities				
Trade and other payables	X		X	
Short-term borrowings	X		X	
Current portion of long-term borrowings	X		X	
Current tax payable	X		X	
Short-term provisions	X		X	
		X		X
Total equity and liabilities		X		X

1.7 Statement of profit or loss and other comprehensive income

The following is a simplified version of the statement of profit or loss and other comprehensive income format provided in IAS 1.

ABC CO
STATEMENT OF PROFIT OR LOSS AND OTHER COMPREHENSIVE INCOME FOR THE YEAR ENDED 31 DECEMBER 20X2
Illustrating the classification of expenses by function

	20X2 $'000	20X1 $'000
Revenue	X	X
Cost of sales	(X)	(X)
Gross profit	X	X
Other income	X	X
Distribution costs	(X)	(X)
Administrative expenses	(X)	(X)
Other expenses	(X)	(X)
Finance cost	(X)	(X)
Profit before tax	X	X
Income tax expense	(X)	(X)
Profit for the year	X	X
Other comprehensive income:		
Changes in revaluation surplus	X	X
Total comprehensive income for the year	X	X

Exam focus point

Questions in the exam may refer to a statement of profit or loss: this means the entries from 'Revenue' to 'Profit for the year'. References to other comprehensive income means the last three lines shown above. However, a reference to statement of profit or loss and other comprehensive income means the whole statement shown above.

Note that the November 2010 and May 2011 exams refer to the 'statement of financial performance', which means the statement of profit or loss and other comprehensive income.

1.8 Notes to the financial statements

Exam focus point

These notes are given as illustrations. For your exam, you only need to know five and these are listed in Section 1.9.

(1) *Accounting policies*

This will generally be the first note to the accounts and is governed by IAS 1 *Presentation of financial statements*. Disclosure of the following policies is likely.

- Depreciation
- Inventories
- Revaluation of long-term non-current assets
- Revenue recognition

(2) *General disclosures*

- Restrictions on the title to assets
- Security given in respect of liabilities
- Contingent assets and contingent liabilities, quantified if possible
- Amounts committed for future capital expenditure
- Events after the reporting period

(3) *Property, plant and equipment*

- Land and buildings
- Plant and equipment
- Other categories of assets, suitably identified
- Accumulated depreciation
- Separate disclosure should be made of leaseholds and of assets being acquired on instalment purchase plans

(4) *Other non-current assets*

- Include, if applicable, the method and period of depreciation and any unusual write-offs during the period
- Long-term investments stating the market value of listed investments if different from the carrying amount in the financial statements
- Long-term receivables
    - Accounts and notes receivable: trade
    - Receivables from directors
    - Other
- Goodwill
- Patents, trademarks, and similar assets
- Development costs capitalised and their movements during the period

(5) *Investments*

For marketable securities, the market value should be disclosed if different from the carrying amount in the financial statements.

(6) *Receivables*

- Accounts and notes receivable: trade
- Receivable from directors
- Other receivables and prepaid expenses

(7) *Cash*

Cash includes cash on hand and in current and other accounts with banks. Cash which is not immediately available for use, for example balances frozen in foreign banks by exchange restrictions, should be disclosed.

(8) *Shareholders' interests*

The following disclosures should be made separately.

- *Share capital*: disclose the following for each class of share capital.
    - Number of shares authorised, issued and partly paid, and issued but not fully paid
    - Par value per share or that the shares have no par value
    - Reconciliation of number of shares outstanding at the beginning and end of the period
    - Rights, preferences, and restrictions with respect to the distribution of dividends and to the repayment of capital
    - Shares in the entity held by itself or related companies
    - Shares reserved for future issue under options and sales contracts, including terms and amounts.
    - Description of the nature and purpose of each reserve
    - Dividends proposed before the financial statements were authorised for issue but not recognised as a distribution during the period
    - Cumulative preferred dividends not recognised
- Statement of changes in equity

(9) *Non-current liabilities*

- Exclude the portion repayable within one year
- Secured loans
- Unsecured loans

A summary of the interest rates, repayment terms, covenants, subordination and conversion features should be shown.

(10) *Other liabilities and provisions*

The significant items included in other liabilities and in provisions and accruals should be separately disclosed. You are unlikely to meet any items of this nature in your syllabus.

(11) *Payables*

- Accounts and notes payable: trade
- Payables to directors
- Taxes on income
- Other payables and accrued expenses

1.9 Examinable notes

For the purposes of your syllabus, you need to be able to **produce the following notes** to the accounts.

(a) Statement of changes in equity (see Chapter 18 of this Workbook)
(b) Tangible non-current assets (see Chapter 16 of this Workbook)
(c) Events after the reporting period (Chapter 21)
(d) Contingent assets and contingent liabilities (Chapter 15)
(e) Research and development (Chapter 17)

Question — Pro forma

Before we go any further, take a blank sheet of paper and write out the 'pro forma' statement of profit or loss and other comprehensive income and statement of financial position shown above. Mark which items are likely to require further disclosure, either by note or on the face of the statements.

1.10 IFRS 18

The IASB issued a new standard IFRS 18 *Presentation and Disclosure of Financial Statements* in 2024. This standard will come into effect in 2027.

IFRS 18 has been issued in response to investors' concerns about the transparency and comparability of companies' financial performance reporting. The main changes are a standardised structure for the statement of profit or loss, disclosure of certain performance measures and enhanced principles of grouping and separating items in the financial statements and notes.

2 Items in the statement of profit or loss and other comprehensive income

2.1 Revenue

There are important rules on revenue recognition and these are the subject of IFRS 15 *Revenue from contracts with customers*. We will look at this in detail in Section 3 of this chapter.

2.2 Cost of sales

This represents the summary of the detailed workings we have used in a sole trader's financial statements.

2.3 Expenses

Notice that expenses are gathered under a number of headings. Any detail needed will be given in the notes to the financial statements.

2.3.1 Managers' salaries

The salary of a sole trader or a partner in a partnership is not a charge to the statement of profit or loss and other comprehensive income but is an appropriation of profit. The **salary of a manager or member of management board of a limited liability company**, however, is an **expense in the statement of profit or loss and other comprehensive income**, even when the manager is a shareholder in the company. Management salaries are usually included in **administrative expenses**.

2.4 Finance cost

This is interest **payable** during the period. This may include accruals for interest payable on loan stock (see Chapter 18).

2.5 Income tax expense

This represents taxation as detailed in Section 2.6 below. Once again this will include accruals for the tax due on the current year's profits. However, it may also include adjustments for any over or under provision for prior periods (see Example 2.6.1).

2.6 Taxation

Taxation affects both the statement of financial position and the statement of profit or loss and other comprehensive income.

All companies pay some kind of corporate taxation on the profits they earn, which we will call **income tax** (for the sake of simplicity), but which you may find called 'corporation tax'. The rate of income tax will vary from country to country and there may be variations in rate within individual countries for different types or sizes of company.

Note that because a company has a **separate legal personality, its tax is included in its accounts**. An unincorporated business would not show personal income tax in its accounts, as it would not be a business expense but the personal affair of the proprietors.

(a) The **charge for income tax on profits for the year** is shown as a **deduction from net profit**.

(b) In the statements of financial position, **tax payable** to the government is generally shown as a **current liability** as it is usually due within 12 months of the year end.

(c) For various reasons, the tax on profits in the statement of profit or loss and other comprehensive income and the tax payable in the statement of financial position are not normally the same amount.

2.6.1 Example: Taxation

A company has a tax liability brought forward of $15,000. The liability is finally agreed at $17,500 and this is paid during the year. The company estimates that the tax liability based on the current year's profits will be $20,000. Prepare the tax liability account for the year.

Solution

TAX LIABILITY ACCOUNT

	$		$
Cash paid	17,500	Balance b/f	15,000
Balance c/f	20,000	SPLOCI	22,500
	37,500		37,500

Notice that the statement of profit or loss and other comprehensive income charge consists of the following:

	$
Under provision for prior year (17,500 – 15,000)	2,500
Provision for current year	20,000
	22,500

Notice also that the balance carried forward consists solely of the provision for the current year.

2.7 Accounting concepts

You will notice from the above that the accounting concepts apply to revenue and expenses. In particular, the matching concept applies and so you should expect to have to adjust for accruals and prepayments.

2.8 Interrelationship of statement of profit or loss and other comprehensive income and statement of financial position

When we were dealing with the financial statements of sole traders, we transferred the net profit to the capital account. In the case of limited liability companies, the net profit is transferred to retained earnings in the statement of changes in equity (SOCIE). The closing balances of the accounts in the SOCIE are then transferred to the statement of financial position. We will deal with this in more detail in Chapter 18.

2.9 Gains on property revaluation

These arise when a property is revalued. The revaluation is recognised in the other comprehensive income part of the statement of profit or loss and other comprehensive income.

For example, an asset originally cost $5,000 and was revalued to $15,000. The $10,000 gain goes to revaluation surplus. However, rather than the SOCIE, the $10,000 transfer to the revaluation surplus is recognised in the statement of **other** comprehensive income.

3 IFRS 15 *Revenue from Contracts with Customers*

FAST FORWARD

IFRS 15 *Revenue from Contracts with Customers* is concerned with reporting the nature, amount, timing and uncertainty of revenue and cash flows resulting from contracts with customers. Generally, revenue is recognised when the entity has transferred control of goods and services to the buyer.

Under IFRS 15, revenue is recognised when goods or services are transferred. This is based upon the **transfer of control** of those goods or services from the seller/provider to the buyer. Control of an asset is defined as the ability to direct the use of and obtain substantially all of the remaining benefits from the asset. IFRS 15 is concerned with reporting 'the nature, amount, timing and uncertainty of revenue and cash flows resulting from contracts with customers'.

(IFRS 15: para.1)

Revenue from contracts with customers arises from fairly common transactions:

- The sale of goods
- The rendering of services

Generally revenue is recognised when the entity has transferred control of goods and services to the buyer. **Control of an asset** is described in the standard as the ability to direct the use of, and obtain substantially all of the remaining benefits from, the asset.

3.1 Introduction

Accruals accounting is based on the **matching of costs with the revenue they generate**. It is crucially important under this convention that we establish the point at which revenue is recognised, so that the correct treatment can be applied to the related costs. For example, the costs of producing an item of finished goods should be carried as an asset in the statement of financial position until such time as it is sold; they should then be written off as a charge to the profit or loss account. Which of these two treatments should be applied cannot be decided until it is clear at what moment the sale of the item takes place.

The decision has a **direct impact on profit** since, it is unacceptable to recognise the profit on sale until a sale has taken place, in accordance with the criteria of revenue recognition under IFRS 15.

3.2 IFRS 15

FAST FORWARD

> The key principle of IFRS 15 is that revenue is recognised to depict the transfer of promised goods or services to customers at an amount that the entity expects to be entitled to in exchange for those goods or services.

IFRS 15 governs the recognition of revenue arising from contracts with customers.

Revenue is income arising in the ordinary course of an entity's activities, such as sales and fees.

This is achieved by applying a **five step model**:

(1) Identify the contract(s) with a customer
(2) Identify the performance obligations in the contract
(3) Determine the transaction price
(4) Allocate the transaction price to the performance obligations in the contract
(5) Recognise revenue when (or as) the entity satisfies a performance obligation

3.3 Definitions

The following definitions are given in the standard.

Key terms

> **Revenue** is income arising in the course of an entity's ordinary activities.
>
> **Income** is increases in economic benefits during the accounting period in the form of inflows or enhancements of assets or decreases of liabilities that result in an increase in equity, other than those relating to contributions from equity participants.
>
> A **contract** is an agreement between two or more parties that creates enforceable rights and obligations.
>
> A **customer** is a party that has contracted with an entity to obtain goods or services that are an output of the entity's ordinary activities in exchange for consideration.
>
> A **performance obligation** is a promise in a contract with a customer to transfer to the customer either: a good or service (or a bundle of goods or services) that is distinct; or a series of distinct goods or services that are substantially the same and that have the same pattern of transfer to the customer.
>
> **Transaction price** is the amount of consideration to which an entity expects to be entitled in exchange for transferring promised goods or services to a customer, excluding amounts collected on behalf of third parties.
>
> *(IFRS 15, Appendix A)*

Revenue **does not include** sales taxes, value added taxes or goods and service taxes which are only collected for third parties, because these do not represent economic benefits flowing to the entity. The same is true for revenues collected by an agent on behalf of a principal. Revenue for the agent is only the commission received for acting as agent.

3.4 Measurement of revenue

This is the transaction price, as defined above in the standard. This will take account of any trade discounts and volume rebates.

3.5 Scope

IFRS 15 covers the revenue from all contracts with customers except:

- Leases within the scope of IFRS 16 *Leases*
- Insurance contracts within the scope of IFRS 4 *Insurance Contracts*

- Financial instruments and other contractual rights and obligations within the scope of IFRS 9 *Financial Instruments*, IFRS 10 *Consolidated Financial Statements*, IFRS 11 *Joint Arrangements*, IAS 27 *Separate Financial Statements* or IAS 28 *Investments in Associates and Joint Ventures*.
- Non-monetary exchanges between entities in the same line of business

3.6 Example: Revenue recognition

TDF is a company that manufactures office furniture. A customer placed an order on 22 December 20X4 for an office desk at a price of $300 plus sales tax at 20% of $60. The desk was delivered to the customer on 25 January 20X5, who accepted the goods as satisfactory by signing a delivery note. TDF then invoiced the customer for the goods on 1 February 20X5. The customer paid $360 to TDF on 1 March 20X5.

Required

How should TDF account for revenue?

Solution

Applying the five step model:

(1) Identify the contract(s) with a customer:

A customer placed an order for a desk. This represents a contract to supply the desk.

(2) Identify the performance obligations in the contract:

There is one performance obligation, the delivery of a satisfactory desk.

(3) Determine the transaction price:

This is the price agreed as per the order, ie $300. Note that sales tax is not included, since the transaction price as defined by IFRS 15 does not include amounts collected on behalf of third parties.

(4) Allocate the transaction price to the performance obligations in the contract:

There is one performance obligation, therefore the full transaction price is allocated to the performance of the obligation of the delivery of the desk.

(5) Recognise revenue when (or as) the entity satisfies a performance obligation:

Since the customer has signed a delivery note to confirm acceptance of the goods as satisfactory, this is evidence that TDF has fulfilled its performance obligation and can therefore recognise $300 in January 20X5.

Note that the timing of payment by the customer is irrelevant to when the revenue is recognised.

For most simple transactions with a single performance obligation, the full transaction price will be recognised when control of goods or services has transferred to the customer.

It gets more tricky however when there are multiple performance obligations, eg, a cell phone network selling a 'free' phone and monthly network service bundled together as a single monthly fee. In this scenario there are two performance obligations; the delivery of the phone at the start of the contract and the network service. The transaction price of the monthly fee would need to be apportioned between these two performance objectives and recognised thereon.

Don't worry about learning this particular example, it is beyond scope of this syllabus but shown here to demonstrate how the standard is applied to more complex revenue arrangements.

PART D FINANCIAL REPORTING, ANALYSIS AND INTERPRETATION

Question
Prudence

Given that faithful representation is the main consideration, discuss under what circumstances, if any, under IFRS 15 *Revenue from Contracts with Customers* revenue might be recognised at the following stages of a sale.

(a) Goods are acquired by the business which it confidently expects to resell very quickly.
(b) A customer places a firm order for goods.
(c) Goods are delivered to the customer.
(d) The customer is invoiced for goods.
(e) The customer pays for the goods.
(f) The customer's cheque in payment for the goods has been cleared by the bank.

Answer

(a) A sale must never be recognised before the goods have even been ordered by a customer. There is no certainty about the value of the sale, nor when it will take place, even if it is virtually certain that goods will be sold.

(b) A sale must never be recognised when the customer places an order. Even though the order will be for a specific quantity of goods at a specific price, it is not yet certain that the sale transaction will go through. The customer may cancel the order, the supplier might be unable to deliver the goods as ordered or it may be decided that the customer is not a good credit risk.

(c) A sale will be recognised when delivery of the goods is made only when:

  (i) The sale is for cash, and so the cash is received at the same time.
  (ii) The sale is on credit and the customer accepts delivery (eg by signing a delivery note).

(d) The critical event for a credit sale is usually the despatch of an invoice to the customer. There is then a legally enforceable debt, payable on specified terms, for a completed sale transaction.

(e) The critical event for a cash sale is when delivery takes place and when cash is received; both take place at the same time.

It would be too cautious to await cash payment for a credit sale transaction before recognising the sale, unless the customer is a high credit risk and there is a serious doubt about his ability or intention to pay. But in that case, why would the business risk despatching the goods?

(f) It would again be over-cautious to wait for clearance of the customer's cheques before recognising sales revenue. Such a precaution would only be justified in cases where there is a very high risk of the bank refusing to honour the cheque.

4 Items in the statement of financial position

4.1 Assets

The assets are exactly the same as those we would expect to find in the accounts of a sole trader. The only difference is that the detail is given in notes and only the totals are shown on the face of the statement of financial position.

4.2 Equity

We will look at share capital and reserves in detail in Chapter 18. Remember that movements must be reported in the SOCIE.

Capital reserves usually have to be set up by law, whereas revenue reserves are appropriations of profit. With a sole trader, profit was added to capital. However, in a limited company, share capital and profit have to be disclosed separately, because profit is distributable as a dividend but share capital cannot be distributed. Therefore, any retained profits are kept in the retained earnings reserve.

4.3 Liabilities

Liabilities are split between current and non-current and this is dealt with in detail in the next section.

4.4 Concepts

The statement of financial position makes use of the accounting equation concept that:

Assets = Capital + Liabilities

The statement of financial position is also prepared according to the **business entity** convention (that a business is separate from its owners).

5 The current/non-current distinction

FAST FORWARD

> You should be aware of the issues surrounding the current/non-current distinction as well as the disclosure requirements laid down in IAS 1.

Current assets and current liabilities of various types have been discussed in earlier parts of this Workbook. Users of financial statements need to be able to identify current assets and current liabilities in order to determine the company's financial position. Where current assets are greater than current liabilities, the net excess is often called 'working capital' or 'net current assets'.

5.1 Alternative views of current assets and current liabilities

IAS 1 lays down rules for entities which choose to show the current/non-current distinction. It also states what should happen if they do not do so.

Each entity must present current/non-current assets and current/non-current liabilities as **separate classifications** in the statement of financial position, except when a presentation based on **liquidity** provides information that is reliable and more relevant. In this case, it should present assets and liabilities broadly **in order of their liquidity**.

In either case, the entity should disclose any portion of an asset or liability which is expected to be recovered or settled **after more than 12 months** after the reporting period. For example, for an amount receivable which is due in instalments over 18 months, the portion due after more than 12 months must be disclosed.

5.2 Current assets

Key term

> An asset is classified as a **current asset** when it:
>
> - Is expected to be realised in, or is held for sale or consumption in, the entity's normal operating cycle;
> - Is held primarily for the purpose of being traded;
> - Is expected to be realised within twelve months after the reporting period; or
> - Is cash or a cash equivalent which is not restricted in its use.
>
> All other assets should be classified as non-current assets. (IAS 1: para. 66)

Non-current includes tangible, intangible, operating and financial assets of a long-term nature. Other terms with the same meaning can be used (eg 'fixed', 'long-term').

The term 'operating cycle' is defined by the standard as follows.

Key term

> The **operating cycle** of an entity is the time between the acquisition of assets for processing and their realisation in cash or cash equivalents. (IAS 1: para. 68)

Current assets therefore include assets (such as inventories and trade receivables) that are sold, or realised as part of the normal operating cycle. **This is the case even where they are not expected to be realised within 12 months.**

5.3 Current liabilities

Key term

> A liability is classified as a **current liability** when it:
>
> - Is expected to be settled in the entity's normal operating cycle;
> - Is held primarily for the purpose of trading;
> - Is due to be settled within twelve months of the reporting period; or
> - It does not have an unconditional right to defer settlement for more than twelve months after the reporting period.
>
> All other liabilities should be classified as non-current liabilities. (IAS 1: para. 69)

The categorisation of current liabilities is very similar to that of current assets. Thus, some current liabilities are part of the **working capital** used in the normal operating cycle of the business (ie trade payables and accruals for employee and other operating costs). Such items will be classed as current liabilities **even where they are due to be settled more than 12 months after the reporting date.**

There are also current liabilities which are not settled as part of the normal operating cycle, but which are due to be settled within 12 months of the reporting date. These include bank overdrafts, income taxes, other non-trade payables and the current portion of interest-bearing liabilities. Any interest-bearing liabilities that are used to finance working capital on a long-term basis, and that are not due for settlement within 12 months, should be classed as **non-current liabilities**.

For the differences between liabilities and provisions, see Chapter 15 of this Workbook.

Chapter roundup

- IAS 1 lists the required contents of a company's statement of profit or loss and other comprehensive income and statement of financial position. It also gives guidance on how items should be presented in the financial statements.

- IFRS 15 *Revenue from Contracts with Customers* is concerned with reporting the nature, amount, timing and uncertainty of revenue and cash flows resulting from contracts with customers. Generally, revenue is recognised when the entity has transferred control of goods and services to the buyer.

- The key principle of IFRS 15 is that revenue is recognised to depict the transfer of promised goods or services to customers at an amount that the entity expects to be entitled to in exchange for those goods or services.

- You should be aware of the issues surrounding the current/non-current distinction as well as the disclosure requirements laid down in IAS 1.

PART D FINANCIAL REPORTING, ANALYSIS AND INTERPRETATION

Quick quiz

1   When is revenue recognised by an entity under IFRS 15 *Revenue from Contracts with Customers?*
    A   When all the significant risks and rewards of ownership have been transferred to the purchaser.
    B   When the purchaser has the ability to direct the use of and obtain substantially all of the remaining benefits from the asset.
    C   When the seller has delivered the goods to the purchaser and the purchaser has agreed to make payment.

2   Managers' salaries in a limited liability company are appropriations of profit.
    A   True
    B   False

3   Which of the following items are non-current assets?
    (i)   Land
    (ii)   Machinery
    (iii) Bank loan
    (iv)   Inventory
    A   (i) only
    B   (i) and (ii)
    C   (i), (ii) and (iii)
    D   (ii), (iii) and (iv)

4   How is a bank overdraft classified in the statement of financial position?
    A   Non-current asset
    B   Current asset
    C   Current liability
    D   Non-current liability

Answers to quick quiz

1. B — Under IFRS 15, revenue is recognised when goods or services are transferred. This is based upon the transfer of control. Control of an asset is defined as the ability to direct the use of and obtain substantially all of the remaining benefits from the asset.

2. B — False. Managers' salaries are an expense charged to the statement of profit or loss and other comprehensive income.

3. B — Item (iii) is a liability and item (iv) is a current asset.

4. C — A bank overdraft is strictly payable on demand and so it is a current liability.

PART D FINANCIAL REPORTING, ANALYSIS AND INTERPRETATION

Accounting ratios

Topic list	Syllabus reference
1 The broad categories of ratio	A5
2 Profitability and return on capital	A5
3 Liquidity, gearing/leverage and working capital	A5
4 Shareholders' investment ratios	A5
5 Presentation of financial performance	A5

Introduction

This chapter looks at **interpretation of accounts**. We deal here with the calculation of ratios, how they can be analysed and interpreted, and how the results should be presented to management.

PART D FINANCIAL REPORTING, ANALYSIS AND INTERPRETATION

1 The broad categories of ratio

FAST FORWARD

> You must be able to **appraise and communicate** the position and prospects of a business based on given and prepared statements and ratios.

If you were to look at a statement of financial position or statement of profit or loss and other comprehensive income, how would you decide whether the company was doing well or badly? Or whether it was financially strong or financially vulnerable? And what would you be looking at in the figures to help you to make your judgement?

Ratio analysis involves **comparing one figure against another** to produce a ratio, and assessing whether the ratio indicates a weakness or strength in the company's affairs.

1.1 The broad categories of ratios

Broadly speaking, basic ratios can be grouped into five categories.

- Profitability and return
- Long-term solvency and stability
- Short-term solvency and liquidity
- Efficiency (turnover ratios)
- Shareholders' investment ratios

Within each heading we will identify a number of standard measures or ratios that are normally calculated and generally accepted as meaningful indicators. One must stress however that each individual business must be considered separately, and a ratio that is meaningful for a manufacturing company may be completely meaningless for a financial institution. **Try not to be too mechanical** when working out ratios and constantly think about what you are trying to achieve.

The key to obtaining meaningful information from ratio analysis is **comparison**. This may involve comparing ratios over time within the same business to establish whether things are improving or declining, and comparing ratios between similar businesses to see whether the company you are analysing is better or worse than average within its specific business sector.

It must be stressed that ratio analysis on its own is not sufficient for interpreting company accounts, and that there are **other items of information** which should be looked at, for example:

(a) The content of any accompanying commentary on the accounts and other statements

(b) The age and nature of the company's assets

(c) Current and future developments in the company's markets, at home and overseas, recent acquisitions or disposals of a subsidiary by the company

(d) Unusual items separately disclosed in the statement of profit or loss and other comprehensive income

(e) Any other noticeable features of the report and accounts, such as events after the end of the reporting period, contingent liabilities, a qualified auditors' report, the company's taxation position, and so on

1.2 Example: Calculating ratios

To illustrate the calculation of ratios, the following **draft** statement of financial position and statement of profit or loss and other comprehensive income figures will be used.

FURLONG CO STATEMENT OF PROFIT OR LOSS AND OTHER COMPREHENSIVE INCOME
FOR THE YEAR ENDED 31 DECEMBER 20X8

	Notes	20X8 $	20X7 $
Revenue	1	3,095,576	1,909,051
Operating profit	1	359,501	244,229
Interest	2	17,371	19,127
Profit before taxation		342,130	225,102
Income tax expense		74,200	31,272
Profit for the year		267,930	193,830
Earnings per share		12.8c	9.3c

FURLONG CO STATEMENT OF FINANCIAL POSITION
AS AT 31 DECEMBER 20X8

	Notes	20X8 $	20X7 $
Assets			
Non-current assets			
Property, plant and equipment		802,180	656,071
Current assets			
Inventory		64,422	86,550
Trade receivables	3	1,002,701	853,441
Cash at bank and in hand		1,327	68,363
		1,068,450	1,008,354
Total assets		1,870,630	1,664,425
Equity and liabilities			
Equity			
Ordinary shares 10c each	5	210,000	210,000
Share premium account		48,178	48,178
Retained earnings		651,721	410,591
		909,899	668,769
Non-current liabilities			
10% loan stock 20X4/20Y0		100,000	100,000
Current liabilities	4	860,731	895,656
Total equity and liabilities		1,870,630	1,664,425

NOTES TO THE ACCOUNTS

		20X8 $	20X7 $
1	*Sales revenue and profit*		
	Sales revenue	3,095,576	1,909,051
	Cost of sales	2,402,609	1,441,950
	Gross profit	692,967	467,101
	Administration expenses	333,466	222,872
	Operating profit	359,501	244,229
	Depreciation charged	151,107	120,147
2	*Interest*		
	Payable on bank overdrafts and other loans	8,115	11,909
	Payable on loan stock	10,000	10,000
		18,115	21,909
	Receivable on short-term deposits	744	2,782
	Net payable	17,371	19,127

PART D FINANCIAL REPORTING, ANALYSIS AND INTERPRETATION

		20X8 $	20X7 $
3	Receivables		
	Amounts falling due within one year		
	Trade receivables	905,679	807,712
	Prepayments and accrued income	97,022	45,729
		1,002,701	853,441
4	Current liabilities		
	Trade payables	627,018	545,340
	Accruals and deferred income	81,279	280,464
	Corporate taxes	108,000	37,200
	Other taxes	44,434	32,652
		860,731	895,656
5	Called-up share capital		
	Authorised ordinary shares of 10c each	1,000,000	1,000,000
	Issued and fully paid ordinary shares of 10c each	210,000	210,000
6	Dividends paid	20,000	–

2 Profitability and return on capital

FAST FORWARD

> Return on capital employed (ROCE) may be used by the shareholders or the Board to assess the performance of management.

In our example, the company made a profit in both 20X8 and 20X7, and there was an increase in profit between one year and the next:

(a) Of 52% before taxation
(b) Of 39% after taxation

Profit before taxation is generally thought to be a better figure to use than profit after taxation, because there might be unusual variations in the tax charge from year to year which would not affect the underlying profitability of the company's operations.

Another profit figure that should be calculated is PBIT, **profit before interest and tax**. This is the amount of profit which the company earned before having to pay interest to the providers of loan capital, such as loan notes and medium-term bank loans, which will be shown in the statement of financial position as non-current liabilities.

Formula to learn

Profit before interest and tax is therefore:

(a) The profit on ordinary activities before taxation; **plus**
(b) Interest charges on loan capital.

Published accounts do not always give sufficient detail on interest payable to determine how much is interest on long-term finance. We will assume in our example that the whole of the interest payable ($18,115, note 2) relates to long-term finance.

PBIT in our example is therefore:

	20X8 $	20X7 $
Profit on ordinary activities before tax	342,130	225,102
Interest payable	18,115	21,909
PBIT	360,245	247,011

This shows a 46% growth between 20X7 and 20X8.

2.1 Return on capital employed (ROCE)

It is impossible to assess profits or profit growth properly without relating them to the **amount of funds (capital) that were employed in making the profits**. The most important profitability ratio is therefore return on capital employed (ROCE), which states the profit as a percentage of the amount of capital employed.

Formula to learn

ROCE	=	$\dfrac{\text{Profit before interest and taxation}}{\text{Total assets less current liabilities}} \times 100\%$
Capital employed	=	Shareholders' equity plus non-current liabilities (*or* total assets less current liabilities)

The underlying principle is that we must **compare like with like**, and so if capital means share capital and reserves plus non-current liabilities and debt capital, profit must mean the profit earned by all this capital together. This is PBIT, since interest is the return for loan capital.

In our example, capital employed = 20X8 $1,870,630 − $860,731 = $1,009,899
20X7 $1,664,425 − $895,656 = $768,769

These total figures are the total assets less current liabilities figures for 20X8 and 20X7 in the statement of financial position.

	20X8	20X7
ROCE	$\dfrac{\$360,245}{\$1,009,899} = 35.7\%$	$\dfrac{\$247,011}{\$768,769} = 32.1\%$

What does a company's ROCE tell us? What should we be looking for? There are three comparisons that can be made.

(a) The **change in ROCE from one year to the next** can be examined. In this example, there has been an increase in ROCE by about 4 percentage points from its 20X7 level.

(b) The **ROCE being earned by other companies**, if this information is available, can be compared with the ROCE of this company. Here the information is not available.

(c) A comparison of the ROCE with **current market borrowing rates** may be made.

   (i) What would be the cost of extra borrowing to the company if it needed more loans, and is it earning a ROCE that suggests it could make profits to make such borrowing worthwhile?

   (ii) Is the company making a ROCE which suggests that it is getting value for money from its current borrowing?

   (iii) Companies are in a risk business and commercial borrowing rates are a good independent yardstick against which company performance can be judged.

In this example, if we suppose that current market interest rates, say, for medium-term borrowing from banks, are around 10%, then the company's actual ROCE of 36% in 20X8 would not seem low. On the contrary, it might seem high.

However, it is easier to spot a low ROCE than a high one, because there is always a chance that the company's non-current assets, especially property, are **undervalued** in its statement of financial position, and so the capital employed figure might be unrealistically low. If the company had earned a ROCE, not of 36%, but of, say only 6%, then its return would have been below current borrowing rates and so disappointingly low.

2.2 Return on equity (ROE)

Return on equity gives a more restricted view of capital than ROCE, but it is based on the same principles.

Formula to learn

$$ROE = \frac{\text{Profit after tax and preference dividend}}{\text{Equity shareholders funds}} \times 100\%$$

In our example, ROE is calculated as follows.

	20X8	20X7
ROE	$\frac{\$267,930}{\$909,899} = 29.4\%$	$\frac{\$193,830}{\$668,769} = 29\%$

ROE is **not a widely-used ratio**, however, because there are more useful ratios that give an indication of the return to shareholders, such as earnings per share, dividend per share, dividend yield and earnings yield, which are described later.

2.3 Analysing profitability and return in more detail: The secondary ratios

We often sub-analyse ROCE, to find out more about why the ROCE is high or low, or better or worse than last year. There are two factors that contribute towards a return on capital employed, both related to sales revenue.

(a) **Profit margin**. A company might make a high or low profit margin on its sales. For example, a company that makes a profit of 25c per $1 of sales is making a bigger return on its revenue than another company making a profit of only 10c per $1 of sales.

(b) **Asset turnover**. Asset turnover is a measure of how well the assets of a business are being used to generate sales. For example, if two companies each have capital employed of $100,000 and Company A makes sales of $400,000 per annum whereas Company B makes sales of only $200,000 per annum, Company A is making a higher revenue from the same amount of assets (twice as much asset turnover as Company B) and this will help A to make a higher return on capital employed than B. Asset turnover is expressed as 'x times' so that assets generate x times their value in annual sales. Here, Company A's asset turnover is 4 times and B's is 2 times.

Profit margin and asset turnover together explain the ROCE and if the ROCE is the primary profitability ratio, these other two are the secondary ratios. The relationship between the three ratios can be shown mathematically.

Formula to learn

Profit margin × Asset turnover = ROCE

$$\therefore \frac{\text{PBIT}}{\text{Sales}} \times \frac{\text{Sales}}{\text{Capital employed}} = \frac{\text{PBIT}}{\text{Capital employed}}$$

In our example:

		Profit margin		Asset turnover		ROCE
(a)	20X8	$\frac{\$360,245}{\$3,095,576}$	×	$\frac{\$3,095,576}{\$1,009,899}$	=	$\frac{\$360,245}{\$1,009,899}$
		11.64%	×	3.07 times	=	35.7%

		Profit margin		Asset turnover		ROCE
(b)	20X7	$\frac{\$247,011}{\$1,909,051}$	×	$\frac{\$1,909,051}{\$768,769}$	=	$\frac{\$247,011}{\$768,769}$
		12.94%	×	2.48 times	=	32.1%

In this example, the company's improvement in ROCE between 20X7 and 20X8 is attributable to a higher asset turnover. Indeed the profit margin has fallen a little, but the higher asset turnover has more than compensated for this.

It is also worth commenting on the change in sales revenue from one year to the next. You may already have noticed that Furlong achieved sales growth of over 60% from $1.9 million to $3.1 million between 20X7 and 20X8. This is very strong growth, and this is certainly one of the most significant items in the statement of profit or loss and other comprehensive income and statement of financial position.

2.3.1 A warning about comments on profit margin and asset turnover

It might be tempting to think that a high profit margin is good, and a low asset turnover means sluggish trading. In broad terms, this is so. But there is a trade-off between profit margin and asset turnover, and you cannot look at one without allowing for the other.

(a) A **high profit margin** means a high profit per $1 of sales, but if this also means that sales prices are high, there is a strong possibility that sales revenue will be depressed, and so asset turnover lower.

(b) A **high asset turnover** means that the company is generating a lot of sales, but to do this it might have to keep its prices down and so accept a low profit margin per $1 of sales.

Consider the following.

Company A		Company B	
Sales revenue	$1,000,000	Sales revenue	$4,000,000
Capital employed	$1,000,000	Capital employed	$1,000,000
PBIT	$200,000	PBIT	$200,000

These figures would give the following ratios.

ROCE	=	$\frac{\$200,000}{\$1,000,000}$	=	20%	ROCE	=	$\frac{\$200,000}{\$1,000,000}$	=	20%
Profit margin	=	$\frac{\$200,000}{\$1,000,000}$	=	20%	Profit margin	=	$\frac{\$200,000}{\$4,000,000}$	=	5%
Asset turnover	=	$\frac{\$1,000,000}{\$1,000,000}$	=	1	Asset turnover	=	$\frac{\$4,000,000}{\$1,000,000}$	=	4

The companies have the same ROCE, but it is arrived at in a very different fashion. Company A operates with a low asset turnover and a comparatively high profit margin whereas company B carries out much more business, but on a lower profit margin. Company A could be operating at the luxury end of the market, whilst company B is operating at the popular end of the market.

2.4 Gross profit margin, net profit margin and profit analysis

Depending on the format of the statement of profit or loss and other comprehensive income, you may be able to calculate the gross profit margin as well as the net profit margin. **Looking at the two together** can be quite informative.

For example, suppose that a company has the following summarised statement of profit or loss and other comprehensive income for two consecutive years.

PART D   FINANCIAL REPORTING, ANALYSIS AND INTERPRETATION

	Year 1	Year 2
	$	$
Revenue	70,000	100,000
Cost of sales	42,000	55,000
Gross profit	28,000	45,000
Expenses	21,000	35,000
Net profit	7,000	10,000

Although the net profit margin is the same for both years at 10%, the gross profit margin is not.

In year 1 it is: $\dfrac{\$28,000}{\$70,000} = 40\%$

and in year 2 it is: $\dfrac{\$45,000}{\$100,000} = 45\%$

The improved gross profit margin has not led to an improvement in the net profit margin. This is because expenses as a percentage of sales have risen from 30% in year 1 to 35% in year 2.

2.5 Historical vs current cost

In this chapter we are dealing with interpretation of financial statements based on historical cost accounts.

It is worth considering how the analysis would change if we were dealing with financial statements based on some form of current value accounting (which we looked at in Chapter 18).

These are some of the issues that would arise:

- Non-current asset values would probably be stated at fair value. This may be higher than depreciated historical cost. Therefore capital employed would be higher. This would lead to a reduction in ROCE.
- Higher asset values would lead to a higher depreciation charge, which would reduce net profit.
- If opening inventory were shown at current value, this would increase cost of sales and reduce net profit.

So you can see that ROCE based on historical cost accounts is probably overstated in real terms.

3 Liquidity, gearing/leverage and working capital

FAST FORWARD

Banks and other lenders will be interested in a company's gearing level.

3.1 Long-term solvency: Debt and gearing ratios

Debt ratios are concerned with **how much the company owes in relation to its size**, whether it is getting into heavier debt or improving its situation, and whether its debt burden seems heavy or light.

(a) When a company is heavily in debt banks and other potential lenders may be unwilling to advance further funds.

(b) When a company is earning only a modest profit before interest and tax, and has a heavy debt burden, there will be very little profit left over for shareholders after the interest charges have been paid. Therefore, if interest rates were to go up (on bank overdrafts and so on) or the company were to borrow even more, it might soon be incurring interest charges in excess of PBIT. This might eventually lead to the liquidation of the company.

These are two big reasons why companies should keep their debt burden under control. There are four ratios that are particularly worth looking at; the debt ratio, gearing ratio, interest cover and cash flow ratio.

3.2 Debt ratio

Formula to learn

> The **debt ratio** is the ratio of a company's total debts to its total assets.

(a) Assets consist of non-current assets at their carrying value, plus current assets.
(b) Debts consist of all payables, whether they are due within one year or after more than one year.

You can ignore other non-current liabilities, such as deferred taxation.

There is no absolute guide to the maximum safe debt ratio, but as a very general guide, you might regard 50% as a safe limit to debt. In practice, many companies operate successfully with a higher debt ratio than this, but 50% is nonetheless a helpful benchmark. In addition, if the debt ratio is over 50% and getting worse, the company's debt position will be worth looking at more carefully.

In the case of Furlong the debt ratio is as follows.

	20X8	20X7
Total debts	$ (860,731 + 100,000)	$ (895,656 + 100,000)
Total assets	$1,870,630	$1,664,425
	= 51%	= 60%

In this case, the debt ratio is quite high, mainly because of the large amount of current liabilities. However, the debt ratio has fallen from 60% to 51% between 20X7 and 20X8, and so the company appears to be improving its debt position.

3.3 Gearing/leverage

Gearing or leverage is concerned with a company's **long-term capital structure**. We can think of a company as consisting of non-current assets and net current assets (ie working capital, which is current assets minus current liabilities). These assets must be financed by long-term capital of the company, which is one of two things.

(a) Issued share capital which can be divided into:
   (i) Ordinary shares plus other equity (eg reserves)
   (ii) Non-redeemable preference shares (unusual)

(b) Long-term debt including redeemable preference shares

Preference share capital is normally classified as a non-current liability in accordance with IAS 32, and preference dividends (paid or accrued) are included in finance costs in the statement of profit or loss and other comprehensive income.

The **capital gearing ratio** is a measure of the proportion of a company's capital that is debt. It is measured as follows.

Formula to learn

$$\text{Gearing} = \frac{\text{Interest bearing debt}}{\text{Shareholders' equity} + \text{interest bearing debt}} \times 100\%$$

As with the debt ratio, there is **no absolute limit** to what a gearing ratio ought to be. A company with a gearing ratio of more than 50% is said to be high-geared (whereas low gearing means a gearing ratio of less than 50%). Many companies are high geared, but if a high geared company is becoming increasingly high geared, it is likely to have difficulty in the future when it wants to borrow even more, unless it can also boost its shareholders' capital, either with retained profits or by a new share issue.

Leverage is an alternative term for gearing; the words have the same meaning. Note that leverage (or gearing) can be looked at conversely, by calculating the proportion of total assets financed by equity, and which may be called the equity to assets ratio. It is calculated as follows.

> **Formula to learn**
>
> $$\text{Equity to assets ratio} = \frac{\text{Shareholders' equity}}{\text{Shareholders' equity} + \text{interest bearing debt}} \times 100\%$$
>
> or
>
> $$\frac{\text{Shareholders' equity}}{\text{Total assets less current liabilities}}$$

In the example of Furlong, we find that the company, although having a high debt ratio because of its current liabilities, has a low gearing ratio. It has no preference share capital and its only long-term debt is the 10% loan stock. The equity to assets ratio is therefore high.

		20X8	20X7
Gearing ratio	=	$\frac{\$100{,}000}{\$1{,}009{,}899}$	$\frac{\$100{,}000}{\$768{,}769}$
		= 10%	= 13%
Equity to assets ratio	=	$\frac{\$909{,}899}{\$1{,}009{,}899}$	$\frac{\$668{,}769}{\$768{,}769}$
		= 90%	= 87%

As you can see, the equity to assets ratio is the mirror image of gearing.

3.4 The implications of high or low gearing/leverage

We mentioned earlier that **gearing or leverage** is, amongst other things, an attempt to **quantify the degree of risk involved in holding equity shares in a company**, risk both in terms of the company's ability to remain in business and in terms of expected ordinary dividends from the company. The problem with a highly geared company is that by definition there is a lot of debt. Debt generally carries a fixed rate of interest (or fixed rate of dividend if in the form of preference shares), hence there is a given (and large) amount to be paid out from profits to holders of debt before arriving at a residue available for distribution to the holders of equity. The riskiness will perhaps become clearer with the aid of an example.

	Company A $'000	Company B $'000	Company C $'000
Ordinary shares	600	400	300
Retained earnings	200	200	200
Revaluation surplus	100	100	100
	900	700	600
6% preference shares (redeemable)	–	–	100
10% loan stock	100	300	300
Capital employed	1,000	1,000	1,000
Gearing ratio	10%	30%	40%
Equity to assets ratio	90%	70%	60%

Now suppose that each company makes a profit before interest and tax of $50,000, and the rate of tax on company profits is 30%. Amounts available for distribution to equity shareholders will be as follows.

	Company A $'000	Company B $'000	Company C $'000
Profit before interest and tax	50	50	50
Interest/preference dividend	10	30	36
Taxable profit	40	20	14
Taxation at 30%	12	6	4
Profit for the period	28	14	10

If in the subsequent year profit before interest and tax falls to $40,000, the amounts available to ordinary shareholders will become as follows.

	Company A $'000	Company B $'000	Company C $'000
Profit before interest and tax	40	40	40
Interest/preference dividend	10	30	36
Taxable profit	30	10	4
Taxation at 30%	9	3	1
Profit for the period	21	7	3

Note the following.

Gearing ratio	10%	30%	40%
Equity to assets ratio	90%	70%	60%
Change in PBIT	–20%	–20%	–20%
Change in profit available for ordinary shareholders	–25%	–50%	–70%

The more highly geared the company, the greater the risk that little (if anything) will be available to distribute by way of dividend to the ordinary shareholders. The example clearly displays this fact in so far as the more highly geared the company, the greater the percentage change in profit available for ordinary shareholders for any given percentage change in profit before interest and tax. The relationship similarly holds when profits increase, and if PBIT had risen by 20% rather than fallen, you would find that once again the largest percentage change in profit available for ordinary shareholders (this means an increase) will be for the highly geared company. This means that there will be greater *volatility* of amounts available for ordinary shareholders, and presumably therefore greater volatility in dividends paid to those shareholders, where a company is highly geared. That is the risk: you may do extremely well or extremely badly without a particularly large movement in the PBIT of the company.

The risk of a company's ability to remain in business was referred to earlier. Gearing or leverage is relevant to this. A highly geared company has a large amount of interest to pay annually (assuming that the debt is external borrowing rather than preference shares). If those borrowings are **'secured'** in any way (and loan notes in particular are secured), then the **holders of the debt are perfectly entitled to force the company** to **realise assets to pay their interest** if funds are not available from other sources. Clearly the more highly geared a company the more likely this is to occur when and if profits fall.

3.5 Interest cover

The interest cover ratio shows whether a company is earning enough profits before interest and tax to pay its interest costs comfortably, or whether its interest costs are high in relation to the size of its profits, so that a fall in PBIT would then have a significant effect on profits available for ordinary shareholders.

Formula to learn

$$\text{Interest cover} = \frac{\text{Profit before interest and tax}}{\text{Interest charges}}$$

An interest cover of 2 times or less would be low, and should really exceed 3 times before the company's interest costs are to be considered within acceptable limits.

Returning first to the example of Companies A, B and C, the interest cover was as follows.

		Company A	Company B	Company C
(a)	When PBIT was $50,000 =	$50,000 / $10,000	$50,000 / $30,000	$50,000 / $36,000
		5 times	1.67 times	1.39 times
(b)	When PBIT was $40,000 =	$40,000 / $10,000	$40,000 / $30,000	$40,000 / $36,000
		4 times	1.33 times	1.11 times

Both B and C have a low interest cover, which is a warning to ordinary shareholders that their profits are highly vulnerable, in percentage terms, to even small changes in PBIT.

Question — Interest cover

Returning to the example of Furlong in Paragraph 1.2, what is the company's interest cover?

Answer

Interest payments should be taken gross, from the note to the accounts, and not net of interest receipts as shown in the statement of profit or loss and other comprehensive income.

	20X8	20X7
PBIT	360,245	247,011
Interest payable	18,115	21,909
	= 20 times	= 11 times

Furlong has more than sufficient interest cover. In view of the company's low gearing, this is not too surprising and so we finally obtain a picture of Furlong as a company that does not seem to have a debt problem, in spite of its high (although declining) debt ratio.

3.6 Cash flow ratio

The cash flow ratio is the ratio of a company's **net cash inflow to its total debts**.

(a) **Net cash inflow** is the amount of cash which the company has coming into the business from its operations. A suitable figure for net cash inflow can be obtained from the statement of cash flows.

(b) **Total debts** are short-term and long-term payables, including provisions. A distinction can be made between debts payable within one year and other debts and provisions.

Obviously, a company needs to be earning enough cash from operations to be able to meet its foreseeable debts and future commitments, and the cash flow ratio, and changes in the cash flow ratio from one year to the next, provide a **useful indicator of a company's cash position**.

3.7 Short-term solvency and liquidity

Profitability is of course an important aspect of a company's performance and gearing or leverage is another. Neither, however, addresses directly the key issue of **liquidity**.

Key term

> **Liquidity** is the amount of cash a company can put its hands on quickly to settle its debts (and possibly to meet other unforeseen demands for cash payments too).

Liquid funds consist of:

(a) Cash

(b) Short-term investments for which there is a ready market

(c) Fixed-term deposits with a bank or other financial institution, for example, a six month high-interest deposit with a bank

(d) Trade receivables (because they will pay what they owe within a reasonably short period of time)

(e) Bills of exchange receivable (because like ordinary trade receivables, these represent amounts of cash due to be received within a relatively short period of time)

In summary, **liquid assets are current asset items that will or could soon be converted into cash, and cash itself**. Two common definitions of liquid assets are:

- All current assets without exception
- All current assets with the exception of inventories

A company can obtain liquid assets from sources other than sales of goods and services, such as the issue of shares for cash, a new loan or the sale of non-current assets. But a company cannot rely on these at all times, and in general, obtaining liquid funds depends on making sales revenue and profits. Even so, profits do not always lead to increases in liquidity. This is mainly because funds generated from trading may be immediately invested in non-current assets or paid out as dividends.

The reason why a company needs liquid assets is so that it can meet its debts when they fall due. Payments are continually made for operating expenses and other costs, and so there is a **cash cycle** from trading activities of cash coming in from sales and cash going out for expenses.

3.8 The cash cycle

To help you to understand liquidity ratios, it is useful to begin with a brief explanation of the cash cycle. The cash cycle describes **the flow of cash out of a business and back into it again as a result of normal trading operations.**

Cash goes out to pay for supplies, wages and salaries and other expenses, although payments can be delayed by taking some credit. A business might hold inventory for a while and then sell it. Cash will come back into the business from the sales, although customers might delay payment by themselves taking some credit.

The main points about the cash cycle are as follows.

(a) The timing of cash flows in and out of a business does not coincide with the time when sales and costs of sales occur. **Cash flows out can be postponed by taking credit. Cash flows in can be delayed by having receivables.**

(b) **The time between making a purchase and making a sale also affects cash flows.** If inventories are held for a long time, the delay between the cash payment for inventory and cash receipts from selling it will also be a long one.

(c) **Holding inventories and having receivables can therefore be seen as two reasons why cash receipts are delayed.** Another way of saying this is that if a company invests in working capital, its cash position will show a corresponding decrease.

(d) Similarly, **taking credit from creditors can be seen as a reason why cash payments are delayed**. The company's liquidity position will worsen when it has to pay the suppliers, unless it can get more cash in from sales and receivables in the meantime.

The liquidity ratios and working capital turnover ratios are used to test a company's liquidity, length of cash cycle, and investment in working capital.

3.9 Liquidity ratios: Current ratio and quick ratio

The 'standard' test of liquidity is the **current ratio**. It can be obtained from the statement of financial position.

Formula to learn

$$\text{Current ratio} = \frac{\text{Current assets}}{\text{Current liabilities}}$$

The idea behind this is that a company should have enough current assets that give a promise of 'cash to come' to meet its future commitments to pay off its current liabilities. Obviously, a **ratio in excess of 1 should be expected**. Otherwise, there would be the prospect that the company might be unable to pay its debts on time. In practice, a ratio comfortably in excess of 1 should be expected, but what is 'comfortable' varies between different types of businesses.

Companies are not able to convert all their current assets into cash very quickly. In particular, some manufacturing companies might hold large quantities of raw material inventories, which must be used in production to create finished goods inventory. These might be warehoused for a long time, or sold on lengthy credit. In such businesses, where the inventory is held for longer than industry standard, so holding period is high (inventory turnover is slow), this means that cash is 'held' in the value of the inventory. Most inventories are not very 'liquid' assets, because the cash cycle is so long. For these reasons, we calculate an additional liquidity ratio, known as the quick ratio or acid test ratio.

The **quick ratio**, or **acid test ratio**, is calculated as follows.

Formula to learn

$$\text{Quick ratio} = \frac{\text{Current assets less inventory}}{\text{Current liabilities}}$$

This ratio should ideally be **at least 1** for companies with a slow inventory turnover. For companies with a fast inventory turnover, a quick ratio can be comfortably less than 1 without suggesting that the company could be in cash flow trouble.

Both the current ratio and the quick ratio offer an indication of the company's liquidity position, but the absolute figures **should not be interpreted too literally**. It is often theorised that an acceptable current ratio is 1.5 and an acceptable quick ratio is 0.8, but these should only be used as a guide. Different businesses operate in very different ways. A supermarket group for example might have a current ratio of 0.52 and a quick ratio of 0.17. Supermarkets have low receivables (people do not buy groceries on credit), low cash (good cash management), medium inventories (high inventories but quick turnover, particularly in view of perishability) and very high payables.

Compare this with a manufacturing and retail organisation, with a current ratio of 1.44 and a quick ratio of 1.03. Such businesses operate with liquidity ratios closer to the standard.

What is important is the **trend** of these ratios. From this, one can easily ascertain whether liquidity is improving or deteriorating. If a supermarket has traded for the last ten years (very successfully) with current ratios of 0.52 and quick ratios of 0.17 then it should be supposed that the company can continue in business with those levels of liquidity. If in the following year the current ratio were to fall to 0.38 and the quick ratio to 0.09, then further investigation into the liquidity situation would be appropriate. It is the relative position that is far more important than the absolute figures.

Don't forget the other side of the coin either. A current ratio and a quick ratio can get **bigger than they need to be**. A company that has large volumes of inventories and receivables might be over-investing in working capital, and so tying up more funds in the business than it needs to. This would suggest poor management of receivables (credit) or inventories by the company.

3.10 Efficiency ratios: Control of receivables and inventories

A rough measure of the average length of time it takes for a company's customers to pay what they owe is the accounts receivable collection period.

Formula to learn

> The estimated average accounts receivable collection period is calculated as:
>
> $$\frac{\text{Trade receivables}}{\text{Sales}} \times 365 \text{ days}$$

The figure for sales should be taken as the sales revenue figure in the statement of profit or loss and other comprehensive income. Note that any **cash sales should be excluded** – this ratio only uses credit sales. The trade receivables are not the total figure for receivables in the statement of financial position, which includes prepayments and non-trade receivables. The trade receivables figure will be itemised in an analysis of the receivable total, in a note to the accounts.

The estimate of the accounts receivable collection period is **only approximate**.

(a) The value of receivables in the statement of financial position might be abnormally high or low compared with the 'normal' level the company usually has.

(b) Sales revenue in the statement of profit or loss and other comprehensive income is exclusive of sales taxes, but receivables in the statement of financial position are inclusive of sales tax. We are not strictly comparing like with like.

Sales are usually made on 'normal credit terms' of payment within 30 days. A collection period significantly in excess of this might be representative of poor management of funds of a business. However, some companies must allow generous credit terms to win customers. Exporting companies in particular may have to carry large amounts of receivables, and so their average collection period might be well in excess of 30 days.

The **trend of the collection period over time** is probably the best guide. If the collection period is increasing year on year, this is indicative of a poorly managed credit control function (and potentially therefore a poorly managed company).

3.11 Accounts receivable collection period: Examples

Using the same types of company as examples, the collection period for each of the companies was as follows.

Company	Trade receivables / Sales	Collection period (× 365)	Previous year	Collection period (× 365)
Supermarket	$\frac{\$5,016K}{\$284,986K} =$	6.4 days	$\frac{\$3,977K}{\$290,668K} =$	5.0 days
Manufacturer	$\frac{\$458.3m}{\$2,059.5m} =$	81.2 days	$\frac{\$272.4m}{\$1,274.2m} =$	78.0 days
Sugar refiner and seller	$\frac{\$304.4m}{\$3,817.3m} =$	29.1 days	$\frac{\$287.0m}{\$3,366.3m} =$	31.1 days

The differences in collection period reflect the differences between the types of business. Supermarkets have hardly any trade receivables at all, whereas the manufacturing companies have far more. The collection periods are fairly constant from the previous year for all three companies.

3.12 Inventory holding period

Another ratio worth calculating is the inventory holding period. This is another estimated figure, obtainable from published accounts, which indicates the average number of days that items of inventory are held for. As with the average receivable collection period, however, it is only an approximate estimated figure, but one which should be reliable enough for comparing changes year on year.

Formula to learn

The inventory holding period is calculated as:

$$\frac{\text{Inventory}}{\text{Cost of sales}} \times 365 \text{ days}$$

This is another measure of how vigorously a business is trading. A lengthening inventory holding period from one year to the next indicates:

(a) A slowdown in trading; or
(b) A build-up in inventory levels, perhaps suggesting that the investment in inventories is becoming excessive.

Generally, the **higher the inventory turnover the better**, ie the lower the holding period the better, but several aspects of inventory holding policy have to be balanced.

(a) Lead times
(b) Seasonal fluctuations in orders
(c) Alternative uses of warehouse space
(d) Bulk buying discounts
(e) Likelihood of inventory perishing or becoming obsolete

Presumably if we add together the inventory holding period and receivables collection period, this should give us an indication of how soon inventory is converted into cash. Both receivables collection period and inventory turnover period therefore give us a further indication of the company's liquidity.

3.13 Inventory holding period: Example

The estimated inventory holding periods for a supermarket are as follows:

Company	$\frac{\text{Inventory}}{\text{Cost of sales}}$	Inventory holding period (days × 365)		Previous year	
Supermarket	$\frac{\$15,554\text{K}}{\$254,571\text{K}}$	22.3 days	$\frac{\$14,094\text{K}}{\$261,368\text{K}} \times$	365	= 19.7 days

3.14 Accounts payable payment period

Formula to learn

Accounts payable payment period is ideally calculated by the formula:

$$\frac{\text{Trade accounts payable}}{\text{Purchases}} \times 365 \text{ days}$$

It is rare to find purchases disclosed in published accounts and so **cost of sales serves as an approximation**. The payment period often helps to assess a company's liquidity; an increase is often a sign of lack of long-term finance or poor management of current assets, resulting in the use of extended credit from suppliers, increased bank overdraft and so on. Under UK legislation, from April 2016, large companies and public companies in the UK are required to publish the average time taken to pay suppliers, ie, the accounts payable payment period, under the Small Business, Enterprise and Employment Act, 2015.

Question — Liquidity and working capital

Calculate liquidity and working capital ratios from the accounts of TEB Co, a business which provides service support (cleaning etc) to customers worldwide. Comment on the results of your calculations.

	20X7 $m	20X6 $m
Revenue	2,176.2	2,344.8
Cost of sales	1,659.0	1,731.5
Gross profit	517.2	613.3
Current assets		
Inventory	42.7	78.0
Trade receivables (note 1)	378.9	431.4
Short-term deposits and cash	205.2	145.0
	626.8	654.4
Current liabilities		
Loans and overdrafts	32.4	81.1
Tax on profits	67.8	76.7
Accruals	11.7	17.2
Trade payables (note 2)	487.2	467.2
	599.1	642.2
Net current assets	27.7	12.2
Notes		
1 Trade receivables	295.2	335.5
2 Trade payables	190.8	188.1

Answer

	20X7	20X6
Current ratio	$\dfrac{626.8}{599.1} = 1.05$	$\dfrac{654.4}{642.2} = 1.02$
Quick ratio	$\dfrac{584.1}{599.1} = 0.97$	$\dfrac{576.4}{642.2} = 0.90$
Accounts receivable collection period	$\dfrac{295.2}{2{,}176.2} \times 365 = 49.5$ days	$\dfrac{335.5}{2{,}344.8} \times 365 = 52.2$ days
Inventory holding period	$\dfrac{42.7}{1{,}659.0} \times 365 = 9.4$ days	$\dfrac{78.0}{1{,}731.5} \times 365 = 16.4$ days
Accounts payable payment period	$\dfrac{190.8}{1{,}659.0} \times 365 = 42.0$ days	$\dfrac{188.1}{1{,}731.5} \times 365 = 39.7$ days

The company's current ratio is a little lower than average but its quick ratio is better than average and very little less than the current ratio. This suggests that inventory levels are strictly controlled, which is reinforced by the low inventory holding period. It would seem that working capital is tightly managed, to avoid the poor liquidity which could be caused by a long receivables collection period and comparatively high payables.

The company in the exercise is a service company and hence it would be expected to have very low inventory and a very short inventory holding period. The similarity of receivables collection period and payables payment period means that the company is passing on most of the delay in receiving payment to its suppliers.

Question — Operating cycle

(a) Calculate the operating cycle for Moribund plc for 20X2 on the basis of the following information.

		$
Inventory:	raw materials	150,000
	work in progress	60,000
	finished goods	200,000
Purchases		500,000
Trade receivables		230,000
Trade payables		120,000
Sales		900,000
Cost of goods sold		750,000

Tutorial note. You will need to calculate inventory holding periods (total year end inventory over cost of goods sold), receivables as daily sales, and payables in relation to purchases, all converted into 'days'.

(b) List the steps which might be taken in order to improve the operating cycle.

Answer

(a) The operating cycle can be found as follows.

Inventory holding period: $\dfrac{\text{Total closing inventory} \times 365}{\text{Cost of goods sold}}$

plus

Accounts receivable collection period: $\dfrac{\text{Closing trade receivables} \times 365}{\text{Sales}}$

less

Accounts payable payment period: $\dfrac{\text{Closing trade payables} \times 365}{\text{Purchases}}$

	20X2
Total closing inventory ($)	410,000
Cost of goods sold ($)	750,000
Inventory holding period	199.5 days
Closing receivables ($)	230,000
Revenue ($)	900,000
Receivables collection period	93.3 days
Closing payables ($)	120,000
Purchases ($)	500,000
Payables payment period	(87.6 days)
Length of operating cycle (199.5 + 93.3 − 87.6)	205.2 days

(b) The steps that could be taken to reduce the operating cycle include the following.

(i) Reducing the raw material inventory holding period.

(ii) Reducing the time taken to produce goods. However, the company must ensure that quality is not sacrificed as a result of speeding up the production process.

(iii) Increasing the period of credit taken from suppliers. The credit period already seems very long – the company is allowed three months credit by its suppliers, and probably could not be increased. If the credit period is extended then the company may lose discounts for prompt payment.

(iv) Reducing the finished goods inventory holding period.

(v) Reducing the receivables collection period. The administrative costs of speeding up debt collection and the effect on sales of reducing the credit period allowed must be evaluated. However, the credit period does already seem very long by the standards of most industries. It may be that generous terms have been allowed to secure large contracts and little will be able to be done about this in the short term.

4 Shareholders' investment ratios

FAST FORWARD

Ratios such as EPS and dividend per share help equity shareholders and other investors to **assess the value and quality of an investment in the ordinary shares of a company**.

They are:

(a) Earnings per share
(b) Dividend per share
(c) Dividend cover
(d) P/E ratio
(e) Dividend yield

The value of an investment in ordinary shares in a company **listed on a stock exchange** is its market value, and so investment ratios must have regard not only to information in the company's published accounts, but also to the current price, and the fourth and fifth ratios involve using the share price.

4.1 Earnings per share

It is possible to calculate the return on each ordinary share in the year. This is the earnings per share (EPS). Earnings per share is the amount of net profit for the period that is attributable to each ordinary share which is outstanding during all or part of the period (see Chapter 18).

4.2 Dividend per share and dividend cover

The **dividend per share** in cents is self-explanatory, and clearly an item of some interest to shareholders.

Formula to learn

Dividend cover is a ratio of: $\dfrac{\text{Earnings per share}}{\text{Dividend per (ordinary) share}}$

It shows the **proportion of profit for the year that is available for distribution to shareholders that has been paid (or proposed) and what proportion will be retained in the business to finance future growth**. A dividend cover of 2 times would indicate that the company had paid 50% of its distributable profits as dividends, and retained 50% in the business to help to finance future operations. Retained profits are an important source of funds for most companies, and so the dividend cover can in some cases be quite high.

A **significant change** in the dividend cover from one year to the next would be worth looking at closely. For example, if a company's dividend cover were to fall sharply between one year and the next, it could be that its profits had fallen, but the directors wished to pay at least the same amount of dividends as in the previous year, so as to keep shareholder expectations satisfied.

4.3 P/E ratio

Formula to learn

The **Price/Earnings (P/E) ratio** is the ratio of a company's current share price to the earnings per share.

A high P/E ratio indicates strong shareholder **confidence** in the company and its future, eg in profit growth, and a lower P/E ratio indicates lower confidence.

The P/E ratio of one company can be compared with the P/E ratios of:

- Other companies in the same business sector
- Other companies generally

It is often used in **stock exchange reporting** where prices are readily available.

4.4 Dividend yield

Dividend yield is the return a shareholder is currently expecting on the shares of a company.

Formula to learn

$$\text{Dividend yield} = \frac{\text{Dividend on the share for the year}}{\text{Current market value of the share (ex div)}} \times 100\%$$

(a) The dividend per share is taken as the dividend for the previous year.
(b) Ex-div means that the share price does *not* include the right to the most recent dividend.

Shareholders look for **both dividend yield and capital growth**. Obviously, dividend yield is therefore an important aspect of a share's performance.

Question — Dividend yield

In the year to 30 September 20X8, an advertising agency declares an interim ordinary dividend of 7.4c per share and a final ordinary dividend of 8.6c per share. Assuming an ex div share price of 315 cents, what is the dividend yield?

Answer

The total dividend per share is (7.4 + 8.6) = 16 cents

$$\frac{16}{315} \times 100 = 5.1\%$$

5 Presentation of financial performance

FAST FORWARD

However many ratios you can find to calculate, **numbers alone will not answer a question**. You **must** interpret all the information available to you and support your interpretation with ratio calculations.

Exam focus point

Examination questions on financial performance may try to simulate a real life situation. A set of accounts could be presented and you may be asked to prepare a report on them, addressed to a specific interested party, such as a bank. The narrative is relevant to your answer as much as calculation of the ratios.

You should begin your report with a heading showing who it is from, the name of the addressee, the subject of the report and a suitable date.

A good approach is often to head up a **'schedule of ratios and statistics'** which will form an appendix to the main report. Calculate the ratios in a logical sequence, dealing in turn with operating and profitability ratios, use of assets (eg holding period for inventories, collection period for receivables), liquidity and gearing/leverage.

As you calculate the ratios you are likely to be struck by **significant fluctuations and trends**. These will form the basis of your comments in the body of the report. The report should begin with some introductory comments, setting out the scope of your analysis and mentioning that detailed figures have been included in an appendix. You should then go on to present your analysis under any categories called for by the question (eg separate sections for management, shareholders and creditors, or separate sections for profitability and liquidity).

Finally, look out for opportunities to **suggest remedial action** where trends appear to be unfavourable. Questions sometimes require you specifically to set out your advice and recommendations.

5.1 Planning your answers

This is as good a place as any to stress the importance of planning your answers. This is particularly important for 'wordy' questions. While you may feel like breathing a sigh of relief after all that number crunching, you should not be tempted to 'waffle'. The best way to avoid going off the point is to **prepare an answer plan**. This has the advantage of making you think before you write and structure your answer logically.

The following approach may be adopted when preparing an answer plan.

(a) Read the question **requirements**.
(b) **Skim through the question** to see roughly what it is about.
(c) Read through the question carefully, **underlining any key words**.
(d) Set out the **headings** for the main parts of your answer. Leave space to insert points within the headings.
(e) **Jot down points** to make within the main sections, underlining points on which you wish to expand.
(f) Write your **full answer**.

You should allow yourself the full time allocation for written answers, that is 1.8 minutes per mark. If, however, you run out of time, a clear answer plan with points in note form will earn you more marks than an introductory paragraph written out in full.

Question — Ratios

The following information has been extracted from the recently published accounts of DG.

STATEMENTS OF PROFIT OR LOSS AND OTHER COMPREHENSIVE INCOME (EXTRACTS) TO 30 APRIL

	20X9	20X8
	$'000	$'000
Revenue	11,200	9,750
Cost of sales	8,460	6,825
Net profit before tax	465	320
This is after charging:		
Depreciation	360	280
Loan note interest	80	60
Interest on bank overdraft	15	9
Audit fees	12	10

PART D FINANCIAL REPORTING, ANALYSIS AND INTERPRETATION

STATEMENTS OF FINANCIAL POSITION AS AT 30 APRIL

	20X9 $'000	20X9 $'000	20X8 $'000	20X8 $'000
Assets				
Non-current assets		1,850		1,430
Current assets				
Inventory	640		490	
Trade receivables	1,230		1,080	
Cash	80		120	
		1,950		1,690
Total assets		3,800		3,120
Equity and liabilities				
Equity				
Ordinary share capital	800		800	
Retained earnings	1,310		930	
		2,110		1,730
Non-current liabilities				
10% loan stock		800		600
Current liabilities				
Bank overdraft	110		80	
Trade payables	750		690	
Taxation	30		20	
		890		790
Total equity and liabilities		3,800		3,120

The following ratios are those calculated for DG, based on its published accounts for the previous year, and also the latest industry average ratios:

	DG 30 April 20X8	Industry average
ROCE (capital employed = equity and debentures)	16.30%	18.50%
Profit/sales	3.90%	4.73%
Asset turnover	4.19	3.91
Current ratio	2.14	1.90
Quick ratio	1.52	1.27
Gross profit margin	30.00%	35.23%
Accounts receivable collection period	40 days	52 days
Accounts payable payment period	37 days	49 days
Inventory turnover (times)	13.90	18.30
Gearing	26.75%	32.71%

Required

(a) Calculate comparable ratios (to two decimal places where appropriate) for DG for the year ended 30 April 20X9. All calculations must be clearly shown.

(b) Write a report to your board of directors analysing the performance of DG, comparing the results against the previous year and against the industry average.

Answer

(a)

	20X8	20X9	Industry average
ROCE	$\dfrac{320 + 60}{2{,}330} = 16.30\%$	$\dfrac{465 + 80}{2{,}910} = 18.72\%$	18.50%
Profit/sales	$\dfrac{320 + 60}{9{,}750} = 3.90\%$	$\dfrac{465 + 80}{11{,}200} = 4.87\%$	4.73%
Asset turnover	$\dfrac{9{,}750}{2{,}330} = 4.18\text{x}$	$\dfrac{11{,}200}{2{,}910} = 3.85\text{x}$	3.91x
Current ratio	$\dfrac{1{,}690}{790} = 2.10$	$\dfrac{1{,}950}{890} = 2.20$	1.90
Quick ratio	$\dfrac{1{,}080 + 120}{790} = 1.52$	$\dfrac{1{,}230 + 80}{890} = 1.47$	1.27
Gross profit margin	$\dfrac{9{,}750 - 6{,}825}{9{,}750} = 30.00\%$	$\dfrac{11{,}200 - 8{,}460}{11{,}200} = 24.46\%$	35.23%
Accounts receivable collection period	$\dfrac{1{,}080}{9{,}750} \times 365 = 40 \text{ days}$	$\dfrac{1{,}230}{11{,}200} \times 365 = 40 \text{ days}$	52 days
Accounts payable payment period	$\dfrac{690}{6{,}825} \times 365 = 37 \text{ days}$	$\dfrac{750}{8{,}460} \times 365 = 32 \text{ days}$	49 days
Inventory turnover (times)	$\dfrac{6{,}825}{490} = 13.9\text{x}$	$\dfrac{8{,}460}{640} = 13.2\text{x}$	18.30x
Gearing	$\dfrac{600}{2{,}330} = 25.75\%$	$\dfrac{800}{2{,}910} = 27.5\%$	32.71%

(b) (i) REPORT

To: Board of Directors
From: Accountant
Subject: Analysis of performance of DG

Date: XX/XX/XX

This report should be read in conjunction with the appendix attached which shows the relevant ratios (from part (a)).

Trading and profitability

Return on capital employed has improved considerably between 20X8 and 20X9 and is now higher than the industry average.

Net income as a proportion of sales has also improved noticeably between the years and is also now marginally ahead of the industry average. Gross margin, however, is considerably lower than in the previous year and is only some 70% of the industry average. This suggests either that there has been a change in the cost structure of DG or that there has been a change in the method of cost allocation between the periods. Either way, this is a marked change that requires investigation. The company may be in a period of transition as sales have increased by nearly 15% over the year and it would appear that new non-current assets have been purchased.

Asset turnover has declined between the periods although the 20X9 figure is in line with the industry average. This reduction might indicate that the efficiency with which assets are used has deteriorated or it might indicate that the assets acquired in 20X9 have not yet fully contributed to the business. A longer term trend would clarify the picture.

(ii) Liquidity and working capital management

The current ratio has improved slightly over the year and is marginally higher than the industry average. It is also in line with what is generally regarded as satisfactory (2:1).

The quick ratio has declined marginally but is still better than the industry average. This suggests that DG has no short term liquidity problems and should have no difficulty in paying its debts as they become due.

Receivables as a proportion of sales is unchanged from 20X8 and are considerably lower than the industry average. Consequently, there is probably little opportunity to reduce this further and there may be pressure in the future from customers to increase the period of credit given. The period of credit taken from suppliers has fallen from 37 days' purchases to 32 days' and is much lower than the industry average; thus, it may be possible to finance any additional receivables by negotiating better credit terms from suppliers.

Inventory turnover has fallen slightly and is much slower than the industry average and this may partly reflect stocking up ahead of a significant increase in sales. Alternatively, there is some danger that the inventory could contain certain obsolete items that may require writing off. The relative increase in the level of inventory has been financed by an increased overdraft which may reduce if the inventory levels can be brought down.

The high levels of inventory, overdraft and receivables compared to that of payables suggests a labour intensive company or one where considerable value is added to bought-in products.

(iii) Gearing

The level of gearing has increased only slightly over the year and is below the industry average. Since the return on capital employed is nearly twice the rate of interest on the loan stock, profitability is likely to be increased by a modest increase in the level of gearing.

Signed: Accountant

Exam focus point

Analysis questions require the exercise of a certain amount of critical judgement. Questions are often set in which the directors propose a course of action and the examiner reports that candidates often agree with the directors' proposals. In which case, why was the question set?

21: ACCOUNTING RATIOS

Chapter roundup

- You must be able to **appraise and communicate** the position and prospects of a business based on given and prepared statements and ratios.
- Return on capital employed (ROCE) may be used by shareholders or the Board to assess the performance of management.
- Banks and other lenders will be interested in a company's gearing level.
- Ratios such as EPS and dividend per share help equity shareholders and other investors to **assess the value and quality of an investment in the ordinary shares of a company**.
- However many ratios you can find to calculate, **numbers alone will not answer a question**. You **must** interpret all the information available to you and support your interpretation with ratio calculations.

Quick quiz

1 List the main categories of ratio.

2 ROCE is $\dfrac{\text{Profit before interest and tax}}{\text{Capital employed}} \times 100\%$

   A True
   B False

3 Company Q has a profit margin of 7%. Briefly comment on this.

4 The debt ratio is a company's long-term debt divided by its net assets.

   A True
   B False

5 The cash flow ratio is the ratio of:

   A Gross cash inflow to total debt
   B Gross cash inflow to net debt
   C Net cash inflow to total debt
   D Net cash inflow to net debt

6 List the formulae for:

   A Current ratio
   B Quick ratio
   C Accounts receivable collection period
   D Inventory turnover period

Answers to quick quiz

1. See Section 1.1.
2. A   True.
3. You should be careful here. You have very little information. This is a low margin but you need to know what industry the company operates in. 7% may be good for a major retailer.
4. B   False (see Section 3.2).
5. C   (See Section 3.6).
6. See Sections 3.9, 3.10 and 3.12.

Statements of cash flows

Topic list	Syllabus reference
1 IAS 7 *Statement of Cash Flows*	A4
2 Preparing a statement of cash flows	A4

Introduction

In the long run, a profit will result in an increase in the company's cash balance but, as Keynes observed, 'in the long run we are all dead'. In the short run, **the making of a profit will not necessarily result in an increased cash balance**. The observation leads us to two questions. The first relates to the importance of the distinction between cash and profit. The second is concerned with the usefulness of the information provided by the statement of financial position and statement of profit or loss and other comprehensive income in the problem of deciding whether the company has, or will be able to generate, sufficient cash to finance its operations.

The importance of the **distinction between cash and profit** and the scant attention paid to this by the statement of profit or loss and other comprehensive income has resulted in the development of the statement of cash flows.

This chapter adopts a systematic approach to the preparation of statements of cash flows in examinations; you should learn this method and you will then be equipped for any challenges in the exam itself.

PART D FINANCIAL REPORTING, ANALYSIS AND INTERPRETATION

Exam focus point

The examiners highlighted statements of cash flows as another area consistently answered badly in the exam. They also recommended practising full questions in this key area. It will not only help you through P1 but is an essential skill at the higher levels.

1 IAS 7 *Statement of Cash Flows*

FAST FORWARD

Statements of cash flows are a useful addition to the financial statements of a company because it is recognised that accounting profit is not the only indicator of a company's performance. Statements of cash flows concentrate on the sources and uses of cash and are a useful indicator of a company's liquidity and solvency.

It has been argued that 'profit' does not always give a useful or meaningful picture of a company's performance. Readers of a company's financial statements might even be **misled by a reported profit figure**.

(a) Shareholders might believe that if a company makes a profit after tax, of say, $100,000 then this is the amount which it could afford to **pay as a dividend**. Unless the company has **sufficient cash** available to stay in business and also to pay a dividend, the shareholders' expectations would be wrong.

(b) Employees might believe that if a company makes profits, it can afford to **pay higher wages** next year. This opinion may not be correct: the ability to pay wages depends on the **availability of cash**.

(c) Survival of a business entity depends not so much on profits as on its **ability to pay its debts when they fall due**. Such payments might include 'profit and loss' items such as material purchases, wages, interest and taxation etc, but also capital payments for new non-current assets and the repayment of loan capital when this falls due (for example, on the redemption of loan stock).

From these examples, it may be apparent that a company's performance and prospects depend not so much on the 'profits' earned in a period, but more realistically on liquidity or **cash flows**.

1.1 Funds flow and cash flow

Some countries, either currently or in the past, have required the disclosure of additional statements based on **funds flow** rather than cash flow. However, the definition of 'funds' can be very vague and such statements often simply require a rearrangement of figures already provided in the statement of financial position and statement of profit or loss and other comprehensive income. By contrast, a statement of cash flows is unambiguous and provides information which is additional to that provided in the rest of the accounts. It also lends itself to organisation by activity and not by statement of financial position classification.

Statements of cash flows are frequently given as an **additional statement**, supplementing the statement of financial position, statement of profit or loss and other comprehensive income and related notes. The group aspects of statements of cash flows (and certain complex matters) have been excluded as they are beyond the scope of your syllabus.

1.2 Objective of IAS 7

The aim of IAS 7 is to provide information to users of financial statements about an entity's **ability to generate cash and cash equivalents**, as well as indicating the cash needs of the entity. The statement of cash flows provides *historical* information about cash and cash equivalents, classifying cash flows between operating, investing and financing activities.

1.3 Scope

A statement of cash flows should be presented as an **integral part** of an entity's financial statements. All types of entity can provide useful information about cash flows as the need for cash is universal, whatever the nature of their revenue-producing activities. Therefore, **all entities are required by the standard to produce a statement of cash flows**.

1.4 Benefits of cash flow information

The use of statements of cash flows is very much **in conjunction** with the rest of the financial statements. Users can gain further appreciation of the change in net assets, of the entity's financial position (liquidity and solvency) and the entity's ability to adapt to changing circumstances by adjusting the amount and timing of cash flows. Statements of cash flows **enhance comparability** as they are not affected by differing accounting treatments used for the same type of transactions or events.

Cash flow information of a historical nature can be used as an indicator of the amount, timing and certainty of future cash flows. Past forecast cash flow information can be **checked for accuracy** as actual figures emerge. The relationship between profit and cash flows can be analysed as can changes in prices over time. All this information helps management to control costs by controlling cash flow.

1.5 Definitions

The standard gives the following definitions, the most important of which are **cash** and **cash equivalents**.

Key terms

- **Cash** comprises cash on hand and demand deposits.
- **Cash equivalents** are short-term, highly liquid investments that are readily convertible to known amounts of cash and which are subject to an insignificant risk of changes in value.
- **Cash flows** are inflows and outflows of cash and cash equivalents.
- **Operating activities** are the principal revenue-producing activities of the entity and other activities that are not investing or financing activities.
- **Investing activities** are the acquisition and disposal of long-term (non-current) assets and other investments not included in cash equivalents.
- **Financing activities** are activities that result in changes in the size and composition of the contributed equity (capital) and borrowings of the entity.

(IAS 7: para. 6)

1.6 Cash and cash equivalents

The standard expands on the definition of cash equivalents: they are not held for investment or other long-term purposes, but rather to meet short-term cash commitments. To fulfil the above definition, an investment's **maturity date should normally be three months from its acquisition date** and the conversion must be into a known amount of cash. It would usually be the case then that equity investments (ie shares in other companies) are **not** cash equivalents. An exception would be where redeemable preference shares were acquired with a very close redemption date.

Loans and other borrowings from banks are classified as financing activities. In some countries, however, **bank overdrafts** are repayable on demand and are treated as part of an enterprise's total cash management system. In these circumstances an overdrawn balance will be included in cash and cash equivalents. Such banking arrangements are characterised by a balance which fluctuates between overdrawn and credit.

Movements between different types of cash and cash equivalent are not included in cash flows. The investment of surplus cash in cash equivalents is part of cash management, not part of operating, investing or financing activities.

1.7 Presentation of a statement of cash flows

IAS 7 requires statements of cash flows to report cash flows during the period classified by **operating, investing and financing activities**.

The manner of presentation of cash flows from operating, investing and financing activities **depends on the nature of the enterprise**. By classifying cash flows between different activities in this way users can see the impact on cash and cash equivalents of each one, and their relationships with each other. We can look at each in more detail.

1.7.1 Operating activities

This is perhaps the key part of the statement of cash flows because it shows whether, and to what extent, companies can **generate cash from their operations**. It is these operating cash flows which must, in the end, pay for all cash outflows relating to other activities, ie paying loan interest, dividends and so on.

Most of the components of cash flows from operating activities will be those items which **determine the net profit or loss of the enterprise**, ie they relate to the main revenue-producing activities of the enterprise. The standard gives the following as examples of cash flows from operating activities.

(a) Cash receipts from the sale of goods and the rendering of services
(b) Cash receipts from royalties, fees, commissions and other revenue
(c) Cash payments to suppliers for goods and services
(d) Cash payments to and on behalf of employees

Certain items may be included in the net profit or loss for the period which do **not** relate to operational cash flows, for example the profit or loss on the sale of a piece of plant will be included in net profit or loss, but the related cash flows will be classed as **financing**.

1.7.2 Investing activities

The cash flows classified under this heading show the extent of new investment in **assets which will generate future profit and cash flows**. The standard gives the following examples of cash flows arising from investing activities.

(a) Cash payments to acquire property, plant and equipment, intangibles and other non-current assets, including those relating to capitalised development costs and self-constructed property, plant and equipment
(b) Cash receipts from sales of property, plant and equipment, intangibles and other non-current assets
(c) Cash payments to acquire equity (shares) or debt instruments of other entities
(d) Cash receipts from sales of equity (shares) or debt instruments of other entities
(e) Cash advances and loans made to other parties
(f) Cash receipts from the repayment of advances and loans made to other parties

1.7.3 Financing activities

This section of the statement of cash flows shows the share of cash which the enterprise's capital providers have claimed during the period. This is an indicator of **likely future interest and dividend payments**. The standard gives the following examples of cash flows which might arise under these headings.

(a) Cash proceeds from issuing shares
(b) Cash payments to owners to acquire or redeem the entity's shares
(c) Cash proceeds from issuing debentures, loans, notes, bonds, mortgages and other short-term or long-term borrowings
(d) Cash repayments of amounts borrowed

1.8 Reporting cash flows from operating activities

The standard offers a choice of method for this part of the statement of cash flows.

(a) **Direct method:** disclose major classes of gross cash receipts and gross cash payments
(b) **Indirect method**: net profit or loss is adjusted for the effects of transactions of a non-cash nature, any deferrals or accruals of past or future operating cash receipts or payments, and items of income or expense associated with investing or financing cash flows. (IAS 7: para. 18)

The **direct method** discloses information, not available elsewhere in the financial statements, which could be of use in estimating future cash flows. However, the **indirect method** is simpler, more widely used and more likely to be examined.

1.8.1 Using the direct method

There are different ways in which the **information about gross cash receipts and payments** can be obtained. The most obvious way is simply to extract the information from the accounting records. The pro-forma is shown below. This may be a laborious task, however, and the indirect method in Section 1.8.2 may be easier.

Formula to learn

	$
Cash receipts from customers	X
Cash paid to suppliers and employees	X
Cash generated from operations	X

1.8.2 Using the indirect method

This method is undoubtedly **easier** from the point of view of the preparer of the statement of cash flows. The net profit or loss for the period is adjusted for the following.

(a) Changes during the period in inventories, operating receivables and payables
(b) Non-cash items, eg depreciation, provisions, profits/losses on the sales of non-current assets
(c) Other items, the cash flows from which should be classified under investing or financing activities

A **proforma** of such a calculation is as follows and this method may be more common in the exam.

	$
Profit before interest and tax (SPLOCI)*	X
Add depreciation	X
Loss/(profit) on sale of non-current assets	X/(X)
(Increase)/decrease in inventories	(X)/X
(Increase)/decrease in receivables	(X)/X
Increase/(decrease) in payables	X/(X)
Cash generated from operations	X
Interest (paid)/received	(X)
Income taxes paid	(X)
Net cash flows from operating activities	X

* Take profit before tax and add back any interest expense

It is important to understand why **certain items are added and others subtracted**. Note the following points.

(a) Depreciation is not a cash expense, but is deducted in arriving at the profit figure in the statement of profit or loss and other comprehensive income. It makes sense, therefore, to eliminate it by adding it back.

(b) By the same logic, a loss on a disposal of a non-current asset (arising through underprovision of depreciation) needs to be added back and a profit deducted.

(c) An increase in inventories means less cash – you have spent cash on buying inventory.

(d) An increase in receivables means the company's receivables have not paid as much, and therefore there is less cash.

(e) If we pay off payables, causing the figure to decrease, again we have less cash.

1.8.3 Indirect versus direct

The direct method is encouraged where the necessary information is not too costly to obtain, but IAS 7 does not demand it. In practice, therefore, the direct method is rarely used. It could be argued that companies ought to monitor their cash flows carefully enough on an ongoing basis to be able to use the direct method at minimal extra cost.

1.8.4 Interest and dividends

Cash flows from interest and dividends received and paid should each be **disclosed separately**. Each should be classified in a consistent manner from period to period as either operating, investing or financing activities.

Dividends paid by the enterprise can be classified in **one of two ways**.

(a) As a **financing cash flow**, showing the cost of obtaining financial resources.

(b) As a component of **cash flows from operating activities** so that users can assess the enterprise's ability to pay dividends out of operating cash flows.

1.8.5 Taxes on income

Cash flows arising from taxes on income should be **separately disclosed** and should be classified as cash flows from operating activities **unless** they can be specifically identified with financing and investing activities.

Taxation cash flows are often **difficult to match** to the originating underlying transaction, so most of the time all tax cash flows are classified as arising from operating activities.

1.9 Components of cash and cash equivalents

The components of cash and cash equivalents should be disclosed and a **reconciliation** should be presented, showing the amounts in the statement of cash flows reconciled with the equivalent items reported in the statement of financial position.

It is also necessary to disclose the **accounting policy** used in deciding the items included in cash and cash equivalents, in accordance with IAS 1 *Presentation of Financial Statements*, but also because of the wide range of cash management practices worldwide.

1.10 Other disclosures

All enterprises should disclose, together with a **commentary by management**, any other information likely to be of importance, for example:

(a) Restrictions on the use of or access to any part of significant cash or cash equivalents;

(b) The amount of undrawn borrowing facilities which are available; and

(c) Cash flows which increased operating capacity compared to cash flows which merely maintained operating capacity.

1.11 Example of a statement of cash flows

In the next section we will look at the procedures for preparing a statement of cash flows. First, look at this **example**, adapted from the example accompanying the standard (which is based on a group and therefore beyond the scope of your syllabus).

1.11.1 Direct method

STATEMENT OF CASH FLOWS (DIRECT METHOD)
YEAR ENDED 20X7

	$m	$m
Cash flows from operating activities		
Cash receipts from customers	30,330	
Cash paid to suppliers and employees	(27,600)	
Cash generated from operations	2,730	
Interest paid	(270)	
Income taxes paid	(900)	
Net cash from operating activities		1,560
Cash flows from investing activities		
Purchase of property, plant and equipment	(900)	
Proceeds from sale of equipment	20	
Interest received	200	
Dividends received	200	
Net cash used in investing activities		(480)
Cash flows from financing activities		
Proceeds from issue of share capital	250	
Proceeds from long-term borrowings	250	
Dividends paid*	(1,290)	
Net cash used in financing activities		(790)
Net increase in cash and cash equivalents		290
Cash and cash equivalents at beginning of period (Note)		120
Cash and cash equivalents at end of period (Note)		410

* This could also be shown as an operating cash flow

PART D FINANCIAL REPORTING, ANALYSIS AND INTERPRETATION

1.11.2 Indirect method

STATEMENT OF CASH FLOWS (INDIRECT METHOD)
YEAR ENDED 20X7

	$m	$m
Cash flows from operating activities		
Net profit before taxation	3,570	
Adjustments for:		
Depreciation	450	
Investment income	(500)	
Interest expense	400	
Operating profit before working capital changes	3,920	
Increase in trade and other receivables	(500)	
Decrease in inventories	1,050	
Decrease in trade payables	(1,740)	
Cash generated from operations	2,730	
Interest paid	(270)	
Income taxes paid	(900)	
Net cash from operating activities		1,560
Cash flows from investing activities		
Purchase of property, plant and equipment	(900)	
Proceeds from sale of equipment	20	
Interest received	200	
Dividends received	200	
Net cash used in investing activities		(480)
Cash flows from financing activities		
Proceeds from issue of share capital	250	
Proceeds from long-term borrowings	250	
Dividends paid*	(1,290)	
Net cash used in financing activities		(790)
Net increase in cash and cash equivalents		290
Cash and cash equivalents at beginning of period (Note)		120
Cash and cash equivalents at end of period (Note)		410

* This could also be shown as an operating cash flow

The following note is required to both versions of the statement.

Note. Cash and cash equivalents

Cash and cash equivalents consist of cash on hand and balances with banks, and investments in money market instruments. Cash and cash equivalents included in the statement of cash flows comprise the following statement of financial position amounts.

	20X7 $m	20X6 $m
Cash on hand and balances with banks	40	25
Short-term investments	370	95
Cash and cash equivalents	410	120

The company has undrawn borrowing facilities of $2,000 of which $700 may be used only for future expansion.

2 Preparing a statement of cash flows

FAST FORWARD

You need to be aware of the **format** of the statement as laid out in IAS 7. Setting out the format is the first step. Then follow the **step-by-step preparation procedure**.

Exam focus point

In essence, preparing a statement of cash flows is very straightforward. You should therefore simply learn the format and apply the steps noted in the example below.

Note that the following items are treated in a way that might seem confusing, but the treatment is logical if you **think in terms of cash**.

(a) **Increase in inventory** is treated as **negative** (in brackets). This is because it represents a cash **outflow**; cash is being spent on inventory.

(b) An **increase in receivables** would be treated as **negative** for the same reasons; more receivables means less cash.

(c) By contrast an **increase in payables is positive** because cash is being retained and not used to settle accounts payable. There is therefore more of it.

2.1 Example: Preparation of a statement of cash flows

Colby Co's statement of profit or loss and other comprehensive income for the year ended 31 December 20X2 and statements of financial position at 31 December 20X1 and 31 December 20X2 were as follows.

COLBY CO
STATEMENT OF PROFIT OR LOSS AND OTHER COMPREHENSIVE INCOME
FOR THE YEAR ENDED 31 DECEMBER 20X2

	$'000	$'000
Revenue		720
Raw materials consumed	70	
Staff costs	94	
Depreciation	118	
Loss on disposal of non-current asset	18	
		(300)
		420
Interest payable		(28)
Profit before tax		392
Taxation		(124)
Profit for the period		268

PART D FINANCIAL REPORTING, ANALYSIS AND INTERPRETATION

COLBY CO
STATEMENT OF FINANCIAL POSITION AS AT 31 DECEMBER

	20X2		20X1	
	$'000	$'000	$'000	$'000
Assets				
Property, plant and equipment				
Cost	1,596		1,560	
Depreciation	318		224	
		1,278		1,336
Current assets				
Inventory	24		20	
Trade receivables	76		58	
Bank	48		56	
		148		134
Total assets		1,426		1,470
Equity and liabilities				
Capital and reserves				
Share capital	360		340	
Share premium	36		24	
Retained earnings	716		514	
		1,112		878
Non-current liabilities				
Non-current loans		200		500
Current liabilities				
Trade payables	12		6	
Taxation	102		86	
		114		92
		1,426		1,470

During the year, the company paid $90,000 for a new piece of machinery.

Dividends paid during 20X2 totalled $66,000.

Required

Prepare a statement of cash flows for Colby Co for the year ended 31 December 20X2 in accordance with the requirements of IAS 7, using the indirect method.

Solution

Step 1 **Set out the proforma statement of cash flows** with the headings required by IAS 7. You should leave plenty of space. Ideally, use three or more sheets of paper, one for the main statement, one for the notes and one for your workings. It is obviously essential to know the formats very well.

Step 2 Begin with the **reconciliation of profit before tax to net cash from operating activities** as far as possible. When preparing the statement from statements of financial position, you will usually have to calculate such items as depreciation, loss on sale of non-current assets, profit for the year and tax paid (see Step 4). Note that you may not be given the tax charge in the statement of profit or loss and other comprehensive income. You will then have to assume that the tax paid in the year is last year's year end provision and calculate the charge as the balancing figure.

Step 3 Calculate the cash flow figures for **dividends paid, purchase or sale of non-current assets, issue of shares and repayment of loans** if these are not already given to you (as they may be).

Step 4 If you are not given the profit figure, open up a **working for the profit or loss account**. Using the opening and closing balances, the taxation charge and dividends paid and proposed, you will be able to calculate profit for the year as the balancing figure to put in the net profit into the net cash flow from operating activities section.

Step 5 You will now be able to **complete the statement** by slotting in the figures given or calculated.

COLBY CO

STATEMENT OF CASH FLOWS FOR THE YEAR ENDED 31 DECEMBER 20X2

	$'000	$'000
Net cash flow from operating activities		
Profit before tax	392	
Depreciation charges	118	
Loss on sale of property, plant and equipment	18	
Interest expense	28	
Increase in inventory	(4)	
Increase in receivables	(18)	
Increase in payables	6	
Cash generated from operations	540	
Interest paid	(28)	
Dividends paid	(66)	
Tax paid (86 + 124 – 102)	(108)	
Net cash flow from operating activities		338
Cash flows from investing activities		
Payments to acquire property, plant and equipment	(90)	
Receipts from sales of property, plant and equipment	12	
Net cash outflow from investing activities		(78)
Cash flows from financing activities		
Issue of share capital (360 + 36 – 340 – 24)	32	
Long-term loans repaid (500 – 200)	(300)	
Net cash flows from financing		(268)
Decrease in cash and cash equivalents		(8)
Cash and cash equivalents at 1.1.X2		56
Cash and cash equivalents at 31.12.X2		48

Working: property, plant and equipment

COST

	$'000		$'000
At 1.1.X2	1,560	At 31.12.X2	1,596
Purchases	90	Disposals (balance)	54
	1,650		1,650

ACCUMULATED DEPRECIATION

	$'000		$'000
At 31.1.X2	318	At 1.1.X2	224
Depreciation on disposals (balance)	24	Charge for year	118
	342		342

Carrying amount of disposals	30
Net loss reported in SPLOCI	(18)
Proceeds from disposals	12

PART D FINANCIAL REPORTING, ANALYSIS AND INTERPRETATION

Question — Statement of cash flows

Set out below are the financial statements of Shabnum Co. You are the financial controller, faced with the task of implementing IAS 7 *Statement of Cash Flows*.

SHABNUM CO
STATEMENT OF PROFIT OR LOSS AND OTHER COMPREHENSIVE INCOME
FOR THE YEAR ENDED 31 DECEMBER 20X2

	$'000
Revenue	2,553
Cost of sales	(1,814)
Gross profit	739
Distribution costs	(125)
Administrative expenses	(264)
	350
Interest received	25
Interest paid	(75)
Profit before taxation	300
Taxation	(140)
Profit for the period	160

SHABNUM CO
STATEMENTS OF FINANCIAL POSITION AS AT 31 DECEMBER

	20X2 $'000	20X1 $'000
Assets		
Non-current assets		
Property, plant and equipment	380	305
Intangible assets	250	200
Investments	–	25
Current assets		
Inventory	150	102
Trade receivables	390	315
Short-term investments	50	–
Cash in hand	2	1
Total assets	1,222	948
Equity and liabilities		
Equity		
Share capital ($1 ordinary shares)	200	150
Share premium account	160	150
Revaluation surplus	100	91
Retained earnings	260	180
Non-current liabilities		
Loan	170	50
Current liabilities		
Trade payables	127	119
Bank overdraft	85	98
Taxation	120	110
Total equity and liabilities	1,222	948

The following information is available.

(a) The proceeds of the sale of non-current asset investments amounted to $30,000.

(b) Fixtures and fittings, with an original cost of $85,000 and a carrying amount of $45,000, were sold for $32,000 during the year.

(c) The following information relates to property, plant and equipment

	31.12.20X2	31.12.20X1
	$'000	$'000
Cost	720	595
Accumulated depreciation	340	290
Carrying amount	380	305

(d) 50,000 $1 ordinary shares were issued during the year at a premium of 20 cents per share.

(e) Dividends totalling $80,000 were paid during the year.

Required

Prepare a statement of cash flows for the year to 31 December 20X2 using the format laid out in IAS 7.

Answer

SHABNUM CO
STATEMENT OF CASH FLOWS FOR THE YEAR ENDED 31 DECEMBER 20X2

	$'000	$'000
Net cash flows from operating activities		
Profit before tax	300	
Depreciation charge (W1)	90	
Interest expense	50	
Loss on sale of property, plant and equipment (45 – 32)	13	
Profit on sale of non-current asset investments	(5)	
(Increase)/decrease in inventory	(48)	
(Increase)/decrease in receivables	(75)	
Increase/(decrease) in payables	8	
Cash generated from operating activities	333	
Interest received	25	
Interest paid	(75)	
Dividends paid	(80)	
Tax paid (110 + 140 – 120)	(130)	
Net cash flow from operating activities		73
Cash flows from investing activities		
Payments to acquire property, plant and equipment (W2)	(201)	
Payments to acquire intangible non-current assets	(50)	
Receipts from sales of property, plant and equipment	32	
Receipts from sale of non-current asset investments	30	
Net cash flows from investing activities		(189)
Cash flows from financing activities		
Issue of share capital	60	
Long-term loan	120	
Net cash flows from financing		180
Increase in cash and cash equivalents (Note)		64
Cash and cash equivalents at 1.1 X2 (Note)		(97)
Cash and cash equivalents at 31.12.X2 (Note)		(33)

PART D FINANCIAL REPORTING, ANALYSIS AND INTERPRETATION

NOTES TO THE STATEMENT OF CASH FLOWS

Note. Analysis of the balances of cash and cash equivalents as shown in the statement of financial position.

	20X2 $'000	20X1 $'000	Change in year $'000
Cash in hand	2	1	1
Short-term investments	50		50
Bank overdraft	(85)	(98)	13
	(33)	(97)	64

Workings

1 Depreciation charge

	$'000	$'000
Depreciation at 31 December 20X2		340
Depreciation 31 December 20X1	290	
Depreciation on assets sold (85 – 45)	40	
		250
Charge for the year		90

2 Purchase of property, plant and equipment

PROPERTY, PLANT AND EQUIPMENT

	$'000		$'000
1.1.X2 Balance b/d	595	Disposals	85
Revaluation (100 – 91)	9		
Purchases (bal fig)	201	31.12.X2 Balance c/d	720
	805		805

Exam focus point

> There may be a question requiring the calculation of the purchase of property, plant and equipment for the statement of cash flows. Make sure you use a working to calculate the figure as shown above.

2.2 The advantages of cash flow accounting

The advantages of cash flow accounting are as follows.

(a) Survival in business depends on the **ability to generate** cash. Cash flow accounting directs attention towards this critical issue.

(b) Cash flow is **more comprehensive** than 'profit' which is dependent on accounting conventions and concepts.

(c) **Creditors** (long and short-term) are more interested in an entity's ability to repay them than in its profitability. Whereas 'profits' might indicate that cash is likely to be available, cash flow accounting is more direct with its message.

(d) Cash flow reporting provides a better means of **comparing the results** of different companies than traditional profit reporting.

(e) Cash flow reporting **satisfies the needs of all users** better.

  (i) For **management**, it provides the sort of information on which decisions should be taken: (in management accounting, 'relevant costs' to a decision are future cash flows); traditional profit accounting does not help with decision-making.

(ii) For **shareholders and auditors**, cash flow accounting can provide a satisfactory basis for stewardship accounting.

(iii) The information needs of **creditors and employees** will be better served by cash flow accounting.

(f) Cash flow forecasts are **easier to prepare**, as well as more useful, than profit forecasts.

(g) They can in some respects be **audited more easily** than accounts based on accrual accounting.

(h) Accrual accounting is confusing, and cash flows are **more easily understood**.

(i) Cash flow accounting should be both retrospective, and also include a forecast for the future. This is of **great information value** to all users of accounting information.

(j) **Forecasts** can subsequently be **monitored** by the publication of variance statements which compare actual cash flows against the forecast.

Question — Cash flow accounting

Can you think of some possible disadvantages of cash flow accounting?

Answer

The main disadvantages of cash flow accounting are essentially the advantages of accrual accounting (proper matching of related items). There is also the practical problem that few businesses keep historical cash flow information in the form needed to prepare a historical statement of cash flows and so extra record keeping is likely to be necessary.

2.3 Criticisms of IAS 7

The inclusion of **cash equivalents** has been criticised because it does not reflect the way in which businesses are managed: in particular, the requirement that to be a cash equivalent an investment has to be within three months of maturity is considered **unrealistic**.

The management of assets similar to cash (ie 'cash equivalents') is not distinguished from other investment decisions.

Exam focus point

You could be asked to consider the usefulness of a statement of cash flows as well as having to prepare one.

Chapter roundup

- **Statements of cash flows** are a useful addition to the financial statements of companies because it is recognised that accounting profit is not the only indicator of a company's performance. Statements of cash flows concentrate on the sources and uses of cash and are a useful indicator of a company's liquidity and solvency.

- You need to be aware of the **format** of the statement as laid out in IAS 7. Setting out the format is the first step. Then follow the **step-by-step preparation procedure**.

Quick quiz

1. What is the objective of IAS 7?
   - A To provide additional information about profit and losses
   - B To provide additional information about generation of cash

2. What are the benefits of cash flow information according to IAS 7?

3. Define cash and cash equivalents according to IAS 7.

4. Which of the following headings is not a classification of cash flows in IAS 7?
   - A Operating
   - B Investing
   - C Administration
   - D Financing

5. A company has the following information about property, plant and equipment.

	20X7 $'000	20X6 $'000
Cost	750	600
Accumulated depreciation	250	150
Carrying amount	500	450

   Plant with a carrying amount of $75,000 (original cost $90,000) was sold for $30,000 during the year.
   What is the net cash flow from investing activities for the year?
   - A $95,000 inflow
   - B $210,000 inflow
   - C $210,000 outflow
   - D $95,000 outflow

6. A company has the following extract from a statement of financial position.

	20X7 $'000	20X6 $'000
Share capital	2,000	1,000
Share premium	500	–
Loan stock	750	1,000

   What is the cash flow from financing activities for the year?
   - A $1,250 inflow
   - B $1,750 inflow
   - C $1,750 outflow
   - D $1,250 outflow

7. When adjusting profit before tax to arrive at cash generated from operations, a decrease in receivables is added to profit before tax.

   Is this statement:
   - A True
   - B False

Answers to quick quiz

1. **B** To provide information to users about the company's ability to generate cash and cash equivalents.

2. Further information is available about liquidation and solvency, on the change in net assets, the ability to adapt to changing circumstances and comparability between entities.

3. See Section 1.5, Key Terms.

4. **C** Administration costs are a classification used in the statement of profit or loss and other comprehensive income, not the statement of cash flows.

5. **C** PROPERTY, PLANT AND EQUIPMENT

	$'000		$'000
Opening balance	600	Disposals	90
Purchases (balancing figure)	240	Closing balance	750
	840		840

Purchase of property, plant and equipment	240,000
Proceeds of sale of property, plant and equipment	(30,000)
Net cash outflow	210,000

6. **A**

	$'000
Issue of share capital (2,000 + 500 – 1,000)	1,500
Repayment of loan stock (1,000 – 750)	(250)
Net cash inflow	1,250

7. **A** True

Practice question bank

FOUNDATION LEVEL

FOUNDATION UNIT

FINANCIAL ACCOUNTING

Practice Question Bank

There is ONE correct answer per question

PRACTICE QUESTION BANK

> Foundation Component subjects cover the following Learning Outcomes (LO's);
> Financial Accounting - LO's A1, A2, A3, A4 & A5

Chapter 1 Introduction to Accounting

1 Which of the following statements about financial accounts is correct?

   A   Financial accounts will always provide a good source of data for future costs
   B   Financial accounts provide historic information about the performance of a business
   C   Financial accounts are designed to meet the requirements of people inside the business
   D   It is not a legal requirement to produce financial accounts

2 Which of the following statements is correct?

   A   Forecasts will always provide a good source of data for historic performance
   B   Financial accounts provide the best source of data for future performance
   C   A good source of data for historic performance are the financial accounting records and financial accounts
   D   It is a legal requirement to produce management accounts

3 Which of the following lists of accounts contains only items that are liabilities?

   A   Cash, accounts payable, buildings.
   B   Accounts payable, bank loans, tax payable.
   C   Accounts receivable, land, wages payable.
   D   Tax payable, accounts receivable, inventory.

4 Management accounting differs from financial accounting in that:

   A   Management accounts are intended for internal users, while financial accounts are primarily for external users
   B   Management accounting tends to be more regulated than financial accounting
   C   Financial accounts are usually prepared on a monthly basis, while management accounts are usually prepared annually
   D   Financial accounting tends to focus on the future, whereas management accounting looks at the past

5 In the list below, who is not an external stakeholder?

   A   Customers
   B   Suppliers
   C   Employees
   D   Bank

6 Which of the following types of business entity benefits from limited liability?

   A   A partnership
   B   A company
   C   A director
   D   A sole trader

7 Which of these financial statements shows the total assets, liabilities and capital?

   A   The statement of profit or loss
   B   The trial balance
   C   The statement of financial position
   D   The statement of cash flows

Chapter 2 The Regulatory Framework

1. Which of the following statements about the regulatory system of financial accounting is incorrect?

    A   Many figures in the financial statements require an accountant to use their judgement, so different conclusions might be reached.

    B   Accounting regulation consists of a mixture of legislation and accounting standards.

    C   The use of IFRS Accounting Standards ensures all figures in the financial statements are calculated in exactly the same way.

    D   Limited companies are required to prepare and publish financial statements each year in most countries.

2. Which of the following is not one of the stages of the IASB standard-setting process?

    A   Initial interpretation
    B   IFRS Accounting Standard issued
    C   Exposure draft
    D   Discussion paper

3. Which of the following statements about the IASB is correct?

    A   The IASB is funded by the governments of the countries who use IFRS Accounting Standards

    B   Prior to 2003, the IASB issues International Standards of Accounting (ISA)

    C   The IASB operates under the oversight of the IFRS Advisory Council

    D   The members of the IASB come from several different countries and have a variety of backgrounds

4. Which of the following are not ways that IFRS Accounting Standards have been used in various ways to improve and harmonise financial reporting around the world?

    A   As an international benchmark for countries developing their own standards
    B   As a basis for some national requirements
    C   To replace national financial reporting standards
    D   To replace national legal requirements

5. Which of the following statements about the ISSB is correct?

    A   The ISSB was formed by the IFRS Foundation in 2021
    B   The ISSB issues IFRS Sustainable Development Standards
    C   One of the objectives of the ISSB is to replace all other sustainability standard setters.
    D   The ISSB is governed by the International Accounting Standards Board

Chapter 3 Accounting Conventions

1. Which accountancy body created the *Conceptual Framework for Financial Reporting*?

    A   GAAP
    B   AIA
    C   IASB
    D   IFRS

2. Which of the following statements about materiality is correct?

    A   Materiality is one of the fundamental qualitative characteristics in the conceptual framework
    B   Materiality is the relative financial value of a figure in the financial statements
    C   Immaterial items can be omitted from the nominal ledger
    D   Some financial balances can be small in financial value but their nature still makes them material

3. Which of the following is not covered in the *Conceptual Framework*?

    A   The objective of general-purpose financial reporting
    B   The qualitative characteristics of useful financial information
    C   Concepts relating to capital and capital maintenance
    D   Political influence

4. The *Conceptual Framework* makes it clear that financial statements should be produced on which basis?

    A   Cash basis
    B   Accruals basis
    C   Financial basis
    D   Materiality basis

5. Financial statements are normally prepared under what important assumption?

    A   The assumption that investment is ongoing
    B   The assumption of prudence
    C   The going concern assumption
    D   The assumption of limited liability

6. The relevance of information is affected by its:

    A   Nature & materiality
    B   Accuracy & nature
    C   Materiality & faithful representation
    D   Nature & comparability

7. Which one of the following is not an enhancing qualitative characteristic of financial information:

    A   Comparability
    B   Verifiability
    C   Understandability
    D   Accuracy

8   Which of the following explanations is the best definition of the business entity concept?

   A   The business entity must be fairly presented
   B   The business is a separate entity from its owners
   C   The transactions of a business entity must be presented in a neutral manner
   D   All transactions between the business entity and shareholders must be reported

9   Which of the following is not a measurement base used in financial statements described in the *Conceptual Framework*?

   A   Fair value
   B   Historical cost
   C   Forecast cost
   D   Current cost

Chapter 4 Sources, Records and Books of Prime Entry

1. Which of the following is not a book of prime entry?

   A Cash book
   B Journal
   C Receivables ledger
   D Purchase day book

2. What is recorded in the sales returns day book?

   A Goods purchased from suppliers
   B Goods sold to customers
   C Details of goods returned by customers
   D Details of goods returned to suppliers

3. Which of the following is not a source document for the cash book?

   A Sales invoice to credit customer
   B Remittance advice from a customer
   C Cheque book
   D Receipt for payment of rent

4. Which of the following would not normally appear on a sales invoice?

   A Delivery date
   B Details of goods or services supplied
   C Details of any discount given
   D Details of sales representative

5. Which of the following is not a source document?

   A Invoice from a supplier
   B Journal
   C Credit note to a customer
   D Paying in slip

6. Which book of prime entry records small cash transactions?

   A Cash book
   B Journal
   C Petty cash book
   D Sales adjustment book

7. A business operates a petty cash imprest system with a float of $200. During the month of December, it spent $150. How much is required to restore it to the imprest level?

   A $50
   B $150
   C $200
   D $350

Chapter 5 Ledger Accounts and Double Entry

1   The books of prime entry are recorded in which ledger?

    A   Payables ledger
    B   General ledger
    C   Receivables ledger
    D   Journal ledger

2   Which of the following is the accounting equation?

    A   Assets = Capital + Liabilities
    B   Assets + Liabilities = Capital
    C   Capital – Liabilities = Assets
    D   Assets + Capital = Liabilities

3   Money taken out of the business by the owner of a sole-trader business is known as:

    A   Wages
    B   Drawings
    C   Dividends
    D   Salary

4   The matching convention requires that revenue earned is matched with the expenses incurred with earning it. What is this also known as?

    A   Relevance
    B   Materiality
    C   Accruals
    D   Prudence

5   Which of the following statements is false?

    A   A debit to an asset account will increase its value
    B   A credit to an expense account will increase its value
    C   A credit to an income account will increase its value
    D   A debit to a liability account will reduce its value

6   Which book of prime entry keeps a record of unusual movements between accounts?

    A   Petty cash book
    B   Sales returns day book
    C   Journal
    D   Cash book

7   What would the double entry be for a cash sale of $1,000?

A	Debit Sales $1,000	Credit Cash $1,000
B	Debit Cash at bank $1,000	Credit Sales $1,000
C	Debit Trade Receivables $1000	Credit Sales $1,000
D	Debit Sales $1,000	Credit Trade Receivables $1,000

8   What would the double entry be for the receipt of cash from a credit customer of $500?

A	Debit Trade receivables $500	Credit Cash at bank $500
B	Debit Cash at bank $500	Credit Revenue $500
C	Debit Cash at bank $500	Credit Trade receivables $500
D	Debit Revenue $500	Credit Trade receivables $500

9   What would the double entry be in the general ledger, for the purchase of office furniture on credit from ABC Ltd for $2,000?

   A   Debit Office furniture $2,000   Credit Cash at bank $2,000
   B   Debit Office furniture $2,000   Credit ABC Ltd $2,000
   C   Debit Office furniture $2,000   Credit Trade payables $2,000
   D   Debit Trade payables $2,000   Credit Office furniture $2,000

10 What would the double entry be in the general ledger, for the sale on credit to XYZ Ltd for $1,500?

   A   Debit Sales $1,500   Credit XYZ Ltd $1,500
   B   Debit XYZ Ltd $1,500   Credit Sales $1,500
   C   Debit Sales $1,500   Credit Trade receivables $1,500
   D   Debit Trade receivables $1,500   Credit Sales $1,500

PRACTICE QUESTION BANK

Chapter 6 From Trial Balance to Financial Statements

1   Beta has the following opening balances on its nominal ledger:

	$
Office Equipment	10,000
Trade Receivables	5,000
Cash at bank	2,500
Loan	5,000

What is the total assets figure?

A $15,000
B $17,500
C $12,500
D $20,000

2   Using the same information, what is the opening figure for capital?

A $5,000
B $17,500
C $12,500
D $10,000

3   In a period, sales are $200,000, purchases are $115,000 and other expenses are $27,500.

What is the figure for net profit to be transferred to the capital account?

A $85,000
B $172,500
C $125,000
D $57,500

4   If the balance carried down on the cash at bank account is a credit of $1,000 is the account:

A   Overdrawn by $1,000
B   Has $1,000 in the account
C   Neither
D   The balance is not correct

5   Which of the following is an error which will cause the trial balance not to balance?

A   An invoice is omitted from the travel expenses account

B   A sales invoice for $2,000 was posted into the relevant accounts as $200

C   A cheque for $500 was banked and posted in the cash at bank account as $5,000 but the entry to trade receivables was recorded correctly

D   A purchase invoice for a computer costing $750 was posted to computer maintenance account

6   Which of the following is not an account that appears on the statement of financial position?

A   Cash at bank
B   Inventory
C   Office Equipment
D   Computer maintenance

7   Which of the following is not an account that appears on the statement of profit or loss?

A   Rent received
B   Carriage inwards
C   Drawings
D   Bank interest

PRACTICE QUESTION BANK

Chapter 7 VAT

1   If input tax exceeds output tax, the tax authorities will:

    A   Look to the business to pay the difference
    B   Do nothing
    C   Refund the difference to the business
    D   Wait for the business to improve their outputs

2   A business has a balance on the trade receivables account of $240,000 (including VAT at 20%). How would this be shown on the statement of financial position?

    A   Current asset of $200,000 and $40,000 (DR) in the VAT payable account
    B   Current liability of $200,000 and $40,000 (CR) in the VAT payable account
    C   Current liability of $240,000
    D   Current asset of $240,000

3   What would the double entry be for the cash purchase of $1,200, including VAT at 20%?

    A   Debit Purchases $1,000   Credit Cash at bank $1,200
          Debit VAT payable $200

    B   Debit Cash at bank $1,200   Credit Purchases $1,000
                                        Credit VAT payable $200

    C   Debit Purchases $1,200   Credit Cash at bank $1,200

    D   Debit Cash at bank $1,200   Credit Purchases $1,200

4   What would the double entry be for the purchase of a car for $24,000 by cheque, including VAT at 20%? VAT on motor vehicles is not recoverable.

    A   Debit Motor vehicle $20,000   Credit Cash at bank $24,000
          Debit VAT payable $4,000

    B   Debit Cash at bank $24,000   Credit Motor vehicle $20,000
                                           Credit VAT payable $4,000

    C   Debit Motor vehicle $24,000   Credit Cash at bank $24,000

    D   Debit Cash at bank $24,000   Credit Motor vehicle $24,000

5   A business in its first period of trading charges $9,000 of VAT on sales and suffers $11,500 of VAT on purchases which include $250 of irrecoverable VAT. What would the closing balance of the VAT payable account show?

    A   A debit balance of $2,250
    B   A credit balance of $2,250
    C   A debit balance of $2,750
    D   A credit balance of $2,750

PRACTICE QUESTION BANK

Chapter 8 Accruals & Prepayments

1. Telephone paid during the year is $34,000. There was an opening accrual of $3,500. A bill for the quarter ended 31 January 20X7 for $3,000 was received in January 20X7. What is the telephone charge in the statement of profit or loss for the year ended 31 December 20X6?

    A $39,500
    B $32,500
    C $35,500
    D $34,000

2. If a business has paid rent of $10,000 for the year to 31 March 20X9, what is the prepayment in the accounts for the year to 31 December 20X8?

    A $2,500
    B $7,500
    C $3,000
    D $7,000

3. What is the correct journal for an electricity prepayment of $2,000?

    A   Debit Electricity $2,000   Credit Prepayments $2,000
    B   Debit Accruals $2,000   Credit Electricity $2,000
    C   Debit Electricity $2,000   Credit Accruals $2,000
    D   Debit Prepayments $2,000   Credit Electricity $2,000

4. What is the correct journal for an electricity accrual of $2,000?

    A   Debit Electricity $2,000   Credit Prepayments $2,000
    B   Debit Accruals $2,000   Credit Electricity $2,000
    C   Debit Electricity $2,000   Credit Accruals $2,000
    D   Debit Prepayments $2,000   Credit Electricity $2,000

5. A company had an opening prepayment for water charges of $4,000 at 1 July 20X5. On 1 September 20X5, the company paid annual water charges of $18,000. What is the expense for water charges in the statement of profit or loss for the year to 30 June 20X6?

    A $17,500
    B $18,500
    C $19,000
    D $17,000

6. Where would a prepayment of rental income be shown on the statement of financial position?

    A   Current Asset – Prepayment of income
    B   Current Liability – Accrual of income
    C   Current Asset – Accrual of income
    D   Current Liability – Prepayment of income

Chapter 9 Bank Reconciliations

1. A bank statement shows a balance of $20,000 in credit. An examination of the statement shows a $500 cheque paid in per the cash book but not yet on the bank statement and a $1,250 cheque paid out but not yet on the statement. In addition, the cash book shows deposit interest received of $500 but this is not yet on the statement. What is the balance per the cash book?

   A $19,750
   B $18,750
   C $19,250
   D $21,250

2. A bank statement shows a balance of $2,000 debit. An examination of the statement shows bank charges of $100 on the statement but not yet in the cash book. In addition, the cash book shows deposit interest received of $500 and a $500 cheque paid in per the cash book that are not yet on the statement. What is the balance per the cash book, prior to correcting for the bank charges?

   A $900 in credit
   B $1,100 in credit
   C $1,100 overdrawn
   D $1,400 overdrawn

3. Which of the following items is not required to go on the bank reconciliation?

   A   A cheque paid to a supplier that has not yet cleared through the bank
   B   Bank charges on the bank statement not yet in cash book
   C   A customer receipt that has been written in cash book but not yet taken to the bank
   D   Rent received written in cash book but has not yet appeared on bank statement

4. Which of the following items is required to go on the bank reconciliation?

   A   A direct debit for the telephone account which is not yet in the cash book
   B   A BACS receipt from a customer not yet in cash book
   C   A standing order payment for rent which has not yet been entered in cash book
   D   Rent received written in cash book but has not cleared through the bank yet

5. Which of the following is not a reason for differences between the cash book and the bank statements?

   A   Timing difference
   B   Error
   C   Contra entry
   D   Omission

Chapter 10 Control Accounts

1 What type of account is a control account?

    A   Impersonal
    B   Personal
    C   Customer
    D   Supplier

2 Which ledger are control accounts found in?

    A   Accounts Receivable Ledger
    B   Nominal Ledger
    C   Accounts Payable Ledger
    D   Purchase Ledger

3 Which of the following accounts is a common control account?

    A   Accounts receivable control account
    B   Purchase control account
    C   Sales control account
    D   ABC Ltd control account

4 Which discount is given to customers who pay early?

    A   Trade discount
    B   Discount received
    C   Discount allowed
    D   Personal discount

5 Which discount is given to a business which makes an early payment?

    A   Trade discount
    B   Discount received
    C   Discount allowed
    D   Personal discount

6 ABC has a trade payables control account balance of $18,500 at the end of the period. However, the extract of balances from the trade payables ledger totals $22,800. Investigation finds the following errors:

- purchases of $5,200 had been omitted from the control account;
- a supplier account of $900 had been omitted from the list of balances.

What is the correct trade payables balance at the period end?

    A $23,700 DR
    B $17,600 DR
    C $22,800 CR
    D $23,700 CR

7 ABC has a trade receivables control account balance of $38,500 at the end of the period. However, the extract of balances from the trade receivables ledger totals $46,650. Investigation finds the following errors:

- sales of $9,900 had been omitted from the control account;
- a customer account of $1,750 had been omitted from the list of balances.

What is the correct trade receivables balance at the period end?

    A $36,750 DR
    B $48,400 DR
    C $40,250 CR
    D $48,400 CR

8 Which of the following items would not be posted to the trade payables control account?

A Credit purchases
B Discount received
C Contra entries
D Discount allowed

Chapter 11 Errors

1. Which book of prime entry records the corrections of errors?

    A   Cash book
    B   Purchase day book
    C   Journal
    D   Sales day book

2. A business paid for a service on the delivery van and this was coded to the motor vehicle cost account rather than the motor repairs expense account.

    What type of error is this?

    A   Principle
    B   Commission
    C   Transposition
    D   Omission

3. A business paid $405 for a service on the delivery van and this was posted as an expense of $405 to the motor repairs account.

    What type of error is this?

    A   Principle
    B   Commission
    C   Transposition
    D   Omission

4. A trial balance has been drafted and the debit column has a total of $125,200 and the credit column has a total of $135,200.

    Which if the following would be appropriate?

    A   Create a suspense account with a debit of $5,000
    B   Create a suspense account with a credit of $10,000
    C   Do nothing
    D   Create a suspense account with a debit of $10,000

5. Purchase returns of $960 have inadvertently been posted to the sales returns, although the correct entry has been made to the accounts payable control. A suspense account needs to be set up for how much?

    A $960 credit
    B $1,920 credit
    C $960 debit
    D $1,920 debit

6. VAT on the sales day book of $520 has inadvertently been posted as the VAT from the purchase day book in the VAT payable account. A suspense account needs to be set up for how much?

    A $1,040 credit
    B $520 credit
    C $520 debit
    D $1,040 debit

PRACTICE QUESTION BANK

Chapter 12 Incomplete Records

1. A business has opening trade payables of $55,000 and closing trade payables of $47,000. Cash paid to suppliers was $52,000 and discounts received $1,000. What is the figure for purchases?

    A $45,000
    B $50,000
    C $47,000
    D $46,000

2. A business usually has a mark-up of 25% on cost of sales. During a year, its revenue was $190,000. What was cost of sales?

    A $47,500
    B $142,500
    C $152,000
    D $150,000

3. A business has opening trade receivables of $105,000 and closing trade receivables of $109,500. Cash received from customers was $99,750 and discounts allowed $2,250. What is the figure for sales?

    A $99,750
    B $97,500
    C $102,000
    D $106,500

4. A business usually has a margin of 25% on sales. During a year, its revenue was $190,000. What was cost of sales?

    A $47,500
    B $142,500
    C $152,000
    D $150,000

5. Which of the following is the correct definition of the business equation?

    A   Profit/Loss = movement in net assets + capital introduced + drawings
    B   Profit/Loss = movement in net assets − capital introduced − drawings
    C   Profit/Loss = movement in net assets + capital introduced − drawings
    D   Profit/Loss = movement in net assets − capital introduced + drawings

6. A business has net assets of $95,000 at the beginning of the year and $112,000 at the end of the year. Drawings were $25,000 and lottery win of $3,000 was paid into the business during the year. What was the profit for the year?

    A $47,500
    B $84,000
    C $34,000
    D $39,000

7. What is the accounting double entry for to record the loss incurred for stolen inventory that is not covered by insurance?

    A   DR Expenses   CR Cost of sales
    B   DR Cost of sales   CR Expenses
    C   DR Insurance   CR Cost of sales
    D   DR Expenses   CR Cash at bank

8   A business has net assets of $75,000 at the beginning of the year and $110,000 at the end of the year and a profit of $45,000 was made. What was the drawings for the year?

    A $12,000
    B $10,000
    C $20,000
    D $27,000

9   Fred's business has an opening inventory of $18,400 at the start of the period, and a closing inventory $19,350. Sales for the year are $180,000, and the business makes a mark-up of 25% on cost for all the items that it sells.

    What were the purchases during the year?

    A $135,950
    B $134,050
    C $143,050
    D $144,950

Chapter 13 Inventory

1. Where is carriage inwards dealt with in the statement of profit or loss?

    A   As part of selling expenses
    B   As part of administration expenses
    C   As part of the cost of purchases
    D   As part of other expenses

2. Which accounting standard contains guidance on the recognition and measurement of inventory?

    A   IAS 2
    B   IFRS 2
    C   IAS 12
    D   IFRS 12

3. What is the accounting double entry to record the value of closing inventory?

    A   DR Statement of profit or loss   CR Cost of sales
    B   DR Inventory   CR Statement of profit or loss
    C   DR Purchases   CR Statement of profit or loss
    D   DR Statement of profit or loss   CR Inventory

4. What is the accounting double entry to transfer the value of opening inventory?

    A   DR Statement of profit or loss   CR Purchases
    B   DR Inventory   CR Statement of profit or loss
    C   DR Purchases   CR Statement of profit or loss
    D   DR Statement of profit or loss   CR Inventory

5. The value of inventory should be calculated as the:

    A   Cost of the item
    B   Higher of cost or net realisable value of the item
    C   Lower of cost or net realisable value of the item
    D   Net realisable value of the item

6. Which of the following techniques to determine the purchase cost cannot be used as per IAS 2?

    A   LIFO
    B   AVCO
    C   FIFO
    D   JIFO

7. An item of inventory was purchased for $5. However, due to a fall in demand, its selling price will be only $2.50. In addition, further costs will be incurred prior to sale of $1. What is the net realisable value?

    A $2.50
    B $1.50
    C $5.00
    D $4.00

8. Which of the following are not allowed to be included in the purchase cost calculation of inventory as per IAS 2?

    A   Import duties
    B   Transport costs
    C   Conversion costs
    D   Administration costs

9   If an item of inventory is regarded as obsolete what should its value be included as?

   A   Nothing
   B   Net realisable value
   C   Purchase cost
   D   Purchase cost + conversion cost

10 Which of the following is the correct calculation of the Cost of Goods Sold?

   A   Opening inventory + Purchases + Closing inventory
   B   Opening inventory – Purchases + Closing inventory
   C   Opening inventory + Purchases – Closing inventory
   D   Opening inventory – Purchases – Closing inventory

PRACTICE QUESTION BANK

Chapter 14 Irrecoverable Debts & Allowances

1   What is the accounting double entry for an irrecoverable debt?

    A   DR Irrecoverable debt   CR Trade receivables
    B   DR Trade receivables   CR Irrecoverable debt
    C   DR Sales   CR Trade receivables
    D   DR Trade receivables   CR Sales

2   If the allowance for trade receivables is decreased, what is the effect on the statement of profit or loss?

    A   Increase in expenses
    B   Decrease in expenses
    C   Increase in other income
    D   Decrease in other income

3   Irrecoverable debts are $8,000. Excluding this amount, trade receivables at the year-end are $150,000. If an allowance for receivables of 3% is required, what is the expense for irrecoverable debts and allowance for receivables in the statement of profit or loss?

    A $8,000
    B $4,260
    C $12,500
    D $4,500

4   An allowance for receivables of 5% is required. Trade receivables at the period end are $350,000 and the allowable for receivables brought forward from the previous period is $14,750. What movement is required this year?

    A   An increase of $2,750
    B   A decrease of $2,750
    C   An increase of $2,500
    D   No adjustment required

5   Irrecoverable debts are $2,500. Trade receivables at the year-end are $183,000, including the irrecoverable debts. If an allowance for receivables of 3% is required, what is the expense for irrecoverable debts and allowance for receivables in the statement of profit or loss?

    A $7,990
    B $5,490
    C $2,500
    D $7,915

6   An allowance for receivables of 2% is required each year. Trade receivables at the period end are $565,000 and the trade receivables brought forward from the previous period are $598,000. What is the movement in the allowance for trade receivables?

    A   An increase of $660
    B   A decrease of $660
    C   An increase of $560
    D   No adjustment required

Chapter 15 Provisions & Contingencies

1 Where would a contingent liability be shown in the financial statements?

    A   On the face of the statement of financial position
    B   On the face of the statement of profit or loss
    C   It would not be included anywhere
    D   In the notes to the financial statements

2 A company has a provision for warranty claims b/f of $35,000. It does a review and decides that provision needed in future should be $30,000. What is the effect on the financial statements?

    A   Increase expenses and increase in the provision
    B   Decrease expenses and increase in the provision
    C   Decrease expenses and decrease in the provision
    D   Increase expenses and decrease the provision

3 Which of the following is not a condition that has to be met to recognise a provision per IAS 37?

    A   The entity has incurred a present obligation
    B   The recoverable amount is less than the carrying amount
    C   A reliable estimate can be made of the amount involved
    D   It is probable that a transfer of economic benefit will be required

4 A company is being sued for $20,000 by a customer. The company's lawyers reckon that it is likely that the claim will be upheld. Legal fees are currently $5,000.

How would this be accounted for?

    A   Provision for $25,000
    B   Provision for $20,000
    C   Accrual for $5,000 and Provision for $20,000
    D   Accrual for $25,000

5 How would this situation change if further legal fees of $2,000 are likely to be incurred?

    A   Provision for $27,000
    B   Provision for $22,000
    C   Accrual for $5,000 and Provision for $22,000
    D   Accrual for $27,000

Chapter 16 Tangible Non-current Assets

1. Which of the following is not capital expenditure?

    A   Purchase of a delivery van
    B   Insurance for the delivery van
    C   Installation of shelving inside the delivery van
    D   Signage on delivery van

2. Which of the following statements about depreciation are true?

    (i)   Depreciation is a way of spreading the cost of the asset over its useful life
    (ii) Depreciation reduces the carrying amount of the asset in the statement of financial position
    (iii) IAS 16 permits different methods of depreciation to be used

    A   (i) and (ii) only
    B   (ii) and (iii) only
    C   (i) and (iii) only
    D   All of the above

3. What is the accounting double entry for depreciation?

    A   DR Depreciation   CR Accumulated Depreciation
    B   DR Accumulated Depreciation CR Depreciation
    C   DR Depreciation   CR Non-current Asset
    D   DR Non-current Asset   CR Depreciation

4. A machine (cost $25,000, depreciation $17,500) is given in part exchange for a new machine costing $45,000. The agreed trade-in value was $8,500. The statement of profit or loss and other comprehensive income will include?

    A   A loss on disposal $1,000
    B   A profit on disposal $1,000
    C   A loss on purchase of the machine of $11,500
    D   A profit on disposal $11,500

5. A tangible non-current asset cost $35,000 and it is estimated to be used for 5 years. At the end of the 5 years it is estimated that it can be sold for $3,500.

    What would the annual depreciation charge be using the straight-line method?

    A $6,700
    B $7,700
    C $7,000
    D $6,300

6. A tangible non-current asset cost $60,000 and it is estimated to be used for 5 years. The company using reducing balance method to calculate depreciation at 25%. What would the carrying value of the asset be at the end of 3 years – to the nearest $?

    A $25,313
    B $24,000
    C $15,000
    D $22,734

PRACTICE QUESTION BANK

7   Which of the following statements about changes in the method of depreciation is true?

    A   The depreciation method can be changed to improve the financial position of the company

    B   The depreciation method can only be changed if it is changed for all assets in the same class

    C   A change in the depreciation method should only be made if there are changes in the expected pattern of use of the asset

    D   A change in the depreciation method from reducing balance to straight-line is permitted, but not the opposite way around.

8   The reducing balance method of depreciating fixed assets is more appropriate than the straight-line methods when:

    A   The expected life of the asset is short

    B   The asset is expected to decrease in value by a fixed percentage of cost each year

    C   The expected life of the asset is not capable of being estimated accurately

    D   The asset is expected to decrease in value less in later years than in the early years of its life

9   What is the accounting double entry for a loss on disposal of a tangible non-current asset?

    A   DR Statement of profit or loss   CR Disposal account
    B   DR Disposal account   CR Statement of profit or loss
    C   DR Disposal account   CR Non-current asset
    D   DR Non-current asset   CR Disposal account

10 A tangible non-current asset cost $135,000 and it is to be depreciated at 10% per annum. It is estimated that it can be sold for $13,500 at the end of its useful life. What would the annual depreciation charge?

    A $14,850
    B $12,150
    C $13,500
    D $10,000

11 A tangible non-current asset cost $90,000 and it is estimated to be used for 7 years, with a scrap value of $1,000. The company uses reducing balance method to calculate depreciation at 25%. What would the carrying value of the asset be at the end of 2 years – to the nearest $?

    A $51,188
    B $50,063
    C $50,625
    D $64,571

12 Which of the following statements regarding tangible non-current asset accounting is not correct?

    A   All tangible non-current assets should be revalued each year

    B   Tangible non-current assets do not have to have a residual value when calculating depreciation

    C   Management can choose which method of depreciation they wish to use

    D   Management can use different methods of depreciation for different types of tangible non-current assets

13   Which of the following is would not be recorded in the non-current asset register?

   A   Date of purchase
   B   Cost of the non-current asset
   C   Who the asset was purchased from
   D   Accumulated depreciation

14   Which of the following is not capital expenditure?

   A   Customs duty charged on the non-current asset when imported into the country
   B   Cost of installation of the new non-current asset
   C   Solicitor fees for the purchase of the non-current asset
   D   Repairs and maintenance of the computer equipment

15   Which of the following is capital expenditure?

   A   Profit on the sale of a building
   B   Annual deprecation of a non-current asset
   C   Installation of air conditioning in the sales office
   D   Wages of the operatives of the new non-current asset

Chapter 17 Intangible Non-current Assets

1   Which of the following is not an intangible asset?

    A   Trademark
    B   Patent
    C   Goodwill
    D   Land

2   Which accounting standard provides guidance on how to recognise and measure intangible assets?

    A   IAS 28
    B   IAS 16
    C   IAS 38
    D   IAS 40

3   What is the accounting double entry for expenditure on research?

    A   DR Research expense   CR Bank
    B   DR Research asset   CR Bank
    C   DR Bank   CR Research expense
    D   DR Bank   CR Research asset

4   An intangible asset with an indefinite useful life should be:

    A   Amortised
    B   Subject to an annual impairment review
    C   Depreciated in the same manner as tangible assets
    D   Left at cost in the accounts

5   Which of the following cannot be a development cost?

    A   Salaries of staff working on development
    B   Depreciation on assets being used in the development
    C   Marketing costs of new product/service being developed
    D   Materials and services used in the development

Chapter 18 Business Entity

1. A limited company is managed by:

    A   Its owners
    B   Its Board of Directors
    C   Its shareholders
    D   Its employees

2. Unlimited liability means:

    A   The owner's liability equates to the amount invested in the business
    B   If the business is unable to pay its debts – it will be insolvent
    C   The owner has to pay the business debts – even if business has the funds to do so
    D   If the business is unable to pay its debts, the owner become personally liable

3. Which of the following is not a disadvantage of a limited liability company?

    A   Limited liability
    B   Compliance with national legislation
    C   Compliance with accounting standards and policies
    D   Formation and annual registration costs

4. The maximum amount of share capital that a company is empowered to issue is known as:

    A   Issued share capital
    B   Ordinary share capital
    C   Authorised share capital
    D   Called up share capital

5. Which type of shares typically have voting rights?

    A   Irredeemable preference shares
    B   Ordinary shares
    C   Treasury shares
    D   Redeemable preference shares

6. Which of the following does not form part of shareholder's equity?

    A   Bonds
    B   Revaluation surplus
    C   Retained earnings
    D   Share premium

7. A company has authorised share capital of 1,000,000 50 cent ordinary shares and an issued share capital of 850,000 50 cent ordinary shares. If an ordinary dividend of 7.5% is declared, what is the amount payable to shareholders?

    A $75,000
    B $50,000
    C $63,750
    D $31,875

8. An appropriation of distributable profits for a specific purpose, is a:

    A   Provision
    B   Accrual
    C   Reserve
    D   Allowance

9 Which of the following is not an advantage of a bonus issue?

    A   Capitalises reserves
    B   Does not raise any cash
    C   Increases capital
    D   Does not dilute current shareholder's holding

The following information relates to Questions 10 – 14:

XYZ Ltd has the following capital structure at 30 June 20X6:

	$
500,000 ordinary shares of 50 cent	250,000
Share premium	75,000
Retained earnings	225,000
Shareholder's equity	550,000

On 1 July 20X6, XYZ Ltd made a 1 for 2 bonus issue. XYZ Ltd use the share premium account where possible when making a bonus issue.

On 1 September 20X6, XYZ Ltd then made a 1 for 4 rights issue at 75c per share. All of the rights were taken up.

10 What is the ordinary share capital balance after the bonus issue on 1 July 20X6?

    A $375,000
    B $500,000
    C $750,000
    D $250,000

11 What is the retained earnings balance after the bonus issue on 1 July 20X6?

    A $200,000
    B $100,000
    C $225,000
    D $175,000

12 What is the ordinary share capital balance at the rights issue on 1 September 20X6?

    A $375,000
    B $468,750
    C $562,500
    D $425,000

13 What is the share premium balance at the rights issue on 1 September 20X6?

    A $75,000
    B $121,875
    C $46,875
    D $42,500

14 What is the total of shareholders' equity after the rights issue on 1 September 20X6?

    A $690,625
    B $468,750
    C $562,500
    D $425,000

15 Which of the following accounts would not be in a sole trader's general ledger?

    A   Drawings account
    B   Dividend account
    C   Wages account
    D   HMRC account

PRACTICE QUESTION BANK

Chapter 19 Preparation of Financial Statements for Sole Traders

1 Which of the following is the correct formula for cost of sales?

    A   Opening inventory + purchases – closing inventory
    B   Sales – Purchases – closing inventory
    C   Sales – (Opening inventory – closing inventory – purchases)
    D   Opening inventory – closing inventory – purchases)

2 Which of the following is the correct formula for gross profit?

    A   Sales + Cost of goods sold
    B   Sales – Cost of goods sold
    C   Sales – (Opening inventory + closing inventory + purchases)
    D   Sales – (Opening inventory - closing inventory – purchases)

3 Where is carriage inwards included in the statement of profit or loss?

    A   Added to sales figure
    B   Deducted from sales figure
    C   Administration and selling expenses
    D   Cost of goods sold

4 If an owner has a personal insurance paid for him by the business, how is this dealt with?

    A   Credited to drawings and debited to insurance
    B   Credited to drawings and debited to bank
    C   Debited to drawings and credited to insurance
    D   Debited to drawings and credited to bank

5 A business starts trading on 1 January 20X0. During the year, it has sales of $1,500,000, purchases of $1,250,000 and closing inventory of $175,000. What is the gross profit for the year?

    A $175,000
    B $675,000
    C $425,000
    D $250,000

The following information relates to Questions 6 – 9:

Below is a list of balances extracted from Fred's trial balance:

	Debit $	Credit $
Trade Receivables	176,800	
Trade Payables		99,570
Inventory	27,450	
Allowance for trade receivables		3,570
Van at cost	32,600	
Fixtures & fittings at cost	14,600	
Bank		5,260
Accumulated depreciation		38,690
Office equipment at cost	11,750	
HMRC	13,420	

6   What is the figure for current assets?

   A $217,670
   B $214,100
   C $221,240
   D $200,680

7   What is the figure for total assets?

   A $234,360
   B $237,930
   C $241,500
   D $220,940

8   What is the figure for current liabilities?

   A $182,060
   B $112,990
   C $118,250
   D $104,830

9   What is the figure for net assets?

   A $52,300
   B $116,110
   C $129,530
   D $121,370

The following information relates to Questions 10 – 15:

Below is a list of balances extracted from Jane's trial balance as at 31st December 2019:

	$
Rent received	16,800
Telephone	4,570
Electricity	6,450
Insurance	3,570

10   The rent includes a receipt of $6,000, for 6 months to 31st March 2020. What will be the amount in the statement of profit or loss for rent received?

   A $16,800
   B $13,800
   C $19,800
   D $10,800

11   An invoice is received after the year end for the telephone account for $1,200 and it relates to the quarter ended 31st January 2020. There is also an accrual bought forward from the previous financial year of $900 included in the account balance.

   What will be the amount in the statement of profit or loss for telephone?

   A $4,470
   B $3,370
   C $4,070
   D $4,670

PRACTICE QUESTION BANK

12 An invoice is received after the year end for the electricity account for $1,800 and it relates to the quarter ended 28th February 2020. There is also an accrual bought forward from the previous financial year of $1,050 included in the account balance.

What will be the amount in the statement of profit or loss for electricity?

- A $6,600
- B $5,400
- C $6,270
- D $6,000

13 The insurance figure includes the annual renewal invoice for year ended 30th April 2020 for $2,400.

What will be the amount in the statement of profit or loss for insurance?

- A $2,970
- B $3,570
- C $2,770
- D $3,170

14 From the answers in the questions 10 – 13, what will be the total accruals figure to be included on the statement of financial position?

- A $600
- B $4,400
- C $800
- D $1,400

15 From the answers in the questions 10 – 13, what will be the total prepayments figure to be included in the current assets on the statement of financial position?

- A $800
- B $600
- C $3,800
- D $2,200

Chapter 20 Preparation of Financial Statements under IAS 1

1. Which of the following is not a current liability?

    A VAT owed to HMRC
    B Trade payables
    C Allowance for trade receivables
    D Bank overdraft

2. Which of the following is not a current asset?

    A VAT owed by HMRC
    B Trade receivables
    C Prepayments
    D Goodwill

3. Which of the following is not correct as per IAS 1?

    A Some items must appear on the face of the statement of financial position
    B A complete set of financial statements includes a statement of changes in equity
    C IAS 1 contains details of all disclosures necessary in a set of financial statements
    D All items of income and expense recognised in a period must be included in profit or loss unless a standard requires otherwise

4. Which accounting standard explains when to recognise revenue?

    A IAS 16
    B IFRS 15
    C IAS 1
    D IFRS 1

5. Which of the following in not a required element for a full set of financial statements?

    A Statement of financial position
    B Trial Balance
    C Comparative information
    D Statement of cash flows

6. Which of the following is 'other comprehensive income'?

    A Profit on disposal of non-current asset
    B Discount received
    C Rent received
    D Gain on revaluation of property

7. A company has a tax liability brought forward of $25,000. The liability is finally agreed at $27,500 and this is paid during the year. The company estimates that the tax liability based on the current year's profits will be $32,000. What would be the amount for tax on the statement of profit or loss and other comprehensive income?

    A $32,000
    B $34,500
    C $29,500
    D $27,500

PRACTICE QUESTION BANK

8 Where do you transfer total comprehensive income for the year on the statement of financial position?

    A   Capital
    B   Shareholders capital
    C   Retained earnings
    D   Dividends

9 Which of the following is not correct as per IFRS 15?

    A   Revenue is recognised when goods/services are transferred
    B   Revenue does include sales taxes
    C   A contract is an agreement between 2 or more parties
    D   Income is defined as both revenue and gains

10 Where on the statement of financial position is a trademark recognised?

    A   In tangible non-current assets.
    B   In long-term financial receivables
    C   In current assets
    D   In intangible non-current assets

11 Which of the following is not an item that would be included on the statement of profit or loss and other comprehensive income for a limited company?

    A   Drawings
    B   Directors' salaries
    C   Adjustment to the allowance for trade receivables
    D   Taxation

The following information relates to Questions 12 – 15:

Below is a list of balances extracted from ABC Ltd's trial balance:

	Debit $	Credit $
Trade Receivables	506,800	
Trade Payables		299,570
Inventory	127,900	
Bank loan ($10,000 due in next year)		150,000
Allowance for trade receivables		13,570
Accumulated depreciation		98,690
Motor vehicles at cost	132,600	
Office equipment at cost	41,750	
Property at cost	249,350	
Patent	80,000	
Accumulated amortisation		5,400
HMRC		33,420
Bank		15,260

12 What is the figure for non-current assets?

    A $399,610
    B $498,300
    C $325,010
    D $249,610

13 What is the figure for non-current liabilities?

    A $0
    B $150,000
    C $140,000
    D $224,600

14   What is the figure for current liabilities?

   A $314,830
   B $324,830
   C $348,250
   D $358,250

15   What is the figure for current assets?

   A $621,130
   B $634,700
   C $636,390
   D $649,960

Chapter 21 Accounting Ratios

1. Which of the following ratios would be used by the shareholders or Board to assess the performance of management?

    A   Gearing ratio
    B   Return on capital employed ratio
    C   Current ratio
    D   Dividend cover

2. Which of the following ratios would be used to measure liquidity?

    A   Gearing ratio
    B   Return on capital employed ratio
    C   Current ratio
    D   Dividend cover

3. Which of the following ratios would be used by the shareholders to assess the value of their investment?

    A   Gearing ratio
    B   Return on capital employed ratio
    C   Current ratio
    D   Dividend cover

4. If a business had a gearing ratio of 80%, this could be interpreted as:

    A   Nothing to be concerned about
    B   It could easily obtain extra finance if required
    C   It will struggle to obtain extra finance if required
    D   It is a very positive indicator of how the business is performing

5. Which of the following is not liquid funds?

    A   Bills of exchange
    B   Fixed term deposit
    C   Short term investments
    D   Bank overdraft

6. The quick ratio can be defined as:

    A   (Current assets less inventory) divided by current liabilities
    B   Current liabilities divided by current assets
    C   Current assets divided by current liabilities
    D   (Current liabilities less inventory) divided by current assets

7. The dividend cover ratio can be defined as:

    A   Dividend per share divided by earnings per share
    B   Earnings per share divided by dividend per share
    C   Profit per share divided by dividend per share
    D   Dividend per share divided by profit per share

8. The inventory holding period ratio is used to assess the company's:

    A   Liquidity
    B   Leverage
    C   Efficiency
    D   Shareholder's investment

9   The return on equity ratio is used to assess the company's:

   A   Profitability
   B   Leverage
   C   Efficiency
   D   Shareholder's investment

10 The P/E ratio is used to assess the company's:

   A   Profitability
   B   Leverage
   C   Efficiency
   D   Shareholder's investment

The following information relates to Questions 11 – 16:

Below is a list of balances extracted from ABC Ltd's trial balance at 31 December 2019:

	Debit $	Credit $
Trade Receivables	506,800	
Trade Payables		299,570
Sales		3,040,800
Purchases	1,652,000	
HMRC		33,420
Opening inventory	133,750	

Closing inventory at 31 December 2019 was:

	$
Raw materials	62,300
Work-in-progress	35,010
Finished goods	42,140

11 Calculate the inventory holding period to the nearest day.

   A   31 days
   B   30 days
   C   32 days
   D   29 days

12 Calculate the accounts receivable period to the nearest day.

   A   61 days
   B   60 days
   C   59 days
   D   62 days

13 Calculate the accounts payable period.

   A   61 days
   B   65 days
   C   67 days
   D   66 days

14 Calculate the operating cycle.

   A   25 days
   B   27 days
   C   26 days
   D   28 days

PRACTICE QUESTION BANK

15 Calculate the current ratio (to 2 decimal places).

A 0.50
B 0.51
C 1.90
D 1.95

16 Calculate the quick ratio (to 2 decimal places).

A 0.66
B 0.65
C 1.53
D 1.65

Chapter 22 Statement of Cash Flows

1 What are the main sections in an IAS 7 statement of cash flows?

    A   Cash flows from investing activities
    B   Cash flows from operating activities
    C   Cash flows from employment activities
    D   Cash flows from financing activities

2 Which of the following is not a cash equivalent?

    A   Current account balance
    B   Short term government bonds
    C   Money market funds
    D   Certificates of deposits

3 Which of the following is not an advantage of cash flow accounting?

    A   Shows the businesses ability to generate cash
    B   Enables a better comparison between the results of different companies
    C   Easier to prepare than profit forecasts
    D   Including cash equivalents gives a realistic picture of the business's liquidity

4 Which of the following headings is a classification of cash flows in IAS 7?

    A   Administration
    B   Investing
    C   Selling
    D   Production

5 Where on the statement of cash flows would a proceeds from the sale of non-current assets be shown?

    A   Administration activities
    B   Investing activities
    C   Operating activities
    D   Financing activities

6 Where on the statement of cash flows would the payment of staff wages be shown?

    A   Administration activities
    B   Investing activities
    C   Operating activities
    D   Financing activities

7 Where on the statement of cash flows would a long-term loan receipt be shown?

    A   Administration activities
    B   Investing activities
    C   Operating activities
    D   Financing activities

8 Where on the statement of cash flows would a tax payment be shown?

    A   Administration activities
    B   Investing activities
    C   Operating activities
    D   Financing activities

9 A company has the following information extract from a statement of financial position.

	20X7 $'000	20X6 $'000
Share capital	3,500	1,500
Share premium	750	–
Loan stock	750	1,500

What is the cash flow from financing activities for the year?

- A $2,000 inflow
- B $3,500 inflow
- C $2,000 outflow
- D $3,500 outflow

The following information relates to Questions 10 – 11:

A company has the following information about property, plant and equipment.

	20X7 $'000	20X6 $'000
Cost	950	875
Accumulated depreciation	115	90
Carrying amount	835	785

Plant with a carrying amount of $55,000 (original cost $100,000) was sold for $62,000 during the year.

10 What is the profit or loss on disposal?

- A $7,000 profit
- B $0
- C $17000 profit
- D $7,000 loss

11 Where would the proceeds from disposal be shown on the statement of cash flows?

- A Administration activities
- B Investing activities
- C Operating activities
- D Financing activities

12 What is the net cash flow on the investing activities?

- A $105,000 outflow
- B $43,000 outflow
- C $105,000 inflow
- D $43,000 inflow

13 An increase in inventory will be shown on the statement of cash flows as a:

- A Positive because it represents a cash inflow
- B Positive because it represents a cash outflow
- C Negative because it represents a cash inflow
- D Negative because it represents a cash outflow

14 An increase in payables will be shown on the statement of cash flows as a:

- A Positive because it represents a cash inflow
- B Positive because it represents a cash outflow
- C Negative because it represents a cash inflow
- D Negative because it represents a cash outflow

15 A decrease in receivables will be shown on the statement of cash flows as a:
    A   Positive because it represents a cash inflow
    B   Positive because it represents a cash outflow
    C   Negative because it represents a cash inflow
    D   Negative because it represents a cash outflow

Practice exam answer bank

FOUNDATION LEVEL

FOUNDATION UNIT

FINANCIAL ACCOUNTING

Practice Answer Bank

There is ONE correct answer per question

PRACTICE ANSWER BANK

> Foundation Component subjects cover the following Learning Outcomes (LO's);
>
> Financial Accounting - LO's A1, A2, A3, A4 & A5

Chapter 1 Introduction to Accounting

1   **The correct answer is B**

   Financial accounts provide historic information about the financial position and financial performance of a business. As such, they are often the most useful source of data for external users.

   The distractors are as follows:

   A   Financial accounts provide little future financial information. This information might be contained in the management accounts in the form of forecast or budget information.

   C   The laws and regulations around the preparation of financial accounts are designed to meet the requirements of external stakeholders such as investor, lenders, customers and suppliers.

   D   It is a legal requirement to produce financial accounts.

2   **The correct answer is C**

   Financial accounts, and the financial accounting records provide information about the historic performance of a business.

   The distractors are as follows:

   A   Forecasts are estimates of future performance which are often based on historic performance, but do not provide a source of data for historic performance.

   B   Financial accounts can be used as a source of data for historic performance, but past performance cannot necessarily be used to determine future performance.

   D   There is no legal requirement to produce management accounts.

3   **The correct answer is B**

   Accounts payable, bank loans and tax payable are all examples of liabilities.

   The distractors are as follows:

   A   Cash and buildings are both assets.
   C   Accounts receivable and land are both assets.
   D   Accounts receivable and inventory are both assets.

4   **The correct answer is A**

   The primary purpose of management accounting is to provide management with information to allow them to plan and control the business. Management accounts are not generally seen by external stakeholders.

   The distractors are as follows:

   B   There is far less regulation for management accounting than for financial accounting as management accounts are for the internal use of the business and can be tailored. Financial accounting tends to be more regulated.

   C   Financial accounting are usually prepared each year to comply with legal and accounting standard requirements.

   D   Financial accounting primarily a record historic information over the last accounting period.

5   **The correct answer is C**

Employees of the company are internal, rather than external, stakeholders.

Customers, suppliers and the bank, as a lender, are all examples of external stakeholders.

6   **The correct answer is B**

A limited company is a separate legal entity and the liability of the owners, the shareholders, is limited to the amount that they paid for their shares.

The distractors are as follows:

- A   In a partnership, the partners together are liable for the debts, but that liability is not limited. You should note that there is a special type of partnership in some countries called a limited liability partnership (LLP) where liability of each partner is limited.
- C   A director is the manager of a business and is not a business entity.
- D   A sole trader is solely liable for the debts of the business.

7   **The correct answer is C**

The statement of financial position shows the assets that are owned, and the liabilities owed by a business at a certain point in time. It also shows the capital (or equity) which represents the amount owned by the shareholders of a business.

The distractors are as follows:

- A   The statement of profit or loss is a record of income generated and expenditure incurred over a given period.
- B   The trial balance is a list of all the account balances at a point in time.
- D   The statement of cash flows shows the cash inflows and outflows of the business over a period of time.

Chapter 2 The Regulatory Framework

1 **The correct answer is C**

Although the purpose of financial reporting standards is to remove some of the subjectivity in financial statements, there are still a number of judgements required in the preparation of financial statements under IFRS Accounting Standards.

The other statements are all correct.

2 **The correct answer is A**

The IASB standard setting process is Discussion paper → exposure draft → IFRS issued.

The IFRS interpretations committee issues interpretations to deal with specific practical accounting issues.

3 **The correct answer is D**

Membership of the IASB board must be spread between a mixture of developed and developing countries to reflect the users of IFRS Accounting Standards. The members are a mix of accountants in practice (such as auditors), accountants in business (preparers of financial statements), users of financial statements and academics.

The IASB is an independent privately funded body. The standards issued prior to 2003 are International Accounting Standards (IAS) not to be confused with the auditing standards currently issued which are the International Standards on Auditing (ISA). The IASB is overseen by the IFRS Foundation.

4 **The correct answer is D**

IFRS Accounting Standards are not used to replace national legal requirements. The other statements are all correct.

5 **The correct answer is A**

The ISSB was formed by the IFRS Foundation in 2021.

The ISSB issues IFRS Sustainability Disclosure Standards. The objectives of the ISSB include working with other sustainability standard setters, not aiming to replace them. The ISSB is governed by the IFRS Foundation and works with the IASB.

PRACTICE ANSWER BANK

Chapter 3 Accounting Conventions

1 **The correct answer is C**

The *Conceptual Framework for Financial Reporting* is set of accounting principles produced by the IASB (International Accounting Standards Board).

The distractors are as follows:

A   GAAP is generally accepted accounting principles, not an accountancy body.

B   AIA: the Association of International Accountants did not create the *Conceptual Framework*.

D   IFRS: IFRS Accounting Standards are the standards issued by the IASB along with the *Conceptual Framework*.

2 **The correct answer is D**

Materiality can relate to either the financial value or nature of an items. A small financial balance can still be material to the users of the financial statements if its misstatement or omission would influence their decisions.

The other balances are all wrong. Relevance and faithful representation are the fundamental qualitative characteristics. Immaterial balances may be amalgamated in the financial statements, but the nominal ledger should contain a list of every balance.

3 **The correct answer is D**

The *Conceptual Framework* does not have a section which covers Political influence. The sections of the *Conceptual Framework* issued in 2018 are:

1. The objective of general purpose financial reporting
2. Qualitative characteristics of useful financial information
3. Financial statements and the reporting entity
4. The elements of financial statements
5. Recognition and derecognition
6. Measurement
7. Presentation and disclosure
8. Concepts of capital and capital maintenance

4 **The correct answer is B**

The *Conceptual Framework* makes it clear that financial statements should be produced on an accruals basis, recognising income and expenses in the period in which they occur, rather than when the cash is paid and received (a cash basis).

5 **The correct answer is C**

The *Conceptual Framework* states that 'financial statements are normally prepared on the assumption that the reporting entity is a going concern and will continue in operation for the foreseeable future'.

Ongoing investment and limited liability are not underlying assumptions in the preparation of financial statements. Prudence is a concept that relates to the characteristic of faithful representation. Prudence is the exercise of caution when making judgments under condition of uncertainty to ensure assets and income are not overstated and liabilities and expenses are not understated.

PRACTICE ANSWER BANK

6   **The correct answer is A**

The relevance of information is affected by its nature and materiality.

The *Conceptual Framework* doesn't define accuracy, but the fundamental qualitative characteristic of faithful representation encompasses the idea of accuracy. To be a faithful representation information must be complete, neutral and free from error.

Materiality is the concept that the omission or misstatement of information could influence the decisions of the user of financial statements.

Comparability is one of the enhancing qualitative characteristics.

7   **The correct answer is D**

The enhancing qualitative characteristics of financial information are comparability, verifiability, timelines and understandability. Accuracy is not one of these.

8   **The correct answer is B**

The concept of the business entity is that it is a separate entity from its owners and the transactions of the owners should never be mixed with the business's transactions.

The other statements are all incorrect.

9   **The correct answer is C**

The four measurement bases set out in the *Conceptual Framework* are: historical cost, fair value, value in use and current cost.

Forecast cost is not a measurement base.

PRACTICE ANSWER BANK

Chapter 4 Sources, Records and Books of Prime Entry

1   **The correct answer is C**

    The receivables ledger is a subsidiary ledger that provides details of the receivables balance for each individual customer.

    The other options are books of prime entry.

2   **The correct answer is C**

    The sales returns day book is used to record details of goods returned by customers.

    The distractors are as follows:

    A   Goods purchased from suppliers are recorded in the purchase day book.
    B   Goods sold to customers are recorded in the sales day book.
    D   Details of goods returned to suppliers are recorded in the purchase return day book.

3   **The correct answer is A**

    A sales invoice to a credit customer would be recorded in the sales day book and not the cash book as it is not a cash transaction.

    A remittance advice, the cheque book and a receipt of payment for rent are all source documents for cash transactions.

4   **The correct answer is D**

    The name of the sales representative would not always appear on a sales invoice. However, the delivery date, details of the goods or services supplied and the price, net of any discount given would be expected on a sales invoice.

5   **The correct answer is B**

    A journal is not a source document, it is the record of prime entry for any transactions which are not recorded in any of the other books of prime entry.

    An invoice from a supplier, a credit note to a customer and a paying in slip are all examples of source documents.

6   **The correct answer is C**

    Small cash transactions are recorded in the petty cash book.

    The cash book and a journal are other books of prime entry. The sales adjustment book does not exist.

7   **The correct answer is B**

    If $150 has been spent during the month, this is the amount that would have be required to restore the float to the imprest level of $200.

    The distractors are as follows:

    A $50 – this is what is left after December's spend
    C $200 – this is the imprest/float amount
    D $350 – this is the float plus the amount spent

PRACTICE ANSWER BANK

Chapter 5 Ledger Accounts and Double Entry

1   **The correct answer is B**

   The books of prime entry are recorded in the general (or nominal) ledger.

   The distractors are as follows:

   A   Payables Ledger – only contains payables
   C   Receivables Ledger – only contains receivables
   D   Journal Ledger – no such ledger

2   **The correct answer is A**

   The accounting equation is Assets = Capital + Liabilities, which can be rearranged as Capital = Assets – Liabilities.

   All of the other options are incorrect.

3   **The correct answer is B**

   When a sole trader removes money from the business, this is referred to as drawings.

   Wages and salaries are payments to employee of the business, dividends are payments to shareholders of a company.

4   **The correct answer is C**

   The matching convention comes from the accruals concept. Income and expenses are recorded as incurred, rather than when the cash is paid or received.

5   **The correct answer is B**

   A   A debit to an asset account will increase its value. TRUE
   B   A credit to an expense account will increase its value. FALSE
   C   A credit to an income account will increase its value. TRUE
   D   A debit to a liability account will reduce its value. TRUE

6   **The correct answer is C**

   The journal is a record of prime entry for transactions which are not recorded in any of the other books of prime entry.

   The petty cash book, sales return day book and cash book are other books of prime entry.

7   **The correct answer is B**

   A cash sale of $1,000 is recorded as: Debit Cash $1,000, Credit Sales $1,000

   Debit Sales $1,000, Credit Cash $1,000 – this is a decrease in sales and cash

   Debit Trade receivables $1,000, Credit Sales $1,000 – this is the recording of a credit sale

   Debit Sales $1,000, Credit Trade Receivables $1,000 is the reverse of a credit sale.

8   **The correct answer is C**

   The receipt of cash from a credit customer is Debit Cash at bank $500, Credit Trade receivables $500.

   Option a is the reversal of the correct journal. Option b is an example of cash sale and option d is the reversal of a credit sale.

9   **The correct answer is C**

The correct answer is Debit Office furniture $2,000. Credit Trade payables $2,000. The debit records the furniture as an asset, and the credit records the payable liability.

10 **The correct answer is D**

A credit sale is recorded as Debit Trade receivables, to create an asset to represent the cash due to the company, and Credit Sales to recognise the sales revenue. The balanced owed by XYZ Ltd will be recorded in the sales ledger, under the XYZ Ltd account. The sales ledger contains a list of balances owed by each client. The trade receivables figure is a single total of amounts owed in the general ledger.

PRACTICE ANSWER BANK

Chapter 6 From Trial Balance to Financial Statements

1 **The correct answer is B**

   Office equipment, trade receivables and cash at bank are all assets, so the total assets are $17,500 ($10,000 + $5,000 + $2,500). The loan is a liability balance.

2 **The correct answer is C**

   Assets = Capital + Liabilities. Therefore, Capital = Assets − Liabilities. In the above example, there were assets of $17,500 less liabilities of $5,000 (the loan) which would give a capital balance of $12,500.

3 **The correct answer is D**

   Net profit = sales − purchases − other expenses = $200,000 - $115,000 - $27,500 = $57,500

4 **The correct answer is B**

   A credit balance of $1,000 carried down will become a debit balance of $1,000 brought down to start the next accounting period, which is a cash asset of $1,000.

   Correspondingly, a debit balance of $1,000 carried down would result in a $1,0000 credit (overdrawn) balance brought down in the next period.

5 **The correct answer is C**

   If a cheque received was recorded as in 'cash at bank' at $5,000 but the trade receivable was only reduced by $500, the trial balance will not balance.

   In option a, if an invoice is omitted, then nothing is recorded so the trial balance will be wrong but it will balance.

   In option b if an invoice is recorded in correctly in both accounts (sales and cash/receivables) then again, the trial balance will be incorrect but will balance.

   In option c, the expense has been posted to the wrong nominal ledger account. This will result on one account being overstated, and one account being understated, but the trial balance will still balance.

6 **The correct answer is D**

   Computer maintenance is an expense and will appear on the statement of profit or loss. The other balances are all asset balances and will appear on the statement of financial position.

7 **The correct answer is C**

   Drawings is a reduction in capital and would appear on the statement of financial position as a reduction to capital.

   Rent received is income, carriage inwards is part of the cost of purchases expense and bank interest is an expense. These balances would all appear on the statement of profit or loss.

Chapter 7 VAT

1 **The correct answer is C**

Input tax represents the tax paid by the company on purchases that they made. Output tax is the tax received on sales. If input tax is greater than output tax, that means the company has paid more VAT than they have collected on sales, and the tax authority will refund the different.

2 **The correct answer is D**

Trade receivables represents the amount a company is due from credit sales, and the balance due includes any VAT. Therefore the full amount of $240,000 would be included as a current asset on the statement of financial position.

3 **The correct answer is A**

The purchase of $1,200 needs to recorded net of VAT. The net amount is:

($1,200/120%) × 100% = $1,000 with $200 VAT

This should be recorded as Debit purchases $1,000, Debit VAT payable $200 and Credit Cash at bank $1,200.

4 **The correct answer is C**

VAT on motor vehicles is not recoverable. Therefore the full amount paid, $24,000 should be capitalised on the statement of financial position. The double entry is Debit Motor vehicles $24,000, Credit Cash at bank $24,000.

5 **The correct answer is A**

VAT on sales is a credit to VAT payable. VAT on purchases is a debit to VAT payable, but irrecoverable VAT is not included.

	$	
VAT on sales (output VAT)	9,000	Debit
VAT on purchases (input VAT)	(11,500)	Credit
Adjustment for irrecoverable VAT	250	Debit
	(2,250)	Credit

Chapter 8 Accruals & Prepayments

1 The correct answer is B

The closing accrual is for the telephone expense in November and December 20X6 as the bill for these months wasn't received until January 20X7 and is $2,000 ($3,000/3 months × 2 months).

TELEPHONE EXPENSE

	$		$
Cash paid	34,000	Bal b/d	3,500
Bal c/d	2,000	SPLOCI (balancing figure)	**32,500**
	36,000		36,000

2 The correct answer is A

If the rental payment covers 1 April 20X8 to 31 March 20X9, then January 20X9 – March 20X9 are prepaid at 31 December 20X8 and the prepayment is ($10,000/12) × 3 = $2,500

3 The correct answer is D

A prepayment is an asset balance in the statement of financial position, so must be a debit. A prepayment reduces the expense for the year, as part of that expense has been prepaid and relates to the next financial year. A credit balance is required to reduce the expense.

The correct entry is: Debit Prepayments $2,000, Credit Electricity $2,000

4 The correct answer is C

An accrual is a liability balance in the statement of financial position, so must be a credit. An accrual increases the expense for the year as part of the expense has not yet been billed or recorded in the financial statements. A debit balance is required to increase the expense.

The correct entry is: Debit Electricity $2,000, Credit Accrual $2,000

5 The correct answer is A

The closing prepayment is for the water charges in July – September 20X6 and is $4,500 ($18,000/ 12 months × 3 months).

WATER CHARGES

	$		$
Balance b/d	4,000	SPL (balancing figure)	**17,500**
Cash paid	18,000	Balance c/d	4,500
	22,000		22,000

6 The correct answer is D

A prepayment of income (commonly referred to as deferred income) is a reduction in income (a debit) which results in a liability (credit) balance in the statement of financial position. Therefore, the correct answer is d.

Chapter 9 Bank Reconciliations

1   **The correct answer is A**

	$
Balance per bank statement	20,000
Add: interest received	500
Adjusted bank statement	20,500
Add: Unpresented cheque	500
Less: Outstanding lodgment	(1,250)
Balance per cash book	**19,750**

2   **The correct answer is A**

	$
Balance per bank statement	(2,000)
Add: Unpresented cheque	500
Add deposit interest	500
Correct balance per cash book	(1,000)
Add: bank charges not yet posted	100
Balance per cash book prior to correction	(900)

3   **The correct answer is B**

The bank charges on the bank statement need to be adjusted for in the cash book. This adjustment would be done prior to completing the bank reconciliation. The other distractors are all genuine timing differences that would appear on a bank reconciliation.

4   **The correct answer is D**

If the rental income has been posted to the cash book, but hasn't yet cleared the bank statements then this is a genuine timing different that would appear on the bank statement.

The other entries are already on the bank statement, and require a corresponding entry to be posted to the cash book prior to completing the bank reconciliation.

5   **The correct answer is C**

A contra entry will not have any impact on cash as it is an adjustment between receivables and payables.

Timing differences, errors and omissions could all create differences between the bank statement and the cash book.

Chapter 10 Control Accounts

1 **The correct answer is A**

A control account is an impersonal account that shows the total balance. The breakdown of this balance, the 'personal' accounts, will be show the individual amounts that makes up the total balance.

2 **The correct answer is B**

Control accounts are found in the nominal ledger.

3 **The correct answer is A**

Control accounts are mainly used for accounts payable and accounts receivables. Therefore, the accounts receivable control accounts would be the most common control account.

4 **The correct answer is C**

The discount given to credit customers who pay early is called a discount allowed. A discount received is a discount given to the company for making an early payment for purchases it has made on credit. A trade discount is given at the time of the transaction and is not conditional on the timing of the payment.

5 **The correct answer is B**

A discount received is a discount given to a business for making an early payment for purchases it has made on credit. A discount allowed is given to credit customers who make an early payment. A trade discount is given at the time of the transaction and is not conditional on the timing of the payment.

6 **The correct answer is D**

	Trade payables control a/c $	Trade payables ledger $
Opening balance	18,500	22,800
Add: purchase omitted	5,200	-
Add: supplier account	-	900
	23,700	23,700

The correct trade payables balance is $23,700 CR as it is a liability balance.

7 **The correct answer is B**

	Trade receivables control a/c $	Trade receivables ledger $
Opening balance	38,500	46,650
Add: sales omitted	9,900	–
Add: customer account	–	1,750
	48,400	48,400

The correct trade receivables balance is $48,400 DR as it is an asset balance.

8 **The correct answer is D**

Credit purchases, discounts received from the supplier and contra entries would all be posted to the trade payables control account.

Any discounts allowed would be posted to the trade receivables control account, therefore the correct answer is d.

Chapter 11 Errors

1 **The correct answer is C**

Errors are corrected with a journal.

2 **The correct answer is A**

Posting an entry to the wrong account code is an error of principle.

3 **The correct answer is B**

Swapping two numbers is a transposition error.

4 **The correct answer is D**

An additional debit of $10,000 is needed so that total debits are $135,200 ($125,200 + $10,000) and equal total credits.

5 **The correct answer is B**

The purchase return should be a credit balance of $960, so total credits are understated by $960. Instead, it has been posted as a sales return (debit balance) of $960, result in total debits which are overstated by $960. Debit balances are $1,920 higher than credit balances ($960 + $960) and so a credit suspense account of $1,920 is required.

6 **The correct answer is A**

VAT on sales should have been a $520 credit but was instead posted as a $520 debit. The net result of the error is that debits are overstated by $1,040, so a credit suspense account of $1,040 is required.

PRACTICE ANSWER BANK

Chapter 12 Incomplete Records

1 **The correct answer is A**

	$
Payments made to suppliers	52,000
Add: closing balance of trade payables	47,000
Less: opening balance of trade payables	(55,000)
Add: discounts received	1,000
Purchases during the period	45,000

The purchase expense can be calculated as payments made during the period (purchases paid for already) plus closing trade payables (purchases made but not yet paid for). The opening trade payables has to be deducted, as some of the payments made during the period relate to purchases made in the prior accounting period.

Discounts received need to be added, as although the discount wasn't paid, the total expense should include the discounted amount.

2 **The correct answer is C**

If there is a mark-up of 25% on cost of sales, this means that gross profit is 25% of the total costs and revenue must be 125% of costs.

		$
Revenue	125%	190,000
Cost of sales	100%	152,000
Gross profit	25%	38,000

$190,000/125% = $152,000

3 **The correct answer is D**

	$
Payments received from credit customers	99,750
Add: closing balance of trade receivables	109,500
Less: opening balance of trade receivables	(105,000)
Add: discounts allowed	2,250
Credit sales in the period	106,500

Discounts allowed are added as these sales were made, and the income must be recognised, but the full amount wasn't received as the customers paid quickly to receive the discount.

4 **The correct answer is B**

		$
Revenue	100%	190,000
Cost of sales	75%	142,500
Gross profit	25%	47,500

5 **The correct answer is D**

The business equation is:

Profit/(loss) = movement in net assets − capital introduced + drawings

6 The correct answer is D

The business equation is:

Profit/(loss) = movement in net assets − capital introduced + drawings
= ($112,000 − $95,000) − $3,000 + $25,000
= $39,000

7 The correct answer is A

The double entry to record stolen inventory that is not covered by insurance is:

Debit Expenses (eg administrative expenses), Credit Cost of sales

This is because the business needs to bear the loss of the of the goods.

8 The correct answer is B

The business equation is:

Profit/(loss) = movement in net assets − capital introduced + drawings
$45,000 = ($110,000 − $75,000) − 0 + drawings

Therefore:

Drawings = $45,000 − ($110,000 − $75,000)
= $10,000

9 The correct answer is D

	$
Cost of sales ($180,000/125%)	144,000
Add: closing inventory	19,350
Less: opening inventory	(18,400)
Purchases	144,950

($180,000/125%) + $19,350 − $18,400 = $144,950

PRACTICE ANSWER BANK

Chapter 13 Inventory

1   **The correct answer is C**

    Carriage inwards is the delivery costs for purchases made. This is included in the cost of purchases.

2   **The correct answer is A**

    IAS 2 *Inventories* is the standard that provides guidance on the recognition and measurement of inventory.

3   **The correct answer is B**

    Closing inventory is recorded by recording the inventory asset (a debit) and crediting the statement of profit or loss (cost of sales account).

    The correct double entry is: Debit Inventory, Credit Statement of profit or loss

4   **The correct answer is D**

    At the end of the accounting period, the opening inventory asset needs to be removed (credited) and taken to the statement of profit or loss.

    The correct double entry is: Debit Statement of profit or loss, Credit Inventory

5   **The correct answer is C**

    IAS 2 requires the value of inventory to be calculated at the lower of cost and net realisable value.

6   **The correct answer is A**

    IAS 2 permits purchase cost to be determined using either FIFO (first-in, first-out) or AVCO (weighted average cost).

    IAS 2 specifically disallows the use of LIFO (last-in, first-out) as a method of determining purchase cost.

    JIFO is not a real acronym.

7   **The correct answer is B**

    Purchase cost – $5

    Net realisable value = selling price less costs incurred to sell = $2.50 – $1 = $1.50

8   **The correct answer is D**

    IAS 2 specifically disallows general administration costs from the purchase cost of inventory.

    However, import duties, transport costs and conversion costs are permitted by IAS 2.

9   **The correct answer is A**

    An obsolete item has no realisable value, and so should be valued at $nil (the lower of cost and $nil).

10 **The correct answer is C**

    Cost of goods sold = opening inventory + purchase costs – closing inventory

Chapter 14 Irrecoverable Debts & Allowances

1 **The correct answer is A**

An irrecoverable debt must be removed from trade receivables (a credit) and an expense (a debit) recorded. The correct double entry is:

Debit Irrecoverable debt, Credit Trade receivables

2 **The correct answer is C**

A decrease allowance for trade receivables is a credit to the profit or loss account. The allowance is decreasing which is a gain (credit) for the business. This would usually be reported in other income.

3 **The correct answer is C**

The expense would be $8,000 + ($150,000 × 3%) = $12,500

4 **The correct answer is A**

($350,000 × 5%) − $14,750 = $17,500 − $14,750 = $2,750

The allowance for receivables was $14,750 and has increased to $17,500, an increase of $2,750.

5 **The correct answer is D**

The allowance for trade receivables can be calculated as ($183,000 − $2,500) × 3%) = $5,415.

The total expense for irrecoverable debts and allowance for receivables is: $2,500 + $5,415 = $7,915.

6 **The correct answer is B**

		$
Current year allowance	= 2% × 565,000	11,300
Prior year allowance	= 2% × 598,000	11,960
Decrease		(660)

Chapter 15 Provisions & Contingencies

1   **The correct answer is D**

    IAS 37 states that a contingent liability should be disclosed in the notes to the financial statements.

2   **The correct answer is C**

    The warranty provision needs to be reduced. A provision is a liability balance, and a reduction in a liability is a debit. The corresponding credit would appear in expenses, which is a decrease in expenses.

    Therefore the correct answer is c – a decrease (credit) to expenses and a decrease (debit) to the warranty provision.

3   **The correct answer is B**

    IAS 37 states that a provision should be recognised when:

    - When an entity has incurred a present obligation
    - When it is probable that a transfer of economic benefits will be required to settle it
    - When a reliable estimate can be made of the amount involved

    The recoverable amount being less than the carrying amount indicated an impairment of assets (IAS 36)

4   **The correct answer is C**

    A provision should only be recognised for the claim, but the legal fees should be accrued, as the fees will need to be paid.

5   **The correct answer is C**

    The additional legal fees are now probable but uncertain, so they would be included in the provision, bringing the total provision to $22,000. The original legal fees will still be accrued.

Chapter 16 Tangible Non-current Assets

1 The correct answer is B

Insurance is an operating expense and not something that can be capitalised. It should be expensed each year.

Purchasing a van, installing shelving needed in the van and putting company signage on the van are all things that are expected to benefit the business over more than one accounting period, and can therefore be capitalised.

2 The correct answer is D

All of the options are correct.

3 The correct answer is A

Depreciation is recorded as an expense (debit) with a credit to accumulated depreciation in the statement of financial position, to reduce the carrying amount of the asset.

4 The correct answer is B

		$
Trade in value		8,500
Carrying amount	($25,000 – $17,500)	7,500
Gain on trade in		1,000

The value given on trade-in of $8,500 is greater than the carrying amount of the machine of $7,500 which results in a gain.

5 The correct answer is D

($35,000 – $3,500)/5 years = $6,300

6 The correct answer is A

		$
Cost		60,000
Dep'n year 1	$60,000 × 25%	(15,000)
NBV year 1		45,000
Dep'n year 2	$45,000 × 25%	(11,250)
NBV year 2		33,750
Dep'n year 3	$33,750 × 25%	(8,437)
NBV year 3		25,313

7 The correct answer is C

IAS 16 only permits a change in depreciation method if the expected patter on use changes. The other options are not correct.

8 The correct answer is D

The reducing balance methods calculates depreciation as a fixed percentage of the carrying amount. Therefore as the carrying amount decreases, so does the depreciation amount. This method is most suited to assets that have a sharper decrease in value at the start of their life.

9 The correct answer is A

Accounting for the loss on disposal of a non-current asset requires a loss expense to be debited to the statement of profit or loss and the disposal account to be cleared with a corresponding credit.

PRACTICE ANSWER BANK

10 **The correct answer is B**

($135,000 – $13,500) × 10% = $12,150

11 **The correct answer is C**

		$
Cost		90,000
NBV year 1	90,000 × 75%	67,500
NBV year 2	67,500 × 75%	50,625

Note that a quick way of calculating the net book value using the reducing balance method is: carrying amount × (100% – reducing balance %)

12 **The correct answer is A**

13 **The correct answer is C**

Non-current assets do not have to be revalued each year under IAS 16.

It is not necessary to know who the asset was purchased from. The date of purchase, cost of the asset and the accumulated depreciation are all necessary.

14 **The correct answer is D**

Repairs and maintenance charges must be expensed under IAS 16 and cannot be capitalised.

The other items can all form part of the purchase and installation cost of the asset which can be capitalised.

15 **The correct answer is C**

Installation of air conditioning is capital expenditure as it is expected to add benefit to the office over a period of time.

Chapter 17 Intangible Non-current Assets

1 **The correct answer is D**

Land is a tangible non-current asset. The others are all examples of intangible assets.

2 **The correct answer is C**

IAS 38 *Intangible assets* is the correct standard. IAS 28 relates to associates and joint ventures, IAS 16 is for tangible non-current assets and IAS 40 deals with investment property.

3 **The correct answer is A**

Research expenditure cannot be capitalised under IAS 38 and must be expensed to the statement of profit or loss. The cash paid would be a credit to Bank.

4 **The correct answer is B**

IAS 38 requires an intangible asset with an indefinite useful life to be subject to an annual impairment review.

An asset with a finite useful life would be amortised each year.

5 **The correct answer is C**

Marketing costs are specifically prohibited in IAS 38 when calculating development costs to be capitalised. The other options are all permitted by IAS 38.

PRACTICE ANSWER BANK

Chapter 18 Business Entity

1 **The correct answer is B**

A limited company is managed by the Board of Directors.

The owners are the shareholders of the company.

2 **The correct answer is D**

Unlimited liability means that the owner becomes personally liable if a business is unable to pay its debts.

If a business has limited liability, then the liability of the owner is limited to the amount that they put into the business.

3 **The correct answer is A**

Limited liability is an advantage not a disadvantage of a limited company.

The other compliance and regulatory options are all considered to be disadvantages.

4 **The correct answer is C**

The authorised share capital is the maximum number of shares that a company can issue.

5 **The correct answer is B**

Ordinary shares typically have voting rights.

Preference shares do not typically have voting rights. Treasury shares are shares bought back by the company, but not cancelled. These also do not have voting rights.

6 **The correct answer is A**

Bonds are a liability. The other options do form part of shareholders' equity.

7 **The correct answer is D**

There are 850,000 shares in issue, and those shareholders will receive a dividend. The amount of dividend payable is:

$850,000 \times 50$ cent $\times 7.5\% = \$31,875$

8 **The correct answer is C**

A reserve is an appropriation of distributable profits for a specific purpose (eg plant replacement) while a provision is an amount charged against revenue as an expense. A provision relates either to a diminution in the value of an asset or a known liability (eg legal claim for damages), the amount of which cannot be established with any accuracy.

Provisions or allowances (for depreciation etc) are dealt with in company accounts in the same way as in the accounts of other types of business.

9 **The correct answer is B**

A bonus issue does not raise any cash, but this is considered to be a disadvantage.

The other options are all advantages of a bonus issue.

PRACTICE ANSWER BANK

10   The correct answer is A

A 1 for 2 bonus issue means that 1 new ordinary share will be issue for every 2 ordinary shares currently in issue.

The increase in share capital will be:

500,000 shares/2 = 250,000 shares × 50 cent = $125,000

Share capital after the bonus issue will therefore be: $250,000 + $125,000 = $375,000

11   The correct answer is D

The bonus issue resulted in $125,000 additional share capital. There is a balance of $75,000 in share premium, so this will be used to create the bonus shares. The balance of $50,000 ($125,000 – $75,000) will be taken from retained earnings.

The retained earnings balance after the bonus issue will be $225,000 – $50,000 = $175,000

12   The correct answer is B

After the bonus issue there were 750,000 shares in issue.

The 1 for 4 rights issue will result in an additional 750,000 shares/4 = 187,500 shares

Therefore share capital after the rights issue will be:

(750,000 + 187,500) × 50 cents = $468,750

13   The correct answer is C

Share premium was reduced to zero after the bonus issue.

The issue of 187,500 50c shares for 75c per share will results in a share premium balance of:

187,500 shares × (0.75 – 0.50) = $46,875

14   The correct answer is A

	$
Ordinary shares	468,750
Share premium	46,875
Retained earnings	175,000
	690,625

15   The correct answer is B

Dividends are paid to equity shareholders of a company. Therefore, a sole trader would not have a dividend account.

They would have a drawings account to record money that they take from the business, and if they have employees, they would have a wages and HMRC account.

PRACTICE ANSWER BANK

Chapter 19 Preparation of Financial Statements for Sole Traders

1. **The correct answer is A**

   Cost of sales = opening inventory + purchases – closing inventory

2. **The correct answer is B**

   Gross profit = sales – cost of sales (cost of goods sold)

3. **The correct answer is D**

   Carriage inwards is the cost of buying goods. This is a purchase cost and is included in the cost of goods sold.

4. **The correct answer is C**

   The insurance cost would have initially been recorded as an insurance expense (debit insurance) and a credit to the business bank.

   As the insurance is a personal expense, this must be recorded as drawings, with a correction to the insurance expense account.

   → Debit drawings, Credit insurance

5. **The correct answer is C**

		$
Sales		1,500,000
Cost of sales	(0 + 1,250,000 – 175,000)	1,075,000
Gross profit		425,000

6. **The correct answer is B**

	$
Trade receivables	176,800
Allowance for trade receivables	(3,570)
Inventories	27,450
HMRC	13,420
Current assets	214,100

   The allowance for trade receivables reduces the trade receivables balance and is not shown as a liability. The HMRC accounts is a debit balance, so would be included in current assets.

7. **The correct answer is A**

	$	$
Current assets		214,100
Van at cost	32,600	
Fixtures & fittings at cost	14,600	
Office equipment at cost	11,750	
Accumulated depreciation	(38,690)	
		20,260
		234,360

8. **The correct answer is D**

	$
Trade payables	99,570
Bank overdraft	5,260
Current liabilities	104,830

   The bank balance is a credit balance, indicating that the bank is overdrawn and is a current liability.

PRACTICE ANSWER BANK

9 **The correct answer is C**

	$
Total assets	234,360
Less: current liabilities	(104,830)
Net assets	129,530

10 **The correct answer is B**

3 months of the rent received relates to the next financial year (an income prepayment or deferred income).

The rental income will need to be reduced by ($6,000 × 3/6) = $3,000

The adjusted rent received balance is: $16,800 – $3,000 = $13,800

11 **The correct answer is A**

The telephone bill for November and December 2019 was only received in January 2020. The expense for these two months will need to be accrued at the year end. The accrual required is: ($1,200 × 2/3) = $800.

	$
Draft telephone expense	4,570
Less: accrual brought forward	(900)
Add: accrual carried forward	800
Telephone expense for the year	4,470

12 **The correct answer is D**

Electricity for December 2019 needs to be accrued at 31 December 2019. The accrual is ($1,800 × 1/3) = $600.

	$
Draft electricity expense	6,450
Less: accrual brought forward	(1,050)
Add: accrual carried forward	600
Electricity expense for the year	6,000

13 **The correct answer is C**

The insurance expense includes prepaid insurance. Insurance for January – April 2020 has been prepaid, and amount of ($2,400 × 4/12) = $800

	$
Draft insurance expense	3,570
Less: insurance prepayment	(800)
Electricity expense for the year	2,770

14 **The correct answer is D**

	$
Q11 accrual	800
Q12 accrual	600
Total accrual	1,400

15 **The correct answer is A**

The only prepayment was the $800 prepayment from Q13. Prepaid income is a liability.

Chapter 20 Preparation of Financial Statements under IAS1

1   **The correct answer is C**

    VAT owed to HMRC, trade payables and a bank overdraft are all considered to be current liabilities under IAS 1.

    Although an allowance for trade receivables is a credit balance, it is deducted from trade receivables and is not a current liability.

2   **The correct answer is D**

    Goodwill is a non-current intangible asset.

    VAT owed by HMRC, trade receivables and prepayments are all current assets.

3   **The correct answer is C**

    IAS 1 does not contain the detail of all disclosure notes, this detail can be found in the individual financial statements.

    IAS 1 does require certain items to appear on the face of the statement of financial position and statement of profit or loss. It also requires a statement of changes in equity to be included in the financial statements and requires all items of income and expense to be includes in the statement of profit or loss unless a standard requires otherwise.

4   **The correct answer is B**

    IFRS 15 *Revenue from contracts with customers* provides guidance on the timing of revenue recognition.

5   **The correct answer is B**

    A trial balance is not part of a set of financial statements.

6   **The correct answer is D**

    A gain on revaluation of property is other comprehensive income, as that gain is recorded as a revaluation surplus rather than through the statement of profit or loss. The other items would all appear in the statement of profit or loss.

7   **The correct answer is B**

	$
Tax paid during the year	27,500
Less: Tax liability brought forward	(25,000)
Prior year under provision	2,500
Tax charge for the current year	32,000
Total tax expense	34,500

8   **The correct answer is C**

    Total comprehensive income is transferred to retained earnings.

9   **The correct answer is B**

    Sales tax is not included in revenue. The other options are all stated in IFRS 15.

10 **The correct answer is D**

    A trademark is an intangible non-current asset.

PRACTICE ANSWER BANK

11 **The correct answer is A**

Drawings would appear in sole trader accounts, but not in limited company accounts.

Directors salaries, taxation and an adjustment to the allowance for trade receivables would all appear in the statement of profit or loss.

12 **The correct answer is A**

	$	$
Motor vehicles at cost	132,600	
Property at cost	249,350	
Office equipment at cost	41,750	
Accumulated depreciation	(98,690)	
		325,010
Patent	80,000	
	(5,400)	
		74,600
		399,610

13 **The correct answer is C**

The bank loan repayable in the next year of $10,000 is a current liability. The balance of $150,000 – $10,000 = $140,000 is a non-current liability.

14 **The correct answer is D**

	$
Trade payables	299,570
Bank loan	10,000
HMRC	33,420
Bank overdraft	15,260
Current liabilities	358,250

15 **The correct answer is A**

	$
Trade receivables	506,800
Less: allowance for trade receivables	(13,570)
Inventory	127,900
Current assets	621,130

Chapter 21 Accounting Ratios

1 **The correct answer is B**

Return on capital employed is often used to assess the performance of management.

The distractors are as follows:

A   Gearing ratio – measures long-term capital structure
C   Current ratio – measures liquidity
D   Dividend cover – measures value of investment

2 **The correct answer is C**

Liquidity is measured by the current ratio.

The distractors are as follows:

A   Gearing ratio – measures long-term capital structure
B   Return on capital employed - measures the performance of management.
D   Dividend cover – measures value of investment

3 **The correct answer is D**

Shareholders might use dividend cover to assess the value of their investment.

The distractors are as follows:

A   Gearing ratio – measures long-term capital structure
B   Return on capital employed – measures the performance of management
C   Current ratio – measures liquidity

4 **The correct answer is C**

A gearing ratio of 80% is a considered to be a high level of gearing and shows that a company has already got substantial debt finance. This means that it will have significant finance costs to pay and will have significant levels of debt to repay going forward. Therefore it is unlikely to receive further debt finance, without very high levels of interest attached to reflect the increased risk to the lender.

5 **The correct answer is D**

A bank overdraft is not liquid funds as the company is in overdraft.

The distractors are as follows:

A   Bills of exchange = liquid
B   Fixed term deposit = liquid
C   Short term investments = liquid

6 **The correct answer is A**

The quick ratio is:

$$\frac{(\text{current assets} - \text{inventory})}{\text{current liabilities}}$$

This is similar to the current ratio which is

$$\frac{\text{current assets}}{\text{current liabilities}}$$

PRACTICE ANSWER BANK

7   **The correct answer is B**

Dividend cover is:

$$\frac{\text{earnings per share}}{\text{dividend per share}}$$

8   **The correct answer is C**

Inventory holding period is used to assess the company's efficiency as one of the working capital ratios.

9   **The correct answer is A**

The return on equity is one of the ratios used to assess profitability.

10   **The correct answer is D**

The P/E ratio, or price/earnings ratio is used by shareholders to compare different companies.

11   **The correct answer is A**

	$
Raw materials	62,300
Work-in-progress	35,010
Finished goods	42,140
Closing inventory	139,500

	$
Opening inventory	133,750
Purchases	1,652,000
Less: closing inventory	(139,500)
Cost of sales	1,646,250

Inventory holding period = (inventory/CoS) × 365 = 30.9 days = 31 days

12   **The correct answer is A**

Account receivables period
= (accounts receivable/sales) × 365
= ($506,800/$3,040,800) × 365 days
= 60.8
= 61 days

13   **The correct answer is D**

Account payables period
= (accounts payables/purchases) × 365
= ($299,570/$1,652,000) × 365 days
= 66.18
= 66 days

14   **The correct answer is C**

	Days
Accounts receivables days	61
Inventory holding days	31
Less: accounts payables days	(66)
Operating cycle	26

PRACTICE ANSWER BANK

15 **The correct answer is D**

	$
Closing inventory	139,500
Trade receivables	506,800
	646,300

	$
HMRC	33,420
Trade payables	299,570
	332,990

Current ratio
= current assets/current liabilities
= $647,560/$332,990
= 1.95

16 **The correct answer is C**

Quick ratio
= (current assets − inventory)/current liabilities
= 506,800/332,990
= 1.53

Chapter 22 Statement of Cash Flows

1 **The correct answer is C**

Cash flows from employment activities is not a section under IAS 7.

2 **The correct answer is A**

The current account balance is 'cash'. The other options are 'cash equivalents' as defined by IAS 7.

3 **The correct answer is D**

The inclusion of cash equivalents has been criticised because it does not reflect the way in which businesses are managed: in particular, the requirement that to be a cash equivalent an investment has to be within three months of maturity is considered unrealistic.

4 **The correct answer is B**

Cash flows from investing activities is one of the headings from IAS 7.

5 **The correct answer is B**

Non-current assets are investment, so the proceeds of selling non-current assets would be included in the cash flows from investing activities.

6 **The correct answer is C**

Payment of staff wages is part of the operating activities of the business. So this cash flow would be included in the cash flows from operating activities.

7 **The correct answer is D**

A long-term loan is part of the financing of a company, so cashflows from the loan would appear in the cash flows from financing activities section of the cash flow statement.

8 **The correct answer is C**

Tax payments are shown in the cash flows from operating activities.

9 **The correct answer is A**

	20X7	20X6	
	$'000	$'000	$'000
Share capital	3,500	1,500	
Share premium	750	–	
	4,250	1,500	
Share issue			2,750
Loan stock	750	1,500	
Loan repayment			(750)
	5,000	3,000	2,000

There has been a $2,000,000 increase in financing for the year, or a $2,000,000 cash flow.

This can be broken down into a $2,750,000 cash inflow from a share issue and a $750,000 cash outflow for a loan repayment.

10 **The correct answer is A**

	$
Proceeds	62,000
Carrying amount	55,000
Profit on disposal	7,000

The items were sold for more than their carrying amount, therefore making a gain on disposal.

PRACTICE ANSWER BANK

11 The correct answer is B

The proceeds from disposal are shown in the cash flows from investing activities.

12 The correct answer is B

	$
Opening carrying amount	785,000
Less: carrying amount of assets disposed	(55,000)
	730,000
Closing carrying amount	835,000
Assets purchased	105,000

	$
Proceeds from disposal	62,000
Purchase of new assets	(105,000)
Net cash outflow	(43,000)

13 The correct answer is D

An increase in inventory means cash has been spent to increase inventory.

This is a cash outflow, which is negative.

14 The correct answer is A

An increase in payables means cash has not been used to pay credit suppliers.

This is a cash inflow and is a positive.

15 The correct answer is A

A decrease in receivables means that credit customers have been paying more.

This is a cash inflow and is a positive.

Exam question bank

FOUNDATION LEVEL

FOUNDATION UNIT

FINANCIAL ACCOUNTING

Exam Question Bank

There is ONE correct answer per question

Pass Exam–November 2021

1. Which of the following is NOT a qualitative characteristic of financial statements?

    A Understandability
    B Relevance
    C Comparability
    D Accruals

2. Which of the following best describes the qualitative characteristic of relevance?

    A Capable of influencing the decisions of users.
    B Complete, neutral, free from error
    C Creditable and reliable
    D Provided within a suitable timescale

3. Which of the following is the definition of an asset?

    A A present economic resource controlled by the entity as a result of past events
    B A present economic resource owned by the entity as a result of past events
    C Tangible resources controlled by an entity as a result of a past event and from which future economic benefits are expected to flow to the entity
    D Resources that will be controlled by an entity in the future and from which future economic benefits are expected to flow to the entity.

4. An owner invests personal cash into their business. What will this do?

    A Decrease assets
    B Decrease liabilities
    C Increase capital
    D Decrease capital

5. Tim Orange has the following items in his business: Cash of £4,750, accounts payable of £14,500, accounts receivable of £22,100 and inventory of £6,500. How much are Tim's assets and liabilities?

    A Assets £4,750   Liabilities £43,100
    B Assets £19,250   Liabilities £28,600
    C Assets £33,350   Liabilities £14,500
    D Assets £25,750   Liabilities £22,100

6. Which of the following is classified as revenue expenditure?

    A Purchase of a motor vehicle
    B Payment of rent
    C Payment of the owner's personal expenses
    D None of the above

7. Apple Ltd has the following information:

Opening receivables balances at 1 January	£18,600
Credit Sales for January	£9,100
Cash Sales for January	£700
Credit Sales returns for January	£800
Receipts from receivables in January	£7,800

    What is the figure for closing receivables at the end of January?

    A £2,500
    B £19,100
    C £19,800
    D £20,700

8   A business is currently showing a loss for the year of £2,350. A reduction in the allowance for doubtful debts of £150 needs to be made, and a further irrecoverable debt of £70 should be written off. After these adjustments what will the loss be?

    A   £2,130
    B   £2,270
    C   £2,430
    D   £2,570

9   A trial balance fails to agree by £27 and the difference is placed in the suspense account. Later, it is discovered that a payment for vehicle repairs of £63 has been entered in the repairs account as £36. Which of these will correct the error?

    A   Debit Suspense £36   Credit Suspense £36
    B   Debit Suspense £27   Credit Vehicle Repairs £27
    C   Debit Vehicle repairs £27   Credit Bank £27
    D   Debit Vehicle repairs £27   Credit Suspense £27

10 At 31 March 2020, rent prepaid was £600. During the year ended 31 March 2021 rent paid was £18,000, including an invoice for £3,000 for the quarter ended 31 May 2021. What is the profit and loss account charge for rent payable for the year ended 31 March 2021?

    A   £18,000
    B   £16,600
    C   £12,000
    D   £15,600

11 Which of the following is not an allowable method for inventory valuation purposes?

    A   First in First out
    B   Standard Cost
    C   Retail Method
    D   Last in First out

12 Which of the following is not included in the valuation of cost for inventory valuation purposes?

    A   Purchase price of raw materials
    B   General administration overheads
    C   Production overheads
    D   Cost of conversion

13 J Smith has an item in inventory which cost £1,000 and can be sold for £1,200. However, before it can be sold it will require to be modified at a cost of £150. The expected selling costs of the item are an additional £100. How should this item be valued in inventory?

    A   £1,000
    B   £1,100
    C   £1,150
    D   £950

14 How often should the residual value and the useful life of an asset be reviewed?

    A   At each period end
    B   When factors suggest that the residual value or useful life has changed
    C   At each month end
    D   When an asset is disposed of

15 A car which cost £20,000 is being depreciated at 30% per annum using the reducing balance method. At the end of three years what will the carrying amount be?

 A £2,000
 B £6,860
 C £13,140
 D £18,000

16 A machine cost £9,000. It had an expected useful life of 5 years and an expected residual value of £1,000. It is depreciated using the straight line method. A full years depreciation is charged in the year of purchase and none in the year of sale. During year 4 it is sold for £3,000. What is the profit/loss on disposal?

 A Loss of £1,200
 B Profit of £1,200
 C Loss of £400
 D Profit of £400

17 Which one of the following would be shown in the Other Comprehensive Income section of the Statement of profit or loss and other comprehensive income?

 A Receipt of rental income
 B Profit on sale of an investment
 C Discounts received
 D Gain on revaluation of a non-current asset.

18 A company has authorised share capital of £500,000, made up of 1 million £0.50 shares. The issued share capital is £300,000. A dividend of 5p per share is declared and approved. At what value will the dividend be included in the financial statements?

 A £25,000
 B £50,000
 C £15,000
 D £30,000

19 A company has opening inventory of £10,000, closing inventory of £9,000, purchases of £40,000, carriage inwards of £800, carriage outwards of £500 and purchases returns of £500. What is the turnover for the period if the company has a mark-up of 20% on cost of sales?

 A £41,300
 B £49,560
 C £51,625
 D £50,260

20 Payments to shareholders would be shown in the financial statements of a company as:

 A A movement in the Statement of Changes in Equity
 B An expense in the Statement of Profit and Loss
 C A current asset
 D Share capital

21 Jade Ltd has non-current assets on 1 January with a net book value of £356,000. During the year an asset was sold for £50,000, generating a profit of £7,000. There were no other disposals. The closing net book value of non-current assets on 31 December was £421,000. What were the additions to non-current assets during the year?

 A £175,000
 B £168,000
 C £132,000
 D £182,000

22 Which of the following is NOT a feature of a limited company?

    A   Separate legal personality
    B   Limited Liability of shareholders
    C   Protection for directors from criminal prosecution
    D   Perpetual succession

23 Which of the following best describes liquidity?

    A   The level of current assets compared to current liabilities
    B   The level of non-current assets compared to non-current liabilities
    C   The level of borrowing compared to equity
    D   The level of total assets to total liabilities

24 Pear plc has a long term loan of £2,500,000 and issued ordinary share capital and reserves totalling £7,000,000. What is the gearing ratio?

    A   34.7%
    B   42.6%
    C   26.3%
    D   52.5%

25 During the year Apple made cash sales of £25,000 and credit sales of £233,000. At the year end closing receivables were £22,400 and other receivables were £12,000. What were the receivables days at the year end?

    A   22.5 days
    B   35.1 days
    C   48.7 days
    D   53.9 days

Pass Exam–May 2022

1. Which of the following is the objective of financial accounting?

   A The objective of financial accounting is to maximise profits and minimise losses.

   B The objective of financial accounting is to form an independent opinion on the financial statements.

   C The objective of financial accounting is to provide reports for internal use.

   D The objective of financial accounting is to record, analyse and summarise financial data.

2. Which of the following is NOT correct in relation to the International Accounting Standards Board?

   A It is an independent private sector body.
   B Its objective is to achieve uniformity in accounting principles used by organisations.
   C It aims to raise the standard of financial reporting
   D It aims to promote individual national standards of financial reporting.

3. Which of the following is the definition of a liability?

   A A present obligation of the entity to transfer an economic resource as a result of past events.

   B A future obligation of the entity to transfer an economic resource as a result of past events.

   C A present obligation of the entity to transfer an economic resource as a result of past or future events.

   D A present or future obligation of the entity to transfer an economic resource as a result of past events.

4. What is the sales return daybook used to record?

   A Sales invoices
   B Sales credit notes
   C Purchase invoices
   D Purchase credit notes.

5. On 1 January Catherine Grey had a van costing $20,000, inventory of $7,000, receivables of $10,000 and payables of $8,000. During the year ended 31 December, Catherine made a profit of $12,000 and took drawings of $5,000. How much capital does Catherine have at 31 December?

   A $29,000
   B $46,000
   C $36,000
   D $41,000

6. What is the double entry to record a credit purchase of $600?

   A Debit payables $600   Credit purchases $600
   B Debit purchases $600   Credit payables $600
   C Debit inventory $600   Credit payables $600
   D Debit purchases $600   Credit cash $600

7. Which of the following is NOT correct in relation to a trial balance?

   A The trial balance is a list of ledger balances shown in debit and credit columns.

   B The trial balance is used as a basis for preparing a statement or profit or loss and other comprehensive income and a statement of financial position.

   C A trial balance can be used to test the accuracy of the accounting records.

   D The trial balance provides information about the cash receipts, cash payments and net change in cash of the balance.

8   A business has a trade receivables control account of $25,000 on 31 December. The list of trade receivables totals $23,500. Investigations find the following errors: sales of $1,500 and credit notes of $750 have been omitted from the control account and a receivables balance of $2,250 has been omitted from the list of balances. What is the correct trade receivables balance on 31 December?

   A $26,500
   B $25,750
   C $25,000
   D $23,500

9   A business has revenue of $100,000 with a mark-up of 25% on cost of sales. If opening inventory is $10,000 and closing inventory is $8,000 what was the purchases figures?

   A $80,000
   B $82,000
   C $73,000
   D $78,000

10 On 31 December 2021, rent of $3,000 had been accrued. The rent paid during the year was $24,000 and on 1 January 2021 there had been an opening prepayment of $2,000.

   What is the rental charge for the year?

   A $25,000
   B $29,000
   C $24,000
   D $19,000

11 Which of the following is NOT an example of an activity associated with research?

   A   Activities aimed at obtaining new knowledge
   B   Search for product or process alternatives
   C   Search for applications of research findings
   D   Design, construction and testing of pre-production prototypes and models

12 A non-current asset with a cost of $20,000 and accumulated depreciation of $5,000 is given in part exchange for a new asset costing $32,000. The company had to pay a balancing payment of $20,000 in addition to the trade in of the existing asset. What will be included in the statement of profit or loss and other comprehensive income?

   A   Profit on disposal of $3,000
   B   Loss on disposal of $3,000
   C   Profit on disposal of $5,000
   D   Profit on disposal of $8,000

13 Which of the following is NOT an example of subsequent expenditure which would be added to the carrying amount of the asset?

   A   Modification to plant extending its useful life.
   B   Modification to plant increasing its capacity.
   C   Upgrade of machine parts to improve the quality of output
   D   Maintenance of plant

14 A company has a policy of making a general allowance of 5% for receivables. The year-end receivables figure was $240,000 and the directors then decide to write off a further $20,000 as bad debts. What will the year end allowance for receivables be?

   A $11,000
   B $12,000
   C $31,000
   D $32,000

15 A cheque paid to you, but not yet passed through the bank statement is which of the following?

   A   A dishonoured cheque
   B   A credit transfer
   C   A standing order
   D   An unpresented lodgement

16 A firm bought a machine for $3,200. It is to be depreciated at a rate of 25 per cent using the reducing balance method. After two years it was sold for $1,200. What is the profit/loss on disposal?

   A   Loss of $600
   B   Profit of $600
   C   Loss of $400
   D   Profit of $400

17 A page in the purchase daybook has been added up to $29,700 instead of $29,250.

   Which of the following would correct this error?

   A   Debit sales $450   Credit receivables ledger $450
   B   Debit purchases $450   Credit payables ledger $450
   C   Debit receivables ledger $450 Credit purchases $450
   D   Debit payables ledger $450   Credit purchases $450

18 A company with an authorised share capital of 25,000 $1 shares and 10,000 issued shares prior to the rights issue makes a rights issue of 1 for 5 at a price of $1.50. What is the correct double entry for the rights issue?

   A   Debit bank $15,000   Credit share capital $10,000   Credit share premium $5,000
   B   Debit bank $3,000   Credit share capital $3,000
   C   Debit bank $3,000   Credit share capital $2,000   Credit retained earnings $1,000
   D   Debit bank $3,000   Credit share capital $2,000   Credit share premium $1,000

19 Given opening capital of $16,500, closing capital of $12,350 and drawings of $3,300 then which of the following is true?

   A   There was a profit for the year of $850
   B   There was a loss for the year of $850
   C   There was a profit for the year of $7,450
   D   There was a loss for the year of $7,450

20 Management salaries would be shown in the financial statements of a company as:

   A   A movement in the statement of changes in equity
   B   An administrative expense in the statement of profit or loss
   C   Finance cost in the statement of profit or loss
   D   Cost of sales

21 Jade Ltd has non-current assets on 1 January with a net book value of $385,000. There were additions during the year of $55,000. During the year an asset was sold for a profit on disposal of $8,000 and depreciation of $45,000 was charged. The closing net book value of non-current assets on 31 December was $360,000. What were the proceeds from the sale of the non-current assets during the year?

    A $27,000
    B $43,000
    C $35,000
    D $70,000

22 A company has 10,000 $1 6% preference shares and the profit after tax for the current year is $12,600. If it retains 40% of its earnings, what will the ordinary dividend be for this financial year?

    A $7,560
    B $4,800
    C $7,200
    D $5,040

23 Which of the following best describes gearing?

    A   The measure of the proportion of a company's capital that is debt.
    B   The level of non-current assets compared to non-current liabilities
    C   The measure of the proportion of a company's capital that is equity.
    D   The level of total assets to total liabilities

24 Profit before interest and tax for the year is $275,000. The total assets of the company are $3,250,000 with current liabilities of $200,000. What is the return on capital employed?

    A   7.97%
    B   8.46%
    C   9.02%
    D   14.6%

25 Which of the following is NOT a liquid asset?

    A   Cash
    B   Non-current assets
    C   Trade receivables
    D   Bills of exchange receivable

Pass Exam–November 2022

1. Which of the following is a possible argument **against** universal adoption of accounting standards?

    A   Accounting standards reduce or eliminate confusing variations in the methods used to prepare accounts.

    B   Accounting standards provide a focal point for debate and discussions about accounting practice.

    C   Accounting standards are a less rigid alternative to enforcing conformity by means of legislation.

    D   Accounting standards may be subject to lobbying or government pressure.

2. Which of the following is NOT correct in relation to the Conceptual Framework?

    A   If there is conflict, the Conceptual Framework overrules any individual IFRS.

    B   It assists the IASB to develop IFRS standards based on consistent concepts.

    C   It aims to assist all parties to understand and interpret IFRS standards.

    D   It assists preparers to develop consistent accounting policies when no Standard applies to a particular transaction or other event.

3. Which of the following best describes faithful representation?

    A   Complete, neutral and free from error.
    B   Capable of influencing the decisions of users.
    C   Provided within a suitable timescale.
    D   Classified, characterised and presented clearly and concisely.

4. What is the process of capturing for inclusion an item that meets the definition of one of the elements of financial statements?

    A   Presentation.
    B   Recognition.
    C   Derecognition.
    D   Measurement.

5. Petty cash is controlled under an imprest system. The imprest amount is $200. At the end of the period, there is $95 remaining in petty cash. How much needs to be reimbursed under the imprest system?

    A $200.
    B $95.
    C $105.
    D $295.

6. Which of these is a ledger for suppliers' personal accounts?

    A   Trade receivables ledger.
    B   Trade payables ledger.
    C   General ledger.
    D   Nominal ledger.

7   Sales of goods for $750 net which are subject to VAT at 20% occur. Which of the following correctly records the credit sale?

  A   Debit receivables $625   Debit VAT $125   Credit sales $750
  B   Debit receivables $750   Debit VAT $150   Credit sales $900
  C   Debit receivables $750   Credit VAT $125 Credit sales $650
  D   Debit receivables $900   Credit sales $750 Credit VAT $150

8   A company's bank statement shows $825 direct debits and $563 interest received, neither of which have been recorded in the cash book. In addition, there are outstanding payments not yet appearing on the bank statement of $367. If the cash book shows a debit balance of $1,024, what balance appears on the bank statement?

  A $395.
  B $1,129.
  C $762.
  D $1,653.

9   A supplier statement shows a balance of $855 and the balance on the purchase ledger shows a balance of $1,235 on the same date. Which of the following may, in isolation, explain this difference?

  A   A settlement discount has been taken by the purchasing company but not yet given by the supplier.

  B   A payment had been made to the supplier, but was in transit, and had not yet been received by the supplier at the given date.

  C   An error had been made when entering an invoice on the purchase ledger and it was entered as $1,200 instead of $1,580.

  D   A credit note has been issued by the supplier but not yet received by the purchasing company.

10 What is the name of an error when two digits in an amount are accidentally recorded the wrong way round?

  A   Error of commission.
  B   Transposition error.
  C   Error of principle.
  D   Error of omission.

11 A business has an opening balance of $24,000 trade payables with credit purchases during the period of $523,000. Cash purchases of $30,000 were also made. If the closing balance of trade payables at the end of the period was $35,000, how much was paid to credit suppliers during the period?

  A $582,000.
  B $534,000.
  C $542,000.
  D $512,000.

12 A business has revenue of $200,000 with a margin of 25% of all sales. If purchases for the period were $120,000 and closing inventory was $20,000 what was the opening inventory at the beginning of the period?

  A $60,000.
  B $50,000.
  C $10,000.
  D $30,000.

13 A firm has the following transactions for its product Qut. There was no opening inventory. Using FIFO calculate the gross profit for the period.

10 January	Purchase 20 units at $20 per unit
15 January	Sell 10 units at $35 per unit
20 January	Purchase 20 units at $22 per unit
24 January	Sell 12 units at £36 per unit
28 January	Purchase 5 units at $21 per unit

- A $320.
- B $303.
- C $444.
- D $338.

14 A company has a policy of making a general allowance of 5% for receivables. The year-end receivables figure was $140,000. The opening allowance for receivables was $9,000. What is the correct entry to record the movement in the allowance for receivables at the year end?

- A Debit allowance for receivables $2,000   Credit expense in SPLOCI $2,000
- B Debit allowance for receivables $7,000   Credit expense in SPLOCI $7,000
- C Debit expense in SPLOCI $7,000   Credit allowance for receivables $7,000
- D Debit expense in SPLOCI $2,000   Credit allowance for receivables $2,000

15 Where a transfer of resources in relation to a material contingent liability is not likely to be remote which of the following should be disclosed?

- (i) Description of the nature of the contingent liability.
- (ii) An estimate of the financial effect.
- (iii) An indication of the uncertainties that exist.
- (iv) The possibility of any reimbursement.

- A (i), (ii) and (iii) only.
- B (i) and (ii) only.
- C (i), (ii) and (iv) only.
- D (i), (ii), (iii) and (iv).

16 A business with a 31 December year end purchased a new asset on 1 June at a cost of $24,000. The expected life of the asset is four years and the residual value is $4,800. Assets are depreciated on a straight line basis and depreciation is calculated on a pro rata basis. What is the depreciation charge for the year for this asset?

- A $2,800.
- B $4,800.
- C $3,500.
- D $1,400.

17 Which of these is the recoverable amount of an asset according in IAS 16?

- A The estimated amount that an entity would currently obtain from disposal of the asset, after deducting the estimated costs of disposal, if the asset were already of the age and in the condition expected at the end of its useful life.

- B The price that would be received to sell an asset or paid to transfer a liability in an orderly transaction between market participants at the measurement date.

- C The amount at which an asset is recognised after deducting any accumulated depreciation and accumulated impairment losses.

- D The higher of an asset's fair value less costs to sell and its value in use.

18 A company with issued share capital of 50,000 shares of $1 each and 10,000 6% preference shares of $1 each made profits after tax of $23,000. The management decided to retain 40% of the profits after tax and preference dividend. What was the amount of ordinary dividend paid?

   A $8,960.
   B $13,800.
   C $14,16.
   D $13,440.

19 Which standard provides guidance on the recognition of revenue which is based upon the transfer of control of goods and services?

   A   IAS 37.
   B   IFRS 15.
   C   IAS 1.
   D   IAS 16.

20 What is the operating cycle for the company based on the following information?

	$
Inventory	200,000
Credit Purchases	800,000
Trade receivables	250,000
Trade payables	160,000
Cost of sales	840,000
Credit sales	1,200,000

   A   162.9 days.
   B   89.9 days.
   C   94.2 days.
   D   93.4 days.

21 A company has earnings of $400,000 and a dividend cover of 5 times. Given that the company has share capital of $50,000 made up of shares with a nominal value of $0.50 each and a current share price of $5.00 what is the dividend yield?

   A   32%.
   B   16%.
   C   8%.
   D   0.16%.

22 A company had property, plant and equipment with an opening net book value of $75,000 and depreciation charge of $15,000 with a closing net book value of $86,000. During the year the company disposed of assets for $23,000 making a gain on disposal of $2,000. What figure would appear in the cash flow statement as payments to acquire property, plant and equipment, assuming all amounts paid during the year?

   A $51,000.
   B $32,000.
   C $47,000.
   D $62,000.

23 An increase in receivables will be shown on the statement of cash flows as a:

   A   Negative because it represents a decrease in cash available.
   B   Negative because it represents an increase in cash available.
   C   Positive because it represents a decrease in cash available.
   D   Positive because it represents an increase in cash available.

24 A debit balance at the start of the year on an expense account indicates which of the following?

- A   A liability and an expense prepaid.
- B   A liability and an expense accrued.
- C   An asset and an expense prepaid.
- D   An asset and an expense accrued.

25 The owner of a business withdraws goods for personal use. What would the double entry for this transaction be?

- A   Debit drawings, credit cash.
- B   Debit drawings, credit purchases.
- C   Debit purchases, credit drawings.
- D   Debit cash, credit drawings.

Pass Exam–May 2023

1. Which of the following is the best definition of financial reporting?

    A   Financial reporting is a way of presenting accounting information in the form most helpful to management.

    B   Financial reporting is a way of planning and controlling the resources of the business.

    C   Financial reporting is a way of analysing data to provide information as a basis for managerial action.

    D   Financial reporting is a way of recording, analysing and summarising financial data in financial statements.

2. Which body produces International Financial Reporting Standards?

    A   International Accounting Standards Board.
    B   Public Company Accounting Oversight Board.
    C   International Auditing and Assurance Standards Board.
    D   Financial Reporting Council.

3. Which of the following is NOT a purpose of the IASB Conceptual Framework?

    A   Assists the development of International Financial Reporting Standards based on consistent concepts.

    B   Assists preparers to develop consistent accounting policies.

    C   Assists the development of highly detailed standards rather than general principles.

    D   Assists all parties to understand and interpret the Standards.

4. What is the process of removing an item that no longer meets the definition of one of the elements of financial statements?

    A   Presentation.
    B   Recognition.
    C   Derecognition.
    D   Measurement.

5. A list of goods that a business has received from a supplier, usually prepared by the business's own warehouse is a:

    A   Goods received note.
    B   Goods despatched note.
    C   Purchase order.
    D   Remittance advice.

6. When might a debit note be issued?

    A   To list all the invoices owed by a customer.
    B   To accompany a payment, detailing which invoices have been paid.
    C   To a supplier as a means of formally requesting a credit note.
    D   To make a written offer to a customer to deliver goods for a certain amount of money.

7. A business in its first period of trading charges $5,000 of VAT on its sales and suffers $2,600 of VAT on its purchases which includes $250 VAT on business entertaining of customers. How will the closing VAT balance be represented?

    A $2,650 liability.
    B $2,650 asset.
    C $2,400 liability.
    D $2,400 asset.

8   When VAT is not recoverable on the cost of a motor car, it should be:

    A   Deducted from the cost of the asset capitalised.
    B   Included in the cost of the asset capitalised.
    C   Deducted from output tax for the period.
    D   Written off to the statement of profit or loss as an expense.

9   Electricity paid during the year is $16,000. There was an opening prepayment of $500. The bill for the quarter ended 31 January 20X2 was received in February 20X2 for $4,500. What is the electricity charge in the statement of profit or loss and other comprehensive income for the year ended 31 December 20X1?

    A $20,000.
    B $21,000.
    C $18,500.
    D $19,500.

10 What is the name of an error when the bookkeeper makes a mistake in carrying out his or her task of recording transactions in the accounts?

    A   Error of commission.
    B   Financial error.
    C   Compensating error.
    D   Error of omission.

11 A bank statement shows money in the bank of $3,500. An examination of the statement shows a $700 cheque paid in per the cash book but not on the bank statement and a $1,650 cheque paid out but not yet on the statement. In addition, the cash book shows deposit interest received of $100 but this is not yet on the statement. What is the balance on the cash book?

    A $2,650.
    B $4,550.
    C $2,450.
    D $4,350.

12 The total of the balances in a company's trade receivables ledger is $900 more than the debit balance on the trade receivables control account. Which one of the following errors could by itself account for the discrepancy?

    A   Credit notes sent to customers totalling $900 have been omitted from the general ledger.

    B   One trade receivables ledger account with a credit balance of $900 has been treated as a debit balance.

    C   The sales day book has been undercast by $900.

    D   The cash receipts book has been undercast by $900.

13 Which of the following are deducted from revenue when it is probable that the customer will avail of the settlement discount?

    A   Trade discounts allowed and settlement discounts given to customers.
    B   Trade discounts received and settlement discounts given to customers.
    C   Trade discounts allowed only.
    D   Trade discounts received only.

14 A company has budgeted sales for the coming year of $240,000. The company achieves a constant gross mark up of 20% and plans to reduce the inventory level by $15,000 over the year. What will the purchases for the year be?

    A $215,000.
    B $185,000.
    C $177,000.
    D $207,000.

15 Included in closing inventory are 6,000 units of Product A at a cost of $42,000 and 4,000 units of Product B at a cost of $52,000. Calculate the closing inventory valuation.

	Product A	Product B
Number of units	6,000	4,000
Cost per unit incurred	$7	$13
Estimated further costs to completion per unit	$6	$9
Estimated selling costs per unit	$2	$4
Estimated selling price per unit	$14	$30

    A $88,000.
    B $94,000.
    C $124,000.
    D $104,000.

16 Irrecoverable bad debts are $4,500. Trade receivables at the year-end are $200,000, before deduction of the irrecoverable bad debts. If an allowance of 5% is required, what is the expense for irrecoverable bad debts and allowance for receivables in the statement of profit or loss?

    A $14,500.
    B $10,000.
    C $14,275.
    D $9,775.

17 A machine with a cost of $45,000 and accumulated depreciation of $15,000 is given in part exchange for a new machine, costing $60,000. The company has to pay a balancing amount of $34,000 by cheque. What will be included in the statement of profit or loss and other comprehensive income?

    A   Gain on disposal of $1,000.
    B   Loss on disposal of $1,000.
    C   Gain on disposal of $4,000.
    D   Loss on disposal of $4,000.

18 An intangible asset with an indefinite useful life should be:

    A   Left as cost in the financial statements.
    B   Depreciated over its useful life.
    C   Amortised.
    D   Subject to an annual impairment review.

19 Which of the following would NOT appear in a Statement of changes in equity?

    A   Dividends.
    B   Issue of share capital.
    C   Revaluation surplus.
    D   Taxation.

20 A company has a balance on the share premium account of $20,000 and on retained earnings of $60,000. The issued share capital is 100,000 50c shares. The company decides to make a bonus issue of one bonus share for every two shares. What are the closing balances on the share premium and retained earnings?

	Share premium	Retained earnings
A	$Nil.	$55,000.
B	$Nil.	$30,000.
C	$20,000.	$10,000.
D	$20,000.	$35,000.

21 Which accounting standard explains when to recognise revenue?

A   IAS 37.
B   IAS 1.
C   IAS 16.
D   IFRS 15.

22 A company had an opening taxation liability of $50,000 and a taxation charge for the period of $35,000. The closing taxation balance liability was $38,000. What figure would appear in the cash flow statement as payments for taxation?

A $53,000.
B $50,000.
C $47,000.
D $38,000.

23 A decrease in inventory will be shown on the statement of cash flows as a:

A   Negative because it represents a decrease in cash available.
B   Negative because it represents an increase in cash available.
C   Positive because it represents a decrease in cash available.
D   Positive because it represents an increase in cash available.

24 Which of the following industries would normally have a low average receivables collection period?

A   A supermarket.
B   A manufacturer of plant and machinery.
C   A construction business.
D   A furniture shop who offers credit deals to customers.

25 A company with 100,000 $1 ordinary shares had earnings for the year of $250,000 and dividends of $50,000. What was the dividend cover?

A   2.5.
B   2.
C   5.
D   1.

Pass Exam–November 2023

1. Which of the following develops IFRSs through an international process that involves the accounting profession, the preparers and users of financial statements and national standard-setting bodies?

    A   IFRS Advisory Council.
    B   IFRS Interpretations Committee.
    C   IFRS Foundation.
    D   IASB.

2. Which of the following are the providers of risk capital for an entity?

    A   Investors.
    B   Lenders.
    C   Suppliers.
    D   Government.

3. Which of the following is **NOT** a disadvantage of the Conceptual Framework?

    A   It is difficult to devise a Conceptual Framework to suit all users.
    B   There may be a need for a variety of accounting standards for different purposes given the diversity of user requirements.
    C   It can bolster standard setters against political pressure from lobby groups.
    D   It is not clear that the Conceptual Framework makes the task of preparing and implementing standards easier than without a framework.

4. What is the characteristic of having information available to decision-makers at a date that can influence their decisions known as?

    A   Comparability.
    B   Verifiability.
    C   Timeliness.
    D   Understandability.

5. A list of goods that a business has sent out to a customer, normally signed by the customer on receipt of the goods is a:

    A   Goods received note.
    B   Goods despatched note.
    C   Purchase order.
    D   Remittance advice.

6. Which of the following is **NOT** a book of prime entry?

    A   Purchase daybook.
    B   Sales daybook.
    C   Sales invoice.
    D   Journal.

EXAM QUESTION BANK

7 A business operates an imprest petty cash system with the imprest amount of $200.00. At the end of the period the three analysis columns of the petty cash book were as follow:

	$
Column 1	28.53
Column 2	73.45
Column 3	52.00

How much cash is required to restore the imprest amount?

A $153.98.
B $46.02.
C $353.98.
D $246.02.

8 From the trial balance shown below, calculate the profit of this business.

	Debit $	Credit $
Bank loan		12,000
Cash at bank	6,000	
Revenue		18,000
Cost of sales	12,000	
Trade receivables	5,000	
Other expenses	2,000	
Trade payables		4,000
Van	8,000	
Bank loan interest	1,000	

A $4,000.
B $3,000.
C $6,000.
D $2,000.

9 If a business paid rent of $10,000 in advance for the year to 30 September 20X3 what is the prepayment in the accounts for the year to 31 December 20X2?

A $2,500.
B $10,000.
C   Nil.
D $7,500.

10 A business recently purchased ten machines originally priced at $2,000 each. A 15% trade discount was negotiated together with a 2% cash discount if payment was made within 10 days. Calculate the total trade discount and settlement discount obtained.

A   Trade discount $3,000   Settlement discount $340
B   Trade discount $300   Settlement discount $340
C   Trade discount $3,000   Settlement discount $400
D   Trade discount $300   Settlement discount $40

11 During a period, a business had the following transactions on the trade receivables control account. Revenue $154,000, cash received $60,000, contras $10,000. The closing balance carried forward was $122,000. What was the opening balance at the beginning of the period?

    A $38,000.
    B $28,000.
    C $18,000.
    D $84,000.

12 A business has the following transactions with its product Z.

Opening inventory: nil

1 July buys 10 units at $300 per unit
3 July sells 7 units at $400 per unit
14 July buys 15 units at $350 per unit
17 July sells 9 units at $500 per unit

Using FIFO calculate the closing inventory at 31 July.

    A $2,700.
    B $3,000.
    C $3,150.
    D $3,500.

13 Which of the following would be included in the cost of bringing inventories to their present location and condition?

    A   Storage costs which are necessary as part of the production process.
    B   Storage costs of finished goods.
    C   Administrative overheads.
    D   Selling costs.

14 At the year end, a business has an additional irrecoverable debt of $10,000 which must be removed from the trade receivables at the period end which are $500,000. The allowance for receivables brought forward from the previous period is $24,000. Calculate the movement in the allowance for receivables if an allowance for receivables of 4% is required.

    A   Increase by $4,400.
    B   Decrease by $4,400.
    C   Increase by $4,000.
    D   Decrease by $4,000.

15 During the year Company A gave a guarantee of certain borrowings for Company B whose financial condition was sound. Which disclosures are required unless the outflow of resources is remote?

    A   Description of the nature of the contingent liability, an estimate of the financial effect, an indication of the uncertainties that exist and the possibility of any reimbursement.

    B   A brief description of the contingent liability along with an estimate of its likely financial effect.

    C   No disclosures are required.

    D   A brief description of the nature of the contingent liability and an indication of the uncertainties that exist.

16 A lorry bought for a business cost $25000. It is expected to last for 5 years and to be sold for scrap for $8,000. Calculate the difference between the depreciation in year 3 calculated on a straight-line method and the reducing balance method using 20%

    A $1,800.
    B $800.
    C $200.
    D $1,224.

17 Which of the following statements is correct?

    A   All non-current assets should be revalued each year.

    B   Management can choose which non-current assets in a class of non-current assets should be revalued.

    C   Non-current assets should always be included at cost not valuation.

    D   Non-current assets may be revalued at the discretion of management. Once revaluation has occurred it must be repeated regularly for all non-current assets in a class.

18 Which of the following is **NOT** correct in relation to preference shares?

    A   Preference shareholders have a priority right over ordinary shareholders to a return of their capital if the company goes into liquidation.

    B   Preference shares confer certain preferential rights on the holder.

    C   If preference shares are cumulative the company must make good any arrears of preference dividends unpaid in previous years.

    D   Preference shares carry a right to vote.

19 Consider the extract from an income statement for a business. Calculate the interest cover.

	$
Profit before interest and tax	200,000
Interest	(50,000)
Taxable profit	150,000
Taxation at 20%	(30,000)
Profit for the period	120,000

    A   2.4 times.
    B   3 times.
    C   5 times.
    D   4 times.

20 A company has the following information about property, plant and equipment.

	20X9 $000	20X8 $000
Cost	600	450
Accumulated depreciation	300	250
Carrying amount	300	200

Plant with a carrying value of $80,000 (original cost $150,000) was sold for $70,000 during the year. What is the net cash flow from investing activities for the year 20X9, assuming all additions were paid in full?

- A $230,000.
- B $300,000.
- C $220,000.
- D $180,000.

21 Which of the following does **NOT** form part of shareholders' equity?

- A Revaluation surplus.
- B Retained earnings.
- C Share premium.
- D Bonds.

22 Which of the following ratios is used to assess the efficiency of a company?

- A Gearing ratio.
- B Quick ratio.
- C Inventory holding period.
- D Dividend cover ratio.

23 A decrease in receivables will be shown on the statement of cash flows as a:

- A Negative because it represents a decrease in cash available.
- B Negative because it represents an increase in cash available.
- C Positive because it represents a decrease in cash available.
- D Positive because it represents an increase in cash available.

24 Which of the following industries would normally have a low gross profit margin compared to the others?

- A A supermarket.
- B A manufacturer of plant and machinery.
- C A construction business.
- D A furniture shop.

25 A company has a mark-up of 20%. During a year its revenue was $240,000 with opening inventory of $20,000 and closing inventory of $30,000. What were the purchases during the year?

- A $190,000.
- B $202,000.
- C $210,000.
- D $182,000.

Exam answer bank

FOUNDATION LEVEL

FOUNDATION UNIT

FINANCIAL ACCOUNTING

Exam Answer Bank

There is **ONE** correct answer per question

Pass Exam–November 2021

1 The correct answer is D

Accruals is an accounting concept, not a qualitative characteristic of financial statements

The distractors are as follows:

- A This is a qualitative characteristic
- B This is a qualitative characteristic
- C This is a qualitative characteristic

2 The correct answer is A

The distractors are as follows:

- B This is faithful representation
- C This is verifiable
- D This is timeliness

3 The correct answer is A

The definition is included in the conceptual framework.

The distractors are as follows:

- B Legal ownership is not required, but control
- C All resources are included, not just tangible
- D The economic resource must be present, not future.

4 The correct answer is C

An investment of personal cash into the business will increase the assets of the business and increase the capital.

The distractors are as follows:

- A An investment of personal cash will INCREASE assets
- B There will be no impact on liabilities
- D The input of personal cash will INCREASE capital

5 The correct answer is C

Cash, accounts receivable and inventory are assets. Accounts payable are liabilities.

The distractors are as follows:

- A Cash, accounts receivable and inventory are assets. Accounts payable are liabilities.
- B Cash, accounts receivable and inventory are assets. Accounts payable are liabilities.
- D Cash, accounts receivable and inventory are assets. Accounts payable are liabilities.

6 The correct answer is B

Rent is a revenue expenditure

The distractors are as follows:

- A The purchase of a motor vehicle is a capital asset
- C Payment of personal expenses are drawings
- D Rent is a revenue expense

EXAM ANSWER BANK

7 **The correct answer is B**

Opening receivables + Credit Sales – Credit Sales returns – Receivables Receipts = Closing receivables

The distractors are as follows:

- A Opening receivables + Credit Sales – Credit Sales returns – Receivables Receipts = Closing receivables
- C Opening receivables + Credit Sales – Credit Sales returns – Receivables Receipts = Closing receivables
- D Opening receivables + Credit Sales – Credit Sales returns – Receivables Receipts = Closing receivables

8 **The correct answer is B**

The loss of £2,350 will be reduced by the reduction in the allowance of £150 and then increased by the further irrecoverable debts of £70

The distractors are as follows:

- A The loss of £2,350 will be reduced by the reduction in the allowance of £150 and then increased by the further irrecoverable debts of £70
- C The loss of £2,350 will be reduced by the reduction in the allowance of £150 and then increased by the further irrecoverable debts of £70
- D The loss of £2,350 will be reduced by the reduction in the allowance of £150 and then increased by the further irrecoverable debts of £70

9 **The correct answer is D**

The vehicle repairs are understated by the difference between £63 and £36 so a debit to vehicle repairs and a credit to remove from suspense.

The distractors are as follows:

- A The vehicle repairs are understated by the difference between £63 and £36 so a debit to repairs and a credit to remove from suspense
- B The vehicle repairs are understated by the difference between £63 and £36 so a debit to repairs and a credit to remove from suspense
- C The vehicle repairs are understated by the difference between £63 and £36 so a debit to repairs and a credit to remove from suspense

10 **The correct answer is B**

Payment of £18,000 less prepayment of 2 months of £2,000 add opening prepayment of £600

The distractors are as follows:

- A Payment of £18,000 less prepayment of 2 months of £2,000 add opening prepayment of £600
- C Payment of £18,000 less prepayment of 2 months of £2,000 add opening prepayment of £600
- D Payment of £18,000 less prepayment of 2 months of £2,000 add opening prepayment of £600

EXAM ANSWER BANK

11 **The correct answer is D**

LIFO is not a permitted inventory valuation method under IAS 2

The distractors are as follows:

A   Allowed as permitted inventory valuation method.
B   Allowed as permitted inventory valuation method.
C   Allowed as permitted inventory valuation method.

12 **The correct answer is B**

General administration overheads are specifically excluded from the cost of production

The distractors are as follows:

A   The cost of purchase is included in inventory, however general administration costs are excluded.

C   Production overheads are included in the cost of inventory, however general administration overheads are excluded.

D   Costs of purchase and costs of conversion are included in the cost of inventory, however general administration overheads are excluded.

13 **The correct answer is D**

The NRV of £1200 - £150-£100 is lower than the cost of £1,000.

The distractors are as follows:

A   The NRV of £1,200 - £150-£100 is lower than the cost of £1,000.
B   The NRV of £1,200 - £150-£100 is lower than the cost of £1,000.
C   The NRV of £1,200 - £150-£100 is lower than the cost of £1,000.

14 **The correct answer is A**

IAS 16 suggests that residual value and the useful life of an asset should be reviewed annually.

The distractors are as follows:

B   IAS 16 suggests that residual value and the useful life of an asset should be reviewed annually.

C   IAS 16 suggests that residual value and the useful life of an asset should be reviewed annually.

D   IAS 16 suggests that residual value and the useful life of an asset should be reviewed annually.

15 **The correct answer is B**

NBV at end of 3 years will be £20,000 - £6,000 - £4,200 - £2,940

The distractors are as follows:

A   NBV at end of 3 years will be £20,000 - £6,000 - £4,200 - £2,940
C   NBV at end of 3 years will be £20,000 - £6,000 - £4,200 - £2,940
D   NBV at end of 3 years will be £20,000 - £6,000 - £4,200 - £2,940

16 **The correct answer is A**

NBV is £9,000 - £1,600 - £1,600 - £1,600 = £4,200. This exceeds the proceeds by £1,200.

The distractors are as follows:

B   NBV is £9,000 - £1,600 - £1,600 - £1,600 = £4,200. This exceeds the proceeds by £1,200.
C   NBV is £9,000 - £1,600 - £1,600 - £1,600 = £4,200. This exceeds the proceeds by £1,200.
D   NBV is £9,000 - £1,600 - £1,600 - £1,600 = £4,200. This exceeds the proceeds by £1,200.

17 **The correct answer is D**

A gain on revaluation is an unrealised gain, so appears separate from profit in other comprehensive income

The distractors are as follows:

A   This is income so appears in the Statement of Profit or loss. A revaluation gain is unrealised and appears in the Other Comprehensive Income

B   This is income so appears in the Statement of Profit or loss. A revaluation gain is unrealised and appears in the Other Comprehensive Income section.

C   This is income so appears in the Statement of Profit or loss. A revaluation gain is unrealised and appears in the Other Comprehensive Income section.

18 **The correct answer is D**

There are 600,000 shares in issue with a nominal value of £0.50 each times a dividend of £0.05 per share.

The distractors are as follows:

A   The dividend must be based on issued share capital of £300,000
B   The dividend must be based on issued share capital of £300,000.
C   The dividend must be based on 6,000,000 share of £0.50 each.

19 **The correct answer is B**

Cost of sales is £10,000 + £40,000 - £500 + £800 - £9,000 = £41,300 Add a mark up of 20% to reach £49,560

The distractors are as follows:

A   Cost of sales is £10,000 + £40,000 - £500 + £800 - £9,000 = £41,300 Add a mark up of 20% to reach £49,560

C   Cost of sales is £10,000 + £40,000 - £500 + £800 - £9,000 = £41,300 Add a mark up of 20% to reach £49,560

D   Cost of sales is £10,000 + £40,000 - £500 + £800 - £9,000 = £41,300 Add a mark up of 20% to reach £49,560

20 **The correct answer is A**

Dividends are a movement in the Statement of Changes in Equity

The distractors are as follows:

B   Dividends are not business expenses therefore do not appear in the Statement of Profit and Loss.

C   Dividends are not assets of the business

D   Dividends are not part of the share capital of the business.

21 **The correct answer is B**

The opening NBV was £356,000 less the NBV of the asset disposed off £43,000 less depreciation of £60,000 to give £253,000. The closing NBV was £421,000 so additions must be £168,000

The distractors are as follows:

A   The opening NBV was £356,000 less the NBV of the asset disposed off £43,000 less depreciation of £60,000 to give £253,000. The closing NBV was £421,000 so additions must be £168,000

C   The opening NBV was £356,000 less the NBV of the asset disposed off £43,000 less depreciation of £60,000 to give £253,000. The closing NBV was £421,000 so additions must be £168,000

D   The opening NBV was £356,000 less the NBV of the asset disposed off £43,000 less depreciation of £60,000 to give £253,000. The closing NBV was £421,000 so additions must be £168,000

22 **The correct answer is C**

Directors of a company can still face criminal prosecution for illegal actions.

The distractors are as follows:

A   Companies do have a separate legal personality from the owners
B   Company shareholders do have limited liability.
D   Companies will continue in perpetual succession.

23 **The correct answer is A**

Liquidity is the ability of the company to pay short term liabilities from funds available to it within a year.

The distractors are as follows:

B   Liquidity is the ability of the company to pay short term liabilities from funds available to it within a year.

C   Liquidity is the ability of the company to pay short term liabilities from funds available to it within a year.

D   Liquidity is the ability of the company to pay short term liabilities from funds available to it within a year.

24 **The correct answer is C**

Debt makes up £2,500,000 from a total capital structure of £9,500,000 which is 26.3%

The distractors are as follows:

A   Debt makes up £2,500,000 from a total capital structure of £9,500,000 which is 26.3%
B   Debt makes up £2,500,000 from a total capital structure of £9,500,000 which is 26.3%
D   Debt makes up £2,500,000 from a total capital structure of £9,500,000 which is 26.3%

25 **The correct answer is B**

£22,400 divided by £233,000 × 365 = 35.1 days

The distractors are as follows:

A   £22,400 divided by £233,000 × 365 = 35.1 days
C   £22,400 divided by £233,000 × 365 = 35.1 days
D   £22,400 divided by £233,000 × 365 = 35.1 days

Pass Exam–May 2022

1 **The correct answer is D**

The objective of financial accounting is to record, analyse and summarise financial data.

The distractors are as follows:

- A   This is one of the objectives of management accounting.
- B   This is the objective of audit.
- C   This is one of the objectives of management accounting.

2 **The correct answer is D**

The aim of the IASB is to eventually bring about global harmonisation of accounting standards.

The distractors are as follows:

- A   The IASB is an independent private sector body.
- B   The IASB aims to achieve uniformity in accounting principles.
- C   The IASB aims to raise the standard of financial reporting.

3 **The correct answer is A**

The definition is included in the conceptual framework.

The distractors are as follows:

- B   The obligation is not future, but present
- C   The obligation must arise from past events, not future events.
- D   The obligation must be present, not future.

4 **The correct answer is B**

The sales return daybook is used to record sales credit notes

The distractors are as follows:

- A   Sales invoices are recorded in the sales daybook
- C   Purchase invoices are recorded in the purchase daybook
- D   Purchase credit notes are recorded in the purchase returns daybook

5 **The correct answer is C**

Opening capital is made up of $20,000 + $7,000 + $10,000 − $8,000 = $29,000. Opening capital $29,000 + Profit of $12,000 less drawings of $5,000 = $36,000

The distractors are as follows:

- A   The opening capital on 1 January is $29,000 so must be adjusted for profit and drawings.
- B   The opening capital on 1 January is $29,000 so profit must be added to the opening capital and drawings deducted.
- D   The opening capital on 1 January is $29,000 so profit must be added to the opening capital and drawings deducted.

6 **The correct answer is B**

A credit purchase increases purchases and increases payables

The distractors are as follows:

- A   A credit purchase increases purchases and increases payables
- C   Entries for purchases should be debited to purchases, not inventory
- D   The credit entry must be to payables not to cash.

EXAM ANSWER BANK

7   **The correct answer is D**

The cash flow statement provides information about the cash inflows and outflows of the business

The distractors are as follows:

The trial balance is extracted from the ledger balances and lists them in two columns, debit and credit.

The trial balance is used as the basis for the financial statements

Errors in the accuracy of the accounting records may be detected as the total of the debits should equal the total of the credits.

8   **The correct answer is B**

The original list of $23,500 must be adjusted by the balance omitted of $2,250 to give $25,750 which agrees to the adjusted control account.

The distractors are as follows:

A   The original list of $23,500 must be adjusted by the balance omitted of $2,250 to give $25,750 which agrees to the adjusted control account.

C   The original list of $23,500 must be adjusted by the balance omitted of $2,250 to give $25,750 which agrees to the adjusted control account.

D   The original list of $23,500 must be adjusted by the balance omitted of $2,250 togive $25,750 which agrees to the adjusted control account.

9   **The correct answer is D**

Cost of sales must be $80,000 and as purchases = closing inventory + cost of sales – opening inventory then purchases = $8,000 + $80,000 - $10,000 = $78,000

The distractors are as follows:

A   Cost of sales must be $80,000 and as purchases = closing inventory + cost of sales – opening inventory then purchases = $8,000 + $80,000 – $10,000 = $78,000

B   Cost of sales must be $80,000 and as purchases = closing inventory + cost of sales – opening inventory then purchases = $8,000 + $80,000 – $10,000 = $78,000

C   Cost of sales must be $80,000 and as purchases = closing inventory + cost of sales – opening inventory then purchases = $8,000 + $80,000 – $10,000 = $78,000

10 **The correct answer is B**

Payment of $24,000 + $3,000 accrual + $2,000 opening prepayment = $29,000

The distractors are as follows:

A   Payment of $24,000 + $3,000 accrual + $2,000 opening prepayment = $29,000
C   Payment of $24,000 + $3,000 accrual + $2,000 opening prepayment = $29,000
D   Payment of $24,000 + $3,000 accrual + $2,000 opening prepayment = $29,000

11 **The correct answer is D**

Design, construction and testing of pre-production prototypes and models is a development activity

The distractors are as follows:

A   Activities aimed at obtaining new knowledge are included as a research activity
B   Search for product or process alternatives are included as a research activity
C   Search for applications of research findings are included as a research activity

12 **The correct answer is B**

The net book value of the trade in is $15,000. The value given to the trade in is $12,000 therefore there is a loss on disposal of $3,000.

The distractors are as follows:

A   The net book value of the trade in is $15,000. The value given to the trade in is $12,000 therefore there is a loss on disposal of $3,000, not a profit.

C   The net book value of the trade in is $15,000. The value given to the trade in is $12,000 therefore there is a loss on disposal of $3,000.

D   The net book value of the trade in is $15,000. The value given to the trade in is $12,000 therefore there is a loss on disposal of $3,000.

13 **The correct answer is D**

The maintenance of plant does not lead to future economic benefits, in excess of the originally assessed standard of performance of the existing asset and so cannot be capitalised.

The distractors are as follows:

A   The modification to the plant, extending its useful life WILL lead to future economic benefits, in excess of the originally assessed standard of performance of the existing asset and so CAN be capitalised.

B   The modification to plant, increasing its capacity WILL lead to future economic benefits, in excess of the originally assessed standard of performance of the existing asset and so CAN be capitalised.

C   The upgrade leading to improved quality of outputs WILL lead to future economic benefits, in excess of the originally assessed standard of performance of the existing asset and so CAN be capitalised.

14 **The correct answer is A**

The remaining receivables will be $220,000 after the bad debt write off and an allowance of 5% of this is required which is $11,000.

The distractors are as follows:

B   The remaining receivables will be $220,000 after the bad debt write off and an allowance of 5% of this is required which is $11,000.

C   The remaining receivables will be $220,000 after the bad debt write off and an allowance of 5% of this is required which is $11,000.

D   The remaining receivables will be $220,000 after the bad debt write off and anallowance of 5% of this is required which is $11,000.

15 **The correct answer is D**

The distractors are as follows:

A   A dishonoured cheque is a cheque from a customer with insufficient funds
B   A credit transfer is an amount paid directly into the bank
C   A standing order is a recurring payment of set amount

16 **The correct answer is A**

NBV is $3,200 less $800 less $600 = $1800. The proceeds are only $1,200 resulting in a loss of $600.

The distractors are as follows:

- B NBV is $3,200 less $800 less $600 = $1800. The proceeds are only $1,200 resulting in a loss of $600
- C NBV is $3,200 less $800 less $600 = $1800. The proceeds are only $1,200 resulting in a loss of $600.
- D NBV is $3,200 less $800 less $600 = $1800. The proceeds are only $1,200 resulting in a loss of $600.

17 **The correct answer is D**

The correction of the casting error is to reduce purchases and the payables ledger by $450.

The distractors are as follows:

- A The casting error is in relation to purchases and payables, not sales and receivables.
- B The casting error has resulted in purchases being too high, therefore purchases must be credited and payables reduced.
- C The receivables ledger is the incorrect ledger as this entry relates to suppliers, not credit customer.

18 **The correct answer is D**

There will be 2,000 new shares each issued at a nominal value of $1 and a share premium of $0.5 per share.

The distractors are as follows:

- A The proceeds will not be $15,000 as $3,000 was received as a result of the issue of 2000 at $1.50 each.
- B An entry must be made to the share premium account as shares are issued above the nominal value of $1.
- C The difference between the nominal value and the consideration must be credited to a share premium account, not retained earnings.

19 **The correct answer is B**

Opening capital of $16,500 less drawings of $3,300 gives $13,200. As closing capital is $850 less than $13,200 there must have been a loss of $850.

The distractors are as follows:

- A Opening capital of $16,500 less drawings of $3,300 gives $13,200. As closing capital is $850 less than $13,200 there must have been a loss of $850.
- C Opening capital of $16,500 less drawings of $3,300 gives $13,200. As closing capital is $850 less than $13,200 there must have been a loss of $850.
- D Opening capital of $16,500 less drawings of $3,300 gives $13,200. As closing capital is $850 less than $13,200 there must have been a loss of $850.

20 The correct answer is B

Management salaries are included in administrative expenses.

The distractors are as follows:

A   Management salaries are an expense in the statement of profit or loss not in the statement of changes in equity.

C   Management salaries are included in administrative expenses, not finance costs.

D   Management salaries are included in administrative expenses, not cost of sales.

21 The correct answer is B

The opening NBV was $385,000 plus additions of $55,000 to reach $440,000 NBV less depreciation of $45,000 to give a NBV before disposals of $395,000. The NBV of the disposal must be $35,000 ($395,000 less $360,000) and as there was a profit on disposal of $8,000, proceeds must be $43,000.

The distractors are as follows:

A   The opening NBV was $385,000 plus additions of $55,000 to reach $440,000 NBV less depreciation of $45,000 to give a NBV before disposals of $395,000. The NBV of the disposal must be $35,000 ($395,000 less $360,000) and as there was a profit on disposal of $8,000, proceeds must be $43,000.

C   The opening NBV was $385,000 plus additions of $55,000 to reach $440,000 NBV less depreciation of $45,000 to give a NBV before disposals of $395,000. The NBV of the disposal must be $35,000 ($395,000 less $360,000) and as there was a profit on disposal of $8,000, proceeds must be $43,000.

D   The opening NBV was $385,000 plus additions of $55,000 to reach $440,000 NBV less depreciation of $45,000 to give a NBV before disposals of $395,000. The NBV of the disposal must be $35,000 ($395,000 less $360,000) and as there was a profit on disposal of $8,000, proceeds must be $43,000.

22 The correct answer is C

Profit after tax $12,600 less preference dividend of $600 = $12,000. 40% is retained therefore 60% is paid out as dividend which is $7,200

The distractors are as follows:

A   Preference dividend of $600 must be deducted which leaves $12,000 and 60% is distributed.

B   40% is retained, therefore 60% is paid out which is $12,600 * 60% = $7,200

D   Preference dividend of $600 must be deducted which leaves $12,000 and 60% is distributed.

23 The correct answer is A

The measure of the proportion of a company's capital that is debt.

The distractors are as follows:

B   The comparison on non-current assets to non-current liabilities is not a measure of gearing.

C   The proportion of a company's capital that is equity does not represent gearing as this part of the capital has been financed by shareholders.

D   The comparison of total assets to total liabilities is not a measure of gearing.

EXAM ANSWER BANK

24 **The correct answer is C**

Total assets minus current liabilities are $3,050,000. $275,000 divided by $3,050,000 is 9.02%

The distractors are as follows:

A   This is incorrect as the current liabilities must be deducted from, not added to total assets before calculating the return on capital employed.

B   This is incorrect as the current liabilities must be deducted from total assets before calculating the return on capital employed.

D   Total assets minus current liabilities are $3,050,000. $275,000 divided by $3,050,000 is 9.02%

25 **The correct answer is B**

Liquid assets are current asset items that will or could soon be converted into cash and cash itself.

The distractors are as follows:

A   Cash is a liquid asset.
C   Trade receivables are liquid assets as they could soon be converted into cash.
D   A bills of exchange receivable is a liquid asset as it could soon be converted into cash.

EXAM ANSWER BANK

Pass Exam–November 2022

1   **The correct answer is D**

    Accounting standards may be subject to lobbying or government pressure which may influence the standard in favour of a particular group.

    The distractors are as follows:

    A   Elimination of confusing variations in methods is an argument for standardisation.
    B   Providing a focal point for debate and discussions is an argument for standardisation.
    C   Less rigidity in enforcement is an argument for standardisation.

2   **The correct answer is A**

    If there is a conflict, the IFRS will prevail over the Conceptual Framework.

    The distractors are as follows:

    B   The Conceptual Framework provides consistent concepts for the development of standards.

    C   The Conceptual Framework provides a basis for explanation of fundamental principles to assist with understanding and interpretation of IFRS.

    D   The Conceptual Framework facilitates the development of consistent and complementary standards.

3   **The correct answer is A**

    To be a faithful representation, information must be complete, neutral and free from error.

    The distractors are as follows:

    B   Relevance means capable of influencing the decisions of users.
    C   Timeliness means provided within a suitable timescale.
    D   Classified, characterised and presented clearly and concisely makes it understandable.

4   **The correct answer is B**

    Recognition is capturing for inclusion in the financial statements an item that meets the definition of an element of the financial statements.

    The distractors are as follows:

    A   Presentation is the communication of information about elements of the financial statements.

    C   Derecognition normally occurs when the item no longer meets the definition of an element of the financial statements.

    D   Measurement is providing monetary information about an element of the financial statements.

5   **The correct answer is C**

    Under an imprest system the petty cash will be reimbursed the $105 spent during the period.

    The distractors are as follows:

    A   The petty cash will only be reimbursed by the amount spent, not the imprest amount of $200.

    B   The petty cash will be reimbursed by the difference between the imprest amount and the amount remaining of $95, which is $105.

    D   The petty cash will be reimbursed by the amount spent of $105, not the sum of the two amounts given.

EXAM ANSWER BANK

6 **The correct answer is B**

The trade payables ledger is a ledger for suppliers' personal accounts.

The distractors are as follows:

- A The trade receivables ledger is a ledger for customers' personal accounts.
- C The general ledger is an accounting record which summarises the financial affairs of a business.
- D The nominal ledger is an accounting record which summarises the financial affairs of a business.

7 **The correct answer is D**

The gross amount is debited to receivables and the net amount to sales, showing the VAT as a liability.

The distractors are as follows:

- A The sale of $750 is net, therefore receivables should be debited with the gross of $900.
- B Sales should be posted net of VAT and receivables recorded gross of VAT.
- C The sale of $750 is net, therefore receivables should be recorded at the gross amount of $900.

8 **The correct answer is B**

The balance per cash book is $1,024. The direct debits must be deducted and the interest added to reach $762. The outstanding payments that do not appear on the bank statement would mean that the bank statement shows a balance of $367 higher at $1,129.

The distractors are as follows:

- A The outstanding cheques should be added to the adjusted balance per the cash book, not deducted.
- C The adjusted cash book balance will differ from the bank statement by the outstanding payments of $367.
- D The direct debits should be deducted and the interest added to the cash book balance before adjustment for outstanding payments.

9 **The correct answer is D**

A credit note in transit would explain the lower balance on the supplier statement.

The distractors are as follows:

- A A settlement discount claimed by the purchasing company would lead to a higher balance on the supplier statement than the purchase ledger.
- B A payment in transit would lead to a higher balance on the supplier statement.
- C This error would lead to a higher balance on the supplier statement.

10 **The correct answer is B**

A transposition error involves two digits being transposed.

The distractors are as follows:

- A An error of commission is a mistake in recording transactions in accounts such as putting a debit and credit entry the wrong way round or making an error in casting.
- C An error of principle involves treating revenue expenditure as capital or vice versa.
- D An error of omission means failing to record a transaction at all or making a one-sided entry.

EXAM ANSWER BANK

11 **The correct answer is D**

Opening balance of $24,000 plus $523,000 less closing balance of $35,000 to give $512,000.

The distractors are as follows:

- A   The closing balance of $35,000 should be deducted to work out payments.
- B   The opening balance should be added to purchases and the closing balance deducted to calculate payments.
- C   The $30,000 of cash purchases should not be included in the payments to credit suppliers.

12 **The correct answer is B**

With a margin of 25% the cost of sales figures must be $150,000. Purchases of $120,000 less closing inventory leaves $100,000 so opening inventory must have been $50,000.

The distractors are as follows:

- A   The margin of 25% results in a cost of sales of $150,000 rather than the mark-up which would lead to cost of sales of $160,000 with opening inventory of £60,000.
- C   Purchases of $120,000 less closing inventory leaves $100,000 so opening inventory must have been $50,000.
- D   Purchases of $120,000 less closing inventory leaves $100,000 so opening inventory must have been $50,000.

13 **The correct answer is D**

Sales (22 units) 10 × $35 + 12 × $36		782
Purchases (45 units)	945	
Closing inventory (23 units)	(501)	
5 × $21 + 18 × $22		
		444
Gross profit		338

The distractors are as follows:

- A   The closing inventory should not all be included at $21 but instead 5 units at $21 and 18 units at $22.
- B   This answer uses LIFO for closing inventory but FIFO should be used.
- C   The cost of sales figures should be deducted from sales to calculate gross profit.

14 **The correct answer is A**

The closing allowance will be $7,000 which is a reduction of $2,000.

The distractors are as follows:

- B   The closing allowance is $7,000 however only the movement should be posted.
- C   The closing allowance is $7,000 however only the movement should be posted and it should reflect a decrease in the allowance.
- D   The journal entry should reflect the decrease in the allowance which should be shown as a debit to the allowance for receivables of $2,000.

15 The correct answer is D

The distractors are as follows:

A It is also necessary to disclose the possibility of reimbursement per IAS 37.

B It is also necessary to disclose the uncertainties and the possibility of reimbursement per IAS 37.

C It is also necessary to disclose an indication of the uncertainties that exist per IAS 37.

16 The correct answer is A

Annual depreciation is £24,000 less £4,800 divided by 4 years which is $4,800 per annum. Seven months depreciation in this year results in depreciation of $2,800.

The distractors are as follows:

B Only seven months depreciation should be charged for the asset rather than a full year.

C The depreciation charge must be based on cost less residual value, not just cost.

D The depreciation charge must be based on cost less residual value and apportioned for the number of months the asset was in use as per the accounting policy.

17 The correct answer is D

This is the definition of recoverable amount contained in IAS 16. *Property, Plant and Equipment.*

The distractors are as follows:

A This is the residual value.
B This is the fair value.
C This is the carrying amount.

18 The correct answer is D

Profits after tax of $23,000 less preference dividend of $600 leaves profits available for distribution of $22,400. Sixty percent were paid out as dividend which is $13,440.

The distractors are as follows:

A The profits available for distribution were $22,400 and as 40% retained, 60% were paid out as dividend which is $13,440.

B The preference dividend of $600 should be deducted prior to calculating the 60% ordinary dividend.

C The preference dividend of $600 should be deducted, not added, prior to calculating the 60% ordinary dividend.

19 The correct answer is B

IFRS 15 Revenue from Contracts with Customers.

The distractors are as follows:

A IAS 37 provides guidance on the treatment of provision and contingent liabilities.
C IAS 1 provides guidance on the presentation of financial statements.
D IAS 16 provides guidance on the treatment of non-current assets in financial statements.

20 The correct answer is B

Inventory days 200,000/840,000 × 365	86.9 days
Receivable days 250,000/1,200,000 × 365	76.0 days
Payable days 160,000/800,000 × 365	(73 days)
Operating cash cycle	89.9 days

The distractors are as follows:

A The payable days should be deducted to arrive at the operating cycle.
C Inventory/Cost of sales is correct ratio rather than inventory/credit purchases.
D Payables/credit purchases is correct ratio rather than payables/cost of sales.

21 The correct answer is B

As dividend cover is 5 times the dividend must be $80,000 which is $0.80 per share. The dividend of $0.80 divided by the share price of $5 gives a dividend yield of 16%.

The distractors are as follows:

A The correct number of shares is 100,000 shares of $0.50 each rather than 50,000 shares.

C As dividend cover is 5 times the dividend must be $80,000 which is $0.80 per share. The dividend of $0.80 divided by the share price of $5 gives a dividend yield of 16%.

D As dividend cover is 5 times the dividend must be $80,000 which is $0.80 per share. The dividend of $0.80 divided by the share price of $5 gives a dividend yield of 16%.

22 The correct answer is C

NBV of assets disposed of must be $21,000. As the company had an opening nbv of $75,000 then after disposal and depreciation removed this leaves a NBV of $39,000. As the closing NBV is $86,000, additions of $47,000 have been acquired.

The distractors are as follows:

A The $2,000 gain on disposal means that the NBV of assets sold is $21,000, not $25,000.

B NBV of assets disposed of must be $21,000. As the company had an opening nbv of $75,000 then after disposal and depreciation removed this leaves a NBV of $39,000. As the closing NBV is $86,000, additions of $47,000 have been acquired.

D NBV of assets disposed of must be $21,000. As the company had an opening NBV of $75,000 then after disposal and depreciation removed this leaves a NBV of $39,000. As the closing NBV is $86,000, additions of $47,000 have been acquired.

23 The correct answer is A

As the company has increased the amount of credit offered there will be less cash available.

The distractors are as follows:

B As the company has increased the amount of credit offered there will be less cash available.

C As the company has increased the amount of credit offered there will be less cash available.

D As the company has increased the amount of credit offered there will be less cash available.

EXAM ANSWER BANK

24 **The correct answer is C**

It indicates a prepaid expense brought forward in this year and an asset.

The distractors are as follows:

- A It indicates a prepaid expense brought forward in this year and an asset.
- B It indicates a prepaid expense brought forward in this year and an asset.
- D It indicates a prepaid expense brought forward in this year and an asset.

25 **The correct answer is B**

Drawings will be debited and the amounts taken removed from business purchases.

The distractors are as follows:

- A Drawings will be debited and the amounts taken removed from business purchases
- C Drawings will be debited and the amounts taken removed from business purchases
- D Drawings will be debited and the amounts taken removed from business purchases

Pass Exam–May 2023

1 **The correct answer is D**

   Financial reporting is a way of recording, analysing and summarising financial data in financial statements

   The distractors are as follows:

   A   Management Accounting as opposed to Financial Reporting is most helpful to management.

   B   Management Accounting as opposed to Financial Reporting is a way of planning and controlling resources.

   C   Management Accounting as opposed to Financial Reporting is a way of analysing data as a basis for managerial action.

2 **The correct answer is A**

   The IASB produces International Financial Reporting Standards

   The distractors are as follows:

   B   The PCAOB oversees the audit of public companies in the US.
   C   The IAASB sets standards for auditing.
   D   The FRC is an independent regulatory body.

3 **The correct answer is C**

   The IASB Conceptual Framework assists the application of general principles rather than detailed standards.

   The distractors are as follows:

   A   The development of consistent standards is a purpose of the IASB Conceptual Framework.

   B   The IASB Conceptual Framework aims to assist preparers to develop consistent accounting policies.

   D   The IASB Conceptual Framework aims to help all parties to understand and interpret the standards.

4 **The correct answer is C**

   Derecognition normally occurs when the item no longer meets the definition of an element.

   The distractors are as follows:

   A   Presentation relates to the overall requirements for the structure and minimum requirements of financial statements.

   B   Recognition is the process for capturing for inclusion in the statement of financial position of the statement of financial performance an item that meets the definition of one of the elements of financial statements.

   D   This is the choice of historic cost or current value in financial statements.

5 **The correct answer is A**

   A goods received note is a list of goods that a business has received from a supplier, usually prepared by the business's own warehouse.

   The distractors are as follows:

   B   A goods despatched note is a list of goods that a business has sent out to a customer.
   C   A purchase order is related to an order for other goods or services from a supplier.
   D   A remittance advice is a document sent with a payment.

6   **The correct answer is C**

    A debit note may be issued to a supplier as a formal means of requesting a credit note.

    The distractors are as follows:

    A   A statement lists all the invoices owed by a customer.
    B   A remittance advice accompanies a payment, detailing which invoices have been paid.
    D   A quotation is a written offer to a customer to deliver goods for an agreed sum of money.

7   **The correct answer is A**

    The output liability of $5,000 less the recoverable VAT ($2,600-250) leaves a liability of $2,650.

    The distractors are as follows:

    B   The output liability of $5,000 less the recoverable VAT ($2,600-250) leaves a liability of $2,650, not an asset.

    C   The output liability of $5,000 less the recoverable VAT ($2,600-250) leaves a liability of $2,650. The VAT on business entertaining is irrecoverable.

    D   The output liability of $5,000 less the recoverable VAT ($2,600-250) leaves a liability of $2,650. The VAT on business entertaining is irrecoverable.

8   **The correct answer is B**

    The VAT is not recoverable so is added to the net cost of the asset capitalised.

    The distractors are as follows:

    A   The VAT is an additional cost and must be added to the cost of the asset, not deducted.
    C   The VAT is not recoverable so cannot be deducted from the output tax for the period.
    D   The VAT is part of the cost of the asset and should be capitalised, not expensed.

9   **The correct answer is D**

    The opening prepayment of $500 is added to the payments made of $16,000 and two thirds of the bill for the quarter ended 31 January 20X2 must be added giving a total of $19,000.

    The distractors are as follows:

    A   The opening prepayment of $500 is added to the payments made of $16,000 and two thirds of the bill for the quarter ended 31 January 20X2 must be added giving a total of $19,000.

    B   The opening prepayment of $500 is added to the payments made of $16,000 and two thirds of the bill for the quarter ended 31 January 20X2 must be added giving a total of $19,000.

    C   The opening prepayment of $500 is added to the payments made of $16,000 and two thirds of the bill for the quarter ended 31 January 20X2 must be added giving a total of $19,000.

10 **The correct answer is A**

    An error of commission is when the bookkeeper makes a mistake in carrying out his or her task of recording transactions in the accounts.

    The distractors are as follows:

    B   This is a general term and not a specific type of error.
    C   Compensating errors are errors which are, coincidentally, equal and opposite to one another.
    D   An error of omission means failing to record a transaction at all, or making a debit or credit entry, but not the corresponding double entry.

EXAM ANSWER BANK

11 The correct answer is A

The bank statement balance is $3,500. To obtain the cash book balance it is necessary to adjust for the entries that have not yet been recorded in the bank statement, therefore the $700 must be added, less the $1,650 plus the $100 giving $2,650.

The distractors are as follows:

- B The bank statement balance is $3,500. To obtain the cash book balance it is necessary to adjust for the entries that have not yet been recorded in the bank statement, therefore the $700 must be added, less the $1,650 plus the $100 giving $2,650.

- C The bank statement balance is $3,500. To obtain the cash book balance it is necessary to adjust for the entries that have not yet been recorded in the bank statement, therefore the $700 must be added, less the $1,650 plus the $100 giving $2,650.

- D The bank statement balance is $3,500. To obtain the cash book balance it is necessary to adjust for the entries that have not yet been recorded in the bank statement, therefore the $700 must be added, less the $1,650 plus the $100 giving $2,650.

12 The correct answer is C

The undercast of the sales daybook would lead to a lower receivables figures than the individual ledgers as the totals are used to post to the trade receivables control account.

The distractors are as follows:

- A The omission of credit notes from the general ledger would lead to a higher receivables figures than the individual ledgers as the totals are used to post to the trade receivables control account, not a lower one.

- B The treatment of a trade receivables ledger account as a debit rather than a credit would lead to a difference of $1,800.

- D The undercast of the cash receipts book would lead to a higher receivables figures than the individual ledgers as the totals are used to post to the trade receivables control account, not a lower one.

13 The correct answer is A

Both trade discounts allowed to customers and settlements discounts given to customers are deducted from revenue.

The distractors are as follows:

- B Trade discounts received from suppliers should be deducted from cost of sales.

- C Both trade discounts allowed to customers and settlement discounts given to customers are deducted from revenue.

- D Trade discounts received from suppliers should be deducted from cost of sales. Settlement discounts given to customers are deducted from revenue.

EXAM ANSWER BANK

14 **The correct answer is B**

The mark up is 20% so the cost of sales will be 100/120 *$240,000 = $200,000. As the inventory is to be reduced by $15,000 the purchases will be $15,000 less than the cost of sales which is $185,000.

The distractors are as follows:

A The mark up is 20% so the cost of sales will be 100/120 *$240,000 = $200,000. As the inventory is to be reduced by $15,000 the purchases will be $15,000 less and will be deducted from cost of sales, not added.

C The mark up is 20% so the cost of sales will be 100/120 *$240,000 = $200,000. As the inventory is to be reduced by $15,000 the purchases will be $15,000 less than the cost of sales which is $185,000.

D The mark up is 20% so the cost of sales will be 100/120 *$240,000 = $200,000. As the inventory is to be reduced by $15,000 the purchases will be $15,000 less than the cost of sales which is $185,000.

15 **The correct answer is A**

Product A has a cost of $7 and an NRV of $6 ($14-$2-$6) so the lower figure of $6 per unit will be used multiplied by 6,000 units to give $36,000. Product B has a cost of $13,000 that is lower than NRV of $17 ($30-$4-$9) which when multiplied by 4000 units gives $52,000. This means that inventory will be $36,000 +$52,000 = $88,000.

The distractors are as follows:

B Product A has a cost of $7 and an NRV of $6 ($14-$2-$6) so the lower figure of $6 per unit will be used multiplied by 6,000 units to give $36,000. Product B has a cost of $13,000 that is lower than NRV of $17 ($30-$4-$9) which when multiplied by 4000 units gives $52,000. This means that inventory will be $36,000 +$52,000 = $88,000.

C Product A has a cost of $7 and an NRV of $6 ($14-$2-$6) so the lower figure of $6 per unit will be used multiplied by 6,000 units to give $36,000. Product B has a cost of $13,000 that is lower than NRV of $17 ($30-$4-$9) which when multiplied by 4,000 units gives $52,000. This means that inventory will be $36,000 +$52,000 = $88,000.

D Product A has a cost of $7 and an NRV of $6 ($14-$2-$6) so the lower figure of $6 per unit will be used multiplied by 6,000 units to give $36,000. Product B has a cost of $13,000 that is lower than NRV of $17 ($30-$4-$9) which when multiplied by 4000 units gives $52,000. This means that inventory will be $36,000 +$52,000 = $88,000.

16 **The correct answer is C**

Trade receivables of $200,000 less $4,500 = $195,500. 5% of $195,500 is $9,775. The total expense will be $9,775 + $4,500 = $14,275.

The distractors are as follows:

A Trade receivables of $200,000 less $4,500 = $195,500. 5% of $195,500 is $9,775. The total expense will be $9,775 + $4,500 = $14,275.

B Trade receivables of $200,000 less $4,500 = $195,500. 5% of $195,500 is $9,775. The total expense will be $9,775 + $4,500 = $14,275.

D Trade receivables of $200,000 less $4,500 = $195,500. 5% of $195,500 is $9,775. The total expense will be $9,775 + $4,500 = $14,275.

17 The correct answer is D

The NBV of the machine is $30,000 and the proceeds are the balancing amount due which is $60,000 less £34,000 which is $26,000. Therefore the machine has made a loss on disposal of $4,000.

The distractors are as follows:

A   The NBV of the machine is $30,000 and the proceeds are the balancing amount due which is $60,000 less £34,000 which is $26,000. Therefore the machine has made a loss on disposal of $4,000.

B   The NBV of the machine is $30,000 and the proceeds are the balancing amount due which is $60,000 less £34,000 which is $26,000. Therefore the machine has made a loss on disposal of $4,000.

C   The NBV of the machine is $30,000 and the proceeds are the balancing amount due which is $60,000 less £34,000 which is $26,000. Therefore the machine has made a loss on disposal of $4,000.

18 The correct answer is D

Intangible assets with indefinite useful lives should be subject to an annual impairment review.

The distractors are as follows:

A   Intangible assets with indefinite useful lives should be subject to an annual impairment review.

B   Intangible assets with indefinite useful lives should be subject to an annual impairment review.

C   Intangible assets with indefinite useful lives should be subject to an annual impairment review.

19 The correct answer is D

Taxation does not appear in a Statement of changes in equity.

The distractors are as follows:

A   Dividends do appear in a Statement of changes in equity.
B   Issue of share capital does appear in a Statement of changes in equity.
C   Revaluation surplus does appear in a Statement of changes in equity.

20 The correct answer is A

The number of shares issued will be 50,000 at 50c each which gives $25,000. This will be allocated against the share premium first reducing it to zero and then the remaining $5,000 will be deducted from retained earnings.

The distractors are as follows:

B   The number of shares issued will be 50,000 at 50c each which gives $25,000. This will be allocated against the share premium first reducing it to zero and then the remaining $5,000 will be deducted from retained earnings.

C   The number of shares issued will be 50,000 at 50c each which gives $25,000. This will be allocated against the share premium first reducing it to zero and then the remaining $5,000 will be deducted from retained earnings.

D   The number of shares issued will be 50,000 at 50c each which gives $25,000. This will be allocated against the share premium first reducing it to zero and then the remaining $5,000 will be deducted from retained earnings.

21 The correct answer is D

IFRS 15 is the standard which deals with Revenue from Contracts with Customers.

The distractors are as follows:

A   IAS 37 is the standard on provisions, contingent liabilities and contingent assets.
B   IAS 1 is the standard on presentation of financial statements.
C   IAS 16 is the standard on non-current assets.

22 The correct answer is C

The opening tax liability of $50,000 plus the taxation charge of $35,000 gives a liability of $85,000. Only $38,000 of this is outstanding, therefore the difference between $85,000 and $38,000 must have been paid which is $47,000.

The distractors are as follows:

A   The opening tax liability of $50,000 plus the taxation charge of $35,000 gives a liability of $85,000. Only $38,000 of this is outstanding, therefore the difference between $85,000 and $38,000 must have been paid which is $47,000.

B   The opening tax liability of $50,000 plus the taxation charge of $35,000 gives a liability of $85,000. Only $38,000 of this is outstanding, therefore the difference between $85,000 and $38,000 must have been paid which is $47,000.

D   The opening tax liability of $50,000 plus the taxation charge of $35,000 gives a liability of $85,000. Only $38,000 of this is outstanding, therefore the difference between $85,000 and $38,000 must have been paid which is $47,000.

23 The correct answer is D

A decrease in inventory will be a positive figure on the cash flow as there is an increase in cash available to the entity.

The distractors are as follows:

A   A decrease in inventory will be a positive figure on the cash flow as there is an increase in cash available to the entity.

B   A decrease in inventory will be a positive figure on the cash flow as there is an increase in cash available to the entity.

C   A decrease in inventory will be a positive figure on the cash flow as there is an increase in cash available to the entity.

24 The correct answer is A

A supermarket will not normally sell on credit to its customers so will have a low average receivables collection period.

The distractors are as follows:

B   A manufacturer of plant and machinery will normally sell on credit to its customers so will have a high average receivables collection period.

C   A construction business will normally sell on credit to its customers so will have a high average receivables collection period.

D   A furniture shop who offers credit deals to customers will normally sell on credit to its customers so will have a high average receivables collection period.

25 **The correct answer is C**

The earnings divided by the dividend gives 5 which represents that the earnings will cover the dividend 5 times over.

The distractors are as follows:

A   The earnings divided by the dividend gives 5 which represents that the earnings will cover the dividend 5 times over.

B   The earnings divided by the dividend gives 5 which represents that the earnings will cover the dividend 5 times over.

D   The earnings divided by the dividend gives 5 which represents that the earnings will cover the dividend 5 times over.

Pass Exam–November 2023

1 The correct answer is D

The International Accounting Standards Board develops IFRSs.

The distractors are as follows:

- A The IFRS Advisory Council puts forward views of members to identify issues that need addressing and prioritise the work of the IASB.
- B The IFRS Interpretations Committee issues guidance where unsatisfactory or conflicting interpretations of accounting standards have developed.
- C The IFRS Foundation is an independent, not-for-profit body that oversees the IASB.

2 The correct answer is A

The investors provide risk capital to an entity.

The distractors are as follows:

- B Lenders provide loans and other forms of credit.
- C Suppliers provide trade credit to a company.
- D Government may provide grants to a company.

3 The correct answer is C

An advantage of the Conceptual Framework is the ability to bolster the ability of standard setters to withstand political pressure from various lobby groups and interested parties.

The distractors are as follows:

- A The difficulty in devising a suitable Conceptual Framework may be considered a disadvantage.
- B The need for various accounting standards for different purposes with different concepts as a result may be considered a disadvantage.
- D It is not clear that the Conceptual Framework makes the task of preparing and implementing standards easier than without a framework and this is a disadvantage.

4 The correct answer is C

Timeliness means having information available to decision-makers in time to be capable of influencing their decisions.

The distractors are as follows:

- A Comparability enables users to identify and understand similarities in, and differences among, items.
- B Verifiability helps assure users that information faithfully represents the economic phenomena it purports to represent.
- D Understandability means classifying, characterising and presenting information clearly and concisely.

5 The correct answer is B

A goods despatched note is a list of goods that a business has sent out to a customer.

The distractors are as follows:

- A A goods received note is a list of goods that a business has received from a supplier, usually prepared by the business's own warehouse.
- C A purchase order is related to an order for other goods or services from a supplier.
- D A remittance advice is a document sent with a payment.

6 The correct answer is C

A sales invoice is primarily a demand for payment, not a book of prime entry.

The distractors are as follows:

- A The purchase daybook is the book of prime entry for credit purchases.
- B The sales daybook is the book of prime entry for credit sales.
- D The journal is the record of prime entry for transactions which are not recorded in any of the other books of prime entry.

7 The correct answer is A

The petty cash spent during the period was $153.98 and this should be replenished to restore the imprest amount.

The distractors are as follows:

- B The petty cash spent during the period was $153.98 and this should be replenished to restore the imprest amount.
- C The petty cash spent during the period was $153.98 and this should be replenished to restore the imprest amount.
- D The petty cash spent during the period was $153.98 and this should be replenished to restore the imprest amount.

8 The correct answer is B

Revenue $18,000 less cost of sales $12,000 less other expenses $2,000 less bank loan interest $1,000 leaves profit of $3,000.

The distractors are as follows:

- A The bank loan interest must also be deducted.
- C The bank loan interest and other expense must also be deducted.
- D Revenue $18,000 less cost of sales $12,000 less other expenses $2,000 less bank loan interest $1,000 leaves profit of $3,000.

9 The correct answer is D

The rent covers the period from 1 October 20X2 to 30 September 20X3 so nine months will be prepaid. The prepayment will be 9/12 × $10,000 which is $7,500.

The distractors are as follows:

- A The rent covers the period from 1 October 20X2 to 30 September 20X3 so nine months will be prepaid. The prepayment will be 9/12 × $10,000 which is $7,500.
- B The rent covers the period from 1 October 20X2 to 30 September 20X3 so nine months will be prepaid. The prepayment will be 9/12 × $10,000 which is $7,500.
- C The rent covers the period from 1 October 20X2 to 30 September 20X3 so nine months will be prepaid. The prepayment will be 9/12 × $10,000 which is $7,500.

EXAM ANSWER BANK

10   **The correct answer is A**

The total amount will be 10×$2,000 which is $20,000. Trade discount will be 15% of $20,000 which is $3,000. The settlement discount will be 2% of $20,000 less $3,000 which is $340.

The distractors are as follows:

B   The trade discount and settlement discount for all ten machines is required.

C   The settlement discount will be 2% of $20,000 less $3,000 which is $340.

D   The settlement discount will be 2% of $20,000 less $3,000 which is $340, and the calculation should be for all ten machines.

11   **The correct answer is A**

The bank statement balance is $38,000. The opening balance plus the revenue of $154,000 less cash received £60,000 less the contra of $10,000 leaves a closing balance of $122,000 therefore the opening balance must be $38,000.

The distractors are as follows:

B   The contra of $10,000 must be included in the calculations.
C   The contra of $10,000 is a credit in the control account not a debit.
D   The closing balance of $122,000 must be included in the calculations.

12   **The correct answer is C**

The number of units in inventory at 31 July will be 25 bought less 16 sold = 9 units. This will be included at the purchase cost of $350 per unit so the inventory will be 9 × $350 = $3,150.

The distractors are as follows:

A   It is incorrect to include the 9 units at a cost of $300.

B   There are 9 units in inventory at the year end, each with a cost of $350.

D   The number of units in inventory at 31 July will be 25 bought less 16 sold = 9 units. This will be included at the purchase cost of $350 per unit.

13   **The correct answer is A**

Storage costs which are necessary as part of the production process are part of the cost of bringing inventories to their present location and condition. The other costs are specifically excluded.

The distractors are as follows:

B   Storage costs of finished goods are a distribution cost.
C   Administrative costs should be expensed in the period.
D   Selling costs are a distribution cost.

14   **The correct answer is B**

The closing receivables are $500,000 less the irrecoverable debt of $10,000 = 490,000. The allowance for receivables will be 4% of $490,000 which is $19,600. This means that the allowance for receivables will decrease by $4,400.

The distractors are as follows:

A   The allowance for receivables will need to decrease to $19,600 which is a decrease of $4,400.

C   The irrecoverable debt must be removed before the allowance is calculated at 4% × $490,000 which is $4,400. This is a decrease of $4,400.

D   The irrecoverable debt must be removed before the allowance is calculated at 4% × $490,000 which is $4,400. This is a decrease of $4,400.

EXAM ANSWER BANK

15 The correct answer is A

IAS 37 requires disclosure of a description of the nature of the contingent liability, an estimate of the financial effect, an indication of the uncertainties that exist and the possibility of any reimbursement.

The distractors are as follows:

- B   The nature of the uncertainties that exist should also be disclosed and the possibility of any reimbursement.
- C   Disclosures are required for this contingent liability unless the outflow of resources is remote.
- D   The disclosures must also include an estimate of their financial effect and the possibility of any reimbursement.

16 The correct answer is C

Depreciation each year on the straight-line basis will be $25,000 less $8,000 divided by 5 years which is $3,400. Using the reducing balance method, the depreciation will be as follows:

Year 1 $25,000 × 20% = $5,000 Year 2 $20,000 × 20% = $4,000 Year 3 $16,000 × 20% = $3,200. The difference in year 3 will be $3,400 less $3,200 = $200.

The distractors are as follows:

- A   The comparison is for year 3, not year 1.
- B   The comparison for year 3, not year 1.
- D   The residual value is not deducted from cost when using the reducing balance method.

17 The correct answer is D

The distractors are as follows:

- A   IAS 16 provides guidance on revaluation of non-current assets and revaluation is at the discretion of management not on an annual basis.
- B   IAS 16 provides guidance that when a revaluation has occurred it must be repeated regularly for all non-current assets in a class not at the discretion of management.
- C   IAS 16 provides guidance that non-current assets can be carried at either cost or valuation at the discretion of management however once revaluation has occurred it must be repeated regularly for all non-current assets in a class.

18 The correct answer is D

Preference shares do not carry a right to vote.

The distractors are as follows:

- A   Preference shareholders do have priority rights over ordinary shareholders in the event of a liquidation.
- B   Preference shares do confer preferential rights on the holder.
- C   Cumulative preference shares means that before a company can pay an ordinary dividend it must make good any arrears of preferential dividends unpaid in previous years.

EXAM ANSWER BANK

19 The correct answer is D

Interest cover is calculated as Profit before interest and tax divided by interest and is expressed as the number of times profit before interest and tax covers the interest expense.

The distractors are as follows:

A   Do not use profit for the period for this calculation.
B   Do not use taxable profit for this calculation.
C   The calculation should be PBIT of $200,000 divided by $50,000 which is 4 times.

20 The correct answer is A

Opening carrying value is $200,000 less $80,000 disposal carrying value gives $120,000. The depreciation charge is $120,000. The closing balance is £300,000 so additions must be $300,000. The proceeds of disposal are $70,000 therefore the net cash outflow is $230,000.

The distractors are as follows:

B   The proceeds of disposal should be deducted from $300,000 to reach the net cash flow.

C   The proceeds of disposal are $70,000 and this should be deducted from additions not the NBV.

D   Opening carrying value is $200,000 less $80,000 disposal carrying value gives $120,000. The depreciation charge is $120,000. The closing balance is £300,000 so additions must be $300,000. The proceeds of disposal are $70,000 therefore the net cash outflow is $230,000.

21 The correct answer is D

Share capital, share premium, retained earnings and the revaluation surplus all form part of shareholders' equity.

The distractors are as follows:

A   Share capital, share premium, retained earnings and the revaluation surplus all form part of shareholders' equity.

B   Share capital, share premium, retained earnings and the revaluation surplus all form part of shareholders' equity.

C   Share capital, share premium, retained earnings and the revaluation surplus all form part of shareholders' equity.

22 The correct answer is C

Inventory holding period is used to assess the company's efficiency.

The distractors are as follows:

A   The gearing ratio is used to assess the company's leverage.
B   The quick ratio is used to assess the company's liquidity.
D   The dividend cover ratio is used to assess the shareholders' investment.

23 The correct answer is D

A decrease in receivables will be a positive figure on the cash flow as there is an increase in cash available to the entity.

The distractors are as follows:

- A A decrease in receivables will be a positive figure on the cash flow as there is an increase in cash available to the entity.

- B A decrease in receivables will be a positive figure on the cash flow as there is an increase in cash available to the entity.

- C A decrease in receivables will be a positive figure on the cash flow as there is an increase in cash available to the entity.

24 The correct answer is A

A supermarket will normally have a low gross profit margin, selling a high volume of products at a low gross margin.

The distractors are as follows:

- B A manufacturer of plant and machinery will normally have a higher gross profit margin than a supermarket.

- C A construction business will normally have a higher gross profit margin than a supermarket.

- D A furniture shop will normally have a higher gross profit margin than a supermarket.

25 The correct answer is C

The revenue is 120% of the cost of sales therefore cost of sales must be $200,000. As the inventory has increased by $10,000 the purchases must be $210,000.

The distractors are as follows:

- A Cost of sales is $200,000 and as inventory increased by $10000 the purchases must be $10,000 higher at $210,000

- B The business marks up the cost at 20%, rather than a margin of 20% so the cost of sales will be $200,000. The increase in inventory should then be added to calculate purchases of $210,000.

- D The revenue is 120% of the cost of sales therefore cost of sales must be $200,000. As the inventory has increased by $10,000 the purchases must be $210,000.

EXAM ANSWER BANK

Mock exam 1 questions and answers

FOUNDATION UNIT

FINANCIAL ACCOUNTING

Question Bank – Mock Exam 1

There is **ONE** correct answer per question

1 Which of the following lists of accounts contains only items that are assets?

- A Cash, trade receivables, buildings cost
- B Trade receivables, bank loans, tax payable
- C Trade payables, buildings cost, income receivable
- D Buildings accumulated depreciation, trade payables, inventory

2 Which of the following is not an objective of the IFRS Foundation?

- A To enforce IFRS Accounting Standards in most countries
- B To develop high quality, understandable, enforceable and globally accepted standards for general purpose financial reporting based on clearly articulated principles
- C To promote the use and rigorous adoption of the IFRS standards
- D To take account of the needs of a range of sizes and types of entities in diverse economic settings

3 Which of the following statements about preparation of financial statements under the accruals basis is correct?

- A The financial statements will show users how the statements have been prepared and if they have any pending cash flow issues.
- B The financial statements will show users the business budgets for future income and expenditure.
- C The financial statements just record all accruals of expenditure and income that the business has made within the financial year.
- D The financial statements will recognise the effect of transactions and other events when they occur, not when the cash is received or paid.

4 Which of the following statements about materiality is correct?

- A Materiality is based on the value of a figure.
- B Items which are not material can be grouped together and presented as a single figure in the financial statements.
- C An items is material if it is probable the item will be misstated.
- D If an items is not material, it can be omitted from the financial statements.

5 What is the primary purpose of an invoice?

- A A demand for goods to be delivered.
- B A demand for payment.
- C An order acknowledgement.
- D Proof of delivery of goods.

6 Which of the following is a book of prime entry?

- A Sales returns day book
- B Purchase ledger account of Mr Smith
- C Sale account
- D Purchases account

7   What would the double entry be in the general ledger, for the sale on credit to ACD Ltd for $2,500?

    A   Debit Trade Receivables $2,500   Credit Sales $2,500
    B   Debit Sales $2,500   Credit ACD Ltd $2,500
    C   Debit ACD Ltd $2,500   Credit Sales $2,500
    D   Debit Sales $2,500   Credit Trade Receivables $2,500

8   Which of the following headings would appear on the statement of profit or loss?

    A   Prepaid income
    B   Gain on disposal of non-current assets
    C   Gain on revaluation of non-current assets
    D   Drawings

9   What is the VAT charged on goods and services sold by a business is referred to?

    A   Input VAT
    B   Irrecoverable VAT
    C   Output VAT
    D   Levied VAT

10 A credit balance at the start of the year on an expense account indicates which of the following?

    A   A liability and an expense prepaid
    B   A liability and an expense accrued
    C   An asset and an expense prepaid
    D   An asset and an expense accrued

11 A bank statement shows an overdraft of $600. Unpresented cheques total $250; outstanding lodgements total $1,000. What is the balance at the bank shown by the cash book?

    A $1,350 Credit
    B $1,350 Debit
    C $150 Credit
    D $150 Debit

12 You have been given the following information for the month of January:

    - Opening accounts payable $25,985
    - Credit purchases made $16,250
    - Purchase returns $798
    - Money paid to suppliers $17,500
    - Discounts received $275

    What is the closing account payables balance for January?

    A $23,662
    B $22,662
    C $23,937
    D $24,460

13 Electricity expenses of $450 paid from the bank have been debited to the bank columns of the cash book and credited to the electricity expenses account. Which of the following entries will correct the error?

    A   Dr Bank $450   Cr Electricity expenses $450
    B   Dr Bank $900   Cr Electricity expenses $900
    C   Dr Electricity expenses $450   Cr Bank $450
    D   Dr Electricity expenses $900   Cr Bank $900

14 A business has the following information:

Cost of sales for the year is $600,000.

Mark-up is 50%

What is the sales revenue for the year?

   A $1,200,000
   B $300,000
   C $900,000
   D $750,000

15 At the year end, the cost and net realisable value of two products are as follows:

Product	Cost	Net realisable value
Product A	$3,500	$3,200
Product B	$7,000	$9,500
	$10,500	$12,700

Which is the correct inventory valuation at the year end?

   A $10,500
   B $12,700
   C $13,000
   D $10,200

16 A company had an opening allowance for receivables of $2,500. At the year end, the trade receivables balance was $140,000 and an allowance for receivables of 1.5% is required.

What is the double entry to adjust the allowance for receivables?

   A   Dr Statement of profit or loss $400, Cr Allowance for receivables $400
   B   Dr Allowance for receivables $400, Cr Statement of profit or loss $400
   C   Dr Statement of profit or loss $437, Cr Allowance for receivables $437
   D   Dr Allowance for receivables $437, Cr Statement of profit or loss $437

17 The draft statement of profit or loss for AZY Ltd has been prepared and shows a loss of $4,350.

Further adjustments are required for a reduction in a legal provision of $150 and a loss on disposal of an asset of $70.

What is the adjusted loss for the year?

   A $4,130
   B $4,270
   C $4,430
   D $4,570

18 AZY Ltd has been told that it is likely to have to pay $10,000 in damages for a product that failed. The business needs to set up a provision at 31 December 20X9.

How is the provision treated in the accounts as at 31 December 20X9?

   A   Dr Damages expense $10,000   Cr Provision $10,000
   B   Dr Provision $10,000   Cr Bank $10,000
   C   Dr Finance costs $10,000   Cr Provision $10,000
   D   Dr Provision $10,000   Cr Retained earnings $10,000

19   Which of the following is not one of the criteria for the recognition of development costs?

   A   The ability to use or sell the intangible asset.

   B   The costs of development exceed the costs of research.

   C   The technical feasibility of completing the intangible asset so that it will be available for use or sale.

   D   The availability of adequate technical, financial and other resources to complete the development and to use or sell the intangible asset.

20   What is the distinguishing factor of the financial statements of a business entity?

   A   Business and owners' transactions are accounted for in the financial statements.

   B   The assets and liabilities of the owner are incorporated into that of the business (they are as one).

   C   An owner pays his personal taxes though the business entity.

   D   The assets and liabilities of the owner are separate to that of the business.

21   A business has a statement of profit or loss which shows a draft profit of $18,900. It has discovered that no adjustments have been made for telephone expenses accrued of $920 and insurance prepaid of $650 at the year end.

   What is the adjusted profit for the year?

   A $19,170
   B $20,470
   C $18,630
   D $17,330

22   What is generally the first note to the financial statements?

   A   Payables note
   B   Accounting policies note
   C   Investments note
   D   Goodwill note

You have been presented with the following figures, this information covers questions 23 and 24:

	Year 1 $	Year 2 $
Revenue	90,000	120,000
Cost of sales	52,000	79,000
Gross profit	38,000	41,000
Expenses	31,000	35,000
Net profit	7,000	6,000

23   What is the gross profit margin in year 1?

   A   18%
   B   42%
   C   22%
   D   73%

24 What is the net profit margin in year 2?

  A 34%
  B 5%
  C 17%
  D 8%

25 What is the aim of a statement of cash flows?

  A To indicate an entity's ability to sell products
  B To indicate an entity's ability to identify its own liquidity
  C To indicate an entity's ability to generate and use cash and cash equivalents
  D To indicate an entity's ability to produce financial statements

FOUNDATION LEVEL

FOUNDATION UNIT

FINANCIAL ACCOUNTING

Answer Bank – Mock Exam 1

There is **ONE** correct answer per question

ANSWER BANK – MOCK EXAM 1

1 The correct answer is A

Cash, trade receivables and buildings cost are all asset items.

In option b, both bank loans and tax payable are liabilities. Trade payables in options c and d are also liabilities.

The income receivable balance (option c) is an asset, it is similar to trade receivables, but is the account used for income due that doesn't come from trade, such as bank interest receivable.

Buildings accumulated depreciation (option d) is a credit balance, but accumulated depreciation is not a liability, it is a reduction in asset value to reflect the use of an asset.

2 The correct answer is A

The objectives of the IFRS Foundation are to:

1   Develop high quality, understandable, enforceable and globally accepted standards for general purpose financial reporting based upon clearly articulated principles;

2   Promote the adoption and rigorous application of those standards;

3   Take account of the needs of varied sizes and types of entities in diverse economic settings; and

4   Promote transparency and comparability.

Enforcement of IFRS is not an objective of the IFRS Foundation, so the correct answer is a).

3 The correct answer is D

Financial statements prepared under the accruals basis recognise the effect of transactions and other events when they occur, not when the cash is received or paid.

Financial statements do not necessarily highlight and pending cash flow issues, as they show information for a historic financial period. They do not include forecast or budgeted data.

4 The correct answer is B

The *Conceptual Framework* states that "information is material if omitting it or misstating it could influence decisions that the primary users of general-purpose financial reports make".

If an item is not material, then it might be grouped together with other 'immaterial' items as providing detail of each balance is not considered to be useful for users of the financial statements. Therefore, option b is correct.

Items can be material due to their size, or due to their nature. It is not just about the value of an item, so option a is not correct.

Option c is not the correct definition of materiality. All balance should be included in the financial statements, including items that are not material. This is necessary for the financial statements to balance. Immaterial items may be amalgamated together for clearer presentation.

5 The correct answer is B

An invoice is a demand for payment that is issued when the goods or services have been delivered.

A demand for goods to be delivered is a purchase order ie a request for goods. An order acknowledgement might be issued by the supplier once they have received the order, before they are dispatched. Proof of delivery of goods is received once they have been delivered.

ANSWER BANK – MOCK EXAM 1

6   **The correct answer is A**

The sales returns day book is one of the books of prime entry.

The purchase ledger account of Mr Smith is a subsidiary ledger account which provides details of all purchase orders placed with Mr Smith and payments made to him for goods/services provided.

The sales account and purchases account are general ledger accounts which should the total sales and purchases made.

7   **The correct answer is A**

A credit sale is recorded as Debit Trade receivables, Credit Sales, so the correct answer is a. This entry creates a trade receivables balance as ACD Ltd will make payment for the sale at a later date. The credit to sales recognised the sales income in the statement of profit or loss.

The individual sales ledger account of ACD Ltd is not held in the general ledger, this will be part of the subsidiary sales ledger.

8   **The correct answer is B**

Gains on disposal of non-current assets do appear on the statement of profit or loss, either as a heading in its own right or as part of other income.

Gains on revaluation are recorded in the revaluation surplus and would appear in the statement of changes of equity. Prepaid income is a heading that would be shown within current liabilities in the statement of financial position. Drawings is a reduction in capital for a sole trader or partnership.

9   **The correct answer is C**

VAT charged on goods and services is referred to as OUTPUT VAT.

Input VAT is the VAT paid on purchases made by a business. Irrecoverable VAT is input VAT that a business is unable to recover from the tax authorities.

10   **The correct answer is B**

A credit balance on an expense account at the start of the year will arise where there has been an accrual in the previous financial period (which will have been recorded as Debit expense, Credit accrual). The reversal of the accrual will be recorded as Debit accrual, Credit expense, and will result in a credit balance in the expense account, until the first invoice is recorded with a debit to expense.

11   **The correct answer is A**

	$
Balance per bank statement	(600)
Add: Unpresented cheque	250
Less: Outstanding lodgment	(1,000)
Balance per cash book	**(1,350)**

The balance per the cash book is a credit of $1,350, an overdrawn balance.

12   **The correct answer is A**

	$
Opening accounts payable	25,985
Less: purchase returns	(798)
Less: discounts received	(275)
Less: cash paid to suppliers	(17,500)
Add: purchases made	16,250
Closing accounts payable	**23,662**

13 The correct answer is D

The correct entry that should have been recorded is:

Debit Electricity expenses $450, Credit Bank $450

The entry that has been recorded is:

Debit Bank $450, Credit Electricity expenses $450

The correcting entry is therefore:

Debit Electricity expenses $900, Credit Bank $900 (option d)

14 The correct answer is C

A mark-up of 50% means that gross profit is 50% of the cost of sales.

		$
Revenue	150%	900,000
Cost of sales	100%	600,000
Gross profit	50%	300,000

15 The correct answer is D

	Cost	NRV	Lower of cost and NRV
	$	$	$
Product A	3,500	3,200	3,200
Product B	7,000	9,500	7,000
	10,500	12,700	10,200

Inventory should be held at the lower of cost and net realisable value. The NRV of Product A is lower than its cost by $300. The total inventory value at the year end is $10,200.

16 The correct answer is B

		$
Closing allowance for receivables	1.5% × $140,000	2,100
Opening allowance for receivables		2,500
Decrease		(400)

A decrease to the allowance for receivables is a debit to the allowance, with a corresponding credit to the statement of profit or loss.

If the closing allowance for receivables was calculated as ($140,000 − $2,500) × 1.5% = 2,063, it would be a decrease of $437.

17 The correct answer is B

	$
Draft loss	(4,350)
Reduction in legal provision	150
Loss on disposal of asset	(70)
Adjusted loss for the year	(4,270)

A reduction in the legal provision is a credit to the statement of profit or loss and the loss on disposal is a debit.

ANSWER BANK – MOCK EXAM 1

18 **The correct answer is A**

To set up a provision, there is a debit to the expense account in the statement of profit or loss and a credit to the provision liability on the statement of financial position. The correct double entry is: Dr Damages expense $10,000, Cr Provision liability $10,000

19 **The correct answer is B**

Development expenditure should be recognised as an asset only when the business can demonstrate all of the following. Where the criteria are met, development expenditure must be capitalised.

- The technical feasibility of completing the intangible asset so that it will be available for use or sale
- Its intention to complete the intangible asset and use or sell it
- Its ability to use or sell the intangible asset
- How the intangible asset will generate probable future economic benefits. Among other things, the entity can demonstrate the existence of a market for the output of the intangible asset or the intangible asset itself or, if it is to be used internally, the usefulness of the intangible asset
- The availability of adequate technical, financial and other resources to complete the development and to use or sell the intangible asset
- Its ability to measure reliably the expenditure attributable to the intangible asset during its development

Option B is not one of these criteria.

20 **The correct answer is D**

The concept of business entity is the concept that the transactions of the business are separate from the transaction of the owner. Only transactions and balances relating to the business should be recorded in the financial statements of the business.

Transactions between the business and its owner(s) are recorded in the capital/equity sections.

21 **The correct answer is C**

	$
Draft profit	18,900
Accrual	(920)
Prepayment	650
Adjusted profit	18,630

The accrual is an expense that needs to be included, which reduces the profit, and the prepayment means that too much expense has been recognised so the expense needs to be reduced which increases profit.

22 **The correct answer is B**

Generally, the first note to the financial statement is the accounting policies.

23 **The correct answer is B**

Gross profit margin = gross profit/revenue = $38,000/90,000 = 42%

24 **The correct answer is B**

Net profit margin = net profit/revenue = $6,000/$120,000 = 5%

25 **The correct answer is C**

The aim of a statement of cash flows is to show how the business generates and uses cash and cash equivalents.

ANSWER BANK – MOCK EXAM 1

Mock exam 2 questions and answers

FOUNDATION UNIT

FINANCIAL ACCOUNTING

Question Bank – Mock Exam 2

There is ONE correct answer per question

1. Which of the following reports lists all of the balances in the nominal ledger, is set out in two columns and checks the accuracy of the accounting system?

   A   The statement of profit or loss.
   B   The statement of financial position
   C   The trial balance
   D   The statement of cash flows

2. Financial statements are used by a range of stakeholders. Which of the following statements is incorrect?

   A   Supplier might use financial statement to assess the liquidity of the business
   B   Employees might use the financial statements to argue for a bigger bonus
   C   Management might use the financial statements to check actual performance against budget
   D   Tax authorities might use the financial statements to calculate the taxation due

3. Which of the following must be disclosed on the face of the statement of profit or loss?

   A   Tax expense
   B   Analysis of expenses
   C   Prepayments and accruals
   D   Non-current assets

4. What is the accounting equation?

   A   Capital + Assets = Liabilities
   B   Capital + Non-current assets = Liabilities – current assets
   C   Assets = Capital + Liabilities
   D   Capital + Non-current liabilities = Assets + current liabilities

5. If an invoice from a supplier is posted twice in the accounting records, what is the likely impact?

   A   An increase in liabilities on the statement of financial position
   B   A decrease in liabilities on the statement of financial position
   C   No effect at all
   D   A decrease in the sales ledger control account

6. What would the double entry be in the general ledger for the purchase of machinery on credit from TBC Ltd for $20,000?

   A   Debit Machinery $20,000   Credit Bank $20,000
   B   Debit Machinery $20,000   Credit TBC Ltd $20,000
   C   Debit Trade Payables $20,000   Credit Machinery $20,000
   D   Debit Machinery $20,000   Credit Trade Payables $20,000

7. Which of the following documents is sometimes used in conjunction with both sales and purchases?

   A   Inventory requisition
   B   Statement of account
   C   Remittance advice slip
   D   Goods received notes

8 The trial balance of TBC Ltd does not balance. The debit column totals $221,472 and the credit column totals £219,648. What will be made in the suspense account to balance the trial balance?

   A $912 Debit
   B $1,824 Debit
   C $1,824 Credit
   D $912 Credit

9 TBC Ltd have discovered an invoice for fuel for the business motor vehicles, the invoice has been debited to the account for motor vehicles cost account. What type of error is this?

   A Omission
   B Principle
   C Commission
   D Compensating

10 TBC Ltd has a balance on the trade payables account of $120,000 (including VAT at 20%). How would this be shown on the statement of financial position?

   A Current asset of $100,000 and $20,000 (DR) in the VAT payable account
   B Current liability of $100,000 and $20,000 (CR) in the VAT payable account
   C Current liability of $120,000
   D Current asset of $120,000

11 Which of the following is an asset?

   A Tax payable
   B Wages accrued
   C Bank overdraft
   D Income accrued

12 When preparing a bank reconciliation which of the following items create a timing difference?

   A Unpresented cheques
   B Direct Debit payments
   C Bank charges and interest
   D BACS receipts

13 You have been given the following information for the year ended 31 August 20X9:

Trade receivables at 1 September 20X8	$53,230
Credit sales	$631,504
Cash received from credit customers	$628,985
Goods returned by credit customers	$2,894
Discounts allowed	$854
Irrecoverable debts written off	$851

   What is the trade receivables balance as at 31 August 20X9?

   A $53,209
   B $56,938
   C $51,650
   D $51,150

14 A trial balance fails to agree by $750; the difference has been posted to the suspense account. It was later discovered that the $750 was for a cash sale which had not been posted to the sales account.

Which of the following journals entries correct the error?

A	Debit suspense account	$750	Credit sales account	$750
B	Debit suspense account	$1,500	Credit sales account	$1,500
C	Debit sales account	$750	Credit suspense account	$750
D	Debit sales account	$1,500	Credit suspense account	$1,500

15 A business has opening trade receivables of $95,000 and closing trade receivables of $98,750. Cash received from customers was $87,650 and discounts allowed $1,150.

What is the figure for sales?

A $98,750
B $87,650
C $90,250
D $92,550

16 A business usually has a margin of 25% on sales. During a year, its revenue was $175,000.

What was cost of sales?

A $58,333
B $131,250
C $140,000
D $218,750

17 A business has the following information:

Cost of sales for the year is $450,000.

Margin is 40%

What is the sales revenue for the year?

A $700,000
B $750,000
C $630,000
D $660,000

18 100 items of inventory were purchased for $95 and a further 20 were purchased for £90. However, due to a new model being released there has been a fall in demand so its selling price will be only $70. In addition, further costs will be incurred prior to sale of $10 per item.

What is the net realisable value?

A $8,400
B $7,200
C $9,600
D $10,000

19 An allowance for receivables of 2.5% is required. Trade receivables at the period end are $995,000 and the allowable for receivables brought forward from the previous period is $23,250.

What movement is required this year?

A An increase of $1,043
B A decrease of $2,206
C An increase of $1,625
D No adjustment required

20 Which of the following words completes the sentence?

A provision is a ……………………… of ……………….. timing or amount.

- A Liability, guaranteed
- B Asset, additional
- C Liability, uncertain
- D Asset, guaranteed

21 Which of the following elements can be included in the production cost of a tangible non-current asset?

- A Purchase price of raw materials
- B Architect's fees
- C Import duties
- D All the above

22 AYZ Ltd has a piece of machinery which is being depreciated using the reducing balance method at a rate of 20% over 4 years. The original purchase price was $20,000.

What will the total accumulated depreciation be as at the end of 4 years?

- A $11,808
- B $8,192
- C $11,200
- D $9,956

23 The owner of an entity withdraws money from the entity for use in personnel matters.

What would the double entry be for such a transaction in the entity's accounts?

- A Debit Drawings   Credit Bank
- B Debit Expenses   Credit Bank
- C Debit Capital   Credit Bank
- D Debit Bank   Credit Drawings

24 A draft statement of profit or loss shows a profit for the year of $28,790. The owner of the business wishes to increase the allowance for receivables by $2,800 and to write off an irrecoverable debt of £2,150. What is the adjusted profit for the year?

- A $23,840
- B $28,140
- C $29,440
- D $28,790

25 The final standard heading used in IAS 7 *Statement of Cash Flows* is?

- A Net current assets
- B Non-current assets
- C Net increase (decrease) in cash and cash equivalents
- D Non-current liabilities

FOUNDATION LEVEL

FOUNDATION UNIT

FINANCIAL ACCOUNTING

Answer Bank – Mock Exam 2

There is ONE correct answer per question

1 The correct answer is C

The trial balance is the report that lists all of the balances in the nominal ledger. It is set out in two columns – a column of debit balances and a column of credit balances. Due to the double entry bookkeeping system, the total debits should equal the total credits, and so the trial balance checks the accuracy of the accounting system.

The distractors are as follows:

A   The statement of profit or loss – lists all income and expenditure
B   The statement of financial position – lists all assets and liabilities
D   The statement of cash flows – lists cash flows

2 The correct answer is C

Financial statements deal with historic information. Management are unlikely to use financial statement to check actual performance to budget, they would use the current management accounts.

Suppliers want to ensure that a business will be able to pay its debts if they provide goods or services on credit, so may use the financial statements to assess financial liquidity.

Employees might argue for increased salary, or a larger bonus if the financial statements show good performance.

The tax authorities may use financial statements to estimate or calculate the tax payable.

3 The correct answer is A

The tax expense must be shown on the face of the statement of profit or loss.

The distractors are as follows:

B   Analysis of expenses – usually shown in the notes to the accounts

C   Prepayments and accruals – shown in the statement of financial position or in the notes to the accounts

D   Non-current assets – shown in the statement of financial position

4 The correct answer is C

The accounting equation is Assets = Capital + Liabilities

5 The correct answer is A

An invoice from a supplier will debit expenses and credit payables. There will be an increase in the liabilities (payables) – option a.

The sales ledger control account is the total of trade receivables, so will not be impacted by the duplicate invoice.

6 The correct answer is D

A purchase of machinery on credit would be recorded as debit machinery cost, credit trade payables (option d).

Option a is the purchase of machinery for cash. In option B the individual supplier account is credited, but the individual balance is maintained on the subsidiary purchase ledger and not posted in the general ledger.

7 The correct answer is D

Goods received notes can be used for both sales and purchases. A customer who receives an order might use a goods received note, or a purchase of goods into the business would also be recorded on a goods received note.

The distractors are as follows:

A Inventory requisition – used in warehouse or stores
B Statement of account – sent to customer summarising their account
C Remittance advice slip – received from customer to identify payment of goods

8 The correct answer is C

The credit column total is $1,824 less than the debit column. A suspense account of $1,824 credit is needed to correct the trial balance.

9 The correct answer is B

An invoice for fuel should be posted as an expense in the statement of profit or loss. It has been debited to the motor vehicles cost account in the statement of financial position instead. This is an error of principle.

The distractors are as follows:

A Omission – completely missed out
C Commission – entered to the wrong persons account
D Compensating – two errors cancelling each other out

10 The correct answer is C

The trade payables balance is recorded inclusive of VAT as a liability. Therefore the correct answer is c.

11 The correct answer is D

Income accrued in an asset. This is similar to trade receivables, it is money owed to the company. Trade receivables relates to income receivable through trading (sales), income accrued relates to 'other income' accrued such as bank interest receivable.

The distractors are as follows:

A Tax payable – this is a liability
B Wages accrued – this is a liability
C Bank overdraft – this is a liability

12 The correct answer is A

An unpresented cheque creates a timing difference, as the cheque payment will have been recorded as a payment in the cashbook, but if the cheque hasn't cleared there will not yet be a corresponding payment in the bank statements.

Direct debits, bank charges and interest and BACS receipts are all cash items which are initiated by the bank and so commonly appear in the bank statements and then have to be adjusted in the cashbook. However, they are not considered to be timing differences, a company should just post them to the cash book as soon as they are seen on the bank statements.

13 The correct answer is D

	$
Trade receivables at 1 Sept X8	53,230
Credit sales	631,504
Less: cash received	(628,985)
Less: goods returned	(2,894)
Less: discounts allowed	(854)
Less: irrecoverable debts	(851)
Trade receivables at 31 Aug X9	51,150

14 The correct answer is A

The missing entry in the sales account would be a credit of $750. There must be a credit in the suspense account of $750, so the correcting entry would be: Debit suspense account $750, Credit sales account $750.

15 The correct answer is D

	$
Payments received from credit customers	87,650
Add: closing balance of trade receivables	98,750
Less: opening balance of trade receivables	(95,000)
Add: discounts allowed	1,150
Credit sales in the period	92,550

16 The correct answer is B

A margin of 25% means that gross profit is 25% of revenue.

		$
Revenue	100%	175,000
Cost of sales	75%	(131,250)
Gross profit	25%	43,750

17 The correct answer is B

A margin of 40% means that the gross profit is 40% of revenue.

		$
Revenue	100%	750,000
Cost of sales	60%	(450,000)
Gross profit	40%	300,000

18 The correct answer is B

Inventory is valued at the lower of cost and net realisable value.

		$
Cost – 100 items	100 × $95	9,500
Cost – 20 items	20 × $90	1,800
Total cost		11,300
NRV	120 × ($70 – $10)	7,200

Net realisable value is the estimated selling price less the estimated costs of completion and the estimated costs necessary to make the sale.

In this case, the estimated selling price is $70 per unit, and there are an additional $10 of costs necessary to make the sale. The NRV per item is $60, or $7,200 for 120 items.

ANSWER BANK – MOCK EXAM 2

19. **The correct answer is C**

		$
Closing allowance for receivables	$995,000 × 2.5%	24,875
Opening allowance for receivables		23,250
Increase required		1,625

20. **The correct answer is C**

A provision is a liability of uncertain timing or amount. A provision is a liability as it will result in the transfer of economic benefits (often cash) to settle. The key difference between a trade payable or accrual and a provision is the uncertainly surrounding a provision.

21. **The correct answer is D**

IAS 16 permits the purchase price plus any directly attributable costs to be capitalised as the cost of a tangible non-current asset.

22. **The correct answer is A**

Year 1	$20,000 × 20% = $4,000
Year 2	$16,000 × 20% = $3,200
Year 3	$12,800 × 20% = $2,560
Year 4	$10,240 × 20% = $2048
Total: Accumulated Depreciation	$11,808

23. **The correct answer is A**

A withdrawal by the owner is recorded as a debit to drawings and a credit to entity bank account. All transactions between the owner and the entity are recorded within capital, drawings is part of the capital balance.

24. **The correct answer is A**

The adjusted profit is: $28,790 – $2,800 – $2,150 = $23,840

The distractors are as follows:

- B $28,140 – incorrectly calculated
- C $29,440 – incorrectly calculated
- D $28,790 – incorrectly calculated

25. **The correct answer is C**

Under IAS 7, the total of the cash flows from operating, investing and financing activities is shown as the net increase (decrease) in cash and cash equivalents.

ANSWER BANK – MOCK EXAM 2

Bibliography

BIBLIOGRAPHY

Department for Business. (2006) *Companies Act 2006*. [Online]. Available from: https://www.legislation.gov.uk/ukpga/2006/46/contents [Accessed 19 September 2024]. http://www.nationalarchives.gov.uk/doc/open-government-licence/version/3/ Contains Parliamentary information licensed under the Open Parliament Licence v3.0.

International Accounting Standards Board. *IFRS Accounting Standards* [Online]. Available at: https://www.ifrs.org/issued-standards/list-of-standards/[Accessed 19 September 2024].

International Sustainability Standards Board. *IFRS Sustainability Disclosure Standards* [Online]. Available at: https://www.ifrs.org/issued-standards/ifrs-sustainability-standards-navigator/ [Accessed 19 September 2024].

International Accounting Standards Board. (2010) *Conceptual Framework for Financial Reporting*. [Online]. Available from https://www.ifrs.org/issued-standards/list-of-standards/conceptual-framework.html/content/dam/ifrs/publications/html-standards/english/2024/issued/cf/ [Accessed 19 September 2024].

BIBLIOGRAPHY

Index

INDEX

Note. **Key Terms** and their page references are given in **bold**

Accounting concept, 16
Accounting equation, 65
Accounting for sales tax, 111
Accounting policy, 357
Accounting record, 315
Accounting standards, 16, 21
Accruals, 120, 125
Accruals accounting, 29
Accruals and prepayments, 180, 192
Accumulated depreciation, 275
Acid test ratio, 384
Allowance for trade receivables, 240, 247
Amortisation, 301
Amortisation of development costs, 303
Asset, 9, 35
Asset turnover, 376
Authorised (or nominal) capital, 316
AVCO (average cost), 223

Balancing ledger accounts, 95
Bank charge, 134
Bank interest, 134
Bank reconciliation, 134, 135, 139
Bank statements, 57
Benefits of cash flow information, 399
Bonus (capitalisation) issues, 326
Books of original entry, 82
Books of prime entry, 52
Business entity concept, 66
Business equation, 193

Calculating ratios, 373
Called-up capital, 317
Capital, 66, 375
Capital expenditure, 264
Capital gearing ratio, 379
Capital income, 264
Capital transaction, 265
Carriage inwards, 214
Carriage outwards, 214
Carrying amount, 286
Cash, 358, **399**
Cash and cash equivalents, 399
Cash book, 52, **55**, 87, 180, 188
Cash cycle, 383
Cash equivalents, 399
Cash flow ratio, 382
Cash flows, 399
Cash transaction, 75

Comparability, 32
Compensating errors, 97, 168, **169**
Contingent asset, 256
Contingent liability, 256
Continuous inventory record, 220
Contract, 362
Control, 36
Control account, 146, 160
Correction of errors, 83, 170
Cost, 286
Cost formulas, 231
Cost of goods sold, 213
Costs of conversion, 229
Costs of purchase, 229
Counting inventory, 220
Credit, 74
Credit note, 51
Credit sales and trade accounts receivable, 180, 182
Credit transactions, 77
Credits, 95
Cumulative weighted average costing, 225
Current asset, 365
Current cost of a liability, 40
Current cost of an asset, 40
Current liabilities, 365
Current liability, 366
Current ratio, 384
Current replacement cost, 221
Current value, 38
Customer, 362

Day book analysis, 84
Debit, 74, 95
Debit note, 51
Debt ratio, 379
Debt/equity ratio, 380
Debtors' payment period, 385
Depreciable amount, 267, 301
Depreciable asset, 267
Depreciation, 267, 288, 292
Depreciation methods, 268
Derecognition, 37
Development, 301
Direct method, 401
Disclosures, 354
Discount, 147
Disposal of a fixed asset, 281, 282
Dividend cover, 389
Dividend per share and dividend cover, 389

INDEX

Dividend yield, 390
Dividends, 323
Double entry bookkeeping, 75, 96
Drawings, 67, 180, 192

Earnings per share, 389
Efficiency ratios, 385
Elements of financial statements, 35
Equity, 35
Error of commission, 168, **169**, 173
Error of omission, 168, 173
Error of principle, 97, 168, **169**
Error of transposition, 168
Errors, 83
Exchange of asset, 287
Expenses, 36

Fair value, 39, 286
Faithful representation, 30, 31
FIFO (first-in, first-out), 223, 224, 231
Financial accounts, 6
Financial capital, 42
Financial reporting, 4
Financing activities, 399, 400
Fixed production overheads, 230
Format of a ledger account, 65
Fulfilment value, 40

GAAP, 19, 27
Gearing ratio, 379
General ledger, 64
Generally Accepted Accounting Practice (GAAP), 19
Going concern, 33
Goods destroyed, 186
Goods received note, 52
Goods stolen, 186
Goods written off, 215
Gross profit margin, 185, 377

Historical cost, 38, 221

IAS 1 Presentation of financial statements, 354, 402
IAS 16 Property, plant and equipment, 286
IAS 2 Inventories, 222, 228
IAS 37 Provisions and contingencies, 254
IAS 38 Intangible assets, 301
IAS 4 Depreciation accounting, 288
IAS 7 Cash flow statements, 398
IASB, 18

IFRS 15 Revenue from contracts with customers, 362
IFRS Sustainability Disclosure Standards, 22
Impairment of development costs, 303
Impersonal accounts, 86
Implications of high or low gearing, 380
Imprest system, 58
Income, 36, 362
Income tax, 360
Incomplete records, 180
Indirect method, 401
Indirect versus direct, 402
Input and output sales tax, 110
Input VAT, 110
Intangible asset, 301
Interest cover, 381
Internal check, 160
International Accounting Standards, 17
International Accounting Standards Board (IASB), 17
International Sustainability Standards Board (ISSB), 21
Interpretation of IASs, 20
Inventory, 229, 292
Inventory destroyed, 188
Inventory holding period, 386
Investing activities, 399, 400
Investment, 358
Invoice, 50
Irrecoverable debt, 238, 245
Irrecoverable sales tax, 111
Issued capital, 316

Journal, 52, **82**
Journal entries, 83, 170

Ledger account, 73
Level of precision, 355
Leverage, 379, 380
Liability, 9, 35, 69, **254**
Limited liability, 315
Limited liability companies, 314
Liquidity, 378, 382, **383**, 384
List of account balances, 94, 160
Loan stock bonds, 319
Long-term solvency, 378

Management (or cost) accounting, 6
Market value of shares, 319
Mark-up, 185
Materiality, 31

INDEX

Need for financial statements, 7
Net profit margin, 377
Net realisable value (NRV), 215, 221, **229**, 232
Nominal ledger, 64
Non-current asset, 267, 357
Non-current liability, 358
Normal capacity, 230

Obligation, 36
Omission of a transaction, 96
Opening and closing inventories, 216, 217
Opening statement of financial position, 180
Operating activities, 399, 400
Operating cycle, 366
Ordinary shares, 318
Output VAT, 110

Paid-up capital, 317
Par value, 316
Payable, 69, 152, 358
PBIT, profit before interest and tax, 374
Performance obligation, 362
Personal accounts, 86
Petty cash book, 52, **58**
Physical capital, 42
Potential to produce economic benefits, 35
Preference share, 317
Prepayment, 120, 122, 124, 127
Presentation of a ratio analysis report, 390
Price/Earnings (P/E) ratio, 390
Primary profitability ratio, 376
Primary users, 28
Profit, 5, 66
Profit analysis, 377, 378
Profit before interest and tax, 374
Profit margin, 376
Profitability, 374
Property, plant and equipment, 286, 357
Provisions, 254, 324
Purchase day book, 52, **53**
Purchase ledger, 160
Purchase order, 50
Purchase returns day book, 52, **54**
Purchases, inventory and the cost of sales, 180
Purchases and trade accounts payable, 180, 183

Quick ratio, 384

Ratio analysis, 372
Real accounts, 291
Receivable, 69, 150, 358

Receivables and payables ledgers, 86
Recognition, 37, 286
Reconciling items, 155
Recoverable amount, 286
Reducing balance method, 270, 272
Relevance, 30
Relevance (qualitative characteristic), 30
Reporting period, 355
Research, 301
Research and development, 300
Reserve, 320, **324**
Residual value, 268, **286**
Retail method, 230
Return on capital employed (ROCE), 375
Revaluation, 288
Revaluation of non-current assets, 278
Revaluation surplus, 322
Revenue, 362
Revenue expenditure, 264
Revenue income, 264
Review of depreciation method, 289
Review of useful life, 289
Right, 35
Rights issues, 327
ROCE, 375
ROE, 376

Sales day book, **53**, 87
Sales order, 50
Sales returns day book, 52, **54**
Secondary ratio, 376
Settlement discount, 148
Share premium account, 321
Shareholders' interests, 358
Short-term solvency, 382
Source documents, 50
Standard cost, 230
Statement of changes in equity, 324
Statement of financial position, 9
Statement of financial position, 9, 100, 101, 160, 241, 355, 364
Statement of financial position disclosures, 357
Statement of profit or loss and other comprehensive income, 10, 111
Statement of profit or loss and other comprehensive income, 10, 111
Stolen goods, 186
Stolen goods or goods destroyed, 180
Straight line method, 271
Substance over form, 32
Supplier statement reconciliations, 154
Suspense account, 172, 173, 174

589

INDEX

T accounts, 65
Taxation, 360
The advantages of cash flow accounting, 410
The disposal of non-current assets, 280
Theft of cash from the till, 191
Time difference, 134
Timeliness, 32
Trade accounts receivable, 69, 70
Trade discount, 147, 148
Trade payables control account, 146
Trade payables ledger, 88
Trade receivable, 69
Trade receivables control account, 146
Trade receivables ledger, 87
Tradings, income and expense account, 98
Transaction price, 362
Transposition error, 161, 172
Trial balance, 94
Two column cash book, 189
Types of error, 168

Understandability, 33
Unlimited liability, 314
Unpresented cheques, 138
Use and application of IASs and IFRSs, 18
Useful life, 267, 268, **301**
Users of accounting information, 7

Value in use, 40
Valuing inventories, 221
Variable production overheads, 230
VAT, 110, 111, **113**
Verifiability, 32

Wages and salaries control, 146
Weighted average cost, 231
Working capital, 366
Wrong account, 96